Democracy for Hire

Democracy for Hire

A HISTORY OF AMERICAN POLITICAL CONSULTING

Dennis W. Johnson

OXFORD
UNIVERSITY PRESS

OXFORD
UNIVERSITY PRESS

Oxford University Press is a department of the University of Oxford. It furthers the University's objective of excellence in research, scholarship, and education by publishing worldwide. Oxford is a registered trade mark of Oxford University Press in the UK and certain other countries.

Published in the United States of America by Oxford University Press
198 Madison Avenue, New York, NY 10016, United States of America.

© Oxford University Press 2017

Library of Congress Cataloging-in-Publication Data
Names: Johnson, Dennis W., author.
Title: Democracy for hire : a history of American political consulting / Dennis W. Johnson.
Description: New York, NY : Oxford University Press, 2016. | Includes bibliographical references and index. | Description based on print version record and CIP data provided by publisher; resource not viewed.
Identifiers: LCCN 2016020566 (print) | LCCN 2016009381 (ebook) | ISBN 9780190272708 (Updf) | ISBN 9780190272715 (Epub) | ISBN 9780190272692 (hardback)
Subjects: LCSH: Political consultants—United States—History—20th century. | Political consultants—United States—History—21st century. | Public relations and politics—United States—History—20th century. | Public relations and politics—United States—History—21st century. | Political campaigns—United States—History—20th century. | Political campaigns—United States—History—21st century. | Political culture—United States—History—20th century. | Political culture—United States—History—21st century. | BISAC: POLITICAL SCIENCE / Political Ideologies / Democracy. | POLITICAL SCIENCE / Political Process / Elections. | POLITICAL SCIENCE / Political Process / Political Advocacy. Classification: LCC JK2281 (print) | LCC JK2281 .J624 2016 (ebook) | DDC 324.0973—dc23
LC record available at https://lccn.loc.gov/2016020566

9 8 7 6 5 4 3 2 1
Printed by Sheridan Books, Inc., United States of America

For Pat, with all my love

CONTENTS

LIST OF TABLES

PREFACE AND ACKNOWLEDGMENTS

My introduction to political consulting three and a half decades ago was abrupt and dismissive. "I don't need no goddamned professor on this campaign," scoffed the frazzled campaign manager. "Trouble is, they can't get off the can, can't make a decision. To them everything is gray; I want black and white. I want to nail our opponent, I want to rip his head off. I want answers, and I want them now!"

For fifty years, one of the US Senate seats from Virginia had been held by the Byrd family, first by Harry F. Byrd, and then his son, Harry F. Byrd Jr. In 1982, "Little Harry" announced his retirement. Here was a great opportunity for both Republicans and Democrats to capture an open seat. I took a leave of absence from my university political science department to work for the Democratic candidate, Owen B. Pickett, a quiet, self-effacing lawyer and member of the Virginia House of Delegates. His Senate candidacy didn't last long: Pickett was tripped up over intraparty bickering and was forced to quit the race. His replacement was the popular lieutenant governor, Dick Davis, who somewhat reluctantly accepted the party's plea to run.

Taking over the fractured campaign was a battle-scarred political operative from Louisiana, James Carville, who was now running his first statewide race. Carville didn't want me to be the issues and research director, goddamned professor that I was, but veteran staffers working for Davis prevailed upon him. Carville, thirty-seven years old, was jumpy, intense, but fiercely focused. He impressed me in two significant ways. First, while he had never worked in a Virginia election campaign before, within a week, forever working the telephones calling political operatives and party influentials, he gained a far better understanding of the peculiarities of Virginia politics and the strengths and weaknesses of our candidate than I would ever have. Second, he made it clear that we were locked in mortal combat with our opponent. Yes, we would do everything possible to rip the head off our Republican opponent, Congressman Paul S. Trible Jr. For Carville this was not an academic study, we were not engaging in a civics lesson: it was political life or death.

One day, Carville and I had a meeting with our Washington-based pollster, and to make our appointment we had just ninety minutes to drive from Richmond to DuPont Circle in Washington, DC. Normally, the trip takes two hours. We jumped in the campaign car, but first Carville stopped for "lunch" at McDonald's. We went directly to the drive-thru lane, and when the order came out the pickup window, Carville threw away the hamburger bun, folded the meat in half, and ate it in three bites. He then wolfed down the French fries and gulped the twenty-ounce Coca Cola—all this before we returned to the street. We made it to our Washington meeting with time to spare.

Our pollster, Peter D. Hart, was one of the established stars of the Democratic consulting world. Hart, thirty-nine, started his polling business in 1971, and had worked for scores of Democratic statewide hopefuls and presidential candidates by the time the Davis for US Senate campaign hired his firm. Calm, cerebral, and gracious, Hart sat down with us to go over the results of the first survey, the benchmark analysis, that he conducted of Virginia voters measuring their attitudes and preferences. I learned quickly why he was one of the best in the business. Hart's analysis was clear and compelling: he summarized the survey data, offering about twenty insightful recommendations on what issues to emphasize, the mood of the voters, where our candidate was known and where he was not, and how voters felt about the candidates.

Dick Davis was a late entry to the race, was outspent two-to-one, and had to contend with a fractured Democratic party; he lost by 2.4 percent. James Carville went on to other races, winning some important gubernatorial and Senate contests, and gaining national and worldwide fame by managing the Clinton for President campaign in 1992. He then focused on international campaigns, speaking engagements, and television and cameo movie appearances, taking on the role of a political celebrity.

Peter Hart spent two more election cycles polling for candidates, then in 1986 turned over the election and candidate side of the business to his partner Geoff Garin, who was later joined by Fred Yang. Hart then concentrated on public polling, teaming up with Republican pollster Robert Teeter in 1989 to create the NBC/Wall Street Journal poll. The Garin-Hart-Yang Research Group remains today one of the most important private polling firms for Democratic and progressive causes.

In 1982, the political consulting business was still relatively new. It began in the 1930s in California, but came into its own in the late 1950s and 1960s. In the early years, many candidates, from president on down, were ambivalent about using outside professional help. But today, consulting is a booming business. During the last presidential-state/local election cycle, candidates, parties, and outside interest groups spent $6 billion to convince voters, and there appears to be no end in sight for the expenditures in future races, especially with super PAC money flooding in. The money buys professional help. Nearly every major race—for president, governor, US Senate and Congress, big city mayor, and nearly every ballot issue—finds a battery of professional political consultants: general consultants, campaign managers, media firms, pollsters, candidate and opposition researchers, time buyers, direct mail and telephone specialists, online communication specialists, microtargeting specialists, and more.

This book is a history of the growing and evolving field of political consulting. Its title is inspired by journalist William Greider's trenchant observations about American business and democracy written nearly a quarter of century ago.[1] Many individuals assisted me in the writing of this work, particularly those scholars and journalists who understand and appreciate the importance of political consultants in the electoral arena and political consultants who have written their memoirs, oral histories, and have sat for interviews with me and others. I am most appreciative of the scholars, consultants, and other keen observers of American politics who have discussed and debated with me the role of professionals in campaigns.

A number of colleagues and friends have read the full manuscript or individual chapters. Thanks in particular to my colleagues and friends at the Graduate School of Political Management of George Washington University: Christopher Arterton, Steven Billet, Lara Brown, Michael Cornfield, Matthew Dallek, Edward Grefe, Roberto Izurieta, Mark Kennedy, Gary Nordlinger, and David Rehr. I am also indebted to a number of campaign and election scholars, especially Michael Burton and Bruce Newman. Political consultants who have toiled in the real world of politics have also given me valuable advice and counsel: Whit Ayres, Doug Bailey, David Beatty, Joel Benenson, Bob Blaemire, Walter Clinton, Walter De Vries, Tom Edmonds, Dale Emmons, Brian Franklin, Jim Innocenzi, Mark Mellman, Phil Noble, Rick Ridder, Ray Strother, Lance Tarrance, and Joe Slade White. Further thanks goes to Grace Guggenheim and my friend and wordsmith extraordinaire, Jane E. Jones. Thanks, too, to the staff of the Gelman Library, George Washington University, who graciously and efficiently handled my research requests and gathered materials from far and wide, especially Patricia S. Greenstein, Zachary Elder, Holley Matthews, Fowzia Osman, and Keliy Zechariah.

This book is dedicated to my wife and best friend, Pat. She has read every word of this project, has been my best sounding board and critic, and has helped this project immeasurably with her cheer and encouragement. An entire summer in paradise was spent with me huddled over my keyboard cranking out the final chapters; through it all, she smiled and understood.

Thanks especially to my editor Angela Chnapko, and the support staff at Oxford, particularly editorial assistant, Princess Ikatekit. My thanks as well to the production team, including copy editor Peter Jasowiak, and the production team at NewGen Publishing, especially project manager Alphonsa James.

Dennis W. Johnson
Denver, Colorado

Democracy for Hire

Introduction

*In a meaningful sense, America is about the
holding of elections.*

—Anthony King (1997)

T HE UNITED STATES is the land of elections; it holds more elections, and
holds them more frequently, than any other democracy. Altogether, there
are more than 1 million elections held for local, statewide, and national
office during a four-year cycle, and there are over 513,000 popularly elected officials in the country. Through their constitutions or laws, states, counties, cities,
and other jurisdictions require frequent elections, usually for terms of two or
four years. Most elections are low profile, with small budgets, and local impact.
But several thousand elections are for much higher stakes, including races for
governor, US senator, US representative, other statewide offices such as attorney general, big city mayor, and, in a growing number of cases, statewide ballot
issues. Of course, the most consequential and visible contests are presidential
elections, held every four years, with pre-primaries, primaries, and the general
election—the nation's unique, cumbersome, and expensive electoral marathon.

The United States is also the land of political consultants. For those few thousand critical and expensive races, from president to city council to ballot initiative, professional consultants are brought in to advise and assist candidates,
political parties, and outside interests. This book is a history of political consulting in America, examining how the consulting business developed, highlighting
the major figures in the consulting industry, and assessing the impact of professional consulting on elections and American democracy. A key focus is on presidential elections, beginning in 1964, and the crucial role played by consultants
and political operatives.

Who are these political consultants? In simplest terms, political consultants
are individuals or firms who provide election skills, strategic advice, and services
to candidates running for office, to political parties, and to interest groups trying

to influence candidate elections or ballot initiatives.[1] In many cases, consultants started their careers working on campaign staffs, for elected officials, or for a political party. Most early political consultants were motivated by ideology or partisanship; others sought out the thrill of competition and the chance to make a living in the rough and tumble of politics. In recent years, "old school" consultants have been joined by specialists with twenty-first-century technological skills, such as data mining, digital communication, and microtargeting.

Today, political consulting is a flourishing multibillion-dollar business, attracting hundreds of firms and several thousand employees. Sparked by sharp ideological tensions in recent years, with increasing amounts of campaign funds available and the nationalization of what were once local contests, consultants now play a bigger role than ever before in the fabric of campaigns and elections.

Political consultants are sometimes vilified as "hired guns" who will do anything to get their candidates elected; as "image merchants" who, through misleading advertising and distortion, appeal to base emotions of voters; or as the "new kingmakers," the purveyors of the black arts of campaign trickery and shenanigans. There certainly are enough examples of political consultants who have behaved badly, and throughout this book, from the very first consultants, we will examine such behavior and practices. Yet, for those 5,000–10,000 professional consultants, it is unfair to tar them with such characterizations. Political consultants, unfortunately, suffer from the same kind of reputational smears as personal injury lawyers, "Washington bureaucrats," Internal Revenue Service employees, nuclear power plant operators, and parking meter readers. They work in an arena that draws controversy and contention. Elections can be brutal: candidates and outside groups often draw sharp distinctions, expose raw edges, and aggressively define their opponents and their policies. In this political warfare, consultants are right in the thick of election strategy and communication.

Why have political consultants? According to Walter De Vries, one of the pioneer consultants featured in this book, "A major reason—if not the only reason—for having campaign consultants is that political parties basically failed to do their job in a changing technological and social environment."[2] And consultants have their defenders. Political scientist David A. Dulio, who has carefully examined the impact of political consultants on American campaigns and elections, argues that consultants "are not the bane of the U.S. electoral system. In fact, their appearance and increased presence in elections can benefit democracy."[3]

I argue that political consultants are essential to modern campaigning and, for the most part, make a positive contribution to democracy and public discourse. Candidates and causes depend on the skill, judgment, and experience of political consultants. Whether candidates are seeking to be president, governor, senator, big city mayor, or even local school board member, professional consultants are brought in to advise them, develop a winning strategy, and manage their campaigns. In addition, twenty-eight states, the District of Columbia, and many local governments have some form of direct democracy, such as initiatives, referenda, or the recall of elected officials. These ballot initiatives, particularly in California, have become lucrative markets for political consultants. American-style democracy is emulated in many parts of the world, and American political consultants and their European or Latin American counterparts have become key factors in the electoral success of candidates for high office. Business interests and advocacy organizations have found that the skills and experience of political consultants are valued resources in their attempts to influence public policy. For several decades, political consulting firms have been small enterprises, with a handful of principals and associates, rarely generating over a few million dollars in revenue. Recently, however, several successful political consulting firms have merged into larger public relations organizations, and become integral parts of national, even global, communications operations.

Political consultants bring experience, skills, and discipline to unpredictable and often volatile electoral and communication battlefields. A campaign for elective office is faced with many unknowns, and much can go wrong: the candidate goes "off message," a friend acting as a surrogate says something stupid, a damaging allegation from thirty years ago resurfaces, the candidate's teenage son posts something salacious on Instagram, an intraparty feud threatens the candidate's success, or fundraising falls far short of the campaign's goals. Meanwhile, the opponent and his team are doing everything they can to raise money, grab attention, sharpen their attack lines, mobilize resources, and convince uninformed and relatively uninterested voters to select him on Election Day. Candidates for major office cannot handle these challenges alone, nor can they simply rely on friends and eager volunteers. All the best intentions, sincere beliefs, and enthusiasm of volunteers can rarely supplant the skill, judgment, and, above all, experience of seasoned campaign veterans, who have seen it all before and have a good understanding of how to cope with the many potential obstacles a campaign might face. The learning curve is too steep and the stakes are too high to learn on the job.

Today, political consulting embraces a wide variety of specialties and niches. Political consulting firms provide quantitative and qualitative research, through a variety of public opinion polls, focus group analysis, and other forms of research. Media firms produce campaign advertising, direct mail firms create messages that try to persuade voters and have them contribute campaign dollars, targeting firms analyze and determine where the campaign should focus its resources, candidate and opposition researchers comb through public records to find weaknesses or lines of attack. Some professionals are campaign managers, while others are devoted to fundraising, telephone persuasion calls, online communication, or television time buying.

A gubernatorial campaign, spending $10 million, may use a wide range of consultants—campaign manager, pollster, media team, candidate and opposition researchers, telephone and direct mail communication, online specialists, fundraisers, and others. A local campaign, spending $50,000 may be able to afford just a campaign manager, a few volunteers, one poll, and some direct mail. Below the $50,000 level, it is very difficult to hire professionals, and such campaigns, almost always for local office, will have to rely on the enthusiasm and shoe leather of committed volunteers.

Elections, of course, have been core elements of American democracy since the beginning of the Republic. During the nineteenth and early twentieth centuries, local political parties and political organizations ran campaigns, augmented by volunteers and friends of the candidates. Professional political consulting is a relatively recent phenomenon. The first political consultants, a husband and wife team, began their work in California during the 1930s; other public relations or advertising firms did political work on the side and emerged during the 1940s and 1950s. By the mid-1960s, a new group of young political operatives had created small political consulting firms, often with just two or three professionals, providing expertise and analysis for a variety of candidates from their respective political parties. In many ways, they were replacing the political party services that for many decades had provided candidates with manpower and strategic advice.

In 1981, political scientist Larry J. Sabato, who wrote the first scholarly book focusing on the emergence of political consultants, noted that "there is no more significant change in the conduct of campaigns than the consultants' recent rise to prominence, if not preeminence, during the election season."[4]

For decades, scholars, especially political scientists, have examined the question of whether or not campaigns (let alone consultants) even matter. For political consultants, the answer is obvious: yes, elections do matter, and moreover, any serious candidate would be a fool to not hire a team of experienced professionals to guide the campaign through the inevitable landmines and challenges. Some political scientists are not so sure, citing the more important effect of fundamentals, such as economic conditions, partisan affiliation, and past judgments and opinions, rather than campaign activities and consultant involvement. For these political scientists, elections and campaigning have had minimal effects on the eventual outcome. Political scientists Karen M. Kaufmann, John R. Petrocik, and Daron R. Shaw argue that both consultants and academics see reality through their own lenses: "Political science tends to produce research that is inaccessible or (especially in the view of those outside the academy) irrelevant. Consultants cherry-pick the good ideas and repackage them while simultaneously proffering their own ideas about what makes the electoral world turn."[5] Political scientist Ken Goldstein and his colleagues Matthew Dallek and Joel Rivlin remind us that most American elections "are driven by partisan turnout, partisan loyalty, and the behavior of swing voters," and that while the fundamentals are central, the marginal effects of turnout and persuasion can be decisive in close contests.[6]

After reviewing several dozen scholarly findings on forecasting elections, and the impact of television and radio advertising, direct mail and telephone calls, door-to-door canvassing, candidate appearances, debates, and nominating conventions, Kaufmann, Petrocik, and Shaw wrote that "electioneering tends to mobilize rather than persuade and typically produces small but discernible effects."[7] Those small but discernible effects, however, can become very significant in tight, heavily contested races.

Daron Shaw, one of the few academics who has had experience working in the field of applied politics alongside political consultants and candidates, argued in another study that scholars started paying much more attention to the role of campaigns after the 1988 presidential election, when George H. W. Bush and his team beat back a seemingly strong challenge from Michael Dukakis, whose efforts collapsed during the final crucial months.[8] The team of Republican veteran campaigners capitalized on focus group research to pinpoint Dukakis's weaknesses. The infamous "Willie Horton" ads bore down on Dukakis and his alleged failures as a governor, and the Dukakis campaign fumbled its response. A clear edge for Dukakis evaporated in a matter of weeks, and Bush, once politically battered and bruised, ended up victorious. A victory for the Democrats was snatched away by aggressive, negative campaigning, the likes of which had rarely been seen before in modern presidential campaiging.

Much of the "minimal effects" literature has focused on presidential general election campaigns, but, as this book will show, there is a much broader reach and impact for political consultancy—into statewide contests, ballot initiatives, issue advocacy, government relations, presidential primaries, and other aspects of politics. Political scientist Gary C. Jacobson explored the range of academic studies conducted in recent years and concluded campaigns do, in fact, matter, in many important ways. Yet the most important questions deal with "when, where, why, how, for what, and for whom" they matter.[9]

Largely their efforts are unseen by the public, but the influence and impact of political consultants often have been far-reaching. A political consultant persuaded Barry Goldwater to run for the presidency, and political consultants helped prepare a political novice, the one-time movie actor Ronald Reagan, in his quest for the governor's office in California. Unfairly or not, other consultants gave voters the lasting impression that Barry Goldwater was trigger-happy, couldn't be trusted on issues of international importance, and wanted to gut key social programs. On his way to the White House in 1980, Reagan's consultants had him concentrate on certain values, crafted by his pollster from a sophisticated hierarchy of values schema. Political consultants helped stop the Clinton health-care initiative, just as they did when Harry Truman proposed similar legislation forty-five years earlier. Political consultants have given presidents valuable insight into the mood of the public, their aspirations, and their interests. A consultant helped build the career of George W. Bush and persuade him to run for the presidency. Consultants have helped set a sharp edge to presidential elections, from Willie Horton to the half-truths and accusations found in the 2016 contest, and, with the collaboration of their clients, they have helped polarize the electorate with their biting messages. In the twenty-first century, political operatives have aided super PACs as they have built massive databases on prospective voters, fielded get-out-the-vote operations, and attacked opponents during Senate races and presidential campaigns.

Whenever a voter opens the mail and reads a direct-mail piece blasting a candidate for office, that piece was written by consultants, and often the exact words and message were tailored to that voter's detailed profile. When television viewers watch the latest 30-second ad mocking an opponent, that ad was researched, created, tested, and placed by consultants. Through social media, political consultants were able to reach millions of new voters for Barack Obama and other candidates. When a young voter opens the Pandora app on her iPhone, and listens to her favorite Delta Rae or Skylar Grey hits, she might also find a political advertisement specifically tailored to her interests. Likewise, while watching Dish TV, a voter might see campaign commercials specifically targeted at his political and demographic profile, while the voter down the street might see political commercials that are quite different in theme and message. Psychographic targeting helped Ted Cruz figure out where to go, what to say, and who to recruit as 2016 Republican primary foot soldiers. These are all products of political consultants and their creative teams. The political consultant of decades ago relied on experience and political horse sense; today's consultants rely on metrics, algorithms, big data, and applied social science. All are seeking the same results: identify likely voters, persuade them, and get them out to vote.

What Follows

Throughout this book, several themes will unfold. First, political consultants emerged, starting in California in the 1930s and then in other parts of the United States in the 1950s and 1960s, because of the crumbling of the political party as a source of manpower and strategic advice, and because of the weakening of traditional party loyalties among voters. Second, political consulting services embrace three broad categories: determining what voters want (survey research), communicating with them (media consulting, direct mail, and telephone specialists), and finding more precisely who voters are and where they reside (targeting and data mining). Third, many of the communications and targeting techniques employed by political consultants had been used for years in commercial advertising and public relations, and only later adapted for campaigns and elections. Fourth, the services of political consultants became all the more imperative because of the complexities of state and federal elections, which have become national in scope, engulfed in 24/7 media, an explosion of online and social media outlets, and seemingly unlimited campaign funds, often fueled by outside sources. Finally, as political consultancy has matured as a business, it has grown more competitive (and for some more lucrative), and firms have often merged with larger media and public relations conglomerates, serving not just candidates, but issue advocacy fights, business, and nonprofits alike.

Part I explores the beginnings of political consulting, the early use of polling, the coming of the television age, and the growth of consulting during the 1950s and 1960s. Chapter 1 focuses on the career of the first political consultants, the husband-wife team of Clem Whitaker and Leone Baxter, who, during the 1930s through the 1950s, worked on candidate elections, ballot initiatives, and issue advocacy campaigns. Chapter 2 looks at the formative years of public opinion research, which suffered a black eye with the wildly inaccurate 1936 *Literary Digest* presidential poll and the polling fiasco during the 1948 presidential election. It introduces several of the pioneer public pollsters as well as the first important private pollster, Louis Harris. Chapter 3 examines the beginning of radio, campaign films, and the birth of television, and how these communications media related to politics. It covers the beginning of television commercials, from the 1952 presidential campaign through the 1960 campaign.

Chapter 4 marks the beginning of the modern era of political consulting, with the emergence of pioneer general consultants, private pollsters, media consultants, and field operations specialists. Biographical sketches are presented of the leading pioneers in each of these fields, together with a look at the first political consulting professional organizations. Chapter 5 begins our discussion of the role of political consultants in presidential campaigns with a look at the role of media and polling consultants, in particular during the 1964 and 1968 presidential campaigns.

Part II of the book examines the expansion and growth of political consulting during the 1970s and 1980s. Chapter 6 looks at the major developments in campaign law and fundraising and introduces the next generation of political consultants, particularly important in general campaign management, media, and polling. Chapter 7 focuses on the evolution of polling, looking at how the science, techniques, and technology of survey research have changed. Several of the leading private pollsters are featured, and there is an examination of private polling done during the administrations of President Johnson through that of George H. W. Bush. Chapter 8 explores the media revolution, the move away from commercial advertising to political media firms, the explosion of cable television, technological advances in communication, and the fragmentation of the communications market. Several prominent media consultants are also profiled. Chapter 9 examines voter contact, through the first efforts at targeting voters, using direct mail and phone banks. Several important targeting and voter contact consultants are profiled.

Chapter 10 looks again at the role of political consultants in presidential elections. Here the presidential campaigns of 1972, 1976, and 1980 are examined. Chapter 11 examines the role of consultants in statewide contests, in congressional races, big-city mayoral contests, and the role of consultants in ballot initiatives. The final chapter in this section, chapter 12, looks at the role of political consultants during the 1984 and 1988 presidential elections.

Part III examines the transformation of political consulting from the 1990s to the present time, and the challenges ahead for consultants, US elections, and democracy. Chapter 13 focuses on the next generation of political consultants, those who became prominent during elections in the 1990s and early 2000s. Chapter 14 looks at the role of political consultants during the 1992 and 1996 presidential elections. Chapter 15 examines the technological and communication advances made during this time period, particularly in data management, microtargeting, and digital communication. Several key political consultants are profiled. Chapter 16 looks at the increasing role of political consultants in issue advocacy campaigns and in corporate and government affairs activities. Many of the features and techniques honed in political campaigns are now being used by corporations, labor unions, and others as they try to persuade the public or elected officials on certain issues. It also looks at the trend of several prominent firms being incorporated into global public relations groups.

Chapter 17 focuses on the role of political consultants during the 2000 and 2004 presidential campaigns. Chapter 18 examines the increasing role of American political consultants going abroad to ply their trade for candidates for high office throughout the world. Chapter 19 looks at the role of political consultants during the 2008 and 2012 presidential races, and chapter 20 examines candidates, outside dark money, and consultants during the 2016 presidential primary season. The final chapter, chapter 21, looks at the challenges and opportunities facing the business of political consulting, the impact of American elections, and the effect on our democratic system of government.

There are two appendixes. The first is a compilation of the major consultants and political operatives in presidential elections, from 1952 through 2012, along with operatives from the 2016 presidential primaries. The second lists the political consultants who were inducted into the American Association of Political Consultants Hall of Fame.

Campaigning in the Early Republic and Nineteenth Century

Campaign operatives and election sloganeering have been around for a long time. We can go back to Roman times for the first recorded evidence of campaign operatives giving advice. In 2012, Princeton University Press reissued what could be considered the first manual on campaign consulting, Quintus Tullius Cicero's campaign handbook, *Commentariolum*, which has been given a modern title of *How to Win an Election*. Quintus Tullius (102–43 BCE) was the younger brother of the famed orator and statesman Marcus Tullius Cicero, and was thought to have written the manual for his brother's electoral benefit. Furthermore, archaeologists have discovered evidence of robust politicking in the ruins of Pompeii. A century after Cicero wrote his handbook, Mount Vesuvius erupted in 79 CE, burying Pompeii and its citizens, along with some 3,000 political campaign inscriptions. As classics professor Philip Freeman described them, many of the tablets or inscriptions were from individuals and groups, hawking their favorite candidates; some were fake endorsements from "runaway slaves, gamblers and prostitutes"; others were from interest groups, like goldsmiths, grape pickers, or bartenders, urging citizens to vote for certain candidates.[10]

Throughout the centuries that followed, popular elections have often gone hand in hand with full-bodied debate and chicanery. From the very beginning of the American Republic, there have been robust and vigorously fought elections.[11] Communications professor Robert V. Friedenberg noted that the first political campaign in America of national scope was the 1787–1789 Constitution Ratification campaign, and the first political debate was between ratification advocate Theodore Sedgwick and anti-federalist John Bacon, who were seeking a seat on the Massachusetts Constitutional Ratifying Convention.[12] During the campaigns in Massachusetts and the other colonies, candidates received help from their friends and supporters who printed campaign literature, helped craft speeches, provided food, and staged events. Soon, this pattern of political assistance was shared with others as they prepared for ratification debates in their own states.[13]

John Beckley, a close friend of Thomas Jefferson and clerk of the House of Representatives, was considered America's first campaign manager, distributing political materials and enlisting surrogates for Jeffersonian Republican candidates. Some candidates for office, like James Madison, who stood for re-election to Congress in 1790, could run from the sidelines, staying in Washington and asking key gentlemen from his home district in Virginia to back him. Others had to work hard to get elected. One Kentucky candidate in 1806 complained that to obtain a seat in Congress a man "must for at least a year before the election totally neglect his private affairs" and perpetually "take the rounds, through the district with the velocity of a race rider."[14]

The 1800 presidential election, with Thomas Jefferson challenging incumbent John Adams, was both "the largest and most heated" election during the first decades of the nation. Historian Robert J. Dinkin stated that, "without question, more people were involved, more literature was distributed, more canvassing went on, and more interstate coordination took place than in any presidential race before the Jacksonian period."[15]

During the Jacksonian era, from 1824 through 1852, there were an extraordinary number of changes in electioneering. Campaigns for president began to be coordinated nationwide, the parties were reinvigorated with nominating conventions, party platforms, and elaborate party organizations. Mass demonstrations, torchlight parades, and other devices became commonplace, and campaign fundraising became crucial for the first time.

The 1828 presidential campaign, the bitter rematch between Andrew Jackson and incumbent president John Quincy Adams, saw a number of advancements in electioneering. The voting population tripled from that of 1824 because of the growth in national population, the extension of the franchise, high interest in the contest, and an emphasis on the popular election of presidential electors. The politically savvy New York senator Martin Van Buren served as Jackson's national campaign manager and before that as William Crawford's campaign manager in 1824.[16] During the election of 1836, William Henry Harrison appealed directly to the public in what might resemble the modern campaign speech.[17] There was also a new way to communicate with mass audiences. On May 29, 1844, word was sent from Baltimore, Maryland, to Washington, DC, over an experimental telegraph that James Knox Polk had been selected as the Democratic Party nominee for president. For the first time, the traditional method of transmission of news, through newspapers, had been bypassed by this experimental use of electronic media.[18]

Following the collapse of the Whig Party in the early 1850s, came the creation of the Republican Party in 1854, and with it the beginning of what Dinkin called the "Golden Age of Parties."[19] When Abraham Lincoln was running for president in 1860, Republicans created military-like organizations, called the Wide

Awakes, to drum up support and rally voters. The clubs were mostly composed of young people, who emphasized old Whig campaign tactics: "they built wigwams, raised flagpoles, displayed Lincoln fence rails, exploded fireworks, ignited bonfires, and held torch-light parades in hundreds of villages, towns, and cities."[20] This was something revolutionary in American political organization. The Wide Awakes electrified the presidential election, developing a grassroots movement with hundreds of thousands of members, from Maine to California.[21] Many of the Wide Awakes were paid by the campaign for their fieldwork. As Emerson D. Fite noted, "many men spoke every day for two or three months; ten thousand set speeches were made for Lincoln in New York State alone, 50,000 throughout the Union."[22] Other political marching clubs, some touting Stephen Douglas—the Little Giants, Ever Readys, Invincibles, and Douglas Guards—also added to the excitement and military flavor of the campaign.

Still, the presidential candidates themselves did little actual campaigning. They did not participate in the nominating process, waited at home for a party delegation to inform them that they had won the nomination, and said little or nothing during the general election campaign. Illinois senator Stephen Douglas broke this tradition in 1860. Sensing that he was trailing badly, Douglas embarked on an extended speaking tour. Another kind of politicking emerged during the 1880s with the "front porch" campaign. It was first used by Republican presidential candidate James A. Garfield, who received many groups and visitors in his hometown of Mentor, Ohio, and spoke to them, and through them, to the gathered reporters and wider public.[23]

During the last decade of the nineteenth century, the old "army-style" campaigning of the torchlight parades and Wide Awakes gave way to a greater emphasis on education and merchandising. Just as modern commercial advertising was beginning to catch on, presidential campaigns began creating campaign buttons, posters, cartoons, lithograph portraits of the presidential candidates, billboard likenesses, pamphlets, and tracts. In addition, electioneering stories proliferated in the 2,200 daily and 10,000 weekly, often partisan, newspapers.[24]

Mark Hanna and William McKinley

Marcus A. (Mark) Hanna is sometimes considered to be the first modern political consultant in the United States. He was a wealthy Cleveland industrialist, who increasingly dabbled in politics. He managed the presidential campaign of US senator John Sherman of Ohio, assisted his close friend William McKinley during his campaigns for governor of Ohio, and then became McKinley's chief adviser. Hanna retired from business in 1895 and turned to politics full time, helping McKinley's drive toward the Republican nomination for president. Hanna served as chairman of the Republican National Committee (RNC) and helped raise for McKinley a staggering $3.5 to $4 million in campaign contributions, mostly from corporate interests.[25]

The 1896 election between McKinley and William Jennings Bryan was fiercely fought and brought out more voters than any other presidential election up until this time. It took place under the cloud of national crisis, with major issues of political unrest, class conflict, economic depression, free silver, tariff, and violence stemming from labor unrest.[26] Hanna efficiently supervised the campaign that McKinley had devised, and thirty-year-old Chicago businessman Charles G. Dawes ran the day-to-day operation.[27] Bryan traveled 18,000 miles by train, reaching about 5 million people in his six hundred speeches. But McKinley decided to run a "front porch" campaign, raised and spent about $7 million, and recruited 18,000 persons to speak on his behalf.[28]

The 1900 re-election campaign, a rematch between McKinley and Bryan, was largely a duplication of the organization and fundraising of 1896. A total of 125 million pieces of campaign literature were distributed, along with 21 million postcards; and 2 million copies of newspaper material were sent out to over 5,000 newspapers.[29] Under Hanna's direction, the Republican Party was able to raise and spend about $2.5 million.[30] However, Hanna wasn't the first operative to collect large funds from corporations. "Boss" Matthew S. Quay, a Republican senator from Pennsylvania, had perfected the art of wresting large amounts of campaign cash from business interests during the previous decade.[31]

Ohio senator John Sherman was chosen as McKinley's secretary of state. Hanna replaced Sherman in the Senate and served in that capacity from 1897 until his death in early 1904.[32] Hanna is remembered today primarily because Republican political consultant and Bush II White House operative Karl Rove called Hanna his political hero.

Over the years, there have been other "president makers," political operatives and persons of wealth and power working behind the scenes, such as Colonel Edward House, George Harvey, and Robert Woolley during the ascendancy of Woodrow Wilson; Harry M. Daugherty for Warren G. Harding; Frank W. Stearns for Calvin Coolidge; Louis M. Howe for Franklin Roosevelt; and Joseph P. Kennedy for his son John.[33]

Public Relations and Presidential Campaigning

> *Political campaigns today are all side shows, all honors, all bombast,*
> *glitter, and speeches. These are for the most part unrelated to the main*
> *business of studying the public scientifically, of supplying the public with*
> *party, candidate, platform, and performance, and selling the public*
> *these ideas and products.*
>
> —Edward Bernays (1928)[34]

The business of public relations began to emerge in America around 1900. Most big corporations at the time were aloof to the press and simply shrugged off bad publicity. But there was growing public concern about the abuses of monopolies and the growth of corporate power. The early twentieth century produced reform-minded journalists like Ida Tarbell, who exposed the abuses of Standard Oil; John Spargo, who wrote about child labor; and Frank Norris, who found corruption and influence in the Southern Pacific railroad. Muckrakers had put corporations on notice that bad publicity was bad for business.[35]

When business interests were harmed, they began to turn to public relations men to repair their public images. Ivy Lee, one of America's pioneer advertising men, opened his publicity firm in 1915 and helped the Rockefeller family restore some of its image following the Ludlow Massacre in Colorado. This was America's most violent labor strike, resulting in at least sixty-nine deaths caused by Colorado National Guardsmen and retaliating coal miners in Rockefeller-owned mines.[36] Lee's work on Rockefeller's behalf was characterized as "more clever and contrived than the typical work of the whitewashers."[37] Journalist Upton Sinclair labeled him "Poison Ivy," and poet Carl Sandburg called him a "paid liar" who was "below the level of hired gunman or slugger."[38]

Lee, who later gave us the iconic image of Betty Crocker and the memorable Wheaties slogan "Breakfast of Champions," also advised the austere John D. Rockefeller to hand out dimes to city urchins to show his kinder and gentler side. Lee never advised candidates for office, but he was a forerunner in another aspect of political consulting—the care and feeding of the image of well-known politicians and others in the public eye. But in the 1930s, Lee's considerable reputation was ruined when it was revealed that he advised Adolph Hitler on how the Nazi government could improve its image in the United States.[39]

Albert Lasker and Warren G. Harding

During the 1916 presidential race, the George H. Batten Company became the first advertising agency to assist a presidential campaign, that of Republican nominee Charles Evans Hughes. As seen below, Batten's firm later merged with that of Bruce Barton, Roy Durstine and Alex Osborn forming Batten, Barton, Durstine & Osborn (BBDO), which became a major commercial firm and an important voice in mid-twentieth century Republican presidential campaigns.[40]

Shortly after Batten assisted the Hughes campaign, another important advertising man began helping presidential candidates. Albert Lasker began by sweeping floors at the advertising firm of Lord & Thomas in 1898; fourteen years later, he owned the company. Under his guidance, Lord & Thomas reached number one in the advertising business.

By 1915, Lasker was time probably the most famous advertising man in the country (and later ranked by *Advertising Age* as the ninth most influential public relations individual in the twentieth century),[41] had made Van Camp's Pork and Beans a household name throughout the country. He was so confident of his skills that he offered one year of free advertising for the cash-strapped Van Camp company. This caught the attention of industrialist William G. Irwin, one of Van Camp's major creditors and, more importantly, Republican National Committeeman from Indiana.

On Irwin's recommendation, Will Hays, the chairman of the Republican National Committee, reached out to Lasker, asking him to help the RNC in the critical 1918 congressional elections. Hays had the thankless task of trying to halt the infighting and lingering hostilities between Taft conservatives and Roosevelt progressives. President Woodrow Wilson had made a strong push for a Democratic-controlled Congress. To counter this effort, Lasker, heading the Republican publicity team, developed this message: Wilson was ungrateful for the contributions and sacrifices made by Republican citizens and the lawmakers they had elected to office, he was power-hungry, and he was intent on depriving the people of their political rights.

Lasker had one more weapon: former Republican presidents Theodore Roosevelt and William Howard Taft, old friends and then political enemies, publicly reconciled just one week before the November elections and urged "all Americans who are Americans first to vote for a Republican Congress."[42] One week later, Republicans swamped the Democrats, and now the GOP was in control of the Senate by a 49–47 margin and the House by a 239–194 margin.

The next prize for the Republicans was to recapture the White House after eight years of Democratic control. The 1920 Republican field reached nine candidates by the time of its nominating convention. California senator Hiram Johnson, retired Army general Leonard Wood of New Hampshire, Illinois governor Frank Lowden, and Ohio senator Warren G. Harding were among those vying for the nomination. Baking in the 100-degree heat in the unventilated Chicago Coliseum, the delegates were hopelessly deadlocked. After four days of the convention and four rounds of balloting, sixteen current and former US senators gathered in Suite 404 of the Blackstone Hotel, in the proverbial "smoke-filled room," and agreed that Harding would be the party's nominee. Yet it took until the tenth ballot on the convention floor before Harding finally had enough delegate support to secure the nomination.[43]

Lasker had backed Hiram Johnson and didn't really like or trust Harding, not only for the senator's support of the League of Nations but also because of his many rumored sexual indiscretions. Nevertheless, Harding was now a client, and Lasker would do his best to help Harding beat his Democratic opponent and fellow Ohioan, Governor James M. Cox. Historian John A. Morello observed that with the 1920 election, a "new alliance had been forged between politics and modern advertising."[44]

The first objective was to create an image of Harding as a down-home, everyday fellow from small-town America—in contrast to the "stuffed shirt" brittleness of departing president Woodrow Wilson. Part of this folksy image was the creation of an old-fashioned front-porch campaign, where supplicants and admirers would visit Harding in his hometown of Marion, Ohio, rather than Harding frenetically traveling from state to state trying to woo voters. The front-porch campaign would also help meet the second objective, to keep Harding from saying something stupid on the political stump. Harding never claimed to be the brightest of candidates, and those that knew him best wanted him reined in. "Don't let him make any speeches," admonished Pennsylvania senator Boies Penrose, "If he goes out on tour, somebody's sure to ask him some questions, and Warren's just the sort of damn fool that'll try to answer them."[45]

Harding, an old newspaperman, along with Lasker and the campaign leaders knew that they had to keep good relations with the press, many of whom were cooped up in Marion. They did so by feeding them tidbits of information, and enough news to keep them satisfied. Radio had not become a major communication medium in 1920, but newsreels, still photography, newspaper ads, billboards, and pamphlets were important vehicles for getting out the message. Reporters were flooded with Harding campaign materials. Lasker also had a team of Hollywood stars, including Mary Pickford, Douglas Fairbanks, and Lillian Gish, form the Harding-Coolidge Theatrical Team and make short films extolling the virtues of the Republican ticket. Al Jolson wrote a little ditty, "Harding, You're the Man for Us."

Lasker had Harding refocus his leisure image from golf (a rich man's sport) to baseball (everyman's sport) and had the Chicago Cubs (Lasker was part owner of the team), make a special junket to Marion, where they played the local team, and Harding threw out the first three pitches. The resourceful Lasker also paid hush money (at least $20,000) to have one of Harding's alleged lovers and her husband leave town. Lasker created a slogan for the campaign, "Let's be done with wiggle and wobble." We might scratch our heads, but "wiggle and wobble" probably meant something like "flip-flop" means today—changing policies or positions for mere political advantage. "Wiggle and wobble" became a standard line in Harding's speeches, was plastered on billboards, and appeared as the cartoon characters "Aunt Wobble" and "Uncle Wiggle" in Hearst newspapers. Lasker created special days for people to gather in Marion, like "Woman's Day" to appeal to the 20 million newly franchised women, or "Foreign Voters Day," "First Voters Day," or "Colored Voters Day."[46] He shipped 15 million pictures of Harding and Harding events to newspapers throughout the country, at the cost of $200,000.[47]

In all, Lasker applied emerging commercial advertising techniques to political campaigns: testimonials, preemptive advertising, market segmentation, a wide variety of media, including the new media of talking motion pictures and, to a lesser extent, radio. Above all, Lasker used a technique honed in his commercial advertising business: the "reason why" strategy, which gives the listener or reader a reason why they should buy a certain product, a message that should be both positive and aggressive.[48] Here, that product was Warren Gamaliel Harding, everyman. Why should you vote for him? Because he's just like you and believes what you believe.

Harding, with the help of Albert Lasker, crushed James Cox and the Democrats. Harding carried thirty-seven states, received 60.3 percent of the popular vote, and gained 404 electoral votes, while Cox received just 127 electoral votes and 34.1 percent of the popular vote.

Bruce Barton and Calvin Coolidge

While the focus was on Albert Lasker, another publicity man was working quietly with Massachusetts governor Calvin Coolidge. In 1919, Bruce Barton, Roy Durstine, and Alex Osborn formed an advertising agency bearing their names, which would soon dominate its field, with blue-chip clients like General Motors, General Electric, Gillette, and Standard Oil of New York.[49] Frank Stearns, a Boston department store baron, and Dwight Morrow, a partner at J. P. Morgan and Company, wanted to boost the chances of their fellow alumnus from Amherst College, Massachusetts governor Calvin Coolidge. They turned to Bruce Barton, another Amherst alumnus. Barton had earlier worked with other advertisers, providing George Creel's Committee on Public Information, the pro-war propaganda bureau set up by the Wilson administration, with screenplays for films.[50] He was also the author of a wildly popular book, *The Man Nobody Knows*, a 1925 biography of Jesus, whom Barton characterized as a man's man and the "founder of modern business."[51]

Barton liked Coolidge, and in late 1919 he began introducing him to the wider public. First through a glowing biographical piece in *Collier's* magazine, Barton worked on the brand and image of Calvin Coolidge. As Kerry W. Buckley notes, Coolidge was introduced "not as a political commodity, not by discussing the issues of the day, but by presenting a personality with whom Americans could identify."[52] Here was Calvin Coolidge: the courageous governor who stood up to the striking Boston policemen, the protector of American values, and a man of "unimpeachable ethnic/racial credentials." Barton crafted the image of Coolidge in his *Collier's* profile: "It sometimes seems as if this great *silent majority* had no spokesman. But Coolidge belongs with that crowd: he lives like them, he works like them, and understands."[53] A half century later we would hear the same themes, a great "silent majority" of Americans, with Spiro Agnew and Richard Nixon as their champion.

Barton had worked with two packaged goods giants, General Mills and Lever Brothers, helping them sell cereal and soap to mass audiences. Barton felt that politicians could be sold in the same way.[54] By early 1920 he not only was a publicist, but also a strategist for Governor Coolidge. He targeted special constituencies, writing pamphlets for teachers and leaflets for the delegates to the upcoming Republican national presidential nominating convention. Barton arranged a nationwide letter-writing campaign so that the popular magazine *Literary Digest* would include Coolidge in a series of interviews about presidential contenders.[55]

While Albert Lasker was burnishing Harding's image and reputation, Barton was doing the same for Coolidge. Using the advertising skills of Barton, along with the money of Frank Stearns and Frank Morrow, Coolidge was able to bypass the Republican Party. The energy and excitement over his 1920 presidential bid came almost exclusively from mass media coverage.[56] Coolidge did not win the presidential nomination that year, but the delegates—going against the wishes of Republican Party bosses—chose Coolidge as Harding's vice-presidential running mate.

While President Harding became increasingly engulfed in scandal, Bruce Barton was called upon to both burnish and protect Vice President Coolidge's image. Harding died in office in 1923, Coolidge became president, and in 1924 Coolidge ran for a full four-year term. The 1924 election has been called the "radio election," because the radio had become a common fixture in American homes. A decade before Franklin Roosevelt's radio "fireside chats," Bruce Barton advised Coolidge to tap this new medium, for "it enables the president to sit by every fireside and talk in terms of that home's interest and prosperity."[57] Barton coached Coolidge on how to use the radio effectively. Now, for the first time in most American's lives, people could sit in their kitchen or living room and listen to the president, talking directly to them. It was an intimate, new form of communication. Barton stressed that on the radio it wasn't the ideas that mattered, but personalities. Barton urged Coolidge to begin his campaign early, in late December 1923, to take advantage of the fact that the Democrats had not picked their standard-bearer. He urged the campaign to strategically place advertising in the right periodicals, and to create a tracking system to focus on the delegates to the July 1924 Republican nominating convention.[58]

During the presidential election campaign, Barton had the Coolidge campaign halt random nationwide door-to-door pamphleteering, and instead concentrate its efforts only on doubtful states. Today, candidates focus on "battleground states," the highly competitive states where the campaign will be won or lost. Barton had the same idea: Coolidge would easily win his home state of Massachusetts, but he would never win the died-in-the-wool Democratic state of Georgia. Stop wasting time and money on unwinnable or easily winnable states, he argued, and instead concentrate on those states where the margins were thin and the effort would pay off with electoral votes. Barton also stressed that campaign messages had to be crafted by professional advertisers, with style mattering more than substance. Barton urged that Coolidge take advantage of photo opportunities—and Coolidge would go out of his way to please photojournalists, even famously donning a Sioux Indian headdress in 1927.[59]

Bruce Barton later entered the arena of politics himself, and he was elected to the House of Representatives in 1937. There, he was a fierce and vocal opponent of Franklin D. Roosevelt—and the feeling was mutual. In the heat of his presidential re-election campaign in October 1940, Roosevelt derisively told an audience at Madison Square Garden that if it were up to "Martin, Barton, and Fish," there would never have been a program to help the British fight against Germany. Martin was the Republican leader Joseph Martin of Massachusetts, and Hamilton Fish of New York was chairman of the House Committee on Foreign Affairs. Barton was finishing his career as a New York congressman and was in the thick of an unsuccessful fight to become a US senator. The next time Roosevelt spoke, in Boston, the audience beat him to it, shouting out the tag line of "Martin, Barton, and Fish." The Democrat's campaign slogan for the 1940 election, thus, came alive during the week before Election Day.[60] Later, Wendell Willkie, the Republican presidential candidate in 1940, lamented, "When I heard the president hang the isolationist votes of Martin, Barton and Fish on me, and get away with it, I knew I was licked."[61]

After losing his Senate race, Barton toyed with some other political opportunities, but he eventually returned to BBDO and public relations. He openly supported Wendell Willkie over Thomas Dewey in 1940, but four years later he became part of a volunteer group, "the highest-paid public-relations minds" who met in New York City to help Dewey's 1944 presidential campaign come up with campaign ideas.[62] Barton helped Dewey again in 1948, and in his 1950 gubernatorial bid. Later, *Ad Age* recognized Barton as the fifteenth most influential public relations person in the twentieth century.[63] As seen in chapter 3, BBDO worked for the Republican National Committee and Dwight Eisenhower during his re-election campaign in 1956, and in presidential campaigns during the 1960s.[64]

Edward L. Bernays, the "Father of Spin"

Also helping Coolidge was the man later dubbed "the father of modern public relations" and the "father of spin," Edward L. Bernays.[65] Born in Austria in 1891, the nephew (twice over) of Sigmund Freud, Bernays began his public relations career in the United States in the 1910s, and was part of George Creel's US Committee on Public Information, the American World War I propaganda effort to "Make the World Safe for Democracy." In the 1920s, he worked for American Tobacco Company, linking Lucky Strike cigarettes to the women's rights movement, by having women marchers in New York City hold up Luckys as "torches of freedom." He also helped Procter and Gamble sell Ivory soap by setting up a nationwide soap-carving contest, with cash awards and plenty of press coverage; that contest lasted more than thirty-five years, until 1961.[66]

The problem with John Calvin Coolidge Jr., as Bruce Barton well understood, was that he seemed cold and aloof. He was "Silent Cal," speaking only when necessary. (An often-repeated story tells of a young woman at a dinner party betting that she could make Coolidge say three words. "You lose," said Coolidge, without looking up).[67] Theodore Roosevelt's irrepressible daughter, Alice Roosevelt Longworth, once said Coolidge was so sour he seemed to have been "weaned on a pickle."[68]

Enter Edward Bernays to help with a presidential personality makeover. Perhaps stealing from Albert Lasker's playbook, Bernays, just weeks before the 1924 election, brought a troop of forty Broadway performers on a midnight train from New York to Washington. Departing from Union Station in Washington, they formed a caravan of Cadillacs, shuttling to the White House, where the Coolidges were awaiting them for breakfast. After a pancake and sausage breakfast, they went out to the White House lawn, where the singer Al Jolson serenaded the president with a rousing song, "Keep Coolidge." And then something remarkable happened: the president smiled, and then he laughed.

The newspapers had a field day: the *New York Times* proclaimed "Actors Eat Cakes with the Coolidges . . . President Nearly Laughs," while the *New York Review* went even further: "Jolson Makes President Laugh for the First Time in Public."[69] In a stroke, Coolidge's image was reshaped (at least for the moment). Who knows if this helped, but Coolidge easily defeated the Democratic candidate, John W. Davis, with Coolidge receiving 382 electoral votes (54.0 percent) to 136 electoral votes (28.8 percent) for Davis. Davis won the old Confederate states, but nothing else. Coolidge won the rest of the country, except for Wisconsin, which went for progressive candidate and favorite son, Robert M. La Follette.

President Herbert Hoover, facing a tough re-election fight, was impressed by what Bernays had done for Coolidge. In October 1932, just a month before the election, Hoover called Bernays to figure out how to beat back the formidable challenge of New York governor Franklin Roosevelt and the constant stream of bad economic news being dumped on his presidency. Bernays wanted to recruit some 25,000 disinterested thought leaders, in a Non-Partisan Fact-Finding Committee, that would get the word out that the economy wasn't as bad as people thought, and that with Hoover re-elected to a second term, things would get better. But the cold, hard facts suggested otherwise, and 13 million people (23.6 percent of the adult population, the highest percentage ever recorded in US history) were out of work. Bernays's public relations magic could only go so far, and the public wasn't buying it or Hoover. The president was crushed by Roosevelt, offering a "New Deal," and capturing 472 electoral votes to Hoover's 59.[70]

At the same time that he helped Hoover, Bernays became public relations adviser to George Z. Medalie, the US attorney in New York, who was running against US senator Robert F. Wagner. Bernays wanted a bright, young liaison between his office and Medalie's, and he was given a young assistant US attorney, Thomas E. Dewey. This was Dewey's "first introduction to public relations, and he liked it," Bernays wrote.[71] Dewey would go on to become a famous US attorney who successfully prosecuted mobsters, was elected governor of New York, and was twice the presidential nominee for the Republican Party. But it took Dewey a long time to warm up to the idea of professional help for his own campaigns.

By 1940 Bernays was using much more sophisticated methods for campaign strategy. His client was William O'Dwyer, the district attorney for Brooklyn, who had become famous in prosecuting Murder, Inc., an organized crime syndicate. O'Dwyer was trying to unseat New York City's two-term mayor, Fiorello La Guardia. Bernays, contacted just two months before the election, gave campaign communications and message advice that was far ahead of its time. "I can only give you advice if I first know what people's attitudes are," wrote Bernays. "What do people expect of the mayor? What do they think of La Guardia? And what are the issues they associate you two men with?"[72]

Bernays had his staff fan out into each of the five boroughs of the city, survey thousands of potential voters, and ask them about their political attitudes. He then broke down the voters into ethnic and religious backgrounds, and conducted a "psychological survey." In his forty-six pages of recommendations, he targeted various audiences and suggested the kind of appeal that should be stressed for each. Targeting, survey research, and message development are done today on a very sophisticated level, but in 1940 campaigns this was unheard of.[73]

Bernays stressed message discipline, encouraging O'Dwyer to stick to basic themes. He also stressed the importance of individual words, giving a list of verbs that should guide the campaign's actions: ask, promise, appeal, urge, hope, advocate, declare, reveal, and others. Some political consultants today specialize in finding the right words for their candidates.[74] O'Dwyer narrowly lost to La Guardia, but he came back in 1944 to win the mayoral race.

Bernays admired James A. Farley, the Democratic Party's chairman who helped sell Roosevelt to the public in 1932. Farley told Bernays that the secret was, above all, that FDR had a great and memorable last name, a wonderful smile, and a great voice. Farley also engaged in a massive letter-writing campaign, sending individual letters to some 3,000 national, state, county, and city Democratic leaders, even to precinct captains. He bought a check-signing machine, signed the letters in green ink, and waited for the flood of letters that came back saying that Democratic leaders were behind Roosevelt.[75]

While earlier presidential campaigns had hired advertising specialists, the Alf Landon presidential campaign in 1936 was the first to hire full-time a commercial advertising agency. That agency, Blackett-Sample-Hummert of Chicago, was known for burnishing the image of Oxydol, Parker Pens, Lava Soap, and Gold Medal flour, and it would try do the same for the Kansas governor. But when word got out about the advertising arrangement, Landon was accused by his opponents of being "sold" through some "well-conceived marketing plan."[76] There may indeed have been a well-conceived marketing plan, but Landon went down to ignominious defeat, winning only Maine and Vermont.

While Lasker, Barton, Bernays, and other ad men dabbled in campaigns and politics, their real bread and butter came from commercial advertising. Yet one husband-wife California public relations agency, beginning in the 1930s, made politics their full-time business, and began what we today know as the business of political consulting.

PART I

The Early Business of Political Consulting, 1930s–1960s

CHAPTER 1

In the Beginning, Whitaker and Baxter

It was no accident that California inspired the first experiment in professional campaign management.
—Greg Mitchell (1992)

More Americans Like Corn than Caviar.
—Whitaker & Baxter, Public Relations Rule No. 10 (1935)

Whitaker & Baxter remain the giants in the field today.
—Robert J. Pitchell (1958)

CALIFORNIA, OFTEN THE trendsetter in fashion, culture, and ideas, was also the home of the first full-time political consulting firms. Why California? Robert J. Pitchell and others[1] have noted several factors. First, Californians amended their state constitution in 1911 to allow direct democracy, giving individual citizens and interest groups a direct voice in lawmaking through initiatives, referendums, and the recall of elected officials. But activists and groups needed help in organizing, collecting signatures on petitions, and communicating their concerns to others in order to pass citizen-driven propositions. With few exceptions, political parties did not become involved in the management of initiatives and referendums, and this vacuum was filled by private consultants.

Second was the immense size of the state, with the population centers of San Francisco, Sacramento, Los Angeles, and San Diego spread apart by hundreds of miles. In many ways, the centers of population were politically and culturally dissimilar to each other. Further, the state experienced a population explosion, particularly in the 1930s and 1940s, with millions of easterners, midwesterners, and southerners—with no ties to California politics and political parties—migrating to the Golden State. Third was the rise of political awareness among Californians, particularly during the 1930s with Dr. Francis Townsend's old-age pension scheme and Upton Sinclair's End Poverty in California (EPIC) movement, both drawing enormous grassroots support. The public had become increasingly aware of its power to affect legislation.

Fourth, political party organizations were nearly nonexistent, thanks in part to California's system of nonpartisan municipal elections. The Democratic and Republican Parties were weak and unable to operate effective political campaigns even for their own candidates.[2] Finally, California was America's new dream factory: Hollywood press agents and their publicity machine hawked talent, elevating the ordinary into the magical, making busboys and waitresses into stars and starlets, and propelling local talent into elective office.

Into this world came Clem Whitaker and Leone Baxter.

"Government by Public Relations"

In 1951, Carey McWilliams, a political reporter for the *Nation* magazine, wrote that Clem Whitaker and Leone Baxter had created something new in American politics. Theirs was "the first public-relations firm to specialize exclusively in political public relations."[3] They had been successfully doing so for fifteen years, under the name of Campaigns, Inc., but were more often referred to simply as Whitaker & Baxter. The firm, McWilliams observed, "evolved a style of operation which makes the old-fashioned boss and lobbyist completely obsolete. Whitaker & Baxter has ushered in a new era of American politics—government by public relations."[4]

In the 1930s, the business of campaign consulting or campaign management was simply unknown. Up until that time, campaigns were, in Leone Baxter's words, "the natural province of broken down politicians and camp followers."[5] Most campaigns had little understanding of strategic planning, few had workable campaign budgets, and for the most part they were without direction.

Before he was eighteen, Clement S. (Clem) Whitaker (1899–1961) became a reporter for the *Sacramento Union*, covering the state capitol. He later worked as the leading crime reporter for the *Union*. His son, Clem Jr., recalled, "Every murder that happened, every hanging that happened, whatever, that was my father's assignment. So we used to get some of the gory details as these things were going on."[6]

After serving a short stint in the US Army during World War I, Whitaker returned to the *Union* as an editor, and he later wrote a daily column for the *San Francisco Call-Bulletin*. From 1921 to 1930, he operated Capitol News Bureau, a news service that provided stories for more than eighty California newspapers, then sold it to United Press. Leone Baxter (1906–2001) was the manager of the Redding, California, Chamber of Commerce, and had been sent to Sacramento to work on a referendum.[7]

Clem Whitaker got involved in politics when his barber complained that his profession was having trouble getting a bill passed to create a state board of barber examiners. The old way of hiring a lobbyist, twisting some legislators' arms, hadn't worked. Whitaker had an idea: rely on barbers themselves, turn them into a grassroots lobby, and have them put pressure on their lawmakers back in their hometowns. The barbers liked the idea, and, for a fee of $4,000, Clem Whitaker had created a new business.[8]

The Central Valley Project

Clem Whitaker decided to continue this new line of business. His next client was John B. McColl, from Red Bluff, whom he helped get elected to the California Senate.[9] Later, the legislature passed a McColl bill that authorized a $170 million bond issue for the Central Valley Project Act, an ambitious plan to provide irrigation and public power. Opposing the Central Valley Project was Pacific Gas & Electric (PG&E), the giant public utility company. PG&E sought to defeat the project through a referendum, and it was ready to pour unlimited amounts of money into accomplishing its goal. On the advice of his friend Sheridan Downey, Whitaker hired Leone Baxter, who was working against the referendum for the Redding Chamber of Commerce.

Whitaker and Baxter called their firm Campaigns, Inc.,[10] and with a budget of $40,000 they bypassed the political parties. Using newspaper advertising and editorials, they went directly to the people to fight against the PG&E-backed referendum. They managed to get their message out to nearly every small-town radio station and newspaper outlet. They also made extensive use of radio, probably the first such use in a statewide campaign, handling everything from scripts to sound effects.[11] Clem Whitaker called this their "toughest" campaign, but they were able to defeat the referendum by 33,063 votes. Five years later, PG&E hired Whitaker & Baxter to oppose the "unfreezing" of the revenue bonds. Now working on the other side of the issue, Whitaker & Baxter was again successful. Pacific Gas and Electric had learned a valuable lesson, and from then on kept Whitaker & Baxter on an annual retainer.[12]

The 1934 California Governor's Race

> *The average American doesn't want to be educated. He doesn't . . .*
> *even want to work, consciously, at being a good citizen. But there are two*
> *ways you can interest him in a campaign. . . . Most every American likes a*
> *contest. He likes a good hot battle, with no punches pulled. So you can*
> *interest him if you put on a fight. Then, too, most every American likes to be*
> *entertained . . . he likes fireworks and parades. So if you can't fight, put on*
> *a show!*
>
> —Clem Whitaker (1934)[13]

In August 1934, California was stunned when Upton Sinclair—the muckraking author of *The Jungle*, avowed socialist, and leader of the End Poverty in California (EPIC) movement—won the Democratic primary for governor. Sinclair had been a Democrat for just a year, and he used the EPIC movement as his springboard to elective office. Sinclair's plan to end poverty involved taking idle land and factories in California and turning them over to cooperatives of unemployed workers. During the depths of the Great Depression, Sinclair's scheme caught fire. There were hundreds of EPIC clubs throughout California, and through his strong grassroots appeal, Sinclair overwhelmed his moderate Democratic opponent in the gubernatorial primary.

Sinclair and his movement were part of a much broader pattern of social unrest and turmoil, from politicians like Floyd B. Olson of Minnesota and Robert M. La Follette Sr. of Wisconsin, who were calling for democratic socialist reforms; to Huey Long in Louisiana, calling for "sharing the wealth"; to Dr. Francis E. Townsend's wildly popular Old Age Revolving Pension Plan, begun in Long Beach.

Conservative and monied interests were alarmed at the thought of Sinclair "Sovietizing" California, and they strongly backed the lackluster lieutenant governor, Frank Merriam, who was the Republican candidate for governor. In southern California, Albert Lasker's advertising agency Lord & Thomas was hired to assist Merriam. Lord & Thomas had created the widely popular radio show *Amos 'n' Andy*, and it used its skills to create anti-Sinclair soap operas. The firm also employed a sophisticated direct-mail program, targeting specific groups, and sent out appeals to out-of-state donors.[14]

Clem Whitaker had been approached to work for the Merriam campaign in northern California. But he balked. Whitaker thought Merriam was an "incompetent fool," and, more directly, he wasn't going to be simply one player in a larger campaign organization—he'd handle a campaign himself and run the whole show, or not play at all.[15] Sinclair was a friend of Whitaker's family, particularly Clem's socialist father, a Baptist preacher. But Clem couldn't abide the radical ideas of their old family friend. Whitaker later admitted that "it's always difficult to fight a campaign against a man you like personally."[16]

Nor would he work for one of his closest friends, Sheridan Downey, who was running for lieutenant governor. Downey, a Democrat, and the man who introduced Whitaker to the woman he would eventually marry, was playing for the wrong team. Instead, Whitaker took on his first major candidate, George Hatfield, a prominent San Francisco attorney, who was running on the Republican ticket for lieutenant governor.

While they nominally worked for Hatfield, Clem Whitaker and Leone Baxter focused their attention on destroying Sinclair. One of the first things they did was hole up in Sacramento, and for three days they poured through the voluminous— and politically charged—writings of Sinclair. They read every one of Sinclair's books and tracts, and lifted juicy quotes that made Sinclair appear radical or would offend voters.[17] Later, Clem Whitaker, when asked why Sinclair lost, said simply, "Upton was beaten because he had written books."[18]

The job was made easy by the astonishing range of institutions that were condemned by Sinclair: he went after the American Legion, the Boy Scouts of America, Christian Scientists, Baptists, the University of California, and the city of San Francisco, among others. The political consultants took phrases out of context and edited quotes to make them more scandalous—for example, they quoted Sinclair as saying that wedded bliss was nothing more than "marriage plus prostitution," and that every religion was a "mighty fortress of graft." If that weren't enough, Whitaker and Baxter excerpted quotes from dialogue spoken by unsavory characters in Sinclair's novels. From a 1910 Sinclair novel, they cobbled together three different lines of dialogue: "The sanctity of marriage . . . I have had such a belief . . . I have it no longer." The words were exact, but chopped from different sentences, and readers of anti-Sinclair editorials and pamphlets had no way of knowing that this was fictional material.[19]

At the same time, the state Republican Party hired Clem Whitaker to create and serve as the publicist for the California League Against Sinclairism (CLAS), a front group for big-money interests in northern California (a similar group, United for California, operated in the southern part of the state). Clem's job, again, was to smear the reputation of Upton Sinclair. Whitaker used direct mail, but he also found a lucrative business in using his Capitol News Service and his own advertising agency. Whitaker was cozy with about 700 newspaper publishers throughout the state: in those lean Depression years, the newspapermen needed every dime of advertising they could get. Clem Whitaker provided the newspapers with professionally written copy, "suggested editorials," and "news stories" about the horrors of Sinclair. His art director provided the newspapers with cartoons, one showing a big boot ready to stamp out an entire town dotted with church steeples; the caption merely read: "SINCLAIRISM." Whitaker shrewdly paid in advance for campaign advertising in these same newspapers. What followed was a relentless barrage of editorials, stories, pictures, and cartoons that savaged Sinclair.[20]

Perhaps for the first time, the motion picture industry became a major player is disseminating political campaign propaganda. One of its leaders, Louis B. Mayer, the president of Metro-Goldwyn-Mayer (MGM), was also the vice chairman of the Republican State Central Committee. Mayer and other studio heads threatened to pull the movie industry out of California if Sinclair were elected governor. During the campaign, the studios raised a half-million dollars to help Frank Merriam, extracting part of the fund from one day's wages from their employees.[21]

Movies and newsreels depicted the horrors of a California filled with the kinds of motley people Sinclair would supposedly attract. One newsreel showed vagrants (actually actors) headed to California to take advantage of Sinclair's supposed welfare schemes. A bearded actor with a thick fake Russian accent said he would vote for Sinclair because "his system vorked vell in Russia, vy can't it vork here?"[22]

But Sinclair's problems extended beyond the constant media attacks orchestrated by Whitaker & Baxter and the Hollywood studios. Sinclair at times was his own worst enemy. He made some off-the-cuff but costly remarks, saying, for example, "I expect half of the unemployed in the U.S. to flock to California if I'm elected."[23] Californians were reminded of this quip when anti-Sinclair forces rented 2,000 billboards across the state and reproduced that impolitic remark on them.[24] Despite Sinclair's urging, President Franklin Roosevelt would not endorse him and his movement, giving many California Democrats the excuse they were looking for to jump to the Republican side. Added to this was another candidate,

Raymond L. Haight of the Commonwealth-Progressive Party, who drained votes away from Sinclair.[25]

Merriam won the election, but not by an overwhelming margin. In a record-breaking turnout, Merriam received 1,138,620 votes to Sinclair's 879,537; Haight received 302,519 votes. This was an extraordinary election, one that journalist Greg Mitchell dubbed the "Campaign of the Century." Political scientist Walt Anderson observed that the "real significance of the Sinclair-Merriam campaign lies in the fact that a candidate—perhaps for the first time in American history, although certainly not for the last—was defeated, not by his opponent, but by a planned and coordinated use of the mass media of communications."[26] Historian Arthur M. Schlesinger Jr. was blunt, calling this gubernatorial contest "the first all-out public relations Blitzkrieg in American politics."[27] That media attack was thanks in no small part to Whitaker & Baxter's efforts.

While Sinclair lost the gubernatorial race, many Democrats were nonetheless elected to the state legislature. One of those swept into office on the EPIC-Democratic ticket of 1934 was Culbert Olson, who won a seat in the California Assembly. Four years later, Olson defeated the hapless Frank Merriam to become governor of California.

How Whitaker & Baxter Operated

At the time that Clem Whitaker and Leone Baxter opened their political campaign firm, campaigns were hardly considered businesses. Whitaker & Baxter would offer something new. The tired old political bosses could never stand up to a modern, hard-hitting public relations campaign, said Whitaker. It was necessary to build public attitudes by analyzing different political markets, employing alternative ways of framing appeals, and a variety of methods to distribute ideas.

Furthermore, they would offer full-service campaign management, a one-stop shop for candidates and their campaigns. "The candidate," wrote journalist Greg Mitchell, "just had to *be*—neither the candidate nor party headquarters had to *do*."[28] The candidate did not have to rely on party bosses for their approval, ward heelers to approve the message, or party hacks to chase after voters.

For a gubernatorial campaign, Whitaker & Baxter would set up an elaborate statewide organization, designed to do what a party organization would do, but without the problems associated with political party dynamics.[29] Their staff, normally about sixteen or twenty, would expand to forty or eighty, with northern and southern chairmen appointed as fundraisers and goodwill ambassadors for the candidate. After that, county, district, and local chairs were chosen, and then volunteer committees were created. The volunteers would be responsible for leaflet and publicity drops, speakers' bureaus, and other grassroots efforts.[30]

In the age before television, Whitaker & Baxter used a variety of communication tools. From a description of its services for a 1948 ballot issue, we see how the firm planned to communicate with the state's 4.5 million voters. Whitaker & Baxter mailed out 10 million pamphlets and leaflets, 4.5 million postcards, and 50,000 letters. It bought 70,000 inches of newspaper advertising in 700 daily and weekly newspapers; showed film trailers in 160 theaters, watched by 2 million people a week; bought 3,000 radio spots on 109 radio stations and twelve 15-minute radio network shows; and purchased 1,000 fourteen-sheet billboards and 20,000 posters. Whitaker & Baxter also used sound trucks, newspaper cartoons, and even skywriting.[31]

They honed in on certain mass communications techniques. For example, issues had to be distilled into themes or slogans, with simplicity and clarity. The appeal had to capture public attention and not simply focus on politics. There also needed to be a "gimmick." For example, during a 1948 referendum to repeal California's railroad full-crew law (what opponents called the "featherbedding" issue), Whitaker & Baxter had a campaign-created song, "I've Been Loafing on the Railroad," sung five to ten times a day for a month over 200 radio stations. For a school-aid initiative, they chose a catchy rhyme: "For Jimmy and me, vote 'yes' on 3." They targeted specific audiences, using market segmentation, to reach various racial, religious, economic, occupational, and sectional concerns.[32]

Whitaker & Baxter also invented the sinister "Faceless Man," the unnamed opponent against whom its candidate or cause could fight. In 1946, San Francisco mayor Roger Lapham was confronted with a recall election. There was no adversary; just his record as mayor. Lapham hired Whitaker, and Clem created an evil, anonymous opponent to fight against. Billboards and newspaper ads would show the shadowy profile of a man. But who was he? What were his intentions? What terrible things was he trying to do against Mayor Lapham? Why won't he come forward? The imaginary enemy, the "faceless man," became the target, and voters in the end refused to kick Lapham out of office.[33]

Journalist Irwin Ross stated that Whitaker & Baxter's "peculiar contribution" had been to make "a precise art of oversimplification, to systematize irrational appeals, to merchandise propaganda through a relentless exploitation of every means of mass communication."[34] In their own defense, and in a more reflective moment years later, Clem Whitaker said that "we search our souls to be sure we are not using tactics that will do damage to society." Leone Baxter reflected on the 1934 battle against Upton Sinclair: "We wouldn't operate like that now, would we, Clem?" she said to her husband.[35]

Working for and against Earl Warren

Clem Whitaker and Leone Baxter were hired to help California attorney general Earl Warren in his 1942 bid to oust Culbert Olson as governor. In the primary election, Warren ran an intensive, tiring, "economy-class" campaign throughout the state, and he had no real opposition on the Republican side. He easily won, pulling in 90 percent of the total Republican vote. On the Democratic side, where Warren was also on the ballot, voters were demoralized. Fewer than 50 percent of eligible citizens came out to vote, and Warren wound up with 404,778 votes, with only 515,144 going to the Democratic incumbent, Governor Olson.

Warren's platform included charges against Olson that sounded faintly like the Willie Horton charges against Governor Michael Dukakis some forty years later. The "darkest chapter" of Olson's administration, Warren charged, was his policy of pardoning criminals. Olson had released 28 percent of convicted criminals, "of whom 207 had been convicted of rape and 285 of other sex crimes."[36]

Until this time, Warren was a cautious politician, projecting a stern law-enforcement persona. But his public image would soon change: Whitaker & Baxter would humanize him. Years later, the reporter Carey McWilliams recalled his reaction: after Warren announced his candidacy for governor, he said, "I still remember the shock." Warren was at a grunion hunt, a uniquely California experience where revelers go down to the beach, build a bonfire, drink beer, and capture and eat the small, slimy fish.

> Here was our candidate for governor in a bathing suit, laughing and running up and down the beach, etc., etc. Now I had never seen a photograph of Warren like this. *Never.* When I first saw it, I said to myself, "That is the hand of Whitaker & Baxter. They are humanizing this man. They are making him a very—you know."[37]

From then on, Warren was photographed with his large and handsome family, smiling, playing together, eating dinner, projecting the image of a warm and friendly father who just happened to be running for governor. Indeed, *Time* magazine noted that Whitaker & Baxter had taught Earl Warren "how to smile in public, and were the first to recognize the publicity value of his handsome family."[38]

Yet, despite Whitaker & Baxter's assistance, it was still Earl Warren in charge of the campaign. As the Republican operative Murray Chotiner remarked, "Warren remained his own campaign manager. Others could set up committees, do the organizing, perform the routine jobs. It was Warren, however, who set the tone and philosophy of his campaign. He either made, or approved, every major decision. I would say that no one ever ran Warren's campaigns except Warren himself."[39]

But in the last week of the campaign, Warren fired Whitaker (whose name Warren consistently misspelled in his memoirs)[40] and totally broke off communications with him. Warren wanted to run a nonpartisan campaign, hoping to draw Independents and Democrats as well as Republicans to his side. In fact as seen above, he filed for both the Democratic and Republican nominations, running under the platform that "partisan politics had no place and must be eliminated, so that we can give President Roosevelt our unqualified support."[41] The trouble was, that Frederick N. Howser, a Los Angeles lawyer, had been chosen as Warren's running mate, and Howser insisted that the two Republicans run as a unified ticket. Warren said no, that this would go against his nonpartisan approach. "Finally," Warren wrote in his memoirs, Howser "personally told me that if I did not announce such a ticket, he would announce his withdrawal from the campaign, and say I had double-crossed him." But Howser didn't withdraw, and Warren was under great pressure to announce the Warren-Howser ticket. Warren remained adamant: he had always viewed the governorship as a bipartisan office, and he ran in the primaries of both parties.[42] Then, just one week before the election, Clem Whitaker announced from Warren's San Francisco campaign office that Warren and Howser would indeed run as a team. A furious Warren, campaigning in another part of the state, called Whitaker, telling him to close down the office and issue no more bulletins. "That was my last personal experience with Whitaker," Warren wrote, "and as far as I know it was his last important political campaign during the years I was governor. This is not to say I injured his business, as I was thereafter indirectly responsible for his making a fortune.[43]

Clem Whitaker and Leone Baxter would indeed reap a fortune, and that fortune came as a result of Warren's health-care proposal, and eventually the American Medical Association's battle against Harry Truman's national health insurance proposal.

The CMA and Warren's Health-Care Proposals

In 1938, Californians elected Culbert Olson as governor. He was the first Democrat elected to this office in decades, and one of his first acts was to propose a statewide health insurance plan that would cover employees with incomes below $3,000 (90 percent of the workforce) on a compulsory basis, while the self-employed could join voluntarily. The state seemed ready for such a bold proposal. In 1935, 1936, and 1937, the California Medical Association (CMA) had backed a form of compulsory state health insurance; then, in 1938, the Democratic platform called for such a program.[44] Olson naively assumed that the Democrats in the legislature would go along with his health insurance proposal, but ultimately the lukewarm reception from Democrats and opposition from doctors and business interests killed his plan.

Earl Warren and Culbert Olson disagreed on many issues, but once sworn into office, Warren decided to move ahead on a state health insurance scheme. In the fall of 1944, Warren had been hospitalized with a kidney infection, and that episode apparently focused his attention on the financial and personal consequences of catastrophic illness.[45] While not acknowledging it in his memoirs, Warren used the Olson plan as his starting point. Warren, usually an adroit politician, stumbled when launching his relatively modest health-care plan. He assumed the public would be on his side and would put pressure on the legislature, but he had not prepared the public for this policy initiative, and the support was simply not forthcoming. Nor did Warren prepare those legislators who were outside his inner circle of advisers on his plan.[46]

One group that was quite concerned about Warren's proposal was the CMA. One decade after its endorsement of a state health insurance program, the CMA was now firmly against such a scheme. In late 1944, Warren met with a contingent of doctors from the CMA to outline his plan. Warren considered this a courtesy call (and perhaps tacit approval from the doctors), but the CMA wanted more. The doctors wanted Warren to speak at their 1945 statewide House of Delegates meeting, and not announce his program until after hearing from the assembled members. But Warren went ahead and announced his plan in late 1944. The CMA, and particularly Dr. John W. Cline (later the president of CMA), were furious.[47]

Cline hired Whitaker & Baxter to handle the campaign against Warren's health insurance plan. Clem Whitaker was still smarting from his sacking at the end of the 1942 Warren gubernatorial campaign. As his son, Clem Jr., allowed, "I know that my father felt very strongly that he did not want to have anything to do with Earl Warren."[48] It would thus be sweet revenge to oppose a major policy initiative of Warren's.

The Whitaker & Baxter–CMA strategy involved attacking Warren's health insurance plan but also proposing an alternative, the California Physicians' Service, a private, voluntary insurance program that later became Blue Shield. Altogether, Warren proposed three versions in the course of three different sessions of the legislature. All were beaten back by the grassroots efforts orchestrated by Whitaker & Baxter: legislators received anti-health insurance letters and editorials from hundreds of groups throughout the state; a 9,000-doctor speaker's bureau was created to send delegations of physicians to Sacramento to lobby lawmakers and visit city and county officials; and 70,000 inches of advertising space in newspapers were purchased throughout the state.[49]

In his memoirs, Earl Warren remembered the struggle and the complete change in attitude of the CMA: "The principle of insurance which was by them [CMA] described as social progress in 1935 had become ten years later, 'socialized medicine, Communist-inspired.' . . . Nevertheless, they [doctors] stormed the legislature with their invective, and my bill[s] [were] not even accorded a decent burial."[50]

As late as 1966, a good twenty years after the California health insurance battles, the firm of Whitaker & Baxter still took credit for "the successful public-opinion campaign in opposition to former Governor Earl Warren's compulsory health-insurance program."[51]

The AMA and National Health Insurance

While the California Medical Association and Whitaker & Baxter were fighting back Warren's compulsory health insurance proposals, the American Medical Association (AMA), based in Chicago, was warily monitoring national legislation in Washington. During World War II, legislation pushed by Representative John D. Dingell Sr. (Michigan), Senator Robert F. Wagner (New York), and Senator James E. Murray (Montana) sought a federal system of hospital and medical coverage, funded through the payroll tax mechanism of Social Security. This Democratic plan, called the Wagner-Murray-Dingell plan, was the first real attempt at a federal health insurance program. It was first submitted to Congress in 1943, and resubmitted in 1945, 1947, and 1949.[52]

When Harry Truman won the 1948 presidential election, many were stunned. Nearly every commentator, pollster, and editorial writer had written off the Harry Truman–Alben Barkley ticket, knowing that there was no way it could stop Thomas Dewey and his running mate, Earl Warren. But not only did Truman retain the presidency, but Democrats also won seventy-five additional seats to regain control of the House of Representatives.

Perhaps most alarmed was the AMA, because with Democrats now in the majority in both the House and Senate, Truman was ready to launch a series of political reforms, including national health insurance. In his State of the Union speech, on January 4, 1949, Truman was emphatic:

> We must spare no effort to raise the general level of health in this country. In a nation as rich as ours, it is a shocking fact that tens of millions lack adequate medical care. We are short of doctors, hospitals, nurses. We must remedy these shortages. Moreover, we need—and we must have without further delay—a system of prepaid medical insurance which will enable every American to afford good medical care.[53]

For years, the AMA had feared that this moment would come. In preparation, it first removed its hide-bound chief spokesman, Dr. Morris Fishbein, and then it hired Whitaker & Baxter to assist it in fighting against any national effort. Whitaker & Baxter moved to Chicago to set up its own war room, and it remained there for the next three-and-a-half years.

In early 1949, Clem Whitaker prepared an overall battle plan for the fight against Truman's health insurance proposal. It sounded familiar themes that were first used in the fight against Earl Warren's California plan: "First, this is an affirmative campaign. Defeating compulsory health insurance is the immediate job, but stopping the agitation for compulsory health insurance, by enrolling the people in sound voluntary health insurance systems, is our most important objective. That's the only way to resolve this."

"Second," Whitaker continued, "this must be a *broad, public* campaign—with leaders in every walk of life participating—not just a doctor's campaign.... *A simple campaign program, vigorously and carefully carried out, is much more effective than an ambitious, complicated program, with some of the bases left uncovered.*"[54]

Clem Whitaker adopted a more acerbic tone at the National Editorial Association (NEA) meeting in Chicago, in November 1949. The assembled 500 members of the NEA heard Whitaker proclaim:

> This isn't a fight for freedom of medicine. This is a fight for freedom of the individual from government domination. The American people must be aroused to come to their own defense. They must be told the blunt truth, that the welfare state is a slave state, and that the cancerous growth of government-dependency is the most dangerous sickness in our world today.
>
> American doctors have become the second greatest force in the nation, second only to the American press, in alerting the people to the danger of socialized medicine.[55]

"Socialized medicine" was the perfect, damning label to wrap around Truman's national health-care plan. It played on the fears of Americans, afraid of some unknown socialist, even communist, menace. It fit in nicely with the red-baiting of the House Committee on Un-American Activities and rising stars in the post–World War II Red Scare, such as the young Richard Nixon of California and Joe McCarthy of Wisconsin. Clem Whitaker and Leone Baxter weren't the first to use the term, but they indeed knew how to exploit it.[56]

Mike Gorman, a newspaper reporter in Oklahoma, was fired from his job for writing an article favorable to the idea of national health in early 1949. Gorman returned to his home in California, and a few days later he received a telephone call from Clem Whitaker, asking him to join Whitaker & Baxter as it geared up to fight Truman's plans. Gorman averred, saying that he didn't think anything could stop the president's plan. "Oh, that's easy," said Whitaker, adding:

> We've been through this fight with Governor Warren's proposal for a state health insurance program and it's a cinch to beat it. In order to do so, there are only two things you have to have. First you have to give the program a bad name and we're going to call it 'socialized medicine' because the idea of socialism is very unpopular in the United States. . . . The second thing you have to have is a devil. You have to have a devil in the picture to paint him in all his horns and we've got that man chosen. We first thought we would center the attack on President Truman, but we decided he is too popular; but we've got a perfect devil in this man Ewing and we're going to give him the works.[57]

Oscar Ewing, the administrator of the Federal Security Agency, the organization that would administer a national health program, would be the devil. The attack wouldn't be against Truman or his plan; instead, it would be against the evils of "socialized medicine" and the threat to American freedom. Leone Baxter wasn't so kind: she called Ewing "the patent medicine man" for his "deliberate attempt to hide from the people the true cost and social consequences of the scheme of socialized medicine which he is proposing."[58]

"Socialized medicine" lived on and became a stock reply for those opposed to federal government intervention into medicine. It was an AMA theme against the creation of Medicare in 1965, and it was resurrected by opponents of President Obama's first-term health-care legislation.[59]

The AMA and Whitaker & Baxter swung into action. During the first several months after Truman announced his plan, the AMA poured out $1.4 million for its grassroots lobbying and publicity effort. Later, in December 1949, in an unprecedented move, the AMA instituted a compulsory annual dues payment of $25 per member to raise another $3 million.[60] For its efforts, Whitaker & Baxter reportedly received $350,000, and altogether during the three-and-a-half year period, some $4.7 million was spent fighting the president's plan. These were astounding, unprecedented numbers; no organization had ever spent so much money to defeat federal legislation.[61]

The Whitaker & Baxter team, now numbering thirty-seven, gathered endorsements from 8,000 nonmedical organizations—groups as diverse as the American Legion, the General Federation of Women's Clubs, fraternal organizations, business groups, and organizations large and small. They all pledged their resistance to national health insurance. Whitaker & Baxter distributed some 40 to 50 million pieces of literature to doctors' and dentists' offices, druggists, insurance agents, and others.

The campaign literature stressed "compulsory versus voluntary health insurance" or "Socialized Medicine versus The Voluntary Way." The message was not subtle. Here is an example of one of the AMA's releases:

> Who is for Compulsory Health Insurance? The answer: The Federal Security Agency. The President. All who seriously believe in a Socialistic State. Every left-wing organization in America ... The Communist Party.[62]

One effective piece of campaign propaganda was a poster featuring a well-known painting by nineteenth-century artist Sir Luke Fildes, showing a kindly family doctor at the bedside of a sick child, while a worried father watches on. The poster's text read:

> Keep Politics Out of This Picture!" .... Would you change this picture? Compulsory health insurance is political medicine. It would bring a third party—a politician—between you and your Doctor. It would bind up your family's health in red tape. It would result in heavy payroll taxes— and inferior medical care for you and your family. Don't let that happen here.[63]

Truman's health-care proposal, announced in his January 1949 State of the Union speech, was stopped cold by November. Whitaker & Baxter stayed on for the next two years to help the AMA fight against any similar proposals coming out of the White House or the Democrats in Congress. They were also instrumental in helping the AMA, doctors' groups, hospital staffs, insurance companies, and pharmaceutical representatives in opposing incumbent federal legislators who supported national health insurance. This three-year battle, the most expensive thus far waged by an interest group, made Clem Whitaker and Leone Baxter wealthy, admired by fellow conservatives, and feared by progressive and liberal policymakers.

Other Campaigns

Between 1933 and 1955, Whitaker & Baxter managed seventy-five campaigns and won seventy of them: thirteen of those campaigns were for major public offices, a few were for minor offices, and the rest were ballot propositions.[64] The firm had several subsidiary operations: Campaigns, Inc. planned and executed the campaign, while Clem Whitaker Advertising Agency placed all the advertising (and took the usual 15 percent agency fee), and their California Features Service provided news copy for some 700 newspapers throughout California.[65] Whitaker & Baxter candidate campaigns were "99 and 44/100ths percent" Republican campaigns, noted Clem Whitaker Jr.[66] The most important candidates, apart from Earl Warren for governor (1942), were Goodwin Knight (lieutenant governor, 1946; governor, 1954; governor and US senator in 1958) and presidential candidates Wendell L. Willkie (1940) and Thomas E. Dewey (1948). Earl Warren was Dewey's running mate, but Whitaker & Baxter did not work for the Warren part of the ticket in 1948. The breach between Clem Whitaker and Warren had not healed. The firm also handled a portion of Richard Nixon's 1960 presidential campaign. Whitaker & Baxter handled the presidential campaign of the Nixon-Lodge campaign in northern California, while Baus & Ross Campaigns handled southern California for the Republican ticket. Nixon won the state by just 36,000 votes, out of a record 6.6 million votes cast.[67]

The firm also handled numerous state initiatives and worked for several corporate clients.[68] Clem Whitaker Jr. summed up the practice: "We ran issue campaigns that didn't have too much of a partisan impact, some of them, and they were of a sufficient mix that we never got into the position where we were viewed as Standard Oil's people or as Southern Pacific's people. We were doing shipping campaigns and school campaigns and a whole variety of things that broke those barriers."[69]

After a 1958 falling out with their candidate Governor Goodwin Knight, Whitaker & Baxter became less of a factor in California politics. Whitaker sold his firm to his elder son, Clem Jr., and two associates, James Dorais and Newton Stearns, in 1958. The new owners assisted the Barry Goldwater for President campaign in California in 1964 and later helped former child movie star Shirley Temple Black in her unsuccessful bid for a congressional seat in 1967.[70] Clem Sr. and Leone then formed Whitaker & Baxter International, which branched out into national and international consulting for government relations. Three years later, in 1961, Clem Whitaker died and was survived by Leone Baxter, who died in 2001.

In summing up his career, Clem Whitaker was optimistic (or was it simply part of his advertising spin?) when he said, "We feel that people in our state are better informed, more alive to the issues, are better citizens because of our activities."[71]

Other California Campaign Firms

Several other public relations firms emerged in California during the late 1940s and 1950s. The California Commission on Campaign Financing concluded that by the 1950s, there were perhaps "dozens" of firms in operation in California, many of which were created by former employees of Whitaker & Baxter.[72] Harry Lerner, who had received his training with Whitaker & Baxter, set up shop in San Francisco. He successfully managed Edmund G. (Pat) Brown's 1950 and 1954 campaigns for state attorney general.[73] In 1956 Lerner defeated his old colleagues during an initiative measure to "unitize" California's oil fields, thus limiting the production of oil in the state (Proposition 4).[74] Thomas S. Page and Robert Alderman, also protégés of Whitaker & Baxter, created separate campaign management businesses. Page worked primarily in city campaigns, particularly for Board of Supervisor races in San Francisco. Alderman had managed Lieutenant Governor Goodwin Knight's re-election campaign in 1950, and several statewide and state legislative contests.[75] Other California campaign management firms included those of H. Harvey Hancock, D. V. Nicholson, and A. Ruric Todd.[76]

The Los Angeles-based firm Baus & Ross Campaigns, headed by Herbert M. Baus (1914–1999) and William B. Ross (1915-2003), was created in 1948. Baus had been publicity director for the Los Angeles Chamber of Commerce, and Ross managed the public relations efforts of the Los Angeles Home Show. When a local proposition calling for the construction of public housing appeared on the ballot, they jointly worked on a campaign to stop the proposition. They were successful, and out of that experience came their business partnership.[77] For the next thirty-five years, Baus & Ross Campaigns served California clients, especially Richard Nixon and Pat Brown. From 1948 through 1980, Baus & Ross managed over 100 campaigns, winning over 90 percent of them.[78] The firm was a pioneer in the use of survey research and direct-mail persuasion.

Herbert Baus and William Ross made the case for having seasoned professionals handle campaigns:

> Political campaigns are too important to leave to the politicians; too rich the prize, too complex and costly the process to entrust the struggle for political power entirely to party chieftains, political bosses, committee chairmen, hopeful candidates, ambitious insiders, and political 'volunteers' (paid or otherwise).
>
> They are all necessary as grains of sand to the final mix, but they require the added cement of professional management pros steeled and battle-readied in the crucible of political combat.[79]

Another campaign consultant was Murray Chotiner (1909–1974), a Los Angeles lawyer and political operative who ran several campaigns, but was most associated with Richard M. Nixon's ascent in California and then national politics. He had been campaign manager for Earl Warren and William F. Knowland, and in 1946 he was campaign manager when Nixon first ran for Congress against five-term incumbent Jerry Voorhis. Historian Stephen Ambrose wrote that this initial Nixon campaign effort was "characterized by a vicious, snarling approach that was full of half-truths, full lies, and innuendoes, hurled at such a pace that Voorhis could never catch up with them."[80]

In 1950 Chotiner was Nixon's campaign manager in the hard-fought, rough-and-tumble US Senate contest between Nixon and congresswoman and former Hollywood actress Helen Gahagan Douglas. Chotiner, a disciple of Clem Whitaker, was a difficult individual to like. Pat Nixon despised him and asked her husband to fire him, but Nixon decided that Chotiner's "hard-line, street-smart political advice was more important to him than his wife's objections."[81] Nixon charged Douglas with being soft on communism, the "Pink Lady" who often voted the same way as leftist congressman Vito Marcantonio of New York, and who could not be trusted to stand up to the forces of evil in the US Senate. She was, Nixon charged, "pink right down to her underwear."[82] Douglas, in turn, labeled Nixon "Tricky Dick," a label that would stick with him throughout his long, checkered career. Nixon was making a name for himself as a fierce anticommunist, committed to aggressively rooting out communist sympathizers. The liberal, sophisticated, but naïve Douglas fell right into the Nixon soft-on-communism, un-American-activities narrative and lost the election.

Chotiner was also a close adviser and campaign manager when Nixon was chosen by Dwight D. Eisenhower as his vice-presidential running mate in 1952. Nixon had been accused of taking money from a secret fund, created by political backers (see chapter 3). Chotiner advised Nixon to make public his side of the story. "Dick, all we've got to do is to get you before enough people talking about this fund, and we will win this election in a landslide," he said.[83] Nixon made a historic, half-hour speech, sponsored by the Republican National Committee, in which he defended his action and then attacked his opponents. This maudlin, self-serving speech, commonly called the "Checkers speech," was important to salvaging Nixon's place on the vice-presidential ballot.

At a May 1956 meeting of the Republican National Committee chairmen's campaign school in Washington, DC, Chotiner gave this hard-hitting advice: the first step toward attaining public office is to tear down your opponent before you start to run. "Like it or not," Chotiner explained, "the American people in many instances vote against a candidate, against a party, or against an issue, rather than for" candidates, parties or issues.[84] Political scientist Totton J. Anderson observed in 1959 that "the traditional Nixon-Chotiner formula for lineage-with-communism has practically become standard operating procedure for Republican campaigning in California."[85]

Nixon and Chotiner parted ways during the mid-1950s, principally because of investigations into Chotiner's alleged influence peddling, but in 1962 he was back assisting Nixon in the California governor's race. The California Democratic state chairman, Eugene Wyman, accused Richard Nixon in 1962 of condoning the "dirtiest" gubernatorial campaign in recent memory.[86] The Nixon campaign again was run by Chotiner. At the heart of Wyman's complaints were two pamphlets containing faked photos of Governor Edmund G. (Pat) Brown Sr., who was running for re-election. One of the photos had been taken several years earlier, and the pamphlet showed Brown in a prayerful attitude, saying: "Premier Khrushchev, we who admire you, we who respect you, welcome you to California." The overline read: "Brown is a Red Appeaser." Chotiner denied any involvement in the pamphlets.[87]

Brown was also attacked by a phony organization set up by none other than Whitaker & Baxter. The consultants employed an appeal that Nixon had used before: *Real* Democrats (that is, conservative Democrats) should be outraged at Brown, who sold out to the ultra-New Dealers and Kremlin-lovers. Voice your opinion and send money to fight against Brown. A half-million Democrats were sent this mailer, at a cost of $70,000, but it yielded just $368.50 from outraged Democrats.[88]

Murray Chotiner continued as an informal adviser to Nixon and became a member of the White House staff in 1969. He died in an automobile accident in early 1974, in the midst of the Watergate scandal.

Another firm, the Joseph Robinson Company, specialized in collecting signatures for qualifying petitions. Political scientist Stanley Kelley noted that from the 1930s through the mid-1950s, the Robinson Company had qualified over 90 percent of all propositions appearing on California ballots. The company charged between 15 and 20 cents per signature (in 2016 the rates were $1.00 and up). On occasion, Robinson also provided his services for both sides of an issue.[89]

In Washington DC, one of the important earlier campaigners was Joseph S. (Smiling Joe) Miller, who helped a number of prominent Democrat senators get elected to office, including Henry M. Jackson (Washington), Warren G. Magnuson (Washington), Wayne Morse (Oregon), Frank Church (Idaho), William Proxmire (Wisconsin), and Philip Hart (Michigan). In 1957, working for the Democratic Senatorial Campaign Committee, Miller was a particularly hot property, having helped six Senate Democrats win office. The *Washington Post* called him the Democrats answer to the Madison Avenue Republicans.[90]

Other advertising or public relations firms, both in California and in other states, worked in candidate or ballot-issue campaigns, but nearly all did so as a sideline to their main business for commercial clients. Writing about money and American politics in 1960, political scientist Alexander Heard surveyed public relations firms and "commercial politicians" that were involved in presidential and other US campaigns.[91] Altogether, 130 firms stated that during the years 1952–1957 they had participated in 554 political campaigns at all levels; further, they claimed to have over-all responsibility for managing 183 campaigns. The services they provided included arranging advertising space in newspapers or airtime for radio or television (57 firms), speech writing and preparing publicity materials (66), fundraising (36), and overall management of the campaign (41).[92] Those 41 campaign management firms were spread among fifteen states, but were mostly located in California, Texas, and New York. In addition to Heard's survey, Whitaker & Baxter estimated that by the 1950s there were probably no more than 30 to 40 firms that had managed political campaigns.[93]

CHAPTER 2

Measuring Public Opinion, 1930s–1960s

Polls go wrong, and that's all there is to it.

—Jim Farley (1938)

Public opinion . . . is the pulse of democracy.

—George Gallup (1940)

*No poll I have ever been witness to has made the candidate
a different man, has changed his position on an issue,
has made him into what he is not.*

—Louis Harris (1963)

W HAT DOES THE public want? What do voters believe? What do they think
about our candidate, our opponent, or about the campaign? For much of
the history of campaigning, that understanding of public opinion came
through educated guesses, reading newspapers and political tracts, and listening
to groups and individuals. But beginning in the 1930s, guesswork and political
horse sense about what the public thinks had been supplanted by rudimentary
survey research. Private polling consultants began their work in the 1930s, with
President Franklin D. Roosevelt seeking out the public's attitudes on a variety of
subjects. In the electoral arena, private polling was first used by John F. Kennedy
as he prepared for the 1960 presidential election. Public polling, conducted by
the media, had to overcome some serious and embarrassing mistakes during the
1936 and 1948 presidential elections, and for much of this time, candidates for
office and officeholders were reluctant to rely on survey results, either from public
sources like newspaper-commissioned studies or from private pollsters hired exclusively by the candidates or political parties.

From the earliest times in American politics, newspaper, organizations, and citizen groups conducted "straw polls" to gauge the opinions and

sentiments of the public. During the 1824 presidential election—that heated four-way contest between John Quincy Adams, Andrew Jackson, Henry Clay, and William H. Crawford, which eventually had to be resolved in the House of Representatives—a variety of opinion surveys were taken, with people raising their hands or marking secret ballots at Fourth of July celebrations, tax gatherings, grand juries, military musters, and special political meetings.[1] The first known American newspaper poll was conducted that year by the *Harrisburg Pennsylvanian*, asking citizens in Wilmington, Delaware, which presidential candidate they preferred. However, this kind of survey of public opinion, conducted throughout the nineteenth and early twentieth centuries, while interesting and perhaps entertaining, was inherently flawed. Nineteenth-century critics of these polls, even without an understanding of statistical analysis and scientific survey methodologies, raised valid objections: the straw polls were not being accurately reported, the groups polled were dominated by supporters of one candidate, respondents were often ineligible to vote, those who voted were unrepresentative of the area, and tallies were inaccurate. As social scientist Tom W. Smith pointed out, the straw polls were "seriously flawed and unscientific." Samples were haphazard with imperfect population targets, data collection was biased, and analysis of the data was too simplistic. Despite these flaws, the 1824 straw polls "did quite well" in their predictions.[2]

By the middle decades of the nineteenth century, straw polls formed an integral part of the partisan debate, and candidates for office took notice. In 1859, Abraham Lincoln observed that "public opinion in this country is everything."[3] In the middle of the nineteenth century, campaigns were often raucous spectator sports. It was not unusual to have high voter turnout in presidential elections, even 70 to 80 percent of eligible men. Straw polls added to the excitement. Newspaper reporters interviewed citizens on trains, at rallies, or at other public gatherings, and citizens polled themselves and reported the results to newspapers.[4]

Straw polling, however, became serious business in 1896, in the presidential contest between former congressman William Jennings Bryan, a Democrat from Nebraska, and William McKinley, a Republican and former governor of Ohio. Many newspapers conducted straw polls, and some were quite accurate. For example, the *Chicago Tribune* and the *Chicago Record* canvassed voters in person or with postcard ballots, and the results closely mirrored the actual results in Chicago.[5] During the first three decades of the twentieth century, presidential straw polls became commonplace among major newspapers, including the Hearst newspapers, the *New York Herald, Cincinnati Enquirer, Chicago Tribune, Columbus Dispatch, Cleveland Press*, and *St. Louis Times*.[6] The most well-known nationwide preference poll was conducted by the popular magazine *Literary Digest*, and from 1920 through 1932 it was remarkably accurate in predicting the presidential outcomes.

The *Literary Digest*

Beginning in 1920, the *Literary Digest*, a national magazine with a large circulation, published a nationwide poll predicting the outcome of the presidential election. Every four years, the *Literary Digest* polls predicted the results correctly, and the magazine congratulated itself over its "uncanny accuracy." Indeed, its 1932 presidential poll (between incumbent Herbert C. Hoover and New York governor Franklin D. Roosevelt) was just one percentage point away from the actual results. James Farley, chairman of the Democratic Party in 1932, was impressed: "Any sane person cannot escape the implication of such a gigantic sampling of popular opinion as is embraced in the *Literary Digest* straw vote.... It is a poll fairly and correctly conducted."[7] These presidential polls, along with the *Literary Digest* polls on other elections and other public policy issues, brought the magazine a great deal of credibility and increased readership. But all this came crashing down with the publication of its 1936 predictions, when the inherent flaws of the polling methodology led to an embarrassing miscalculation.[8]

In 1936 Roosevelt was running for re-election; his Republican opponent was Kansas governor Alf Landon, with North Dakota lawyer William Lemke, the candidate of Father Charles Coughlin's Union Party, as a third-party opponent. In late summer, the *Literary Digest* sent out 10 million straw-vote ballots (it had sent out about twice that number in 1932), drawn from telephone listings and automobile registrations; 2.5 million ballots were returned. Four hundred clerks spent September and early October tabulating the results, which were then published shortly before the November election. The poll results were clear: Landon would handily beat Roosevelt, 55–41 percent, with Lemke receiving 4 percent.[9]

The actual vote showed quite the opposite: Roosevelt overwhelmed Landon, 61–37 percent, with Lemke receiving just 2 percent; Roosevelt won 523 electoral votes, and all but two states. It was the most lopsided presidential contest in modern history up to that point.[10] The results crushed the reputation of the *Literary Digest*, which had been losing readers before 1936, and after the bungled poll changed ownership, it declared bankruptcy and folded. How could this happen? There were cries of foul: Had the *Literary Digest* been dishonest? Had its editors rigged the poll in favor of Landon? Was there some connivance to deny Roosevelt a second term? Pollster George H. Gallup, who in 1936 was just earning a national reputation, later remarked, "Disaster lay in the *Digest's* cross section and its sampling methods, not in the morals of its organizers."[11]

In fact, Gallup challenged the *Literary Digest* poll even before it came out. In a July 1936 newspaper column, using a 3,000-person sample drawn from the same automobile registration and telephone lists used by the *Literary Digest*, Gallup forecast that, based on that sample, Landon would get 56 percent of the vote, and that result would be far off the true mark, not anywhere near the actual results. The *Literary Digest* editor, Wilfred J. Funk, shot back an indignant response in the *New York Times*: "I am beginning to wish that the esteemed Dr. Gallup would confine his political crystal-gazing to the offices of [Gallup's own] American Institute of Public Opinion and leave our *Literary Digest* figures politely and completely alone." Never before had anyone—particularly an upstart competitor—dared to say in advance that the *Literary Digest's* methods of prediction might be wrong.[12]

Actually, others had criticized the methodology, but not so publicly. Long before the 1936 poll results, some academics and professional pollsters had warned that the straw poll methods were flawed. A study by a Columbia University sociologist showed that there were at least eight sources of potential error, including class bias in the *Literary Digest* poll.[13]

What then had gone wrong? First, there was a sampling problem: the addresses of the 10 million persons who received ballots from the magazine came from telephone numbers and automobile tags. The middle class and well-off (mostly Republicans) were overrepresented, and those who could not afford a telephone or an automobile (mostly Democrats) during the Depression years were underrepresented. Political scientist Peverill Squire notes, however, that even respondents who both owned an automobile and had a telephone were solidly for Roosevelt, and if all 10 million had returned the ballots, Roosevelt still would have been the predicted winner, albeit with a far smaller margin.[14] Second, there was a nonresponse problem. The better educated and wealthier respondents (Republicans) were more eager to fill in the ballot and return them than were Roosevelt supporters.[15]

In early elections, the sampling and nonresponse problems were masked by the Republican victories in 1920, 1924, and 1928. With the 1932 election, there was a rare crossover of upper-income voters choosing Roosevelt over Hoover, and the sampling problems were not detected. But then came the 1936 fiasco, a black eye for the nascent survey research industry, and the demise of a popular magazine.[16]

Crossley, Gallup, and Roper

Survey research became a growing business after World War I. By 1932, there were at least eighty-five polling organizations, mostly regional or local, that were conducting public opinion surveys. The *Literary Digest* poll was the most well-known at the national level, but there were three other organizations, all coming out of a background in market research, that also were gauging the mood of the public nationwide.

The leading pollster of the day was Archibald M. Crossley (1896–1985), who entered the market research business in 1918, and created his own research firm, Crossley, Inc., in Princeton, New Jersey, in 1926. He had also developed the Crossley Radio Survey, which published the results of telephone interviews on the preferences of listeners in fifty cities. By the 1936 presidential election, Crossley was conducting polls for the Hearst newspapers; he relied on personal interviews, rather than mail-in questionnaires, for election forecasting. Crossley predicted a Roosevelt win in the 54–55 percent range, but the fiercely anti-Roosevelt Hearst papers muted (and downplayed) the results: "Roosevelt in Lead but Crossley Poll Finds Landon Victory Quite Possible" read one headline.[17] But he wasn't always right. As noted below, Crossley, along with Gallup and Roper, predicted wrongly that Thomas E. Dewey would defeat Harry Truman in the 1948 presidential election. Crossley was a pioneer in developing psychological dimensions for questionnaires, and he was particularly interested in the wording of survey questions and the intensity of answers.

The second prominent pollster was George H. Gallup Sr. (1901–1984). Gallup earned his BA, MA, and PhD degrees from the University of Iowa, then taught journalism at the University of Iowa, Drake University, and Northwestern University. During the late 1920s and early 1930s, he conducted research for the *Des Moines Register, Des Moines Tribune, Cleveland Plain Dealer*, and *St. Louis Post-Dispatch*.[18] In 1932, he joined the advertising agency of Young & Rubicam as head of marketing and director of research. Gallup's interest in public opinion and politics was partly inspired by the desire to assist his mother-in-law, Ola Babcock Miller, a Democrat, in winning an election (and then re-election) to the office of secretary of state in Iowa.[19] Mrs. Miller may have been the first candidate for American elected office to benefit from private polling, which showed that, while being a Democrat, she nevertheless had a good chance of winning in that traditionally Republican state.[20]

Gallup founded the American Institute of Public Opinion (AIPO) in 1935 in Princeton, New Jersey. His first syndicated public opinion poll, "America Speaks" debuted on October 20, 1935, and was featured in at least twenty-five newspapers across the United States.[21] Gallup was "creating newspaper content that would interest the common man, convince more of them to buy newspapers, lead interested readers to advertising, and thus please publishers."[22] Each weekly segment of "America Speaks" presented one question, the poll results, and articles by the newspaper reporters. The inaugural question, asked during the depths of the Depression, was timely: "Do you think the expenditures by the government for relief and recovery are too little, too great, about right?"[23]

Gallup predicted that Roosevelt would win in 1936 with 54 percent of the popular vote and 477 electoral votes (his actual win was 61 percent and 523 electoral votes). Yet Gallup also made some big errors in the 1936 election forecast: he was 28 points off in Arizona and 24 off in Minnesota, with a median error rate of 12 percent in the states where he was wrong.[24]

The third competitor was Elmo Roper (1900–1971), who began his career in the family jewelry business in Iowa, but then pioneered in the fields of market research and public opinion analysis. From 1935 through 1970, he was director of the Fortune Survey, sponsored by *Fortune* magazine, the first nationwide poll based on sampling techniques. Roper's *Fortune* survey during the fourth quarter of 1936 wasn't a direct forecast, but it showed that Roosevelt was the "favorite," with 61.7 percent, less than a 1 percent deviation from the actual vote results.[25]

Roper's surveys during the 1940 and 1944 presidential elections proved to be the most accurate of the three. During World War II, Roper was recruited by William (Wild Bill) Donovan to be deputy director of the Office of Strategic Services (OSS), charged with finding the best recruits for the new intelligence agency. Roper later became a "dollar-a-year" man for the Office of War Information, Office of Production Management, the Army, and the Navy, surveying the public on wartime issues and the transition to a peacetime economy. Just after World War II, with the cooperation of George Gallup, Roper established the

Roper Center at Williams College. Now housed at Cornell University, the Roper Center for Public Opinion Research is the world's largest archive of public opinion surveys, representing the work of more than 150 polling firms in the United States.[26]

Quota and Probability Sampling

Instead of surveying millions of people by using mail-in ballots (the method used by the *Literary Digest*), Crossley, Gallup, and Roper contacted just a few thousand voters who were identified and selected to represent the population as a whole.[27] They were interviewed in person, a time-consuming and expensive method, but one that proved to be far more accurate than the straw vote methods of prescientific polling.

George Gallup used the technique of quota sampling in his surveys. Census data were used to determine the population characteristics of those to be surveyed. The census data determined, for example, that x-number of men over fifty should be surveyed, along with y-number of women living in a defined geographic part of the state, z-number of women under thirty, and so forth. The choice of who should be questioned, however, would be left up to the interviewer. The key advantage of quota sampling was cost savings: interviewers would not have to go block to block, could interview the most convenient persons, and could avoid costly and time-consuming legwork. But there were drawbacks: the crucial element of randomness was lost when the interviewer selected the subject, resulting in over- or underrepresentation of particular groups of individuals. After the 1948 presidential election, the quota sampling method fell into disrepute.[28]

It is generally agreed that while the theoretical roots of sampling theory extend back to the late nineteenth century, the first use of probability sampling came during the mid-1930s and was improved upon during the next two decades.[29] The sampling process identifies, selects, and then contacts individuals from a given population, using some form of random selection. The first large-scale use of probability sampling in the United States was undertaken by the federal government, through the Works Projects Administration in 1939, seeking to determine estimates on unemployment and the size of the labor force.[30]

Both Crossley and Gallup conducted small surveys, using the techniques of probability and quota sampling, and correctly predicted the election outcome. These techniques, wrote Martin R. Frankel and Lester R. Frankel, "provided a clear repudiation of the generally accepted notion that quantity in the number of respondents provided the ultimate measure of data quality and accuracy."[31]

The 1948 Presidential Polling Fiasco

In 1940, public polls performed better in predicting the outcome of the presidential campaign than they had in 1936.[32] The Roper organization, with a staff of eighty-one trained interviewers, focused on attitudinal scales, which permit respondents to express gradations of opinion. Roper conducted its polls for the Fortune Survey, and its results of forecasting the popular vote were characterized as "amazingly accurate." The American Institute of Public Opinion (Gallup

Poll) used 1,100 part-time interviewers, mostly trained through the mail, for its state-by-state analysis. The Crossley poll was also correct in predicting the outcome of the 1940 presidential election. All three polling organizations relied on expensive and time-consuming personal interviews, rather than the less reliable mail-in ballots.

There were, however, some major embarrassments in 1940. Franklin Roosevelt's first private pollster, Emil Hurja (see below), conducted a poll for *Pathfinder* magazine, which relied on mail-in ballots and gave Wendell Willkie a heavy electoral victory and a narrow popular vote victory over Roosevelt. Roger Dunn of Dunn Surveys relied on neither mail-in ballots nor personal interviews, but on secondary estimates of public opinion, like newspaper circulation and amount of WPA employment. Dunn predicted a landslide for Willkie. In the end, Roosevelt won 449 electoral votes and 54.7 percent of the popular vote, while Willkie had just 82 electoral votes and 44.8 percent of the popular vote.[33]

During the 1944 presidential election, the public polls performed credibly, with the Roper Fortune Survey again the most accurate. The Gallup and Crossley polls, on average, were within 2 or 3 percentage points of the actual vote in their state-by-state analyses. Yet, as social psychologist Daniel Katz explained, the 1944 record was "less a reflection of recent scientific advances in public opinion research than an indication of the increasing skill in the use of old techniques."[34]

Still, the memory of the 1936 polling errors lingered on. Writing in 1948, political scientist Earl Latham observed, "The memory of the *Literary Digest* poll of 1936 must lie in the nostrils of today's commercial poll-takers like the odor of coffin flowers, a mixture of fragrance and fright."[35] As Latham wrote this, the second big polling fiasco was about to unfold: the misreading of the 1948 presidential election.

Hardly anyone in the know expected President Harry Truman to beat Thomas E. Dewey in the 1948 presidential election. Democrats were split badly, demoralized, and in a sour mood. Deep South conservatives had bolted from the party, forming their own Dixiecrat movement under the banner of South Carolina governor Strom Thurmond. Northern liberals and radicals sided with Henry Wallace, Truman's former secretary of commerce and Roosevelt's former vice president, who was running under the banner of the Progressive Party. There was speculation that Dwight Eisenhower, just beginning his service as president of Columbia University, might be drafted for the Democratic nomination instead of Truman. Few political commentators respected Truman. The fiercely Republican *Chicago Tribune* called him a "nincompoop"; others were less kind. No political commentator worth his salt would have predicted that the ticket of Harry Truman and seventy-year-old Alben Barkley from Kentucky had a chance against the 1948 version of the "dream team," New York governor Thomas Dewey, who had put up a good fight for president against Roosevelt in 1944, and his running mate, the popular governor of California, Earl Warren.

During the summer of 1948, the three national pollsters—Gallup, Crossley, and Roper—each reported that Dewey was ahead of Truman by a wide margin. On September 9, roughly eight weeks before Election Day, Elmo Roper announced that he would no longer publish polls on the presidential race. "Thomas E. Dewey is almost as good as elected," Roper declared. "That being so, I can think of nothing duller or more intellectually barren than acting like a sports announcer who feels he must pretend he is witnessing a neck and neck race."[36] Roper's announcement had special significance: he had been the most accurate of the major pollsters in 1936, 1940, and 1944, and now he was telling the world that further polling wouldn't be needed.

But, in the end, undecided voters began breaking Truman's way, farmers and rural voters also turned to Truman, and the president was able to hold on to most of the South, despite the threat from the Dixiecrats. One of the most famous photos in American political history is a beaming Harry Truman holding aloft the *Chicago Tribune*, which recklessly proclaimed "Dewey Defeats Truman." Pollsters were just as embarrassed as Robert R. McCormick's Chicago newspaper and its wishful thinking. A month later, Daniel Katz wrote that "to the world of applied research the poor predictive performance of the polls was as much of an upset as the election of President Truman was to the newspaper world."[37]

Truman won the popular vote with 49.5 percent, carried twenty-eight states, and received 308 electoral votes. All three pollsters predicted that he would lose, with Gallup predicting a popular vote of 44.5 percent, Crossley predicting 44.8 percent, and Roper predicting 37.1 percent. The three pollster overestimated Dewey's popular vote (45.1 percent) by 4.4, 4.8, and 7.1 percent, respectively.[38] Thomas Dewey's own analysis of why he lost in 1948 was direct and simple: "You can analyze figures from now to kingdom come, and all they will show is that we lost the farm vote which we had in 1944 and that lost the election."[39] But why didn't the pollsters pick up on this?

Survey researcher Albert H. Cantril, son of pollster Hadley Cantril, later wrote that the 1948 election would "serve as a reminder of how far removed the polls were from the rough and tumble of the campaign."[40] Unlike today, when poll results are published daily (even hourly) throughout the crucial final weeks, there were no tracking polls or exit polls on Election Day to explain why voters chose Truman.

A thoroughly deflated Elmo Roper, the pollster with the best reputation in predicting past elections, conceded, "I could not have been more wrong. I don't know what happened."[41] Wilfred Funk, who was ridiculed for his *Literary Digest* poll of 1936, was asked for his reaction. "I do not want to seem malicious," he said, "but I couldn't help get a good chuckle out of this."[42] Comedian Fred Allen also got a chuckle, saying that Truman "was the first president to lose in a Gallup, but win in a walk."[43]

One poll was right on target: Just before the election, the Staley Milling Company in Kansas City conducted an informal survey—a straw poll—of farmers who came to buy feed bags. They could choose a sack of feed with an elephant on it (Dewey), or one with a donkey (Truman). On the day before the election, the results were announced, and Truman won, 54 to 46 percent. The chicken feed was called Pullet Atoms, and from then on the Staley Milling Company's survey was called the Pullet Poll.[44]

The Pullet Poll provided some comic relief, but the serious, professional poll-sters were deeply embarrassed. Just like in 1936, there were charges of fraud and calls for investigations. One obvious problem was that the pollsters stopped sur-veying opinion too soon. They simply didn't appreciate last-minute decisions by voters. Experts weighed in, condemning the polls as careless, with unintentional bias, errors of judgment, and the use of outmoded survey techniques. The Social Science Research Council, in a special report on the 1948 election surveys, con-sidered eight methods for measuring polling error, and concluded that the failure to accurately predict the outcome created "widespread confusion and misgivings about the reliability of the polls.["][45] Cabell Phillips of the *New York Times* put it another way: "Now that they have suffered a major defeat, the once rather cocky poll-takers have been confessing the vulnerability of their methods."[46]

But just two years later, George Gallup boasted that his company's predic-tions in the 1950 congressional elections had been the most accurate forecast in its fifteen-year history, with a vote deviation of just 0.7 percent.[47] The AIPO had learned valuable lessons from the 1948 embarrassment, and it used new survey techniques during the 1950 cycle to improve its predictions. Gallup saw three problems in 1948. First, pollsters failed to capture last-minute shifts in voter senti-ment; in fact, his firm had stopped polling 10–12 days before the election. Second, undecided voters in 1948 were assumed not to be interested, and thus would not vote. However, as later surveys found, a sizeable group of the electorate, 8.7 per-cent, moved from undecided to Truman. Third, there was a failure to determine who would turn out to vote and who would not. This had been a low-turnout election, with a million fewer people voting than in 1940, despite the population increase. Gallup was convinced that by polling until just before election day (and sending the results by telegram), and by probing the choices of undecided voters and determining who would vote and who would stay at home, the survey results would have produced far more accurate surveys. In 1949 surveys in the governor's race in New Jersey, the US Senate race in New York, and the 1949 Canadian gen-eral election, AIPO, using refined techniques and more probing questions, was able to achieve more accurate surveys.

Other media polling firms took root in the 1940s and 1950s. The Texas Poll, established by Joe Belden in 1940, became the first statewide public opinion sur-vey. The *Des Moines Register* developed the Iowa Poll in 1943, and the *Minneapolis Tribune* began the Minnesota Poll in 1944. In 1947, Mervin Field established the California Report, now called The Field Report, which publishes approximately thirty to fifty media polls annually. Field drew attention to his surveys when he correctly predicted that the 1948 presidential election would be a virtual dead heat, rather than an easy Dewey victory.[48] In addition, the *Boston Globe, Detroit Free Press, New York Daily News, Chicago Tribune,* and *Portland Oregonian* began sponsoring statewide and local public opinion surveys in the late 1940s and early 1950s.[49]

Today, media and other public polls seem to appear nonstop throughout the primary and general election season. In recent presidential elections, some forty or so organizations regularly published public opinion survey results. Straw polls, despite their unreliability, certainly have not faded away. Rather, they have proliferated—on television, the Internet, and in social media. Recent presidential elections have been replete with straw votes, testing the strength, likeability, and electability of candidates. Other elected officials have also gotten involved. Members of Congress frequently post straw polls on their websites, asking citizens about policy issues and posting the results, often without any disclaimer that such votes have no scientific validity.

Private Polling

Public polling receives a lot of attention because it appears in newspapers and other communication outlets, and is meant to inform (or entertain) the reader. Another side of survey research is private polling, which is not shared with the public, but instead is meant to give the client valuable information about customers or the public. Since the early part of the twentieth century, companies have been conducting private market research studies, trying to determine the tastes and preferences of potential consumers. All three major public opinion researchers—Crossley, Gallup, and Roper—got their start conducting market research on consumer preferences for various products. Soon, private survey research extended to election campaigns and public policy.

Public (or media) polling and private polling have different purposes. Louis Harris, who was the first important private presidential campaign pollster (see below), and later became an influential media pollster, explained the difference between public and private survey research. The biggest difference is that for the private pollster, the "precise percentage point standing is far less important than the extent to which the poll clearly shows an understanding of the dynamic elements at work in the election itself." Newspapers are far more interested in who is ahead, who is catching up, and who fell behind, rather than understanding why voters decided the way they did. Published polls, Harris argued, usually have "statistical validity, but often lack the full reporting that gives a reader an understanding of what forces really are at work in an election. Technically, private and public polling are likely to differ little. The private poll, however, will have concentrated more on probing the reasons that lie behind the voter's choices. It will leave far more room for free expression."[50]

Except for George Gallup's surveys for his mother-in-law in Iowa, private polling did not emerge until the mid-1930s. Private polling for candidates for president did not begin until the 1940 campaign, but earlier, Franklin Roosevelt and the Democratic Party used pollsters to assist them in probing public opinion.

Franklin Roosevelt and Private Polling

Franklin D. Roosevelt was the first president to make systematic use of private public opinion polling when he used the surveys of Emil Hurja (1892–1953), and later those of Hadley Cantril (1906–1969), to advance his legislative and policy agendas. Thanks to these polls, Roosevelt had "a secret weapon" that he could use to become a stronger and more adept president.[51]

A former Air Force captain, Emil Hurja served the Democratic National Committee and the White House from 1933 through 1936 as a polling analyst and political consultant.[52] Hurja had taken classes on polling and politics at the University of Washington, became a mining industry journalist in Alaska and Texas, and later worked as a mining stock analyst at a Wall Street brokerage firm. He was versed in statistical techniques, particularly those known today as random sampling, quotas, weighting, and representative cross-sections. None of these concepts, however, had been used before to predict presidential elections.[53]

Hurja tried to persuade New York governor Alfred E. Smith's 1928 presidential campaign to use statistical methods for forecasting results, but Democratic National Committee (DNC) chairman John J. Raskob would have none of it, characterizing Hurja as a crank with a crackpot idea. The would-be pollster tried again in 1932, when Franklin D. Roosevelt was the Democratic candidate. Hurja sent a memorandum to the DNC outlining a statistical method for analyzing "political sentiment" for the upcoming presidential election.[54] This time, the DNC agreed to see what Hurja could do.

Hurja set up a program to systematically monitor American newspapers. From the 12,964 dailies and weeklies, he focused on the 175 leading newspapers and created a system that allowed Democratic chairmen and precinct workers to carefully monitor the size of the story, where it was placed, and the paper's political affiliation. Hurja also monitored radio stations' editorial "attitudes."[55] Further, he systematically tracked all state polls and vote returns from the past election. He gave the sage advice that "borderline" states (what we would later call "battleground" states) should be given the most attention. Hurja also helped the Democratic Party determine the rewarding of patronage jobs, by identifying areas of the country with pockets of Roosevelt loyalists.[56] *Collier's* magazine described Hurja as the "prophet extraordinary of the Democratic party."[57] The *Saturday Evening Post* called him the Democrat's "political doctor" who collected all kinds of straw votes, "including tests of sentiments at barbecues, picture houses and hog-calling contests," and translated the data into "colored cubes, pyramids, cylinders, curves and zigzag lines."[58]

Hurja's own polls were conducted under the cover name of National Inquirer. He emphasized that a poll is not something that just hits the nail on the head, but its value comes in detecting the direction and speed of change.[59] He developed a method that later would be called "trend analysis" to track the changes in the course of an election. He also used what political scientists Lawrence R. Jacobs and Robert Y. Shapiro later would call "priming"—using popular policy issues to influence (or prime) the electorate's standards for evaluating a candidate or office holder's personal attributes—as seen in the polling conducted for Presidents Kennedy, Johnson, and Nixon.[60]

Hurja's 1936 predictions showed a heavy Landon drift in certain areas of the country. But Jim Farley, Roosevelt's campaign manager, who correctly predicted that Landon would win just two states, Maine and Vermont, knew that something was amiss with Hurja's numbers: "Having unshaken belief in his figures like all poll operators, [Hurja] disregarded my constant warnings that the figures were so far wrong as to be positively worthless."[61] Farley's exact prediction was so remarkable that one leading pollster in the inaugural issue of *Public Opinion Quarterly* said that Farley was "the best predictor of them all."[62] But was it based on optimism, good luck, political horse sense, or scientific sampling? Undoubtedly it was a combination of the first three. Hurja finally broke with Roosevelt over the president's decision to seek a third term in 1940.

The second private pollster used by Roosevelt was Hadley Cantril. In 1940 Cantril created and became director of the Office of Public Opinion Research at Princeton University. (Princeton, New Jersey, became the epicenter of public opinion research in the United States, with the polling firms of Cantril, Gallup, Roper, together with Claude Robinson's Opinion Research Corporation). Cantril began conducting surveys to determine public attitudes on politics and social issues.[63] Soon he was providing the White House with the results of public opinion surveys. While the administration had access to Gallup, Roper, and other pollsters, Gallup was not in favor, because he was thought to have strong Republican sentiments. Cantril, on the other hand, was a loyal Democrat who publicly backed the president.[64]

At first, Cantril relied on survey data provided by Gallup's organization and funding from the Rockefeller Foundation. But in 1942, Cantril, assisted by a financial angel, millionaire Gerard Lambert, created the Research Council. Lambert's family business made a famous household product, Listerine, and much of the product's success came from using the best of consumer polling to test the effectiveness of its advertising and slogans ("cures halitosis.") Lambert wanted to get involved in public service, and that led him to financially assisting Hadley Cantril.[65] Over the next two years, Cantril supplied Roosevelt's senior advisers with a flow of public opinion studies. They met in Washington, at Lambert's house on Kalorama Circle, and the advisers later passed the polling information on to Roosevelt himself.[66] The Research Council had carte blanche on what to survey: the economic health of the country, progress of the war, postwar issues and concerns, and so on. In 1977 the *New York Times* revealed that during its decade of existence, the Research Council had also been covertly funded by the Central Intelligence Agency.[67]

In 1941 Roosevelt wanted to help Britain as it courageously fought against the Axis powers. However, he did not want to get too far ahead of American public opinion. Once a month, during the six-month period from May through October 1941, Cantril asked Americans this question: "So far as you personally are concerned, do you think President Roosevelt has gone too far in his policies of helping Britain, or not far enough?" Some 70 percent of the respondents approved of what Roosevelt was doing, while just 22 percent disapproved.[68]

On March 1, 1944, toward the end of the extraordinarily difficult and costly Italian campaign, Roosevelt worried that the bombing of Rome would hurt his standing with American Catholics. One morning, around 9:00 a.m., Lambert received a telephone call from the White House: could he and Cantril find out, quickly, what the reactions of American Catholics would be?[69] Cantril asked this question: "If our military leaders believe it will be necessary to bomb Rome but take every precaution to avoid damage to its religious shrines, would you approve this decision?" Among Catholics, 66 percent approved, while 27 percent disapproved; Protestants approved in higher numbers, 81 percent, with 13 percent disapproval. Two days later, on March 3, Rome was heavily bombed, with railroad yards and airports heavily damaged, but not religious sites.[70]

Cantril also conducted survey research on domestic issues. For example, in a 1943 survey of 2,000 farmers, Cantril asked whether farmers approved or disapproved of subsidies. What he found was a "widespread ignorance" on the part of farmers about Roosevelt's farm program.[71]

Private Polling after Roosevelt

Since Roosevelt, every president has used private polling to test the mood of the country, prime voters, and take action. Truman had "serious doubts" about the accuracy of polling, particularly with the 1948 election in mind. Writing in his memoirs in 1956, Truman noted that he "never paid any attention to the polls myself because in my judgment they did not represent a true cross section of American opinion."[72] Dwight D. Eisenhower used polling on a limited basis, but there is evidence that he did follow public attitudes toward North Korea and the activities of Senator Joseph McCarthy of Wisconsin.[73] Both the Truman and Eisenhower administrations minimized the use of polls, but Truman's White House had quietly and behind the scenes reached out to survey research firms. Both administrations used secret State Department/National Opinion Research Center (NORC) surveys that concluded that the White House should be independent of party benefactors.[74] The Republican National Committee (RNC), which had hired the advertising firm of Batten, Barton, Durstine & Osborn (BBDO) to produce television commercials for the 1952 campaign, also signed a four-year contract with BBDO to provide weekly tracking polls, analyzing the opinions of about 1,200 persons each week. The results were shown to Eisenhower.[75]

The primary source of public opinion analysis for the Eisenhower team in 1952 came from Sigurd (Sig) Larmon, then the president of the advertising firm Young & Rubicam. Larmon was well placed, having been a mentor to George Gallup and a friend of both Dwight Eisenhower and his chief of staff, former New Hampshire governor Sherman Adams. Larmon provided the White House with advice on public opinion and public information not only during the 1952 campaign, but throughout Eisenhower's eight years in office.[76]

Private presidential polling came of age during the 1960s and beyond, and will be explored further in chapter 7. As survey researcher Charles Roll observed in 1982, the private pollster had displaced party chairmen, like the Democrat's Jim Farley or the Republican's Leonard Hall. "Old style political advice—subjective, arguable, derived from intuition, gut-feeling, and past experience—has given way to the objectivity and finality of cold, hard figures, vividly presented and perceived as realities in their own right."[77]

While the White House sought public opinion analysis, very few members of the US Congress conducted or commissioned polls during the 1930s and 1940s, and lawmakers had mixed feelings about the usefulness of public opinion surveys. By 1953, only 48 out of 438 members of the House of Representatives had conducted surveys, and most of those did not use random samples.[78]

John Kennedy and Louis Harris

The first presidential candidate to use private polling data was Thomas Dewey in 1940. The polling was financed by the same Gerard Lambert who had assisted Hadley Cantril and the Roosevelt White House. After Dewey lost the Republican Party nomination to Indiana businessman Wendell Willkie, Lambert financed opinion polls for Willkie, who became the first presidential candidate in a general election who had the benefit of survey research advice (which he ignored). Jacob K. Javits, running for Congress in New York in 1946, was the first congressional candidate to commission a private poll, from the Roper organization.[79]

During the 1952 presidential campaign, Dwight Eisenhower's advertising agencies, Ted Bates and Company and BBDO, had consulted with Gallup about possible themes for their television ads—"Eisenhower Answers America!"—but the Gallup organization did not conduct polls specifically for the Eisenhower campaign.[80] Further, Gerard Lambert conducted a number of polls during the fall campaign, and Joseph E. Bachelder did some polling for the 1952 and 1956 campaigns.[81]

During the 1950s, few candidates for office conducted private polls. When they did, it was usually late in the contest and served more as a check to see how things were going, not as a principal element of strategy.[82] Charles Roll had a small number of private contracts with Republican candidates, and in the early 1960s, Frederick Currier's firm, Market Opinion Research (MOR), worked for auto executive George W. Romney in his bid to become governor of Michigan. But because of the visibility of the Kennedy presidential campaign, Louis Harris became the best known of the early private pollsters, and, according to William R. Hamilton, another important early pollster, it was Harris "who truly spawned a new industry or profession in 1960."[83]

Louis Harris (b. 1921) began working at the American Veterans Committee shortly after the conclusion of World War II, and there he met Elmo Roper. After the 1948 election and the black-eye that it gave the polling business in general and Roper in particular, Harris went to work for Roper and was put in charge of political polling. In 1954 Harris caught peoples' attention when he wrote a book, *Is There a Republican Majority?*,[84] the first in-depth national political analysis of the 1952 Republican presidential and legislative victories.

Harris was having a difficult time working for Roper, and in July 1956, much to Roper's bitter disappointment, Harris left the firm, took several key clients, and started his own business, Louis Harris & Associates.[85] Harris was already making a name for himself, and Washington syndicated columnists Stewart and Joseph Alsop repeatedly praised his polling skills. The Alsops were conducting their own informal surveys throughout the country, and they praised Harris's techniques and methods.[86] One of Harris's early clients was Richard C. Lee, the mayor of New Haven, Connecticut, and some of the questions asked in a survey commissioned by Lee involved a probable 1960 presidential contest between Vice President Richard M. Nixon and Senator John F. Kennedy of Massachusetts. Lee liked the way Harris conducted his survey and suggested to his friend, John Kennedy, that Harris might come in handy.[87] Harris was thirty-six when he first began working for Kennedy. He also caught the eye of journalist Theodore White, who characterized Harris as a "young, shrewd, vibrant, a man who found subtleties in statistics" and who became "so entranced by the Kennedy personality" that he became a Kennedy "zealot."[88]

While Dewey had private polling available to him, John F. Kennedy became the first presidential candidate to take advantage of private survey research analysis.[89] Two years before the West Virginia primary, in the summer of 1958, the Kennedy campaign sent Harris to that state to assess public opinion.[90] The Kennedy campaign adopted two innovations suggested by Harris: to poll in separate states rather than undertaking national surveys, and to integrate polling research into the campaign's strategic considerations.[91]

In 1960 there were just sixteen Democratic primaries, starting, as usual, with New Hampshire on March 8, which Kennedy easily won. The real test would be the Wisconsin primary, held on April 5, with Kennedy and one of his chief rivals, Minnesota senator Hubert H. Humphrey, meeting head to head. Wisconsin had a complex system of choosing delegates, and it was an open primary, allowing anyone, not just Democrats, to vote. Kennedy announced he would run in the Wisconsin primary on January 21, and then moved his entire operation to Wisconsin for the next two months. Harris conducted a series of polls reaching 23,000 voters, all conducted door-to-door, statewide and in selected congressional districts, in what probably was the largest person-to-person political survey research ever conducted up until that time.[92]

One of the major issues Harris wanted to explore was how voters felt about a Catholic running for president. From the surveys, Harris determined that Wisconsin Catholics believed that in order for Kennedy to win in the state, he would need every possible Catholic vote he could garner. As Shaun A. Casey observed, "Catholics identified with Kennedy and felt they must rally to one of their own, since if they didn't, no one would."[93] Harris also concluded that Kennedy should do everything possible to avoid the appearance of a pro-Catholic bias: no church-state speeches, no appearances at Catholic churches, and no photo opportunities with Catholic clergy. But in other states, the message would be tailored according to local public opinion. Harris recommended that Kennedy attack the religious issue on television in Minnesota, and tell of his belief in separation of church and state in Maine.[94] In West Virginia, Harris and seventeen of his workers polled in a swing district weeks before the primary, and found virulent opposition to the notion of a Catholic president. Armed with that news, Kennedy bought television time on all West Virginia stations. Flanked by Franklin Roosevelt Jr., and while placing his hand on a Bible, he declared that his presidency would not be influenced by the Catholic Church or by the pope. Follow-up polling by Harris showed that Kennedy's message had mollified many undecided primary voters.[95]

Irwin Ross of the *New York Post*, writing two major articles on Harris just a week before the 1960 election, contrasted the "newer" techniques used by Harris with the old methods used by Gallup and Roper: "Lou Harris or the Alsops can . . . tell you what working class voters in Seattle or hog farmers in Iowa are thinking—what their grievances, prejudices, aspirations are, as well as how they are likely to vote." By contrast, with Roper and Gallup polls, "one gets only a skimpy impression of the real concerns that are moving broad masses of people."[96]

By studying the interconnection between Harris's innovative polls and the Kennedy election campaign, political scientists Lawrence Jacobs and Robert Shapiro argued that Kennedy used the Harris policy and issue findings to shape his candidate image.[97] As Jacobs and Shapiro confirmed in their quantitative analysis of polling and policy issues, Kennedy responded to the issues that were raised in the public opinion polls taken by Harris. The polls showed that the public was particularly interested in social issues (increasing Social Security, passing healthcare legislation, reforming education), the economy (fighting unemployment, worried about the high cost of living), and security and foreign affairs (bolstering America's military spending and reputation abroad). Not only did Kennedy emphasize the issues found salient in Harris' polls, but "the frequency and strength of his stance was congruent or consistent with the public's preferred *direction* for policy."[98] Altogether, the Kennedy campaign commissioned Louis Harris to conduct fifty polls during the Democratic primaries and twenty-seven during the general election.[99] Kennedy "was the easiest client I ever had to communicate with," Harris later remembered.[100]

The Kennedy campaign reached out to other public opinion sources as well. Computer analysis of survey research findings was just coming of age, and Robert F. Kennedy, managing the campaign of his brother, was intrigued with the polls and computer simulations performed by Simulmatics Corporation, an organization created by political scientist Ithiel de Sola Pool and psychologist Robert Abelson. The academics collated 66 polls and 100,000 voter surveys, developed 480 distinct voter types, and generated voter-driven profiles of Kennedy and Nixon.[101] But the Simulmatics data did not play an important role in the Kennedy campaign, because the Democratic National Committee doubted the usefulness of the meta polling data.

Following the success of the Kennedy campaign, Louis Harris was at the top of his game. He was not a dispassionate bystander, but an enthusiastic participant in the game of politics. In his later years, Harris reflected:

I earned a reputation for polling candidates partly because. . . . See, there are certain things you can't fake. You can't fake politics, you can't fake sports. . . . A lot of people claim to be experts. I made myself an expert in politics, and I worked in politics as well as poll-taking. And I felt that [George] Gallup and I totally disagreed. Gallup never registered to vote, never voted. He was a eunuch, he got to be so remote from the political process.[102]

But in April 1963, Louis Harris announced that he would no longer conduct private polling for political candidates or political parties. His firm began with five full-time employees and fifty part-time field workers and grew to thirty full-timers and a network of 3,000 part-time field operators nationwide.[103] In February 1963, Harris abandoned private polling in favor of public opinion consulting for the Columbia Broadcasting System, under a six-year contract with CBS News. Harris was just forty-one years old when he made this decision, and his firm, Louis Harris and Associates, founded in 1956, had been the most important in the fledgling business of private polling. But he was exhausted. During its eight years of operation, Harris's firm had conducted 214 election campaigns, including campaigns for forty-five US senators, twenty-five governors, New York mayoral candidates, and, most famously, Kennedy in 1960. During the 1962 election cycle, Harris had polled for candidates in forty-four states. His principal partner, Oliver Quayle III, left the firm, chiefly because of the decision to drop political polling for private clients, and set up his own firm, Oliver Quayle & Company, in Bronxville, New York.[104]

In 1969 Harris sold Louis Harris and Associates to a brokerage firm, and in 1975 it was sold to the media giant Gannett Company. During this time, Harris stayed on as head of the polling organization. In 1992 he left Gannett to form his own polling firm, L.H. Research. In 1996 the Gordon S. Black Corporation acquired Louis Harris and Associates from the Gannett Corporation.[105]

In these early days, despite Kennedy's use of Harris's polls, survey research still played only a minor role in campaigns. Pollster Douglas E. Schoen summed up the attitude of campaigns and candidates: "No one believed polls should be an important part of day-to-day political campaigning, much less orchestrate every aspect of a campaign." The idea that polls could be used "to monitor a race or determine tactics in midstream was simply unheard of."[106]

CHAPTER 3

Radio, Television, and Campaigning, 1920s–1960

This is the worst thing I've ever heard of, selling the presidency like cereal.
Merchandising the presidency. How can you talk seriously
about issues with one-minute spots!
> —Adlai E. Stevenson II, presidential candidate (1952)

What Truman achieved in months of whistle-stop campaigning,
Kennedy and Nixon, in 1960, could achieve with one televised speech or one
Sunday morning interview on national television.
> —Gary A. Donaldson (2007)

Without television, Kennedy would have been neither nominated nor elected.
> —W. J. Rorabaugh (2009)

A T THE BEGINNING of the twentieth century, candidates and political causes relied on newspaper advertisements, magazine articles, pamphlets, fliers, billboards, and direct mail. In 1900 some candidates for Congress began experimenting with a new technology, the graphophone, honing their public speaking voices and having them recorded on wax cylinders and played back through a brass funnel. But the usual form of campaign advertising remained the printed page. About half of the money spent on campaigns during the early decades of the century went for print advertising, and candidate ads were beginning to look more and more like the pleas and come-ons found in commercial advertising.[1] Writing in 1927, political scientist Edward M. Sait observed that running for office "is a great selling campaign. The parties advertise their wares—platforms and candidates— just as the manufacturer of a breakfast food or shaving cream . . . present[s] [the candidate's] case to consumers through the medium of newspapers and magazines."[2]

By the early 1920s, other forms of mass communications were being developed. Radio was coming into living rooms, and in movie theaters, patrons soon discovered the new sensation of the "talkies," motion pictures with synchronized sound. Even before the October 1927 premier of *The Jazz Singer*, the first full-length picture with synchronized dialogue, sound had been introduced in short-subject movies, a medium that was soon discovered by officeholders and candidates. Then came television. In 1941 the first commercial television station was established in New York City, and by midcentury, candidates for governor, the US Senate, and the presidency were experimenting with these revolutionary new media, taking their cues from public relations and advertising consultants. They adjusted how they spoke, what they said, what clothes they wore, and how they presented themselves to the public. With the advent of radio, campaign films, and especially television, Edward Sait would undoubtedly have agreed, we were entering a whole new chapter in the great selling campaign.

Radio, Campaign Films, and Politics

The first time that presidential election results were transmitted by radio was in 1920, by the Pittsburgh, Pennsylvania, station KDKA. By 1924 the national political conventions were broadcast by radio. However, this new medium proved a disaster for the Democratic Party, as its convention dragged on through a record 103 ballots, with bitter fights between candidates and over divisive issues, like the role of the Ku Klux Klan. All this political dirty laundry was heard by radio audiences throughout the nation. The eventual winner of the Democratic nomination, John W. Davis, proved to be no match for the incumbent president, Calvin Coolidge.

The first president to broadcast messages over the radio was Warren G. Harding, in 1923, but Coolidge was the first to use it effectively. Coolidge's first message to Congress, in December 1923, was heard live by listeners over stations in Missouri and Texas.[3] In fact, "Silent Cal" had a good radio voice. "I am very fortunate that I came in with the radio. I can't make an engaging, rousing, or oratorical speech as you can," he once said to Senator James Watson of Indiana, "but I have a good radio voice, and now I can get my message across to [audiences] without acquainting them with my lack of oratorical ability."[4] Coolidge's second inaugural address, on March 4, 1925, was carried by twenty-one radio stations throughout the country, with an audience of about 15 million people. All the previous presidents, in all of their public addresses, did not have a combined audience as large as this.[5] Coolidge, however, did miss an opportunity, declining to take up Bruce Barton's suggestion that he periodically report to the American people through "fireside chats."[6] By the 1928 presidential election, radio had become a familiar household fixture, and the majority of Americans could now hear the voices of candidates directly, without intermediaries.[7]

Senator Huey Long of Louisiana, pushing his "Share the Wealth" scheme and other populist ideas, was one of the first politicians to grasp the power of the radio in reaching average citizens, not only in his home state, but throughout the nation.[8] Another public figure was Father Charles Coughlin, "the radio priest," who in his heyday reached 30 million radio listeners, roughly one in every three radios in the United States. Coughlin started out in 1926 with religious messages, but during the Depression turned to economic themes and social justice. He initially supported Roosevelt, but later became a vocal critic of the president.[9]

On March 12, 1933, just eight days after his inauguration, Franklin Roosevelt began the first of what would become thirty-one "fireside chats," on issues ranging from the banking crisis to the tribulations of World War II. Roosevelt would often begin with "My friends" or "Good evening, friends." He spoke in a clear, direct, conversational tone for fifteen to forty-five minutes, often ending with a request that listeners "tell me your troubles." By the millions, Americans from all walks of life wrote to the president, often responding within hours of his radio message.[10] Gaining an even wider audience, the fireside chats were filmed and distributed to movie theaters.[11]

In 1934, Republican senator Arthur Vandenberg of Michigan complained that Roosevelt was dominating the airwaves and stifling criticism of his New Deal programs. The following year, the National Broadcasting Company (NBC) and Columbia Broadcasting System (CBS) gave free radio time to senators on 150 occasions, to members of Congress more than 200 times, and to governors more than 50 times. Critics got their chance, but many elected officials who took advantage of this free air time spoke in support of the New Deal programs.[12]

During the 1936 presidential election, both Republicans and Democrats put considerable emphasis on foreign-language radio stations and made an estimated 2,000 such broadcasts. The Democrats, for whom the immigrant vote was becoming increasingly important, used Italian, Polish, Hungarian, German, Greek, and Yiddish messages to reach voters. Republicans reached voters through 100-word radio spots and thirty-minute speeches delivered in twenty-nine languages.[13] During that same year, the Alf Landon presidential campaign was supported by radio spots prepared by the Liberty League, a conservative, anti-Roosevelt citizens group.[14]

By 1944, nearly 90 percent of American homes had radios. During the presidential campaign of that year, the Republican nominee, Thomas E. Dewey, possessing a strong baritone voice and clear diction (he once considered a career as a professional singer), demonstrated that he was a good communicator over the radio. The Republicans turned to an advertising agency radio expert, Henry Turnbull, for advice and direction. The two political parties spent roughly $1.5 million combined in radio advertising, and one study indicated that 56 percent of persons interviewed believed that radio was the most accurate source of political information.[15] Despite all the money spent on advertising, most compelling was the voice of the public, which wanted to keep the ailing Roosevelt in the White House for a fourth consecutive term.

The 1948 presidential election marked the end of radio as the only mass broadcasting vehicle; by 1952, presidential candidates would be packaged and sold through television ads, and by 1956, the amount of campaign money spent on television ads surpassed that spent on radio.[16] Nevertheless, radio was still an important tool for political communication: Richard Nixon in 1968 and 1972,

Gerald Ford in 1976, and Jimmy Carter in 1980 relied on radio for long addresses to the public.[17]

While Grover Cleveland was the first president to appear on film, it was Theodore Roosevelt who first understood its value as a tool of persuasion. Roosevelt invited two camera operators to accompany him and his Rough Riders as they charged up San Juan Hill, and he halted at a particular spot so that the pose would be just right for the cameras.[18] In 1918 Michigan senatorial candidate Truman H. Newberry spent $8,788 to produce and distribute a film showing him inspecting a warship as part of his duties as lieutenant commander of the US Navy Fleet Reserve. A little artistic license was used, however. Commander Newberry posed in front of an imitation battleship in a New York City park, certainly not in a Navy shipyard.[19]

In 1923 William Fox produced a sixteen-minute silent film, *The Life of Calvin Coolidge*, which used still photos, some on-location shots of his New England home, his activities as governor, and his selection as vice president—even Mrs. Coolidge was shown expertly knitting. The following year, communications pioneer Lee DeForest created the first presidential talking picture, a four-minute film with Coolidge on the White House grounds discussing policy issues.[20]

Herbert Hoover, Franklin Roosevelt, Alf Landon, and Wendell Willkie were all subjects of campaign films, often showing the personal side of the candidates, as well as newsreel footage of their campaigns and speeches. Newsreels and films were also used against candidates and officeholders. As seen in chapter 1, the motion picture industry used newsreels to attack Upton Sinclair in the 1934 California gubernatorial race, and *The March of Time*, a US weekly news series shown in movie theaters, got Louisiana senator Huey Long to cooperate in the making of a newsreel, but then used Long's own words to ridicule and condemn him.[21]

In 1948, Louis de Rochemont, producer of the *March of Time* films, created a newsreel called *The Dewey Story*, praising the career and accomplishments of Thomas Dewey. Actors were dressed like gangsters in the segment portraying Dewey's crime-fighting accomplishments. The Republican National Committee bought 900 copies of the film, with the intent of releasing it in movie theaters two weeks before the election. The movie audience was huge: there were about 20,000 theaters throughout the United States, with a weekly audience of about 65 million. Jack Redding, head of publicity for the Democratic Party, demanded that Hollywood produce an equally flattering Truman documentary or face congressional hearings on their involvement in the Dewey film. Universal Pictures, which represented the motion picture industry, bowed to the pressure, and produced *The Truman Story*, a quickly assembled ten-minute film, with footage of Captain Truman from World War I, Truman meeting world leaders, and Truman acting "presidential." The film aired during the last six days of the campaign in movie theaters, and according to Redding "it was probably the most important, most successful publicity break in the entire campaign. The motion picture industry, to this day, is convinced that their film elected Harry S. Truman, President."[22]

The Birth of Commercial Television

*Conceived in 1940, embryonic in 1944 and 1948, television
as a viable political force was born in 1952.*

—Stephen C. Wood (1990)[23]

While there had been earlier experiments with televised news coverage, July 1, 1941, marks the birth of commercial television in the United States. In the 1930s, the Columbia Broadcasting System (CBS) aired a news discussion program called *Bill Schudt's Going to Press*, which covered the 1939 World's Fair and the 1940 Republican Party presidential nominating convention. On July 1, 1941, the Federal Communications Commission (FCC) permitted two New York television stations to run commercials, but it required them to meet a strict set of standards and provide at least fifteen hours of programming a week. In June 1941, when Germany invaded the Soviet Union, and later when Japan bombed Pearl Harbor, television was just learning how to manage breaking news stories, live on the air. In January 1942 the New York CBS affiliate, WCBW, broadcast the first live televised war bond sale, featuring boxing champion Jack Dempsey, and raising more than $100,000.[24]

However, very few people owned television sets, there was a limited supply of television equipment, and many of the television broadcast personnel had been sent to war. In June 1942, WCBW dropped its daily newscasts, and by December of that year it shut down its studio. Not until May 1944, just before the Allied invasion of France, did CBS reopen its studio.

The 1948 Nominating Conventions

In 1948, television was the new broadcast medium, still in its infancy. By September of that year, there were just thirty-four television stations broadcasting from twenty-one cities, with an audience of 1 million television sets.[25] The Republican Party had already chosen Philadelphia as the site of its nominating convention, and with San Francisco making a strong bid for the Democratic convention, the general manager of television station WFIL-TV in Philadelphia made a pitch to the Democratic National Committee. With coaxial cable soon to be laid out by American Telephone &Telegraph (AT&T), nine cities on the East Coast, from New York to Richmond, Virginia, would be able to receive live television broadcasts. The nine cities had seventeen television stations, and supposedly would reach a viewing audience embracing one-third of the country's electoral votes. The rest of the nation would rely on next-day broadcasts of kinescopes (movies made of television action) that would be airmailed to outlying television stations.[26] The Democrats were convinced, and decided to hold their convention in Philadelphia and take advantage of this new medium.

Just 1 percent of American families enjoyed this expensive new device, in its cumbersome big box, with a seven-inch oval black-and-white screen. The picture was often grainy, the sound poor, and the black-and-white images sometimes gave off a ghostly glow. If a family were lucky enough to live in a big city, it might be able to pick up three channels. In our age of 60-inch flat screens and 500+ channels, the bulky Philco and DuMont televisions seem to have come from the Stone Age, but during the postwar years, television was a marvel to behold.

The outcome of the Republican convention, held earlier in July, in Philadelphia, was a foregone conclusion. New York governor Thomas E. Dewey and California governor Earl Warren were nominated for president and vice president, respectively, without much excitement or drama. Everything was carefully stage-managed and anticlimactic, and the television cameras caught that manufactured atmosphere. The television cameras, tethered to thick cable, were heavy and hard to move, and the lights installed to brighten the arena gave off tremendous amounts of heat and caused highly unflattering images. Governor Dwight H. Green of Illinois, the temporary chairman of the Republican convention, decided he'd better put on makeup so that he wouldn't look so ghostly on television. In the end, no one really cared about Green, but they certainly cared about their standard-bearer, Thomas Dewey, who chose not to have his brow powdered. Hollywood makeup artist Hal King, who was hired by the Democrats to burnish their television images, remarked that Dewey "looked as if he had a bad case of five o'clock shadow."[27]

The Democrats met two weeks later. They were despondent, dejected, and on the verge of certain defeat. Few thought Truman could win, and the party was about to break apart, with southerners under South Carolina senator Strom Thurmond bolting to form a third party and progressives rallying around former vice president Henry Wallace. Truman and the Democrats were faced with the bleak prospect of going up against the dream ticket of Dewey and Warren. To make matters worse, the delegates were stuck in the stifling heat of a Philadelphia summer, in an un-air-conditioned auditorium, with the glaring hot television lights making them even more miserable.

On the day of his nomination, Truman watched the convention proceedings on a twelve-inch television screen in the White House. He then boarded the train at Washington's Union Station with his entourage and arrived in Philadelphia at 9:15 in the evening. Earlier in that day's marathon twelve-hour session, Senator Alben W. Barkley of Kentucky, soon to be the party's choice for vice president, spoke for sixty-eight minutes without looking at his text. Representative Sam Rayburn of Texas droned on, focusing on the written text before him, rarely looking at the television cameras. Truman had to wait patiently in the wings through four hours of seconding speeches and the agonizingly slow nominating process.

Finally, at 1:45 in the morning, the band struck up "Hail to the Chief," and Truman, resplendent in his white linen suit (perfect for the television cameras), came to the podium. In contrast to Dewey's stilted acceptance speech, Truman gave a plain-spoken, fiery address, in which he predicted victory, defended his record, blamed the Republicans for most of the ills of the country, and, most audaciously, called the 80th Congress back into session, daring Republicans to put up or shut up. While this electrified the conventioneers, few Americans were awake at this hour.[28] The concept of "prime time" was still years away, and only certified night owls or political junkies saw this live performance.

Madison Avenue advertising man Rosser Reeves tried to persuade Dewey to use television advertising. The 1948 election would be very close, Reeves warned, and television advertising in key markets might make the difference. Dewey turned the adman down, saying, "I don't think it would be dignified."[29] Nevertheless, the film *The Dewey Story*, sponsored by the Republican National Committee, did air on one NBC affiliate in New York City just days before the election.[30]

After losing the presidency in one of the closest races in history, Thomas Dewey returned to his office as governor of New York. However, when it came time for his re-election campaign, Dewey became a believer in television. He was one of the first politicians to use this new medium, which he did in his 1950 gubernatorial campaign.[31] With the assistance of Batten, Barton, Durstine & Osborn (BBDO), Dewey held an eighteen-hour televised "talkathon" on the last day of the campaign, where he answered hundreds of questions from New York citizens from all over the state, often in "awe-inspiring" detail, reeling off facts and figures about the state budget and problems throughout the state.[32] Four women on camera answered the telephone calls and passed the questions on to Dewey. In addition, a member of his staff was at a phone booth in a corner drugstore, with a pile of nickels, ready to ask questions if no one else did.[33]

The Dewey campaign also used a man-on-the-street format. Entertainer Happy Felton interviewed passersby on the streets of New York, under the marquee of the Astor Hotel. The citizens would indicate what they were concerned about, and then Dewey, watching from a monitor in a studio, would respond. However, it was all staged. Dewey's staff had, the day before, selected the passersby, gave them the questions to ask, and rehearsed them. As seen below, a version of this man-on-the-street format reappeared in 1952 with Eisenhower's twenty-second spots.

These devious theatrics baffled advertising man David Ogilvy, who in 1985 wrote, "Dewey, the ex-district attorney, the battler against corruption, the governor of the state, thought of himself as an honorable man. It never occurred to him that he was involved in deception. I doubt that it would occur to anyone, honorable or dishonorable, to pull such a play today. . . . Times change."[34]

In describing the preparations for the 1950 congressional campaigns, the Republican-leaning *New York World-Telegram*, under the headline "The Hucksters Take Over GOP Campaign," wrote that "the politicians are beginning to apply all the smart advertising techniques used by mass production America to merchandise autos, bath salts, and lawn mowers."[35]

In 1950, in Connecticut, Republican challenger Prescott S. Bush used the televised audience participation format in his unsuccessful campaign against incumbent senator William Benton. One year earlier, Connecticut governor Chester Bowles had appointed Benton to the US Senate seat; ironically, years earlier they had been business partners in the New York advertising agency Benton & Bowles, a pioneer agency that created the radio (and later, television) soap opera. The *New York Times* wrote that Bush and Benton "are men of means, and each is making a vigorous campaign without regard to expense for radio and television time," and noted particularly that Bush made a hit "by his songs on television appearances."[36] James Hagerty, a *New York Times* correspondent who had been Dewey's press secretary and later was press secretary for President Eisenhower, characterized the Connecticut elections for senator and governor as unprecedented in the use of radio and television, calling the governor's race a "battle of press agents."[37] Still, it was too early for television to have much of an impact. There were no television stations in Connecticut, and the commercials and speeches of the Connecticut candidates had to be broadcast from New York, Rhode Island, and Massachusetts stations, wasting much of the effort on viewers who could not vote in the Nutmeg State.[38]

Others seeking political office—including Senate Majority Leader Scott Lucas of Illinois (who lost to former representative Everett M. Dirksen), Senator Robert A. Taft of Ohio, and Representative Richard M. Nixon (who defeated Representative Helen Gahagan Douglas in California)—experimented with television in their campaigns.[39] Elected officials took notice in 1951, when Democratic senator C. Estes Kefauver from Tennessee became a nationwide celebrity. Kefauver chaired the Senate Crime Investigating Committee and agreed to televise the committee's provocative hearings. He then took them on the road, first to New Orleans, then to Detroit, St. Louis, San Francisco, and Los Angeles. By the time they ended in New York three months later, some or all of the hearings were seen by 20 to 30 million television viewers. The FBI had denied that there was a nationwide criminal conspiracy, and through the hearings Kefauver brought before television audiences unsavory mob figures pleading the Fifth Amendment and allegations of widespread organized crime.[40] It was great drama, with the crusading senator taking on the mafia—the kind of attention-getting device that most politicians could only dream about.

The hearings propelled Kefauver into presidential politics. In the 1952 New Hampshire Democratic primary, Kefauver defeated incumbent president Harry Truman, whose name had been placed in nomination by a New Hampshire loyalist, without the permission or knowledge of the White House. In March, Truman finally declared publicly that he would not seek re-election. Kefauver formally entered the race and then won twelve primary states, but in the end he was defeated for the Democratic nomination by Illinois governor Adlai E. Stevenson II.

The 1952 Presidential Campaign

By 1952, television was coming into its own. In July of that year, in the midst of the presidential nominating conventions, there were some 17 million television sets receiving signals from 110 television stations located in 66 cities. In large urban areas, 62 percent of homes owned television sets.[41] With the advent of television, there began a fundamental change in the way candidates would communicate with voters. The Truman 1948 whistle-stop campaign aboard the presidential railroad car, the *Ferdinand Magellan*, was an anachronism by 1952, as quaint as the front-porch campaign of Warren Harding and torchlight parades in Abraham Lincoln's time.

Radio, the dominant form of mass communication in the 1920s, was still the most common source, but it would soon be eclipsed by television. Heated political oration that worked well in front of open-air crowds had to be tempered to fit radio audiences. Likewise, politicians had to find a comfortable voice and adapt to the demands of the small screen. The long-winded thirty-minute televised campaign speech was also on its last legs. Nixon's "Checkers" speech was an anomaly; essentially a radio speech, he delivered it on television to a national audience. The speech was the first and only one of its kind, the national party paid for it and intended it as a defense of its vice-presidential choice. In this new age of television, the five-minute campaign advertisement and the twenty-second spot ad were born, created by the same advertising agencies that had advised presidents in the past, along with a few new firms. Further, television advertising would now cost money. By the beginning of the 1952 primary season, the television networks and stations had decided that they would sell advertising time to candidates; in the past, they had donated some or all of the time and absorbed the lost revenue themselves.[42]

In 1952, on the Republican side, the focus was on Ohio senator Robert A. Taft, "Mr. Republican," the leader of the conservative wing. It was his third attempt at the presidential nomination, against Dwight D. Eisenhower, the former Supreme Allied Commander in Europe during World War II and president of Columbia University, on leave as NATO commander in Europe. There had been a flurry of speculation that Eisenhower might jump into the presidential race in 1948, but nothing came of the draft movement. However, historian William B. Pickett has argued that recently discovered documents at the Eisenhower Library suggest that Eisenhower and his friends, beginning in July 1948, were "deeply involved in promoting his presidential fortunes" for 1952, that the country needed his experience and knowledge, and that the leading contender for the Republican race, Taft, was not right for the job.[43] In late 1951 the situation was becoming increasingly awkward: Eisenhower was still in Europe and serving as supreme allied commander of NATO—he hadn't even declared his party affiliation, and the filing date for the New Hampshire primary was drawing near. His supporters put his name on the ballot, and when Eisenhower, in absentia, handily defeated Taft, the die was cast. He began assembling his team of advisers. Chief among them was Herbert Brownell, the Republican Party's most able and experienced campaign manager, who had organized Dewey's 1944 and 1948 presidential campaigns and had served as Republican national party chairman.[44]

The contest grew bitter between Taft, who was trying one more time to plant the conservative imprint on the Republican nomination, and Eisenhower, the successor of the Dewey moderate, internationalist wing. While Eisenhower was still in Europe, he and Taft each won several primaries. Eisenhower finally resigned from the NATO position and returned home to Abilene, Kansas, to announce his candidacy on June 4. His announcement was the first such televised event, but it did not go very well. It was held at an unsheltered grandstand at the town's rodeo, the crowd was drenched by a sudden cloudburst, and Eisenhower, with the wind blowing his text and his hair, continued reading an unmemorable announcement. The next day, Eisenhower redeemed himself with an indoor press conference, where he was able to smoothly handle questions from the national press.[45]

The Republican and Democratic nominating conventions, held between July 7 and July 26, were the first conventions to be carried in their entirety—"gavel to gavel"—over a nationwide hookup, and were seen by 65 or 70 million people.[46] The Republican convention, held in Chicago, was a contest between Eisenhower and Taft. It also made a television star out of Illinois senator Everett Dirksen, who in his fiery speech defending Taft pointed his finger directly at Thomas Dewey and charged him with leading the Republican Party twice down the road of defeat. In the opinion of some critics, Eisenhower came across at the convention as good-natured, sincere, and honest, the professional soldier turned statesman.[47]

But the advertising professionals at BBDO, the New York agency on retainer for the Eisenhower campaign, were not impressed; in fact, some of them were "appalled" at Eisenhower's inability to communicate on television. He was stiff, awkward, spoke too fast, and, though he was only sixty-one, looked old and tired under the glare of television cameras.[48] The contrast was most evident with the mellifluous Democratic candidate Adlai Stevenson of Illinois.

Both presidential candidates were helped by media professionals. Eisenhower was coached by actor Robert Montgomery (whose own popular television show was sponsored by a BBDO client), while the CBS newscaster Edward R. Murrow helped Stevenson.[49] However, on the air, the more aloof Stevenson did not come across as well as Eisenhower. Surveys in California and Ohio and commentaries at the time concluded that Ike was more telegenic.[50] As communications scholars Edwin Diamond and Stephen Bates put it, "If Ike was everyone's father, then Stevenson was everyone's brother-in-law, and a smart one at that."[51]

Citizens for Eisenhower hired Roy O. Disney of the Disney Studios to create a sixty-second black-and-white spot, "I Like Ike," using a bouncing jingle, cartoon characters on parade, and Uncle Sam, who was followed by an elephant holding a banner with the word "Ike." They were followed by farmers, a businessman, a chef, a nurse, a housewife, and a mother and father with a baby carriage. The family dog held an Ike sign. They all marched to Washington, while Adlai and a donkey marched in the opposite direction.[52]

"Ike for President"

[*Text*: A Paid Political Announcement. Paid for by Citizens for Eisenhower.]
[*Text*: Eisenhower for President]

Group (singing): Ike for president, Ike for president,
Ike for president, Ike for president.

You like Ike, I like Ike,
Everybody likes Ike—for president.

Hang out the banners, beat the drums,
We'll take Ike to Washington.

We don't want John or Dean or Harry.
Let's do that big job right.
Let's get in step with the guy that's hep.
Get in step with Ike.

You like Ike, I like Ike,
Everybody likes Ike—for president.
Hang out the banners, beat the drums,
We'll take Ike to Washington.

We've got to get where we are going,
Travel day and night—for president.
But Adlai goes the other way.
We'll all go with Ike.

You like Ike, I like Ike,
Everybody likes Ike—for president.
Hang out the banner, beat the drums,
We'll take Ike to Washington.
We'll take Ike to Washington.

Ike for president, Ike for president, Ike for president, Ike for president...

[*Text*: Vote for Eisenhower]

Male Narrator: Now is the time for all good Americans to come to the aid
of their country. Vote for Eisenhower.

The production quality, by current standards, was primitive, but it did drive home a consistent, simple message: "I Like Ike," which has to be one of the best presidential slogans ever created. (It's a little harder to believe that the former Supreme Allied Commander-Europe and five-star general was the "guy that's hep"—1950s slang for "cool," usually associated with jazz musicians.) Americans from all walks of life—farmers, business, housewives, and even the family dog—would carry him to Washington to "do the big job right."

In addition to this catchy jingle, the Eisenhower campaign became pioneers in the thirty- or twenty-second television spot advertisement. Such advertising was not new: it had been used in radio during several of the past presidential election cycles, but it had never appeared before on television.

Other ads showed a beaming Dwight Eisenhower surrounded by adoring fans. Mamie Eisenhower also appeared in the campaign ads, and this was more than mere coincidence. It was a calculated gesture to show Ike, the family man and fatherly figure, in contrast to Stevenson, the divorced man. In this era, a divorce was a major liability for an aspiring public servant.[53]

Two advertising executives, Alfred Hollender of Grey Advertising and Rosser Reeves of Ted Bates and Company, volunteered their services to help the Eisenhower effort.[54] A group of Texas oilmen approached Reeves to see what his advertising agency could do to counter Harry Truman's boast that the country "never had it so good." Under the guise of Citizens for Eisenhower, the oilmen were willing to raise money to develop a slogan for the Republicans to counter Truman. Reeves had a better idea: instead of coming up with slogan, he put up $2 million for a series of twenty-second spots featuring Eisenhower answering questions from average voters.[55]

By this time, Rosser Reeves was a partner at Ted Bates and Company, a New York advertising firm with a reputation for the "hard sell" approach to advertising. The firm had annual billings of $35 million, with clients such as Kool cigarettes, Minute Maid frozen orange juice, Colgate dental cream, and Carter's Little Liver Pills.[56] Reeves was a proponent of the doctrine of the "Unique Selling Proposition" (USP): tell why the product is different, then repeat, repeat, repeat. As an example, M&Ms, the chocolate candy with a hard sugar coating, "melts in your mouth, not in your hands."[57]

Eisenhower, reluctant to engage in campaign pandering, gave Reeves just one day to film his part of the spots. Accompanied by his brother Milton, Ike came into the Transfilm, Inc. studio in Manhattan, read his two or three lines for each spot from cue cards, and then, as the day wore on, started to relax and be more comfortable with his lines. Reeves was able to get forty usable Eisenhower responses that day. "On cue," wrote Kathleen Hall Jamieson, "Ike played either Santa or Scrooge. He appeared as all things to all people."[58] Still uncomfortable with the whole format, Eisenhower at one point shook his head and said, "To think that an old soldier should come to this."[59]

The Eisenhower answers were then spliced together with the questions asked by citizens, picked by Reeves' film crew from tourists visiting Radio City Music Hall. The tourists—real people, with their own regional accents and clothes—were asked to come to a film studio and read questions from cue cards. Altogether, twenty-eight of the forty twenty-second "Eisenhower Answers America" spots were actually shown, along with three one-minute spots.[60] The format for the twenty-second spots were all the same: an announcer began by saying, "Eisenhower Answers America," then a citizen asking a short question, then a cut to Ike, giving a succinct, punchy answer. Here are two examples:

"Eisenhower Answers America"

Narrator: Eisenhower Answers America
Housewife: You know what things cost today, high prices are just driving me crazy.
Ike: Yes, my Mamie gets after me about the high cost of living. It's another reason why I say, it's time for a change. Time to get back to an honest dollar and an honest dollar's worth.

Narrator: Eisenhower Answers America

Man: I'm a veteran, General, what's wrong down in Washington? Graft,
    scandal, headlines, how can you fix it?

Ike: Here's how. By your votes, we'll get rid of the people who are too small
    for their jobs, too big for their britches, too long in power.

Reeves had been impressed by the recently published book *The Future of
American Politics* by Samuel Lubell, which offered an early analysis of ethnic voting in the United States.[61] Michael Levin, a disciple of Lubell's, developed a plan
for airing the "Eisenhower Answers America" spots during the last critical days
of the campaign. Levin's plan spelled out the strategy: "This campaign . . . is a
special, all-out effort to switch 49 counties in 12 states and with them the election
to Eisenhower."[62] To help focus the spots, the campaign turned to pollster George
Gallup, who identified three themes—corruption, high taxes, and war—and the
"Eisenhower Answers America" spots honed in on those topics. This, according to journalist Robert Spero, was the first use of survey research to determine
"scientifically a political campaign strategy."[63] In addition, Albert Cole of the
Reader's Digest Corporation volunteered his company's extensive mailing list;
three sets of 10,000 addresses were chosen, and questionnaires sent to them, asking what Eisenhower should stress in the campaign.[64]

Reeves explained the thinking behind the twenty-second spots: "I think of
a man in a voting booth who hesitates between two levers as if he were pausing
between competing tubes of tooth paste in a drugstore. The brand that has made
the highest penetration on his brain will win his choice."[65]

But Reeves had difficulty placing the ads. Frank Stanton and Joseph
McConnell, the presidents of CBS and NCB, respectively, opposed spot advertising, regarding it as "undignified, excessively abbreviated and only a caricature of
the candidate's views." It took the considerable persuasive powers of BBDO to get
the networks to air the spots.[66]

The reaction from the Stevenson campaign was predictable. George Ball, a
Stevenson staffer, complained, "They have invented a new kind of campaign—
conceived not by men who want us to face the crucial issues of this crucial day,
but by the high-powered hucksters of Madison Avenue."[67] Adlai Stevenson hated
the idea of creating twenty-second or one-minute spots. Despite his protestations, however, the Stevenson campaign was not above using its own spots. They
didn't feature Stevenson, but they did get their message across. This jingle tried to
convince voters that Republicans had broken their promises:

"The farmer's farming every day, making money and that ain't hay.
[*Clap! Clap!*]
Don't let 'em take it away."
"They'll promise you the sky! They'll promise you the earth! But what's a
Republican promise worth?"[68]

Altogether in the last month of the 1952 presidential campaign, Democrats
bought only $77,000 of airtime, compared to $1.5 million for the Republicans.[69]

Joseph Katz, the head of the Baltimore-based advertising agency that bore his name, was working for Stevenson and didn't want to give the Republicans all the credit: "We had the idea for a saturation spot campaign long before the Republicans, but we couldn't get the money."[70] Political scientist Alexander Heard noted that three Democratic campaign committees—Stevenson-Sparkman Forum, Volunteers for Stevenson, and the Democratic National Committee— paid nearly $1 million to the Joseph Katz Company, while three Republican campaign organizations—Citizens for Eisenhower, the Republican National Committee, and the Republican Senatorial Campaign Committee—paid more than $1.2 million to the Manhattan-based Kudner Agency.[71]

Most of the television budget of the Democrats went to eighteen half-hour speeches given by Stevenson, Harry Truman, and other Democrats. To save money, the thirty-minute speeches were set for 10:30 to 11:00 p.m. on Tuesday and Thursday nights, and the idea was that once voters saw the first one or two, they'd be used to tuning in at the same time of night to watch the others as the campaign unfolded. While the audiences were not insignificant, averaging about 3.8 million, the ads probably reached already committed Stevenson voters and few others.[72]

From our twenty-first-century aesthetic, the ads produced for Eisenhower and Stevenson were unsophisticated, even laughable. The pictures were grainy, the production quality was poor, the question-answer set up was corny, with the stentorian voice-overs tried to sound like the voice of God. Neither the candidates nor their ad agencies completely understood that the standard thirty-minute stump speech loses its effectiveness and impact when shown on television, and that a candidate sitting in his home study, like Stevenson, awkwardly trying to converse with his family and then talk about presidential politics, loses much appeal, particularly when the candidate doesn't know when to stop talking. They soon learned that it would be very difficult to compete with hugely successful commercial broadcasts like *The Milton Berle Show* or *I Love Lucy*; they also learned that few people wanted their favorite television show preempted for a boring thirty-minute candidate performance.

And above all, the candidates themselves were still not sold on the idea of presenting themselves like soap detergent or car wax. But they were warming to it. Political scientist Stanley Kelley, who wrote one of the first books on the intersection of politics and public relations, noted that the "strategy, treatment of issues, use of media, budgeting, and pacing of the Eisenhower campaign showed the pervasive influence of professional propagandists."[73] Democrats had fewer resources, and their public relations consultants had less of a voice in the campaign. One analysis of the 1952 presidential election concluded that a "Republican Cadillac" was pitted against a "Democratic horse-and-buggy." The Republicans simply were able to use campaign methods and techniques in a much better way than Democrats.[74]

While candidates may have been reluctant to embrace television, broadcast executives were ecstatic. As veteran television news director Sig Mickelson described it, the executives believed that a new day had dawned: thanks to television there would be better candidates, better informed audiences, and the old whistle-stop campaigns would be a thing of the past. And think of the advertising revenue that would come in from the campaigns! CBS chairman William S. Paley, in 1953, even advocated federal legislation limiting future presidential campaigns to eight or nine weeks; television, he reasoned, would make long, drawn-out campaigns no longer necessary.[75]

Nixon and the Checkers Speech

The television spot ads, the longer biographical ads, and the jingles were novelties, brought to an eager viewing public by Madison Avenue advertisers. The other historic use of television during the 1952 election was Richard Nixon's "Checkers speech," a thirty-minute soliloquy, televised nationwide, in which Nixon defended his honor, lashed out at critics, and hoped to retain his place on the Republican ballot. Nixon was in trouble because a number of wealthy California businessmen had created a special fund to help reduce the financial pressures on Nixon during the election. "They are so poor that they haven't a maid, and we must see to it that they have a maid," said Dana Smith, one of the organizers of the fund.[76] As a US senator, Nixon was living on $12,500 a year, and the cost of Christmas cards alone that he sent to constituents came to $4,237.54 during a two-year period. Nixon's longtime political adviser Murray Chotiner suggested that the fund become permanent and that individual donors be limited to $500 each.[77] Others, including Adlai Stevenson, were receiving similar help from supporters, in what might be characterized as an early form of unregulated personal political action committee (PAC) money. But the focus clearly was on Nixon and the $18,235 fund. "SECRET RICH MEN'S TRUST FUND KEEPS NIXON IN STYLE FAR BEYOND HIS SALARY" blared the *New York Post*.

Eisenhower's people were in a predicament. Ike was campaigning on a platform of cleaning up the mess in Washington, and here was a potential mess on his own team. James Hagerty, Eisenhower's press secretary, wouldn't comment: it would be up to Nixon to explain himself. The pressure built, and well-placed Republicans (including Eisenhower's brother Milton) wanted to dump Nixon; journalists covering the campaign placed their own bets and overwhelmingly thought Ike would dump Nixon. Eisenhower kept quiet, but the silence was deafening, and it looked like Nixon's place on the Republican ticket was very much in jeopardy. But most average voters didn't see it that way. A private poll conducted by Gerard Lambert's organization showed that fewer that one-fifth of those interviewed saw anything wrong with the fund, and just 10 percent said the revelations would make them less likely to vote for Nixon.[78]

Nixon felt he had to respond. Party chairman Arthur Summerfield and publicity chief Bob Humphreys were given the task of raising $75,000 on behalf of the Republican National Committee for a nationwide television and radio hookup. On September 23, right after the Milton Berle comedy show, Nixon went live from the NBC studio in the El Capitan Theater in Hollywood, reaching 64 NBC television stations, 194 CBS radio stations, and nearly all 560 radio stations in the Mutual Broadcasting System. There was no advance text for reporters (or Eisenhower's aides) to scrutinize; a battery of stenographers was hired to transcribe his words from an improvised television screen at the Ambassador Hotel, thus providing an "official" text.[79]

Nixon acknowledged that it would be morally wrong to accept $18,000 for his own personal gain, but that he had not done so; the money went only to pay political expenses. He told people what he owed and what he owned: "It isn't very much. But Pat and I have the satisfaction of knowing that every dime that we have got is honestly ours." Then repeating a line he had used in his campaigns, Nixon added, "I should say this, that Pat doesn't have a mink coat. But she does have a respectable Republican cloth coat, and I always tell her that she would look good in anything."

The thirty-minute apologia has been forever known as the "Checkers" speech. In one of the more maudlin moments, Nixon explained that a man down in Texas heard that his children loved dogs, and he sent them a little cocker spaniel, "black, white and spotted." Trisha, their six-year old daughter, called him Checkers. Then Nixon declared, "And you know, the kids, like all kids, loved the dog, and I just want to say this, right now, that regardless of what they say about it, we are going to keep it."[80]

Critics laughed, heaping big-city sophisticate scorn on Nixon's unctuous performance, but many Americans embraced the embattled, courageous young senator. Two hundred thousand letters poured into Republican headquarters during the next five days, with $62,000 in contributions, mostly $10 or less. After some hesitation, Eisenhower saw that he had no choice, and at a stop in West Virginia, Eisenhower, with a big grin, embraced his running mate. "You're my boy!" he exclaimed.[81] Scholars Edwin Diamond and Stephen Bates argue that from a purely technical point of view, the "Checkers" speech was "a model of political advertising."[82]

Television was often the nemesis of Richard Nixon during his long and at times painful public career. But at that moment, in the first nationwide paid political announcement, and fighting for his political life, television was his lifeline, his way to reach out to and connect with millions of curious and ultimately sympathetic viewers.

The 1956 Presidential Campaign

By 1956 television was becoming a familiar, indispensable entertainment fixture in many living rooms. The number of television sets grew from 17 million in early 1952 to 40 million in 1956; television stations grew from 110 in 1952 to nearly 500 in 1956. By 1956 every state had at least one television station; four years earlier, fifteen states had no station of their own.[83] There was little in the way of innovation in television advertising during the 1956 presidential election, which again pitted incumbent Dwight Eisenhower against Adlai Stevenson. But, for the first time, television advertising expenditures exceeded radio expenditures.

The Democrats began the general election campaign with a prime-time address by Stevenson on September 13. A total of 354 television stations on three networks, and 1,230 radio stations on four networks, carried the speech, from 9:30 to 10:00 p.m. Stevenson's speech was popular, ending up the fourth most-watched show that week.[84]

Republican presidential and congressional candidates spent roughly $4 million on campaign broadcasts, with three quarters of that going to television advertising. Republicans even targeted African American voters, buying approximately 150 spot announcements on black-oriented radio stations during a nine-week period before the election.[85] Democrats spent $3 million on broadcasts, with $2.1 million going to television advertising.[86]

The Republican Party was again aided by BBDO, under Carroll Newton. The Citizens for Eisenhower Committee hired Young & Rubicam and Ted Bates. Democrats, however, had a difficult time finding an advertising agency that would take their business. Madison Avenue firms, with their large corporate (and mostly Republican) clients, didn't want to attach themselves to a poorly funded and undoubtedly losing campaign. Finally, a medium-sized agency, Norman, Craig & Kummel, a rare Democratic firm, was hired, and staffers were borrowed from other agencies to fill in. Thirty-four-year-old account executive Chester Herzog, who had worked on the Blatz beer account, headed the Stevenson operation.[87]

The twenty-second spot ads of 1952 caught the public's attention; televised half-hour speeches, however, were no longer used. What was new in 1956 was the five-minute ad: not too long, not too expensive, long enough to include a good deal of substance, and short enough so that viewers weren't turned off. Democrats credit Reggie Scheubel, the veteran time buyer working with Norman, Craig & Kummel, for creating the five-minute ad concept, while Republicans credit NBC president Robert Kintner. The five-minute ads were called "hitchhikes": free rides attached to somebody else's commercial audience. They weren't really free rides, costing about $10,000, but they were a lot cheaper than the $60,000 for a half-hour commercial and $20,000 for the preemption of a regularly broadcast show.[88]

Democrats used the four- and five-minutes spots as well, scheduling eighty-nine such advertisements on television and radio.[89] Stevenson's campaign relied on its television adviser, William Wilson, and a young documentary film producer, Charles Guggenheim, to produce them. Lou Cowan, who had been the television advisor for Stevenson in 1952, was not available in 1956, because of his new responsibilities as president of CBS. But Cowan recommended a one-time employee, Charles Guggenheim.[90] A resident of St. Louis, Guggenheim was first involved in political filmmaking, working for forces advocating a 1956 bond issue in that city. His work came to the attention of Stevenson's campaign and he was recruited to produce Stevenson's four- and five-minute documentaries. (Guggenheim's role as a political consultant is discussed in greater detail in chapter 4.) Wilson and Guggenheim produced the four-minute "Man from Libertyville" (Stevenson's Illinois hometown), perhaps copying the 1952 Republican ad, "The Man from Abilene" (Eisenhower's Kansas hometown). The language was stilted, with Stevenson insisting on rewriting the scripts until the last minute. There were also no retakes, and the candidate often went over the allotted time, though he delivered only about two-thirds of what he was supposed to say. One scene had Stevenson, dressed in a suit, carrying a bag of groceries, talking about policies and his aspirations, then saying, "Oh, I forgot to deliver the groceries and made a speech instead." Years later, Guggenheim acknowledged that these 1956 campaign films were "quite bad."[91]

For the most part, candidate advertising on television was still trial and error. Sig Mickelson observed that "the 1952 and 1956 campaigns represented an era of testing the water, trying out new ideas, experimenting with visual appeals, determining how best to exploit the power of the visual medium."[92]

The Democrats, trying to defeat the popular Eisenhower, had little money, a candidate who had lost to Eisenhower previously and was disinterested in communicating over television, and were faced with international crises in the Suez, Hungary, and Israel that only reinforced the public's trust in the incumbent president.

Gearing up for the election, the Republicans acknowledged that they were in a new "electronics age." Eisenhower would rely on the mass media to get his message across, and he became more comfortable, accepting advice on makeup, lighting, and television delivery. Actor and television host Robert Montgomery again was chosen as "special consultant on TV and public communications," and served, as he did in 1952, as Eisenhower's adviser.[93]

Thus far in the era of television, it seemed that the Republicans and their Madison Avenue ad agencies had come up with the innovative ideas and methods of delivery. Negative campaigning had certainly been a staple of elections since the beginning of the Republic, but in this new age of television, voters did not see a negative TV ad until the Democrats launched one in 1952, called "Platform Double-Talk," which accused the Republicans of holding diametrically opposite positions on Korea, aid to Europe, and other issues.[94] The first negative ad directed at a presidential candidate came in 1956 in an ad called "How's That Again, General?," produced by Norman, Craig & Kummel. In it, the Democrats used Eisenhower's own words from one of his 1952 "Eisenhower Answers America" spots against him ("We must bring back integrity and thrift to Washington"). The ad featured Estes Kefauver, the Democratic candidate for vice president, laying out charges of corruption and cronyism against several Republican officeholders and public officials.[95]

A more punchy negative ad came in the last days of the campaign. Dwight Eisenhower had suffered a heart attack in September 1955 and had surgery for ileitis in June 1956. There was a growing concern about Ike's health. In addition, there were public grumblings within the Republican Party about whether Nixon should be on the 1956 ticket. Norman, Craig & Kummel produced this thirteen-second anti-Nixon spot:

"Nervous about Nixon"

[*Video: A still black and white photo of Nixon, looking shifty-eyed; over the screen, in big white letters, that look like they were written by a ghost, is the word* "NIXON?"]

Announcer: Nervous about Nixon?

<u>President</u> Nixon?

Vote Democratic. The party for you—not just the few.[96]

During the 1968 presidential campaign, Democratic ad maker Tony Schwartz reprised this theme—the horrible thought that an unprepared vice president could take over from a president. This time, the president was Richard Nixon and his running mate was Maryland governor Spiro T. Agnew (see chapter 5).

From this new technology of television, candidates for office, and politicians in general, were soon to learn important lessons. Media consultant Chester Burger examined television as a tool of communication. Writing in 1955, he argued that one of the most important features of television news is its informational brevity: ideas are presented in small bites, sentence structure is simplified, words should be familiar and conversational, and, above all, "pictures are the language of television." For Burger, "pictures don't illustrate the story; they are the story."[97] One of the early pollsters, Claude Robinson, president of Opinion Research, Inc., saw television as the important new communication medium, but he also saw a "cultural lag" in the use of television. Most television commercials, Robinson surmised, were being crafted as though they were written for radio, not for the visual medium.[98] Candidates and their commercial advertising firms still had much to learn, but they would soon begin catching on.

The 1960 Presidential Election

Without TV, Nixon had it made.

—Marshall McLuhan (1964)

We wouldn't have had a prayer without that gadget [television].

—John F. Kennedy (1960)[99]

By 1960, television was a familiar household commodity, reaching into 88 percent of American homes. Further, the American public was now becoming more familiar with the role of advertising firms in shaping the message and image of candidates on television. The *Saturday Evening Post* in 1959 had declared that the "sinister sorcerers" of Madison Avenue had replaced the financiers of Wall Street as the villains of campaigns and politics.[100] Vance Packard, in his 1957 best-selling exposé of the advertising world, *The Hidden Persuaders*, warned of "a strange and rather exotic new area" of American life where, unknowingly, citizens were being manipulated by advertising agencies that used insights gleaned from psychiatry and social sciences. Packard devoted an entire chapter of his book to politics and image builders, noting that, particularly since the 1956 presidential campaign, advertisers and manipulators "have made spectacular strides in changing the traditional characteristics of American political life.[101] On the academic side, Stanley Kelley Jr., in his seminal book *Public Relations and Political Power,* detailed the growing use of advertising agencies and public relations in presidential and other political campaigns.[102]

By 1960 Richard Nixon was a well-known quantity, with nearly eight years of service as vice president. John Kennedy, on the other hand, was relatively unknown, with an undistinguished career as a three-term congressman and two-term senator from Massachusetts. Kennedy, however, did receive a boost when his name was put forth for the vice-presidential nomination in 1956. In an extraordinary move, Adlai Stevenson threw open the choice of vice president, letting the Democratic delegates decide. Kennedy lost to Estes Kefauver, but he gained an enormous amount of free publicity from a nationwide audience.

The 1960 presidential campaign put television front and center, and image became an important ingredient in the outcome. Historian Gary A. Donaldson argued that "television changed American politics, making the 1960 presidential campaign the first modern campaign."[103] Indeed, John F. Kennedy, days after his razor-thin victory, concluded that "It was TV more than anything else that turned the tide.[104]

Minnesota senator Hubert H. Humphrey, running against Kennedy in the Democratic primaries, was outmaneuvered by Kennedy's combination of money and glamour. Throwing nearly all his campaign money into the Wisconsin primary, Humphrey chugged along, riding in an unheated campaign bus, while Kennedy crisscrossed the state in a private plane. Humphrey had his charming wife, Muriel, in tow, but Kennedy was joined by his glamorous wife, Jackie, plus other Kennedy women, Peter Lawford, and Sergeant Shriver. Even Frank Sinatra sang a Kennedy campaign commercial based on the crooner's popular tune "High Hopes."[105] Wisconsin voters flocked to the Kennedys, who sent out engraved invitations to Wisconsin Democrats. Historian W. J. Rorabaugh compared the Kennedy Wisconsin primary effort to Allied saturation bombing during World War II, writing that the "organization was superb, and nothing was left to chance."[106] Money and celebrity became a tough combination to beat, and Kennedy was able to defeat Humphrey in his own Upper Midwest backyard.

Out of money, Humphrey should have gracefully pulled out, but he insisted on battling Kennedy in the West Virginia primary. There, in a state that was 96 percent Protestant, the issue of Kennedy's religion became a factor. Polls taken by Louis Harris showed that once West Virginians knew that Kennedy was Catholic, support for him slipped and Humphrey gained. Kennedy decided to take the issue on directly, and on May 8, in a thirty-minute broadcast to the people of West Virginia, in what campaign chronicler Theodore White recalled as "the finest TV broadcast I have ever heard any political candidate make," Kennedy peered into the camera and spoke directly about the role of religion and the greatest of all constitutional decisions: to separate church from state.[107] After having won the Democratic nomination, Kennedy once again addressed the issue of religion, speaking before the Greater Houston Ministerial Association on September 12. Kathleen Hall Jamieson considers that speech "the most eloquent he made either as candidate or president," and it was soon used by the Kennedy campaign: a thirty-minute tape produced from the speech was later aired in thirty-nine states.[108]

In West Virginia, the greatest impact came in the ground game—the arduous, time-consuming effort to reach individual voters, woo courthouse political bosses, and register new supporters. But Kennedy and Humphrey both used television; Kennedy spent about $34,000 on his television buys, but Humphrey, in the last desperate days decided to hold a half-hour telethon, opening the telephone lines to anyone who wanted to talk, on any subject. Humphrey's campaign had no money left, and the candidate himself pulled out a personal check for $750. Unlike the scripted and controlled telethon of Thomas Dewey in 1950, Humphrey listened and responded to every call. It was both comic and sad: people asked harebrained, nasty, or off-the-wall questions, and some rambled on forever. Topping it all off, the line had to be cleared because someone on a party line had an emergency, trying to summon a doctor. It was all televised and proved to be disastrous for poor Hubert Humphrey.[109]

In the general election, with Kennedy facing Richard Nixon, one of the principal tasks of the Kennedy campaign was to get the relatively unknown senator's name before the American people. What helped was a bouncy one-minute ad that hammered home the name "Kennedy" (twenty-seven times), along with still photos and cartoons of Democratic themes and icons, including Eleanor Roosevelt and Harry Truman. Ranked as one of the ten best political commercials in history by *Time* magazine, the commercial was simply known as "Jingle."[110]

"Jingle"

> *Group* (singing): Kennedy, Kennedy, Kennedy, Kennedy, Kennedy, Kennedy, Kennedy for me, Kennedy! Kennedy! Kennedy! Kennedy!
> Do you want a man for President who's seasoned through and through,
> But not so dog-goned seasoned that he won't try something new?
> A man who's old enough to know, and young enough to do?
> Well, it's up to you, it's up to you, it's strictly up to you.
> Do you like a man who answers straight, a man who's always fair?
> Well measure him against the others and when you compare,
> You'll cast your vote for Kennedy and the change that's overdue.
> So it's up to you, it's up to you, it's strictly up to you.
> Yes, it's Kennedy, Kennedy, Kennedy, Kennedy, Kennedy, Kennedy, Kennedy for me, Kennedy! Kennedy! Kennedy! Kennedy! Kennedy! Kennedy! Kennedy!
> KENNEDY!

Altogether, some 200 commercials were produced for Citizens for Kennedy-Johnson and the Democratic National Committee (DNC) by Jack Denove Productions and Guild, Bascom and Bonfigli. One, entitled "Debate 2," highlighted Kennedy's performance during the presidential debates. For the DNC, African American singer Harry Belafonte talked with Kennedy about issues of justice, with the announcer asking citizens to "Vote for a leader like Roosevelt. Vote for John F. Kennedy for president." Also for the DNC, Guild,

Bascom and Bonfigli produced a one-minute spot called "Mrs. JFK," which had Jacqueline Kennedy speaking in careful schoolgirl Spanish, asking citizens for their support. Another celebrity, actor Henry Fonda was featured in a four-minute, sixteen-second commercial talking about the courage that Franklin Roosevelt demonstrated, and about the same kind of courage shown by John Kennedy.

The Nixon campaign used Carroll Newton from BBDO, Ted Rogers (who had produced the "Checkers" telecast in 1952), and Gene Wyckoff. Nixon didn't want his campaign associated with a big Madison Avenue firm, so he asked Newton to set up a separate organization.[111] Newton then formed an ad hoc advertising agency called Campaign Associates, and used Ruth Jones from J. Walter Thompson as the television time buyer. Many of the commercials for Nixon featured him sitting comfortably on a desk, wearing a dark suit, speaking clearly and forcefully talking about "Peace" or "The Most Important Issues." In the parlance of television, Nixon was a "talking head"—formal, sincere, dignified, and reassuringly boring.[112]

The television networks provided five-minute time periods for paid political advertising during prime time. Regularly scheduled shows were shortened to accommodate the campaign commercials. Nixon's Campaign Associates bought thirty five-minute time slots during the last few weeks, and most featured Nixon talking directly into the camera.[113]

For most of the 1960 campaign, the sitting president was absent. But the Democrats used Eisenhower's own words to cast doubt on Nixon's credibility as presidential material. In a one-minute spot, "Nixon's Experience?," produced by Guild, Bascom and Bonfigli, Eisenhower is seen at a news conference, where he is asked what major ideas Nixon had contributed. Here is part of the text:

"Nixon's Experience?"

> *Male Reporter*: I just wondered if you could give us an example of a major idea of his that you had adopted in that role as the, as the decider and, and final—
>
> *Eisenhower*: If you give me a week I might think of one. I don't remember. [*Eisenhower and crowd laughing.*][114]

Later in the commercial, Eisenhower's blunt answer is repeated: "If you give me a week I might think of one. I don't remember."

This forced the Nixon campaign to rebut with a commercial of its own, again using Eisenhower's words. In a one-minute spot, Eisenhower speaks from a podium at a Republican rally, and is captured in this advertisement, produced by Campaign Associates:[115]

"Best Qualified"

> *Male Narrator*: Here is President Eisenhower's decision on who is best qualified to follow him in the White House.

Eisenhower: Dick Nixon is superbly experienced, maturely conditioned in the critical affairs of the world. For eight years he has been a full participant in the deliberations that have produced the great decisions affecting our nation's security and have kept us at peace. He has shared more intimately in the great affairs of government than any vice president in all our history. He has traveled the world, studying at firsthand the hopes and the needs of more than fifty nations. He knows in person the leaders of those nations, knowledge of immeasurable value to a future president. By all odds, Richard Nixon is the best qualified man to be the next president of the United States.

Male Narrator: Along with the president, all America is going for Nixon and Lodge. Vote for them November 8th. They understand what peace demands.

The Nixon campaign made no paid television appearances in the three months from July 25 through October 25. Then, Campaign Associates flooded the airwaves with commercials and appearances. During the week before the election, Nixon's campaign purchased fifteen-minute prime-time slots each night, at 7:00 p.m. in the East. Eisenhower was finally engaged in the race, attracting huge crowds on behalf of Nixon, and television coverage. On the afternoon before the election, Nixon's campaign replaced all regular programming on the ABC-TV network, holding a four-hour telethon, with Nixon talking directly to the people. Actor Lloyd Nolan and actress Ginger Rogers were the co-hosts of "Dial Dick Nixon," with people from throughout the country calling in, the phone calls screened, and then given to Nixon to answer.[116]

Altogether, the Nixon and Kennedy campaigns broadcast television commercials 9,000 times during the general election period, and aired commercials 29,000 times on radio. Four years later, in the contest between Lyndon Johnson and Barry Goldwater, there would be a marked escalation of political advertisements over the airwaves.[117]

The Presidential Debates

For the first time in American presidential history, the two major party candidates would face each other in four televised debates held during the closing weeks of the Fall campaign. It took a special act of Congress to allow for an exemption to the FCC equal time rule, repealing Section 315 of the 1934 Communications Act, which required that *all* of the declared presidential candidates (there were sixteen candidates from fringe parties) would be eligible for equal time and an equal footing in the debates. Eisenhower thought the debates were a bad idea: why give Kennedy the exposure, why give him equal billing? But Nixon was confident that he could best the upstart senator, and he was not willing to face criticism that he was afraid to defend the Eisenhower administration's record. Kennedy forces were ecstatic: in a joint appearance with Nixon, Kennedy had nothing to lose, and everything to gain.[118] Finally, after lengthy negotiations, over the course of fifteen sessions, the Kennedy and Nixon camps agreed to four debates, the first held in Chicago on September 26, followed by a second in Washington on October 7, a third, with Nixon answering from Los Angeles and Kennedy answering from New York, on October 13, and then a final debate.

At the end of August, Nixon banged his knee while getting out of a campaign car in Greensboro, North Carolina. The pain was so bad and the doctors so worried, that he was sent to Walter Reed Hospital in Washington for a fluid tap. Then the knee became infected, and Nixon was ordered to stay in the hospital for two weeks. Back on his feet by September 12, Nixon pushed himself too hard, obsessed over sticking to a grueling scheduled and determined to fulfill an earlier pledge to visit each of the fifty states. On the evening of the first debate, September 26, the physical and emotional toll on Nixon was evident: he was exhausted, he'd lost ten pounds, and he looked sickly. His shirt collar was now too big, but Nixon refused to change into a better-fitting one.[119] At the worst possible time, as he exited his campaign car to enter the WBBM-TV studios in Chicago, he banged the same knee. He was in excruciating pain, and to make matters worse, he would have to stand up throughout most of the debate. Nixon's suit was a medium grey, which blended in too much with the grey-scale background of the studio, making Nixon look even more unappealing. CBS's best makeup artist was on hand to help, but neither candidate used her. To try to hide Nixon's heavy beard, his television consultant Ted Rogers applied a pasty powder, called Lazy Shave, to Nixon's jowls. Seeing Nixon up at the podium, Chicago mayor Richard J. Daley blurted out, "My God, they've embalmed him before he even died."[120]

Kennedy, on the other hand, was tanned, rested, and relaxed. He wore a dark suit that looked sharp on the television screen, and exuded confidence. Kennedy's opening words, echoing his acceptance speech, were strong and assertive, essentially a restatement of the campaign theme, "Let's get America moving again." Nixon's opening remarks were defensive and understated: "I subscribe completely to the spirit that Senator Kennedy has expressed tonight, the spirit that the United States should move ahead." The candidates bobbed and weaved their way through the questions asked by the four reporters and moderator Howard K. Smith of CBS.

Looking at substance alone, the first debate was probably a tie. Many felt that Nixon did better, particularly those who listened to the debate on the radio, and the positive effect for Kennedy most likely came from undecided voters. But on television, before that unblinking eye, the triumph was Kennedy's.[121] Image and appearance mattered, and for John F. Kennedy, this was his moment of victory. Nixon did better in the subsequent three debates; he even drank milk shakes to gain weight.[122] But it didn't matter: the first impression was the lasting impression. Henry Cabot Lodge, Nixon's running mate, blurted out after watching Nixon during the first debate, "That son of a bitch just lost us the election."[123]

The irony for Nixon is that television already had helped save his career, when he delivered his Checkers speech. Eight years and three days later, to an America now fully comfortable with television, Nixon was doomed by the more telegenic and confident John Kennedy. For *New York Times* columnist

Russell Baker, writing thirty years later, September 26, 1960 was a moment of transition: "That night, image replaced the printed word as the natural language of politics."[124]

Political communication scholar Robert V. Friedenberg argued that the 1960 Kennedy campaign was the "first major blow that weakened the parties. It illustrated that candidates could put together their own organizations and win nomination and election with relatively little help from the major parties."[125] The political parties, once dominant in orchestrating election strategy and execution, were being replaced by campaigns that focused on the candidates themselves. Those candidates brought in their own advisers and friends to help win elections. But with the growing complexity and sophistication of political campaigns, individual political operatives, many of whom once worked in advertising or public relations, began to establish their own firms, and to use their skills and experience to assist a variety of candidates. They followed in the footsteps of Clem Whitaker and Leone Baxter, Herbert Baus and William Ross, Louis Harris, and others. By the late 1960s, as seen in the next chapter, the first true generation of political consultants emerged on the landscape of American campaigns and elections.

CHAPTER 4

The Pioneers

Reporter: *How can you work for candidates with such different convictions?*
Bill Roberts: *We are mercenaries.*

—Walt Anderson (1966)

I sold insurance, I sold Britannicas, I sold cars for my
father. I needed to do that to make a living—until I met John Kennedy.

—Matt Reese (1989)

Campaign consultant firms are mostly
small, marginally profitable, and constantly on the
edge of collapse. Politics is not a good business.

—Ithiel de Sola Pool (1976)

WHILE CLEM WHITAKER, Leone Baxter, and a few others were forerunners in the business of political consulting in the 1930s and 1940s, it would be another fifteen or twenty years before campaigns routinely sought out the advice of political consultants. By the 1960s, statewide, congressional, and big city campaigns were becoming more complicated and more special-ized. Candidates therefore turned to professional consultants, such as advertis-ing agencies, pollsters, or even the new breed of campaign managers to supplant party operatives and political amateurs.[1] "Politics," said a member of the political consulting firm Spencer-Roberts in the mid-1960s, "has become too expensive and too complicated to leave to the amateur."[2] There was even a new name for it, the "new politics." As Joseph Napolitan, one of the first midcentury consultants, remarked, "the new politics is the art of communicating a candidate's message directly to the voter without filtering it through the party organization."[3] The new specialists, the political consultants, saw themselves not as party operatives; rather, they were business professionals, whose business happened to be cam-paigning and political communication.[4]

As noted in chapter 1, by the mid-1950s, about forty public relations firms were providing services to political campaigns. Around the same time, a small number of campaign operatives or public relations specialists began carving out businesses dedicated almost exclusively to campaigns and elections. They honed their skills and expertise, and worked for a variety of candidates. Some in this generation fell into the business by chance or luck, others were fueled by ideology or partisanship, or simply the opportunity to make a living.

They came from various parts of the country—western Massachusetts, southern California, Louisiana, Detroit, Missouri, West Virginia, and Florida. Except for one, they all had their start in local or regional, rather than presidential, politics. Each of these consultants would have an important part to play in the presidential primaries and general elections from the start of the modern era of political consulting.

General Consultants

A political consultant is a specialist in political communication. That's all there is to it—it's not very Machiavellian.

—Joseph Napolitan (1981)[5]

Political consulting is an art form, not a science.

—Stuart Spencer (1988)[6]

The first group of consultants were generalists. They had their hands in a variety of campaign functions, including overall management, writing press releases, conducting polls, shooting campaign commercials, and advising candidates on how to prepare for debates. The campaign generalists were jacks-of-all-trades, learning as they went along, and becoming savvy to the ways of increasingly sophisticated modern campaigning.

Joseph Napolitan (1929–2013), a one-time sports and politics reporter from Springfield, Massachusetts, was the first campaign operative to call himself a "political consultant." After spending ten years writing for the *Springfield Union*, Napolitan decided to open a public relations office in his hometown.[7] He was inspired by reading one of the first books on the subject, Stanley Kelley's *Professional Public Relations and Political Power* (1956).[8] Two weeks after opening his office, a young state representative, Tom O'Connor, came to Napolitan. He wanted to run for mayor; could Napolitan help him? "I said sure," Napolitan later remembered, "and tried to figure out what to do."[9] Under Napolitan's guidance, O'Connor campaigned aggressively, used television heavily, and soundly defeated the six-term incumbent mayor of Springfield, Dan Brunton.

In 1958, one of Napolitan's candidates, Matthew Ryan, was short of cash and wasn't receiving much help from the three local newspapers. The newspapers collectively had decided to cut way back on stories of politicians running for office; henceforth, coverage would run no more than two paragraphs, with no pictures. "The less print about politicians, the better," proclaimed a memo posted in one of the papers' city room. The papers, all owned by the same employee benefit and retirement funds, were particularly upset over a bill sponsored by Massachusetts senators Leverett A. Saltonstall and John F. Kennedy to legalize employee trust funds.

Napolitan knew that the best way to introduce Ryan, who was running for state district attorney, was through the Sunday edition of the *Springfield Republican*, but the newspaper wouldn't cover the race. As a former sports reporter, Napolitan knew his way around the newspaper business. He called the advertising manager, an old friend, and asked if there were any restrictions on typeface used in advertisements. No, there weren't. Napolitan submitted an ad just seven minutes before the deadline on Friday. It was a full-page ad, using the same typeface and font size as the *Republican* regular text, with glowing praise for Ryan, a cartoon, and a sketch. In tiny type at the top of the page it said "paid political advertisement" and at the bottom, "paid for by Matthew Ryan for District Attorney . . . Bernard O'Connor, chairman."

The ad fooled a lot of people into thinking that the newspaper had fully endorsed Ryan. Ryan's opponent, Eddie Donovan, was not so amused, however. He called Napolitan at 7:30 Sunday morning, complaining, "You son-of-a-bitch, that ad's going to beat me. But I have to tell you that's the best political ad I've ever seen in my life." Donovan was defeated, and the twenty-nine-year-old Joseph Napolitan made national news when *Time* magazine picked up the story.[10]

Napolitan went on to win his first thirteen local races in a row, before losing in a primary election while working for Endicott Peabody, who was vying for the Democratic gubernatorial nomination in Massachusetts. Up until that defeat, Napolitan wrote, "I considered myself invincible."[11] In 1960, he became a campaign staff assistant to Lawrence F. O'Brien Jr., another native of Springfield, ten years his senior, who was the director of organization for the Kennedy for President campaign.[12] Then Napolitan worked as a pollster, helping George McGovern's Senate campaign in South Dakota, and he managed Thomas J. McIntyre's successful Senate campaign in New Hampshire in 1962. Later, Napolitan was called upon to conduct at least two polls for the Kennedy White House, one in April 1963 on political attitudes in Pennsylvania, and another in June 1963 in Massachusetts, asking voters about probable 1964 Republican presidential candidates.[13] Napolitan epitomized the work of some of the earlier consultants: generalists who served as campaign managers or media experts, who knew how to do field work, and even conduct survey research.

By the mid-1960s, Napolitan was working for a variety of candidates, from Milton J. Shapp, running for governor in Pennsylvania, to Maurice R. (Mike) Gravel, running for the US Senate in Alaska in 1968. As seen in chapter 5, Napolitan's big break into presidential politics came in 1968, when he, together with O'Brien, took over the fledgling Hubert Humphrey campaign during the Fall general election. Napolitan was also one of the first political consultants to work internationally, when he was hired immediately after the Humphrey campaign by Ferdinand Marcos, who was seeking re-election as president of the Philippines. Altogether, he worked in elections in over twenty countries.

Napolitan, who ended his consulting career in 2004, was particularly important in creating professional organizations both in the United States and internationally, where political consultants could meet, discuss new techniques and practices, and set a minimum standard of ethical and normative behavior for campaigning and elections. In 1968, he cofounded the International Association of Political Consultants (IAPC), and the following year he was one of the founders of the American Association of Political Consultants (AAPC). In 1991 Napolitan was elected to the first class of the AAPC Hall of Fame, together with F. Clifton White. (For a complete list of AAPC Hall of Fame honorees, see Appendix B). Democratic direct-mail veteran Richard Schlackman was one of many to assess Napolitan's role in campaigns and elections: "There would not be a political consulting industry without Joseph Napolitan. Period." On the news of his death in 2013, fellow pioneer consultant Raymond Strother remarked that Napolitan was the "rock on which we built modern political consulting."[14]

Stuart K. Spencer (b. 1927) came from a politically active family. His father was one of the committee of 100 that in 1946 selected Richard Nixon to run for Congress, and his mother was the president of the influential California Parent-Teachers Association. William Roberts (1925–1988) was active in the California Young Republicans during the 1950s. The two began working together as organizers for the Los Angeles County Republican Central Committee, and in 1960 they established Spencer-Roberts & Associates, one of the first full-service political consulting firms in the country. By the end of their careers, they had helped manage approximately 400 political campaigns. Their first high-profile client was California senator Thomas H. Kuchel, a Republican running for re-election in 1962. By 1964, they had a highly enviable track record, winning thirty-six out of forty congressional and other contests. *Washington Star* political reporter David Broder called the Californians the "current 'hot firm.'"[15] Their clients included New York governor Nelson A. Rockefeller, who was running for the Republican presidential nomination in 1964 and needed their assistance during the California primary.

Their big break came in 1965, when Ronald Reagan was getting ready to run for governor of California. Reagan's wealthy backers, particularly auto dealer Holmes Tuttle and oilman Henry Salvatori, wanted the very best consultants to shepherd their novice candidate through the Republican primary. They sought out Spencer and Roberts. Reagan met with them in May 1965, and during the course of their conversation, one of the consultants reminded Reagan that they had worked for Rockefeller, while Reagan had supported Goldwater, in 1964. Stuart Spencer recalled Reagan's answer: "He said, 'I was out in Phoenix visiting in-laws and I saw Barry and I told him I was thinking of running for governor and he said, "if I were running in California I would get those sons of bitches Spencer and Roberts."'"[16]

Veteran political reporter Lou Cannon wrote of California during the mid-1960s: "In no other populous state of the nation at this time could a handful of millionaires and a political consultant so easily have decided on their own to run an aging actor for governor without consulting with party leaders."[17] But that was California and one of the legacies of progressive governor Hiram Johnson, who smashed the political grip of the Southern Pacific railroad and its control of the state parties.

Spencer and Roberts provided a full-service approach as Reagan first went up against San Francisco mayor George Christopher in the Republican primary, and then against incumbent governor Edmund G. (Pat) Brown Sr. in the general election. To counter claims that Reagan lacked any experience in governing, the Spencer-Roberts team boasted that their candidate was a "citizen politician," the uncorrupted amateur fighting against Sacramento and the inherent entrenched evils of politics. Reagan's weaknesses (a lack of experience and political knowledge) became his strength.[18] Spencer-Roberts controlled nearly all aspects of the campaign, including organization, scheduling, and the selection of issues and themes, while leaving the fundraising to Reagan's own money people.

To help candidate Reagan bone up on the many policy issues facing him, Spencer-Roberts hired two psychology professors, Stanley Plog and Kenneth Holden and their firm Behavior Science Corporation of Los Angeles. They formed Reagan's "brain trust," working behind the scenes to convince voters that their relatively uninformed candidate had the policy gravitas to become the state's elected leader.[19] The psychologists developed a list of eighteen policy areas, and put the information together in eight separate books, with basic numbers and facts stored on 8-by-5-inch cards; Reagan would then take that information, write his own speeches, and put them on 3-by-5-inch index cards. According to Stuart Spencer, the speeches Reagan crafted were well-written and persuasive. "I say to this day," Spencer remembered in 2001, "he's the best speechwriter I've ever seen in all this period of time."[20] This assessment was echoed by James A. Baker III, who worked both for and against Reagan starting in 1976 and throughout his presidency: "In my opinion, the best presidential speechwriter who ever worked in the White House—at least since Lincoln—was Ronald Reagan himself."[21]

As for his ability to handle television, Reagan was a natural. "We just put Ron in front of the camera and let him talk," said Spencer.[22] As public relations specialist James Kelleher argued in 1956, the politician on television must be an actor, not a policy expert.[23] Ronald Reagan, who left his film career in 1954, began an eight-year stint as spokesman for General Electric, and as the host of the weekly television show *General Electric Theater*. He traveled throughout the United States and met with nearly all 250,000 GE employees, visiting every company plant and facility. Reagan soaked in Middle American values and, with his easy telegenic manner and everyman, neighborly persona, proved to be the ideal spokesman for his conservative corporate employers.[24] Spencer and Roberts brought in the advertising firm of McCann Erickson, whose California office was headed by Reagan's brother, to produce and place the television advertising.[25]

While running for governor, Reagan and Spencer never talked about the possibility of an eventual run for the White House. But within a few months of meeting him for the first time, Spencer sensed "a subtle, yet strong desire" on Reagan's part "to be president of the United States someday."[26]

On the Democratic side, the Brown campaign used two public relations firms: Baus and Ross, which managed the Goldwater victory over Rockefeller in the California presidential nomination of 1964, was hired on an adjunct basis, while Harry Lerner and Associates produced some blistering attack ads against

Reagan, characterizing him as an extremist.[27] Bill Roberts, looking back at the campaign, thought it was a big mistake for Brown's campaign to attack Reagan that way: "I would never have attacked Reagan. . . . I would have killed him with kindness, I would have said he's a decent, fine person and no doubt has a future in politics, but maybe he should start at a local level. . . . The extremist issue . . . was a mistake. That's an over-the-hill issue; it worked in '62 and '64 but not in '66."[28]

During its first decade, Spencer-Roberts branched out into public policy and strategic planning for corporate clients and associations, such as the American Medical Association. Stuart Spencer became the sole owner of the firm in 1974, and, as seen in upcoming chapters, was an influential campaign adviser for Gerald Ford and Ronald Reagan. He also teamed up with Bill Hecht to form a Washington, DC–based lobbying firm, Hecht, Spencer & Associates. In 1989 his daughter, Karen Spencer, joined the firm and expanded its public policy and political strategic planning services.[29] Spencer was inducted into the AAPC Hall of Fame in 1992.

F. Clifton White (1919–1993) owned a business consulting firm that assisted U.S. Steel, Standard Oil of Indiana, General Electric, and other corporations, but as a hobby, he was heavily involved in Republican politics. "My political career," White wrote in his memoirs, "began back when I was too young to know any better."[30]

One of White's first battles, and the one he felt was most instructive, was the fight over control of the American Veterans Committee (AVC). White, who later was best known for his support of Barry Goldwater, found himself allied with socialist leader Gus Tyler and David Dubinsky, head of the International Ladies' Garment Workers' Union (ILGWU), fighting for control of the AVC against communist activists. White explained that he had "no problem whatsoever working with liberals, Trotskyites, and democratic socialists in an alliance against Communists and Fascists."[31] For White, the fundamental ideology centered on the idea of freedom.

White was approached in 1946 by a group of dissident New York Republican Party leaders to run for Congress against conservative Republican incumbent W. Sterling (Stub) Cole. White ran and lost, but he learned valuable lessons about the rough-and-tumble world of politics. During the 1950s, he became leader of the National Federation of Young Republicans. He became a "technician in politics,"[32] as journalist Theodore H. White described him, "one of the finest in America." He was a specialist in the arcane, but vital, elements of politicking: petitions, organizing, registration of voters, convention tactics, and the like.

As seen in the next chapter, White stepped into the national scene by convincing a reluctant Barry Goldwater to run for the presidency in 1964. Working from behind the scenes, from 1961 until the announcement of a Draft Goldwater campaign in summer of 1963, White used his skills at organizing and his knowledge of the delegate selection process to create the grassroots movement.

White was one of the founders of the American Association of Political Consultants, and of the International Association of Political Consultants, and he worked at times with Democrat Joseph Napolitan on international campaigns.

One of White's clients was Carlos Andrés Pérez, president of Venezuela, who was first elected in 1973. White also worked on the 1972 Senate campaign of Jesse Helms in North Carolina, headed the 1970 Senate campaign of James L. Buckley in New York, and advised corporations, offering training sessions for business executives on how to understand and deal with politics, governmental affairs, and organizations.[33] In 1987 White founded the International Foundation for Electoral Systems (IFES), a nonpartisan, nonprofit organization headquartered in Washington, DC, to promote democracy and democratic institutions throughout the world. By 2013, IFES had assisted organizations and institutions in some 135 countries.[34] Along with Napolitan, White was inducted into the first class of the AAPC Hall of Fame in 1991.

Born in Queens, New York, Joseph R. Cerrell (1935–2010) moved to California in 1951 for health reasons, and enrolled in the University of Southern California as a political science major. Politics was in his blood, and he drew attention nationwide when he led a demonstration against a southern governor in 1955, which led to the governor's censure by his own state's legislature.[35] He worked as a volunteer for California assemblyman Jesse Unruh in 1954, and as Unruh rose in power, he brought Cerrell along, appointing him executive secretary of the California Democratic Party in 1959. Ten years later, Cerrell commented that, had he still been in New York, "I'd be maybe an assistant precinct captain somewhere," rather than executive director of the state party.[36] Such was the power vacuum in California politics, that Cerrell, at twenty-four, was the youngest of all state party directors.

Cerrell managed the Kennedy 1960 presidential campaign effort in California, and he was active in many presidential, California, and local races. In 1966 he established Golden State Consulting with his colleagues Don Simonian and Chuck Winner, but the firm, probably the first Democratic consulting firm established in California, was short-lived. The following year it became Cerrell, Winner & Associates, and once Winner left to form his own firm in 1975, Cerrell and his wife, Lee, became the sole owners of Cerrell & Associates in Los Angeles. In 1983 he created an East Coast branch with political consultant Ben Palumbo, called Palumbo & Cerrell, in Washington, DC. His firm worked for Hubert H. Humphrey, Al Gore, John Glenn, Willie Brown, Jesse Unruh, Pat Brown, and Brown's son, Edmund G. (Jerry) Brown Jr.

In 1978, about thirty judges, mostly appointed by Governor Jerry Brown, were facing election challenges. Cerrell signed up nine judicial candidates in Los Angeles County at $7,500 each during that year, and won every race. He then sponsored a conference on judicial campaigning the following year, targeting local judges who were up for re-election. One session on the conference agenda was "Campaigning with Dignity: Maintaining the Judicial Image."[37] From then on, Joe Cerrell became known as the consultant to turn to for judges facing challengers in California's elected judicial system. Since 1978, Cerrell & Associates has handled over 375 judicial clients, scoring over a 90 percent win rate.[38] The firm, which in its early days worked solely on political campaigns, had evolved into public affairs, public relations, crisis management, and a special events firm.[39]

Cerrell, who was once the president of the American Association of Political Consultants, was inducted into the AAPC Hall of Fame in 1997.

Walter De Vries (b. 1929) became interested in politics through one of his professors at Hope College in Michigan. Following a stint in the US Army, De Vries ran as a delegate for both the Republican and Democratic state conventions in Michigan, and was elected to both. As part of his graduate training in political science at Michigan State University, he was required to work fifteen hours a week in the office of an elected official. He ended up working for a politician who was also of Dutch ancestry, George van Person, the Speaker of the Michigan House of Representatives. De Vries was tucked into a makeshift office space in van Person's marble bathroom, where he wrote speeches. During the next several years, he ran the House staff while finishing his PhD.[40]

In 1960, George W. Romney, the president of American Motors Corporation, proposed changing or rewriting the Michigan state constitution. Romney headed up the constitutional convention, and De Vries, now a twenty-six-year-old instructor at Adrian College, was elected as a convention delegate from Grand Rapids. During the course of that convention, De Vries took a leave of absence and became full-time director of research and strategy, devising the campaign plan for Romney, who was increasingly being talked about as gubernatorial material. In November 1962, Romney defeated incumbent John B. Swainson, becoming the first Republican governor in fourteen years. Romney was re-elected, with increasing popular support, in 1964 and 1966. De Vries then became Romney's chief of staff. "What was neat" De Vries recalled, was that Romney said in effect, "you have carte blanche to do whatever you want to win this campaign," including research, polling, and the new technique of focus group analysis.[41]

De Vries developed the concept of "ticket splitting," and later coauthored, with Republican pollster V. Lance Tarrance Jr., a book on the subject, called *The Ticket-Splitters*.[42] De Vries found that many Democrats were not voting a straight Democratic ticket, splitting off to vote Republican, and that Independents didn't necessarily split their tickets. At the time, the idea of ticket splitters went against political science theories of voter behavior, but De Vries dismissed the academic arguments: "We never would have won had we followed the traditional concepts of political science."[43]

Also working with the Romney campaign was Frederick P. Currier, head of a Detroit-based public opinion firm, Market Opinion Research (MOR). With the blessings of Romney, Currier was willing to try a variety of new polling techniques. The campaign did a baseline poll, a survey well in advance of Election Day to establish a starting point of public opinion and determine the challenges and opportunities facing the campaign.[44] MOR also conducted tracking polls, although, as De Vries concedes, "we didn't know it was tracking."[45] The television commercials produced for the campaign were also pretested using an early form of a focus group, with union workers, Catholics, suburbanites, and others in the test audience. During Romney's 1966 bid for re-election as governor, De Vries noted that the campaign had "probably made more use of in-depth polling on issues than any other political organization in the country."[46] Writing two years later, James M. Perry observed that "the 1966 election in Michigan will stand for years to come as one of the first thoroughly modern statewide political campaigns."[47]

When Romney dropped out of the 1968 Republican nomination fight, De Vries shifted gears. Through professor Richard Neustadt, De Vries was able to obtain a fellowship at the Harvard University Institute of Politics, staying there about a year and a half. At Harvard he worked on his first important book, *Ticket-Splitters*. Still associated with MOR in 1968, De Vries worked with about twenty-five US Senate and congressional candidates, translating polling data into electoral strategy. The following year, De Vries set up his own polling firm and was made a full professor at the University of Michigan.[48]

DeVries was a "true believer" in the new techniques of campaigning: "I find nothing Machiavellian about asking what problems bother people, or asking what they think ought to be done about these problems. Once I find out, I don't think it Machiavellian to find the best media to inform people what the candidate intends to do or not do about these problems, or why he is better able to handle them than his opponent."[49] The new techniques of using private surveys and commercial advertising had succeeded "only because the two traditional political parties have failed. . . . The new politics are a service to this Republic—not a disservice."[50]

Four other individuals fall into this category of pioneer general consultants: Hal Evry, Hal E. Short, Sanford Weiner, and Roy Pfautch. Evry worked on the gubernatorial campaigns of Democrats David Trapp (Kentucky) and George P. Mahoney (Maryland).[51] During his first decade of consulting, Evry won thirty out of thirty-nine campaigns, working mostly in California for candidates, especially Los Angeles mayor Sam Yorty and governor Goodwin Knight.[52] Evry also authored a book on campaign techniques, *The Selling of a Candidate*, in 1971.[53] David L. Rosenbloom described him as one of the "most colorful and outspoken" campaign managers, who discouraged candidates from making public appearances or speeches during a campaign, preferring to hide the candidate behind mass media advertising.[54]

Hal E. Short worked for Republican senators Thruston Morton (Kentucky), Louis Nunn (Kentucky) and James C. Gardner (North Carolina). Short also worked for the election of Earl Warren as California governor and for a variety of Republican candidates. Sanford (Sandy) Weiner, a California consultant, worked for Paul N. (Pete) McCloskey (who defeated Shirley Temple Black for Congress), George Murphy, George Christopher, and Richard Nixon. Roy Pfautch, an ordained Presbyterian minister, formed Civic Service, Inc., in St. Louis, Missouri, and was active in a number of Missouri campaigns and other races. Pfautch created his political consulting business in 1963, but he abandoned candidate campaigns after becoming involved in one of the Watergate spin-off scandals, the "Townhouse Operation," which laundered campaign money to Nixon-backed candidates.[55]

One insight into the wide variety of operations of early professional consultants comes from a lawsuit that Hal Short filed against Claude R. Kirk, who was running for a US Senate seat in Florida against eighteen-year incumbent Spessard

Holland in 1964. Short claimed that he was owed money by the Kirk campaign for his services over the course of twelve months. While he had other clients, Short stated that he spent two-thirds of his time on the Kirk campaign in Florida, doing a variety of campaign activities: studying Holland's voting record, doing background material, writing all the speeches and campaign literature, briefing the candidate on issues, and even going to public meetings of Holland before he was recognized as being with his opponent. Holland easily won the election, and the Circuit Court on DuVal County determined that Short's contract with Kirk was not enforceable.[56]

Private Pollsters

The people that I most admire are the people like
Stu Spencer, like Bob Teeter, like Dick Wirthlin, who are masters
of their craft, but also believed in the principles of democracy.
—Peter D. Hart (2007)[57]

During the 1930s and 1940s, the public pollsters George Gallup, Elmo Roper, Archibald Crossley, Hadley Cantril and others came into their own, predicting election outcomes, spotting important national issues, and having their findings published in syndicated columns in prominent newspapers. During the 1950s and 1960s, private pollsters Louis Harris, then Oliver Quayle, John Kraft, and Charles Roll began serving candidates for office with survey analysis. It was a growing business. Political communications scholar Dan Nimmo identified forty private polling firms that assisted candidates during the 1960s.[58] Louis Harris estimated that two-thirds of the candidates for the US Senate in 1962 had private polls conducted, along with three-fourths of the gubernatorial candidates, and about one in ten congressional candidates. The disparity between senatorial and congressional candidates, Harris wrote, was "primarily one of finances, rather than desire."[59] By 1968 the number of US senators and representatives using private pollsters had steadily increased.[60]

During the late 1960s and early 1970s, several individuals began making a career out of private campaign-related survey research. Oliver A. Quayle III (1921–1974) took over political clients from Louis Harris in 1963 when Harris decided to stop conducting private polls for candidates. Quayle, described by the *New York Times* as a "zestful, handsome, square-shouldered man,"[61] established Quayle & Company and worked for Presidents John Kennedy and Lyndon Johnson, Vice President Hubert Humphrey, and scores of governors, members of Congress, and others. He also frequently contributed to newspapers and magazines, and directed public opinion research for NBC News. Johnson was so enamored with the results that Quayle produced that he offered a rare compliment: "That boy seems to know what he is doing."[62] Unfortunately, when the polling news was not so encouraging, Johnson's assessments of Quayle were caustic and disparaging.

Robert M. Teeter (1939–2004) was an assistant professor at Adrian College in Michigan when he was offered a part-time position as an advance man with George Romney's gubernatorial re-election campaign. After Romney was re-elected in 1966, Teeter joined Fred Currier, Romney's pollster, and Walter De Vries at Market Opinion Research (MOR). He directed the political research division of the company and helped extend its reach outside of Michigan to campaigns in neighboring Ohio and other parts of the Midwest. In 1968, Teeter and Fred Currier bought the firm. MOR did political survey research, but most of its work was for business clients, especially automobile companies and Stroh's beer. Teeter insisted that political work pass the same tough criteria as commercial work, meaning it had to provide the same level of profit margins. Because of the cyclical nature and higher risk of political business, Teeter and MOR wanted campaign research to be no more than 20 percent of their entire business.[63]

In 1972 Teeter left MOR to help William D. Ruckelshaus organize the new Environmental Protection Agency in Washington. He returned to MOR, but was soon asked to become the research director for the Nixon Committee to Re-elect the President. His role was to analyze the survey research numbers rather than to make decisions about campaign strategy.[64] Teeter later became president of MOR and principal pollster for Gerald R. Ford's 1976 election, and he was later the pollster and strategist for George H. W. Bush in his quest for the 1980 presidential nomination. During the 1980 presidential general election, Reagan's chief pollster was Richard Wirthlin, but Teeter also conducted polls for the campaign in both 1980 and 1984 . He became the chief pollster for Bush in 1988, and later chaired the Bush re-election campaign in 1992. In his book on the private polling business, David W. Moore wrote that "of all the presidential pollsters, Robert Teeter has the most extensive experience and the most solid reputation among journalists and political observers."[65] In 2013 Teeter was posthumously inducted into the AAPC Hall of Fame.

Richard B. Wirthlin (1931–2011) first became involved in politics "absolutely by chance."[66] He had completed his PhD in economics at the University of California, Berkeley, and was teaching at Brigham Young University, when a friend who wanted to run for governor of Utah asked him if he knew anything about survey research. Dick Wirthlin hesitated at first, but then decided to help, using some graduate students and recruiting his wife, Jeralie, to write up the survey findings using an old Smith-Corona typewriter at their kitchen table. The friend lost, by about the percentage that Wirthlin predicted, but Wirthlin was now committed to a new career in professional survey research. "Politicians from all over the West flew into Provo to see what this professor and his students were doing politically," Wirthlin recalled.[67] He took a sabbatical from BYU in 1966, and by 1968 he was completely devoted to the new field of private polling.

One of Wirthlin's early customers was Barry Goldwater, who was attempting to regain his senate seat in Arizona in 1968 after losing the 1964 presidential campaign against Lyndon Johnson. At the time, Wirthlin was a visiting professor of economics at Arizona State University in Phoenix. There he teamed up with Bruce D. Merrill, an ASU political scientist, to conduct private polling through their firm, Merrill/Wirthlin. Lance Tarrance, who at the time was with the Republican National Committee, recalled that Merrill was the better known of the two, and more of the salesman for their services.[68] Goldwater recommended Wirthlin to

Reagan in the fall of 1968, and Reagan's people sent out feelers.[69] As Wirthlin recalled in his memoirs, a "Mr. Green" from New York wanted him to conduct a survey of Californians' attitudes toward selective policy issues and political leaders.[70] When he finished the survey, Wirthlin met with the mysterious Mr. Green (California political operative Tom Reed) at the International Hotel near the Los Angeles Airport, and they took a limousine up into the California hills, when Reed finally confessed that Wirthlin would be meeting with none other than the governor of California, Ronald Reagan.

Before the meeting, Wirthlin had thought Reagan was "politically to the right of Attila the Hun!" But after meeting with Reagan, discussing politics and issues that he cared about, Wirthlin was charmed: "My preconceptions of a heavy-handed, right-wing Hollywood actor had been wrong from the start." Further, Wirthlin discovered that it was a "synergy of words, values, and vision" that would "forever change the way I viewed political strategy and leadership."[71]

In 1969 Wirthlin started his firm, Decision Making Information (DMI) in Los Angeles. The firm was a subsidiary of the Spencer-Roberts Group and employed Wirthlin's friend, marketer Vincent P. Barabba, then president of Datamatics, Inc., who enticed him to come to California.[72] Working with Wirthlin and Barabba was Vince Breglio. During the decade of the 1970s, DMI handled between sixty and seventy campaigns each election cycle.[73] Wirthlin polled for Reagan's gubernatorial re-election campaign in 1970 against Democrat Jesse Unruh. Through a series of "what if" scenarios asked of voters, it was readily determined that Unruh had no chance of defeating Reagan. This allowed Reagan to reallocate much of his resources during the last four months of the campaign to help other Republicans get elected; Reagan, as predicted, was easily re-elected. Then in 1972, Reagan, who had flirted with a run for the presidency in 1968, asked Wirthlin to conduct a national study in preparation for a possible second run for the presidency in 1972.[74] But Reagan decided not to challenge Richard Nixon's re-election effort that year.

With Gerald Ford assuming the presidency in August 1974, and soon struggling, Wirthlin was brought in to conduct several polls on national issues, particularly the problems of inflation and the economy. He then signed on for Reagan's bid for the Republican 1976 presidential nomination. After Reagan won the presidency in 1980, Wirthlin moved his firm from Los Angeles to the suburbs of Washington (Republican consulting firms almost always choose the Virginia suburbs rather than the District of Columbia itself), and renamed his company The Wirthlin Group. Wirthlin's work is given further analysis in subsequent chapters. Democratic pollster Mark S. Mellman, among many to praise Wirthlin's career, wrote that Wirthin's "creative mind, interpretative genius, personal grace and commitment to his core values were unsurpassed."[75] In 2009, Wirthlin was inducted into the AAPC Hall of Fame.

In 1964, William R. Hamilton (1938–2000) established what has now become the longest-standing private partisan survey research firm in the United States. Hamilton, who held a master's degree in political science and did postgraduate work in research design at the University of North Carolina-Chapel Hill, began his career at the age of twenty-three in his native Florida with just one client, who was running for a state cabinet office. Hamilton was a truth-teller, and he could be both forthright and direct: when his first (and at that time only) candidate asked what his chances were, Hamilton said they were hopeless. The candidate dropped out, and Hamilton had no other clients. The next client was a gubernatorial candidate, who thought he might end up in second place, and thus become eligible in a run-off. Hamilton burst that bubble, telling the candidate he'd only come in fourth place. The candidate basically fired Hamilton, but learned a valuable lesson: he came in fourth place, as his pollster had predicted.[76]

Despite the inauspicious start, Bill Hamilton's business grew. In 1969 Jimmy Carter was assembling a team of campaign consultants for a run at the Georgia governorship. Carter had made an unsuccessful run for governor three years earlier, and he was now reassembling his team, which included Hamilton Jordan, Joseph L. (Jody) Powell, media consultant Gerald Rafshoon, and Bill Hamilton.[77] Several years later, Hamilton conducted a poll to determine whether Carter would be viewed as a credible vice-presidential running mate for George McGovern in 1972. Then, when Carter started thinking about a run for the presidency himself, Hamilton backed away. Over drinks at a bar in Chicago in 1975, Bill Hamilton was blunt with Jody Powell: Carter was not cut out to be president. "I didn't want to work for a candidate who was a long shot," Hamilton reminisced twenty years later.[78]

During his long career, Hamilton's clients have included Democratic senators John Glenn (Ohio), Lloyd Bentsen (Texas), Bob Graham (Florida), Adlai Stevenson III (Illinois), Paul Sarbanes (Maryland), and Tom Eagleton (Missouri), gubernatorial candidates John Y. Brown (Kentucky), Bruce Babbitt (Arizona), and Carter; and five presidential candidates: Hubert Humphrey (1968), Edmund Muskie (1972), Birch Bayh (1980), John Glenn (1984), and Bruce Babbitt (1988).

Hamilton also worked abroad, in twenty-two countries, introducing new techniques in telephone survey research; he also assisted with the survey research that supported the "Harry and Louise" television ads used against the Clinton administration's 1993 health-care proposal. In 1999 Hamilton was inducted into the AAPC Hall of Fame.

Media Consultants

> *The best thing about radio is that people were born without earlids. You can't close your ears to it.*
>
> —Tony Schwartz[79]

At the presidential level during the 1950s, television advertising continued to be dependent on major commercial advertising agencies, mostly based in New York. However, political media specialists began appearing in the 1960s, and they were influential in crafting and portraying candidates for office, especially candidates running for governor or the US Senate.

Charles E. Guggenheim (1924–2002), a native of Cincinnati, was first involved in political filmmaking when he worked for groups advocating a 1956 bond issue in St. Louis, Missouri. His advocacy film, showing the decaying infrastructure of St. Louis, was broadcast on all three network television stations at 8:00 o'clock in the evening. The bond issue passed, and Guggenheim's work was noticed by the Adlai Stevenson 1956 presidential campaign. After working for Stevenson, Guggenheim aided a candidate running against incumbent Orville Faubus in the 1958 Arkansas gubernatorial election. George McGovern, running for the US Senate in South Dakota, called next in 1962, and Guggenheim worked on his successful campaign.[80] After Stevenson, Guggenheim worked for four other Democratic candidates for president; altogether he worked in seventy-five campaigns.[81] His ads for Robert F. Kennedy's 1964 senatorial bid in New York, and then for his short-lived, chaotic presidential bid in 1968, represented some of his finest work. Of particular interest were the television spots made in Indiana. Kennedy, dressed in a suit and tie, was seen with farmers, factory workers, and children. In 2008, Ann Hornaday of the *Washington Post* wrote that "to watch Guggenheim's ads four decades later, it's possible to see the creation, almost in real time, of the grammar of political advertising—the elements of style that are still evident today, at a time when emerging technologies and political passion are merging again to revolutionize political communication."[82]

Guggenheim used a small, lightweight 16mm camera and a portable Nagra sound recorder, and in cinéma vérité fashion, captured small groups of people surrounding Kennedy, and asking tough questions. Kennedy was at once charming ("I'm doing a tremendous amount just personally for the farmer, with 10 children"), tough spoken ("I've seen children here in the United States *starving*"), and flippant (when asked how could he beat Nixon in Indiana, Kennedy responded, "Well, I know President Kennedy had some trouble with that").[83]

It wasn't clear if the 1968 Democratic nominating convention would accept the documentary film Guggenheim had created paying tribute to Robert Kennedy. Kennedy was assassinated on June 6, and the Democratic convention was held nine weeks later. The wounds of the Democratic Party were still raw due to the horrific losses of Kennedy and Martin Luther King Jr., the rift between Kennedy loyalists and Humphrey supporters, and the fact the Lyndon Johnson was still president. The memorial film was narrated, at Ethel Kennedy's request, by the actor Richard Burton, who recorded it in one take. "It was the greatest piece of narration I ever had since I've been in my business," observed Guggenheim.[84]

After having worked for the 1972 presidential campaign of George McGovern and the 1980 campaign of Edward Kennedy, Guggenheim decided to leave the business of political advertising in 1986, with his last client being his friend Senator Ernest (Fritz) Hollings of South Carolina. "The process now calls for using tactics and for using methods that are demeaning. You're in the process of creating half-truths, and trying to trick people on behalf of a candidate who may be very good. But if you don't do that, you won't win for him."[85] He found himself using "all kinds of half-truths" about other candidates, saying "I wasn't liking myself very much."[86]

Guggenheim was also well known for his four Academy Award-winning films: *Nine from Little Rock* (1964), *Robert Kennedy Remembered* (1968), *The Johnstown Flood* (1989), and *A Time for Justice* (1995). Near the end of his life, Guggenheim, together with his daughter Grace Guggenheim, produced a documentary, *Berga: Soldiers of Another War* (2002), about 350 America soldiers, from his own unit, who were captured by the Nazis during the Battle of the Bulge and sent to slave labor camps because they were Jewish or "looked Jewish."[87]

At the age of ten, Raymond D. Strother (b. 1940) was painting picket signs and handing out literature for US Senate candidate Ralph Yarborough. Strother's father was a union organizer in Port Arthur, Texas, who wanted his son to become a labor lawyer.[88] But Ray had another dream, to go to journalism school and become a political reporter. He worked for the Associated Press and completed a master's thesis at Louisiana State University in 1965 on propaganda and its use in politics. In his thesis, he predicted that media, and not political organization, would dominate future campaigns.[89] In the mid-1960s, Strother joined a relatively new ad agency operated by Gus Weill in Baton Rouge, Louisiana. Weill's upstart firm had pulled off a major upset by helping John J. McKeithen win the governor's race in 1963.[90] Now Strother was at the right place at the right time, when elected officials were looking at television as the new medium of communication. In 1968 Strother wrote in his memoir that "candidates had a great fear of political television."[91] Many were convinced that Kennedy beat Nixon in 1960 because of his skillful use of television. Gus Weill, the smooth salesman, convinced potential clients that young Strother was a "budding genius" who could solve their television communication problems. The only trouble was that Strother, while armed with a freshly minted master's degree, had no understanding of how television production worked. As he later confessed, "I only knew enough about television to turn on the black-and-white set."[92] But he was able to fake his way through and learn quickly on the job.

Strother's first client was McKeithen's handpicked candidate for state treasurer, Mary Evelyn Dickerson Parker—Miz Parker, or as she was later called "Hatchet Mary" because of her reputation as McKeithen's television attack dog. His work with Parker made Strother well known in the world of political consultants and operatives in Louisiana, and launched his career as one of the pioneer media and general consultants.

Strother created his own consulting firm and became media producer and consultant for successful US Senate candidates, including Lloyd Bentsen (Texas), Russell Long (Louisiana), John Stennis (Mississippi), Dennis Deconcini (New Mexico), Gary Hart (Colorado), Al Gore (Tennessee), Mary Landrieu (Louisiana), and Blanche Lincoln (Arkansas), along with a number of governors, including Bill Clinton, and several members of Congress. As seen in chapter 12, he was also principal adviser to Senator Gary Hart's two presidential campaigns, in 1984 and 1988. In 2008 Strother was inducted into the AAPC Hall of Fame.

Douglas L. Bailey (1933–2013) and John Deardourff (1943–2004) were moderate Rockefeller Republicans, who, according to the *Washington Post Magazine* in 1977, were "the two hottest hired guns the Grand Old Party can boast."[93] But moderate Republican candidates were becoming increasingly hard to find. In the 1970s, after the disastrous years of Watergate and the downfall of Richard Nixon, the Republican Party was tilting toward the right. But Deardourff remained optimistic, stating in 1980, "It's a mistake to believe that moderate Republicanism is on the way out. We go out and look for those candidates. We can offer our services to the people we want and the rest we can forget."[94]

John Deardourff grew up in a household filled with politics. His father ran a smalltown newspaper in Greenville, Ohio, and local politicians liked to get to know the editor and share their stories. After graduating from Wabash College, a small liberal arts school in Crawfordsville, Indiana, Deardourff went to the Fletcher School of Law and Diplomacy at Tufts University, and then moved to Washington to work as a staff aide for several members of Congress.[95] He became research director for the New York Republican State Committee, and was lent out to the John V. Lindsay campaign for mayor of New York City in 1965. Then he worked on the re-election campaign of New York governor Nelson A. Rockefeller. At the Rockefeller campaign, he met Doug Bailey.

Doug Bailey, born in Cleveland, received a bachelor's degree from Colgate University, served in the US Army for a year, and then earned a master's degree and PhD, also from the Fletcher School. Bailey's first taste of politics was working for George C. Lodge in his unsuccessful fight against Edward Kennedy for the US Senate in a Massachusetts special election in 1962. Bailey then worked in Washington as the research director for the Wednesday Group, an informal organization of moderate Republicans in the House of Representatives.

In 1966, Bailey and Deardourff, along with David B. Goldberg, created a firm called Campaign Consultants, Inc.,[96] with Goldberg's office in Boston, Deardourff's in New York City, and Bailey's in Washington, DC. Goldberg was the national director of the Draft [Henry Cabot] Lodge Committee in 1964, and primarily responsible for Lodge's victory in the 1964 Republican presidential primary in New Hampshire. Campaign Consultants was hired to run Nelson Rockefeller's unsuccessful presidential bid in 1968. After the 1968 election cycle, the consultants decided that having three separate offices was not working very well, and that they should concentrate their efforts in Washington; Goldberg decided to stay in Boston, however, and thus the firm was dissolved. In 1969 Bailey and Deardourff created their own firm, Campaign Systems, Inc., in Washington, and then in 1970, became Bailey, Deardourff and Bowen, with former advertising man John Bowen joining the firm.[97]

Richard Nixon tried to hire Bailey and Deardourff, but they refused. Doug Bailey recalled that in 1968, both he and Deardourff were recently married, and that their wives would have kicked them out of the house had they signed up with Nixon.[98] However, they did work for a string of moderate Republican candidates, including the US Senate campaigns of Edward Brooke (Massachusetts), John Chafee (Rhode Island), and Richard Lugar (Indiana), plus the gubernatorial races of Thomas Kean (New Jersey), Lamar Alexander (Tennessee), and Richard Thornburgh (Pennsylvania). In the mid-1970s, eleven of the nineteen Republican governors were clients of their firm. These candidates fit into their comfort zone: "We are one of the centers of moderate Republicanism," Deardourff said in 1979.[99]

The firm was best known for helping embattled president Gerald Ford run for a full term in 1976. Ford, who had suffered the most calamitous drop in the history of presidential approval ratings when he pardoned Richard Nixon in September 1974, was battling against a strong challenge from former California governor Ronald Reagan in the Republican primary, and he then faced former Georgia governor Jimmy Carter in the general election. As seen further in chapter 10, Republicans had been beaten down by the Watergate scandal, and Ford was not expected to retain the presidency. Bailey and Deardourff were hired at the Republican convention, and, at the time, Ford was down by 32 percentage points. In the end, with the help of upbeat media created by Bailey and Deardourff, Ford lost by just 2 percentage points in the popular votes, and by fifty-seven Electoral College votes.

In 1987 Doug Bailey decided to leave the firm (Deardourff would leave in 1992). He formed a partnership with direct-mail specialist Roger Craver, establishing *Hotline,* a daily political insiders newsletter, which they then sold to *National Journal* in 1996. Bailey also created several voter-oriented organizations during the 2000 and 2004 presidential campaigns: Rolling Cyber Debate, Freedom Channel, and Youth-e-Vote. Bailey then teamed up with former Clinton administration White House press secretary Mike McCurry to launch Freedom's Answer, an organization to help turn out young voters.

Together with Republican operative Jim Jonas and Democrats Hamilton Jordan, Gerald Rafshoon, and Roger Craver, Bailey created Unity08, a short-lived attempt to put together a unity ticket, with a Democrat and a Republican on the ticket. If things went as planned, Unity08 would have had the first online nominating convention.[100]

David Garth[101] (1930–2014) began his career in New York City at ABC-TV producing a weekly sports program and a weekly public affairs program, *Adlai Stevenson Reports.* He was nominated three times for Emmy Awards for the sports programs and won a Peabody Award for the Stevenson show. Throughout his career, Garth produced some 500 television shows. He did not get involved in politics until he was thirty years old. In 1960 he and several others, on their own, established a draft Adlai Stevenson club in New York. Once Eleanor Roosevelt joined the organization, it gained considerable publicity, and at the Democratic convention the Stevenson boomlet was a momentary stumbling block to John Kennedy's nomination. In the end, Stevenson decided not to jump into the presidential sweepstakes for a third time.

Garth's breakthrough into political consulting came with the New York City mayoral candidacy of John V. Lindsay in 1965. Under Garth's directions, Lindsay, the lean and photogenic congressman from Manhattan's "silk stocking" district, loosened his tie and draped his tailored suit coat over his shoulder, then ventured into poor sections of the city, talking with average voters, and showing his concern.[102] Garth helped Lindsay in his successful re-election campaign (1969), then assisted three other New York mayoral aspirants, Edward I. Koch (1977, 1981,

1985, 1989), Rudolph Giuliani (1993), and Michael Bloomberg (2002). In all, the New York City mayors he helped elect served forty years.

Garth also helped Tom Bradley win the mayoral race in Los Angeles three times (1973, 1977, and 1982), H. John Heinz III win three US Senate races in Pennsylvania (1976, 1982, and 1988), Adlai E. Stevenson III in Illinois (1974), and John V. Tunney in California (1971). He also was the lead consultant for Independent presidential candidate John B. Anderson in 1980. In 1978 the *Los Angeles Times* called him the "nation's hottest political consultant."[103] His early style, called the "Garth spot," showed candidates, like Lindsay, out with real people, with no script, natural lighting, and outdoor settings. But once other media consultants began copying his style, Garth adopted a news-style approach, making his ads deceptively simple.[104] Altogether, Garth participated in more than 150 political campaigns. Robert Shrum, who later became one of the most important Democratic consultants and is profiled in chapter 13, commented that Garth was "one of the two people most responsible for the central role of television in modern politics," the other being Charles Guggenheim.[105] In 2014, Garth was inducted into the AAPC Hall of Fame.

David Garth was also known for his gruff personality and barbed tongue. *New York Times* reporter Joseph Lelyveld captured the famous Garth temperament: "Garth . . . can wrap a barb in an insinuation with the loving finesse of a pastry chef filling a tart."[106] He also became the model for the rumpled, garrulous political consultant Marvin Lucas, in the 1972 movie *The Candidate.*

Robert Goodman (b. 1929) had an early love of music, not advertising, and he dreamed of being the next Irving Berlin.[107] "Ever since I was young, I wanted to be a song writer," he remembered.[108] He wrote a few jingles and musical scores, but did not have what it takes to make it on Broadway. Instead, he began a career in advertising at the Joseph Katz Agency in Baltimore. Katz had worked on the Adlai Stevenson campaign for president in the 1950s and was working for the Democratic National Committee. Goodman considered Katz, who had just an eighth grade education, "one of the greatest copywriters in America," whose basic style was simplicity, never using big words when short, punchy text would do. Goodman worked on Amoco Oil Corporation ads, wrote radio ads for Edward R. Murrow, and worked with Eleanor Roosevelt on Democratic Party advertisements.

Shortly after he opened his own agency in Baltimore in 1966, Goodman was approached by an obscure Republican candidate for governor, Spiro Agnew. Agnew won an upset victory over Democrat George P. Mahoney, whose race-tinged message was embodied in the slogan, "Your home is your castle." Agnew was considered the voice of reason, a moderate in civil rights matters, and some 80,000 Democrats crossed party lines to vote for him. With a singer mimicking Frank Sinatra's version of "My Kind of Town," we learned from Goodman's commercial how swell Agnew would be for Maryland: "My kind of man, Ted Agnew is, my kind of man, Ted Agnew is. A bright new talent for, governor, and what's more, he's your kind of man."[109]

Goodman became, in the words of *New York Times* reporter Bernard Weintraub, an "influential and provocative figure" in political advertising.[110] By the time he handled his first presidential account in 1980 for George H. W. Bush, Goodman had worked in sixty-four Republican statewide contests in thirty-one states. He became known as the "jingle man"—approvingly by his admirers, disdainfully by some of his competitors. "In politics I saw an incredible outlet," Goodman recalled in 1999. "I saw politics as a drama and the candidates were the stars in my musical comedies."[111]

He once hired a seventy-eight-piece orchestra to back up a commercial for Minnesota senator Rudy Boschwitz.[112] Goodman noted that he wasn't all that great at directing spots, but that he hired great people to do that work. "Actually what I did was paste pictures over my music, for years. . . . I think I helped sing a lot of people into office."[113] For Goodman, music captured the feeling of the campaign and the state or region where the campaign was being fought.[114] In 1998 Goodman was inducted into the AAPC Hall of Fame.

Roger E. Ailes (b. 1940) was born in Warren, Ohio, graduated from Ohio University in Athens, then began his multipronged media career, as a producer and director of a Cleveland-based television variety show, the *Mike Douglas Show*. The show then became syndicated nationally, and Ailes received two Emmy Awards for producing it. In 1967, one of the guests on the show was Richard Nixon, who had his own checkered experienced with television. Nixon, soon to be the presidential candidate for the Republican Party, asked Ailes to produce television commercials for his campaign. Ailes's involvement in preparing Nixon for debates and telethons is richly described in Joe McGinniss's tell-all, *The Selling of the President 1968*,[115] as described in chapter 5.

Ailes originally planned to return to network television, but, perhaps thanks to the notoriety of the McGinniss book, he was "swamped with offers" to run political campaigns in the 1970s.[116] As his brother Robert observed, Roger's career was "started not by Richard Nixon but by Joe McGinniss."[117] Ailes was essentially frozen out of the Nixon White House and turned to private political consulting. He founded Ailes Communications, Inc. in New York in 1969, and consulted with a variety of businesses as well as political candidates. He worked with a wide range of Republican senatorial and congressional candidates for office in the 1970s and 1980s—about 140 campaigns according to his own reckoning, winning about nine out of ten.[118] He helped prepare Ronald Reagan for his debates in the 1984 election, and his aggressive ads in 1988 helped George Bush defeat Michael Dukakis. During the 1980s, Ailes and Democratic media consultant Bob Squier would debate each other on NBC's *The Today Show*. Biographer Zev Chafets wrote that the 1988 election made Ailes into "the first superstar political consultant, so famous and infamous that his mere participation in a campaign became an issue."[119] However, in 1992, following the disastrous 1991 campaign of Richard Thornburgh for a US Senate seat in Pennsylvania, Ailes withdrew from political consulting to concentrate on television.[120]

He had earlier worked as a television executive producer and had tried his hand in theater production. After leaving political consulting, Ailes produced the Rush Limbaugh television show, consulted on Paramount Television's tabloid show *Inside Edition*, and became president of the CNBC cable television network. In 1996 he became chief executive officer of Fox News. Ailes also is the author, with Jon Kraushar, of *You Are the Message: Secrets of the Master Communicators.*[121]

Following his graduation from the Pratt Institute in 1944, Tony Schwartz (1923-2008) began recording the sounds of his native New York City, from the giggles and screams of children playing in the parks, the screeching of subway cars, to conversations with taxicab drivers. From 1945 to 1976, he produced a weekly radio program on the people and sounds of his city.

Schwartz, described by Randall Rothenberg of the *New York Times* as having a "face like a potato, all soft bulges and small eyes," was reclusive (suffering from agoraphobia) and somewhat eccentric. A native New Yorker, he rarely left his Hell's Kitchen home, jam-packed with electronic equipment and sound recording devices. In his old townhouse on Fifty-Sixth Street and Tenth Avenue, the bathroom had two toilets, one labeled "Republicans," and the other labeled "Democrats."[122] Schwartz was dubbed the "American advertising world's acknowledged King of Sound,"[123] and he estimated that his collection of sounds included more than 20,000 samples. Schwartz was the first to use children in advertisements; before this, adult females faked the voices of children. Schwartz believed that shame was a tool that should be used in commercials. One of his most notable advertisements was one of the first anti-smoking commercials, with children dressed up in their parents clothing. The commercial voice-over said this: "Children learn by imitating their parents. Do you smoke cigarettes?"[124]

Throughout his career, Schwartz produced over 200 ads for political candidates, but none was more famous or controversial than his first, the "Daisy" commercial for the Lyndon Johnson 1964 presidential campaign (see the following chapter for more on this historic commercial). His other clients included Jimmy Carter's 1976 presidential election campaign; the US Senate campaigns of Abe Ribicoff (Connecticut), Daniel P. Moynihan (New York), Edward Kennedy (Massachusetts), and Mike Gravel (Alaska); and the campaigns of House leader Tom Foley (Washington) and Representative Andrew Young (Georgia).

Schwartz was a disciple of the media theorist Marshall McLuhan, and later shared teaching responsibilities with McLuhan at Fordham University.[125] In his influential 1974 book *The Responsive Chord*,[126] Schwartz argued that he did not want to package candidates; rather, he wanted to package voters. Television, in Schwartz's view, was the ideal medium for "surfacing feelings voters already have." The best campaign commercials were similar to Rorschach patterns: "They do not tell the viewer anything. They surface his feelings and provide a context for him to express his feelings."

In the pre-online age, Schwartz was also a pioneer: he lectured to students at various universities and conducted seminars throughout the world without leaving his Hell's Kitchen home. He was visiting electronic professor at Harvard, and taught for New York University, Columbia, Emerson College, and Fordham University. In 2001 Schwartz was inducted into the AAPC Hall of Fame.

Field Operations

While the use of television ads in the 1952 presidential campaign caught the attention of most campaign watchers, another critical factor involved strategic field operations. Republicans, who did it best, put together a strategic campaign plan, laying out how Eisenhower would address issues, where and when he would go, and how media would be used to communicate the message. The plan also focused on targeting the base of Republican voters, some 20 million, and then going after those who favored Eisenhower but had not registered or cast their votes in the previous presidential election. The Republican operation clicked, and millions of new voters were registered, while the Democrats, often at cross-purposes with one another, were "ill-equipped strategically, philosophically and organizationally" to take on Eisenhower.[127]

Much like the Eisenhower strategists, the Kennedy operatives in 1960 decided to make a major effort to capture those citizens who were not registered and had never voted before. They estimated that of the 107 million people old enough to vote in 1960, 40 million were not registered; and they surmised that seven out of ten of those nonregistered voters would be Democrats. The goal was to increase Democratic registration by 10 million; this turned out to be unrealistically high, but the party was able to sign up over 8.5 million new voters by October 1960, and that effort probably made the difference in closely contested states like New York.[128]

Lawrence F. O'Brien Jr. (1917–1990), director of organization for the Kennedy campaign, was principally responsible for the voter registration plan, but he was also critical in the early quiet days of lining up delegates in state after state. Larry O'Brien spent much of 1959 on the road, going to each of the primary states—Indiana, California, Nebraska, Montana, Wyoming, Colorado, New Hampshire, Oregon, Maryland, Wisconsin, and West Virginia—and talking up Kennedy, getting to know local leaders, and securing their commitment. "The thing that amazes me," O'Brien later wrote in his memoirs, "is that we had the field almost entirely to ourselves."[129] There were no representatives from the Adlai Stevenson, Hubert Humphrey, Stuart Symington, or Lyndon Johnson campaigns. Johnson biographer Robert A. Caro writes of the uncharacteristic indecision of Lyndon Johnson, and of the unease that it caused his closest advisers. Johnson, the master of the Senate, thought that since he controlled his Senate colleagues, they controlled their state delegations and could be counted on to support him; Kennedy forces knew better, and wholly outmaneuvered Johnson.[130]

In 1960, the Kennedy campaign was following the O'Brien Manual, a sixty-four-page grassroots fieldwork and volunteer plan first put together by O'Brien for Kennedy's 1952 Massachusetts Senate race. It went out to volunteers and party officials throughout the country, outlining the role of coordinators, preparation of mailings, telephone banks, handing out literature, and get-out-the-vote efforts. It was used with particular effectiveness in West Virginia, where an eager young volunteer was ready to help.

Twenty-six-year-old Matthew A. Reese (1927–1998) came to Washington in the mid-1950s after helping one of his Marshall University professors successfully run for Congress. Two years later, when his boss Representative Maurice Gwinn Burnside (Democrat-West Virginia) lost in the Eisenhower presidential sweep of 1956, Reese became involved in a political organization, the Young Democrats. One day, he happened to meet Senator John Kennedy on the US Capitol steps. Kennedy, recently ill, was on crutches, but made a good impression on the young man from Huntington, West Virginia. In the fall of 1959, Reese received a card from the Democratic National Committee seeking volunteers, and he checked the name of John Kennedy as the person he would like to help. "This was the reason I was picked to do a little early volunteer work for the senator," Reese recalled.[131]

From the basement of the Kanawha Hotel in Charleston, West Virginia, Matt Reese joined other Kennedy volunteers, working the telephones eighteen hours a day, persuading Democratic voters to choose Kennedy over Hubert Humphrey.[132] Every morning, the gregarious, 300-plus-pound Reese brought cartons of Coca-Cola and huge bags of potato chips, appeasing his appetite as he worked the phones for long hours.[133]

Reese was asked to put on an event in Huntington, his hometown. He thought he could get 600, maybe 700 people, but in the end over 5,000 attended. Reese learned from the Kennedy organizers a valuable lesson in campaign psychology and planning. The Kennedy staffers asked twenty-four women to serve on the committee for the Huntington event, and asked them to bring their lists of friends and neighbors from club memberships, PTAs, and Christmas card mailings. The fancy invitation read: "West Virginians for Kennedy cordially invite you to meet Senator and Mrs. Kennedy." The results were "monstrous," Reese recalled: 15,000 invitations sent, and over 5,000 people came. This was an unheard-of positive response rate, and at the cost of just 19 cents per person for the room, the mailing, the cookies, and tea. "I would never have thought of this," Reese recalled.[134] This, however, was a long-established tactic of the Kennedy campaign operatives, particularly Larry O'Brien. In Kennedy's 1952 Senate campaign against incumbent Henry Cabot Lodge Jr., tens of thousands of women were sent engraved invitations, addressed by hand, to meet Kennedy and his family.[135]

Reese, who was Kennedy's only paid worker in West Virginia, took the O'Brien Manual and used it to assemble Kennedy chairmen in thirty-nine of the state's fifty-five counties. Out of that organization came a potent volunteer base.[136]

Despite all the fears of a Hubert Humphrey triumph, John Kennedy prevailed in West Virginia, by a margin of 61–39 percent, carrying forty-eight of the state's fifty-five counties. Reese was sent to work on the Tennessee delegation at the Democratic convention, then work in North Carolina during the general election.

For Matt Reese, this was the beginning of the political consulting career as one of the founders of the industry. After the 1960 election, he ran the voter registration division of the DNC, and is credited with having boosted voter registration for the 1964 presidential election by 4 million voters. He went back to a government job in West Virginia, and in 1966 he formed Matt Reese & Associates, which later became Reese Communications Companies.[137] Reese was a supreme field organizer and a specialist in voter contact. Long before computer technology, Reese was able to put together instant coalitions, recruit hundreds of block captains, and utilize telephone banks; these were demanding and labor-intensive efforts, but absolutely critical to campaigns.

As an example, during the Democratic presidential primaries of 1968, Matt Reese was assisting the Robert F. Kennedy campaign. For the crucial Indiana primary, Reese set up phone banks and a get-out-the-vote effort for the ten or twelve days before the May 1968 primary. Reese's firm recruited 15,000 block campaigns in five major Indiana cities, energized participants with receptions, callbacks to remind them to attend, and visits from the extended Kennedy family at rallies.[138] Reese was also a pioneer at voter targeting, using sophisticated methods to determine likely supporters.[139]

Altogether, Reese and his firm worked in more than 450 political campaigns both in the United States and internationally. The *Washington Post* in 1989 observed that Reese had "changed politics forever, and in the process, transformed political consulting from a backroom fraternity of cutthroat hacks into a bona fide billion-dollar industry of influence."[140] By 1982, Reese had waged his last candidate campaigns. He then went into the much more lucrative field of corporate work, before selling his business to an international public relations conglomerate. In 1992 Reese was inducted into the AAPC Hall of Fame.

In 1972, the Campaign Communications Institute for Politics, a New York–based communications firm, compiled a list of campaign consultants; it tallied 278 firms and individuals that provided campaign services, from campaign management, to survey research, to lobbying.[141] Writing in 1980, journalist Nicholas Lemann summed up the job of the top consultants: "The consultants' most important function—the job of the people at the top of the field, and the centerpiece of modern American political campaigning—was taking public opinion polls and then designing television advertising based on the results. To put it more generally, what they did was try to determine what it was that would make people vote for a candidate, and then find a way to present that argument directly to the voters it was meant to sway."[142]

The IAPC and AAPC

In the mid-1960s, Joseph Napolitan, somewhat restless with American campaigns, began spending time in Europe during off-election years, visiting capital cities, and meeting with political party leaders. Napolitan had read in a 1967 *New York Times* article that a French political consultant, Michel Bongrand (1921–2014), had been using American campaign techniques in European elections.[143] In 1967 Napolitan and Bongrand met in Paris and came up with the idea of establishing an international club of political consultants. Thus was born the International Association of Political Consultants (IAPC) which held its first meeting in Paris immediately following the November 1968 US presidential election, with representatives from fifteen countries in attendance.[144]

Two months later, in January 1969, an American counterpart to the IAPC was formed. Led by Napolitan, fifty-eight political consultants met at the Plaza Hotel in New York City to discuss the creation of a professional organization. Out of that meeting came the American Association of Political Consultants (AAPC), and Napolitan was elected the president, with F. Clifton White as vice president, Walter De Vries as secretary, and Martin Ryan Haley, a New York-based general consultant, as treasurer. Bill Hamilton, who later became president of the AAPC, remarked that "you couldn't quite fit us all in a phone booth," but within several years, the membership had grown to 100 consultants.[145] The organization's leadership was equally divided along partisan lines, with a Democratic chosen as president one year, followed by a Republican the next year. One of the early issues involved the creation of a code of ethics for the organization. Napolitan confessed that it was impossible to come up with a workable code; Martin Haley suggested that there was nothing wrong with adopting the Ten Commandments.[146] Republican consultant Tom Edmonds, who later became president of both the AAPC and IAPC, warned against self-regulation, principally because politics and campaigning deals largely with issues of free speech:

> We cannot restrict trade; we cannot restrict the First Amendment to the Constitution; we cannot penalize those who choose not to be AAPC members. We've got to be very, very careful that we don't put the organization in the position of being liable or trying to restrict or be exclusive in terms of who may practice in this profession and who may not.[147]

The AAPC now has a code of ethics, adopted unanimously at its annual meeting in Las Vegas, Nevada, in 1994, though it is rarely enforced. See chapter 21 for further discussion of campaign ethics and political consultants.

Other regional political consultant organizations were later created. The European Association of Political Consultants (EAPC) was formed in 1996, and, more recently, the Asia Pacific Association of Political Consultants (APAPC), the Brazilian Association of Political Consultants (Associação Brasileira de Consultores Políticos), the Canadian Association of Political Consultants, and the Latin American Association of Political Consultants (Asociación Latinoamericana de Consultores Políticos, or ALACOP).

CHAPTER 5

Consultants and Presidential Campaigns, 1964 and 1968, and Consulting Abroad

Your job, Mr. President, is to tell us what to say.
Our job is to tell you how to say it.
Advertising executive William Bernbach to Lyndon Johnson (1964)

Someday we'll elect a Republican president who is worth
electing. In the meantime, we'll make lots of money.
—A Republican campaign manager (1969)

PRESIDENTIAL ELECTIONS, HELD every four years, are the centerpiece of American democracy. We rightly focus on the candidates themselves, their character, experience, temperament, and policy preferences. We measure them against the performance of the economy, our own prejudices and insecurities, and our hopes and aspirations. We put them through an arduous, time- and energy-consuming process that often begins two or more years before Election Day, that requires them to woo party insiders and grub for money, convince a relatively small group of enthusiastic and often sharply partisan voters to choose them in primary and caucus contests in states throughout the country, and assemble in state after state a core of volunteers willing to do the legwork for the all-important ground game.

No candidate can do this alone, not even outsiders like Ross Perot or Donald Trump. And particularly when devising the campaign's strategy, crafting its message, and implementing its tactics, the candidate must rely on key advisers. For much of the history of American campaigning, candidates relied on national, state, or local political party operatives or persons tied to them by friendship or political loyalty. At the presidential level, several such individuals stood out.

Democratic Party chairman James A. Farley and Louis Howe served as chief campaign advisers during Franklin Roosevelt's 1932 campaign (as well as his earlier campaigns for governor of New York); Farley aided Roosevelt again in 1936, but Howe died before the end of Roosevelt's first term. Herbert Brownell Jr. twice served as Thomas Dewey's campaign manager for president (and as Republican Party chairman), and he helped convince Eisenhower to run in 1952; he then became attorney general during the Eisenhower administration. Clark Clifford, Truman's strategist in the come-from-behind 1948 race, became a lawyer-lobbyist, and later secretary of defense and Washington *éminence grise*. Robert F. Kennedy was his brother's chief political adviser in the 1960 campaign, and then became attorney general, US senator from New York, and presidential candidate in 1968. Lawrence F. O'Brien Jr. was a key campaign operative for Kennedy throughout his career, particularly in the 1960 presidential election, and he was campaign manager for Lyndon Johnson in 1964 (he then became US postmaster general, and later commissioner of the National Basketball Association). These individuals led the campaign efforts, while party workers and volunteers assisted with the many thousands of details.

But by the mid-1960s, there had been an important change in the conduct of presidential campaigns. The old way of electing presidents had given way to a new electoral system. Political scientist Darrell M. West sums up what had changed in his book *Making Campaigns Count*. In the old system, from the 1930s to the 1960s, he states, the nominating process was predictable:

> There were few primaries; most delegates were selected through caucuses where party leaders exercised considerable influence. Presidents generally had a free ride to renomination. . . . Dark horses were rare. Party identifications in the electorate were strong and stable from election to election. . . . Campaign technologies were relatively unsophisticated.[1]

In the new electoral system, however, there were many changes:

> With the proliferation of primaries, nominating contests have become long and unpredictable. In-party challenges are the rule, not the exception. Dark horse candidates have multiplied. Party loyalties are weak; short-term campaign forces (like personal campaigning, media appeals, and clever symbolism and rhetoric) enable candidates to build momentum. Party leaders have lost influence while specialists in new technologies have gained.[2]

During the presidential campaigns in the 1960s, private polling was in its infancy, Madison Avenue firms continued to be the main focus of media advertising, and grassroots activism was still directed mostly by volunteers. Yet by 1964, and especially 1968, new players, including some of the key pioneers in political consulting, were now helping to craft campaign messages, develop strategy, and communicate to voters through the new medium of television.

The 1964 Presidential Election: Lyndon Johnson v. Barry Goldwater

*I want you to know that some day, people are going
to look back at '64 and say that we changed
the Republican Party.*

—Pollster V. Lance Tarrance Jr., speaking to Barry Goldwater
about the 1964 presidential election (1964)[3]

Lyndon B. Johnson, who had become president on November 22, 1963, ran unopposed as the 1964 Democratic nominee, and he chose Minnesota senator Hubert H. Humphrey as his vice-presidential running mate. On the Republican side, there was a political and ideological scramble for the presidential nomination. Conservative Arizona senator Barry Goldwater was competing against New York governor Nelson A. Rockefeller and Pennsylvania governor William W. Scranton II. At first, Goldwater was reluctant to run, but he was persuaded by admirers and close associates to challenge Rockefeller, Scranton, and three other candidates.

With the death of Ohio senator Robert A. Taft in 1953, the conservative wing of the Republican Party had lost its most influential voice. For a time, Richard Nixon looked to be the one to fill the vacuum. But Nixon was defeated by Kennedy in 1960, then lost the California gubernatorial race in 1962, bitterly telling journalists that they "wouldn't have Nixon to kick around anymore." Many Republicans assumed that the 1964 nomination would go to Nelson Rockefeller, who had won a resounding re-election as governor of New York in 1962. Behind the scenes, Rockefeller was eagerly courting Goldwater, trying to keep him from running for the nomination. Both Rockefeller and Goldwater distrusted Nixon, and they spoke of the need for party unity; but unity would never come.

The Role of F. Clifton White

The most important person instrumental in drumming up support for Goldwater was also one of the pioneer political consultants, Clif White.[4] Through a series of secret meetings with like-minded conservatives, White emerged as the leader in the Draft Goldwater movement. As the movement picked up support, and thousands of Goldwater supporters were mobilized, it became nearly impossible for the senator to ignore this growing national political force. Journalist Robert D. Novak observed that during the delegate selection process, White "exercised a degree of personal control . . . not seen before in American politics."[5] By August 1963 the Draft Goldwater forces, under White and Peter O'Donnell, the Republican Party chairman from Texas, had become the "combat troops" of the Goldwater movement, with a permanent headquarters in Washington, DC.

White had help in creating the movement, but later was brushed aside. John Grenier, from the Republican National Committee (RNC), was brought in to manage Goldwater's campaign during the primaries. Then one of Goldwater's closest confidants, mining lawyer Denison Kitchel, was brought in to manage the general election and White was shunted to the corner. Stephen Shadegg, described by journalist Rick Perlstein as "swarthy, intense, standoffish,"[6] had managed Goldwater's Senate campaigns in 1952 and 1958, but this veteran operative was also passed over in the presidential race. A disappointed White later wrote that "Denny Kitchel was a nuisance and a hindrance from the start," and knew "next to nothing about politics."[7] Joining Kitchel were Richard Kleindienst, Dean Burch, and others dubbed the "Arizona mafia." They were a "bunch of cowboys," as they called themselves, "proud, almost, of what they didn't know."[8] The Goldwater inner circle, indeed, was one of sincere amateurs, with little experience in campaigning, and none at the presidential level, driven by loyalty to Goldwater and admiration of his conservative ideology. William J. Baroody, head of the American Enterprise Institute, a conservative think tank, tried to help by bringing in several of his associates, including Edward McCabe, who became director of research, and Karl Hess who became Goldwater's speechwriter.[9]

Television, now a prominent fixture in most homes, became an important communication tool in the 1964 election season. Leading up to the presidential year, television had been key in capturing the realities and tensions of the times: the civil rights marches, the beating of protestors, urban riots, the unfolding of conflict in Vietnam, and the assassination of a president. Television coverage, too, was seen more and more in the presidential primaries.

Through the early primaries, Goldwater was blunt, forthcoming, and controversial: he was against the popular Medicare proposal working its way through Congress, and he would not support the landmark Civil Rights Act of 1964. His view on nuclear weapons got him into hot water; he even suggested to an enthusiastic group of supporters in California that nuclear weapons be used to defoliate Vietnam. In a last-gasp effort to stop Goldwater during the crucial California primary, the consulting firm of Spencer-Roberts, working for Rockefeller, mailed 2 million fliers to registered Republicans with the simple message: "Who Do You Want in the Room with the H Bomb?," accompanied by some of Goldwater's most extreme statements.[10] Spencer-Roberts also produced a half-hour film called *The Extremist*, but Rockefeller considered it too much like "McCarthyism-in-reverse" and decided not to use it. Then Spencer-Roberts hired 1,200 telephone operators to set up a phone bank to persuade Republican voters to oppose Goldwater. Despite all the efforts of California's best-known consulting firm, and bags full of Rockefeller money, Goldwater won the California primary with 51.5 percent of the vote, and the Rockefeller drive for the nomination effectively came to an end.[11]

The General Election

During the general election, the Republican and Democratic campaign teams took different approaches to their television advertising. Goldwater, still relatively unknown to many voters, relied on thirty-minute television ads, featuring the candidate himself defending his position against charges by Democrats. But

Goldwater had helped to dig his own negative image, with reckless statements about what he would do as president. Also not helping were the scenes from the raucous Republican nominating convention, covered gavel-to-gavel on network television, of Rockefeller being jeered, and Goldwater delivering his memorable words, "Extremism in the defense of liberty is no vice! Moderation in the pursuit of justice is no virtue!" As Stephen Shadegg, Goldwater's long-time campaign adviser, wrote, "the phrase about extremism, which for any other candidate in any other context might have been greeted with loud approval, ripped open old wounds and erected barriers which were never broken."[12]

Goldwater, with another self-inflicted wound, was now the "the Extremist" presidential candidate, and his attempts to clarify and explain what he meant missed the mark. The Democrats, with a series of short negative ads, pounced on Goldwater. Doyle Dane Bernbach (DDB), the Madison Avenue advertising firm handling the Johnson account, used props and visuals to get across the basic theme: Goldwater could not be trusted. In one television spot, seen more often than any other Johnson ad, a Social Security card was slowly torn apart and voters were warned about what would happen if Barry Goldwater got his way.[13]

"Social Security"

> *Male Narrator*: On at least seven different occasions, Barry Goldwater has
>   said he would drastically change the social security system.
> [*Video: as each source is mentioned, the newspaper, speech, or tape is
> slapped down on a table, building up to a tall pile*]
>
> *Male Narrator*: In the Chattanooga *Tennessee Times*, in a "Face the
> Nation" interview, in the *New York Times Magazine*, in a Continental
> Classroom TV interview, in the *New York Journal American*, in a
> speech he made only last January in Concord, New Hampshire, and
> in the *Congressional Record*. Even his running mate, William Miller,
> admits that Barry Goldwater's voluntary plan would wreck your Social
> Security.
>
> *Lyndon Johnson* (AT DEMOCRATIC CONVENTION): Too many have worked
>   too long and too hard to see this threatened now by policies which
>   promise to undo all that we have done together over all these years.
> *Male Narrator*: For over thirty years President Johnson has worked to
>   strengthen Social Security. Vote for him on November 3rd. The stakes
>   are too high for you to stay home.[14]

In another ad, a Styrofoam map of the United States floated in a body of water, and from underneath the water a saw was cutting off the Eastern Seaboard. The sawing began, with no commentary, and continued for 24 seconds. All the viewer heard was scraping sound of the saw and the gurgling of the water beneath it. Then the male narrator spoke.[15]

"Eastern Seaboard"

> *Male Narrator*: In a *Saturday Evening Post* article dated August 31st, 1963, Barry Goldwater said, "Sometimes I think this country would be better off if we could just saw off the Eastern Seaboard and let it float out to sea." Can a man who makes statements like this be expected to serve all the people, justly and fairly?
> [*Sound of the Eastern Seaboard sawed off, breaking away from the rest of the map, and floating away.*]
>
> *Male Narrator*: Vote for President Johnson on November 3rd. The stakes are too high for you to stay home.

The last sentence—"The stakes are too high for you to stay home"—was particularly important, because the campaign feared that Democratic voters would become too complacent, assume that Johnson would win, and would decide not to vote. As noted below, Democrats feared (and Republicans hoped) that there was hidden support for Goldwater that was not showing up in the public polling.

DDB, Tony Schwartz, and the "Daisy" Ad

Goldwater, trigger-happy; Goldwater, too eager to use nuclear bombs. That was the message Nelson Rockefeller tried to fix in the minds of California primary voters; now the Johnson campaign would take that theme nationwide against Goldwater. The "Daisy" ad was but the opening salvo. This most famous, or infamous, Democratic political spot was shown only once, on September 7, at 9:50 p.m. eastern time, during a commercial break for NBC's *Monday Night Movies*, the 1951 biblical drama *David and Bathsheba*. "Daisy" made such a jolt that it was covered on all the morning newscasts of the three networks the next day, and it also was featured on the cover of *Time* magazine. The one-minute spot gained a place in campaign history and has become required viewing in college courses on political communication and campaigns ever since. *Advertising Age* rated it the second most important political commercial ever created.[16]

In September 1963, John Kennedy asked his newly appointed re-election campaign director, Stephen Smith, to talk with Doyle Dane Bernbach (DDB), one of the most successful and talked-about New York ad agencies. In 1959, DDB had created the memorable "Think Small" campaign for Volkswagen, revolutionizing the way print ads presented their message; it turned the VW from the peoples' car of Nazi Germany into a Beetle, a cute little bug. In 1960, DDB crafted the "We Try Harder Because We're Number 2" message for Avis Rental Cars. Kennedy saw the humor in the auto commercials, liked that DDB was a solidly Democratic shop, and thought the agency would help his re-election.[17] Yet DDB had never handled a political account before.

Lyndon Johnson began gearing up for the 1964 election in February of that year. He turned to DDB, but there was serious opposition to using an advertising firm coming from the Democratic National Committee, particularly from chairman John Bailey and Richard Maguire, who thought the cost of an advertising agency wasn't worth it, considering the president's ability to gather in free television time any time he wanted. But in the end, DDB was hired, and thirty-year-old presidential assistant Bill D. Moyers was put in charge of all media and speech coordination for the upcoming campaign.

Out of the 800-member agency, Bill Bernbach and account executive James Graham selected forty Democrats to work on the campaign.[18] Aaron Ehrlich, a producer at DDB, called Tony Schwartz, to see if his one-time collaborator would help the Johnson campaign and DDB in producing a one-minute advertisement based on a five-minute outline that the agency had created. The outline was about Soviet missiles and began with a voice-over of an American missile countdown. Could Schwartz make a one-minute version? Thus was born one of the most controversial political commercials in American history, "Peace, Little Girl," as DDB labeled it, but "Daisy" to the world of political consulting and political communications history.[19]

"Daisy" ("Peace, Little Girl")

[*Video: Camera focuses on a little girl in a field, picking petals off a daisy*].

[*Audio: Birds chirping.*]

Little girl: "One, two, three, four, five, seven, six, six, eight, nine, nine . . ."

[*Video: Girl looks up and is startled. Freeze frame on her, the camera focuses on her right eye, until the screen goes blank.*]

[*Audio: A man's loud, authoritative voice, as if over a loudspeaker: "Ten, nine, eight, seven, six, five, four, three, two, one—"*]

[*Video: Atomic bomb explodes, then to a close up of the explosion.*]

[*Audio: Sound of the explosion.*]

Lyndon Johnson (in voice-over): These are the stakes—to make a world in which all of God's children can live, or to go into the dark. We must either love each other, or we must die.

[*Video: White letters on a black background: "Vote for President Johnson on November 3."*]

Announcer (in voice-over): Vote for President Johnson on November 3. The stakes are too high for you to stay home.

The ad never mentioned Goldwater and Johnson's voice (but not his image) came in only toward the end. White House aide Bill Moyers reported that Lyndon Johnson was "very pleased" with the commercial. Understandably, the Republican Party and Goldwater fumed. Dean Burch, chairman of the RNC, filed a complaint with the Fair Campaign Practices Committee, charging that the ad amounted to "libel against the Republican nominee."[20]

Barry Goldwater later reflected that the "Daisy" commercial was the start of "all this dirty ten-second advertising" seen on television, and in his memoirs he wrote, "Every time I saw that hideous Johnson TV commercial with the little girl, it saddened me to realize that all involved—the reporter, the spot writer, the producer, the advertising agency, and the candidate who was then incumbent president of the United States—valued political victory more than personal honesty."[21]

Tony Schwartz, understandably, saw it differently. It was one of his fundamental insights that "the most meaningful aspect of recall in electronic media is not what you recall after you see the commercial, but what is evoked while you're seeing the commercial." "Daisy" affirmed this concept, according to Schwartz, because it reminded television viewers of their fear that Barry Goldwater was "trigger happy."[22] Indeed, in both Republican and Democratic private polls, respondents feared that Goldwater might begin a nuclear war.[23] In his later years, during an MSNBC interview in 2000, Schwartz reflected on "Daisy": "For many years, it's been referred to as the beginning of negative commercials. There is nothing negative about it. Frankly, I think it was the most positive commercial ever made."[24]

Ironically, the protests from the Republican side kept the issue alive for the public, with the networks replaying the ad as a news feature. Charles M. Lichenstein, Goldwater's media strategist acknowledged, "We gave the 'Daisy' ad so much publicity that it was shown over and over again on news and commentary programs so a lot of people saw it who wouldn't have ordinarily seen it."[25]

"Daisy" was copied by candidates and independent groups in later campaigns, but, as historian Robert Mann noted, "never with the same degree of success" as achieved in 1964.[26] Variations of the "Daisy" commercial were shown in the 1996 and 2000 presidential campaigns and in the 2010 congressional races. There was, however, ongoing controversy over who was responsible for the ad's creation. DDB and Schwartz both claimed to be the creators, and as the advertisement went from famous to legendary, the contention over who should get ultimate credit grew greater.

After the "Daisy" ad came the next round of commercials on the theme of nuclear destruction and Goldwater. On September 12, on *NBC Saturday Night at the Movies*, "Little Girl, Ice Cream Cone," a Democratic National Committee ad, produced by the DDB team and Tony Schwartz, was aired. It featured another little girl and the health dangers of nuclear testing that Goldwater wanted to restart. A little girl with long brown hair, wearing a jumper, is licking an ice cone, and continues to do so throughout the 30-second video. The dialogue was very simple, with a voice-over by a woman (a first in presidential commercials).[27]

"Little Girl, Ice Cream Cone"

Female Narrator: Do you know what people used to do? They used to explode atomic bombs in the air. Now children should have lots of vitamin A and calcium, but they shouldn't have any strontium 90 or cesium 137. These things come from atomic bombs, and they are radioactive.

They can make you die. Do you know what people finally did? They got together and signed a nuclear test ban treaty. And then the radioactive poison started to go away.

But now there's a man who wants to be president of the United States, and he doesn't like this treaty. He fought against it. He even voted against it. He wants to go on testing more bombs. His name is Barry Goldwater, and if he is elected they might start testing all over again.

Male Narrator: Vote for President Johnson on November 3rd. The stakes are too high for you to stay home.

Several other spot ads followed, warning against Goldwater's reckless statements on nuclear weaponry and his poor judgment on the use of such weapons.

Goldwater and RNC Ad Campaigns

The Goldwater campaign and the Republican National Committee tried to fight back with a series of one-minute commercials, produced by Interpublic: Erwin, Wasey, Ruthrauff & Ryan. In August 1964, Interpublic replaced the Chicago-based Leo Burnett ad agency as Goldwater's lead agency. Leo Burnett, famous in the commercial advertising world for creating the iconic Jolly Green Giant, Tony the Tiger, Charlie the Tuna, and the Marlboro Man, made just one lasting contribution to Goldwater's television advertising with this tag line: "In your heart, you know he's right."

The Interpublic ads carried several themes: corruption in Washington, big government attempting to take over, the lack of moral responsibility, and the threat of communism. "Ike at Gettysburg" featured the former president sitting at an outdoor table at his Gettysburg, Pennsylvania, retirement farm, with Eisenhower saying that the charges that Goldwater was a "warmonger" were nothing but "actual tommyrot." In three different spots, Goldwater turned to Hollywood actors. Raymond Massey vented his anger against the Johnson administration's Vietnam policies, while John Wayne and, most famously, Ronald Reagan stood up for Goldwater. Reagan's was by far the most polished of the three performances.[28]

He also made a half-hour speech endorsing Goldwater, which served to catapult Reagan into the larger public eye. The speech, according to Clifton White and William J. Gill, was almost accidental. It had been vetoed by several of Goldwater's key advisers, including William Baroody and Denison Kitchel, as "too emotional and unscholarly." Further, it did not air until October 27, just a week before the election, as the Goldwater campaign frantically tried to buy air time. The speech, written by Reagan himself, was a version of the conservative message that he had been delivering for years. White and Gill summed it up: "Ronald Reagan switched thousands of voters from the Democratic fold that night. Many of them never returned."[29]

Republicans had their own nasty television advertisement, a documentary called "Choice." Produced by Russ Walton and Robert Raisbeck, the film was filled with "beer cans (Johnson's favorite), speeding black limousines (another LBJ favorite), white women in topless bathing suits, drunken college students, and blacks rioting and looting in the streets."[30] The film, which was never shown nationwide, was previewed before the press by an undercover Democratic National Committee operative. It was supposed to show two sharply contrasting views of America: Lyndon Johnson's immoral America, on the one hand, and the patriotic, upright world of Barry Goldwater, on the other. Ostensibly, the sponsor of the film was Mothers for a Moral America, a newly created division of Citizens for Goldwater-Miller. The film was to be shown on October 22, 1964, just weeks before the election, but at the last minute Goldwater himself decided to temporarily withdraw the film, saying "It's nothing but a racist film."[31]

Both the Goldwater and the Johnson campaigns used private survey research to help guide them. Goldwater turned to Opinion Research Corporation (ORC) for assistance. One nagging question was whether there was a bloc of "silent voters," persons who would vote for Goldwater on Election Day, but would not admit it to public pollsters, like Gallup. Thirty-seven percent of respondents in one of ORC's polls said they knew of friends or associates who would vote for Goldwater, but wouldn't publicly say so. Yet that silent vote never materialized. Rather, Thomas W. Benham, vice president of ORC, wrote that many Goldwater supporters "were infected with 'defeatism.'"[32] Charles Lichenstein later admitted that Goldwater's staff had realized from even the early polls that the campaign was over before it began.[33]

The Johnson campaign used Oliver Quayle for its private polling. The polls were taken mostly to assure Johnson that he was well ahead of Goldwater, determine what strategy might be needed, see how various campaign issues were being received by the public, and evaluate the chances of other Democratic candidates. Bruce E. Altschuler, writing on Johnson's use of polls, noted that "the more favorable polls Johnson received, the more he wanted to see."[34] Then came a minor crisis, and the need for a last-minute, emergency take on public opinion. Just three weeks before the election, President Johnson and the entire Democratic campaign apparatus were shaken by the news that Walter Jenkins, a senior White House aide, was arrested for "disorderly conduct" in a men's room at a District of Columbia YMCA. This revelation could play directly into the Republicans' hands, another sign of the immorality and moral corruption in Washington. Johnson ordered an immediate FBI investigation to see if Jenkins had been framed (he had not been, the report said), and he woke Quayle from his sleep to get a quick read on public opinion. His telephone survey showed that few people would change their intended vote because of the Jenkins matter.[35]

In the end, Goldwater was trounced by Johnson, winning only his home state of Arizona and the Deep South states of Mississippi, Louisiana, Alabama, Georgia, and South Carolina. For the southern states, who had always voted Democratic, Goldwater's appeal was his opposition to federal civil rights legislation and his advocacy of states' rights. The liberal Republican organization, the Ripon Society, labeled the Goldwater campaign as "one of the most inept and unprofessional campaigns in American history."[36]

The 1968 Presidential Election: Hubert Humphrey v. Richard Nixon v. George Wallace

I'm not going to have any damn image experts
telling me how to part my hair.

—Richard Nixon (1968)[37]

The time has come for political campaigning—its techniques
and strategies—to move out of the dark ages and into
the brave new world of the omnipresent eye.

—H. R. Haldeman (1967)[38]

A few days before shocking the world by announcing that he would not seek a second full term as president, Lyndon Johnson had commissioned a poll that showed that he would have beaten all probable rivals—including the quixotic Minnesota senator Eugene McCarthy—and would be re-elected. But the Vietnam War was weighing him down, and on March 31, Johnson made his surprise announcement.[39] Four days later, Martin Luther King Jr. was assassinated in Memphis, Tennessee, and the country was in anguish. In mid-March, New York senator Robert F. Kennedy announced that he would compete in the May 7 Indiana Democratic primary against Indiana governor Roger D. Branigin (standing in for Hubert Humphrey) and McCarthy. Vice President Hubert Humphrey had not yet made his formal announcement to run for president, waiting until April 27.

Kennedy enlisted veteran campaigner Larry O'Brien to run his primary campaign. For the May 7 Indiana primary, O'Brien called on his old friend Matt Reese for grassroots help. Thanks to the efforts of thousands of volunteers and Reese's organizational skills, Kennedy won with 42 percent of the vote, gaining momentum for the upcoming Nebraska and California primaries.[40] But following Kennedy's assassination on June 6, the Democratic Party was utterly demoralized and adrift. Yet to come were the riots and policemen beating protesters in the streets of Chicago, and the name-calling and taunting in the International Amphitheater as Democrats tore each other apart. What was left of the Democratic Party leadership stepped in: Humphrey, who had won no primaries, was nominated on the first ballot. The political and emotional wounds in the Democratic Party were deep and long-lasting. Amid all the turmoil of the Chicago convention, on the last day of the proceedings the delegates and the television audience fought back tears as they watched one of the best political documentaries ever created. *Robert Kennedy Remembered*, commissioned by the Kennedy family, was produced by Charles Guggenheim, and the following year it was honored with an Academy Award.

In sharp contrast was the Republican nomination process. Richard Nixon faced Michigan governor George W. Romney and Nelson Rockefeller, and then came a late challenge from California governor Ronald Reagan. Romney dropped out in early 1968, following his candid but ill-suited comment that he had been "brainwashed" while making a fact-finding trip to Vietnam. Rockefeller, winning only the Massachusetts primary, failed to capture the voters' attention, and Reagan, while winning the California primary, was unable to advance. Nixon won nine of the twelve primaries. The nominating convention, held in Miami Beach, was everything the Chicago melee was not: scripted, tightly controlled, and without contention.

Alabama governor George C. Wallace, who briefly ran for president as a Democrat in 1964, returned as a third-party candidate. Wallace certainly would be most persuasive in the Deep South, but Nixon hoped to capture enough southern support to reach the White House. Nixon courted South Carolina senator Strom Thurmond, a 1964 convert to the Republican Party, spoke to hundreds of groups in the South, and developed his "southern strategy." This required Nixon, wrote Wallace biographer Dan Carter, to "walk a precarious ideological tightrope—to distance himself from Goldwater's explicit appeal to southern white racism while reaping the benefits of such a strategy."[41] Nixon's courting of southerners helped to quash the primary challenge from Ronald Reagan, and later in the general election it helped Nixon gain southern votes as the Wallace alternative faded.[42]

Private Polling

Humphrey did not conduct any private polls while considering whether or not to enter the race, and overall he made limited use of private survey research. For the Oregon primary, the campaign hired the Waterhouse firm to assess the strengths and weaknesses of the candidates, but in other primary states, like South Dakota and California, the campaign did not have access to private polling.[43] In May the Humphrey campaign hired college professor Gerald D. Hursh to supervise the general election polling; the team recruited to analyze the polls included fellow political scientists Evron and Jean Kirkpatrick. But by mid-August it was still unclear what the scope and, more importantly, the cost of the polls would be. Hursh argued strongly that at least $500,000 should be spent on polls. No business would blindly launch a plan or product without research and testing, Hursh argued; likewise, the Humphrey campaign should not go forward with its advertising strategy and scheduling plans without knowing the lay of the land.[44] Indeed, as media coordinator Joseph Napolitan readily admitted, at the beginning of the general election, during the last week of August, the campaign still had no media strategy.[45]

The Humphrey campaign commissioned polls in eighteen key states, and parceled out polling to several public survey organizations, including Oliver Quayle and Company (Illinois, Michigan, Missouri, and Wisconsin), Independent Research Associates (Kentucky, Maryland, and North Carolina), Belden Associates (Texas), and Mid-Continent Surveys (Minnesota). One problem was that the polls would take about three weeks to complete and have the results tallied, leaving only five weeks for the campaign to adjust strategy and tactics. In the end, the private polls supplemented the political instincts of the candidate and his senior staff, and were used to counter some of the less favorable results coming from the public polls of Gallup, Harris, and others.[46] "You're playing catch-up ball or trying to," recalled Larry O'Brien, "You're desperate to create a climate that this election isn't over. . . . You try to place the best face on it you can."[47]

The Nixon campaign, under campaign manager John N. Mitchell, a law partner of the candidate, began assembling its team. For Mitchell, who began his duties on May 18, this was his first experience at running a political campaign of any kind.[48] Nonetheless, he would be starting at the top. It was a top-down management team, headed by Mitchell, then his deputy Peter Flanigan, then campaign veteran Maurice Stans, Leonard Garment, Frank Shakespeare, Harry Treleaven, Herbert Klein, Thomas Evans, and John Sears. In June, Mitchell brought in professor David R. Derge, a political scientist from Indiana University, to analyze polling data. Derge worked with Opinion Research Corporation (ORC) of Princeton, New Jersey, a firm that had a long-standing relationship with the Republican Party and recent presidential campaigns. It was a commercial firm, known mostly for doing survey research for General Motors, Campbell Soup, Standard Oil, and others. ORC had conducted polls in thirty-eight states for Republicans in 1964 and had worked for Nixon during the 1960 campaign.

ORC devised a set of panel studies in thirteen key states; 500 individuals would be surveyed several times over the course the campaign. They were interviewed in September, in early October, and again in late October. ORC also arranged for instant telephone polls, following certain late-breaking events.[49]

The Wallace campaign relied almost exclusively on fellow Alabamians, such as Seymour Trammel, the national campaign chairman; Cecil Jackson, national campaign director; and Ed Ewing and Bill Jones, campaign coordinators. Wallace also relied on Roy Harris for outreach and grassroots, thus relying on old friends and carefully chosen former Alabama officeholders—a "good ol' boy" network.[50]

Selling the Candidates on Television

Soon after he announced his presidential bid, Humphrey signed up New York advertising agency Doyle Dane and Bernbach (DDB), the same agency that worked for Democrats in the 1964 election. The senior account representative was Arie Kopelman, a twenty-nine-year-old vice president of the firm, whose principal work at DDB was the Heinz soup account. What's the difference between a can of soup and a presidential candidate? Not much, Kopelman remarked: "When I wrote the media plan, we looked at it as if we were marketing a product for Heinz or Procter & Gamble [where Kopelman used to work]."[51] By the time of the Democratic nominating convention in August, Kopelman had assembled fifty-seven people to work on the Humphrey ads, and he went to Chicago with fifteen copywriters, film directors, and others, just waiting for word to begin. Altogether, DDB was planning to spend $6 or $7 million, and the agency had been preparing fall spot advertisements since early May.[52] The trouble was, there simply wasn't anywhere near that kind of money available to spend, not just on advertising, but on the entire campaign.

Larry O'Brien had planned to leave the campaign after the convention and was looking forward to considering a number of lucrative private offers. But Humphrey, with slumping poll numbers, no cash available, and the bitter aftertaste of the calamitous Chicago nominating convention, persuaded O'Brien to stay. O'Brien left Washington, bringing with him Ira Kapenstein and Joe Napolitan, his lieutenants at the Democratic National Committee. Napolitan, on his flight out to the Humphrey Minneapolis headquarters, began sketching out the campaign plan for the general election. The thirty-nine-year-old political consultant was beginning to receive national attention. Writing in the *New York Times* in mid-October 1968, Thomas J. Fleming described him as "abrupt" and "monosyllabic," an operative who is "just beginning to emerge from the political shadows as one of the most formidable professional campaign managers in the nation."[53] He was unafraid to speak his mind, even urging Humphrey to resign the vice presidency, declare his misgivings about Johnson's war policies, and have Humphrey state that it would not be right to remain in the White House. "If it works you're president, if it doesn't, you still lost." According to Napolitan, Humphrey replied that his consultant was probably right, but that he just couldn't resign.[54]

It didn't take long for the culture of Madison Avenue to clash with the rough and tumble of political campaigning. DDB produced a storyboard and spot on Social Security, with an elderly woman talking about why Social Security had to be preserved. The woman was gorgeously dressed, straight from the beauty parlor, with diamonds from luxury jeweler Harry Winston. One of Humphrey's top moneymen, Jeno Paulucci, a fellow Minnesotan and owner of Chung King foods and Jeno's pizza rolls, was furious. According to Napolitan, "Jeno yells out, 'are you guys out of your fucking minds?'" There wasn't anything wrong with what the actress said, but she was coming out of Harry Winston's and sitting in the lobby of the Pierre Hotel. It was just wrong. "So," Napolitan remembered, "we decided to fire Doyle, Dane." [55]

The firing was abrupt and unexpected. In the presence of senior partner William (Bill) Bernbach, Napolitan, disgusted with a DDB commercial, shouted out, "That's not an effective use of television, and I think it's terrible." One DDB underling complained, "You just don't talk to Mr. *Bernbach* that way." Napolitan admitted later that he didn't know who Bernbach was, but he stuck to his guns. Another factor in firing DDB was that the advertising agency was more interested in ideological principle than in the nuances of political strategy. A number of the DDB creative people had earlier done volunteer work for Eugene McCarthy, and had pushed hard on social justice and liberal Democratic ideas. Napolitan pushed back: "I don't want to see any black faces in this stuff. I don't want to argue about it. No black faces!"[56] In DDB's place, Napolitan hired another Madison Avenue agency, Lennen & Newell, a firm he'd worked with in earlier campaigns, along with Tony Schwartz, Shelby Storck, Charles Guggenheim, and a newcomer, Robert Squier.[57]

The campaign planned to air its first nationwide spot advertisement on September 16, but with the firing of DDB and the readjustments in the ad campaign, there just wasn't any suitable material. The first ad from the post-DDB team appeared in the last week of September, during the *Jerry Lewis Show*. It was hurriedly put together and constituted a series of clips showing average citizens saying nice things about Humphrey. One reporter commented, "It looked like a leftover 'Lark' [cigarette] commercial."[58]

Schwartz produced one of the more memorable ads, a spot ridiculing Spiro Agnew as Nixon's choice for vice president. Called "Laughter," the twenty-second spot focused on the corner of a television set, then slowly took in the full screen, which had these simple words: "Agnew for Vice-President?" No narration, no music, just a man laughing for fifteen seconds, increasingly hysterical, then superimposed on the screen was this text: "This would be funny if it weren't so serious." The man coughed again, wheezed, and coughed once more.

"Laughter" was vintage Tony Schwartz: unusual, grabbing the viewers' attention, and spiced with vicious humor. It also fit voters preconceptions: Maine senator Edmund Muskie, Humphrey's running mate, was widely considered to be competent and qualified; not so Agnew, who was little known to the public outside of his home state of Maryland, and what the public did know was none too favorable.[59] The question "Spiro who?" was often repeated that summer.

Napolitan called on Shelby Storck, a St. Louis-based documentary film producer who had worked earlier in 1968 with him on a campaign film for their US Senate client Mike Gravel in Alaska. Storck, who had worked for Charles Guggenheim, was busy working for his friend, thirty-two-year-old Republican John Danforth, who was running for attorney general in Missouri. Just nine weeks before the election, Napolitan summoned Storck up to Waverly, Minnesota, Humphrey's hometown. There, Storck and his crew produced a thirty-minute Humphrey documentary, *What Manner of Man*, about Humphrey's earlier accomplishments. Napolitan argued that this documentary, "was the single most important vehicle in Humphrey's meteoric rise in the final weeks of the campaign."[60] Yet it was hardly aired—the campaign simply did not have any money.

Nixon's lead looked insurmountable, and potential donors were shying away. Money was always a problem for the Humphrey-Muskie ticket. They were constantly down in the public media polls. Smart money was following the long-standing advice of Chicago mayor Richard J. Daley: "Don't back no losers."[61] Sometimes, however, the money was just not worth the price. For example, deep-pocketed Texas oil barons might have been persuaded to give $700,000, but they needed Humphrey's assurance, in writing, that he would protect their oil-depletion allowance. Humphrey wouldn't agree, and the Texans' money stayed in their own pockets.[62]

"We're broke, Hubert," Larry O'Brien said to the candidate. "We don't have money and we can't get credit. We're not going to have the materials we wanted, and the television campaign has to be cut to the bone. The money just isn't there."[63] There was no state or regional television advertising during mid-October for Humphrey—there was simply no money. Napolitan and others went without salary. Nixon was outspending Humphrey nearly two-to-one on television and more than four-to-one on radio.[64] Altogether, Humphrey was able to spend just $3,525,000 on television.

Humphrey's key moneyman, Dwayne Andreas, soon to be CEO of the food processing giant Archer-Daniels-Midland, brought together a dozen or so wealthy New Yorkers in his Waldorf Astoria apartment, begging for their last-minute support. "This is not a contribution. It's a loan. Would you help us? We're desperate," Larry O'Brien remembered Andreas pleading.[65] Another Humphrey fundraiser, Robert Short, was busy securing loans and donations wherever he could, mostly from wealthy donors. At last, the campaign was able to secure enough loans to do last-minute television commercials and a telethon.

Bob Squier, thirty-four years old, was brought into the Humphrey campaign, after working very briefly for Johnson's abortive re-election campaign. O'Brien decided, three weeks before Election Day, to produce a telethon for Humphrey. Nixon had done the same in 1960, and it seemed to be an effective way to reach voters in the waning days of the campaign. At the ABC television studios in Los Angeles, the Humphrey-Muskie campaign put on a four-hour, $300,000 telethon. It was a deliberately messy affair, noisy, unscripted, with large cable wires snaking across the floor, and paper coffee cups tossed about. Humphrey answered screened phone calls directly from voters. It was supposed to look real, not antiseptic and scripted like the Nixon telethon (see below) that was held just miles away. Celebrities like Frank Sinatra, Danny Thomas, Joanne Woodward, and Burt Lancaster lent their support. Bob Squier, while initially opposed to the idea of a telethon, produced the show, which reached about 14 million viewers.[66]

At the same time, George Wallace was on three separate half-hour programs, on each of the major networks. The polling firm Sindlinger and Company reported that two-thirds of the national audience watched; 79.3 percent saw both Nixon and Humphrey, and 54.4 percent saw Wallace.[67]

The irony was that, though desperate for money, the Humphrey campaign, after the election was over, received a refund check from their advertising agency Lennen and Newell for $318,000. Knowing how fragile some campaign finances are, the ad agency didn't want to get burned by not getting paid its fees, so it over-billed the Humphrey campaign every time it placed an ad. This might be acceptable for a commercial client, but the agency violated one of the basic principles of campaigning: never end the campaign with extra funds. Napolitan was furious, stating that if the Democrats had that extra money, they could have shown more ads in swing states and won.[68]

Richard Nixon formally declared his candidacy for the Republican nomination on February 1, 1968. The New York advertising agency Feeley and Wheeler produced several television spots touting Nixon's electability and knowledge of international affairs, along with a thirty-minute film highlighting Nixon's personal characteristics. There was also a series of television programs, thirty minutes to an hour in length, focused on Ohio, Illinois, California, and Michigan, called "The Nixon Answer," in which citizens would ask Nixon questions. The California show even added a five-minute conversation between Nixon and African American basketball star Wilt Chamberlain. The shows were produced by Frank Shakespeare of CBS, who was soon to be the lead television adviser for the Nixon campaign.[69]

Also working on the Nixon account was Fuller & Smith & Ross, a New York advertising agency that had sixty people focusing full-time on marketing the Nixon account. The Nixon advertising budget was roughly $8 to $10 million, concentrated in a two-month window during the general election months. That sum, according to one of the ad agency's senior vice presidents, was equivalent to what General Motors, General Foods, or Procter & Gamble might spend for their annual advertising.[70]

Enter Joe McGinniss

While Theodore White's *Making of the Presidency 1968*, the third volume of his chronicles of presidential elections, was sure to be a bestseller, another surprise best-selling book was written by an unknown twenty-six-year-old sports columnist, Joe McGinniss. McGinniss wanted to write about campaign advertising and approached Doyle, Dane and Bernbach, then the Humphrey agency. Could he tag along and follow the campaign? Absolutely not, said the agency. Then McGinniss turned to Harry Treleaven and Leonard Garment of the Nixon campaign, who said yes—no questions asked, no ground rules. Garment later confessed, "We foolishly allowed ourselves to be lulled by his friendly assurances and our own gullibility—plus at least a touch of vanity." Little did they know that McGinniss was, in Garment's characterization, a "sworn enemy of [their] campaign."[71]

The *Selling of the President 1968* was McGinniss's funny, audacious, behind-the-scenes account of the Nixon presidential campaign, and of the role that advertising men had in trying to shape the candidate into a viable television product.[72] The book's dust jacket showed Nixon's brooding, enigmatic face on a package of cigarettes, with the clear message that the Republican candidate for president was being presented, packaged, and sold like an everyday commercial product. The book was wildly popular, staying on the *New York Times* bestseller list for six months.

The McGinniss book featured television ad makers Harry Treleaven and Frank Shakespeare, who were responsible for creating Nixon's television ads, and Leonard Garment and Roger Ailes, who managed the televised town hall meetings that were produced for Nixon in ten different media markets. McGinniss called the quartet of Nixon aides the first to adapt, in the word's of Leonard Garment, "the manipulative techniques of commercial advertising on a large scale to presidential politics."[73]

The twenty-seven-year-old Ailes, who recently had been a producer for the *Mike Douglas Show*, knew that they had their work cut out for them in remaking the image of Richard Nixon. There was to be a "new" Nixon, not the self-pitying, defeated Nixon of 1962, or the "Tricky Dick" of the late 1940s, or the maudlin, grasping Nixon of the Checkers speech, or the Nixon who, perhaps thanks to televised debates, had lost to Kennedy in the razor-thin 1960 contest. Nixon in 1968 was fifty-four years old, and a new approach had to be tried.

There had been earlier attempts to humanize Nixon. In 1963, on the *Jack Paar Show*, the popular late night precursor to the *Tonight Show*, Nixon showed off his very modest skill at piano playing, laughing along with his host.[74] When the 1968 general election had just kicked off, Nixon appeared on the comedy show *Rowan & Martin's Laugh-In*. As journalist Rick Perlstein described it, one of the long-running gag lines on the show was the "innuendo-laden non sequitur," "Sock it to me." One of Nixon's old joke writers, Paul Keyes worked for the television show, and arranged for Nixon to make a cameo appearance on the show, saying, in mocking tones, "Sock it to *me*?" Suddenly, it was Nixon who momentarily seemed hip, cool, and in tune with the youth culture.[75]

But in this election year, the Nixon handlers had their work cut out for them. Ailes was in charge of assembling town hall audiences, with participants carefully screened in advance. What Ailes was trying to do was present Nixon in an informal, but tightly controlled, situation, with no surprises and little chance for miscues.

"Let's face it," said Ailes to McGinniss in one of the most memorable descriptions in campaign history, "a lot of people think Nixon is dull. Think he's a bore, a pain in the ass. They look at him as the kind of kid who always carried a book bag. . . . He looks like somebody hung him in a closet overnight and he jumps out in the morning with his suit all bunched up and starts running around saying, 'I want to be president.' I mean this is how he strikes some people. That's why these shows are important. To make them forget all that."[76]

Selling of the President 1968 was an eye-opener to the behind-the-scenes activities of admen and professional consultants. Richard Nixon, however, writing twenty years later, argued that the "myth" of this campaign was that it was "the first where media advisers reigned supreme and that it consisted entirely of television commercials and staged question-and-answer sessions with voters."[77] "The truth," Nixon wrote, was that between Labor Day and Election Day, "I gave 178 speeches in person, on radio, and on television." It was not style over substance, he wrote, because he gave "detailed statements or proposals on agriculture, education, NATO, the Supreme Court, crime, foreign aid, urban renewal, taxes, the budget, Vietnam, and other issues."[78] Equally pathbreaking in the McGinniss book were the eighty-two pages of memos, strategy plans, and campaign notes written by campaign staffers.[79]

Harry W. Treleaven (1922–1998) had earlier worked at the J. Walter Thompson ad agency in New York on accounts for Ford automobiles, Lark cigarettes, Pan American Airlines, and Singer sewing machines. His first political consulting job was for George H. W. Bush's successful congressional campaign in Houston, Texas, in 1966 against popular Democratic incumbent Frank Briscoe. During the 1968 presidential campaign, Treleaven's most lasting contribution was the double-edged campaign slogan, "Nixon's the One!"

During the general election drive, the Nixon advertising was produced by Leonard Garment, Harry Treleaven, and Frank Shakespeare. Eugene Jones, meanwhile, made the commercials. Jones, a former combat Marine photographer, had never directed a political campaign before,[80] but he skillfully combined still photographs and rapid-fire collages to make for powerful visuals. A number of one-minute spots focused on the discord and strife in the United States: bloody protestors, burned buildings, riots, crime, and rag-tag hippies, accompanied by blaring, discordant, even weird music. To counter this turmoil and dissonance, Richard Nixon was the voice of reason. In "The First Civil Right," Nixon acknowledged the right to protest, but called on a more fundamental right: "Let us recognize that the first civil right of every American is to be free from domestic violence. So I pledge to you, we shall have order in the United States."

Three years before the ratification of the Twenty-Sixth Amendment to the Constitution, giving eighteen-year-olds the right to vote, Nixon appealed to young voters. In "Youth," Nixon narrates:[81]

[*Video: Montage of decidedly hippie and weird-looking young people.*]

(Rock music)

Nixon (voice-over): American youth today has its fringes but that's part of the greatness of our country. I have great faith in American youth.

[*Video: pictures of productive, well-scrubbed young people.*]

(Upbeat music)

Nixon (voice-over): The youth of today can change the world. And if they understand that, I think that we're going to go forward to a great age, not just for Americans, but for peace and progress for all the people in the world.

(Peaceful music)

The Nixon one-minute ads ended with this tag line: "This Time Vote Like Your Whole World Depended on It . . . Nixon."

The Nixon campaign scheduled a four-hour telethon, like Humphrey, the day before the election. The smooth and telegenic Oklahoma football coach Bud Wilkinson served as moderator, with softball questions phoned in from around the country, screened, and given to Nixon. Some of his advisers said such a telethon would be too costly and tiring, but Nixon overruled them. Writing in his memoirs, Nixon said he remembered his razor-thin defeat in 1960 and vowed to do everything possible to make a difference in 1968. "It was my best campaign decision," Nixon wrote. "Had we not had that last telethon, I believe Humphrey would have squeaked through with a close win on Election Day."[82]

The Wallace campaign's spots, produced by the Alabama-based advertising firm of Luckie & Forney, had Wallace standing behind a podium, talking directly to voters, with video spliced in. In one commercial, the male narrator asks: "Why are more and more millions of Americans turning to Governor Wallace?" Then Wallace focuses on the evils of forced busing of school children, crime in the streets, and hard-earned tax dollars going to unfriendly foreign countries. In another ad, Wallace promises to use conventional weapons to bring victory in Vietnam. (No doubt this was to counter the fear of a nuclear war, seen first with Goldwater four years earlier, and with Wallace's own running mate, former Air Force general and head of the Strategic Air Command, Curtis LeMay).

What Ifs

In this bitter, three-way race, Nixon bested Humphrey by just 500,000 votes out of 63 million cast; Wallace garnered the remaining 9.9 million votes. Nixon won in thirty-two states and received 301 electoral votes; Humphrey carried thirteen states and the District of Columbia and received ninety-one electoral votes. Wallace carried five Deep South states and forty-six electoral votes. Humphrey lost Missouri, New Jersey, Ohio, Alaska, and Illinois, all by less than 3 percent.[83] Americans did not know who their new president would be until the vote count was completed in California, Illinois, and Ohio on early Wednesday morning.[84]

Democrats started out in a deep hole: unpopular war, chaos among Democratic contenders, the riots in Chicago, the usual clamor for change after a party had been in power for several administrations in a row. What if Humphrey broke with Johnson on the Vietnam War sooner? What if the Democratic convention had not been in riotous Chicago? What if it were held in early July rather than wait to coincide with Lyndon Johnson's birthday in late August? What if the Democrats could have raised more money? What if the ad agency hadn't sat on last-minute precious funds? What if Johnson's last-minute peace proposal had come earlier? Larry O'Brien was convinced: "I am absolutely persuaded that if we had been able to implement fully our campaign program as we developed it, Hubert Humphrey would have been elected."[85]

Several major political consultants were involved in this election: Larry O'Brien, working his third presidential campaign; Joseph Napolitan, playing a major part in a presidential campaign for the first time; Charles Guggenheim and Tony Schwartz again producing Democratic media; and Bob Squier, who later became one of the most important media consultants during the 1970s–1990s. On the Republican side, Roger Ailes, now famous after the McGinniss book, would be in demand during the 1970s as a political consultant.

This time around, Nixon's luck had changed. After losing by a hair's breadth in 1960, and then losing badly in the California governor's race in 1962, he had returned triumphant. His re-election campaign four years later would be quite unlike his battle against Humphrey and Wallace.

Turning to Americans for Campaign Advice

The participation of political consultants in the 1968 presidential election caught the attention of another president seeking re-election. In 1969, Philippine president Ferdinand Marcos wanted to accomplish what no other leader of his country had done, win re-election to office. His opponent, Sergio Osmeña Jr., was relatively weak and should have been easily defeated, but Marcos wasn't taking any chances. To make sure he would be re-elected, Marcos sought out two American political consultants, the veteran Joe Napolitan and the young Bob Squier. Marcos admired and envied American power politics and he intended to use the best resources available to thoroughly defeat his opponent.

Philippine political image-making was truly in its infancy, usually portraying politicians as threatening and overbearing, given to bombastic and long-winded speeches before enormous crowds of rabid supporters. The American consultants came into the presidential race and recast the wooden and stiff Marcos with a new image. Napolitan used his media savvy to refocus the campaign message, to repackage Marcos and present him as a "warm, popular, progressive, dynamic leader—not as a hatchet man," and to assist in overall campaign strategy.[86]

The Napolitan and Squier media campaign had to conform to the realities of mass communications in the Philippines. Few people outside Manila and other urban areas had access to television, but nearly everyone listened to the radio; thus, radio became the most useful form of paid media throughout the country. Yet the video image of Marcos was powerful and appealing. In the remote rural areas, the Marcos campaign resorted to a very old-fashioned delivery system. It secured fifteen flatbed trucks, outfitted them with movie screens and projectors, and drove them from village to village. Every night campaign operatives showed two hours of Marcos campaign commercials to enthralled villagers.[87]

For their work in shaping the Marcos media image and reshaping the campaign's major themes, Napolitan and Squier were paid $240,000, not counting film-production costs and travel expenses. "In a presidential election in a country of 40 million people that's not a significant expense," Napolitan later wrote.[88] Apparently, it was quite a bargain for Marcos. Raymond Bonner, who portrayed in devastating detail America's twenty-year alliance with Marcos,[89] wrote that the 1969 election cost Marcos "a staggering $50 million" which was $16 million more than Richard Nixon had spent on his 1968 presidential race. For Marcos, the campaign weapons of choice were bribe money and political muscle. Bonner stated that Marcos's campaign manager, Ernesto Maceda,[90] dispensed millions of dollars of "walking around" money to barrio captains, mayors, and favorite congressional candidates throughout the Philippines. Bonner concluded that "what votes Marcos couldn't buy, he stole, not very subtly."

Marcos overwhelmed his opponent, gave generous credit to Napolitan, and the international political consulting business was born. Bribery, intimidation, and favoritism had far more to do with Marcos's victory than the work of his American consultants, but for the first time a presidential race in another country got a taste of American message development, campaign strategy, and media manipulation.

The Marcos re-election campaign illustrates what would become a recurring theme throughout many international elections, particularly in emerging democracies: enormous sums of money were raised and spent with little or no accountability; Americans were called in for their strategic advice to assist a campaign that had little experience in sophisticated campaign techniques; and the American consultants had limited, but sometimes crucial, impact on the outcome of the elections.[91] Did Napolitan regret working for Marcos? In 1999 he said, "I have no apologies for the Marcos election; it's like all the people who worked for Richard Nixon and his campaigns didn't expect he would disgrace the office."[92] But at the time of his death in late 2013, Napolitan's daughter, Martha, said that her father indeed regretted working for Marcos. "He never said that publicly, but I know he did. He said he didn't know he would become a dictator."[93]

Joseph Napolitan became a trailblazing international political consultant, working throughout the world both openly and secretly for presidential candidates and political parties. Robert Squier, while concentrating on American elections, also branched out to presidential clients abroad, particularly in Spain and Latin America. As seen in chapter 18, these pioneers were followed by a trickle, then a steady stream of American consultants during the following decades.

PART 2

The Expansion and Growth of Consulting, 1970s–1980s

CHAPTER 6

Money, Campaigns, and the Next Generation of Consultants

Money is the mother's milk of politics.

—Jesse M. Unruh (1966)

There is nothing better than a scared, rich candidate.

—Matt Reese (1997)

JOHN C. STENNIS HAD served in the US Senate representing Mississippi since 1947. He never had to campaign seriously, nor did he ever have to raise more than $5,000 for any election. Then came a major challenge in 1982 from Republican Haley Barbour, a thirty-six-year-old Yazoo City lawyer. Mississippi, like much of the rest of the South, was experiencing a change in partisan affiliation, with conservative white voters flocking to the Republican Party. Stennis, an old-school Democratic politician and campaigner, turned to media consultant Ray Strother for help.

> "I'm being abused by this Mr. Barbour," the eighty-one-year-old senator
>   told Strother, "and I think we should run a campaign."
> "OK, Senator," replied Strother.
> "How much will this cost?"
> "Senator, I think about $2 million."
> "$2 million? I only have $5,000. . . . That's always been enough."
> "Senator, it's not enough any longer."
> Stennis replied, "Well, I best go out and raise some money."[1]

This was a race, the *New York Times* reported, between a "young man who is liked," and an "elderly one who is revered."[2] Stennis easily won, but he had to spend over a million dollars to defeat Barbour, who later became governor of Mississippi and a prominent national Republican figure. "Big-time campaigning—I've never been in it much," Mr. Stennis exclaimed, slapping a table for emphasis. "But it's a whiz with all this television and everything."[3]

Big-time campaigning had not always been the norm. In 1922 the US Senate formally condemned the spending of $195,000 in a Senate primary campaign as "contrary to sound policy, harmful to the honor and dignity of the Senate, and dangerous to the perpetuity of a free government."[4] Converted to 2015 dollars, that would have been $2,760,236—not an unusual amount to spend in any state-wide primary, but considered small change for some of the more competitive big state races. (In the 2014 Mississippi Republican primary for the US Senate, a total of $17.4 million was spent, with a considerable amount coming from thirty super PACs. Most of the money backed Tea Party candidate Chris McDaniel, trying unsuccessfully to defeat long-time incumbent Thad Cochran).[5]

In 1958, Maine governor Edmund S. Muskie defeated incumbent US senator Fred Payne, and in the process spent just $37,350.86 ($307,336 in 2015 dollars). Muskie's budget allowed $3,500 ($28,779) for television, but that translated into heavy coverage. It was possible to get a half hour of Maine television time for only a few hundred dollars. By contrast, in 2008, incumbent Maine senator Susan M. Collins spent a little over $8 million defeating Tom H. Allen, who spent just less than $6 million.[6]

For much of the twentieth century, campaign financing was on a cash-and-carry system. Funds were unreported, there were no spending limits, and no public scrutiny. In vivid detail, historian Robert Caro wrote about Senate majority leader Lyndon Johnson's extraordinary cash machine, where his congressional aides and cronies would fly back to Washington from Texas with their suit coat pockets bulging with oil money, ready to be distributed to Johnson favorites.[7]

When George Wallace was running for president in 1968, the Mississippi Citizens' Council, a white supremacist group, raised a quarter-million dollars, but it tried to conceal the big-dollar donors by having more than 300 individuals write checks for $1,000 or less. Several wealthy contributors gave as much as $30,000 each; actor John Wayne was reported to have given three checks, each for $10,000. In a Jackson, Mississippi, rally in June 1968, some $450,000 was collected through cash and small checks. Wallace biographer Dan T. Carter observed that the campaign finance director "commandeered an ex-Mississippi State football player to 'stomp down' on the checks and cash so that they could squeeze the booty into twelve oversized mail bags."[8]

The 1972 presidential election became, according to campaign finance expert Herbert E. Alexander, the "high water mark for large donors."[9] Insurance magnate W. Clement Stone contributed $2.1 million (nearly all to Richard Nixon), heir to the Mellon banking and oil empire Richard Mellon Scaife gave $1 million to Nixon, and General Motors heir Stewart R. Mott contributed $400,000 to George McGovern and another $422,000 to other Democratic candidates and causes.[10] At the time, these were all extraordinary, headline-making amounts, but nothing compared to the mega-donors in the post-*Citizens United* world, as seen in chapter 20.

Congress decided it was time to respond. The Federal Election Campaign Act (FECA) of 1971, as amended in 1974, was designed to curb the influence of the super rich, require disclosure of funds, put ceilings on the amount of money that could be spent on campaigns, and provide public financing for presidential elections. In 1976 the Supreme Court struck down parts of FECA that restricted total spending for all federal races, independent spending on behalf of federal candidates, and spending by the candidates themselves.[11] Wealthy candidates, like James L. Buckley, would now be allowed to spend as much of their own money as they wanted. Ever since, wealthy candidates have popped up, spending their own money and sometimes getting elected. While multimillionaires like Herbert Kohl (Wisconsin) and Rick Scott (Florida), and billionaire Michael Bloomberg (New York City), have been successful, many others have failed. Money alone certainly doesn't buy the love of voters.

Most candidates running for office don't have millions of their own money to throw around. Super-wealthy presidential aspirants Ross Perot, Pete DuPont, Steve Forbes, and Donald Trump are the outliers. Indeed, one of the biggest obstacles for candidates for their party's presidential nomination is the inability to attract funds, despite assistance from federal financing. Money is the surrogate for a campaign's success, and second- or third-tier candidates often simply run out of funds. For example, two weeks before the 1976 Democratic presidential primary in Wisconsin, Congressman Morris K. Udall's campaign was completely out of money. Out came Udall's personal American Express card: hotel bills, chartered airplane, meals, a barge ride down the Hudson River, and more. The total bill, coming directly to the candidate, was $142,000.[12] The Udall campaign limped along, but it was hampered by a chronic shortage of funds.

During that same year, the Reagan presidential campaign was down to its last dollars. Reagan aide Peter Hannaford remembered how desperate they were in March 1976 while running against incumbent Gerald Ford for the Republican nomination: "We were poor as church mice." The campaign had chartered a United Airlines flight very early in the morning from California to Salisbury, North Carolina. All the traveling campaign staff was on board, but the plane wouldn't take off. What was the matter? Aide Michael Deaver said, "We're waiting around for the office in Washington to open the mail to see if there are enough checks to pay for the airplane today."[13] Fortunately for Reagan, the money came in, the plane took off, and he was able to defeat Ford in the crucial North Carolina primary. With the Reagan campaign re-energized, money soon started flowing its way.

The 1976 presidential campaign was the first conducted under the amended federal campaign law. The candidates were relying on public money, in this case $21.8 million during the general election. "It was terrible," remembered Stuart Spencer, Ford's senior campaign adviser. "We got 21 million bucks each. In the end, we spent 18 million on media, the rest on overhead and organization. What did it mean? We didn't have any troops . . . we had no way to motivate them. We cannot put a headquarters in without it being applied against my budget. So I said, 'No headquarters.'"[14]

Soft Money and Political Action Committees

Number one, money is the Lord your Savior.
You, both candidate and manager, shall have no other Lord.
—Democratic consultant Jeffrey Pollock (2006)[15]

For many campaigns strapped for funds, it was also "no" to bumper stickers, campaign signs and buttons, funds for volunteer activities, get-out-the-vote drives, and other traditional forms of campaign activity. To address this, Congress amended the FECA in 1979 to exempt certain, specific activities from the "expenditure" and "contribution" definitions. The political parties were now allowed to spend unlimited amounts of money on grassroots activities for voter registration and get-out-the-vote activities, under the guise of "party building."[16] Moreover, the Federal Election Commission (FEC) in 1978 changed rules that governed political party fundraising, determining that at the state level, the political parties could accept corporate and union funds (both of which were prohibited at the time by federal campaign law) to finance voter registration drives. Separate bank accounts would have to be established between "hard money," or funds raised and spent according to the requirements and restrictions of FECA and used in connection with federal campaigns, and "soft money," or funds not covered by the requirements or restrictions of federal law. Soft money could be contributed in unlimited amounts.

At first, soft money came in slowly, but over the next few cycles, it exploded. in 1980, the total of Democratic and Republican soft money was just $19 million; in 1984, it was $21 million; in 1992, it was $86 million, and in 1996, it was $263 million. Republicans generally out raised Democrats in soft money, but both were aggressively seeking corporate and big donor funds.[17]

During the 1970s, political action committees (PACs) became much more commonplace, and by 1995 there were a total of 4,016 such organizations. The most common kind of political action committee was the "connected" PAC, which was affiliated with a labor union, a corporation, or a membership organization. A second kind, the "unconnected" PAC, was not affiliated with a parent organization and was most likely an ideological or policy-oriented committee. The third kind of PAC was the individual or "leadership" PAC, which was created to give congressional leaders (often self-appointed) a vehicle to raise money to help other candidates. By mid-1998 there were some seventy-four such leadership PACs in Congress, and by 2012 that number had swelled to 456, making nearly every member of Congress (and some former members as well) a "leader."[18]

Most PACs depended on funds from employees, shareholders, or union or trade association members. But one influential PAC stood out in its aggressive solicitation of disaffected voters. Begun in 1972, the Raleigh, North Carolina–based National Congressional Club (NCC) was a rather modest fundraising vehicle to help retire the $100,000 campaign debt of Jesse Helms, who had just been elected to the US Senate from that state. Together with Raleigh attorney and long-time friend Tom Ellis, Helms turned to direct-mail specialist Richard Viguerie to create a larger base of donors for this new organization. The NCC became an extraordinary money machine. Helms biographer William A. Link wrote that the NCC was able to refine donor lists, use polling results developed by consultant Arthur Finkelstein to learn about the demographics of their contributors. "They discovered, to their surprise, that donors came in different categories: some gave frequently, others only once a year, and the club learned whom to ask and when to ask them."[19]

Most money, with no strings attached, came in small amounts, often $10 or $15; much of it came from the 100,000 out-of-state contributors loyal to Helms and his hard-edged brand of conservatism. Mike Dunn, a consultant who joined the NCC in 1977, began expanding the North Carolina donor base. Soon, the NCC had hundreds of employees, raking in millions of dollars in contributions. Writing in 1990, reporter Charles Babington noted that Helms's direct-mail operation "remains among the nation's biggest, boldest, and wealthiest."[20] In 1990 the Helms for Senate Committee, just one part of the NCC, raised $5.6 million, mostly in $10 and $20 checks, with less than 20 percent coming from North Carolina.

Jesse Helms played to the fears and prejudices of his admirers: he warned against AIDS activists, homosexuals, and lovers of "perverted art." According to Babington, "nearly every Helms letter describes a black person or institution as part of the enemy."[21] One letter declared, "Since Jesse refuses to compromise conservative principles, the union bosses, Jesse Jackson's crowd, the radical feminists, and the homosexuals are all out for Jesse's political hide." The letters were sent with a sense of urgency: "If I have inconvenienced you in any way, I sincerely apologize. But I need your help urgently." There would be a new campaign crisis every week, and, according to Babington, Helms would "ask the same people for money often enough to make a televangelist blush . . . and lace nearly every letter with racial code words."[22]

By 1981 the NCC had become the largest political action committee in the United States.[23] Nearly 70 percent of its regular contributors were from outside of North Carolina.[24] Helms and his operatives created about a half dozen other political organizations, including Jefferson Marketing, a political advertising and consulting business for like-minded conservative candidates.[25]

Political action committees mostly give to incumbent legislators, rather than challengers. During the 1996 election cycle, PACs collectively gave $243 million, averaging $288,000 for winning House candidates and $1.1 million to winning Senate candidates.[26] By 2009 a total of 4,611 political action committees were operating, and in the election cycle of 2007–2008, PACs had invested some $1.2 billion in candidates and independent expenditures.

There were many attempts to amend or totally reform FECA during the 1990s, particularly because of the unforeseen growth of soft money spending. During this time, the US Senate held 29 hearings, with 522 witnesses, 17 filibusters, and 113 votes on campaigning finance reform—and all attempts failed. Then came legislation introduced by Senators John S. McCain III (Arizona) and Russell D. Feingold (Wisconsin), who proposed a comprehensive reform, the Bipartisan Campaign Reform Act (BCRA) of 2002, known as the McCain-Feingold Act.

"Hell is going to freeze over first before we get rid of soft money," warned Kentucky senator Mitch McConnell in 1999.[27] But Congress responded, and through BCRA unlimited soft money for national political parties was banned, and the use of soft money by state party committees was restricted. Hundreds of millions of unreported soft-money dollars from corporations, labor unions, advocacy groups, and wealthy individuals were now prohibited. BCRA also required "electioneering" communications by labor unions or business interests to be restricted to within sixty days of a general election or thirty days of a primary. But, in a curious omission, Congress restricted communications delivered by broadcast, cable, or satellite, but not by newspapers or online, such as through websites (and as the technology developed, text messaging, podcasting, Twitter, and other platforms). Further, BCRA increased the amount of money an individual could donate to a candidate, from $1,000 to $2,000 for each primary, run-off, or general election (raised to $2700 in 2016). Individuals could give a total of $95,000 over a two-year cycle to candidates and political action committees. (Later, that ceiling would be ruled unconstitutional, and with the *Citizens United* ruling in 2010, much of the federal election law has become ineffective. This will be discussed in chapter 20).

But there is nothing as creative as campaign finance lawyers looking for ways to circumvent BCRA restrictions. One solution was found in section 527 of the Internal Revenue Code, which allows partisan political organizations to accept contributions without paying taxes on them. Section 527 had been in the tax code for a quarter of a century, but only after BCRA's restrictions on soft money took effect did those in the campaign arena seriously start looking at this new source. The 527 organizations, as they were soon called—whether associated with an ideological cause, labor union, or business interest—could receive unlimited amounts of money, and, until July 2000, no names of donors had to be disclosed.

The 2004 presidential election saw a major push by newly formed 527 groups; in all, $612 million poured into these groups. Twenty wealthy individuals gave a total of $146 million to 527 groups. (Clement Stone and Stewart Mott would have been proud). The pro-Democratic Service Employees International Union (SEIU) poured in the most, $51.5 million; Swift Boat Veterans for Truth (anti-Kerry) spent $13 million, and Media Fund (pro-Democratic), MoveOn.org (pro-Democratic), Progress for America Voters Fund (pro-Republican) were among the largest 527 advocacy groups. However, during the 2008 presidential election, total spending by 527 organizations dipped to $480 million.[28]

A total of 795 organizations created under the 527 provision participated in the 2012 election cycle, collecting $548.8 million from backers and spending $539 million on campaigns. The Republican Governors Association topped the list, spending $101 million, followed by the Democratic Governors Association ($50.1 million), and the AFSCME Special Account ($44 million).

While much attention has been given to the 527 organizations, other groups—501(c)(4) social welfare organizations, 501(c)(5) labor unions, and 501(c)(6) business organizations—spent more than three times what 527 groups did during the 2008 presidential election.[29] (There will be more on the ramifications of 501(c) group spending in chapter 20.)

The Growth of Political Consulting

> *The modern campaign is the bailiwick of hired guns—political*
> *gypsies skilled in the mechanics of polling, fundraising, media buys,*
> *and driving a message. The process has become so complex*
> *that anyone who tried to do it without people like me is a fool.*
> —Ed Rollins (1996)[30]

In the later 1960s and early 1970s, some candidates, particularly long-time incumbents, still were reluctant to use consultants. As Jill Buckley, a pioneer Democratic consultant remembered, in those days consultants "had to work very hard to convince candidates, any candidate, that they needed somebody from outside."[31] But, as John Stennis found, candidates needed professional help, and they needed to raise money to pay consultants and the campaigns they would put together.

More spending on campaigns meant more work for political consultants and the campaign industry: more polls taken, more television advertising created and aired, greater use of direct-mail and telephone communication, more attention to grassroots and get-out-the-vote efforts. And with more available money came an increase in the number of individuals and firms in the political consulting business.

Several leading political consultants began practicing their trade during the late 1960s and early 1970s. Some got into politics by chance, others were born to it. All of them made an important impact on presidential and statewide races during the next two decades.

General Consultants

Charles R. (Charlie) Black Jr. (b. 1947) didn't plan to get into politics. A native of North Carolina, he nonetheless fell in love with politics during high school and college at the University of Florida. He graduated from American University Law School, practiced for ten years, and then gave up on the law. He was inspired by Barry Goldwater and became active in college and law school Republican politics, volunteering for Nixon and US Senate candidates in Florida. His first paying job was working on the US Senate race in North Carolina for Jesse Helms. "Helms was my next version of Goldwater," Black later remarked.[32] He helped start the National Conservative Political Action Committee (NCPAC) in 1974, with Terry Dolan and Roger Stone. The conservative movement at the time, Black observed, was mostly intellectual, centered on William F. Buckley Jr. and Russell Kirk. In contrast, NCPAC would be composed of conservative political activists. NCPAC, copying what several liberal organizations were doing, began using direct mail, phone banks, and particularly independent expenditures.

Black was one of the first paid staffers for the Reagan presidential bid in 1976, and he was active in the primaries for Reagan in 1980. He formed a Republican consulting firm with Paul Manafort and Roger Stone—Black, Manafort & Stone—and later added Peter G. Kelly, a Democratic operative. In 1984 Lee Atwater, whom Black had known since the early 1970s, joined the firm as a named partner working on campaigns, but not lobbying. Black later became the official spokesman for the Republican National Committee during the time of Atwater's illness.

The firm branched out into lobbying, and its list of clients included the government of Somalia; Jonas Savimbi the guerilla leader seeking to overthrow the Angolan government; the Tobacco Institute; Trans World Airlines, and the Puerto Rico Federal Affairs Administration. Black was inducted into the American Association of Political Consultants Hall of Fame in 2010. He now heads Prime Policy Group, a Washington-based lobbying firm that was created with the merger of BKSH & Associates and Timmons and Company.[33]

Roger J. Stone Jr. (b. 1952), one of Black's partners and a protégé of Richard Nixon, engaged in Watergate dirty tricks and had the reputation of being both cocksure and controversial. He dropped out of George Washington University after a few semesters, and worked on a variety of campaigns, for Goldwater, Nixon, Reagan, and a series of Republican or conservative candidates throughout the 1970s through the 1990s. A 1985 cover story profile in the *New Republic* labeled him as "Washington's slickest operator," with the headline "State-of-the-Art Sleazeball."[34] Such a label would usually devastate a political operative, whose reputation is of paramount importance. Stone, instead, was busy mailing out copies of the profile to friends and potential clients.[35] Having dabbled in eight presidential contests, by 2000 Stone was helping his friend and longtime client Donald Trump explore a presidential candidacy under the Reform Party banner. In 2015 Stone was again an adviser to Trump, but he was either fired or quit in a July 2015 shake-up of Trump's presidential campaign.

Harvey LeRoy (Lee) Atwater (1951–1991) was at the peak of his political career when he died of brain cancer in 1991. Born in Georgia, Atwater spent most of his youth in South Carolina. He earned a bachelor's degree from Newberry College and a master's degree from the University of South Carolina. He had hoped to become a teacher, or perhaps play in a rhythm-and-blues band. Whatever his aspirations, politics was in his blood, and his early mentor was Senator Strom Thurmond. Lee Atwater became active in the College Republicans National Committee and was campaign manager for Karl Rove, who was running for chair of the CRNC. After Rove won, amid confusion and controversy in the vote, he appointed Atwater executive director. One day Atwater bumped into George H. W. Bush, the RNC chair, and blurted out that he had a few ideas for Bush to consider. Bush invited him into his office, and after twenty minutes, he asked the twenty-two year old, "What do you want to do in politics?" "Someday," Atwater replied, "I'd like to be sitting in your chair right here."[36]

Atwater made a name for himself when he worked on Thurmond's tough re-election fight in 1978. Arthur Finkelstein and his aide Roger Stone were in charge, but Atwater was an important part of the campaign. After Thurmond easily won, Lee claimed the credit for victory; the notoriously secretive Finkelstein kept quiet.[37]

Atwater came to national attention in 1980 when he was regional political director (South Carolina, Georgia, Alabama, and West Virginia) for Reagan's presidential bid. Once Reagan was in office, Thurmond used his considerable influence to recommend Atwater for a job in the White House Office for Political Affairs.

Atwater was particularly impressed by Clark Clifford's strategic advice to Harry Truman in his come-from-behind re-election victory in 1948. Clifford was thirty-nine at the time, roughly Atwater's age when he worked for Reagan and Bush. Clifford had shown that the Democrats could carry the Solid South and western states, ending up with 216 of the then required 266 electoral votes. In March 1983, Atwater devised his own "southern strategy," in a seventy-two-page single-spaced memo, showing how the Republican Party could achieve a similar victory in 1984.[38] He served as Ed Rollins's lieutenant, as political director, in the Reagan re-election campaign of 1984, but in many ways he was the driving force of the campaign strategy.

Following the 1984 elections, Atwater became a full partner in the consulting firm of Black, Manafort & Stone. His primary task was to sign up George Bush as his personal client. By December 1985, Atwater had become the chair of the Fund for America's Future, the political action committee that helped launch Bush's presidential bid. In 1988 Atwater would be at the center of the Bush presidential election, while Rollins was shunted aside. As a reward for successfully managing his 1988 presidential campaign, Bush appointed Atwater chair of the Republican National Committee. At thirty-seven, Atwater was one of the youngest chairs in Republican Party history, fulfilling that wish he had blurted out to Bush on their first meeting.

Atwater died at the age of forty. In his last agonizing months, his face and body swollen by steroids and anti-cancer drugs, his left arm was useless; many could not recognize him in his last photo. In his final days, Atwater reached out to several opponents who were on the receiving end of his cut-throat politics. In a February 1991 article in *Life*, Atwater wrote, "In 1988, fighting Dukakis, I said that I 'would strip the bark off the little bastard' and 'make Willie Horton his running mate.' I'm sorry for both statements: the first for its naked cruelty, the second because it makes me sound racist, which I am not."[39] Mary Matalin, who worked for Atwater, described him as "a genius, a best friend, and one of the most wonderful people the world has known."[40]

Atwater was the subject of an award-winning 2008 documentary, *Boogie Man: The Lee Atwater Story* and a 1999 biography, *Bad Boy*.[41] In 2013 the American Association of Political Consultants posthumously elected him to its Hall of Fame.

Jill Buckley, one of the first female political consultants, got involved in politics "absolutely by accident." While living in Colorado during the mid- and late 1960s, Buckley heard on her car radio of a woman bemoaning the fact that she and her husband had bought a lot of doughnuts, but not enough people showed up at her political caucus meetings. Buckley and her husband decided then and there to go to a subsequent precinct caucus. From that point on, she was "sucked into politics."[42] Her first introduction to professional consulting came when she worked on the 1972 US Senate campaign of Floyd Haskell, running against three-term incumbent Gordon Allott. Bob Squier, Pat Caddell, and Joe Rothstein were brought out from Washington to consult on the Haskell campaign. After the Haskell victory, Buckley joined Rothstein in creating a consulting firm in 1973 to assist progressive Democrats.

Joe Rothstein, after graduate school at UCLA, moved to Alaska, and for five years served as executive editor of the *Anchorage Daily News*. When Mike Gravel won an upset US Senate victory in 1968, Rothstein left Anchorage to join him as chief of staff in Washington. Buckley and Rothstein worked for the US Senate campaigns of George McGovern (South Dakota), Patrick Leahy (Vermont), Tom Harkin (Iowa), and Quentin Burdick (North Dakota), and they were part of the team of Democratic consultants who would work on various campaigns for the National Committee for an Effective Congress.

Eventually, Buckley spun off and created her own media consulting firm, becoming the first woman with a nationally based, nationally focused political media business. However, Buckley became disillusioned with the deception, manipulation, and mean-spiritedness of candidate campaigns, and with what it was doing to her personally. She decided to concentrate on advocacy work for organizations like the Sierra Club, and eventually joined the US Agency for International Development (USAID). Rothstein kept his consulting business until 2011, but he also became editor of EIN News, an Internet news service based in Washington, DC, in 1996.

Media Consultants

> *I used to do ads for C. B. Fleet enemas and Massengill douches,*
> *so making the transition to political advertising wasn't*
> *particularly difficult.*
>
> —Tom Edmonds (2005)[43]

Robert D. Squier (1934–2000) began his media career when he was a senior at the University of Minnesota and was director of television for Minnesota governor Orville Freeman's re-election campaign in 1956. He then worked at the National Educational Television network as assistant to the president. Squier's break into national politics came when Lyndon Johnson called him to the White House in March 1968 to be his television adviser for the upcoming re-election campaign. Just two days later, however, Johnson announced he would not run again. Squier then worked with Joe Napolitan for Hubert Humphrey in the 1968 general election, where he was in charge of the Humphrey-Muskie telethon.

Napolitan had plenty of campaign opportunities, and he was happy to throw some work Squier's way. Three weeks after the 1968 presidential election, "some guy called and he was running for sheriff in Wilkes Barre, Pennsylvania, or something like that"; Napolitan suggested Squier take the job.[44] While his first candidate lost, Squier went on to be one of the most important Democratic media consultants.

In early 1969, Squier opened up The Communications Company, working on a Virginia gubernatorial primary, the mayoral race in Philadelphia, and a few other campaigns. That same year, he joined Napolitan in helping President Ferdinand Marcos get re-elected in the Philippines, as described in chapter 5. In 1970 Squier worked on eight major races, and he developed a close relationship with Maine senator Edmund Muskie, who was widely considered the favored candidate for the 1972 Democratic presidential nomination. Muskie's campaign imploded during the snowy primaries. Squier became the scapegoat, was fired by the Muskie campaign, and it appeared that his budding career might be over.[45]

By the late 1970s, Squier had rebounded. The *Washington Post* labeled him the "Kingmaker of the 30-Second Spot," with a hot streak of winning thirteen out of fourteen primary and general election campaigns. "When you ask people about Bob Squier," wrote journalist Bill Peterson, "they tell you he is part hustler, part political operator, who has weathered his share of defeats. He is clever, glib and likable. He is tough and competitive, a man willing to go for the jugular."[46]

Among his many clients were US senators Christopher J. Dodd (Connecticut), John D. (Jay) Rockefeller IV (West Virginia), Dale Bumpers (Arkansas), Tom Harkin (Iowa), Paul Simon (Illinois), Gary Hart (Colorado), Robert C. Byrd (West Virginia), Joseph R. Biden (Delaware), Bob Graham (Florida), and Charles S. Robb (Virginia). In one of his most memorable media plans, Squier persuaded Bob Graham, who was running for the Florida governor's office, to devote himself to working at 100 different jobs, like bellhop, chicken plucker, and dairy cow herder. Gimmicky, no doubt, but Graham grabbed considerable free media attention and won the race.[47]

Squier decided to stay away from presidential campaigns starting in 1980. From a business standpoint, it was far more lucrative for his firm to concentrate on US Senate or gubernatorial candidates than on presidential candidates. But Squier jumped back into presidential campaigning, working for Al Gore in 1992, the re-election of Bill Clinton in 1996, and for a time with the Gore presidential campaign in 1999, before his death in early 2000. His media firm also included several important partners, especially Carter Eskew, with whom Squier had a bitter falling out in the early 1990s; Bill Knapp, who was in charge of media for the Gore 2000 general election; and Anita Dunn, who served in senior positions in the Bill Bradley presidential drive in 2000 and in the Obama presidential campaign in 2008.

Along with his political media work, Squier was known for his documentaries, including award-winning works on William Faulkner and Herman Melville. His son, Mark Squier, also became a well-regarded media consultant.

Joe Slade White (b. 1950) began his career working with several pioneer Democratic consultants. He grew up in Iowa, came to Washington in 1968 to attend Georgetown University, where he "majored in English and minored in tear-gas."[48] He first worked for Iowa senator Harold Hughes, and when Hughes was up for re-election, White helped put together thirty-second sound bites for radio commercials. While he didn't realize it, he was helping invent a new form of political communication—radio actualities. White was then hired by the 1972 McGovern presidential campaign, becoming, at twenty-one, the "kid with the microphone." After the McGovern defeat, White briefly stayed with his Senate staff job, but at age twenty-three struck out on his own. Matt Reese gave White his first job, working for the re-election of Senator Claiborne Pell of Rhode Island. Then he was introduced to Tony Schwartz, the master of radio and sound recordings, and became his protégé. Schwartz, the author of *The Responsive Chord*, told him, "you know how to make a recording. Now I'll teach you a whole new way of thinking."[49]

In his early years, White worked with pioneer Democratic media consultants, including David Sawyer, Squier, and Napolitan. "The first guys—Squier and Sawyer—were filmmakers," White remembered. "They knew how to edit, knew lighting, and so forth. This started to change as campaign consultants became media consultants" who just handed over the shoot to editors and didn't bother to look at how the work was created.

White worked for Democratic senators, such as McGovern, Pell, John Culver (Iowa), and Frank Church (Idaho), for New Jersey congressman Peter Rodino, and for Michigan governor Jennifer Granholm. White has also been the media strategist for Vice President Joe Biden, beginning with his 1996 bid for re-election as a senator from Delaware. During his long career, he has worked extensively in initiative campaigns and for corporate clients, including AT&T, T. Boone Pickens, the Seattle Mariners, and Planned Parenthood. Altogether, Joe Slade White's firm has engaged in 400 campaigns over its more than forty years of operation, and White was named Democratic Strategist of the Year by the AAPC in 2014.

David Sawyer (1936–1995) and Scott Miller founded the Sawyer/Miller Group in 1979. Scott Miller graduated from Washington and Lee University, then began his career in public relations and advertising, serving as creative director of McCann-Erickson, working for clients like Coca-Cola, Miller Brewing, and Exxon. David H. Sawyer, born in Boston, is a graduate of Princeton University, and he also studied filmmaking at City College of New York. He made a full-length documentary, *Other Voices,* a cinéma vérité examination of the treatment of mentally ill patients. The cinéma vérité technique was in vogue during the 1960s, and soon, politicians began looking for a realistic, unvarnished image that could counter the "politician in dark suit behind the podium" look. Milton Shapp, who had hired Joe Napolitan in 1966 in his successful primary fight for the Pennsylvania governorship (but lost in the general election), was back, and wanted a thirty-minute cinéma vérité biography for his successful 1970 run for the governor's office. Shapp was Sawyer's first important political client. In 1972, with two staffers from Capitol Hill, Sawyer opened D. H. Sawyer and Associates, specializing in half-hour biopics.[50] Miller joined Sawyer in 1979 to form Sawyer/Miller Group, and specialized in Democratic candidates for governor and senator. In

1988 the firm handled the media for Daniel Patrick Moynihan (New York), John D. Rockefeller IV (West Virginia), Edward Kennedy (Massachusetts), and John Glenn (Ohio), plus six gubernatorial candidates, as well as candidates for president in Israel and the Philippines.[51] Altogether, Sawyer/Miller advised over forty candidates for governor or senator, and several presidential campaigns.[52]

In 1988 the Sawyer/Miller Group was acquired by True North (now Interpublic Group), and Scott Miller founded the Core Strategy Group with Sergio Zyman. By 1990, however, the firm was backing away from domestic political campaigns. One of its last was the bitter fight between their client Harvey Gantt and incumbent US senator Jesse Helms. Scott Miller worked on his own more and more, and the firm began reaching out to corporations and international political clients. Miller teamed up with pollster Pat Caddell in assisting Coca Cola in its bumpy launch of New Coke. Soon, Sawyer was bought out by four of the firm's partners. By 1993, Sawyer/Miller was bought out by a larger public relations firm, Robinson, Lake, Lerer & Montgomery, which itself was part of the advertising giant Bozell, Jacobs, Kenyon & Eckhardt. Robinson, Lake was hired by former junk-bond king Michael Milken, attempting to burnish his reputation after his imprisonment stemming from the junk bond scandals of the 1980s.[53]

Clients of Sawyer/Miller Group included presidential candidates Corazon Aquino (Philippines), Vaclav Havel (Czech Republic), Boris Yeltsin (Russia), Lech Walesa (Poland), Virgilio Barco Vargas (Colombia), and, as described further in chapter 18, Mario Vargas Llosa (Peru). Later, at Core Strategy, Miller assisted campaigns of Kim Dae-jung (South Korea), and Vicente Fox (Mexico).

Frank Greer (b. 1947) was born and raised in Alabama, educated at the University of Maryland, and became the Labor Department spokesman during the Carter administration before launching his media consulting business for progressive candidates and causes. He had earlier worked for the 1976 Fred Harris for President campaign, and then, after the Carter years, he worked for Mondale for President in 1984. He made his mark in 1986, helping three Democratic challengers—Brock Adams (Washington), Wyche Fowler (Georgia), and Kent Conrad (North Dakota)—defeat incumbent Republican senators. Greer helped L. Douglas Wilder of Virginia become the first African American governor in the country since Reconstruction. By 1990 Greer was considered the "hot political consultant" of the year.[54] He then became part of the consulting team that helped elect Bill Clinton president in 1992. Following that election, he was invited to South Africa to assist Nelson Mandela and the African National Congress (ANC) in the historic 1994 all-race elections. (See chapter 18 for more on Greer's role in the South African race).

Greer and his firm, GMMB (Greer, Jim Margolis, David Mitchell, and Annie Burns), also played lead roles in the advertising and placement of media ads for the Obama for President campaigns of 2008 and 2012. GMMB is now a "specialty brand" of Fleishman-Hillard, which, since 1997, has been a part of the global advertising conglomerate Omnicom.

Republican media consultants J. Brian (Jay) Smith (1950–2014) and Mark Harroff (1948-1989) created their firm, Smith & Harroff, in 1973, serving about

100 candidates, and had the reputation of taking on clients with difficult election battles. Jay Smith graduated from Loyola College in Baltimore, Maryland, and worked with the Republican National Committee (RNC) through the 1972 presidential campaign. Soon after creating his media firm, Smith took a leave of absence to work as the press secretary to House Republican leader John J. Rhodes of Arizona. Later, Smith wrote a well-received biography of Rhodes.[55] Mark Harroff grew up in Ohio, graduated from Dennison University, and also began his career working for the RNC and the Committee to Reelect the President. Together, Smith and Harroff would tour college campuses, defending Richard Nixon and debating student leaders who supported George McGovern. Among their candidates were New Jersey congresswoman Millicent Fenwick, Arizona senator John McCain, and Maine senator Olympia Snowe. With over 100 victorious campaigns, Smith & Harroff had one of the best won-lost records in the business. Their political consulting firm was one of the first to transition over to corporate clients, while still keeping ten to fifteen candidate clients until the early 2000s.

Don Ringe (b. 1946) began his media career as a copy boy at Long Island's *Newsday* while he attended Hofstra University. He also did graduate work at Columbia University. His first media consulting job came in the early 1970s, working on three ballot initiatives in California, while working for pioneer consultant Stuart Spencer. In 1978, he founded Ringe-Russo (with partner Bill Russo), and worked for gubernatorial candidate William Clements (Texas), and for senatorial candidates John Warner (Virginia), Edward Brooke (Massachusetts), and John Chafee (Rhode Island). In 1985 he worked on selling the benefits of the Strategic Defense Initiative (SDI, or "Star Wars") for a private organization, High Frontier. In a simplistic, stick figure animation of a child, a dog, and the sun, Ringe portrayed the SDI as critical to national defense. His ads became the centerpiece of the SDI program, and as journalist Lloyd Grove noted, it "redefined the debate and radically streamline the discussion—in all of 27 seconds."[56] Three years later, he worked on the rocky Bob Dole presidential campaign. Ringe worked for Republican candidates and causes for forty years, but in 2008 he left the party and voted for Barack Obama.

Thomas N. Edmonds (b. 1943) began his career in a commercial advertising agency, but he was soon attracted to politics.[57] In 1980 he started his own sole proprietorship and was "blown away" at his early success: in his first year, he worked for one Senate campaign, two congressional campaigns, the Bob Dole for President campaign, the Fund for a Conservative Majority, and the National Conservative Political Action Committee (NCPAC). By 1982 he had seventeen full-time employees, working for Republican and other conservative candidates and causes. Edmonds's two biggest mentors were direct-mail specialist Brad O'Leary and media consultant Roger Ailes. As seen in chapter 17, one of Edmonds's most significant contributions was leading the National Rifle Association (NRA) effort in West Virginia, along with other states, to defeat Al Gore in the 2000 presidential election. Edmonds has been a frequent commentator on political events, is a past president of the AAPC and the IAPC, and produced the official documentary on the Reagan presidency, *Ronald Reagan: An American President*. From 2001 to 2004, Edmonds was in a business partnership with Arthur Hackney, a Republican consultant from Anchorage, Alaska, who in 2014 became the president of the American Association of Political Consultants.

Alex Castellanos (b. 1954) was born in Havana, Cuba, and came to the United States with his family in 1960. He graduated with honors from the University of North Carolina and became involved in North Carolina politics, particularly working with Arthur Finkelstein and his client Jesse Helms. Over the years, Castellanos has worked with many Republican heavyweights: US senator Strom Thurmond (South Carolina), Florida governor Jeb Bush, and presidential candidates George H. W. Bush (1992), Bob Dole (1996), George W. Bush (2000 and 2004), and Mitt Romney (2008). Castellanos was a fellow at the Institute of Politics at Harvard's Kennedy School, and has lectured widely and been a regular political commentator on television. He has been called the "father of the attack ad," a label that Castellanos proudly wears, and which appears in his own biographical material.[58] For years, Castellanos worked with Robin Roberts in the Republican firm National Media. In 2008 he cofounded Purple Strategies, a bipartisan media and strategic consulting firm based in the Virginia suburbs of Washington, DC, with Democratic consultant Steve McMahon. One of its first clients was the US Chamber of Commerce. Following the 2010 Deepwater Horizon oil spill, Purple Strategies was hired to assist BP in its media and public relations efforts.

Candidate and Opposition Research

Campaigns are won and lost in the library.

—Ken Khachigian (1984)[59]

When done wrong, opposition research can cause your campaign headaches, including fatal headaches. Done right, though, opposition research will be a major contributing factor in your victory.

—consultant Terry Cooper (n.d.)[60]

Another crucial aspect of political campaigns is candidate and opposition research. Under the glare of the campaign spotlight, a candidate's record is fair game, including promises made when running for office, voting records, tax and financial information, and even personal and family information. Invariably, the information gathered about a candidate is true—it makes little sense to make up facts and figures, and if caught doing so, the researcher and his candidate will be the first ones to suffer. The real sin is how facts, often unrelated, are put together to create a false narrative or accusation.

An early, infamous example came during the 1950 US Senate race in California. The Richard Nixon campaign produced the "pink sheets," a list of 354 votes in Congress in which Nixon's opponent, Helen Gahagan Douglas, agreed with known leftist congressman Vito Marcantonio. Nixon's campaign, led by Murray Chotiner, published the list of votes, on pink paper, and confronted Douglas at rallies, charging her with being "the Pink Lady." It was a flagrant attempt at guilt by association. Being soft on communism, being the "Pink Lady" during this time of loyalty oath hysteria, was probably the most damaging charge that could be leveled against Douglas.[61] Guilt by association has often been used to berate an opponent: conservatives would howl when their Democratic opponent "votes just like Ted Kennedy" or, more recently, "Nancy Pelosi" or "Harry Reid." Democrats would scoff at an opponent who is "in bed with Newt Gingrich" or, more recently, "the Tea Party crazies," or "Ted Cruz and Rand Paul."

Incumbents are particularly vulnerable to promises they made but did not keep. Certainly the most visible (and it took no research to unearth this one) was George H. W. Bush's pledge in 1988 of "read my lips, no new taxes" at the Republican nominating convention. When he reneged on that boast, conservative Republicans, led by Newt Gingrich, revolted, and voters punished Bush in 1992. During the same 1988 presidential campaign, Democratic nominee Michael Dukakis was attacked for his supposed failures to keep promises. Republican Party researchers, under James Pinkerton, unearthed the information, and it was transformed into a hard-hitting negative ad:

Voice-over: Michael Dukakis promised not to raise taxes. But, as governor, he imposed the largest tax increase in Massachusetts's history. He promised jobs, but since 1984 Massachusetts lost ninety thousand blue-collar jobs. He promised less spending, but spent at a greater rate per capita than any other governor in America. And now he wants to do for America what he's done for Massachusetts. American can't afford that risk.[62]

The infamous "Willie Horton" ad in that same 1988 presidential race depended on opposition research which was used to create an attack on Dukakis, which was characterized as "Dukakis on crime." Chapter 12 goes into greater detail on the creation and implications of this attack ad.

Candidates for office have to be very careful when putting together their resumes. Candidates and incumbents often stretch the truth regarding their accomplishments ("he fought hard against crime"), but they must be extremely careful on matters that can be verified. Republican congressman Wes Cooley, running for re-election in Oregon, lied about being married (allegedly so that he could fraudulently continue collecting benefits as a widower of a deceased Marine). He also lied about his residency in central Oregon, about being selected to Phi Beta Kappa, and about having a law degree. Then he lied one too many times, stating on a campaign brochure that he had served in the Army in Korea. That was news to the Army. It was also against the Oregon election law to lie on an official voter pamphlet. In a plea agreement, Cooley was found guilty, required to serve 100 hours of community service, and was fined $7,100. (In 2005 Cooley was convicted in a bogus Internet auction scheme. He was charged, and along with his associates, required to pay over $2.1 million to bilked investors.)[63] This is a highly unusual example, but occasionally other candidates for office have been caught padding their resumes, usually with nonexistent college degrees or awards.

How far back in one's career might a researcher go? While Arkansas governor Bill Clinton had served over ten years as his state's chief executive,

Bush I campaign researchers were much more interested in Clinton's early years, when he was at Oxford, when he allegedly visited Russia, and how he sought to avoid the draft. John Kerry's long record in the Senate was of secondary importance to Bush II researchers, who honed in on Kerry's supposed strength, his Vietnam War record. Democratic researchers were most interested in Mitt Romney's business activities at Bain Capital, rather than his governorship in Massachusetts. No doubt researchers continued searching for the "truth" about Barack Obama's birth certificate throughout his 2008 and 2012 campaigns.

Incumbent candidates need to know how they might be attacked in a campaign by their opponents or outside interest groups. For them, researchers prepare "vulnerability studies." The studies will warn the public official of possible shortcomings, but they also can be used to highlight accomplishments. A vulnerability study might ask these questions (and prepare the answers): What were the ten most important things you promised to accomplish when you were first elected? Why did you support President Obama on the Affordable Care Act when the majority of voters in the state opposed it? In what specific ways did you oppose the president? How much money will it cost taxpayers to support the projects you have voted for?

On any major campaign, candidate and opposition research is one of the first tasks undertaken. George H. W. Bush's senior strategist, Lee Atwater, remarked that "the only group I was very interested in having report to me directly was opposition research."[64] While attention is often given to "oppo" research, candidate research is probably more important. A campaign must know the strengths, and particularly the weaknesses, of its candidate. James Carville remarked that if he had two staffers or consultants doing research, he'd put the best one on his own candidate.[65]

Candidate and opposition research is often conducted by the political parties, or by staff members on a campaign. However, several specialists in candidate and opposition research opened up their own consulting businesses during the last decades of the twentieth century.

One of the first political consultants to specialize in research was Phil Noble (b. 1951). Noble's interest in politics went back to when he was nine years old and living in Anniston, Alabama. His father called him over to watch the Kennedy-Nixon debate on television. "Who do you like?" his father asked. "Kennedy," replied young Phil. "Well then," said his father, "why don't you go work for him." Phil got on his bicycle and went down to the local Kennedy headquarters, expecting to see Kennedy himself. No Kennedy, but Phil was excited by the mimeograph machine and all the bustle of the campaign. An amused office volunteer gave Phil a packet of brochures to hand out; Phil handed them out, asked for more, and became hooked on politics.[66]

Noble worked for a variety of Democratic clients, both on his own and for the established firms of Matt Reese and Rothstein/Buckley. He opened his firm, Phil Noble and Associates, in 1979 and continued working on domestic campaigns until 1992. He then turned his attention to international campaigns and the growing importance of online communications and campaigns. Noble's career is also noteworthy for his early application of the Internet and digital communications, and there is more on his profile in chapter 15, on technological advances.

Averell (Ace) Smith (b. 1961) has been described as "genteel, soft-spoken and bespectacled," but also as "Doctor Death" and as "one of the nation's most feared opposition researchers." While a student at U.C. Berkeley, he took time off to help in his father's 1979 campaign for San Francisco district attorney. That experience peaked his interest in politics and campaigning. Smith established himself as an exacting and resourceful opposition researcher working for Democratic candidates. During the late 1980s, he was political director for the Democratic Congressional Campaign Committee (DCCC), and produced "vulnerability studies" for Governor Bill Clinton as he prepared for the 1992 presidential run. "I've seen him walk into a room, and the opposition candidate will literally start mumbling," said former consultant Clint Reilly.[67] Smith moved away from the subspecialty of candidate and opposition research when he became the campaign manager for Antonio Villaraigosa's successful mayoral campaign in Los Angeles. He also helped Hillary Clinton in her 2008 primary campaign in California and Texas. He is a partner in the San Francisco-based consulting firm of SCN Strategies, with partners Sean Clegg and Dan Newman.

On the Republican side, one of the most prominent research consultants has been Terry Cooper, a graduate of Princeton and the University of Virginia Law School, and before entering politics full-time, he worked on Wall Street and held executive positions at three Fortune 500 companies. But he was drawn by politics, and opened his candidate and opposition research firm, Terry Cooper Research, in 1985. Cooper has worked for Republican candidates and conservative causes in all fifty states, for Senate and gubernatorial candidates, and for others down-ballot. "My goal in my opposition research," Cooper wrote, "is to find a way to make the strengths of my client and the weaknesses of my opponent as vivid in voters' minds as the Willie Horton ad made the asininity of Dukakis's furlough policy."[68]

Beyond individual researchers and those affiliated with political parties, independent organizations are also getting into the opposition research business. One of the most significant is American Bridge 21st Century, an opposition research clearinghouse for Democrats. American Bridge prepared opposition research reports on many Republicans running competitive races in 2012 and 2014, and it released an early media guide on the foibles of the prospective 2016 Republican presidential candidates. American Bridge researchers have recorded thousands of events attended by Republican hopefuls, and have made the video library accessible to media, candidates, and consultants.[69] As seen in chapter 20, the Koch brothers also set up their own sophisticated research and analysis unit, examining not only candidate records, but also the activities of other outside political organizations active in the 2016 presidential campaign.

CHAPTER 7

The Evolution of Polling

Just give me the numbers, Lou . . . I know what they mean.
—John F. Kennedy to Louis Harris (1960)

Every major innovation in political survey research in
the past forty years has Bob [Teeter's] DNA in it.
—Peter D. Hart (2004)

A pollster is both an objective observer and a campaign
consultant. We try to make the differences understood between
survey data and our own instincts.
—Patrick Caddell (1979)

The media have made pollsters into philosopher kings. We're not.
There's no science in the questions. There's no science in the interviews.
And there's more art than science in the results.
—Irwin (Tubby) Harrison (1984)

D URING THE 1950s and 1960s, it was hard to convince many candidates that they needed private polling. Incumbents seeking re-election and newcomers alike were wary, for they remembered the polling failures that occurred in 1936 and 1948. Incumbents wondered why they needed polling when they could rely on, as they had done in past elections, their own gut instinct or understanding of their constituents; while challengers wondered whether it was worth it to invest precious campaign money in survey research. Bill Hamilton remembered that, even in the late 1960s, "you had to sell the idea to politicians that they needed polling before you could sell them on the fact that you were the one to do it."[1]

When pollsters were hired, they usually came in during the last several weeks to give a snapshot of how the candidates were doing. Candidates didn't use polling research as a tool for guiding them throughout their campaigns; they just wanted to know how they were doing during the last crucial weeks. As pollster Douglas E. Schoen noted, "the notion of using polls to monitor a race or determine tactics in midstream was simply unheard of."[2] As an example, in the mid-1960s, a US senator from the Midwest, just one week before the election, insisted that Oliver Quayle conduct a "quickie" poll. Quayle protested, saying it would be unscientific and invalid—a useless exercise and a waste of money. "Do it anyway," said the senator. "I just want to know."[3]

In the late 1950s and early 1960s, private pollsters simply provided the numbers. The Kennedy epigraph quote neatly summarized the attitude: just give us the numbers; we'll know what to do with them. Pollsters were not an integral part of the strategy team during this period, as they would become in the decades to follow. But Louis Harris, the pioneer private campaign pollster, did find a place at the strategy table, perhaps not with Kennedy, but with other clients. "I was certainly the first [poll] taker," Harris recalled in 1984, "who . . . served on a super-strategy committee."[4]

But as the business of private survey research grew, pollsters were able to give some very compelling reasons why candidates should hire them. When starting with a benchmark poll—the first poll taken, often ten to twelve months before the election—candidates could determine whether or not to run for office, understand the issues most important to the electorate, and determine which groups were supportive. Surveys taken during the campaign itself could help determine how the candidates should project their images or the effectiveness of television advertising. Favorable poll results could be used to bolster fundraising or be leaked to the press. During the final weeks of the campaign, nightly tracking polls could help determine the last-minute impact of advertising and the trends as voters made up their minds.[5] As campaigns evolved during the 1970s and 1980s, pollsters were able to offer these research services. In addition, pollsters began using qualitative research techniques that had been crafted earlier for commercial and marketing purposes, such as focus group research and dial meter analysis.

The Transformation of Polling

> [*Private polling*] *is a phenomenal growth industry.*
> [*Polls*] *are more sophisticated, accurate, informative, succinct,*
> *and timely—all for substantially less money.*
>
> —Journalist Beth Bogart (1987)[6]

Up until the 1970s, survey research was slow, cumbersome, relatively expensive, and conducted only in the latter stages of a campaign. Surveys were conducted in person, with interviewers going door-to-door, asking questions, marking responses on answer grids, and then mailing the results back to the polling center, where the information would be transferred to computer punch cards and run through a mainframe computer. Then the results were analyzed. Bob Teeter and his firm Market Opinion Research (MOR) used field directors and trained interviewers, and he spent considerable time on the road, meeting with staffers and collecting data. Until the early 1970s, the idea of receiving a telephone call from a pollster, who then would ask a series of questions "was kind of a strange thing," Teeter remarked.[7] Peter Hart recalled that when he started his firm in 1971, about 95 percent of his polls were conducted door-to-door. His interviews, whether conducted in Montana or New Jersey, were done in peoples' homes or on their doorstep.[8]

Data processing was also slow, cumbersome, and expensive. In the 1960s, data were tabulated by running IBM punch cards through sorters, often with a large group of employees working with hand-cranked calculators. In 1965, Market Opinion Research purchased a new IBM computer, specifically designed for its research business. The bulky computer had 8K of storage capacity, which MOR upgraded to 16K, and cost $70,000 ($528,455 in 2015 dollars). In our world of terabytes and hand-held computing, this may seem hard to believe, but at the time, the IBM computer was considered a marvel. Computing was an expensive proposition. Polling firms had to either rent computer time on a mainframe or, like MOR, spend an extraordinary amount of money for their own computing operations. Further, many of the statistical instruments now widely used, such as multivariate analysis, were not available to pollsters in the 1960s.[9]

Democratic pollster Mark S. Mellman remembered that he would send raw polling data by Federal Express from his New Haven, Connecticut, office to a data key punch company in Philadelphia, which would then deliver the punched cards back to New Haven to be run through the mainframe computer. The results and analysis were written up and only then delivered overnight to the client. In those days, in the early 1980s, even fax machines were not widely in use.[10]

The time needed to process and analyze the polling data also sped up dramatically. "If you did something inside a week," recalled Peter Hart, "it was almost unheard of; if it was done in two weeks it was considered terribly quick."[11] Kathleen Frankovic, director of surveys at CBS, noted that it took the Gallup Poll two weeks to announce to the country whom the American public thought won the 1960 Kennedy-Nixon debates. By contrast, the public's response was released within fifteen minutes of the second presidential debate in 1992.[12]

For two pollsters, basic knowledge of computers and a little ingenuity sped the process along. Mark Penn and Doug Schoen were hired in 1975 by media consultant David Garth to work on the New York mayoral campaign of Edward I. Koch. The young pollsters, just out of college, input data onto punch cards. Penn said, "I can buy a computer kit, build it, program it and process this stuff for nothing." Schoen remarked, "Nah, I don't want a computer. It's too big an investment." Undeterred, Penn bought a kit-built personal computer, called SAL processor technology, programmed it, and the two were able to turn polls out instantly. "At that time," Penn recalled, "no one had that capability."[13]

Now, with inexpensive computer software and hardware, even the most complex survey analysis can be done quickly. David Beattie, who now heads the firm founded by Bill Hamilton, recently observed that "what pollsters can now do in four or five days used to take four or five weeks back in the 1960s and early 1970s."[14]

It was not until the 1972 presidential election that telephone interviewing became widespread. Up until that time, it was considered "radical" to use telephones for nationwide personal interviews.[15] With the introduction of telephone surveys, polling firms created in-house call centers, with perhaps hundreds of telephone books lining their walls. Telephone numbers were dialed manually on rotary-dial phones (push-button phones were just starting to be used in the 1970s). In the years to come, many polling firms contracted out the interview process to established marketing telephone centers.

Bob Teeter used telephone interviewing from call centers in Detroit (where MOR was headquartered), Los Angeles, or another metropolitan area close to where the surveys were to be conducted. This was at the beginning of the 800-number service, and long-distance calls still were incredibly expensive. Interviewers would manually dial the telephone number and write down the answer on paper. It was a heavily labor-intensive activity.[16]

Technology helped speed up the process and make polling less expensive and more responsive. Low-cost long-distance service became commonplace; speed dialing was introduced. Computer-assisted telephone interviewing (CATI) systems were developed, with interviewers sitting at a computer, the survey questions displayed on the video terminal; they would use a telephone headset to ask questions, and input answers directly into a computer file. At great expense, Teeter's firm created its own CATI system, but in later years, with powerful and sophisticated personal computing, CATI systems became readily available and inexpensive. Also important to polling was the development in the 1970s of random digit dialing (RDD), by which telephone numbers were dialed automatically and randomly. Thus all numbers, including unlisted, business, and nonworking numbers, could be called. In order to get a completed survey from about 600 individuals, it might take ten times that number of calls, and the technological advances of CATI and RDD made the process less time-consuming.

While telephone calling was more efficient and less expensive than person-to-person interaction, the nature of the interview changed. Peter Hart observed that "if I am sitting in your living room or on your door stoop, the answers I am getting are probably a little more reflective than you and I talking over the telephone. There's a different sense of interchange."[17]

Private polling was mostly conducted late in the campaign, with little early strategic polling being done. "In those days [late 1960s]," remarked Bill Hamilton, "there was a lot of seasonality to our business. We were really busy during the last five months of every campaign period." But twenty years later, "polls are done for politicians even when they're not running for office so that they won't have to do them later during campaigns."[18]

Pollsters also began experimenting with several qualitative research methods, particularly focus group analysis and dial meters. Initially labeled as "focused interviews," the focus group was first used in the Office of Radio Research at Columbia University in 1941. Professor Paul F. Lazarsfeld invited his colleague Robert Merton to evaluate audience responses to radio programs. The audience members were asked to press a red button when they heard something that they thought was negative, and a green button for something they heard that was positive. After World War II, Merton used the techniques to analyze US Army training and morale films.[19] By the 1950s, focus groups were being introduced into market research to test commercial products. A focus group consists of between ten and fourteen participants, carefully selected, who are guided through a series of open-ended questions by a moderator, usually over a two-hour period of time. Often the participants are grouped by gender, race, or past voting preferences. By the late 1970s, political campaigns began using focus group analysis to give them further insight into the mood and preferences of the electorate, and to test messages and advertising.

The electronic versions of focus groups are "perception analyzers" or dial meters. Long used in testing commercial products, dial-meter testing brings together carefully selected groups of voters, perhaps fifty or more. In the 1950s, television talent shows sometimes used "applause meters" to gauge the audience's enthusiasm for a contestant. From that crude beginning, "perception analyzers" are able to determine in real time what individuals and groups of individuals think about a candidate, a debate performance, or a candidate commercial. Each participant is given a hand-held dial meter, which can be turned from 0 to 100, with 0 representing complete disagreement or absolute negative response, and 100 representing complete agreement or total positive response. Responses are simultaneously fed into a computer, and it is possible to tell in real time how the twenty females under 35 years old, or the several men aged 50 to 65, reacted. Dial-meter groups often are used to pretest words, phrases, and campaign commercials, much to the chagrin of ad makers, who often feel that the creative process is being compromised by citizens who don't like the color of the dress that the spouse is wearing, think the ad is too negative, or wince when the candidate says he's a Republican.

Polling Consultants

Today, there are probably no individuals in America
who have been in more campaigns that the six top pollsters.
—William Hamilton (1984), referring to Peter Hart,
Pat Caddell, Richard Wirthlin, Robert Teeter, Lance Tarrance, and himself.[20]

With Lou Harris leaving private polling in 1962, the retirement of John Kraft, and the death of Oliver Quayle III in 1974, the field of polling on the Democratic side was largely wide open, making room for several consultants who would become important players in presidential and statewide campaigns for years to come. Bill Hamilton, profiled in chapter 4, was joined by Peter D. Hart and his business partner Geoff Garin, Patrick Caddell, and Irwin (Tubby) Harrison.

Peter D. Hart's family had been active in politics, with his maternal grandmother working for Socialist candidates Norman Thomas and Eugene Debs, and his mother an active Adlai Stevenson supporter. After graduating from Colby College, Hart (b. 1942), not really set on a career path, began working as a coder for pollster Louis Harris for the munificent sum of two dollars an hour. During the 1966 congressional elections, Hart was a researcher for the Harris CBS election unit and traveled to about twenty states to cover the elections. In 1968 he took a leave of absence to work for former Ohio congressman John J. Gilligan, who was running for a US Senate seat against William B. Saxbe. While Gilligan lost, Hart found work with Democratic consultants Joseph Napolitan and Charles Guggenheim. He also got his next big lead from another Gilligan campaign staffer, Mark Shields, then a political operative who later became a journalist, who recommended Hart to the Democratic National Committee. Hart was hired as the political research director under DNC chairman Senator Fred R. Harris of Oklahoma.[21]

Hart then went to work for Oliver Quayle in 1970 and conducted private polls in twenty-two Senate and gubernatorial contests, the lion's share of the Democratic campaign business that year. He was lured back to the Louis Harris firm when Harris was considering reopening a political shop; in the end, however, Harris decided not to reopen, and he urged Hart to open up his own polling firm.[22]

Hart created his polling firm, Peter D. Hart & Associates, in Washington, DC, toward the end of 1971, offering his services to a series of congressional candidates. After noting that the *New York Times* had done exit polling in Florida during the 1972, Hart walked over to the *Washington Post* and convinced the newspaper to hire him to conduct poll reports. "Obviously, that took me from being, 'who's the new guy,' to the pollster for the *Washington Post* four months into my business."[23]

By 1974, Hart's firm had conducted polls in seventeen statewide campaigns. Democrats won big in 1974, and fourteen of the seventeen clients that Hart assisted won. Hart became one of the most sought-after private pollsters for Democratic candidates running for statewide office, such as the US Senate and governorships, and presidential candidates. His clients included senators Hubert H. Humphrey (Minnesota), Henry M. (Scoop) Jackson (Washington), Warren Magnuson (Washington), Frank Church (Idaho), Robert Byrd (West Virginia), John D. (Jay) Rockefeller IV (West Virginia), Edward M. (Ted) Kennedy (Massachusetts), and John Glenn (Ohio). In the 1976 presidential primary, he was the pollster for Morris K. Udall (Arizona), and in 1984 he was the pollster for Walter Mondale (Minnesota).

One of the lessons Hart learned early in his career was the importance of knowing how many candidates his firm could effectively serve. He decided that fourteen candidates during an election cycle was the limit. Many more candidates sought his services, but they had to be turned down. He also learned that a key to good business was satisfied clients and repeat business.[24]

By 1986, however, Hart had tired of the vicissitudes of campaign life. At the age of forty-four, he moved out of the candidate side of private polling to focus on public and media polling. In 1989 he partnered with Republican pollster Robert Teeter, and later with Bill McInturff of Public Opinion Strategies (POS). Hart's colleague Geoffrey Garin (b. 1953), who joined the firm in 1978, became lead partner of the political division, which was renamed Garin-Hart Research Group. Later, Fred Yang was added as a name partner, and the firm became Garin-Hart-Yang Research Group.

Geoff Garin, a graduate of Harvard College, began his career working for Republican congressman H. John Heinz III, who was running for the US Senate seat in Pennsylvania in 1976. There he met Peter Hart, and was hired two years later. Garin became president of Hart Research Associates in 1984. His clients have included a long list of Democratic senators and Senate candidates, including Hillary Clinton (New York), Richard Durbin (Illinois), Charles Schumer (New York), Patrick Leahy (Vermont), Kent Conrad (North Dakota), and Dianne Feinstein (California). He was called on to rescue the faltering Clinton presidential nomination in 2008, replacing Mark Penn as senior strategist. During the 2012 election cycle, he was pollster and strategic adviser for the super PAC Priorities USA, which supported the re-election of President Obama. In a 2008 feature in *Time,* Karen Tumulty characterized Garin as "one of the most well-regarded and sought after" pollsters for Democratic candidates.[25]

Patrick H. Caddell (b. 1950) became an overnight success, and at the age of twenty-one was the pollster for George McGovern's 1972 presidential campaign. While still in high school in Florida, Caddell designed a math project that correctly predicted the winners of local elections in the Jacksonville area. Precocious, arrogant, temperamental, and whip-smart, Caddell made his mark while still a student at Harvard College. During his sophomore year in 1969, Caddell and two classmates, John Gorman and Daniel Porter, created Cambridge Survey Research. A guest lecturer, former congressman John J. Gilligan, who was running for governor of Ohio, met Caddell and learned about his Florida polling. Soon Gilligan and former astronaut John Glenn, who was running for an Ohio Senate seat, became clients of Caddell's fledgling company.[26]

Caddell, who befriended McGovern's campaign manager Gary Hart, became the youngest pollster for a presidential nominee when he signed on to George McGovern's 1972 presidential campaign. By 1975, when he joined the Carter presidential campaign, Caddell had already served as pollster in some thirty Senate campaigns and dozens of gubernatorial campaigns.

Caddell was focused, perhaps fixated, on finding a candidate who would appeal to the new generation of voters and to those who were alienated by the political process. Who would be the new Democratic John F. Kennedy, the young new face who would reach out to a new generation of voters, pursue progressive ideas, call for campaign finance reform, and appeal to the growing independent and distrustful electorate? Shortly after joining up with McGovern in 1972, Caddell wrote a memo, describing a fictitious, perhaps mythical "Senator Smith," who would embody all these attributes. He kept searching for that perfect candidate, but they all somehow came up short. Following his polling for Carter in the 1976 and 1980 presidential races, Caddell worked for Gary Hart in 1984, Joe Biden in 1988, and was an unpaid adviser to Jerry Brown in 1992.[27]

Caddell's most important contribution, according to political reporter Joe Klein, was his "newly aggressive type of questioning, designed not only to test existing attitudes but also to figure out ways to change them." He helped transform polling from "mere reporting" of people's attitudes to "an active, strategic weapon." For example, on the politically sensitive issue of abortion and privacy,

Caddell would test different phrases and approaches. Out of this came a winning policy statement for Democratic clients: "Abortion is a decision of a woman, her clergyman, and her doctor."[28]

Caddell dropped out of political campaigning and made headlines when he and Scott Miller teamed up to help Coca-Cola launch a new product, New Coke. But the launch was a public relations nightmare. Upon occasion, Caddell resurfaces with commentary on politics and advice for presidents, but his service as a political consultant essentially ended in 1988.

Irwin (Tubby) Harrison (1930–2012). After graduating from Harvard University Law School, Tubby Harrison (who was slim as a rail in his adult life) and his classmate David Goldberg joined Doug Bailey and John Deardourff to form one of the first Republican consulting firms. Later, Harrison worked with John Becker, became the pollster for the *Boston Globe*, and then settled into campaign consulting with Goldberg, creating their own firm.[29] Harrison, based in Boston, was best known for his work with Michael Dukakis, beginning with his 1982 successful attempt to regain the governorship that he had lost in 1978. Harrison served as pollster for Dukakis's 1986 re-election campaign, then as his pollster during the 1988 presidential drive. Harrison could be blunt and forceful, but getting Dukakis to listen "was never easy."[30] Summing up his life's work, journalist J. M. Lawrence described Harrison as a "smoke detector": for his clients over a thirty year period, "he sounded alarms long before anyone saw smoke. Candidates who heeded his warnings and retooled their messages got elected, political strategists say, while those who dismissed him as a dour curmudgeon usually wound up giving concession speeches."[31]

Also founded in the 1970s was the Boston-based polling firm of Marttila and Kiley. John Marttila, a union organizer's son, originally from Detroit, began his political career in 1970 as campaign manager for Father Robert Drinan, SJ, the antiwar candidate and dean of the Boston College Law School, who successfully ran for the US House of Representatives. Thomas Kiley, also from Detroit, had been studying for the priesthood when he learned of Drinan's bid for public office. Also from Detroit was Dan Payne, a onetime classmate of Marttila's. David Thorne, John Kerry's college classmate and brother of Kerry's first wife, was the fourth member of the firm Marttila, Payne, Kiley & Thorne, which was created in 1972 and became a leading Boston political consulting firm. Long associated with progressive candidates and causes, Marttila and Kiley have assisted senators Joe Biden (Delaware), John Kerry (Massachusetts), and Thomas Eagleton (Missouri), as well as a number of big city mayors. Like many firms, they split apart over the years, with Payne leaving in the 1970s, and Kiley and Marttila branching out with their own firms.[32]

On the Republican side, there were two well-established private consultants, Robert Teeter and Richard Wirthlin. Joining them in the 1970s were V. Lance Tarrance Jr. and Arthur J. Finkelstein.

By the time he was thirty years old, V. Lance Tarrance Jr. had climbed high in Republican circles. Before graduating from Washington and Lee University in Virginia, with a major in modern European history, Tarrance had no idea that he would become involved in politics.[33] But then someone gave him a copy of Barry Goldwater's book *Conscience of a Conservative*, which made a huge impression upon him. Tarrance went home and enrolled at the University of Texas Law School, but legal studies bored him. He volunteered at the Texas Republican Party headquarters in Austin, which in the 1960s was a small operation. But the Goldwater nomination caught fire in Texas, and Tarrance was at the right place at the right time. At twenty-three, he became research director for the Texas Goldwater for President Committee. He was heavily involved in the John Tower US Senate race in 1966, and the next year, RNC chairman Ray C. Bliss began rebuilding the national party, and he asked Tarrance to come to Washington as second in command of the RNC research department. With Nixon elected president in 1968, Tarrance was elevated to research director of the RNC; at twenty-eight, he was the youngest ever to hold that position. He modernized the operation, bringing in computers, software, and technology to transform the research activities.

The 1970 census was just becoming available, and because of the Supreme Court's 1964 one-man, one-vote mandate, the political implications for redistricting and reapportionment were becoming increasingly clear. The Nixon White House assigned Tarrance to the US Census Bureau, creating a special political appointment reporting directly to the commissioner, so that he could analyze census data in preparation for state and local redistricting fights. Then, in 1973, Tarrance received a fellowship to the Kennedy School of Government at Harvard.

Tarrance had considered working for both of the established Republican research firms, Wirthlin and Barabba's DMI and Currier and Teeter's MOR, but he made a "geopolitical decision" (better to go to sunny California than frigid Detroit), and accepted Vince Barabba's offer to work at DMI. Being low man on the totem pole, Tarrance was handed three long-shot Senate races, pitting Republican challengers against Democratic incumbents: Malcolm Wallop against Gale W. McGee in Wyoming; Harrison H. Schmitt against Joseph Montoya in New Mexico; and S. I. Hayakawa against John V. Tunney in California. All three Republicans won, and Tarrance had the best record in the firm.

After spending three years at DMI, Texas beckoned, and eventually Tarrance made the leap, going back home and opening V. Lance Tarrance Associates. As business picked up, his firm expanded to include partners David Hill, Frank Newport, and Richard (Rick) Ryan, and then to expand the business with a Washington, DC, office, headed by Edward A. (Ed) Goeas, III. After ten years of polling for Republican Senate, congressional, and gubernatorial candidates, Tarrance sold his business to the Gallup Organization. He then became a member of the board of directors of the Gallup Organization, and then was managing director and president of Gallup-China, based in Beijing, from 1993 to 1995. After years in the private sector, Tarrance made something of a political reprise by working in 2008 for Senator John McCain's political action committee, Straight Talk America, and later working for Texas senator Kay Bailey Hutchison in 2012. In 2013 Tarrance was inducted into the AAPC Hall of Fame.

Arthur J. Finkelstein (b. 1945) first worked for Irwin A. (Bud) Lewis, the head of survey research for NBC News, and he volunteered at the New York headquarters of the Draft Goldwater Committee, which was set up by Clifton White. While studying at Columbia University, Finkelstein produced a radio show and interviewed conservative writer Ayn Rand. Eventually, he completed his undergraduate degree at Queens College. In 1969 Finkelstein wrote a lengthy letter to James L. Buckley outlining how he could win an upcoming US Senate race, but only if he ran on the Conservative Party ticket.[34] Buckley was intrigued, hired White and Finkelstein, and won the US Senate seat from New York in 1970, defeating Republican incumbent Charles Goodell. Finkelstein was one of several pollsters recruited for the Nixon re-election campaign in 1972, and that same year he helped Jesse Helms win a Senate seat from North Carolina. Finkelstein was also a key factor in helping Ronald Reagan win the important North Carolina primary during the 1976 Republican presidential primary season.

Finkelstein helped Helms associates Tom Ellis and Carter Wrenn establish the National Congressional Club (NCC), a national organization based in North Carolina designed to promote conservative causes and candidates. (See chapter 6 for more on NCC.) Finkelstein was also instrumental in the strategy behind the National Conservative Political Action Committee (NCPAC), which was created 1975 and dedicated to defeating national liberal candidates. Among Finkelstein's clients were US Senate candidates Orrin Hatch (Utah), Strom Thurmond (South Carolina), Jesse Helms (North Carolina), John East (North Carolina), Don Nickles (Oklahoma), and Alphonse D'Amato (New York). Finkelstein was controversial, even among admiring Republicans, particularly for his demands to control campaigns in their entirety. As journalist Alicia Mundy characterized him in a 1996 profile, "Finkelstein wants to be all: strategist, tactician, media adviser, and pollster."[35]

In 1995, D'Amato became chairman of the National Republican Senatorial Committee (NRSC) and Finkelstein became his principal pollster. Finkelstein's signature attack line accused his client's opponent of being too liberal: "Hey Buddy. You're a Liberal" (against Buddy McKay in Florida, 1988); "Bob Abrams: Hopelessly Liberal" (against Abrams in New York, 1992); or "Paul Wellstone: Embarrassingly Liberal" (against Wellstone in Minnesota, 1996). Democratic pollster Mark Mellman commented on what he called the Finkelstein formula: "just brand somebody a liberal, use the word over and over again, engage in that kind of name-calling."[36]

In 1996 *Boston* magazine published a report that the famously reclusive Finkelstein was a homosexual (a decade later, he married his partner of forty years). This caused some embarrassment among his more virulent antigay clients, and some backpedaling and hair-splitting by others who saw this as a private matter.

During the 2000s, Finkelstein increasingly turned his attention to international clients, including clients in Israel, Albania, Austria, the Czech Republic, Ukraine, and Hungary. In 2013 he was inducted into the American Association of Political Consultants Hall of Fame.

Private Polling for Presidents Johnson through Bush I

If President Johnson does not have poll fever,
he has a good stiff case of the poll sniffles.

—William M. Honan (1966)[37]

I don't think that any political man who has any sense of
responsibility at all can change his position every time he takes a poll.

—Richard M. Nixon (1968)[38]

Presidential polling is a staple of the modern presidency.

—Kathryn Dunn Tenpas (2003)[39]

As seen in chapter 2, every president since Franklin Roosevelt has used private polling to some degree or another. John F. Kennedy was the innovator, however. As political scientists Lawrence R. Jacobs and Robert Y. Shapiro have noted, "starting with John Kennedy . . . the White House's sensitivity to public opinion became an enduring institutional characteristic of the modern presidency; it no longer simply mirrored the personal inclinations of the sitting president."[40]

Kennedy used Louis Harris both in his 1960 presidential campaign, conducting fifty polls during the primaries and twenty-seven during the general election, and during his term of office, conducting sixteen surveys.[41] Despite conducting the polls while Kennedy was in the White House, Harris later declared that he had never been paid for that work.[42] Kennedy also had polls conducted on his behalf by Joe Napolitan and others, but the president didn't want others to know that he was polling and kept the data locked in a safe in his brother's office at the Justice Department.[43]

Polling for Lyndon Johnson

When Harris left private polling, his second-in-command, Oliver A. Quayle III, set up his own shop in 1963; by 1964, Quayle was a key figure in analyzing public opinion for the Johnson White House. Lyndon Johnson, earlier in his career, was generally not impressed with pollsters or their conclusions—he had seen how the polls of Joe Belden in Texas were too often off the mark. But both Harris and Quayle caught Johnson's attention. Quayle coined the term "frontlash" for the 1964 Johnson presidential campaign: it described Johnson's appeal to moderate Republicans who would vote for the president, in contrast to the much more talked about "backlash" of conservative, southern Democrats who would vote for Goldwater.[44] Quayle was also the most accurate of pollsters, convincing Johnson that he was not just lucky, but was skilled at polling: "That boy seem to know what he's doin'," the president remarked.[45]

White House staffer Walter Jenkins commissioned private polls on the Maryland primary, then in Indiana and Wisconsin. Johnson, in the words of one historian, was "not only converted, but close to transfixed" on the value of polling research, with his pockets stuffed with polling research data.[46] Quayle provided Johnson with 130 separate surveys, paid for by the Democratic National Committee, with thirty-nine of them conducted in connection with the 1964 election.[47] In addition, John Kraft prepared eleven polls and Joseph Napolitan conducted ten. Beyond the Quayle polls, some fifty-four were conducted, but a number of them were forwarded to the White House unsolicited.[48] Johnson elevated polling in the White House by creating a "stand alone" polling operation, with Bill Moyers and W. Marvin Watson responsible for evaluating the Quayle polls, along with Albert H. (Tad) Cantril, Fred Panzer, Hayes Redmon, and Richard Nelson.[49]

One of Quayle's most interesting polling reports concerned Johnson's 1964 choice for running mate. Quayle concluded that Johnson was running so strong, it was more a question of who among the vice-presidential candidates would hurt him the least. The polls showed that Robert F. Kennedy—who Johnson had no desire to choose, and whose hatred for each other was palpable—would have "seriously weakened" Johnson's chances among southerners and business interests. Johnson, afraid that sentiment for Kennedy among many 1964 delegates was strong, and that the convention could be swept up in an emotional undertow, was determined to end the speculation and gossip. On July 29, just weeks before the convention, Johnson met with Kennedy, informing him that he would not be chosen, and then telling the press that no one in his cabinet (which everyone knew meant Kennedy) would be recommended as his running mate.[50]

Quayle also conducted frequent polls on Vietnam, asking citizens whether America was on the right course, whether they were "Pure Hawks" (disagreeing with US policy, not going far enough), an "LBJ Hawk" (agree with policy, but should do more to claim victory), an "LBJ Dove" (agree with policy, but do more to bring about negotiations), or a "Pure Dove" (disagree with current policy, shouldn't be in Vietnam, should pull troops out). Citizens were asked if taxes should be increased to pay for the war, or if domestic spending should be cut to compensate for the costs.[51]

The determination of the White House was, according to Jacobs and Shapiro, to "refocus public attention away from Vietnam by raising the salience of other policies and to change public preferences toward its Vietnam policy."[52] As opposition to the war increased, this became an increasingly more difficult task.

Quayle also conducted surveys of voter attitudes toward civil rights. He compiled a "Backlash Index," which sought to measure how many white Democratic voters would abandon their party and vote Republican because of their racial attitudes.[53]

In August 1966, *New York Times* reporter William Honan wrote a lengthy essay titled "Johnson May Not Have Poll Fever, But He Has a 'Good Case of the Poll Sniffles.'" Quayle had boasted to the reporter that he was Johnson's private pollster and that the White House devoured his research. The White House took great exception, for the work done by Quayle was supposed to be confidential—for the eyes of the president and his advisors only. Soon thereafter, Quayle's work for the White House was minimized.[54]

Johnson, as Louis Harris cryptically wrote, was "the truest believer of polls, but only when they tended to support what he was doing."[55] When Johnson's popularity sank, the White House tried to counter the poll results by a variety of means, such as attacking the poll results, leaking the results of their own private surveys, and courting the pollsters. In the end, however, none of these tactics could erase the reality of sinking popularity and public support.[56]

Polling for Richard Nixon

> Since Nixon, all presidents have internalized the
> lessons learned on the campaign trail.
>
> —Diane J. Heith (2004)[57]

Political scientist Kathryn Dunn Tenpas observed that "Nixon's use of pollsters marked a turning point in the history of presidential polling because it signaled the birth of White House–commissioned polls. No longer tethered to the timetables and agendas of public pollsters like Lou Harris and George Gallup, presidents began to direct both the timing and the substance of their polls."[58]

Nixon's White House dramatically increased the number of private polls taken during his 1972 re-election effort and during his first years in office. Nixon's first private polling analyst was David Derge, a professor of political science at Indiana University. Derge would contact private polling firms to conduct White House surveys, then analyze the results.[59]

Nixon was reluctant to share survey findings with allies, even the Republican National Committee, which was picking up the tab. White House chief of staff H. R. (Bob) Haldeman was the gatekeeper, ensuring that the polls were seen only by key White House advisers; otherwise, they were locked in a safe.[60] Nixon used Claude Robinson's Opinion Research Corporation (ORC) for internal White House polls and Bob Teeter's Marketing Opinion Research (MOR) for campaign work. Robert M. Eisinger observed that the "genius of President Nixon's polling operation lay in the ability to amass and interpret polls from a variety of allies, all of whose loyalty to the president overrode their allegiance to the GOP."[61]

The Nixon team also drilled down into the technical aspects of polling—insisting on complete printouts of the surveys; requesting additional information; and questioning the wording, the timing, and even the location of where polls were conducted. There was also secret polling conducted by the Committee to Re-elect the President to figure out how to handle the disgraced vice president, Spiro Agnew.[62]

Polling for Gerald Ford

The Republican National Committee had completed a major national survey of 12,000 respondents in June 1974, just two months before Nixon's resignation, and Bob Teeter did a follow-up to that survey for the Ford White House in September 1974.[63] Teeter conducted seventy-five surveys for Ford, but only three national surveys before the 1976 election. Teeter, while the pollster for the president, did not serve in a central advisory role.[64] Richard B. (Dick) Cheney, White House chief of staff, oversaw the White House public opinion operation, but polls were not conducted for strategic purposes. Richard Wirthlin also provided at least eight polls, from October 1974 through April 1975, on broad topics such as Ford's clumsy Whip Inflation Now (WIN) program. But when the 1976 primaries began shaping up, Wirthlin cast his lot with Ronald Reagan, and his services for Ford ceased.

The first and most important test of Ford's leadership came just weeks into his term of office, when he decided to pardon Richard Nixon. Public opinion surveys showed that a clear majority of those interviewed wanted Nixon to go to trial. In his memoirs, Ford told his aide Robert Hartmann that he was aware that he could be hurt politically by the pardon, but that he would go ahead with it. "It could easily cost me the next election if I run again," Ford wrote, "But damn it, I don't need the polls to tell me whether I'm right or wrong."[65]

Ford, unlike Nixon and Johnson, was not a heavy consumer of public opinion polls. The Ford White House received many public opinion polls, regularly getting Harris and Gallup polls, and, like the Nixon and Johnson White Houses, received advanced copies. The private polling was mostly done by Robert Teeter, and as the 1976 election loomed, the public opinion research branched out into focus group and dial-meter analysis. Teeter's polling showed that the American people liked Gerald Ford, thought he was a nice guy, but didn't think he was much of a national leader. The White House took a page out of the Nixon campaign book from 1972 by having Ford adopt a Rose Garden strategy—highlight the president signing bills, greeting dignitaries, holding ceremonies—looking presidential, in other words.[66]

The polls Teeter conducted on Ford's behalf were paid for by the Republican National Committee, but the RNC apparently played no role in determining when the polls would be taken or in interpreting the results.[67] The polling reports went mainly to chief of staff Dick Cheney and the head of the President Ford Committee, Bo Callaway. Robert M. Eisenger notes that two major polling-oriented themes developed during the Ford years. First, the concept of a presidential pollster became institutionalized, using the services of Teeter. The pollster met with Ford thirty-eight times during 1976, and Cheney or his aide reviewed the private polls. Second, the private polls "were now unadulterated political vehicles designed to help the president get re-elected."[68]

Polling for Jimmy Carter

A month after the 1976 presidential election, Patrick Caddell gave the new president-elect a sixty-two-page, 10,000-word memo, titled "Initial Working Paper on Political Strategy." In it, he gave Carter advice on policy problems that the Democratic administration would face, but also on how Carter should conduct the presidency in the new age of television. It required a "continuing political campaign." As journalist Joe Klein observed, this was a key insight into how the White House would be run: "All future presidents would run their administration from a consultant's-eye view." Polling would be continuous, and short-term success would matter more than long-term planning.[69] Thus was born the new reality, the "permanent campaign."

Caddell and his firm, Cambridge Survey Research, provided the Carter White House with detailed polling analyses, over 300 pages each, on a quarterly basis from 1977 through 1979.[70] Unlike the Nixon White House, where control over private survey research was highly restricted, the Carter White House staffers, cabinet members, and domestic policy staff had "virtually unrestricted" access to Caddell's poll data.[71] His most notable memo to Carter noted a "crisis in confidence," among American citizens. Taking that theme, Carter spoke to a nationwide audience in July 1979, in what was later characterized as the "malaise" speech (although Carter never used that word).

Polling for Ronald Reagan

> Politics and government are inseparable.... Polling is important
> to know the politics of a decision. And politics is inseparable from
> technique.... Campaign experience is good experience for
> a job like this. You have got to judge how an action will be received
> and what the optimal responses are.
>
> —Reagan chief of staff James Baker (1981)[72]

Richard Wirthlin, the pollster for the Reagan presidential campaign, continued that role when Reagan took office. Preparing for the first months of the new Reagan administration, Wirthlin developed a strategic plan for the first 180 days. It envisioned strong actions on cutting the federal budget and on reducing taxes. "The idea," wrote Reagan adviser Edwin Meese, "was to exploit the force of public opinion—to remind the legislators of who had elected them—and thereby counter the special interest pressures we knew would be mounted in opposition to the Reagan program."[73]

Wirthlin's firm, Decision Making Information (DMI, later the Wirthlin Group), conducted cross-national polls once or twice each month, seeking to find out how the president was doing in the view of citizens.[74] During the first twenty-nine months, Wirthlin met with the president more than twenty-five times to discuss polls and politics, and sent over forty public opinion memoranda to top aides James Baker, Michael Deaver, and Edwin Meese.[75] Altogether, Wirthlin met with Reagan ninety-six times during the eight-year administration, or about once a month.[76]

Wirthlin's polls helped Reagan policymakers spot both real and potential trouble. Right after Reagan offered a Social Security reform proposal with a negative impact on millions of retirees, there was immediate blowback in the polls. A cabinet-level advisory board suggested several reforms to the immigration law, including a controversial national counterfeit-proof identity card. But survey respondents, liberals and conservatives alike, balked at the ID card and it was dropped in subsequent White House proposals. After the collapse of the Reykjavik summit in 1986, where Soviet leader Mikhail Gorbachev unexpectedly offered a nuclear arms peace proposal, Reagan's team was worried about public reaction. The press had criticized Reagan for walking away from the proposal, but Wirthlin polls immediately afterward showed that Americans blamed Gorbachev, not Reagan, for the breakdown.[77]

David Gergen, the director of communications, emphasized message discipline, crafting talking points for the days news, and policy points for the administration to follow weekly or monthly. Using dial-meter analysis, Wirthlin was able to determine which phrase and words were most powerful, and which received the best responses, and those were incorporated into subsequent speeches, messages, and even policy. As an example, Reagan's lengthy speech to the United Nations, preceding his visit to Reykjavik was tested, and key words and phrases were captured in a subsequent televised address to Congress.[78]

The Reagan White House collected public opinion polls from television and newspapers, with summaries collected for the president and his top aides in the White House News Summary. Further the White House Office of Planning and Evaluation collected and reported on major public opinion polls, carrying summaries in a regular report called *Public Opinion Digest*. Public opinion news also came from the government itself. This included the Consumer Price Index and unemployment rate, determined by surveys conducted by the Bureau of the Census and the Bureau of Labor Statistics. Special interest groups, like the National Rifle Association, and others regularly let the White House know the results of surveys they took. Reagan also received polls from members of Congress and from US embassies around the world.[79]

Polling for George H. W. Bush

> Bush was not a greater user of polls.
>
> —Robert Teeter (1998)[80]

The idea of a "permanent campaign," advocated by Carter's Pat Caddell, was anathema to George H. W. Bush. The bruising 1988 presidential election (see chapter 12) saw the Bush campaign use focus-group research to redefine and then attack Michael Dukakis. Out of the Paramus, New Jersey, focus groups and the opposition research conducted by Jim Pinkerton's team, came the evidence that Dukakis could be cut off at the knees. Soon came Willie Horton and the charges and countercharges of racism and fearmongering. The rough and tumble of the campaign trail left a bitter taste in Bush's mouth.

Communications specialist Wynton C. Hall argued that there were four factors in Bush's reluctance to use private polling. First, he had a belief that campaigning and governing should be distinct and separate entities. Governing was not to be simply an extension of campaigning. Second, Bush disliked being scripted and stage-managed. Third, he had a "disdain for rhetoric" and the process of speech making. Finally, his authoritarian chief of staff, former New Hampshire governor John Sununu, shared Bush's disdain and had a bruising relationship with pollster Bob Teeter.[81]

What Bush got, then, was "an administration driven less by polls, less scripted, and not reliant on rhetorical performances."[82] But polls were taken, principally by Teeter and his firm, MOR, by RNC director of surveys David Hansen, and by Reagan's pollster, Richard Wirthlin and the Wirthlin Group. When Bush was at his most popular, right after the 1991 Gulf War, he enjoyed an 88 percent approval rating, but soon other events crowded out the memory of the war. Most seriously was the eroding economy, with Bush's approval rating on how he handled the economy sagging into the 40 percent range. "We were in a hell of a lot of trouble," said pollster Ron Hinckley, "and nobody wanted to listen."[83]

Another reason that the White House did not order many private polls, according to Teeter, was the proliferation of public polls, far more than in past decades, that could give the White House a sense of where the president and his policies stood. But public polls, helpful as they might be, do not provide the kind of depth of coverage and specificity that private polls can deliver. This meant that Bush and his top advisers did not, according to political scientists Shoon Kathleen Murray and Peter Howard, have the kind of "current, in-depth information" needed to "follow how daily events affected the president's image and standing with particular segments of the public, to know how the public responded to breaking events and thereby craft their spin, to pretest policy initiatives and spot potentially controversial issues, or to test the public's response to phrases in order to craft successful speeches.[84]

The Next Generation of Pollsters

During the 1980s, private survey analysis became a growth business, and soon the pioneer Republican and Democratic private pollsters had competition. On the Republican side, several new polling firms were created.

Neil Newhouse, Bill McInturff, and Glen Bolger are partners and cofounders (in 1991) of Public Opinion Strategies (POS). Newhouse, a graduate of Duke University, previously had been executive vice president of the Wirthlin Group. He is probably best known as the lead pollster for the Romney/Ryan 2012 presidential campaign, but also has extensive experience in the international arena and in studying the needs and desires of swing voters, such as "Walmart Moms." Newhouse also participated as the Republican pollster on the NBC/Wall Street Journal poll. He was honored as "pollster of the year" by the AAPC for his work on the 2010 special Senate election that saw Scott Brown score an upset victory in Massachusetts. McInturff specializes in health-care analysis, having completed over 500 focus group sessions and over 200 national surveys on the subject, and was instrumental in creating the "Harry and Louise" commercials in 1993 that helped cast doubt on Clinton's health-care proposal. (See chapter 16 for more on the health-care fight). McInturff also partnered with Democratic pollster Peter Hart in the NBC/Wall Street Journal public polls; he took over the Republican side after Bob Teeter died. He was also lead pollster for John McCain during the 2008 presidential campaign. Bolger, a graduate of American University, was director of survey research for the National Republican Congressional Committee before cofounding POS. He was honored in 2009 by the AAPC as "pollster of the year" for his help in getting Robert McDonnell elected governor in Virginia.

Since its founding in 1991, POS has been one of the most important fixtures in Republican campaigning and politics. It boasts of being the largest political polling firm in the country, having helped elect seventy-five new members to the House of Representatives; six governors, including Susan Martinez (New Mexico) and Bob McDonnell (Virginia); and fifteen US senators, including Scott Brown (Massachusetts), Rand Paul (Kentucky), Roger Wicker (Mississippi), and Saxby Chambliss (Georgia). When Republicans made their historic gains in the 2010 House races, POS was involved in fifty-six of the sixty Republican victories, either working for the candidates themselves or for independent expenditures. The firm has conducted over 14,000 polls and has interviewed seven million individuals, throughout the fifty states as well as abroad.

First-generation pollster Lance Tarrance (see chapter 4 for his profile) opened the Tarrance Group in 1977, and hired Edward A. (Ed) Goeas III to open a Washington office in 1987. Goeas had recently completed two election cycles as national campaign director at the National Republican Congressional Committee (NRCC). That same year, Brian C. Tringali, who had been research director at the NRCC, joined the firm. The following year, David Sackett, who had also been research director at the NRCC and a media specialist, joined the firm. The polling firm was purchased by SRI/Gallup in 1988, and Lance Tarrance left to become a member of the Gallup Board. Three years later, Goeas, who had been elevated to be CEO and president, Tringali, and Sackett purchased the firm from SRI/Gallup.[85]

The Tarrance Group is one of the premier Republican polling firms today, having helped elect more than eighty Republican governors, US Senators, members of Congress, and a number of state office candidates. It also has worked on a wide variety of ballot issues, and it assists corporate clients with crisis management and public image issues. Since 2001 it has teamed with Democratic pollster Celinda Lake in providing the bipartisan Battleground Poll, in conjunction with the George Washington University.

Bob Moore, based in Portland, Oregon, began his firm in 1981. A graduate of Oregon State University, Moore was also executive director of the National Republican Senatorial Committee (NRSC) from 1977 to 1980. The Republican takeover in the Senate in 1980 was significantly aided by Moore's research efforts. His firm, Moore Information, has conducted survey research for many Republican candidates for governor, US Senate, and US House of Representatives, particularly in the West. His clients have included governors Jan Brewer (Arizona) and Butch Otter (Idaho), and Alaska senator Lisa Murkowski, as well as a long list of ballot issues, corporate clients, and advocacy groups.[86]

On the Democratic side, several pollsters created their firms during this era.

Stanley B. Greenberg (b. 1945) was born in Philadelphia, but he spent his formative years in Washington, DC, and its Maryland suburbs. He became immersed in Democratic politics while at Miami (Ohio) University and at graduate school at Harvard, where he received his PhD in political science. While a young assistant professor at Yale, he founded The Analysis Group, a survey research firm. After leaving Yale, his first real effort as a political pollster came in 1982 when he, along with young media consultant Frank Greer, helped M. Robert (Bob) Carr win back his congressional seat in Michigan. Greenberg worked closely with the new Democratic organization, the Democratic Leadership Council, and in 1988 he helped elect his close political friend Connecticut attorney general Joseph I. (Joe) Lieberman to the US Senate, in an upset over incumbent Lowell P. Weicker Jr. Next came Greenberg's involvement in Bill Clinton's quest for the White House in 1992, described in chapter 14.

Greenberg became the White House pollster in 1993 and served in that capacity until after the 1994 congressional elections. After Democrats were thoroughly beaten in the 1994 elections, Bill Clinton turned to Dick Morris, Doug Schoen, and Mark Penn, abandoning Greenberg and James Carville. For a time, Greenberg's business partner was pollster Celinda Lake (see below). In 1994, Greenberg and Frank Greer were principal consultants in the historic South African all-race election won by Nelson Mandela. Later, Robert Shrum, James Carville, and Stanley Greenberg teamed up to form an international political consulting firm and worked together in Israel and the United Kingdom.

In 1999 Greenberg teamed up with James Carville to form the Democracy Corps. The organization, designed to help progressive groups and candidates, was born "out of outrage over the impeachment of President Clinton when the leadership in Congress preferred radical partisanship to addressing the issues that really matter to American families."[87] It provides free survey research and strategic political advice to Democratic candidates. Greenberg's firm today, Greenberg Quinlan Rosner Research (GQR) is one of the foremost research and strategic communications organizations, with offices in Washington, DC, New York, Buenos Aires, and London. The firm has a wide range of political and corporate clients in the United States and throughout the world.[88]

Mark J. Penn (b. 1954) and Douglas E. Schoen (b. 1953) began their polling business in 1977, working for David Garth and helping Representative Edward I. Koch run for mayor of New York City. They worked for Jay Rockefeller in West Virginia (1980, 1984), Frank Lautenberg in New Jersey (1982), Richard Shelby in Alabama (1986), Evan Bayh in Indiana (1988), Jon Corzine in New Jersey (2000 and 2005), and Michael Bloomberg in New York City (2000, 2005).

When Dick Morris was hired by President Clinton following the 1994 congressional elections, he brought along Penn and Schoen to conduct polling research. Yet after Morris publicly turned against the Clintons, Schoen in his memoirs described Morris as a "discredited and tragic figure."[89] Mark Penn stayed on during Clinton's second term, polling for the president and for the Democratic National Committee. Penn also assisted Hillary Clinton in her 2000 Senate race in New York, and later was the chief strategist during her 2008 presidential nomination bid, before being replaced by veteran pollster Geoff Garin (see chapter 19). In 2007, journalists John F. Harris and Jim VandeHei described Penn as "easily the most influential political strategist to both Clintons," and as "the Democrats closest equivalent to Karl Rove."[90]

Penn and Schoen began doing corporate work in the 1980s, and their clients have included AT&T, Eli Lilly, Texaco, and Microsoft. In 2001, Penn Schoen Berland (PSB) was acquired by the British-based WPP Group, and Penn retained the presidency of PSB. In 2005 Penn was made CEO of Burson-Marsteller, the 2,000-employee public relations firm. Michael Berland, the third partner, began working for the firm in 1987 and left in 2006, only to return later after resolution of a noncompete dispute to become president of PSB. In a game of musical chairs, Douglas Schoen left PSB to write and provide commentary for news outlets, including Fox news.

Penn Schoen Berland is currently headed by Don Baer, a former Clinton White House senior speechwriter who is now worldwide chair and CEO of Burson-Marsteller, a WPP Group company.[91] Michael Berland left PSB in 2012 to become CEO of Edelman Berland; in July 2012, Mark Penn stepped down from Burson-Marsteller to become executive vice president for advertising and strategy at Microsoft, one of PSB's longtime clients. Just two years later, he left Microsoft and formed The Stagwell Group, an investment advisory company financed in part by former Microsoft CEO, Steve Ballmer. In 2015, Stagwell acquired SKDKnickerbocker, a firm that was originally founded by media consultant Bob Squier.

Harrison Hickman began his polling career working with Bill Hamilton, and in 1985 he left Hamilton & Staff to start a polling company with Paul Maslin. Maslin began his career with Cambridge Research, Pat Caddell's survey research firm. In 1990 Hickman and Maslin split, with Maslin joining the California-based firm of Fairbank, Maslin Maullin (now Fairbank, Maslin, Maullin, Metz & Associates) in 1992. Hickman then joined with Kirk Brown to form Hickman Brown Research; then Brown left after the 2002 election cycle to work as policy director for Wisconsin governor Jim Doyle. Hickman Research and Global Strategy Group merged in 2003, creating what journalist Chris Cillizza called a "powerhouse polling firm."[92] Since 2010, Hickman's firm has been Hickman Analytics. His clients have included US senators Mark Pryor (Arkansas) and Ben Nelson (Nebraska), and governors Mike Beebe (Arkansas), Jim Hunt (North Carolina), and Ann Richards (Texas). Hickman also served as a presidential campaign pollster for Al Gore (2000), Bob Kerrey (1992), and John Edwards (2004, 2008).[93]

Mark S. Mellman (b. 1955) and Edward Lazarus began their careers while both were graduate students at Yale University. In 1984 a young legal aide lawyer, Bruce A. Morrison, given little chance of winning, sought out Yale University professor F. Christopher Arterton, asking for help in his run for Congress. Arterton (who later would become the founding dean of the Graduate School of Political Management at George Washington University) had other obligations, but he turned over the opportunity to his graduate students, Mellman and Lazarus. Morrison defeated Lawrence J. (Larry) DiNardi in 1984 by less than 2,000 votes, and a polling firm was launched. Soon, Mellman and Lazarus had other Washington-based clients, like Michigan senator Carl Levin and Tennessee Senate candidate Al Gore Jr. Initially, they conducted the polls out of their dormitory room.[94]

In Washington, Mellman and Lazarus became a key Democratic consulting firm, signing up many members of Congress and gubernatorial candidates, and working for a wide variety of advocacy issues. Celinda Lake (see below) became a partner, but then later split off to form her own firm, and

Mellman and Lazarus ceased their partnership. The Mellman Group continues to be an important, award-winning survey firm. Its clients have included senators Harry Reid (Nevada), Barbara Boxer (California), Maria Cantwell (Washington), John Glenn (Ohio), and Frank Lautenberg (New Jersey), along with many corporate, advocacy, and international organizations and political parties.

Celinda Lake, who received her undergraduate education from Smith College and a master's degree in survey research from the University of Michigan, is one of the more prominent pollsters working today. Earlier in her career, Lake was research director at the Institute for Social Research in Ann Arbor, Michigan, and political director of the Women's Campaign Fund. Lake worked for pollster Peter Hart during the mid-1980s, then in 1988 she joined Stanley Greenberg in forming Greenberg-Lake. She then joined Mark Mellman and Ed Lazarus in the firm Mellman-Lazarus-Lake, then formed her own polling firm in 1994. Lake Research Partners (LRP) includes long-time pollster Robert Meadow, whose own San Diego-based firm, Decision Research, had been established in 1984 but was subsequently sold to LRP. Lake has worked with a wide variety of progressive, Democratic candidates for the US Senate and House of Representatives, and for the Democratic National Committee, the Democratic Governor's Association, a variety of national labor organizations, EMILY's List, NARAL, the Human Rights Campaign, and others. She was also pollster for Senator Joe Biden in his 2008 presidential bid. Lake has worked for numerous female candidates, including US senators Barbara Mikulski (Maryland), Blanche Lincoln (Arkansas), and Carol Moseley-Braun (Illinois), and for Arizona governor Janet Napolitano. She is considered one of the foremost experts on electing women candidates and framing issues important to women, and she has a long record in defeating incumbent Republican officeholders.[95] With Republican pollster Kellyanne Conway, she coauthored *What Women Really Want*.[96]

John Fairbank, Paul Maslin, and Richard Maullin founded their California-based survey research firm, Fairbank, Maslin, Maullin & Associates, in 1981, and were later joined by David Metz, forming Fairbank, Maslin, Maullin & Metz (FM3). FM3 has focused heavily on clients in California, ballot issues, and local government. The firm has polled for candidates for president (Bill Richardson, Howard Dean, Al Gore) down to local school boards in California. FM3 provides up to 300 surveys and 150 focus groups annually for its wide range of political, corporate, and advocacy candidates.[97]

CHAPTER 8

The Media Revolution

This is the beginning of a whole new concept. This is it.
This is the way they'll be elected forevermore.
The next guys up will have to be performers.
> —Roger Ailes, advising presidential candidate Richard Nixon
> on his television presentation skills (1968)

Like every form of political rhetoric and persuasion,
television advertising is schizophrenic. It has a face of
illusion and a face of substance. . . . It is neither
all imagery, nor all reason, but a perplexing mixture of both.
> —Thomas E. Patterson and Robert D. McClure (1976)

AT MIDCENTURY, TELEVISION was the new magical form of mass communication, and during those early years, campaign ads went through a period
of creative transformation. Communications scholar L. Patrick Devlin
found that during the 1952 and 1956 presidential contests between Eisenhower and
Stevenson, television spots were "primitive ads," with the candidates somewhat
ill at ease, lighting and background uninspiring, and the announcer's stentorian
voice (fine for the 1930s movie theater videos) inappropriate for the intimate
screen of television. With the Kennedy-Nixon campaign in 1960 came "talking
heads," with a serious Richard Nixon and a more informal John Kennedy. The
1964 Johnson-Goldwater contest was best known for its negative ads, particularly
Tony Schwartz and DDB's "Daisy" ad. In 1968, during the Humphrey-Nixon-
Wallace contest, color was used in commercials for the first time, and there was
an emphasis on the visual quality of the ads. In the 1972 Nixon-McGovern race,
there was an increased use of "production idea spots," to convey important ideas
about the candidates, like Nixon being the first president to visit China and
the Soviet Union. Also in 1972, there were cinéma vérité ads showing George
McGovern interacting with real voters. In the 1976 Ford-Carter race, the presentation of the candidates changed: Ford began as the Rose Garden candidate, with

the president busy doing his job, but he ended the campaign as a more personable, approachable candidate wearing a cardigan sweater. Carter, meanwhile, went from a farmer in a plaid shirt leaning on a fence post to an executive in a business suit. In addition, during the 1976 and 1980 presidential campaigns, media consultants revived the 1950s "man on the street" format, with voters being asked what they thought of the candidates.

The 1980 contest, between incumbent Jimmy Carter, Ronald Reagan, and independent John Anderson, saw the Reagan media team using "documentary ads," showing the candidate as a working governor, not merely as an actor. Throughout the campaigns, but especially in 1980, there were "testimonial ads" featuring prominent celebrities, like television star Carroll O'Connor ("Archie Bunker"), praising a candidate. (The most important celebrity, the actor Ronald Reagan, appeared in a testimonial for Barry Goldwater in 1964.) There was also an increase in the number of independent ads, sponsored by the National Republican Congressional Committee or the National Conservative Political Action Committee (NCPAC) during the 1980 election.[1]

When presidential television ads were first made in the early 1950s, the political parties, candidates, and outside groups turned to commercial ad agencies, mostly in New York, for help. While welcoming the business, commercial agencies soon discovered that there were downsides to working on political campaigns. Compared to multimillion-dollar, multiyear commercial accounts for Heinz Ketchup or Chrysler automobiles, the sums earned from presidential, statewide, or big city campaigns, in those days, could be paltry. In addition, being identified as a Republican or a Democratic agency might not be good for business.

Edward Ney, president of Young & Rubicam, at the time the second-largest ad agency in the United States, handled Citizens for Eisenhower-Nixon during the 1952 campaign and John Lindsay for mayor of New York City in 1969. But in 1972, Ney publicly declared that Y&R would no longer make 30-second or 60-second commercials for political candidates. "We feel so strongly that the whole system is wrong.... We would not accept any political candidates in the United States in 1972," wrote Ney, adding, "It is a perversion of our skills to attempt to use the techniques of a 30-second or 60-second commercial to discuss an issue or character of a candidate for high political office." John O'Toole, president of Foote, Cone & Belding, also denounced 60-second spots, saying, "I'm urging all of us in the advertising business not to be beguiled into making commercials that confuse a candidate and an office with a deodorant and an armpit."[2]

Political media consultant Charles Guggenheim begged to differ with Ney: "Go back and look at Ney's list of clients. He's selling gas that pollutes, cars that are unsafe, cereals without nutrients or calories. He's so conditioned to being fraudulent that he thinks if you take a candidate you have to say something fraudulent, so the best way to handle what you believe in is to stay away from it."[3]

By the 1980s, while commercial firms were getting out of the campaign business, political consultants were pushing to grab the increasingly lucrative media campaign business for themselves. Veteran consultant Stuart Spencer argued there were three reasons why political media consultants were pushing out commercial ad agencies. First, commercial ad agencies sometimes get stiffed by politicians; it's a historic problem. Second, "a lot of people in my business have convinced the politicians—the candidate-type—that there is a major difference, that we can [make political commercials] better. It's not true." Third, "I don't think that the big agencies that do the commercials stuff have the stomach for what you have to go through in the political process, in convincing the wife, the brother, the cousin that this is a good ad."[4]

Indeed, there are major differences in the goals and challenges of selling commercial products versus selling candidates for office. The ultimate goal for a commercial product is to increase market share. For example, going from 10 percent to 14 percent of the market for a certain product over the course of a twenty-month advertising campaign might well be considered a victory. For political campaigns, the goal is not market share, but straight-out winning—gaining enough votes to be declared the winner on Election Day. Political marketing has to contend with clear deadlines, in the form of primary and general election days. While commercial marketers also have deadlines, like third-quarter profits and market-share reports, they do not have the same consequences. Commercial products may find themselves compared and contrasted with others, but nothing like the battle-like sharp negativism found in political communication. And for decades, commercial advertising has depended on sophisticated and expensive qualitative and quantitative research, which is often not available in political campaigns.

In the 1960s, the new political media consultants were lauded by the press, accorded the heady status of kingmakers. But as competition increased, some of the magic seemed to have rubbed off.[5] Some of the best-known ad makers lost races: Harry Treleaven, who conducted Nixon's 1968 presidential advertising, found his candidates losing in four out of five Senate races (one of those losses was Congressman George H. W. Bush who was running in Texas for the US Senate). Bailey & Deardourff, the once hot Republican firm, had several major candidates with more money to spend than their opponents, but they still did not have a winner. Charles Guggenheim lost five major races, while winning just four. A new generation of media consultants was stepping forward, and more and more candidates for the US Senate and gubernatorial offices sought them out for their campaigns.[6]

Television was becoming the indispensable medium of communication. The typical household in America in 1976 had its television set turned on for six hours and twenty-six minutes each day, on average, with about 20 percent viewing devoted to sports. By 1980, some 99 percent of all American homes had at least one television set.[7]

The Transformation of Television

> *Television has caused a more radical change in political communication than has any other development since our Republic was founded. Nothing before television altered so drastically the techniques of mass persuasion. No other medium has brought the ideal of an informed electorate so close to reality, yet poses so serious a threat to reducing our politics to triviality.*
>
> —Journalist Robert McNeil (1968)[8]

Political media has changed so much, so fast, and new
technologies and advertising platforms are promising to create
even more changes in the years to come.
—Democratic media consultant Peter Fenn (2009)[9]

Does slick and clever television advertising produce winners? During the late 1960s, it appeared that television might provide that magic formula. Joe Napolitan attributed two important wins—Milton J. Shapp in the Pennsylvania gubernatorial primary in 1966 and Maurice (Mike) Gravel in the Alaska US Senate primary in 1968—to the power of television. Shapp, described as "an eccentric radio manufacturer,"[10] had polled at just 6 percent of the vote three weeks before the primary. Shapp's campaign produced a half-hour political documentary, conducted a nine-day television blitz, and ended up winning the three-way primary. Further, it succeeded in increasing voter turnout in the primary by 15 percent over the comparable primary numbers in 1962. Charles Guggenheim produced the Shapp documentary and Shelby Storck directed it. Shapp won the primary, but was later defeated by Republican Raymond P. Shafer in the general election.[11]

Ernest Gruening, the incumbent Alaska senator, was running ahead of challenger Mike Gravel by two-to-one with just nine days to go. Then the Gravel campaign showed a half-hour documentary, simulcast on all three Anchorage television stations. The next day, polls showed that Gruening's lead had evaporated, and Gravel led 55–45 in Anchorage. Gravel's campaign adviser, Joe Napolitan, surmised that since nothing had occurred except the television simulcast, it had to be the impact of that show that turned the numbers around.[12]

Charles Guggenheim recalled that in the early days of candidate television spots, in the 1960s and early 1970s, television commercials, including the thirty-minute film, could have an enormous impact. Guggenheim saw swings of 20 to 30 percent in poll numbers within two weeks, the time it took to analyze the results.[13]

Those were the simple days, when television meant three or four channels at most, black-and-white seventeen-inch screens, and no competition except from radio, newspapers, billboards, and direct mail pieces. All this began to change with the advent of cable television, which by the mid-1970s was becoming an increasingly important vehicle for communication.[14] The three national networks—NBC, CBS, and ABC—were caught flatfooted; they had been bought out by corporate interests unfamiliar with broadcasting and were unable to adjust to or take immediate advantage of the new cable revolution. In his aptly named book, *Three Blind Mice*, media critic Ken Auletta chronicled how in the 1980s, as cable increased its foothold, NBC, CBS, and ABC managed to lose a third of their audiences and half of their profits.[15]

From 1990 to 2006, prime-time viewing on networks dropped from 74.8 percent to 43.7 percent, while total network viewing dropped from 71.5 percent to 38.9 percent. At the same time, cable television increased from 16.4 percent to 45.8 percent of prime-time viewers.[16] In 1976 the average viewer had a choice of seven channels; today it is in the hundreds. Channels abound to fill virtually every interest, including cooking, travel, history, sports, redneck reality TV, cop shows, and more. There are at least twenty-seven shows devoted to Alaska alone.

The Nielsen Company, which tracks television viewing habits, noted that in 2010, the average American family watched thirty-five hours of television each week; two hours of that was time-shifted, using TiVo (found in 35 percent of American homes) or digital video recorders.[17]

But even in the digital age, with so many tablets, smart phones, and other platforms, television remains the dominant medium. In recent presidential campaigns, for example, television dominated as the means to persuade and inform voters, especially those voters living in battleground states. Pity the poor voters (and their families) in places like Ohio or Florida, crucial swing states, who are inundated with political ads during the frenetic last few weeks of the general election. During the 2004 campaigns, from president down to local races, there were more than 3 million political commercials shown in the 210 American media markets, twice the number shown during the 2000 presidential campaign.[18] From 2004 through the early months of 2014, some 50,000 separate political commercials were shown on network and cable television stations. The most aired campaign ad ever came from the 2008 Obama presidential campaign; called "Unravel," it was shown roughly 24,000 times.[19]

Television remains so important, because that's where most voters get their news. In a 2008 Harris Poll, 70 percent of American adults said they rely on local television for their political news; 66 percent said they also turn to cable news, like Fox, MSNBC, or CNN, for their information.[20] During the day, when is the best time to air a campaign ad? A prime (and the most expensive) spot is right before, during, or after the local news. But other times, such as during daytime talk shows or sporting events, might be just as fruitful for a campaign. As seen in subsequent chapters, the art of ad placement has become quite sophisticated. And particularly during the 2012 Obama campaign, commercials were targeted to ever more specific audiences, often at odd times and on unlikely cable shows.

Radio, that once dominant source of communication, is still a factor in campaign commercials. In 1968 there were approximately 6,500 stations throughout the United States; by mid-2014, there were 15,425 licensed full-power stations.[21] This increase has come primarily through FM stations. Further, there has been growth in high-definition (HD) radio; satellite radio, principally Sirius XM, had some 27.3 million subscribers in December 2014.[22] Like the proliferation of television choices and online platforms, radio gives audiences far more choices. This fragmentation has made it increasingly difficult to reach a broad swath of an audience, but easier to reach a particular audience.[23]

Garry South, veteran political consultant and president of EarWorks, Inc., a Los Angeles-based company that produces radio commercials, was understandably bullish on the built-in advantages of radio. Writing in 1992, he noted that radio was in 99 percent of American homes, in 95 percent of all automobiles, and 61 percent of workplaces, reaching 96 percent of all adults every week. For political campaigns, radio can "roust voters out of bed in the morning, even join them in the shower. Poke voters in the ribs as they drive to work, to shop, or to the beach. Bend voters' ears as they jog down the sidewalk or hike through the woods. Work side by side with voters at the office or factory without diverting their attention or reducing productivity."[24] Yet, like other forms of communication, radio has seen much of its impact diminished by competing sounds downloaded on MP3 players, smart phones, and other devices.

Newspapers have seen fundamental, transformative changes. The industry lost one of its most reliable streams of income when Internet entrepreneur Craig Newmark began a modest online want-ad website in 1995. Craigslist became a nationwide (indeed, worldwide) phenomenon, offering advertising space free of charge, and cutting into the heart of newspapers' classified ads revenue. In addition, newspaper circulation dropped precipitously, while online news sources (including platforms for newspapers) proliferated. Google News, Yahoo News, Bing News, and other aggregators of news sources, along with sites like the *Drudge Report, Huffington Post*, political blogs, Twitter, and others have dramatically increased the bandwidth of information for voters. Never have citizens had the opportunity to have available to them so much information—good, bad, in-depth, superficial, biased, and straightforward.

Media Consultants

Our job is to make stars out of our clients.
We are paid to make them look good, to give them the credit,
to advance their ideas and careers.
  —Democratic media consultant John Franzén (1999)[25]

On the Republican side, several media consultants began to practice their craft during the 1980s.

Steve Sandler (1941–2006), a graduate of Penn State and Johns Hopkins, worked on the ad team for the Republican National Committee during the Reagan for President campaign in 1980. He later worked for the pioneer Republican media firm Bailey-Deardourff in its Ohio office, assisting Midwest gubernatorial candidates. Jim Innocenzi (b. 1954), a graduate of Ohio State University, was media director for the National Republican Congressional Committee for four years before opening up his own media firm.[26] Sandler and Innocenzi created the powerful ad slogan for the 1980 Reagan presidential campaign: "Vote Republican. For a Change." In 1984 the two formed their own media firm, Sandler-Innocenzi. They worked on the upset victory of Kirk Fordice, who became the first Republican governor in Mississippi since Reconstruction. Another major upset was electing Dave Heineman governor of Nebraska. Other recent candidates have included governors Butch Otter (Idaho) and Jim Gibbons (Nevada). In 2011 Innocenzi assisted Texas governor Rick Perry in his bid for the Republican presidential nomination. Jim Innocenzi sits on the board of directors of the AAPC. Sandler-Innocenzi has been the media consultant for over 100 political campaigns, and boasts a 75 percent win ratio in its campaigns.

Michael E. (Mike) Murphy (b. 1962) has had a long career working for many of the top elected Republican officials, including gubernatorial candidates John Engler (Michigan), Christine Todd Whitman (New Jersey), Jeb Bush (Florida), Arnold Schwarzenegger (California), and Mitt Romney (Massachusetts). His firm, founded in 1988, included partners Cliff Pintak, John Gautier, and Mike Hudome. Murphy worked for the presidential nomination campaigns of Lamar Alexander (1996) and John McCain (2000). When two of his former clients, Romney and McCain, battled for the 2008 Republican nomination, Murphy remained neutral. But during the final weeks of McCain's 2008 campaign, Murphy was highly critical of his longtime friend and former client; he was soon *persona non grata* with both McCain and his beleaguered campaign staff. In 2012, on his Twitter feed, Murphy described himself as a "semi-defrocked senior GOP political consultant."[27] He is now partner in Revolution Agency, a Washington, DC–area media advocacy firm, but given his long interest in the arts, he lives in California and is a screenwriter and producer.[28] Yet the temptation to get back into the political saddle were great, and when former Florida governor Jeb Bush entered the 2016 presidential race, Murphy, working through Bush's Right to Rise PAC, emerged as one of his principal advisers.

Donald (Don) Sipple (b. 1950), a graduate of the University of Utah, began his media consulting career working for Bailey and Deardourff. In 1996, the *Los Angeles Times* dubbed him "the GOP's first baby boomer successor to the early Republican image makers."[29] In 1994, California governor Pete Wilson decided to put $2 million of his own campaign money to support Proposition 187, a measure to halt nearly all government aid to illegal immigrants to California. In one of the most provocative commercials, produced by Sipple, shadowy figures are seen running across a highway late at night as the narrator intones, with ominous music in the background, "They keep coming. Two million illegal immigrants in California."[30] Sipple worked for Wilson, later for Arnold Schwarzenegger, and then, in an unusual twist, for Democratic gubernatorial candidate Jerry Brown. Sipple also served as Bob Dole's chief media consultant (one of several) during the rocky 1996 presidential election. He then assisted George W. Bush; Attorney General John Ashcroft; senators Orrin Hatch (Utah), Kit Bond (Missouri), and Pete Domenici (New Mexico); and a variety of congressional and gubernatorial candidates. He boasts a 92 percent winning record for his clients.[31] His career was partially derailed amid allegations that he had beaten two of his former wives, charges that Sipple vehemently denied.[32]

John Brabender began his political career by helping Tom Ridge win his first congressional race in Erie, Pennsylvania. His most important and long-standing client was Rick Santorum, first in his congressional bid, then his US Senate and 2012 and 2016 presidential bids. Brabender, a graduate of Gannon University and Cleveland State University, branched out, with business partner Jim Cox, to other gubernatorial and senate candidates. In 1995, Washington political handicapper Charlie Cook dubbed BrabenderCox "one of the hottest" Republican media firms.[33] In 2000 the firm split apart, with Brabender continuing to concentrate on political clients. Brabender worked for senate candidates David Vitter (Louisiana) and Shelley Capito (West Virginia), along with governors Linda Lingle (Hawaii) and Tom Corbett (Pennsylvania).

Robin D. Roberts, together with Alex Castellanos, Kathleen Jones, John Stewart, and Peter Pessel, created National Media, Inc., in 1985 and specialized in advertising, media placement, and electronic opposition monitoring. Also established in the 1980s were Brockmeyer Media Group, founded by full-service media specialist John Brockmeyer; The Farwell Group, the New Orleans-based media firm founded by James P. Farwell; and Wilson Grand Communications, founded by Paul Wilson and Steve Grand.

On the Democratic side, several media consultants began their careers at this time.

Robert Shrum (b. 1943) has had a long career in Democratic politics, from his early days as a gifted speechwriter to a media consultant in successive presidential campaigns.[34] He grew up in Culver City, California, the son of a tool-and-die maker, and fell in love with politics in high school. When the 1960 Democratic convention was held in nearby Los Angeles, Shrum volunteered for the campaign, and was smitten with both John F. Kennedy and politics. He was a National Merit Scholar, completed his undergraduate work at Georgetown, then went to Harvard Law School. He was a speechwriter for New York City mayor John V. Lindsay, replacing Jeff Greenfield. During the 1972 Democratic primaries, media consultant Bob Squier got Shrum a job as speechwriter for Maine senator Edmund Muskie; then Shrum went to work for George McGovern, penning his memorable "Come home, America" acceptance speech. After the disastrous 1972 campaign, Shrum and his close friend Patrick Caddell wrote a column for *Rolling Stone*. Shrum then worked on the McGovern Senate staff.

Shrum was then recruited by Caddell to work on the 1976 Carter presidential campaign, but he lasted just ten days, resigning in protest over Carter's waffling on liberal issues held dear by Shrum. During the 1980 Democratic primary, a defeated Ted Kennedy delivered the ringing words, written by Shrum, "For all those whose cares have been our concern, the work goes on, the cause endures, the hope still lives, and the dream shall never die." Shrum partnered with Caddell and David Doak to form a media consulting firm. Shrum and Caddell were soon at each other's throats, but Doak and Shrum were able to establish one of the powerhouse Democratic media firms of the 1980s. Shrum worked for a succession of losing presidential aspirants: Richard Gephardt (1988), Bob Kerrey (1992), Al Gore (2000), John Kerry (2004), and Hillary Clinton (2008).

After the Doak-Shrum partnership dissolved in a bitter dispute, Shrum teamed up with consultant Tad Devine and later Mike Donilon.[35] This new firm, Shrum, Devine & Donilon, worked for US candidates but also gained a strong reputation internationally, working for Ehud Barak (Israel), Tony Blair (UK), and the presidents of Ireland, Colombia, and Bolivia. Shrum also partnered with Democratic consultants Stanley Greenberg and James Carville to work on international election campaigns.

Shrum retired from active political consulting after the 2008 election cycle, became a senior fellow at New York University's Graduate School of Public

Service, contributed articles to a number of outlets, and wrote his memoirs, *No Excuses: Concessions of a Serial Campaigner.*[36]

David M. Axelrod (b. 1955), born in New York and educated at the University of Chicago, spent eight years as a political reporter for the *Chicago Tribune* before joining the successful US Senate campaign of Paul Simon in 1984, where Simon unseated Republican incumbent Charles Percy.[37] The following year, he created his own consulting firm, Axelrod & Associates. The firm's first major client was Chicago mayor Harold Washington, who was running for re-election in 1987; later he worked as a communications consultant for Chicago mayor Richard M. Daley. Axelrod gained a reputation for working for big city African American candidates for mayor, including Dennis Archer (Detroit), Michael R. White (Cleveland), Anthony Williams (Washington, DC), Lee P. Brown (Houston), and John F. Street (Philadelphia).[38]

Axelrod also headed the short-lived Simon for President campaign in 1988, hoping this would propel him into a national role. "We want to become a national firm," Axelrod noted, like Squier, Doak and Shrum, David Sawyer, or David Garth.[39] In 1992 he was approached by the Clinton presidential campaign, and later by the Al Gore campaign in 2000. Both times, Axelrod declined, citing the heavy toll these campaigns and the long absences from home would impose on his family. Axelrod's daughter was suffering from debilitating epileptic seizures and needed constant attention, and later his wife, Susan, would have to face breast cancer. The 1992 Clinton campaign, now on its way to victory, would be a hard one to turn down, but in rejecting the offer, Axelrod reached a "watershed moment" in his life. "As driven as I was," Axelrod wrote in his 2014 memoir, "I discovered that there was something more important to me than the job of my dreams. As imperfect a husband and father as I had been, I loved my wife and children. Leaving them at such a critical time would have been a shameful thing to do."[40]

But in 2003–2004, Axelrod got his chance to work for a presidential candidate, North Carolina senator John Edwards, albeit for a short and unpleasant period of time. He also worked for gubernatorial candidates Eliot Spitzer (New York) and Deval Patrick (Massachusetts) in 2006, and for Democratic Congressional Campaign Committee chair Rahm Emmanuel. Altogether, Axelrod had worked for over 150 state, local, and national candidates and causes. Reporter Ben Wallace-Wells described Axelrod as "lumbering, sardonic, and self-deprecating."[41]

In 2002, state senator Barack Obama sought out Axelrod about running for a US Senate seat in Illinois. Axelrod told Obama he should skip the Senate race and wait for a chance to run for mayor, but Obama was determined not to wait. "My involvement was a leap of faith," Axelrod later told Obama biographer David Mendell.[42] When it came time for the 2008 presidential election, the Democratic crowded field was filled with former Axelrod clients: former Iowa governor Tom Vilsack, John Edwards, Hillary Clinton, Connecticut senator Chris Dodd, and Illinois senator Barack Obama. Axelrod was tempted to sit out the 2008 contest. He wouldn't work with Edwards, and the idea of working with Hillary Clinton's chief strategist Mark Penn "was unthinkable."[43] He would only work for the junior senator from Illinois.

Axelrod, his partner David Plouffe, and his firm, now called AKPD, was at the center of Obama's 2008 and 2012 presidential campaigns, as seen in chapter 19. In January 2009, when Obama became president and Axelrod moved to the White House, he sold AKPD Message and Media to longtime partners John Del Cecato, John Kupper, and Larry Grisolano, who was brought in as a partner.[44] Following the 2012 campaign, Axelrod became the founder and director of the Institute of Politics at the University of Chicago and frequent elections commentator on cable television.

Karl Struble began his consulting career thirty-five years ago. He was the deputy national field director for the Carter re-election campaign in 1979, and has been a longtime consultant to former Senate majority leader Tom Daschle (South Dakota).[45] Over the years, Struble has done media work for a number of Democratic senators, including Tim Johnson (South Dakota), Patty Murray and Maria Cantwell (Washington State), Mark Pryor (Arkansas), Max Cleland (Georgia), Mary Landrieu (Louisiana), and Joe Manchin (West Virginia). He has also assisted a number of Democratic candidates for governor, including Tim Kaine (Virginia), Mike Beebe (Arkansas), and Brian Schweitzer (Montana). Struble currently heads Struble Eichenbaum Communications, with partner David Eichenbaum.

Peter H. Fenn (b. 1947), a graduate of Macalester College and the University of Southern California, was the first executive director of Pamela Harriman's Democrats for the '80s, and then served as chief of staff for Idaho senator Frank Church.[46] He was the lead media consultant for the Democratic Congressional Campaign Committee, and then went into the consulting business with Tom King in the late 1980s. Their firm, Fenn-King Communications, became one of the major Democratic media firms, specializing in incumbent congressional campaigns. Fenn also partnered with consultants Steve Murphy and Mark Putnam. The firm is now Fenn Communications Group, and has worked in over 300 campaigns, including presidential, congressional, international campaigns, and it has increasingly been involved in corporate and nonprofit work.

Murphy and Putnam were business partners from 1996 through 2011, and were joined for a period of time by Philadelphia-based media consultant Saul Shorr. Murphy and Putnam worked for a variety of members of Congress and were part of the 2008 Obama media team. Putnam produced and wrote the most watched television commercial in American history, a thirty-minute Obama prime-time infomercial that was watched by 35 million people. Murphy also worked on the Obama 2012 media team.

While working on his law degree from George Washington University, Gary Nordlinger (b. 1950), at twenty-five, opened his own consulting business. He first worked with Mike McClister, one of Matt Reese's early employees, and moonlighted for pollster Bill Hamilton.[47] His career began to take off when working for the Colorado AFL-CIO, through their coordinated campaigns. Nordlinger helped determine which races the union should get involved in. Early on, he worked for the West Virginia Education Association, and then was invited to work for the National Education Association (NEA) and twenty-eight of its state education associations. Nordlinger was one of the early American media consultants to work abroad, and he has worked in twenty-eight countries on six continents helping candidates for office. Over the years, his firm's print and media campaigns for candidates, governments, associations, and labor unions have won more than 120 major awards. He has served on the boards of trustees of the AAPC, the IAPC, and the Latin-American Association of Political Consultants, lectured widely, and taught as a visiting professor at a number of American universities.

Several other Democratic consultants started their own media firms during this time. John Franzén began his career working as George McGovern's press secretary during the 1972 New Hampshire primary. He helped design a new television production studio at the Democratic Party national headquarters, and won national attention for his work on the re-election of Louisiana senator J. Bennett Johnston, who was challenged by white supremacist David Duke. He also developed a generic television ad program and produced a library of campaign spots that were used by more than 300 Democratic candidates for Congress.[48] Bill Carrick, a native of South Carolina, did most of his consulting business in California, specializing in candidates, ballot initiatives, and advocacy, and was chief strategist for Dianne Feinstein's gubernatorial bid in 1990 and her Senate bid in 1992. Before moving to California, he was Senator Edward Kennedy's political director and was campaign manager for Dick Gephardt's presidential nomination bid. At one time he was partner with Hank Morris, a New York-based consultant best known for helping Charles Schumer defeat incumbent New York senator Alfonse D'Amato in 1998. In 2011 Morris pled guilty in a pay-to-play scheme involving the New York State pension fund, directed by state comptroller Alan G. Hevesi, one of Morris's clients. Morris spent twenty-six months behind bars and paid millions in fines before being released in 2013.[49]

Henry (Hank) Sheinkopf, a consultant based in New York, has advised candidates at every level, from Bill Clinton's re-election in 1996, to Alabama judicial candidates, to clients in South Africa, Germany, and several Latin American countries. He began Sheinkopf Communications in 1981 and is a veteran of over 700 campaigns. Sheinkopf is probably the only American political consultant who is also a rabbi.[50] Will Robinson founded a national political advertising firm in 1990, together with Tom Cosgrove, Matthew MacWilliams, and Tina Smith. Robinson's current firm is New Media Firm, which specializes in the integration of television, radio, and new media for progressive Democratic candidates and causes. Robinson was honored as AAPC Democratic Strategist of the Year in 2012. Neil Oxman, Thomas (Doc) Sweitzer, and Bill Wachob created The Campaign Group, a Philadelphia-based media firm in 1980, specializing now in electronic media placement.

Television Advertising

The thirty-second spot, the HIV of American politics.
—CBS News executive Edward Fouhy (1995)[51]

Ads are having much less impact than they did a decade ago. I find this in focus groups. People are so skeptical about political ads.
—Republican media consultant John Brabender (2003)[52]

Each election cycle, millions of dollars are spent on campaign advertising, not just by the candidates themselves, but increasingly by outside interest groups. The often-heard complaint is that media consultants are making a fortune from political advertising. For years, the standard fee collected by media consultants was up to 15 percent of the advertising buy, in addition to production fees (and often bonuses for winning races). Sometimes consultants have been accused of producing and airing more ads than needed, just to rack up bigger fees.

One well-known example came in 1998, when wealthy businessman Al Checchi hired an all-star team of consultants, headed by media consultant Robert Shrum and pollster Mark Penn. Checchi's goal was the California governor's office, and in a crowded three-way Democratic primary, he spent $40 million of his own money, a record amount at the time for a nonpresidential candidate. He was up against another wealthy Democrat, US representative Jane Harman, who poured in about $16 million of her own money. But both Harman and Checchi were trounced by California lieutenant governor Gray Davis, a man of modest means who relied on individual contributions and PAC money. The extravagant spending led to charges that Checchi's famous consultants were greedy, that what was good for their bottom line was good for the campaign.[53] The bitterness between former partners Robert Shrum and Patrick Caddell resurfaced as Caddell urged Checchi not to hire Shrum, and then secretly handed the candidate a memo stating that the expensive television ad campaign wasn't working. Checchi, with the help of his expensive consultants, had staked out the position that voters wanted change, that they were disillusioned with politics as usual. "If you like the status quo, don't vote for me," Checchi told voters. But voters in the three-way primary apparently were satisfied with the status quo, and they chose Gray Davis.[54] Shrum's other former partner, David Doak, with whom he also had a bad breakup, worked for Davis, and came up with a stinging rebuttal to the free-spending Checchi: "Davis: Experience money can't buy."

Democratic media consultant Peter Fenn observed that one of the striking trends in recent years has been the substantial increase in costs for campaign ads. "Even as the audience has grown smaller and smaller, the cost of primetime television commercials has increased dramatically."[55]

But Jim Margolis, senior partner at the Washington, DC–based Democratic media firm GMMB, argued that the culprits often were local television stations, not media consultants. In a 2007 interview with the Center for Public Integrity, Margolis explained this. Picking the media market of Green Bay, Wisconsin, at random from the previous election, Margolis noted that there had been a competitive governor's race with a considerable amount of independent expenditures; there also was a competitive attorney general's race, also with independent expenditures; a tough congressional contest, with the Democratic Congressional Campaign Committee (DCCC) and National Republican Congressional Committee (NRCC) pouring in money. "And they [the station owners] just continued every week to jack up the prices, and further, and further, and further for the same exact spot," noted Margolis. "Now, I don't know whether they tripled it or not from the beginning to the end. But it's amazing what they were able to do."[56] He found the same price increases in competitive television markets in Ohio, Pennsylvania, and Missouri. "The people who make out like bandits each year are stations that are operating in competitive states or competitive districts."[57]

The Science of Ad Placement

The guy who figures out which TV shows are watched by Democrats and which by Republicans is going to make a fortune.
  —Democratic media consultant Bob Squier (1988)[58]

A fundamental question that has perplexed media consultants and media time buyers has been where to place a candidate's ads so that they reach the most receptive audience. Was a popular nighttime western the best place to place an advertisement, or perhaps an equally popular daytime game show? Popular nighttime shows usually cost more than daytime shows, but which would give the best bang for the buck, which would capture the right audience? Pollster Richard Wirthlin pondered these questions in 1970: "We haven't refined this enough yet to tell a candidate he should put his television spot on 'Bonanza' rather than 'The Newlywed Game' but with enough polling, there's no reason why we can't.[59] Eighteen years later, Bob Squier pondered that same basic question: Why can't we better figure out the political preferences of television viewers?

In the 1990s, pollsters and media consultants began refining their analysis of likely voters, and gave far more granularity to the question of where to place ads. During the 1996 presidential campaign, Clinton pollsters Mark Penn and Doug Schoen conducted a "neuro-personality poll" to determine the lifestyle and habits of Clinton versus Dole supporters. In a memo to the campaign, the pollsters noted that Clinton voters are

> more likely to enjoy running or jogging while Dole voters are more likely to be found watching hockey or tennis or enjoying hunting and guns, and Swing voters watch baseball, football, bowling and enjoying the outdoors.
>
> When choosing radio stations, Clinton voters will be listening to Classical, Rap and Top 40, while Dole supporters enjoy Talk Radio and '70s/Classic Rock, and Swing voters turn their dial to News/Sports and '50s Music.
>
> Television is another source of lifestyle differences. Clinton voters are more likely to watch HBO, MTV, Oprah (or similar TV talk shows) and soap operas, while Dole supporters turn to sports and "Home Improvement," and Swing voters watch "Seinfeld" and "Friends."[60]

With sophisticated microtargeting, media buyers learned far more about the television habits of voters during the 2000s. As noted in chapter 19, the Obama 2012 campaign refined television targeting to its most productive level yet, through its program called "The Optimizer." But what if televisions could be targeted individually with the same precision as direct mail? This would be the holy grail, and it is just on the horizon.

While watching an NFL exhibition game on ESPN in August 2014, I noticed something peculiar. A local car dealership advertised just the car I had been looking at on its website a few weeks earlier; and a local mom-and-pop foreign car auto repair shop advertised that they fixed the same model car that was registered to me. Could it be that my cable company, Comcast, was doing a bit of microtargeting of my household? How did ESPN, a nationwide network, know that my local merchants were interested in me? I was used to having ads pop up on my iPad and computer screen, but now were these ads following me on TV as well? Indeed, the commercial world had discovered my buying and viewing habits. How long would it be before political commercials also discovered my individual television set? They already had.

In early 2014, DIRECTV and DISH Network announced that they would allow participating statewide political campaigns to target their television ads at the household level, reaching potentially more than 20 million homes. Called "household-addressable advertising," DIRECTV and DISH Network would use the same methodologies employed by direct mail specialists to reach their desired audience.[61] The political commercials sent to Household A watching *Deadliest Catch* might carry a completely different message from the political commercials sent to Household B, also watching the indomitable Alaskan fishermen. Household C might not see the commercial at all. "We've been waiting for this for a long time," said Danny Jester of GMMB, the Democratic media firm that pioneered the highly targeted ad strategies for the 2012 Obama re-election campaign.[62]

Another example of the use of advanced technologies is the geo-targeting employed by the Michele Bachmann 2010 congressional campaign in Minnesota. Bachmann's campaign deployed ads on mobile devices, in what consultant Eric Frenchman called "hyper-local targeting" or a "mobile surge." Bachmann's opponent allegedly supported taxes on beer, corn dogs, and deep-fried bacon. Wouldn't it be great to point this out to voters who were going to the Minnesota State Fair? Frenchman, with the Republican media firm of Connell Donatelli, created a thirty-second ad, placed it on YouTube, and then targeted the ad to mobile phones located within a ten-kilometer radius of the fairgrounds. Sixty-one percent of the views of the video came from the mobile devices around the fairgrounds. Frenchman noted that click-through rates were much higher than would be expected on a desktop campaign, and the cost-per-click was much lower.[63]

Campaign Ads: Negative, Funny, and Memorable

> I shall refrain from false or misleading attacks on an opponent or
> member of his or her family, and shall do everything in my power to
> prevent others from using such attacks.
>
> —From the Code of Professional Ethics of the
> American Association of Political Consultants

> *The only reason campaigns are negative in the first place is because we have found out that it works. . . . If it didn't work, we wouldn't use it. There's nobody more pragmatic than a politician in the end.*
>
> —Republican media consultant Stuart Spencer (2005)[64]

Political scientists and political communication scholars have made almost a cottage industry of examining negative campaign ads. Since the 1970s, they have been looking at the impact and effectiveness of televised political advertising. Early studies have shown that political advertising can be helpful in getting messages out to persons who otherwise might not seek out campaign information, and in persuading undecided voters and those not highly involved in politics.[65] Researchers have found that voters who are exposed to television ads are more likely to remember candidates' names, in comparison to voters who are not exposed to ads. Those ads that focus on image and character seem to be particularly effective. Campaign ads have been seen as more effective than television news in helping voters gain knowledge about candidates, and political ads that emphasize issue content are most effective in increasing voters' positive attitudes toward the candidates.

Considerable research has been done on negative political advertising. Voters often decry negative or attack ads, but they are used by campaigns for the very simple reason that they are effective. Negative advertising can lead to a higher level of voter knowledge, can punch holes in the reputation or image of an opposing candidate, and, above all, negative ads demand a response from the targeted candidate to negate or soften the blow of the original charge.[66] As Democratic consultant Paul Begala stated in 1992, "The purpose of a campaign is not to respond to every attack, it's to make the other son of a bitch respond to your attacks."[67]

Campaign commercials, from presidential on down, have had their share of hard-hitting and factual attacks against their opponents. Other ads have crossed over an ethical line by presenting misleading information, playing on the fears and prejudices of voters, and sinking to innuendo and guilt by association. In some cases, reputations are smeared, facts are loosely played with, and voting records or actions are distorted or not presented in context. But candidates (and their consultants) have to be careful: negative advertising can backfire. "Going negative is like juggling a hand grenade," observed Democratic media consultant Ray Strother. "You never know if it's going to blow up in your face."[68]

In many cases, the most vicious attack ads come not from the candidates, but from their surrogates, the political parties, or the so-called independent expenditures. Charles Guggenheim emphasized this point many years before the current proliferation of super PACs and other outside voices. Actors are hired, voice-over artists emphasize the point, and media consultants put together the hard-hitting thirty-second commercial. "It's not the candidate who is saying these things," wrote Guggenheim. "It's the surrogate. The candidate does not get blamed for the meanness. He doesn't get blamed for the half-truth, the rabbit punch, the lie, the deceptiveness."[69] Two of the most egregious examples were the racially tinged "Willie Horton" ads in 1988 targeted at Michael Dukakis and the Swift Vote Veterans for Truth ads in 2004 aimed at John Kerry; both are examined in subsequent chapters.

Of the thousands of campaign ads that have been produced over the years, a few stand out because they were unusual, provocative, funny, or simply exceptionally well-crafted. A number of these ads are featured in the chapters on presidential campaigns, but a number were also produced for nonpresidential contests as well.

McConnell "Hound Dog" ad by Roger Ailes and Larry McCarthy. In the 1984 Kentucky Senate race, incumbent Walter (Dee) Huddleston, a Democrat, was being challenged by Jefferson County judge/executive Mitch McConnell. Behind in the race, the McConnell campaign's media consultant Roger Ailes and his associate Larry McCarthy put together a series of humorous but deadly ads against Huddleston, chastising him for missing too many "big votes" and for missing votes while collecting speaking fees at luxury venues. In a thirty-second ad called "Hound Dog," a guy in a plaid flannel shirt, pulling on the leashes of a pack of sniffing bloodhounds, goes looking for the missing senator. The ads were funny, but with a serious point: Huddleston was not performing his duty and was lining his pockets. Maybe we should "Switch to Mitch," went the tag line, with dogs barking in the background.[70] McConnell prevailed, winning by just 5,200 votes, or 0.4 percent, and the Ailes-McCarthy ad earned a spot on an *Ad Age* list of the "Top 10 Game-Changing Ads of All Time."[71]

McCarthy and Ailes parted ways in 1987, but during the 1988 presidential campaign, McCarthy was responsible for the creation of the Willie Horton ad. (In 2008, while working on behalf of Mitt Romney, McCarthy and other members of Romney's media team planned a variation of the Willie Horton ad. An attack ad accused Mike Huckabee, when he was governor of Arkansas, of granting parole to a criminal who then raped and murdered a young woman. The media team was enthusiastic about the ad, but Romney, who would have to say on the ad that he "approved this message," decided it was going too far and the ad was never aired.)[72]

Helms "White Hands" ad by Alex Castellanos. In the 1990 race for US Senate in North Carolina, incumbent Jesse Helms was running against former Charlotte mayor, Harvey Gantt. Helms was well-known for his deep opposition to the civil rights movement, federal legislation, and progressive ideas. He once called the 1964 Civil Rights Act the "single most dangerous piece of legislation ever introduced in Congress," and he referred to the University of North Carolina as the "University of Negroes and Communists."[73] Now he was running against Gantt, a prominent and respected African American.

In her research on attack campaigning, communications scholar Kathleen Hall Jamieson argued that "television has made it possible to show what cannot be said."[74] This observation applied to the Helms campaign commercials aimed at Gantt, where Jamieson argued that "ads subtly priming consciousness of Gantt's blackness began to appear." In one ad, a white North Carolina woman charges that Gantt favored abortion for sex selection, a charge Gantt denied. The ad ended with this voice-over: "Harvey Gantt denied he ever said that. Harvey Gantt, extremely liberal with the facts." Another ad accused Gantt of favoring a mandatory gay rights law, and being a "dangerous liberal. Too liberal for North Carolina." The recurrent words "too liberal" "dangerous liberal" came from Alex Castellanos, a protégé of Arthur Finkelstein, who made a career out of using such phases against Democratic opponents.

In the most provocative of the ads, called "White Hands," a white man in a plaid shirt and wearing a wedding ring opens an envelope, reads an employment rejection letter, then crumbles it. The announcer then says:

> You needed that job. You were the best qualified. But they had to give it to a minority, because of a racial quota. Is that really fair? Harvey Gantt says it is. Gantt supports Ted Kennedy's racial quota law that makes the color of your skin more important than your qualifications. You'll vote on this issue next Tuesday. For racial quotas: Harvey Gantt. Against racial quotas: Jesse Helms.[75]

The creator of the ad, Alex Castellanos, was proud of his work: "Well that spot sure did cause a lot of trouble, didn't it? I'm very proud of it. I believe every bit of it. You know, my name is Castellanos. My son is named Castellanos. It may be, you know, one day he could get a job or he could get some deal because he is of some ethnic minority and all of that. I hope he never does. I think that lessens you when you do that."

"The message in that spot's very clear and that is nobody should get a job, or be denied a job because of the color of their skin. The vast majority of Americans believe that. And if it's wrong for us to discriminate that way, it's wrong for our government to discriminate that way."[76]

After the 1990 election, Carter Wrenn, one of Helms's chief political operatives, said that according to internal polling, the "White Hands" commercial, which was run only for a few days during the final days of the election (but which became infamous, nonetheless), did little to move voters' opinions. What resonated more, according to Wrenn, was a commercial that charged that Gantt had made a big profit on the purchase and resale of a television license by using the federal minority preference provisions.[77]

Humor in ads. Campaigns have used humor, even outrage, in campaign ads to get their point across. One of the earliest, as seen in chapter 5, was the ad created by Tony Schwartz for Hubert Humphrey in the 1968 presidential contest. The ad, called "Laughter," ridiculed Republican vice-presidential choice Spiro Agnew, with a man laughing uncontrollably at the thought of Agnew as a candidate, ending with the tag line: "This would be funny if it weren't so serious."[78]

During his 1998 gubernatorial campaign in Minnesota, former professional wrestler Jesse Ventura posed as Rodin's *The Thinker*, in an ad called "Jesse the Mind." The ad had Ventura, nearly naked, curled up on a pedestal like the Thinker, with soft operatic music playing in the background. The pedestal revolved slowly, as the narrator extolled his biography, "Navy Seal . . . union member . . . volunteer teacher . . . outdoorsman . . . a man who will fight to return Minnesota's tax surplus to the taxpayers . . ." At the end of the twenty-second commercial, Ventura, still coiled like a statue, stares directly at the camera and winks.[79] (When this ad was shown at the 1999 International Association of Political Consultants world congress in Milan, many of the European and Latin American consultants in attendance were aghast, shaking their heads).

This attention-grabbing ad was the product of Bill Hillsman and his Minneapolis-based North Woods Advertising, which boasted in the early 2000s that "Most advertising is like SHIT; Ours is like MANURE."[80] Hillsman, who had started in commercial advertising, caught the attention of the political world with his 1990 award-winning ads for US Senate candidate Paul Wellstone of Minnesota. One of Wellstone's funny spots, "Fast-Paced Paul," emphasized his average guy up against the establishment: "Unlike my opponent, I don't have six million dollars, So I'm gonna have to talk fast." Then, in quick frames, he breathlessly introduces his wife and family, his house in Northfield, and his son's farm and work for farmers; makes a plea to stop poisoning the environment; pledges to lead the fight for national health care; and notes his career as a labor-endorsed teacher—all in a hurried eighteen seconds. In another funny and groundbreaking two-minute ad, "Looking for Rudy," Wellstone searches high and low for opponent Rudy Boschwitz—at his campaign office, his business, on the telephone—trying to get him to join in a campaign debate.[81]

In the 2000 presidential election, third-party candidate Pat Buchanan turned to a small Texas advertising firm, Love Advertising, and its creative director David Harrison. In a thirty-second spot called "Meatballs," a chubby middle-aged white man chokes on a meatball when he hears on the radio that the president has signed a (fictional) executive order declaring that English is no longer the national language. In a panic, he reaches for his telephone, dials 911, and the automated response says, "For Spanish, press 1; for Korean, press 2." The voice-over interrupts: "Do you ever miss English? Immigration is out of control. Bush and Gore are writing off English for good. What can you do? Vote for the third party that puts America first. Vote Buchanan for president." By now, the choking man is slumped on the floor, nearly passed out. The recorded message then concludes: "For Swahili, press 12." In the last frames, the man's dog is licking meatball sauce off his face.[82]

In a final example, in 2014 a relatively unknown Republican candidate, Joni Ernst, vaulted to the top of the race for her party's nomination for the US Senate in Iowa, thanks to an ad called "Squeal." The 30-second ad opens with "I'm Joni Ernst. I grew up castrating hogs on an Iowa farm. So when I get to Washington, I'll know how to cut pork. . . . Cut wasteful spending. Repeal Obamacare. Balance the budget." Ernst, talking directly to the camera, says she's running because "Washington is full of big spenders." Her tag line is "Let's make them squeal."[83] The ad was created by Todd Harris and his colleagues at Something Else Strategies. A second ad shows Ernst, a lieutenant colonel in the Iowa Army National Guard, wearing a black leather jacket and riding a Harley-Davidson motorcycle. She stops, takes a handgun out of her purse, and expertly fires several rounds at a shooting range. The announcer says that she is taking aim at Obamacare. She then says, "Give me a shot, I'm Joni Ernst."[84] In November, Ernst defeated Democrat Bruce Braley. Harris has also worked for Florida senator Marco Rubio, former Florida governor Jeb Bush, John McCain, and California governor Arnold Schwarzenegger.[85]

These ads, like the infamous "Daisy" commercial of 1964 or "Willie Horton" of 1988, gained new life with stories written about them, commentary about them on television, and in college courses devoted to political communication. In 1988, then-media consultant Roger Ailes observed that most candidates are boring, and receive little coverage as a consequence. How do you attract free media attention: "You've got to find a different approach. You've got to create some interest in your language, in the words and pictures you create. If a candidate can't give a 10-minute speech and have reporters reaching for their pens in the first 90 seconds, he probably shouldn't be running."[86] And if candidates cannot have catchy, memorable ads, they will also fail to attract attention.

YouTube, Web Videos, and Cinéma Vérité Production

The first effective use of web videos came during the 2004 presidential campaign. Bush's media director, Mark McKinnon, contacted Justin Germany and Laura Crawford, two young, tech-savvy media consultants. Germany shot footage, digitized it on his laptop, edited it, and added music and graphics, and within twenty-four hours it appeared on the Bush website. The message could then be sent via e-mail to supporters. Crawford produced web videos for the RNC, attacking Kerry.[87]

Much of what appears on web videos is of the cinéma vérité style: handheld cameras, with rough cuts from one angle to another, creating an amateurish and presumably authentic production. Justin Germany observed that "old school guys wouldn't do this, but we have a different mindset now. We mix and match styles, and put our work on YouTube, reality television, and web videos."[88]

Soon web videos became standard fare in the arsenal of campaign communications. As seen further in chapter 19, Hillary Clinton announced her official 2008 candidacy through a high-production web video ("I'm in it to win it"), while John Edwards, wind-blown, with shirt-sleeves rolled up in New Orleans, tried to produce a more rugged and authentic look to his announcement. Several 2016 presidential candidates, including Hillary Clinton, used web videos, Twitter, and other social media to let voters know they were running.

One of the most original (and funny) web videos came from the 2011 mayoral race in San Francisco. An independent organization created by tech mogul Ron Conway, San Franciscans for Jobs and Good Government, released a 2-1/2 minute remix rap video titled "Ed Lee is 2 Legit 2 Quit" two weeks before the November 2011 mayoral race in San Francisco. Conway worked with political consultants Aaron McLear and Josh Ginsberg of the Ginsberg McLear Group, Brian Brokaw of Brian Brokaw Consulting, and Portal-A Interactive to develop a new media advertisement for interim mayor, and ultimate winner in a crowded field, Ed Lee. Posted on YouTube, the video featured local tech and sports personalities (Twitter cofounder Biz Stone, Marissa Mayer of Google, San Francisco Giants pitcher Brian Wilson, San Francisco 49ers star Ronnie Lott), former mayor Willie Brown, Will.i.am of the Black Eyed Peas, and M.C. Hammer. The video was a remix of Hammer's 1991 "2 Legit 2 Quit," and the personalities, simply by their presence, and their rapping and dancing, affirmed that Lee should be elected. This ad was dubbed the "best campaign video of the year" by *The Atlantic*, and it showed that political advertising had come along way since the primitive, grainy, black-and-white ads called "Eisenhower Answers America."[89]

CHAPTER 9

Voter Contact

Targeting, Direct Mail, and Phone Banks

Make a perfect list of all the voters in their
respective districts, and to ascertain with certainty
for whom they will vote.

—Abraham Lincoln (1840)

There are only two mail-donating segments in our society.
The right fringe and the left fringe.

—Morris Dees (1981)

The telephone is the most essential mechanism
to facilitate the conversation between office-seeker
and potential supporter.

—Walter D. Clinton and Anne E. Clinton (1999)

I N PRESIDENTIAL, US Senate, and other high profile campaigns, attention is often focused on television advertising. But for most other campaigns and ballot initiatives, the preferred vehicle for communicating with voters is through direct mail, telephone messages, and, in more recent times, online communication.

Direct Mail

Direct mail is like a water moccasin—silent, but deadly.

—Richard A. Viguerie (2003)[1]

The best direct mail package in the world is worthless
if sent to the wrong mailing list. If there is any "science"
in direct mail, it rests with the way in which mailing lists are drawn up.

—Roger Craver (1988)[2]

Commercial companies have long used the mail to deliver messages, catalogues, and information about products they sell. In the last part of the nineteenth century, two general merchandise retailers, Montgomery Ward & Company and Sears, Roebuck & Company became giants in the direct mail order business. By the end of World War I, direct mail was a $500 million commercial enterprise.[3] Candidates for public office were slow to see the benefit of direct mail communication, but during the 1916 presidential election, William Jennings Bryan, running for the presidency for the third and final time, sent out 1 million letters asking for contributions; 20,000 persons responded, a credible 2 percent response rate. However, Bryan's campaign was barely able to cover the costs of mailing the letters.[4]

Thirty-four years later, in 1950, the *Reader's Digest* direct mail specialist, Walter H. Weintz, was loaned out to the US Senate re-election campaign of Ohio Republican Robert A. Taft.[5] Labor organizations were attacking Taft because of his authorship of the Taft-Hartley Act, legislation they vehemently opposed. The Taft campaign, with the assistance of Weintz, sent out hundreds of thousands of letters to blue-collar workers in Ohio's industrial cities explaining his legislation, and found a warm reception as workers voted overwhelmingly for him, despite the union campaign against him. Two years later, Weintz assisted the Eisenhower for President campaign in developing its basic campaign theme. The campaign sent out ten different issue-based letters, each going to 10,000 voters; the response showed that most voters thought that ending the war in Korea was the most important issue in the election. The campaign followed up, sending a letter to everyone on its mailing list emphasizing Eisenhower's efforts to end the war. After that letter was sent, 300,000 contributors sent money to the campaign.[6] The Eisenhower campaign discovered the strengths of direct mail: if properly targeted, it can become a potent tool for advocacy and fundraising.

The Richard Nixon presidential campaign of 1960 was able to muster about 40,000 to 50,000 contributions through direct mail.[7] However, the breakthrough for presidential elections came in 1964, again on the Republican side. The Barry Goldwater campaign sent fundraising letters to 12 million potential voters, developed a donor list of 221,000 contributors, and was able to raise $4.7 million. The campaign also received many small donations thanks to last-minute television appeals.[8] Goldwater asserted that there were around 661,500 individual contributions to his campaign, generated from direct mail, telephone calls, and television appeals, and this campaign has been characterized as the "first mass campaign in modern American history" in terms of number of people involved in it, and the "first popularly financed campaign in modern American history."[9]

Direct mail had its second champion in the McGovern for President campaign in 1972, although initially neither McGovern nor his senior staff were convinced that direct mail would be beneficial. Morris S. Dees Jr. met George McGovern at one of the senator's speaking engagements in Indiana, before he announced his presidential candidacy. Dees, an Alabama book publisher and businessman, had used direct-marketing mail-order techniques in his business and thought that they could apply in the political arena. The McGovern campaign wanted to send out a mailing to key supporters and to the press announcing that the senator was running for the presidency. It would be just a letter, and not a request for campaign funds. Why not ask for money at the same time, Dees asked. Gary Hart, McGovern's campaign manager, said that a solicitation for money coupled with the announcement wouldn't be dignified.[10]

Dees said he would play around with the idea of a letter, and with the help of New York direct mail writer Tom Collins, put together a seven-page letter. The letter was not standard business size, but smaller, like personal stationery, and was to be sent in an envelope with the senator's name and an embossed seal of the Senate (which is now illegal to do). While this technique is now commonplace, in 1970 it was considered radical.[11] The McGovern staff complained that the letter, dated January 15, 1971, was too long and was sent to far too many people. At first, McGovern was irritated, but once the money started flowing in, at an incredible 15 percent response rate, he saw the light. Dees was even complimented by his ideologically opposite, Richard Viguerie.

At the end of the presidential campaign, McGovern had some 700,000 donors, who had given $24 million, and the campaign was left with a surplus.[12] The political direct mail piece in the early days stood out because it was unique. No one else was sending a letter, and certainly not from a politician or a major national organization.[13]

Then during the 1976 Democratic primaries, nearly all the candidates were copying the voter contact techniques of the failed McGovern campaign.[14] They were now using direct mail, list brokers, and copywriters to seek out donors through the mail. Republican consultant John Deardourff noted that because of the new federal campaign finance law and its contribution limits, candidates had to appeal to a large number of small donors, making direct mail an attractive tool.[15]

The Appeal of Direct Mail

Candidates and causes discovered that there were distinct advantages to using direct mail to either ask for money or advance a point of view, or usually to do both. For just the cost of a third-class postage stamp, campaign literature can get into the hands of likely voters; postal workers, going from mailbox to mailbox, become very cheap extensions of the campaign effort. The mail is also invisible and under the radar screen. Millions of letters, often spewing out pointed, even vitriolic, messages, can be mailed, and there will not be a peep on the television news about how negative the messages were. Further, the opposition won't know if a letter is sent to ten people or 10 million.[16] Mail can go places that a campaign canvasser cannot, including inside apartment complexes or gated communities.

Direct mail is most effective in urban areas, where the alternative form of communication might be high-priced television or radio. For most campaigns below the state or the presidential level, direct mail, not television, has become the biggest aggregate cost item. *Campaigns & Elections* magazine in 1997 calculated that direct mail was more in demand than television or radio as a form of communication.[17]

The key to direct mail is the ability to target people geographically, and when combined with the data-rich demographic and consumer-based information, it becomes highly effective in spotting the right person, with the right message, at the right time. When used properly, according to direct mail specialists Richard Schlackman and Jamie (Buster) Douglas, it is "the most precise weapon in a candidate's arsenal."[18] Direct mail is especially important for down-ballot candidates in major media markets. It would be both extraordinarily expensive and fool-hardy for a city council candidate, or a candidate competing in a suburban state legislature contest, to spend money on big-city television ads. For example, a candidate running for the Illinois House of Representatives seat in District 36 (Palos Hills and Oak Lawn, just south and west of Chicago) who wanted to advertise on television would be paying a premium for big-city rates, and the message would be viewed by millions of voters in both Illinois and northwest Indiana who do not live in the 36th District. This would be a foolish waste of resources. Direct mail targets specific ZIP codes, not straying beyond the boundaries of the 36th District, and not wasting postage and effort on voters living in another district, city, or state.

With more and more sophisticated targeting techniques, direct mail messages can be finely tuned, delivering the right message to just the right individual. The fundraising letter going to the Republican female, under thirty, and pro-life voter in Apartment 602 might be quite different from the letter going to the Republican male, retired, gun-owning voter in Apartment 603.

At the local level, Democratic pollster Douglas Schoen remembered his first job as an independent political consultant, when he worked for Father Louis Gigante, who was running for city council in New York in 1973. Schoen was a junior at Harvard, and working with him was E. J. Dionne Jr., also a Harvard student who later became a well-respected *New York Times* reporter and *Washington Post* syndicated columnist. Gigante, the charismatic activist priest, had a brother, Vincent "The Chin" Gigante, the top capo of the Genovese crime family in New York. The family tie wasn't the problem for Schoen and Dionne, it was how to gain votes in a district that spanned the South Bronx, East Harlem, and a tiny portion of the Upper East Side and Queens. It was "almost like running in Mississippi, Puerto Rico, and the Hamptons all at once," wrote Schoen. They did it through targeted direct mail, still a novelty at the time. For conservative neighborhoods, Gigante ("Father G") was the "patriot priest," a defender of traditional values; in East Harlem and South Bronx, Gigante was depicted as the fighter and activist; for Upper East Side voters, he was the reformer and champion of recycling. Somehow, it all worked, and Gigante won the Democratic primary.[19]

Direct Mail Pioneers

Richard A. Viguerie (b. 1933) became executive director of the Young Americans for Freedom, a conservative activist group, in 1961, and he launched his own direct marketing firm, American Target Advertising in 1965. Viguerie learned the direct mail trade from the innovative Marvin Liebman (1923-1997), who created his own firm in 1957 and amassed some 50,000 names of conservative contributors.[20]

After the 1964 Goldwater defeat, Viguerie stepped in to capture the names of Goldwater contributors. He went to the office of the clerk of the House of Representatives, and with the help of a half-dozen women he had hired, he was able to copy by hand the names of 12,500 of the 15,000 persons who had contributed at least $50 to the Goldwater campaign. That list formed the basis for Viguerie's multimillion-dollar empire in direct mail. "It was my treasure trove" Viguerie later wrote, "as good as the gold bricks deposited at Fort Knox."[21] He brought the contributor names to two friends, Tom Martin and Charles Hamby, who transferred the handwritten list to magnetic tape. The old-fashioned 3-by-5 index cards and lists of names on legal pads were about to be transformed by computer technology. During his first year of operations, Viguerie purchased lists from two early direct mail pioneers: 50,000 names from John Swain, then another 50,000 names from Marvin Liebman. Soon, Viguerie had a total file of over 150,000 conservative donors.

Viguerie turned down offers to raise money for the National Republican Congressional Committee (NRCC). Wyatt Stewart and Steven Winchell, who had worked for Viguerie, accepted the Republican work, and were about to increase the number of Republican Party donors from 25,000 in 1977 to 2 million by November 1980. Viguerie turned down the Republican offer because he wasn't happy with the moderate ideological drift of the party and didn't want to be co-opted by it.[22] For Viguerie, while there was definite overlap, the Republican Party and the conservative movement were not one in the same; and he was steadfastly pushing the conservative movement.

Direct mail came into its own with three presidential candidates—all considered outside of the mainstream of their parties—Barry Goldwater, George McGovern, and George Wallace. In his 1968 Senate race, McGovern tried to recruit Viguerie, but the king of direct mail turned him down.[23] Viguerie opposed McGovern's ideology, and if there is any category of campaign specialist that is sensitive to ideological purity, it is the direct mail consultant.[24] In 1976 Viguerie had no trouble working for the presidential campaign of George Wallace.

Viguerie was also active in founding conservative action groups. Together with Paul Weyrich and Howard Phillips, he was a principal founder of the Moral Majority in 1979. With Phillips he founded the Conservative Caucus and the *Conservative Digest* magazine (and he served as its publisher for ten years). Viguerie also served on the national advisory board of the American Freedom Coalition, an organization financed by the Rev. Sun Myung Moon's operation.

By 2004, Viguerie's direct mail firm had mailed more than 2 billion letters over its forty years of business. Still active, Viguerie heads ConservativeHQ.com, which he dubbed as "the online news source for conservatives and Tea Partiers committed to bringing limited-government constitutional conservatives to power."[25]

Morris S. Dees Jr. (b. 1936) was born in Shorter, Alabama, and graduated from the University of Alabama, with both an undergraduate and a law degree. Dees and Millard Fuller created a book-publishing business, Fuller & Dees Marketing Group, but sold it in 1971. With the proceeds, Dees created the Southern Poverty Law Center (SPLC) and Fuller created Habitat for Humanity. In 1972 Dees served as the finance director for George McGovern's presidential bid, and he later served in the same capacity for Jimmy Carter's 1976 presidential bid. In 1980 he worked as finance director for Senator Edward Kennedy, who was running in the Democratic primaries against President Carter. Dees later worked for Senator Gary Hart's presidential campaign in 1984.

Working with Roger Craver, Dees designed a direct-response development program for nonprofits, including Planned Parenthood, Public Citizen, Common Cause, Habitat for Humanity, and the American Civil Liberties Union (ACLU). The Southern Poverty Law Center is now supported by over 300,000 direct response donors. Its lawyers have filed lawsuits and have bankrupted some of the worst hate crime groups, including the United Klans of America and the Aryan Nations. The SPLC has an education division that provides anti-bias resources to over 75,000 schools and 400,000 teachers. Roger Craver called Dees a "gut fighter against the crazies . . . a guy who won't let up . . . a real junkyard dog."[26] In 2011 Dees was inducted into the American Association of Political Consultants Hall of Fame. He is the author, with James Corcoran, of *Gathering Storm: America's Militia Threat* (1997), and coauthor, with Steve Fiffer, of *Hate on Trial* (1993) and two autobiographical works.

"You need a streak of outrage. You need a sense of injustice. Without outrage, I don't know the hell how you could do this work," said Democratic fundraiser Roger Craver in 1993.[27] Craver, who graduated from Dickinson College and received his law degree from George Washington University, began his career as a major gifts and capital campaign professional at George Washington. When he shifted over to fundraising through direct mail, his colleagues thought he'd "gone mad."[28] In 1970 Craver joined John Gardner in creating Common Cause, and he learned from veteran direct-mail marketer Lester Wunderman how to apply direct mail to nonprofit causes.[29] In 1972 he left Common Cause to help create the National Organization for Women (NOW), then to resuscitate the ACLU, Sierra Club, Amnesty International, Greenpeace, Southern Poverty Law Center, and help dozens more nonprofits gain traction through direct mail fundraising.

Craver built the direct mail programs for the Democratic National Committee (DNC), the Democratic Senatorial Campaign Committee (DSCC), and the Democratic Congressional Campaign Committee (DCCC). But Craver's company, Craver, Mathews, Smith & Company (CMS), resigned after working with the DNC for six years and building its donor base from 60,000 to 750,000. Craver discovered that DNC chairman Charles Manatt and former vice president Walter Mondale were lobbyists for the Alyeska Pipeline Company, and that this constituted a conflict of interest with a CMS client, the Sierra Club. After working with the DCCC for ten years, CMS resigned because its client Common Cause had filed a conflict of interest complaint against Speaker of the House Jim Wright, who was ex-officio chair of the DCCC. After twelve years, CMS resigned from the DSCC. CMS had helped raise "millions and millions of dollars on the promise that this Committee would help elect a Democratic Senate that would protect the interests of women," wrote Craver. "And when the Anita Hill controversy broke out, the Democratic Senate was far too slow in responding to the charges of sexual harassment against Clarence Thomas. So we walked away from that."[30]

CMS "walked away from very big fees" when it resigned from the Democratic committees, but Craver explained that "you have to decide what you're in the business for. Are you in the business just to make money—or are you in the business to affect change. And if you're in the business to affect change, that stuff doesn't wash. You've got to walk away from it."[31] In the late 1970s, his firm raised record amounts for Democratic Senate candidates, including Frank Church (Idaho), George McGovern (South Dakota), Birch Bayh (Indiana), and John Culver (Iowa), and for presidential candidates Morris Udall, Edward Kennedy, and John Anderson during the mid-1970s and in 1980. By the early 1990s, Craver, Mathews, Smith & Company had 110 fundraising professionals working for liberal and progressive clients. Roger Craver brought Greenpeace and World Wildlife to Europe in the early 1980s and in the mid-1990s he founded an advocacy group in the Netherlands called Delphi.[32] Craver founded Public Interest Communications in 1975 and teamed with Republican Doug Bailey in 1987 to create *The Hotline*. In 2011, Craver was inducted into the American Association of Political Consultants Hall of Fame.

A second wave of direct mail specialists began working in the 1970s and 1980s, both on the Republican and Democratic sides.

Bruce W. Eberle and his wife, Kathi, started their own direct mail firm in 1974 in the basement of their home, working exclusively for conservative causes, political action committees, and candidates. The most important early client of Bruce W. Eberle & Associates was Ronald Reagan in his 1976 run for the Republican presidential nomination. The direct mail fundraising efforts in 1976 raised more net dollars for Citizens for Reagan than had ever been raised in a presidential campaign to that point through direct mail. Eberle noted that a direct mail appeal sent out after Reagan's unexpected victory in the North Carolina primary that year was one of the most successful in political fundraising history: 85,000 donors, generating $800,000 in net income (more than $3 million today).[33] Over the years, the firm, now called Eberle Associates, has raised millions of dollars for conservative causes, such as the James Watt Legal Defense Fund, the Stacey Koon Defense Fund (Koon was one of the police officers implicated in the 1991 Rodney King beating); Sheriff Joe Arpaio (the controversial sheriff of Maricopa County, Arizona); and the effort to recall Gary Davis (Davis was governor of California and removed from office through a successful recall effort).[34] A protégé of Eberle's was Richard Norman. During the 1994 election cycle, Norman took a one-year sabbatical from his firm to design and administer the fundraising program for Lt. Col. Oliver L. North's US Senate race in Virginia. Over $24 million was raised from 277,000 contributors; both numbers set political fundraising records at the time. Norman's organization has worked for a number of conservative causes, including Herman Cain for President, the Tea Party Patriots, and the Foundation for Moral Law (created by former Alabama Supreme Court Judge Roy Moore, who was removed for office after failing to uphold a federal court ruling to remove the Ten Commandments from an Alabama judicial building).[35]

Bradley (Brad) O'Leary can boast to having raised a billion dollars for conservative candidates and causes throughout his career.[36] Much of it came through direct mail. At twenty-four, he got his start as an advance man for Nixon's 1960 presidential campaign. O'Leary's first big break was as finance director for Texas senator John Tower's 1972 re-election campaign, where he was asked to raise $1 million but took in over $3 million, an extraordinary amount at the time. His biggest clients over the years for his firm PM Consulting were the National Rifle Association, the Republican National Committee, Ronald Reagan, Bob Dole, Dan Quayle, and many conservative US senators or senatorial candidates. Flamboyant, pugnacious, and controversial, O'Leary basically invented the concept of a "big event," often bringing in celebrities (like President Reagan or Bush) and spending lavishly on fundraising events, but in the end producing the funds necessary. "Before Brad, people used to think you could raise twenty-five thousand bucks off a dinner," observed Republican consultant Charlie Black. "He showed them how to raise a million or more."[37]

Much of O'Leary's fundraising and grassroots advocacy communication came through direct mail. O'Leary was one of the early users of poll-driven mail. In John Tower's 1972 re-election campaign, O'Leary produced 200 pieces of targeted mail, all with a basic message, but all talking about the issues that were relevant to the specific audience. O'Leary was the author of eleven books, a former president of the American Association of Political Consultants, had a ten-year run as a radio talk show host on NBC's *The O'Leary-Kamber Report* (with Democratic consultant Vic Kamber) with 2 million listeners daily in 250 radio stations, and he has done over two dozen television specials. In 2008 he wrote *The Audacity of Deceit*, a screed that charged that Obama policies "could destroy America."[38]

One of the best-known political consultants today, Karl Rove, began his career as a direct mail consultant. Because of his larger role as a general consultant, he will be profiled in chapter 13.

Dan N. Hazelwood formed Targeted Creative Communications (TC2) in 1993, after spending a year in the communications department of the National Republican Congressional Committee (NRCC). He has worked for over seventy members of the House of Representatives, the Bush-Cheney 2004 re-election campaign, and for a number of Republican senators and governors; altogether, he has worked on over 250 election campaigns.

On the Democratic side, four of the important consultants began their work during this time: Richard Schlackman, Tony Fazio, Charles (Chuck) Pruitt, and Frank Tobe.

Richard Schlackman was born and raised in metropolitan New York City, but he began his political career on the Democratic field staff of statewide and local races for the Northern California Democratic Party. Schlackman became familiar with the mechanism of direct mail by working with pioneer Bill Daly. Along with another major Democratic direct mail consultant, Tony Fazio, he opened up a direct mail firm, Schlackman, Fazio & Associates. They parted in 1985, with Schlackman setting up the Campaign Performance Group that year. Schlackman used his direct mail and political strategy skills to build one of the major direct mail firms on the Democratic side. He later created a partnership with veteran consultants Hal Malchow (see chapter 15 for his profile), Jim Crounse, and was later joined by Trish Hoppey, forming Malchow, Schlackman, Hoppey & Crounse (MSHC). Since 2011, he has headed RMS Associates, specializing in general consulting, direct mail, Internet advertising, and telephone town hall sessions.

Schlackman, long active in Democratic politics and the political consulting industry, is credited with inventing what has been called the "California Style" of direct mail, which combines an "innovative visual mix of graphics and emotions, backed with intensive demographic strategies."[39] He was given a Lifetime Achievement Award from the AAPC.

Tony Fazio worked as a grocery clerk in Rhode Island and a longshoreman on the Oakland docks. He was a union organizer for the Service Employees International Union (SEIU), and director of the political action committee for the San Francisco Labor Council. He was educated at San Francisco State University, and began his direct mail business in 1981 with Rich Schlackman, then founded the direct mail firm of Winning Directions in 1989. His firm has worked for a long list of Democratic statewide and local candidates, labor causes, and ballot issues, and boasts on its website of being the first, and only, union shop political consulting firm.[40] His firm has won over 200 industry awards. Fazio served two years as president of the American Association of Political Consultants (2008–2010).

Charles (Chuck) Pruitt began his direct mail business in Milwaukee in 1980, and by 2014, the firm, ABD Direct, became an international firm with more than 350 employees. Pruitt, who received his undergraduate education at Macalester College, and an MA and PhD in political science from Harvard University, once taught at St. Olaf College in Northfield, Minnesota. He has provided direct mail and fundraising services to a long list of Democratic candidates, including the 2008 and 2012 Obama for President campaigns. In those two campaigns, ABD Direct helped raise more money through direct mail than any campaigns in US political history.[41] Pruitt and his firm have worked for a variety of non-profits, including the Environmental Defense Fund, United to End Genocide, US Holocaust Memorial Museum, and the Wilderness Society.

Frank Tobe along with Bill Below created one of the most important direct mail firms, Below, Tobe & Associates, in 1971 in southern California. Tobe worked for more than twenty-five years in the direct mail and computer services business, serving the DNC; presidential, senatorial, congressional, and mayoral candidates; and ballot initiatives throughout the United States, Canada, and other international campaigns. After retiring, Tobe turned to studying and writing about robotics and robots as business opportunities. He now is publisher of the *Robot Report* and cofounder of Robo-Stox LLC, a tracking system to follow the robotics industry.[42]

Most direct mail specialists would be happy with a 2 percent rate of return—that is, two persons responding out of 100 letters sent for fundraising purposes. But the rate of return also depends on targeting, as Karl Rove once commented, on sending the direct mail to "the right list, with the right message and the right time. It has to grab attention and it has to be based in fact and need."[43] Rove claimed to get up to 24 percent response to his direct mail solicitations. Better targeting means better understanding of potential donors or potential audience for advocacy messages. The fundamentals start with up-to-date and accurate voting profiles and the aggregation of useful consumer, cultural, and ideological information about voters.

With so many means of modern online communication, direct mail still has much to offer. Direct mail consultant Liz Chadderdon makes the case for the tried-and-true mailbox: a voter may have a smart phone and a landline, two or three e-mail addresses, watch 100 or so cable channels, and surf the web for hours at a time, but that voter will mostly likely have only one mailing address. It is the address recorded with the state board of elections and is one of the most important sources for political communication.[44]

Voter Files and Targeting

Voter files are the poor man's television.

—Bill Daly (1990)[45]

The registered voter file . . . the DNA of the electorate.

—John Aristotle Phillips (2012)[46]

"Matt Reese began the whole theory of targeting," observed his former associate Walter D. Clinton. Reese developed a system for identifying persuadable voters, high turnout precincts, and switch-split voters.[47] Reese also identified "hardcore voters"—those individuals, especially in low-turnout elections, who will go to the polls, regardless of who the candidates are or issues happen to be. Such voters are extremely important in low-visibility races, particularly primaries. In contrast are "softcore voters"—those who only go to polls in elections they are interested in, like a presidential contest. The information about hardcore and softcore voters is readily obtainable from online voter files today, but in the early 1970s it was laborious, costly, and time-consuming to program the information into computer format. It wasn't until the late 1980s that voter lists became standardized across the country, and before this much of the voter data was done county by county, with different states on different formats. It was, in Clinton's words, a "nightmare."[48]

Targeting firms often used reverse telephone directories, which listed street addresses first, then matched them with customer names. This was a much more efficient way of reaching people. Yet, voter registration files with telephone numbers simply didn't exist in the 1970s.[49]

Reese would analyze precinct-by-precinct behavior in a jurisdiction, like a congressional district or a mayor's race, or a statewide contest. He and his team would identify the precinct's performance—are the voters ours, theirs, or is it a swing precinct. Reese used six or seven criteria. All these data would be punched into hand-held calculators, and the precinct's performance would be analyzed statistically based on this information. "We would have a sweat room set up with people and calculators at card tables for weeks punching this data into it and analyzing it all by hand before there were computers," remembered Clinton.[50]

The US Post Office implemented the Zone Improvement Plan (ZIP) codes in 1963, and the US Census Bureau made great strides in its computerization of data in the 1970 US decennial census. Social scientist and entrepreneur Jonathan Robbin was able to make an important breakthrough in marketing analysis by creating a system that classified all US ZIP codes, census tracts, enumeration districts, and blocks into forty geodemographic "life-style" clusters. He gave the clusters catchy names, like "Money and Brains," "Shotguns and Pickups," or "Blue Collar Nursery." Robbin developed a ZIP Quality (ZQ) index to rank the forty lifestyle clusters, from most affluent (ZQ1—Blue Blood Estates) to least affluent (ZQ40—Public Assistance). His company, Claritas Corporation, which he founded in 1971, then developed the PRIZM system (Potential Rating Index by ZIP Markets) which linked the forty lifestyle clusters to a broad range of consumer information, such as magazine and newspaper subscriptions, buying habits, television and radio ratings, automobile registration, and others. Robbin became known as the "King of the ZIP Codes."[51]

The Claritas system was designed for commercial marketing, and while it looked intriguing as a tool for politics, it was both expensive and not precise enough for campaign use.[52] That turned around when the Claritas Corporation gave exclusive campaign rights to its product to Targeting Systems, Inc., a subsidiary of Matt Reese's company. In 1978 Reese and pollster Bill Hamilton applied Claritas clusters for the first time to a political campaign, when they were hired by a consortium of labor unions in Missouri to defeat a right-to-work initiative. Hamilton's poll results were used with the geodemographic groupings to identify "leaning persuadables" and the most effective message to reach nine different, and mutually exclusive, groups of voters. Over a half-million telephone calls were made, millions of pieces of mail were delivered, and canvassing was done house-to-house. The campaign tried to do this under the radar screen so that they would not tip off their opponents. Television advertising was at a minimum; they poured their efforts into telephone calls, direct mail, and shoe leather. Earlier polls showed the labor unions losing by 60–40 percent, but by Election Day that number had reversed to a 60–40 percent win.

The geodemographic clusters and tactics employed by Reese and Hamilton, along with the Claritas system, were immediately dubbed the "New Magic." In the 1980 presidential campaign, Indiana senator Birch Bayh, running for the Democratic nomination, was the first candidate to use the Claritas system.[53]

But Claritas was not widely adopted by political campaigns. By the beginning of the twenty-first century, a whole new set of precise targeting techniques was emerging. Called "microtargeting," it took data analysis to a whole new level of sophistication and depth. As seen in chapter 15, microtargeting combines hundreds of data points to draw up a picture of the preferences and habits of likely voters. At the core of microtargeting data, however, are voter files, the public information held by state and county election offices about voters. No matter how many lifestyle data points a campaign may have about an individual voter (she reads *Marie Claire* magazine, her favorite television show is *Two Broke Girls*, and she drives a Chevrolet Cruze), far more important is the knowledge that she is a registered Democrat, voted in the past two statewide elections, and her current address is correct. This critical information comes from voter files. Until the mid-1970s, most of this information was kept only in paper files at state, county, or city election offices. But with the growing computerization of files, the vital information found in voter files was finally becoming accessible to campaigns.

Two consultants stand out, one a pioneer in the field of voter contact, and the other one of the leading vendors today.

Bill Daly (1935–2010) had a master's degree in electrical engineering from MIT, but when a business venture he was involved in went bankrupt, he fled the day-to-day office life. He didn't know much about politics, but when a friend was running for office, he looked at the haphazard voter lists, knew he could produce far better results, and immediately recognized a business opportunity. He created Voter Contact Services (VCS), based in Honolulu, Hawaii, and developed sophisticated targeting services, including a precinct ranking systems. He added more information to voter files, including telephone numbers and ethnicity, and used mathematical models to determine such things as family structure. This was all twenty-five years before microtargeting became a standard feature in voter contact. Daly also developed some of the first computer-based delivery systems for voter data, creating a bulletin board system in 1985. By 2011, when VCS was sold to Labels & Lists, Inc., the company had amassed a database of 181 million voters from all fifty states.[54]

John Aristotle Phillips (b. 1957) made a splash in national news while he was still a twenty-year-old junior at Princeton University. As a physics class project, Phillips, using publically available information, wrote a paper demonstrating how any group could build a suitcase-size nuclear bomb. He became an instant celebrity, with US senators calling for an investigation on why it was so easy to use public documents for evil purposes, an agent from Pakistan trying to buy the information from Phillips, television appearances, and potential movie deals.[55] Once his Warholian fifteen minutes of fame faded, Phillips ran unsuccessfully twice for Congress from his home state of Connecticut.

Together with his computer science–trained brother Dean, John Phillips founded Aristotle, Inc., in 1983. In 2004, *Time* called the twenty-year-old company, now Aristotle International, "one of the most influential, if invisible, private-sector players in politics."[56] Aristotle offers its services to candidates and causes, regardless of political party or affiliation. It supplies vital demographic, voter contact, and other information for clients. This includes access to a database of voter files that includes over 190 million records of voters. In a lengthy

2007 profile of Phillips in *Vanity Fair*, his company was described as having an "Orwellian database of voter records [that] has been an essential campaign tool for every president since Ronald Reagan."[57]

Today, Aristotle is the leading vendor in its field, going beyond voter files to providing campaign, political action committee, and grassroots services. It also has constituency services software, giving legislative offices assistance in managing their constituency files, and has an extensive international voter data management business as well.

Telephone Communications

In an age demanding "warm and fuzzy," the
political dialogue is cold and barren.

—Walter Clinton (2002)[58]

Another important form of communication is the telephone call from a campaign (or a telemarketing vendor) to likely voters. Pioneer phone bank specialist Walter (Wally) Clinton has argued that telephone contact is a superior form of communication: "When we are on the telephone, people talk back to us. That is the real value of the telephone."[59] During the 1960s and early 1970s, political telephone calling was still a volunteer and somewhat haphazard operation in campaigns. During the 1972 George McGovern primaries, for example, Clinton would set up a phone center specifically for a campaign, install the telephones, train volunteers to make the calls, and develop a list of people to call. Clinton also experimented with recorded calls, which became the forerunner of today's so-called robocalls. In his living room, Clinton had built a device that held three eight-track tapes and had three telephone lines coming into it. A volunteer would dial a telephone number, and while the phone was ringing, the volunteer would dial another number; if someone answered the first phone, the volunteer would then touch the "play" button on the eight-track, and a message came out urging the listener to vote for McGovern. Perhaps twenty listeners an hour could be contacted. By the late 1990s, with computerization and professional phone banks rather than volunteers, Clinton's team could make sixty or seventy calls each hour.[60]

Over the years, Clinton has observed that "too many political managers have neglected the 'listening' cycle of effective communication," relying totally on polls for citizen input.[61] Candidates and campaigns need to foster two-way communication, building a relationship with the voters, just like consumer-centric businesses have done with their customers. From his thirty-five years of experience, Clinton advises that a relationship with voters must be seen as ongoing. must have a combination of communications channels ("radio, television, mail, Internet, telephone, conversations, and visits"), and must recognize and use the voters' favorite channels of communication; further, the most effective relationship occurs when voters are asked to participate in a tangible way.[62]

Political scientists Alan S. Gerber and Donald P. Green remind us of both the value and the limitations of phone calls. In a special edition on voter mobilization in the *Annals of the American Academy of Political and Social Science*, they note that field experiments showed that during the 2000 presidential election, "local non-partisan phone banks staffed by volunteer callers increased turnout among the young voters they targeted." In addition, volunteer phone banks increased turnout in 2002 of "low-propensity Latino voters." "Even commercial phone banks proved successful in 2002 when a special premium was paid to train and supervise callers reading longer, more interactive scripts," they concluded. But the problem is "not that phone calls are ineffective. The problem seems to be that mechanically delivered phone scripts are ineffective."[63]

Automated political telephone calls, commonly called "robocalls," have been with us since the mid-1970s. Here is a sample of a recorded message:

> Hi. This is [insert name] calling from Vote '98, a nonpartisan group working with the League of Women Voters. We just want to remind you that elections are being held this Tuesday.[64]

Recorded political messages, from get-out-the-vote alerts to advocacy messages from celebrities, have become staples of political communication. The barrage of commercial robocalls led to the Telephone Consumer Protection Act (TCPA) of 1991 and the creation of the Do Not Call Registry. Political messages, however, are exempt from this federal legislation. However, the TCPA prohibits prerecorded and predictive-dialed calls to cell phones, no matter whether they are for commercial purposes or political. In May 2014, gopcalls.com and Dialing Services LLC were hit with $2.9 million in fines for violating the cell phone provision. The AAPC considered this provision a "clear violation" of the First Amendment and pledged to support a lawsuit to overturn this provision.[65]

In recent election cycles, a majority of American voters received robocalls from candidates, political parties, and third-party interest groups.[66] One robocall vendor, Voice Broadcasting Corporation, boasts having placed 1.5 billion automated calls (not necessarily all political) since 1987, emphasizing the low price of between 1 and 7 cents per completed call.[67] "Automatically dial 12,000 people, all at once," Voice Broadcasting pitches on its website. "Don't cold call . . . use our dialer instead."

The following thirty-second automated voice recording was sent by the Republican National Committee and the McCain-Palin campaign during the 2008 general election:

> Hello. I'm calling for John McCain and the RNC because you need to know that Barack Obama has worked closely with domestic terrorist Bill Ayers, whose organization bombed the US Capitol, the Pentagon, a judge's home, and killed Americans. And Democrats will enact an extreme leftist agenda if they take control of Washington. Barack Obama and his Democratic allies lack the judgment to lead our country. This call was paid for by McCain-Palin 2008 and the Republican National Committee at 202-863-8500.[68]

The American Association of Political Consultants (AAPC) estimated in 2008 that 129 firms were in the business of providing robocalls, but that no more than 10 to 20 of those firms were professional political consulting firms.[69] There have been several federal attempts to require disclosure and further transparency of robocalls, and at least twenty-three states have developed regulations to limit political robocalls.

Do such robocalls work? Gerber and Green looked into the question of whether such calls increase voter turnout. In a large-scale field experiment during the 1998 general election involving more than 17,000 registered voters in West Haven, Connecticut, they found that phone canvassing "did not seem to affect voter turnout." Later tests in Iowa and Michigan further suggest "minimal positive effect."[70] Later, Gerber and Green, looking at the 2000 elections, concluded that "robocalls have a minimal effect on [voter] turnout . . . robocalls might help you to stretch your resources in ways that allow you to contact the maximum number of people, but don't expect to move them very much, if at all."[71]

One of Green and Gerber's suggestions— personal invitations from friends and neighbors—comes right out of the 1948 Larry O'Brien campaign playbook, and was used effectively in John Kennedy's congressional campaigns and, as seen in chapter 4, employed in the 1960 West Virginia primary to rally Kennedy supporters.

Green and Gerber summarized the cost effectiveness of several types of get-out-the-vote activities: door-to-door (one vote per 14 contacts; $19 per vote gained); partisan direct mail (one vote per 177 contacts; $59 per vote gained); commercial telephone calls from trained callers (1 vote per 30 completed calls; $45 per vote gained). Robocalls had no detectable effect, nor did e-mails.[72]

Not everyone, particularly political consultants, agreed with the rather dismal conclusions found in the field experiments. For example, Gerry Tyson, a Democratic consultant whose firm conducts robocalls, argues that the effectiveness of robocalls cannot be measured in isolation. "Statistically speaking," Tyson wrote, "[robocalls] probably have little effect when used in isolation. But used in combination with other forms of outreach, there is little doubt robocalls are effective."[73]

Telephone Communication Pioneers

Walter D. (Wally) Clinton (b. 1940), raised in Detroit, first got involved in politics working for the Robert Kennedy presidential campaign in 1968. Matt Reese left the Democratic National Committee and opened up his own consulting business in 1966. Clinton's sister worked at the DNC and she introduced her brother to Reese. Soon, Clinton was in the thick of politics and campaigning. "I walked in the door [of his firm], met Matt, and then I was on a plane the very same day working on a campaign," Clinton remembered.[74] Clinton worked for Reese for four years, then in 1971 he set up his own political telemarketing business, the Clinton Group. One of his first clients was the George McGovern campaign during the 1972 presidential primaries. Many hundreds of clients followed as the Clinton Group flourished in the business of political telephone communication.

Today, Clinton's firm is known as American Directions Group (ADG), and it has branched out to grassroots advocacy and targeting, mobilization of volunteers, market research, and campaign communications. ADG boasts of having recruited and mobilized more than 2 million grassroots activists, made 14 million survey calls, and worked on thousands of ballot initiatives and political campaigns in all fifty states, Canada, South and Central America, and Europe.[75] ADG also has substantial nonpolitical and government business. Clinton was inducted into the AAPC Hall of Fame in 2003.

On the Republican side, one of the most prominent phone bank and grassroots specialists is Jack Bonner. He is known mostly for his work in corporate grassroots and advocacy work, and is profiled in chapter 16.

CHAPTER 10

Consultants and Presidential Campaigns, 1972, 1976, and 1980

[The Nixon re-election campaign was] one of the
most spectacularly efficient exercises in political technology
in the entire postwar era.
                                                    —Theodore H. White (1973)

Forgive me, Mr. President, but as much as you love it,
you're a [expletive] campaigner.
                                        —Stuart K. Spencer to Gerald Ford (1976)

If you leave him alone and let him do what he wants to do,
what he feels comfortable with, we won't have any problems.
The problem is you guys, not him. Let Reagan be Reagan.
                              —Clifton White to assembled Reagan advisers (1979)

D
URING THE THREE presidential elections covered here, political consultants assumed an increasingly important role in helping shape the strategy
and message of presidential candidates. The Nixon 1972 re-election campaign extensively used private polling, under the direction of Robert Teeter. The
campaign invested in an extraordinary voter contact program headed by Fred
Malek, and under Jeb Stuart Magruder it ran an efficient, well-planned campaign. While defeated soundly, the McGovern campaign was important in the
history of political consulting: through Morris Dees, the campaign showed the
potential for direct mail solicitation; with Charles Guggenheim, it displayed the
artistry of a seasoned media consultant; and it launched the career of pollster
Patrick Caddell. John P. Sears III, working for Ronald Reagan in 1976, ran his first
national campaign for a presidential nomination; likewise, Doug Bailey and John
Deardourff became the principal media consultants for their first presidential

general election, working with Gerald Ford. Stuart Spencer assisted the Ford re-election, but in doing so he alienated his most important previous client, Ronald Reagan. Dick Wirthlin and Bob Teeter became major pollsters for Republican presidential candidates. Ed Rollins was selected as the campaign manager for Reagan's landslide victory in 1984, though it was primarily run out of the White House under James A. Baker III. On the Democratic side, Jerry Rafshoon followed his long-time client Jimmy Carter and became his media consultant, while Patrick Caddell worked in his second and third presidential campaign, this time for Jimmy Carter. In 1980, New York media consultant David Garth teamed up with independent candidate John Anderson. Other consultants, like Robert Squier, Peter Hart, Robert Shrum, Arthur Finkelstein, and Lee Atwater, also worked on presidential campaigns, but in secondary roles.

George McGovern surprised his better-known Democratic rivals but was no match for Richard Nixon, running for re-election. Nixon, with the memory of a razor-thin loss in 1960 and a close win in 1968, was taking no chances in 1972. His campaign was thorough, relentless, and clearly outmatched McGovern's efforts. The 1976 election featured a fierce intraparty fight between Reagan and Ford for the Republican nomination, a virtually unknown former Georgia governor, Jimmy Carter, who brilliantly defeated better-known rivals for his party's nomination, and the extraordinary comeback of Ford, from more than thirty points down to nearly defeat Carter. Ford, the accidental president, became the first chief executive since Hoover to be defeated. In 1980, Carter, dogged by the Iranian hostage crisis, sour economic times, and an intraparty challenge from Massachusetts senator Edward M. Kennedy, followed Ford into the defeat column. Reagan, sixty-nine years old and trying for the presidency for the third time, handily defeated Carter and third-party challenger John Anderson.

The 1972 Presidential Election: Richard Nixon v. George McGovern

> *Until the moment that one of the networks gave Ohio to the president,*
> *I personally felt that we were going to win that election.*
> —Gary Hart, campaign manager for George McGovern (1972)[1]

Kevin B. Phillips, a young aide to John Mitchell during the 1968 Nixon presidential campaign, wrote a best-selling book in 1970 arguing that the Republican Party was poised to become the dominant party for years to come. In *The Emerging Republican Majority*, Phillips noted that 57 percent of the American electorate had rejected the Democratic Party in 1968; Nixon was president, and there was now a golden opportunity for the Republican Party.[2] Phillips laid out his case, state by state, region by region, on how the Republican Party could prevail. His basic message was that the Republican Party should reach out to white southerners and suburbanites, shifting its focus away from the dwindling liberal, northeastern portion of the party. *Newsweek* called his book "The Political Bible of the Nixon Era." Another prescient book was Ben J. Wattenberg and Richard M. Scammon's *The Real Majority*, which warned that the Democratic Party was not focusing on average voters, on those who are "the unpoor, the unblack, and the unyoung."[3]

The Committee to Re-elect the President

Despite Phillips's optimism, Nixon campaign operatives were worried. Eighteen months before the 1972 election, the president's popularity was only in the mid-40s, and the war in Vietnam continued to beleaguer him. Jeb Stuart Magruder, heading up the re-election effort, said that the Nixon campaign feared that a centrist Democrat would be difficult to beat, and the "most formidable" would have been Maine senator Edmund Muskie, Humphrey's running mate in 1968.[4] Working for Muskie were Bob Squier and Bob Shrum, young operatives who would become influential consultants for Democratic candidates in the decades to come. But Muskie stumbled, and from a crowded field of Democratic challengers, South Dakota senator George McGovern emerged as the party's choice.[5]

The Nixon re-election committee was a separate operation from the Republican National Committee. Robert Odle Jr., one of those assigned to create the re-election committee, argued that while some were critical of Nixon going outside the national party, it was necessary because of two possible intraparty challenges, one from John Ashbrook, a conservative congressman from Ohio, and the other from a moderate-liberal congressman from California, Paul N. (Pete) McCloskey. More importantly, the decision to run a separate re-election campaign also gave Nixon's advisers free reign. Odle, given the task of coming up with the committee's name, went to wordsmith William Safire, who came up with the Committee for the Re-election of the President. But, Odle later confessed, "we never realized the acronym CREEP would arise. I always kidded Bill about that."[6]

For the Nixon re-election effort, John N. Mitchell once again was the titular campaign manager. While Mitchell was still attorney general, and before he resigned to take up his new duties, he asked Jeb Magruder to run the campaign. In his memoirs, Magruder assured the reader that he was in charge of everything: "Nothing was done in the campaign that I did not basically initiate. I formed the advertising agency, the November Group; I set up the polling situation; we set up the group that developed the campaign strategy; we set up every group, and everything, that related to a political campaign."[7] This blanket assertion, however, overlooks the supervisory role of Mitchell, the fundraising efforts of Maurice Stans, the fieldwork and get-out-the-vote efforts headed by Frederic V. (Fred) Malek, and the work of several political consultants.

Private polling. For the first time, a presidential campaign invested heavily in private polling. Robert M. Teeter, the thirty-three-year-old vice president of Market Opinion Research (MOR), headed the polling effort and coordinated the work of four national polling firms—MOR of Detroit, Decision Making Information (Richard Wirthlin's firm) along with Datamatics (Vince Barabba) of Los Angeles, and Opinion Research Corporation (Tom Henry and Harry

O'Neill) of Princeton, New Jersey. Teeter also recruited pollster Fred Steeper, and together they introduced new statistical and measurement techniques, including multivariate analysis.

Teeter designed the overall polling strategy and wrote memos on the findings of national and local issues. "We were able to hire everybody and try everything," Teeter remembered, "because we had so much money."[8] Money was not going to be a problem for the Committee for the Re-election of the President. On April 7, 1972, the new Federal Election Campaign Act, with its restrictions and reporting requirements, went into effect. The day before, according to journalist Rick Perlstein, "suitcases full of cash and negotiable securities were flying in [to the Nixon campaign office] in a frenzy."[9]

There were four separate "waves" of polling, starting in December 1971 and finishing with continuous telephone polling in targeted states during the last six weeks of the campaign, in what would be, in Magruder's estimation, "the most extensive polling program ever undertaken for a presidential candidate," spending some $1.3 million (not including secret funds).[10] During the election year 1972, the White House (not the re-election committee) commissioned 153 private surveys, three times as many polls they had commissioned in the previous year, and more than Kennedy and Johnson combined during their entire terms as president.[11]

The Nixon campaign wanted to know why Americans weren't warming up to the president, and they wanted to know voters' attitudes on policy issues.[12] The polls showed that voters saw Nixon as "informed, experienced, competent, safe, trained, and honest," he was not perceived to be "warm, open-minded, relaxed, or having a sense of humor." But one piece of character baggage that the campaigning didn't have to worry about anymore was the old "Tricky Dick" label: voters now thought that he was an honest statesman.[13] This, of course, was before the full implications of the Watergate scandal were known.

But for all the polling, the candidate was not always pleased. Late in the campaign, Nixon complained bitterly about Teeter's work: "Teeter's polling is a disaster," H. R. Haldeman wrote in his diary, reflecting Nixon's anger, because the pollster had focused "on our old constituency in the fashionable suburbs instead of the [Charles] Colson hardhats and blue collar types . . . [and has] ignored . . . the military, amnesty, [and] busing."[14] Despite Nixon's concerns, his campaign committee had set a high mark in private polling that was unmatched by any of his rivals.

The media campaign. Nixon's chief-of-staff, Haldeman, who in his earlier career was an executive at the advertising firm J. Walter Thompson, brought in his friend and fellow adman Peter H. Dailey to create a special advertising firm, with just one goal, the re-election of the president. The ad hoc firm was called the November Group, and, according to Dailey, it was "a fully staffed advertising agency from scratch for the sole purpose of working for the president. We planned to dissolve it after the election, which we did."[15] Dailey began working for the re-election campaign in October 1971; the November Group began its operation in February 1972. At its peak, the November Group had forty-five loyal

Nixon ad executives, borrowed from Madison Avenue agencies, working in its Manhattan offices.[16] An ad hoc agency served two purposes: First, it would assure tighter reign over the creative side. Granted the 1968 Nixon television commercials of Harry Treleaven and Roger Ailes were brilliant, but perhaps stung by the Joe McGinniss exposé, it was time to tighten up on outside creative types. Second, it was a chance to save the 15 percent commission that normally went to outside agencies, and turn it around to be used for more commercials.[17]

Dailey explained that the strategy of the media team was to "never allow the public to get the impression that there were two candidates for the office of president."[18] There was the Democratic *candidate* and the Republican *president*. This election would be a vote of confidence on Nixon's performance as president. In addition, the November Group ads were unique because, for the first time, they had been fully pretested: the various designs, slogans, and concepts were all screened to see which best resonated with Nixon-leaning voters.[19] The November Group aired no ads during the primary season and did not start its national advertising until September 25, fifteen days after the McGovern campaign began its television ads.

The McGovern Campaign

> The most exciting aspect of the 1972 election for me was that
> McGovern's perverse treatment of the traditional Democratic power
> blocs that had been the basis of every Democratic presidential
> victory for the last forty years had made possible the creation of a
> New Republican Majority as an electoral force in American politics.
> —Richard Nixon (1978)[20]

Senator George McGovern's primary campaign, improbable at the beginning, was successful against a tough Edmund Muskie, a still popular Hubert Humphrey, the well-liked former North Carolina governor Terry Sanford, and a tenacious George Wallace, now running in his third consecutive presidential race.[21] The 1972 Democratic nomination process marked a turning point: it was playing with a new set of rules. Following the tumult of the 1968 Democratic primaries, the Democratic Party established the Commission on Party Structure and Delegate Selection, called the McGovern-Fraser Commission, named after McGovern and Minnesota congressman Donald M. Fraser. From 1969 through 1972, the committee established a series of rules that opened up the nomination process, encouraged candidates to run in as many primaries as possible, and generally democratized the nomination and selection process.[22] The number of Democratic primaries increased from seventeen in 1968 to twenty-three in 1972, and as first chair of the commission, George McGovern was intimately familiar with its rules and its strategic implications.

McGovern's top aides were Frank Mankiewicz, forty-seven, a veteran of the 1968 Robert F. Kennedy campaign and a Washington political columnist; film producer Charles Guggenheim; Patrick Caddell, the twenty-one-year-old wunderkind pollster, who was still in college; direct mail specialist Morris Dees; and

Richard (Rick) Stearns, the director of research and delegate organizer. Working for the campaign in its Texas field operations were two Yale law school students, Bill Clinton and his girlfriend Hillary Rodham.[23] The campaign manager was Denver lawyer Gary Hart, thirty-four years old when he began working for McGovern in 1970. Hart had earlier worked in the 1968 Robert Kennedy campaign, then volunteered on the Democratic Party reform commission.[24] But one campaign insider insisted that McGovern, himself, was the real architect of the campaign. "Implicit in McGovern's choice of Hart was his decision to run his own campaign," wrote Gordon L. Weil, McGovern's executive aide. "In effect, Hart became McGovern's assistant, and the senator remained his own manager."[25]

Guggenheim, who had produced campaign ads for McGovern in two of his Senate races, wanted to portray him as the candidate for Middle America. McGovern's natural appeal was to young voters and liberals, but "the vast throng of hard-working urbanites, the fellow who pays most of the taxes, reads the *Reader's Digest*, and is on the cutting edge of most of today's social reforms, really doesn't know what to make of George McGovern," Guggenheim wrote in an August 1969 memo. McGovern's coalition didn't include "the people that Norman Rockwell painted."[26] That had to change.

Starting at the beginning of 1972, and throughout the campaign, Guggenheim did nearly all of the television and radio production for the campaign. The Guggenheim-produced advertising showed McGovern talking with ordinary citizens, sharing their frustrations over the futility of the Vietnam War.

The McGovern campaign entrusted its polling to an untested rookie. Gary Hart met Patrick Caddell in the fall of 1971 while on an organizational trip to Florida. At the time, Caddell was a twenty-one-year-old Harvard senior, with very limited polling experience, but driving ambition and enormous self-confidence. At Harvard he formed a survey research company with two other students and conducted statewide polls for candidates in Ohio, Florida, and other states. According to Hart, Caddell was certain that with the right kind of campaign, McGovern would win. The McGovern campaign had no money to pay Caddell, but the pollster came anyway to work on the New Hampshire primary.[27]

Another operative, Robert Shrum, was just getting his feet wet in politics. Shrum had worked as speechwriter for New York City mayor John V. Lindsay, then briefly worked for Edmund Muskie's 1972 primary campaign. When Muskie suspended his campaign, Shrum went over to the McGovern camp to help craft McGovern's speeches.[28]

The McGovern campaign was outgunned on all fronts: Nixon was the incumbent president, fresh from his historic visit to China; he had an experienced, savvy, and tightly disciplined campaign staff; and he had more campaign money (legal and otherwise) than McGovern could ever hope to obtain. One area, however, where the McGovern campaign was able to go up against Nixon was in direct mail fundraising. As seen in the previous chapter, direct mail became an important element in presidential campaigns beginning with the Goldwater campaign of 1964, and particularly with the emergence of Richard Viguerie on the conservative ledger of politics. For progressives and liberals, there was Morris Dees in the McGovern campaign.

McGovern sent out his first fundraising letter on January 15, 1971, set to coincide with his very presidential announcement. "Nobody's ever done this before," the letter went, "I want to run a campaign financed by tens of thousands of small contributions. That's how I want to build my organizational base, not with a lot of money from a few big contributors."[29]

Working with New York ad agency man Tom Collins, Dees crafted this seven-page letter, based on McGovern's Senate speeches. Some objected to its length, but Dees insisted that, based on his experience, the longer letter was more compelling than a shorter one. The letter, sent to 240,000 names that had been gathered over the years by McGovern, had to be trimmed along the edges, in order to get it under one ounce of weight, thus avoiding higher postage rates.[30] With a remarkable 15 percent return rate (a 2 percent return now is considered very successful), Dees was able to focus on loyal contributors, who would make a $10 or so commitment every month. Through the direct mail approach, the McGovern campaign was able to have an assured income of $50,000 a month.[31] Much of the McGovern campaign was day-to-day, depending on what money would come in. Media consultant Charles Guggenheim, whose commercials wouldn't get aired without campaign funds, commented, "I would call Morris and say, 'How much money do we have?' And he would say, 'Well, we haven't opened the mail yet.'"[32]

As it became evident that McGovern would win the Democratic nomination, many party leaders were having considerable misgivings about November. Consultant Joe Napolitan urged Democratic governors, assembled at the annual national governor's meeting, to forego a nationwide battle against Nixon, but concentrate their meager resources on just twenty states, which held 318 electoral votes (48 more than were needed to win) and concede the rest. The reaction from the governors was swift and negative: Napolitan was dead wrong, and they resolved to take the fight to every state. Napolitan's strategy would have written off all the southern states, except Texas. This led Georgia governor Jimmy Carter to declare, "There are not many things that would make me withdraw from the Democratic Party but the adoption of this program is one of them."[33] Napolitan was right, however: scarce resources had to be parceled out to the most winnable battleground states. But there wasn't much that was winnable. The McGovern campaign indeed ignored the South; the South (and the rest of the country) returned the compliment.

Watergate and Eagleton

Two episodes colored the presidential campaign. The first was the Watergate break-in and its subsequent fallout. Watergate, of course, became an all-consuming issue during 1973 and 1974, with its own cast of characters, subpoenas, special congressional investigations, an eighteen-minute gap in the Nixon taping system, and the real threat of the impeachment of the president. Late in the campaign, McGovern charged that Nixon was the most deceitful president and headed the "most corrupt administration in history."[34] But Watergate—the presidential crime story of the century—was just not on the radar screen of journalists or voters during the presidential election. When asked about the impact of the early Watergate revelations, Caddell said that it had very little impact on voters. Rick Stearns observed that most voters viewed Watergate as "nothing exceptional" but for the fact that "the perpetrators were caught."[35]

Even opinion leaders, through their newspaper columns, overlooked the biggest story they would ever cover. A study by Robert C. Maynard of 500 opinion columns written from June 1972 (when the Watergate break-in occurred) to November 1972, showed that fewer than two dozen articles featured the Watergate break-in.[36] The McGovern team late in the campaign put together a commercial, "Break-In," to highlight Watergate (without ever mentioning "Watergate"), but voters simply weren't concerned. Further, Nixon was sounding tough and presidential and urging law enforcement to get to the bottom of this "third-rate burglary." At an October news conference, Nixon pointed out that some 133 FBI agents had been assigned the task of getting to the bottom of the Watergate episode. The president approved of their work: "I wanted every lead carried out to the end because I wanted to be sure that no member of the White House Staff and no man or woman in a position of major responsibility in the Committee for the Re-election had anything to do with this kind of reprehensible activity."[37]

What caught voters' attention, however, was the Eagleton affair. McGovern had considerable difficulty in convincing well-known Democrats to run with him. Edward Kennedy, Edmund Muskie, and, as it turned out, twenty-two others rejected McGovern's offer.[38] Then McGovern found his running mate, Missouri senator Thomas F. Eagleton; but the McGovern-Eagleton ticket lasted just eighteen days. Eagleton was found to have undergone treatment for mental illness, and the electorate just wasn't ready to accept his condition. McGovern publicly announced that he was "1,000 percent for Tom Eagleton" and "had no intention of dropping him from the ticket." He repeated the 1,000 percent remark personally to Eagleton the night before he unceremoniously dropped him from the ticket.[39] Eagleton's condition was not a secret: Congressman Thomas B. Curtis, running unsuccessfully against Eagleton in 1968 for the US Senate seat from Missouri, knew of but refused to make an issue of Eagleton's mental condition.[40] The damage to McGovern's reputation was considerable: until this time, the usual criticism was that he was "too liberal," but now an overwhelming number of critical voters thought that McGovern was "weak and vacillating and a man who did not keep his promises."[41] The *Washington Post* commented on McGovern's steep decline after the Eagleton episode: "Seldom has the public perception of a major political figure changed so rapidly."[42]

The General Election

Despite having far less money to spend, the McGovern campaign invested far more on television ads than did the Nixon team. In all, Nixon's November Group spent only $4 million on campaign ads, about two-thirds of what the Nixon campaign had spent in 1968. The McGovern campaign, heavily banking on television commercials, spent $6.2 million.[43] Nixon's commercials were short spots, emphasizing his experience and the vital duties of the president: Nixon the peacemaker visiting Russia, China, and India, signing treaties, and meeting world leaders. The commercials ended with the same tag line: "President Nixon: Now More Than Ever."

To show the more human side of Nixon, the November Group produced a two-minute bubbly montage of a smiling Nixon in crowds of young people, blue-collar workers, foreign leaders, and political gatherings, with a chorus of men and women singing in the background. The repeated refrain was

> Nixon now, Nixon now.
> He's made the difference,
> He's showed us how.
> Nixon now, Nixon now,
> More than ever, Nixon now.
> Listen, America, Nixon now.

In another ad, Nixon smiles and plays "Happy Birthday" on the piano in a celebration for jazz legend Duke Ellington.

But the Nixon advertising also went after McGovern. Probably the most memorable of the November Group's negative ads was called "McGovern's Defense Plan."[44] Toy soldiers, airplanes, and ships on a table represented the American military.

[*Video: Camera focuses on toy soldiers.*]

[*Audio: Military drumbeat.*]

Announcer (voice-over): The McGovern defense plan.

[*Video: A hand sweeps several soldiers away.*]

Announcer: He would cut the Marines by one-third.

[*Video: More soldiers are taken off the table.*]

Announcer: The Air Force by one-third.

[*Video: More soldiers are taken off the table.*]

Announcer: He would cut the Navy personnel by one-fourth.

[*Video: Toy airplanes, removed from table.*]

Announcer: He would cut interceptor planes by one-half,

[*Video: Toy ships, removed from table.*]

Announcer: the Navy fleet by one-half, and

[*Video: Toy carriers; removed from table.*]

Announcer: carriers from sixteen to six.

[*Video: Toys in a jumble on the floor.*]

Announcer: Senator Hubert Humphrey has this to say about the McGovern proposal: "It isn't just cutting into the fat. It isn't just cutting into manpower. It's cutting into the very security of this country."]

[*Video: Nixon onboard a naval ship.*]

Announcer (with "Hail to the Chief" played in the background): President Nixon doesn't believe we should play games with our national security. He believes in a strong America to negotiate for peace from strength.

[*Text*: Democrats for Nixon]

In the future, similar ads would target Michael Dukakis, in his infamous tank ride, in 1988, and John Kerry in 2004.

But perhaps the most damaging news of all for the McGovern peace plank was the announcement late in the general election by Henry Kissinger, the master of high-stakes legerdemain and shuttle diplomacy. After years of toiling to get an agreement between North and South Vietnam forces, Kissinger announced, "We believe peace is at hand."[45] Kissinger's October 26 announcement came four days after Nixon announced a cessation of all bombing.

Voter contact. The Nixon campaign also invested heavily in voter contact, having a total budget of $12 million, with $5 million devoted to direct mail and another $3 million to telephone banks—record amounts for a presidential campaign.[46] The Nixon committee, now headed by former Minnesota congressman Clark MacGregor and his deputy Fred Malek, worked closely with the Republican National Committee to put together a data bank of voters for its voter identification and get-out-the-vote activities. By October 1, just five weeks before Election Day, Malek's operatives had established 2,000 Republican campaign storefronts throughout the country and operated 250 phone banks. In California alone, there were 170 storefront campaign offices, 30,000 precinct-walking volunteers, and 40 telephone centers.[47] Computer technology, as primitive as it was in 1972, sorted out US census data to identify likely voters. One of the young operatives identifying probable Nixon pockets of support was twenty-seven-year-old Arthur J. Finkelstein, who would later go onto his own major career as a Republican strategist (see chapter 7 for a biographical sketch).

The big Chicago mail order firm R. R. Donnelley printed and mailed 17 million pieces—far more than was ever printed in past presidential elections, with slightly different messages to different groups. In the letters that went to New Jersey addresses, for example, different letters were sent to "Democrats for Nixon, Italian," "Democrats for Nixon, Veteran," "Democrats for Nixon, Middle Income," "Older Republican," "Democrats for Nixon, Older Peripheral Ethnic," "Democrats for Nixon, Peripheral Urban Ethnic," and "Concerned Citizens."[48] Altogether, the campaign directly contacted 15.9 million voters, either through the mail or through personal visits.[49]

Jeb Magruder, writing in his memoirs, was not above self-congratulations: "I may be prejudiced, but I believe the 1972 Nixon campaign was the best-planned, best-organized, best-run presidential campaign in American history, and there was no way that Senator McGovern, with the time and money at his command, could come close to equaling it."[50] Magruder's observations may have been self-serving, but they were also true. McGovern was simply outmanned, outmaneuvered, and outspent. Reporters Jack W. Germond and Jules Witcover agreed, calling the Nixon effort a "technically masterful campaign," in which the president's managers "controlled to an exceptional degree what their candidate said and did, where he went, what the television cameras were able to reveal of him, and the results were almost invariably self-serving."[51]

McGovern's media campaign, directed by Guggenheim, featured the candidate talking with factory workers and wounded veterans in hospitals, emphasizing his opposition to the war, finishing with the tag line: "McGovern. Democrat. For the People." But some Democratic leaders, particularly Larry O'Brien, chair of the DNC, were "increasingly unhappy" with the McGovern spots. They were, in O'Brien's words "low-keyed films," the same kinds of spots used during the primaries.[52] But now, during the last stretch of the campaign, with McGovern twenty points down, it was time to try a more hard-hitting approach. O'Brien called in veteran ad maker Tony Schwartz. Schwartz produced five spots, all attacking Nixon, but just two were eventually aired. Schwartz bragged that his works were "masterpieces," but even his wizardry had little impact, if any, on the ultimate crushing of the McGovern campaign.[53]

Did any of the ads—Nixon or McGovern—make a difference? Scholars Thomas E. Patterson and Robert D. McClure analyzed the effectiveness of the 1972 campaign ads and found that the ads influenced about 3 percent of the total electorate and roughly 16 percent of those voters who were making up their minds during the general election.[54] But 1972 was a blowout, and no matter the efforts of the media teams, it really made no difference.

Guggenheim was discouraged by the whole process: "You become . . . so involved in winning that you no longer discuss issues and character of their merits. You are sparring, looking for ways to jab and get out. . . . They're not bad people. They're fundamentally in a bad business. . . . I think the system is sick."[55] Guggenheim found that polling research was increasingly driving the content of television advertising, driving out the inherent creative process of ad making. "I became more irrelevant," he confessed. "If you play a piano in a house of ill repute, it doesn't make any difference how well you play the piano."[56]

The opening of this section on the 1972 election quotes Gary Hart clinging to a thread of hope for victory on Election Day. Assuming he was saying this with a straight face, it is almost impossible to believe that an astute campaign manager would be so confident as his client headed toward one of the most lopsided defeats in twentieth-century presidential elections. Election Day found 60.7 percent of the votes cast for Nixon, and only 37.7 percent for McGovern, with Nixon winning 520 electoral votes and McGovern winning just Massachusetts (14 electoral votes) and the District of Columbia (3). McGovern couldn't even win his home state, South Dakota. In the twentieth century, only Republican candidate Alf Landon in 1936 gained fewer electoral votes, when he won a total of 8 from Maine and Vermont. Just as lopsided would be the 1984 campaign, with President Reagan winning forty-nine states and 525 electoral votes with former vice-president Walter F. Mondale just barely winning his home state of Minnesota (10) and the reliably Democratic Washington, DC (3).

Bob Shrum, then a twenty-eight-year-old operative working for the McGovern campaign, was given the unenviable task of explaining to the candidate during the final days of the campaign that he was going to lose, and lose big time. Frank Mankiewicz and Gary Hart (clearly ambivalent) were concerned that McGovern might think he still had a chance, and on the Sunday before Election Day, Shrum was dispatched to McGovern's suite to lay out the reality of his inevitable loss. In his memoirs, Shrum wrote, "McGovern asked me to sit down on the couch and went over and poured us each a vodka on the rocks. He handed me one, thanked me, and said, 'Bob, I know, I know. But I just need to believe for one more day.' "[57]

The 1976 Presidential Election: Gerald Ford v. Jimmy Carter

> *In 1976 Ford and Carter ran the first presidential race in which*
> *outside consultants weren't simply known but celebrated.*
> —Journalist and former campaign consultant Victor Gold (1996)[58]

> *Wirthlin's polls said we had a shot at it.*
> *We all said "Go for it."*
> —Lyn Nofziger, Reagan campaign adviser (1974)[59]

Nixon was triumphant in the 1972 re-election campaign, but by late 1974 his party was in shambles. The Watergate scandal, Nixon's ignominious resignation, Ford's controversial pardon, and the debilitating congressional election defeats in November 1974 left the Republican Party reeling. Party chair George H. W. Bush left office in September 1974 to head the US liaison office in Beijing, and Mary Louise Smith stepped in as chair just as the Republicans suffered disastrous defeats in the November midterm elections. Eddie Mahe, the newly appointed RNC executive director, wanted to know the damage done to his party, so he scraped together some money for a poll conducted by Market Opinion Research, Bob Teeter's firm. The news was not good: after Watergate and the pardoning of Richard Nixon, only 18 percent of Americans self-identified as Republicans. Teeter observed, "We are no longer the minority party, we are now a minor party, much like in Canada, because when you drop below 20 percent, you are no longer a minority party, you are then a minor party." Around Thanksgiving 1974, Mahe was forced to close down the RNC building for a month, because he didn't have enough money to pay for it to stay open.[60]

The Republican Primary: Ford v. Reagan

> *Primary fights are a lot more emotional,*
> *corrosive, and painful than general elections.*
> —Mary Matalin (1994)[61]

It was an especially challenging time for President Gerald R. Ford. In December 1973, Ford, the long-serving minority leader in the House of Representatives, was sworn in as vice president, taking over from the disgraced Spiro T. Agnew. On August 9, 1974, following the resignation of Richard Nixon, he was sworn in as president. Immediately following the presidential swearing-in ceremony, Ford addressed a nationwide television audience, saying, "I am acutely aware that you have not elected me as your president by your ballots, and so I ask you to confirm me as your president with your prayers."[62] The Gallup Poll gave Ford a 71 percent approval rating the week after he became president, but this approval rate fell precipitously to 50 percent following his controversial pardon of Nixon in early September. Soon, he would face a strong challenge from within his own party, and his approval rating would fall to just 37 percent in March 1975, during the thick of the Republican primaries.[63]

The poll results troubled Ford's White House staff and his campaign team. Even more worrisome was the fact that Ford had no experience in running for a state-wide or national office. Pollster Bob Teeter reflected on Ford's weaknesses: First, Ford had been a congressman throughout his political career, and the only time he had ever been seriously challenged was during the 1948 Republican primary when he first ran for office. Second, Ford didn't understand how to run against another Republican, particularly the popular Ronald Reagan, who was positioning himself as the true conservative alternative. Ford was the first modern president who had never been through a presidential general election process, and he didn't really understand who made up a potential winning constituency. Third, not only was Ford untested, but his White House staff also had little national campaign experience. Further, Ford was unknown to most people: Teeter's surveys showed that voters didn't know whether he was moderate, liberal, or conservative; most didn't know he was a lawyer; and, particularly worrisome, voters had no strong psychological commitment to him as president.[64]

Ford had been handpicked by Nixon, not by the American people, and certainly not by conservative Republicans. Conservatives were particularly upset when Ford chose their nemesis, Nelson A. Rockefeller, to be his vice president. The overwhelming choice for conservative Republicans was Ronald Reagan, who was about to complete his second term as governor of California in January 1975. Yet Reagan didn't make a firm decision to run until the end of September 1975. His pollster, Richard Wirthlin, had taken surveys exploring the idea of a Reagan candidacy as early as July 1974, a month before Nixon resigned and while Ford had been vice president for less than seven months. In a September 1975 poll, Wirthlin sought to determine the answers to four questions: First, what were Reagan's chances of winning the Republican nomination? Second, would a Reagan nomination split the Republican Party, and if it did, could the party come back during the general election? Third, what were the major issues? And finally, what might a winning coalition look like?[65] The poll showed that Ford gathered only a slim majority, that Reagan would be a stronger candidate, that an outsider would have a very good chance, and that there was a probable winning coalition of the Republican base, southern support, "soft" Democrats, and middle-income nonprofessionals, who were increasingly irritated at increased taxes and what they saw as wasteful welfare payments.[66]

As the Reagan team prepared for the announcement, it didn't merely rely on public opinion polls. In October 1974, even before Reagan had completed his second term as governor, aides Michael Deaver and Peter Hannaford developed a media plan to promote Reagan through speeches, radio commentary, and newspaper columns. Then Deaver and Hannaford set up their own public relations shop to handle the private citizen Ronald Reagan.[67] To communicate Reagan's ideas to a larger public, they used five-minute commentaries, under the banner "Viewpoint," which were aired nationwide over 286 radio stations. They also used opinion columns, published in 226 newspapers, which reached 20 million Americans weekly.[68] Reagan's views reached sympathetic audiences, particularly in the South and Midwest, where many voters agreed with his tough stand against welfare cheaters, his plea for traditional moral values, and his not too subtle denouncing of the Ford administration's policies.[69]

Campaign operatives were also coming on board. In the spring of 1974, Reagan staff assistant Robert Walker and Washington office head James Lake began discussions with John P. Sears III, the thirty-four-year-old campaign operative who had assisted Nixon in 1968. Reagan was impressed with Sears because of his knowledge of Washington and prescient observation that Nixon would soon resign. Together with other Reagan insiders—Lyn Nofziger, Hannaford, Deaver, Ed Meese, Jim Jenkins—they began planning a Reagan run for the nomination.[70]

Armed with positive polling data and a successful communication outreach program, lining up his political team, and gathering key political support from fellow conservatives, Reagan was ready. He announced his candidacy for the Republican nomination at the National Press Club in Washington, DC, on November 20, 1975.

Gerald Ford's campaign was doing its own pre-primary analyses. In November 1975, just before Reagan's announcement, Teeter outlined to Dick Cheney, White House chief of staff, what President Ford had to do to be prepared not only for the fight against a yet unknown Democratic opponent, but also against a probable challenge from within his own party, from Ronald Reagan.[71] As for Reagan, Teeter argued, while only half the voters felt they knew much about him, Republicans had a "very positive" perception: he was "bold, decisive, strong, intelligent, and competent," and without any discernible negatives. However, while Ford led Reagan in almost every state, his support was soft, and there was no "aura of being president." Ford's strong points were that he was warm, friendly, and honest. He shouldn't sound strident and "should not say things that most people don't think are true." The president, Teeter wrote, "needs to appear more presidential," and the White House "badly needs" to find some positions for the president that are outside of the usual Republican stereotype, such as Nixon going to China, or Jerry Brown talking about cutting spending in California. Further, Ford was "failing to communicate with a large share of the voters." He should talk in simple terms about how his programs benefit people, not how it affects institutions of government.[72] Clifton White, who served as Ford's manager at the Republican convention, put it bluntly: "On the campaign trail he comported himself more like a man struggling to retain his seat in Congress than like an incumbent president."[73] The campaign even hired Don Penny, a former television comedian, to coach Ford on how to deliver his lines.[74]

The Ford strategists determined that the campaign should adopt a "Rose Garden" strategy: showing the president signing bills and officiating over award ceremonies in the Rose Garden of the White House, not attacking his opponents, and not overtly campaigning, but just looking and acting presidential. It worked for Nixon in 1972; perhaps it would work for Ford in 1976.[75]

The "Rose Garden" strategy might hide the reality that Ford was not a particularly good campaigner. Stuart Spencer had a low opinion of Ford's campaign skills; Teeter noted that when Ford campaigned strenuously, he wasn't effective. The president became more strident as he became increasingly tired after having given five or six speeches during the course of a campaign day. "I think that any president would probably do better as president than as a candidate, but it had to be doubly or triply true with President Ford because he's a very, very poor stump speaker."[76]

The first Ford campaign manager was former Georgia congressman and secretary of the Army Howard H. (Bo) Callaway. But Callaway was soon implicated in an influence-peddling scheme involving a Colorado ski resort. His replacement was former Maryland congressman and Ford secretary of commerce Rogers C. B. Morton. What the campaign really needed, however, was a tested campaign veteran, and it was fortunate in persuading Stuart Spencer, Reagan's two-time gubernatorial consultant, to be Ford's campaign manager. Spencer was available because of a simmering feud with Michael Deaver that kept him away from Reagan. In his memoirs, California operative Lyn Nofziger wrote that Deaver's decision to exile Spencer "may well have cost Reagan the nomination."[77]

In early 1975, Donald Rumsfeld, then Ford's chief of staff, called Spencer in California, saying "we're having all kinds of problems" with the Ford campaign. According to Spencer, the Ford campaign "conned" him into coming in for the primaries but staying for the general election. He was only supposed to be for the New Hampshire and Florida primaries, two of the early contests, he said. Spencer was ready to go home, but Washington veteran Bryce Harlow convinced him otherwise: "You're not going home." Spencer replied, "What do you mean I'm not going home?" Harlow said, "No, you're not going to go home." That night, Spencer had dinner with President Ford and realized, indeed, he wasn't going home. "Hey, I need you, you stay," Ford told the consultant.[78] Why would he jump from Reagan, the candidate who made Spencer-Roberts famous, and work for Ford? Years later, Spencer reflected on that decision:

> I had an opportunity here. I liked Gerald Ford. I've always had the philosophy that you don't run against a sitting incumbent in your own party. . . .
> It wasn't a matter of being vindictive. It was an opportunity professionally to go national with a sitting president in my own party, knowing full well I was never going to be invited into the primary process any other way.[79]

The Reagans, and certainly the Reagan palace guard, didn't see it that way: they thought Spencer was, in Spencer's words, "a big traitor."[80] They were even more incensed when they were on the receiving end of Spencer's campaign barbs. "It was Stu getting even," said Deaver. "He knew exactly what would make Ronald Reagan blow, what would get to him. And when he finally used it in '76—Reagan blew."[81]

Reagan was on the defensive right before the New Hampshire primary, forced to defend his proposal to cut $90 billion in federal programs and transfer (or eliminate) them at the state level. This proposal, written for Reagan by conservative activist Jeffrey Bell, at first drew little press scrutiny, but Stuart Spencer recognized "the potential for mischief" immediately and worked the press.[82] As the devilish details—that a state like New Hampshire would have to raise its taxes to offset the federal cuts—became reality, the $90 billion proposal became an albatross around Reagan's neck, and it was ridiculed by opponents and the press alike.[83]

Richard Wirthlin was again the lead pollster for Ronald Reagan. For some time, commercial firms had done tracking polls or rolling samples, and Wirthlin had used this technique with his client Maxwell House Coffee in the late 1960s. Now, for the first time in a political campaign, he used the technique of calling a relatively small number of people each day and averaging the results over time. He did this in the 1976 New Hampshire primary; unfortunately for his client, the tracking polls showed Ford pulling ahead during the last week before the primary.[84]

When Reagan answered a reporter's hypothetical question, saying he could imagine a circumstance where the United States would join a UN peacekeeping delegation to Rhodesia, the Ford campaign, and particularly Stuart Spencer, was ready to strike. Spencer prepared a devastating commercial, on the eve of the California primary, which had this tag line: "When you vote Tuesday, remember: *Governor* Reagan couldn't start a war. *President* Reagan could." When told about the commercial, Reagan "went into a rage slamming his fist into the bulkhead wall" of the campaign's airplane, according to aide Michael Deaver.[85] In her memoirs, Nancy Reagan confessed that "it was quite a while before I could forgive Stu for that one."[86]

Reagan fared poorly in the early primaries, losing to Ford in New Hampshire, Vermont, Massachusetts, and Illinois. Reagan also lost in Florida, where Spencer had sent his partner Bill Roberts to assist the campaign, and "cut Reagan into little pieces."[87] Not wanting any further embarrassment to her husband's reputation, Nancy Reagan grabbed consultant Lyn Nofziger, who had recently joined the team after campaign manager Sears had been fired, and said, "Lyn, you know you've got to get Ronnie out of this race. We can't embarrass him any further." But Nofziger was saved from going against Mrs. Reagan's wishes when the candidate popped into the room and declared "Lynwood, I'm not going to get out of this race. I am going to stay in this through Texas."[88] Then came the North Carolina primary, the critical turning point in Reagan's fortunes.

Tom Ellis, a conservative political operative working with the recently elected US senator from North Carolina, Jesse Helms, and pollster Arthur J. Finkelstein ran a hard-hitting, aggressive campaign on Reagan's behalf in the North Carolina primary, and Reagan was able to notch his first victory.[89] The campaign featured the "carnivorous conservatism" of the North Carolina Republican right wing, not the "statesmanlike moderation" of John Sears; in fact, the Sears people were told to stay out of North Carolina.[90] Under the direction of Finkelstein and Ellis, Carter Wrenn produced a list of Republican primary voters—something never done before in that state—some 80,000 names that were key to Reagan's ultimate victory. Ford spent two lukewarm days campaigning in North Carolina, while Reagan spent nearly two weeks, aided by Jesse Helms and his operatives, and an avalanche of direct mail.[91]

The North Carolina victory was sweet, but there was still much to do for the Reagan team. Running short of campaign money and needing an issue to grab the attention of conservatives, both Wirthlin and Finkelstein saw in their polling data that the Panama Canal "giveaway" was an opening. Ford was among five recent American presidents who endorsed a treaty returning control of the canal to the government of Panama. Reagan saw it otherwise: he reminded conservative audiences that spring that "We built it, we paid for it, it's ours, and we are going to keep it." The red-meat comments were poll-driven, much like Reagan's muted responses toward the canal issue years later when he was president.[92]

During the hard-fought primaries, the Reagan campaign turned to Harry Treleaven, the former J. Walter Thompson Company advertising executive, who had overseen the television advertising for Richard Nixon's 1968 presidential campaign. The campaign faced an important issue: How do you present the photogenic, veteran former actor? One side of the campaign said, just let him get in front of the camera and talk. The other side, led by Treleaven, wanted Reagan to interact with citizens, not other actors, and to present something of a cinema vérité quality to the ads. The Treleaven approach had Reagan answering questions from voters at what were called Citizens' Press Conferences, shot in New Hampshire. Reagan stood before a lectern, folks would ask questions, and he would reply. Treleaven's crew filmed the events, then edited the material down to thirty- or sixty-second spots. It turned out that Treleaven's fear—that Reagan would remind voters of an actor if he just spoke in front of a camera—didn't materialize. When Wirthlin asked, it turned out that voters didn't care or mind that Reagan had been a former actor.[93]

Reagan's closest political advisers—Nofziger, Edwin Meese, Deaver, Martin Anderson, Hannaford, and Wirthlin—were all westerners. John Sears, the campaign manager, however, was an easterner, an outsider. Deaver wanted to bring Sears in to manage the Reagan primaries in order to give the campaign national credibility: "We were very sensitive to the fact that the eastern establishment still dominated elite thinking in America, and Reagan was never its ideal candidate. Sears especially would give us an in with the East Coast graybeards, we figured," wrote Deaver.[94] Sears, a native New Yorker, had helped Nixon gain the 1968 Republican nomination for president.

This certainly wouldn't be the last time a candidate tried to enhance his credibility by showcasing his high-profile consultants. But there were problems: while he was impressive, savvy to the ways of Washington, and right in his estimation that Nixon was on borrowed time, Sears rubbed many of the Reagan loyalists the wrong way. He drank too much, and his ultimate loyalty to Reagan was in question. Wirthlin, in his memoirs, wrote that the problem with Sears "was that he didn't understand Ronald Reagan. . . . Sears didn't seem to share our passion for Reagan's vision of what American could become under his leadership, and it wasn't always clear whose interests he was serving."[95] Yet, at times, Sears was a brilliant campaign strategist.[96] But at the nominating convention, he was simply too clever by half: Sears convinced Reagan to announce as his vice-presidential running mate Pennsylvania senator Richard S. Schweiker, a moderate centrist. It was a gamble to break up the eastern establishment resistance to Reagan.[97] But the gambit upset conservatives, changed no votes, and cost Reagan the momentum he needed to defeat Ford on the first ballot.

What saved Gerald Ford and secured him the nomination was his trump card: he was the president. His general election media adviser, John Deardourff, remarked, "The president was the president. If it had been Reagan against Ford and Ford had not been president, [Ford] would have lost."[98]

In the end, Reagan fell 70 votes short of the required 1,070 delegates to win the Republican nomination. He then put on the politician's smiling face, pledged his support for Ford, but campaigned only halfheartedly on the president's behalf. The bitterness lingered just below the surface, while Reagan's operatives immediately began planning for the 1980 campaign.

The Democratic Primary and Jimmy Carter

Georgia governor Jimmy Carter had tried before: he sought the vice-presidential nomination in 1972 when George McGovern was nominated. Pollster Bill Hamilton surveyed Georgia voters and found, not surprisingly, that McGovern would be much better in the South if he had a Georgian (Carter) on his ticket. But when Carter's name came up in McGovern strategy meetings, "some vile language was used and my name was immediately rejected," Carter recalled in his memoirs.[99] It was soon thereafter that Carter began preparing for his own presidential bid. The presidential campaign in 1972 was hardly over before Hamilton Jordan, Carter's chief strategist, prepared a seventy-two page memorandum outlining a Carter presidential victory plan for 1976.[100] Jordan recommended concentrating efforts in selected states, but Carter decided to enter as many as possible.

Carter hit the campaign trail in earnest in 1975, reaching out to local contacts and friends in forty-six states. At his side was his traveling companion and press aide, Joseph L. (Jody) Powell. Thirty-two years old, Powell was described by journalist Martin Schram as a man of "mature judgment and candid, self-effacing style" whose counsel had the "attention and respect" of Carter. The former Georgia governor couldn't get the attention of the national media, but the

Carter campaign began sending out a nationwide newsletter, with clips from all the places Carter visited and the contacts he had made.[101]

In 1976, for the first time, the Iowa caucus became an important launching platform for the presidential candidates.[102] Carter astutely and doggedly spent many months in Iowa, cultivating the support of Democratic loyalists, literally one person and one coffee hour at a time. It paid off: in a Gallup Poll taken right before the Iowa caucus, just 4 percent of national Democrats said they would likely support Carter.[103] But Carter had done his homework and legwork. He won the Iowa caucus, garnering fewer than 14,000 votes (27.5 percent) from the 50,000 Democrats who showed up during that cold evening of January 19, with Indiana senator Birch E. Bayh Jr. coming in second and former Oklahoma senator Fred R. Harris coming in third (ironically, "undecided" beat everyone with 37.16 percent).[104] The next morning, Carter was in the studios of the New York morning television shows, where he was hailed the "front-runner."

The next crucial test was the New Hampshire primary, held on February 24; it was a "must win" for Carter to show that the Iowa victory was not a fluke. According to Gerald (Jerry) Rafshoon, Carter's media adviser, "we made New Hampshire a showcase for presenting Jimmy Carter as the candidate from outside Washington, as the centrist, as the Democratic candidate who could win the election."[105] Jody Powell remarked that the Carter camp was successful "in creating the one candidate opposition—us against everybody else—by painting Congressman [Morris K.] Udall and Senator Bayh as being all of one piece."[106]

The Democratic primary campaign had thirteen candidates vying for the nomination, but Carter was the only Democratic candidate to pursue a "run everywhere" strategy.[107] After his Iowa caucus and New Hampshire primary victories, probably the most important win was Florida, where Carter fended off both George Wallace and Jesse Jackson. In the end, Carter won twenty-one of the thirty-two primaries or caucuses, fighting off a last-minute "stop Carter" movement launched by Udall and California governor Edmund G. (Jerry) Brown Jr. *Time* magazine gushed over Carter, the heretofore unknown former governor with little national visibility, calling him "one of the most phenomenal politicians to rise on the American political scene in this century."[108] Republican consultant Stuart Spencer later applauded the Carter primary campaign as "was one of the best campaigns I've ever seen in my lifetime."[109]

Recent presidential nomination conventions had witnessed a divided and bitter Democratic Party versus a unified and harmonious Republican Party.[110] But 1976 was different. Carter won fairly early, despite a futile last-minute challenge. On the Republican side, however, the nomination was not settled until the end of the rancorous first ballot.

The General Election

The Ford campaign team, under the direction of Richard Cheney, along with Michael Duval, Jerry Jones, Foster Chanock, and pollster Bob Teeter, developed a 120-page election strategy memo. Journalist Martin Schram characterized it as "one of the most remarkable presidential memos ever prepared in a White House" and "remarkably accurate in pinpointing" Carter's vulnerabilities.[111] The Ford team was inspired by Harry Truman's seemingly impossible battle for election in 1948. That year, Truman's aide Clark Clifford prepared a prescient forty-three-page campaign strategy memo. The Ford team, while understanding the many differences between the 1948 and 1976 campaigns, actually went to the Truman Library in Independence, Missouri, to obtain a copy of the famous memo.[112] The basic message of the Ford campaign message was laid out in stark terms: "No president has overcome the obstacles to election which you will following the convention this August." But "we firmly believe that you can win in November." The campaign plan proved to be "remarkably accurate" in showing where Carter was strong (religious, ethical, conservative, a regular Democrat), but also how he could be attacked, showing him to be inexperienced, arrogant, lacking a record of accomplishment, vague and unspecific, and "devious and highly partisan."[113]

The campaign image-makers decided that Ford needed to project a more friendly, down-to-earth look. The earlier suit-and-tie presidential image was replaced during much of the general election advertising with a casual slacks-and-cardigan look. (Carter's image went in just the opposite direction: from the peanut farmer, wearing an open-collar plaid shirt—a first in presidential television ad history—to Carter the serious presidential candidate, wearing a dark suit and sober tie.)[114]

During the primaries, Ford called on ad maker Peter H. Dailey of Los Angeles, who four years earlier had created the November Group for the Nixon campaign. Working for Dailey was Bruce Wagner. However, both Dailey and Wagner resigned because of strong disagreement over the ads that were being run for Ford during the California primary. Those ads came from the New York agency BBDO and its executive Jim Jordan. Two different ad campaigns, two different approaches, and the Ford team was not pleased with either.

It was time for a new media team. In August, after Ford defeated Reagan at the nomination convention, Doug Bailey and John Deardourff were brought in to handle the campaign's general election media. Bailey and Deardourff, along with Boston-based Malcolm MacDougall, were starting from scratch: there was no general election media plan and no staff to support it. As Edwin Diamond and Stephen Bates observed, "No one had looked beyond the convention fight with Reagan; the Ford people had acted as if there was no tomorrow, and now it was here."[115]

Ford's general election media campaign did not start until September 26, three days after his first debate with Jimmy Carter. Bailey and Deardourff, using fresh polling material from Bob Teeter, scrapped all of the commercials created by Dailey and Wagner, which stressed Ford as the incarnation of the presidency, and instead emphasized his personal qualities. Bailey and Deardourff planned a remarkably short television campaign of just five weeks. (By contrast, in 1972,

Nixon started his television ads seven weeks before Election Day, and McGovern started eight weeks before).[116]

The new Ford theme was peace and good times, as seen in the sixty-second Bailey/Deardourff-produced ad called "Peace." The happy, inspiring shots of Americans working, smiling, enjoying life were interspersed with images of Ford, looking sober and presidential in a dark suit, all to the bouncy campaign theme song written by Robert Gardner called "I'm Feelin' Good About America."

"Peace" ("I'm Feelin' Good About America")[117]

[*Video: Farmhouse, a man raises the American flag in front of a rural post office; a child is eating; a man with a hard hat is working; black children are laughing.*]

[*Audio: men and women singing:*]

There's a change that's come over America,
a change that's great to see.
We're living here in peace again,
we're going back to work again,
it's better than it used to be.
I'm feeling good about America,
and I'm feeling (good about me)

[*Video: Family with a baby on the father's back.*]

Ford (over singing): Today America enjoys the most precious gift of all. We are at peace.

[*Video: cute baby, man picking apples, woman smiling, smiling old guy with a cigar; a woman nodding her head in agreement.*]

Male Narrator (over singing): We're at peace with the world and at peace with ourselves. America is smiling again. And a great many people believe that the leadership of this steady, dependable man can keep America happy and secure.

[*Video: Ford at his desk, working; with his hands folded behind his neck, in rocking chair; talking and gesturing; Ford in back seat of his limousine writing on a pad of paper.*]

Male Narrator: We know we can depend on him to work to keep us strong at home. We know we can depend on him to work to ease tensions among the other nations of the world. We know we can depend on him to make peace his highest priority.

[*Video: Older couple, hugging, kissing; young boy, smiling.*]

Male Narrator: Peace with freedom. Is there anything more important than that?

But smiling kids, American flags, and bouncy jingles wouldn't be enough. Ford had to expose Carter's weaknesses. The Bailey-Deardourff team hammered away at Carter, hoping to raise doubts about his effectiveness and leadership potential. Through a series of man-on-the-streets interviews, the Ford media team tried to sow doubts. One of the best remembered, called "Man on the Street—Democrats," featured five Democrats and one Independent: among them a white man from Georgia, a young white woman who actively campaigned for McGovern, a black woman who is switching to Ford, and a white woman with a definite southern lilt to her voice: "I've been a Democrat all my life, but this time I'm going to change."[118]

The Carter campaign relied on his "Georgia mafia," including Jody Powell, Jerry Rafshoon, Hamilton Jordan, Charles Kirbo, and Greg Schneiders. Journalist Kandy Stroud described the Georgia mafia as coming from two different political subsets: "One was mostly liberal, gentlemanly, soft-spoken, nonaggressive, pinstriped and polished." The other "disdained the intellectual, harbored a grudge against the Eastern Establishment, preferred open shirts, blue jeans and cowboy boots to suit and tie."[119]

One outsider added to the campaign was pollster Patrick Caddell, the precocious veteran of the McGovern 1972 campaign who, in the intervening years, had worked on the campaigns of a who's who of Democratic governors and senators. For all their differences in temperament and age, Caddell and Carter got along quite well, with Caddell become the "indispensable catalyst" for the campaign.[120]

Gerald Rafshoon, who had worked with Carter during his gubernatorial campaigns in 1966 and 1970, was the Carter campaign's media consultant. Rafshoon's ads were unique. Carter, dressed in a blue or plaid working shirt, or a short sleeve pullover, spoke from a farmer's field or up against a fence post. This is the first time in presidential television ads that a candidate appears in casual clothes. The image was clear: here was the true outsider, the authentic, honest representative of the people, not the cynical and corrupted Washington insider. One ad has Carter saying, "Now listen to me carefully. I'll never tell a lie. I'll never make a misleading statement. I'll never avoid a controversial issue. Watch television, listen to the radio. If I ever do any of those things don't support me." His ads ended with the tag line "A leader, for a change."[121]

New York media consultant Tony Schwartz was called in to assist the Carter media team in the last weeks. His ads were in direct contrast to the Washington outsider, rural scenes, and work shirts of Rafshoon's commercials. In a Schwartz ad, "Reality," Carter faces the camera, with a dark background, no music, and no props. The candidate is dressed in a dark suit with a conservative tie.

> *Carter:* The Republicans in their TV commercials are saying that the economy is healthy, employment is high, our place in the world is honored, our leadership is great. I've always felt that if something told to me went against my own experience, there was something wrong. And there is. Because when I look around, this is what I see:

Eight million people, every one of them out of work. Every trip to the supermarket—a shock. Cities collapsing, suburbs scared, hospitals closing, teachers fired, crime growing. Police departments—cut. Fire department—cut. Daycare centers—shut. Welfare skyrocketing, energy in foreign hands.

That's our reality. It won't disappear because the Republicans say it's not there. But that doesn't mean we can't face it and work together, and change it. Americans have had to do it before, and we'll do it again. It's a long, tough job. It's time we got started.

During the last weeks of the campaign, Ford, beaten up in the primaries, was now within inches of victory. Carter, or for that matter any Democrat, should have been able to walk away with victory given the abysmal condition of the Republican Party. The Ford campaign team made an incredible comeback, being over thirty points behind immediately after the nominating conventions, but in the end came up short, losing by a little over 2 percentage points in the popular vote. It was, in the summation of journalist Lou Cannon, "the most remarkable comeback in the history of American presidential politics."[122] Republican strategist Clifton White was not so generous: he saw Carter as beatable, but "Ford ran a dismal campaign . . . Carter did not *win*; Ford *lost* the election largely through his own ineptitude."[123] Reflecting on the campaign a decade later, Gerald Ford summed up his feelings toward Stuart Spencer and the campaign: "With Stu, you ignore the language. He understands what the public wants and can turn that into campaign results. The evidence is pretty good that his advice to me was first class. We were trailing by thirty-three points; we lost by two."[124]

In the end, Jimmy Carter and his running mate, Minnesota senator Walter F. Mondale, defeated Gerald Ford and his running mate, Kansas senator Robert Dole. Carter carried twenty-three states and the District of Columbia for 297 electoral votes, while Ford carried twenty-seven states and won 240 electoral votes. The shift in just a few thousand votes in Ohio and Mississippi to the Republicans would have turned the election. This would be the last time any Democratic candidate for president would carry every southern state (except Virginia). It would be another twenty years, and four presidential election cycles, before the Democrats again tasted victory.

The 1980 Presidential Election: Jimmy Carter v. Ronald Reagan v. John Anderson

> *The American people are not going to elect a seventy-year-old, right-wing, ex-movie actor to be president.*
>
> —Hamilton Jordan (1980)[125]

> *These elements—strength, optimism, traditionalism—were naturals for Reagan.*
>
> —Richard Wirthlin (1980)[126]

Several prominent political consultants worked during the 1980 presidential race. Carter, running for re-election, had his seasoned, well-functioning team of pollster Patrick Caddell, advertising man Gerald Rafshoon, and strategists Hamilton Jordan, Jody Powell, and Greg Schneiders. Also working for Carter, but in a relatively minor role, was Robert Squier, whose job was to create a half-hour documentary on the life of the president. Carter's Democratic rival, Edward Kennedy, first approached David Garth, but the New York ad maker turned him down; then Kennedy turned to Charles Guggenheim. On the Republican side, Ronald Reagan again used John Sears, before firing him in the early primaries, retained Richard Wirthlin as his pollster and senior adviser, and again used Peter Dailey and Philadelphia ad maker Elliott Curson. George Bush hired ad maker Robert Goodman, pollster Bob Teeter, and his friend James Baker, while Howard Baker employed Bailey and Deardourff, and John Connally hired Eddie Mahe, Roger Ailes, and, briefly, Richard Viguerie. Independent candidate John Anderson turned to Democratic ad maker David Garth and direct mail specialists Roger Craver and Thomas Mathews. During the general election, newcomer Lee Atwater worked for the Republican ticket as southern states coordinator.

Reagan and the Republican Primaries

In 1964, one of Barry Goldwater's television advisers was Neil (Moon) Reagan, vice president at the advertising firm of McCann-Erikson. Moon Reagan was friends with a young Washington-based national politics reporter for the Copley newspapers, Lyn Nofziger. When Reagan's movie actor brother was looking for a press secretary for his first gubernatorial bid, he recommended Nofziger.[127] The reporter averred, but finally came on board, and helped Ronald Reagan in Sacramento and in his bid for the White House. In 1977 Nofziger used the $1 million left over from the 1976 presidential nomination campaign to set up Citizens for the Republic, a political action committee designed to help Reagan conservatives take over the Republican Party. Now a prominent private citizen, Reagan continued giving speeches, radio broadcast, and penned a syndicated newspaper column to keep his views and himself in the public eye.[128]

Conservative Republicans were ready to listen. They had endured the turmoil of Nixon's presidency, the Watergate scandal, Reagan's near miss at the 1976 nominating convention, and Ford's defeat. New conservative voices were emerging, like Terry Dolan and the National Conservative Political Action Committee (NCPAC); Karl Rove at the College Republicans; Paul Weyrich; Howard Philips and his Conservative Caucus; Richard Viguerie and Bruce Eberle, the direct mail specialists; the Moral Majority, and "New Right" candidates Gordon Humphrey (New Hampshire), Roger Jepsen (Iowa), and Bill Armstrong (Colorado), who all won US Senate seats in 1978.[129] It was a propitious time for Ronald Reagan.

But the 1980 Reagan presidential campaign got off to a difficult start, with infighting between Reagan loyalists and campaign manager John Sears. Sears began his consulting career with the 1968 Nixon delegate selection process (but once the primaries were completed, he was fired by John Mitchell). He then served as campaign manager for Reagan's 1976 Republican nomination bid, and was chosen to be the campaign manager for Reagan's 1980 bid. As Nancy Reagan described him, Sears was the "wonder boy of 1976, and at the time he seemed like the best man to lead us to victory in 1980."[130] However, Sears did not get along with Reagan's former chief of staff, Edwin Meese, who joined the campaign as a senior adviser. Sears dismissed Meese as being out of his league in big-time politics; in addition, Reagan aides Lyn Nofziger, Martin Anderson, and Michael Deaver were all side-stepped.

Sears wanted Reagan to employ a "front-runner" strategy in the early Iowa caucus, New Hampshire primary, and other early contests. That is, Reagan should avoid debates and stay out of the sights of the national media.[131] As Meese complained, Sears believed that Reagan "needed to be packaged, programmed, and kept away from the voters as much as possible."[132] This strategy backfired when former congressman and RNC chairman George H. W. Bush won Iowa, gathering 32 percent of the votes, with Reagan coming in second with 30 percent.

With the assistance of ad maker Robert Goodman, political organizer David Keene, and campaign manager and longtime friend James A. Baker III, Bush "began his campaign earlier, conducted it with greater preparation, and carried it out with more persistence than any other Republican candidate."[133] He copied Jimmy Carter's 1973–1976 campaign primary states nomination plan. During 1978 alone, in preparation for the 1980 primaries, Bush had visited forty-two states, logged 96,000 miles, and sent out more than a million pieces of mail on behalf of his candidacy.[134] Goodman polished his television image, brashly saying, "we're going to make George Bush a TV star." Goodman urged Bush to "show your vulnerable side. Look at Hubert Humphrey. He cared. He was loving. That's what people want."[135] Bush, who served as director of the Central Intelligence Agency (1976–1977), also had a loyal cadre of former CIA personnel helping him, so much so that David Keene remarked at Bush's presidential announcement on May 1, 1979, that "half the audience was wearing raincoats."[136]

Before the first vote had been cast in New Hampshire, Sears had spent his way through much of the Reagan money devoted to the primaries, some 74 percent, in Wirthlin's estimation, of the total allowable budget.[137] Sears became the target of Meese, the California team, and particularly Nancy Reagan. In one memorable event on the eve of the New Hampshire primary, Sears arranged for a Republican nominees' debate in Nashua, where Reagan, off the cuff, famously groused, "I paid for this microphone," when the Bush team tried to limit the number of candidates speaking. That gave Reagan something of a "leadership" boost, but it was too late for Sears. He had annoyed too many Reagan loyalists, and Reagan fired Sears and his aides Jim Lake and Charlie Black on the night of his New Hampshire victory.[138] Both Lake and Black, who'd been supporters of Reagan since 1975, later returned in the Reagan White House and were instrumental in the 1984 re-election campaign. On Sears, Black put it this way, "Reagan would never have become president had he not hired John in 1975 . . . and fired John in 1980."[139] Ed Rollins, writing in his memoirs, pulled no punches in his assessment of Sears, saying "he'd alienated just about everyone with his attitude, which was: I'm so smart I can even get that dumb shit Reagan elected president."[140]

Gerald Carmen, running the Reagan campaign in New Hampshire, later commented that 1980 was "the only election I've ever been in where the campaign manager was more of an issue than the candidate," and that the disruption extended "all up and down the chain."[141] Meese thought he would become the new campaign manager, but instead that role went to sixty-seven-year-old New York lawyer William Casey, a former chair of the Securities and Exchange Commission. Neither Casey nor Meese had any national campaign experience, and aides soon started complaining about the "Casey problem."[142] Reagan quickly started getting into trouble, stumbling and going off message. Nancy Reagan intervened and, ignoring the advice of both Casey and Meese, brought back Stuart Spencer.[143]

Spencer, who first nurtured Reagan in his 1966 gubernatorial campaign, had been a pariah in the Reagan camp when he worked for Ford's re-election in 1976. But that was the past. As journalist Lou Cannon observed, "Nancy Reagan was not one to allow old grudges to stand in the way of her husband's election."[144] Michael Deaver rejoined the campaign and with Stuart Spencer formed an alternative Reagan team on the campaign plan, called LeaderShip '80. On the plane, they reassured the candidate, swapped stories, and made him feel at ease.[145] Deaver took control of the schedule and the candidate. "That was the end of the battle," Deaver remembered, "because whoever controlled the schedule and the body was going to control, pretty much, the campaign."[146]

Yet the two groups sparred with each other and vied for Reagan's attention: Meese and Casey, running the campaign from Arlington, Virginia, and Deaver and Spencer on the plane with the candidate. Meese and Casey thought Deaver was no more than a Reagan sycophant and Spencer just a political hack; Deaver and Spencer returned the compliment by characterizing Meese and Casey as bureaucrats and ideologues.[147] Also on the campaign plane was Ken Khachigian, Nixon's old speechwriter, now writing for Reagan, and furtively passing on campaign advice from Nixon, now in exile at San Clemente.[148]

Stuart Spencer believed that his biggest contribution to the campaign was recognizing how Reagan operates. "I made him feel comfortable. Reagan's a rhythm candidate; you let him get out of rhythm, and he screws up. Once he get in rhythm, he's tough. He gets into rhythm in his speeches, he gets into rhythm in his jokes, he gets into rhythm in his body language. He says, I'm a winner, I'm the number one guy, you've got to take it away from me."[149] When he was working for Ford in 1976, Spencer used that insight against his old boss, getting Reagan out of his rhythm—tripping him up in New Hampshire when Reagan announced a $90 billion package, for example.[150]

Polling for Reagan. Richard Wirthlin, Reagan's chief pollster, was also given the title of deputy campaign director for planning and strategy. He was given $1.4 million to conduct his own polls, and had access to at least another $1 million in polling done by others for the campaign.[151] One of the key contributions that Wirthlin made was to focus the survey research on the values and aspirations of several key voter groups. Beginning in June 1979, Wirthlin's firm, Decision

Making Information (DMI), conducted several such national studies and found that Reagan, more so than any other candidate, polarized voters, when measuring personality and interpersonal style variables.[152] Wirthlin wrote that "we were somewhat surprised to learn that our key win coalition reflected certain values more strongly than the average. We grouped these values under three headings: the traditional ethics factor, the strong-leader appeal, and a 'Can Do, America' vision." Carter's "malaise" speech "provided almost the perfect foil for these specific leadership themes."[153] Of all the Republican candidates, Reagan had the most sophisticated polling operation.[154]

The Reagan media team. Before the primaries began, the C.T. Clyne Company of New York produced several ads, which were fairly uninspiring, but at least held the germ of the theme that would be ultimately used against Carter: that "this great country was not 'being run' like a great country."[155] Campaign manager John Sears replaced the Clyne group with Elliott Curson, head of a Philadelphia agency bearing his name. Curson shot a number of commercials, with Reagan facing directly at the camera, outlining the basic Reagan philosophy: strong national defense, cut taxes, cut spending, but don't leave people behind. These ads were shown throughout the primaries, though once Sears was fired, Curson had no further contact with the campaign.[156]

The Republican nomination field was crowded, with a total of seven candidates running in the primaries. But with Reagan winning seven of the first nine primaries, it seemed to be all over by March 19, when he won the Illinois primary. Former president Gerald Ford announced a week earlier that he would not seek the nomination. Senate minority leader Howard Baker of Tennessee, who at one time was considered the most formidable of candidates, dropped out. So did long-shot conservative Illinois congressman Phil Crane. Former Texas governor John B. Connally spent $12 million during the primaries, was able to get just one lonely Arkansas delegate, and probably set a record for wasting campaign money. Of the $12 million, he spent $10 million on expensive hotel rooms, private planes, consultants, and staff, while only $2 million went into the campaign advertising.[157] Direct mail and fundraising consultant Richard Viguerie worked first for Crane, pulling in $2.5 million (and pocketing most of it in fees), then moved over to assist Connally.[158] Bob Dole had spent a year flying around the country, promising to cure the country's economic woes. But he had no campaign organization; everything was seat of the pants, straight from Dole. He ended up getting just 600 votes in New Hampshire, and made a quick exit.[159] Finally, George Bush dropped out on May 26, after carrying just six states.

Illinois congressman John B. Anderson, who made an early splash in the Iowa debates but did not win a single primary, decided to stay in the race, running as an independent. Anderson retained the direct mail team of Roger Craver and Thomas Mathews, who were just beginning to make their mark in fundraising for progressive causes. Anderson tried, but failed, to land the media firm Bailey & Deardourff. Then his campaign landed its biggest catch, David Garth, by this time one of the best-known (and most expensive, at $35,000 a month) media specialists, who had a reputation for boosting the fortunes of underdogs, but also demanding total control. By having Garth on board, the Anderson campaign hoped that the media would recognize that its efforts were serious.[160] The problem was that the campaign did not have the funds to launch and sustain the kind of advertising campaign Garth was used to. Anderson was in a financial bind. During the general election, both Carter and Reagan received $29.4 million in public campaign funds under the rules of the Federal Election Commission; Anderson, not being a candidate representing either of the two major parties, received no federal funds.[161] Anderson had spent nearly all of his money, $2.5 million, on gaining ballot access, gathering far more names than needed in some states, and pursuing access in states where he had little chance of winning. By the time Garth had gained full control of the campaign's media, it was a million in debt. "When we blew that money," Garth would later say, "we blew any real chance of keeping up there."[162]

Who should Reagan choose as his running mate? Reagan had a "short list" of George Bush, Howard Baker, former Treasury secretary William Simon, Indiana senator Richard Lugar, New York congressman Jack Kemp, Michigan congressman Guy Vander Jagt, and Nevada senator Paul Laxalt. But the one who stood out in Richard Wirthlin's polling was Gerald Ford. Wirthlin laid out to the campaign higher command the positives of having Ford as a running mate, and feelers were sent out to the former president. But Stuart Spencer, now back in the Reagan camp, was emphatic: "Ron, Ford ain't gonna do it, and you're gonna pick Bush."[163] But Reagan really did not like Bush.

At the Republican nominating convention held in Detroit, former president Gerald Ford delivered a strong, fiery speech on July 14, the opening Monday night of the convention. Reagan instructed his aides to find out if Ford might be available for the vice-presidency slot. This was a repeat, but a reversal, of the "dream ticket" talk four years earlier, when the possibility of a Ford-Reagan team in 1976 was briefly floated. But a 1980 Reagan-Ford ticket soon collapsed. Two days later, on July 16, Dick Wirthlin was in Reagan's Detroit hotel room watching Walter Cronkite interview Ford. The former president, when asked about a possible Reagan-Ford ticket, described something that sounded almost like a co-presidency. "When Reagan heard that, he literally jumped out of the couch, pointed at the television, and said to those of us in the room: 'Did you hear what he said about his role? Sounds like he wants to be co-president!' Wirthlin wrote, And at that moment, we knew that the discussion was really ended."[164] Reagan quickly chose Bush, despite the lingering animosity from the New Hampshire microphone episode, Bush's lambasting Reagan's economic policies as "voodoo economics," and the fact that they never got along that well.

Carter, Kennedy, and Brown

It is never good news when an incumbent president is challenged for his party's nomination. In Carter's case, he was challenged by two Democrats, Massachusetts senator Edward M. Kennedy and, to a lesser degree, California governor Edmund

G. (Jerry) Brown Jr. Neither mounted a serious challenge with a stable of top flight consultants and bags full of money; nevertheless, they were a distraction to Carter's drive for re-election. Brown could not win his home state of California, nor any primary state for that matter, and ended up mostly as a footnote. After a string of primary defeats, the Kennedy campaign was about to give up the battle against Carter. Kennedy's campaign, managed by his brother-in-law Stephen Smith, was plagued with friction, and couldn't select a single media advertiser who could drill home a coherent message. A frustrated Joe Napolitan, not a part of the campaign, privately complained to Smith: "The early stuff you produced was an embarrassment, probably the worst television ever produced for a presidential candidate in American history. Teddy deserves better than that."[165] Bob Shrum, Kennedy's speechwriter, had drafted a withdrawal speech, and Kennedy was prepared to give it. Kennedy had won the March 4th Massachusetts primary, but that was to be expected; he lost in Iowa, New Hampshire, and the six states that came next in the Democratic primary calendar. Then came the Connecticut and New York primaries, both on March 25, and both significant victories for Kennedy. Jody Powell recalled that "the New York primary was something we did our damnedest and successfully to throw away."[166]

Kennedy hung on, but in all won only eleven primaries, and would not concede until the Democratic convention. There, on August 12, 1980, he gave one of his most impassioned and long-remembered speeches, ending with these words: "For me, a few hours ago, this campaign came to an end. For all those whose cares have been our concern, the work goes on, the cause endures, the hope still lives, and the dream shall never die."[167] Bob Shrum, who drafted these words, would fight on in many more presidential contests. The nomination would go to the president, but as reporter George J. Church observed, "Not since Harry Truman has a president received such a grudging, unenthusiastic nomination from a Democratic Convention."[168]

For all the difficulty the president was having with the economy, the Iranian hostage situation, the energy crisis, and other problems, Carter had a cohesive and experienced campaign team of Hamilton Jordan, Jody Powell, Greg Schneiders, Gerald Rafshoon, and Patrick Caddell. This was in stark contrast to the bickering, back-channeling, and indecisive Reagan team.

The General Election

In his memoirs, Dick Wirthlin wrote that when devising political strategy, "I always start by studying my opponent. I want to know him better than he knows himself."[169] This became easier for Wirthlin when a number of 1976 campaign memoranda for the Carter team were made public, showing the political assumptions, strategy, and tactics of the campaign. Wirthlin was convinced that both Jimmy Carter and his pollster Patrick Caddell were tough men who "played for keeps." But what he could not imagine—"not in a million years"—was that Carter personally would take on the role of attack dog, going directly after Ronald Reagan.[170]

Attacking Reagan was part of the Carter strategy, although at times Hamilton Jordan tried to dampen Carter's criticisms. Patrick Caddell, who sat in on every major staff meeting, determined which states Carter should visit and who to see, and helped set the strategic message.[171] After the campaign, Caddell outlined the message against Reagan: First "and foremost," the campaign had to be about the future, and not the past; it should not be a referendum on Carter. Second, the incumbency had to be used to its advantage, and Carter had to be portrayed as a better president in his second term than in the first. Third, Carter had to be portrayed as being in the mainstream of American political beliefs, while Reagan was the outsider, especially on the issue of war and peace. Finally, Democrats had to be united, and the South and northern industrial states had to be the core of the winning electoral package.[172]

Carter's attack got under Reagan's skin. On a local Dallas, Texas, television show, Reagan voiced his frustrations: "Criticizing each other belongs in a campaign . . . but I think Carter has lowered himself to a personal type of attack against me. And it's an attack based on falsehoods and distortions. . . . I can hardly have a warm feeling in my heart for someone who's been attacking me on a personal basis for many months now in the campaign."[173]

The Reagan campaign also responded with a tough sixty-second ad, with Nancy Reagan excoriating Carter for his personal attacks against her husband. Sitting alone in a studio, Nancy Reagan spoke forcefully about her husband and her resentment of Jimmy Carter's attack ads.

> *Nancy Reagan:* I deeply, deeply resent and am offended by the attacks that President Carter's made on my husband. The personal attacks that he's made on my husband. His attempt to paint my husband as a man he is not. He is not a warmonger, he is not a man who is going to throw the elderly out on the street and cut out their social security. That's a terrible thing to, to do and to say, about anybody. That's campaigning on fear.
>
> There are many issues that are at stake in this campaign. I would like Mr. Carter to explain to me why the inflation is as high as it is, why unemployment is as high as it is. I would like to have him explain the vacillating, weak foreign policy so that our friends overseas don't know what we're going to do, whether we're going to stand up for them, or whether we're not going to stand up for them. And the issue of this campaign is his three and a half year record.
>
> *Male Narrator:* The time is now for strong leadership.[174]

This ad was produced by Campaign '80, the group of advertising specialists assembled by Peter H. Dailey. The ads were not particularly memorable, but they were thoroughly tested through focus groups and survey research.

Both campaigns relied heavily on survey research results from their private pollsters. From late August until Election Day, Pat Caddell conducted 133 different surveys in thirty-nine states, had fourteen national studies, three waves of open-ended qualitative surveys, and two before-and-after media market tests of commercials. Dick Wirthlin, for Reagan and the Republican National Committee, conducted sixty-four separate polls in twenty-six states, at least six national surveys, several brush-fire (quick, short) polls, and tracked 10,500 voters.[175]

Wirthlin's tracking technique caused "quite a stir" in the polling community. Starting in mid-October 1980, some 500 randomly selected nationwide voters were contacted by telephone and asked a small number of questions, as well as how they intended to vote. A second set of 500 voters were called the next night, then 500 the following night, for a total of five nights of calling. The results from these 2,500 voters were analyzed, and on the sixth night another 500 voters were called, the 500 from the first night were dropped, and this new set of 2,500 was analyzed. During the final three days of the campaign, Wirthlin increased the tracking figures to 1,000 voters per evening.[176]

Also used heavily, but not for the first time, were focus groups and dial-meter analysis. Commercial firms had used these qualitative research techniques for decades to test products and to assess radio programs, army training films, and television audiences.[177] Carter's team used these qualitative research techniques to determine how well Carter did against Reagan during the first presidential debate. About fifty persons were selected in a dial-meter group in Spokane, Washington; half were pro-Reagan, half favored Carter. They watched the television monitor, and while seated in a testing studio turned the knob on a small box in the laps from 0 (highly disagree or disapprove) to 100 (absolutely agree with or approve). Caddell's firm, Cambridge Research, looking at the highs and lows, found that Carter was strongest when he emphasized keeping social security sound, and Reagan was strongest when he emphasized a strong military and mentioned the Misery Index.[178]

The Reagan campaign, according to Wirthlin, had two major concerns going into the final month. The first was that Carter would "mount a campaign of fear," raising the risk of war and concern about Reagan as a leader; the second, and most important, was the concern over an "October surprise"—some dramatic foreign policy development, perhaps the release of the Iranian hostages, that would vault Carter into the lead for good.[179] Carter's campaign ads did sharply call into question Reagan's foreign affairs leadership ability, but there was no announcement from Iran or no other late-campaign "October surprise."

Carter decided not to debate John Anderson, so the first nationwide debate featured Reagan versus Anderson. Though persuasive and articulate, this would be Anderson's swan song, as voters were lining up behind the two major party candidates, not going over to an independent. Just one week before Election Day, on October 28, Carter debated Reagan in Cleveland. Carter was prepared, handled himself adequately, and if the exchange were based solely on debate pints, he probably would have won. But Carter jumped off the tracks when answering a question on nuclear weapons. He said that he was talking to his young daughter Amy, asking her what she thought was important. For many viewers, Carter trivialized the question and opened the door to media ridicule. More damaging, however, was Reagan's mastery of words, image, and television presence. This was not surprising to Stuart Spencer: "I've seen him do it so many times. He rises to the occasion. So much in a debate is style, and he has style and class."[180] Reagan ended the debate by asking the rhetorical question that resonated deeply with voters (as seen through Wirthlin's research): "Are you better off than you were four years ago?" Reagan continued: "Is it easier for you to go and buy things in the stores than it was four years ago? Is there more or less unemployment in the country? . . . Do you feel that our security is safe, that we're as strong as we were four years ago?"[181] Mitt Romney in 2012 would use the same rhetorical device, but without the same success.

The night before the election, Reagan did what he did best: broadcast a half-hour speech, delivered on all three television networks nationwide, describing America as mankind's "last best hope." Ken Khachigian wrote the emotion-laden, soothing, and evocative speech.[182] It was frosting on the cake for a campaign that was coming to a resounding conclusion.

For the Reagan-Bush campaign, William Timmons organized the largest get-out-the-vote drive in American history, employing some 500,000 committed Republicans. The drive employed phone banks, personal visits to voters' homes, rides to polling stations, television and radio advertising, and direct mail to encourage Republicans and disaffected Democrats to get to the polls and vote for Reagan.[183]

Exit polls by ABC News found that more than one in four voters had settled on a choice during the last week of the election, with 44 percent going for Reagan and 38 percent for Carter.[184] Reagan's debate performance, the inability of Carter to get the Iranian hostages released, Reagan's last-evening speech, and the extraordinary get-out-the-vote drive were decisive. Two groups in particular had abandoned Carter: "weak" Democrats and independents. The weak Democrats were almost all white voters, mostly middle-class, both blue- and white-collar, and heavily Catholic.[185] Carter was soundly repudiated, winning only six states, including the home states of Georgia and Mondale's Minnesota, plus the District of Columbia. Carter could gain only 41 percent of the popular vote (and 49 electoral votes), while Reagan gained 50.8 percent (and 489 electoral votes) and John Anderson received 6.6 percent of the popular vote and no electoral votes.

Stu Spencer, along with Nancy Reagan and Michael Deaver, conspired to get James A. Baker III named as the new president's chief of staff, rather than Reagan's longtime gubernatorial chief of staff, Ed Meese. Baker had been brought to Washington in 1976 to work at the Commerce Department, and he quickly became a delegate hunter for the Ford campaign; he then became Bush's campaign manager in the 1980 primaries, and later worked on the Reagan general election campaign. As journalist Lou Cannon noted, "No president had ever chosen his former adversary's campaign manager as chief of staff."[186] But Reagan agreed with Spencer and Deaver, and Baker was chosen to this most senior post in the White House.

CHAPTER 11

State and Local Elections, Ballot Issues

Years ago, a client who hired an out-of-state consultant tried to hide the consultant because he feared it could be a potential issue in his campaign. A candidate had to really want professional advice to take that risk. Now, a candidate will hire a consultant and hold a news conference to announce it. Even the party does not think you are serious if you don't have the right consultant.

—Doug Bailey (1990)

W HILE MUCH OF the national spotlight is on presidential and US Senate contests, campaigns for governor, other statewide officials, local contests, and ballot initiatives have also been fertile ground for political consulting. Some political consultants prefer working in these races rather than in presidential contests. "It's a crapshoot," said media consultant Bob Squier about presidential contests. "You can end up at the [nominating] convention with nothing."[1] For top consultants like Squier, it is often more lucrative and more secure to work on gubernatorial or senatorial races than to take a chance on a presidential primary.[2] However, Squier and his firm did venture into presidential politics when they aided Clinton's re-election in 1996 and Al Gore's run for the presidency in 2000.

State and Local Campaigns

The use of political consultants in statewide races started around the time that presidential campaigns were beginning to use them, in the mid-1960s. The Michigan gubernatorial race of 1966 stands out as one of the first professionalized statewide campaigns, with Walter De Vries as the major consultant for George Romney. Since then, professional political consultants have become essential forces in gubernatorial campaigns.

Working in state politics can be lucrative. The National Institute on Money in State Politics noted that from 2000 to 2010, a total of $9.5 billion was raised and spent on candidates for statewide office, state legislatures, and for state supreme court and appellate courts.[3] Altogether, there were 50,010 candidates for state office during this period. Most of the candidates raised and spent relatively small amounts of money, but the top 1,000 candidates (just 2 percent of the total) raised and spent more than half of all the money, $5.4 billion.[4]

In its report covering the 2009–2010 election cycle, the amount of money raised and spent in state campaigns reached $3.8 billion, including $2.5 billion raised by 16,724 candidates for office, $627.1 million raised by state parties and legislative caucuses, and $628.3 million for committees supporting or opposing ballot measures. Even candidates not up for re-election during this time raised $103.3 million.[5] All this means that political consultants, more than ever, are seeing boom times in the business of politics and electioneering.

Some recent gubernatorial contests have mushroomed in costs, particularly when wealthy candidates have dipped into their own pockets and purses. In 1998, Al Checchi spent $40 million of his own funds, losing in the gubernatorial primary in California; in 2002, Tom Golisano spent $47 million of his own money running, unsuccessfully, in the Republican primary for governor of New York. In 2005, Jon Corzine dipped into his own funds three times: once for US senator from New Jersey ($60 million in 2000), and twice for governor of New Jersey ($43 million in 2005, and $27 million in 2009, when he was defeated for re-election). The leader in self-funded statewide campaigns thus far is Meg Whitman, the former CEO of eBay (and later head of Hewlett-Packard). In 2009–2010, running for governor of California, Whitman raised $176.6 million, with 82 percent ($144 million) coming from her own resources; nonetheless, she lost decisively to former governor Jerry Brown, whose campaign spent $40.5 million, less than one-quarter of the amount spent by Whitman, and zero dollars from his own pocket.[6] Businessman Rick Scott, successfully running for governor in Florida in 2010, poured in well over $75 million of his own money; millions more went into his hotly contested re-election against former governor Charlie Crist in 2014.

Table 11.1 shows the amounts of funds raised by the top gubernatorial candidates during the 2009–2010 election cycle. Altogether, the candidates spent nearly a half-billion dollars on their campaigns; these amounts do not include political party sources, super PAC funds, or other independent expenditures.

When federal or state quarterly campaign reports are made public, the press usually focuses on which candidate has raised the most money and where the money came from. Fundraising figures act as surrogates for a campaign's progress. Political operatives look to see where the money was spent. However, more important than the fact that a campaign raised $1,150,000 during the last ninety days is the understanding of what the campaign can do with the money: pay campaign staffers, afford another round of tracking polls, send out another direct mail solicitation, have several more rounds of telephone persuasion calls, buy extra television time for a saturation of 30-second spots, and pay mounting consultant bills.

TABLE 11.1 Fundraising by Top Ten Gubernatorial Candidates, 2009–2010

Candidate, State, Party	Status	Total Raised	Percent Own Money
Meg Whitman, California–Republican	Lost	$176,684,951	82%
Rick Scott, Florida–Republican*	Won	$85,000,000	90%
Jerry Brown, California–Democrat	Won	$40,556,608	
Rick Perry, Texas–Republican	Won	$39,328,540	
Jon Corzine, New Jersey–Democrat	Lost	$30,583,881	90%
Tom Corbett, Pennsylvania–Republican	Won	$28,561,987	
Steve Poizner, California–Republican	Lost Primary	$26,660,173	91%
Bill White, Texas–Democrat	Lost	$26,291,532	
Andrew Cuomo, New York–Democrat	Won	$26,047,733	
Dan Onorato, Pennsylvania–Democrat	Lost	$25,116,397	
Total		$487,253,745	

Source: National Institute on Money in State Politics.

* Updated estimate from Scott Powers, "It's Official: Rick Scott is the All-Time Big Spender," *Orlando Sentinel*, February 2, 2011.

Local Contests

> *There's hardly a county council race that doesn't have a consultant involved.*
> —consultant Brad O'Leary (1990)[7]

If candidates spend more than $50,000 on a campaign, chances are, professional consultants will be hired; below that figure, candidates most often rely on volunteers, friends, and political associates to help them get elected. Many thousands of campaigns at the local level fall below the threshold of $50,000, but campaigns are increasingly raising more funds and hiring more professional assistance. General campaign management, polling, and direct mail are most in demand at the lowest level, just as they are in multimillion-dollar contests. Table 11.2 illustrates how a typical $6 million campaign and a $100,000 campaign might allocate its funds

Nearly all serious candidates for gubernatorial, other statewide, and congressional contest use consultants; so, too, do state political parties and legislative caucuses. In addition, candidates for state legislature, mayor, city council, sheriff, tax collector, and even school board are using consultants. The annual won-lost list of political consultants published by *Campaigns & Elections* magazine shows consulting firms serving a wide variety of local candidates, legislative caucuses, independent expenditures and state political parties. When the stakes are high, such as when the control of a city council or the state legislature are in the balance, then local races, which were once low-budget operations, can balloon in costs as outside interests get involved.

TABLE 11.2 Use of Consultants in $6 Million Race and $100,000 Race

$6 Million Race and Estimated Expenses

Media consultant	$200,000 in production costs
	10% of media buy ($350,000)
	In-house media buying ($150,000)
Television advertising	$3,500,000
Direct mail consultant	$500,000
Telephone consultant	$200,000
Online advertising	$70,000
Polling and Research	$250,000
General consultant	$280,000 (plus $50,000 bonus if victorious)
Staff	$200,000
Office, travel, overhead	$300,000
Total	$6,000,000

$100,000 Race and Estimated Expenses

Campaign manager	$30,000
Polling consultant	$15,000
Direct mail consultant	$15,000
Staff	$20,000
Office, travel, overhead	$20,000
Total	$100,000

For example, when the Virginia state senate was at stake in 1997, professional consultants were brought into rural southwest Virginia to join the fight between Democratic lawyer and eventual winner Roscoe Reynolds, who was running against Republican banker Allen Dudley. Consultants from Washington, Richmond, and Raleigh came in with polling, focus groups, telephone banks, and voter turnout models. The candidates bought television commercials, which were poll tested, they brought in direct mail specialists who blanketed the small towns of Rocky Mount and Martinsville and Henry and Franklin counties with sharply worded warnings: "When our children needed Allen Dudley, he just wasn't there"; "Don't let politicians like Allen Dudley sell out our families."[8] The normally placid, low-keyed contest became a pitched battleground, with spirited but friendly politicking replaced by slash-and-burn techniques.

In Minnesota, state legislative races used to be low-profile, low-budget affairs; but campaign costs have exploded in the twenty-first century. In 2002, candidates, parties, and political action committees spent a combined total of $12 million for Minnesota House and Senate campaigns; by 2012, the expenditures had doubled to nearly $24 million. In 2012, nine legislative campaigns spent more than $500,000 each, while twenty-nine spent at least $200,000; one of the contests set a record of $870,000. Most of the money was raised and spent by the political parties and independent expenditures, not the candidates themselves.[9]

Some consultants have made a career out of assisting candidates and causes strictly at the state and local levels. For example, one of Kentucky's most successful political consultants, Dale Emmons, has won over 650 state and local campaigns since opening his firm, Emmons and Company, in 1990. Emmons explained why professional consulting is invaluable, particularly at the local level: Many candidates have good ideas, or money, and have the ambition to run, but they are usually not equipped to develop a consistent, compelling message, and they typically have no idea what kind of landmines are out there to trip them up. With outside voices—interest groups, labor unions, national organizations, and others—involved, it becomes even more difficult for a first-time candidate to weave through all the clutter. That's where a political consulting firm, such as Emmons's, which is a full-service firm, can be of great assistance.[10] Having been through races, election cycle after election cycle, building up alliances, knowing everyone who needs to be known—that's what consultants can do.

For Emmons, county and city battles over alcohol have provided steady consulting opportunities. While the Twenty-First Amendment to the US Constitution halted Prohibition, that fight continued in Kentucky, Texas, and some other states. In Kentucky, for example, there are thirty-nine "dry" counties, where alcohol cannot be sold; thirty-two "wet" counties, where alcohol can be sold with a state license; and forty-nine "moist" counties—dry counties where one or more cities have voted to allow the sale of alcohol off premises. The public policy battle goes on, the issue does not dry up, and Emmons fights for clients intent on repealing local prohibition.

Candidates in big-city mayoral contests have also been assisted by political consulting firms. Before his association with Barack Obama, David Axelrod was known as a specialist in assisting African American Democratic mayoral candidates, including Dennis Archer (Detroit), Anthony Williams (District of Columbia), Lee P. Brown (Houston), Michael White (Cleveland), and John F. Street (Philadelphia). As the *Economist* wrote in a profile, Axelrod was adept at "packaging black candidates for white voters."[11] He also assisted Chicago mayor Richard M. Daley.

Recent mayoral contests in big cities have seen large sums of money—sometimes as big as statewide gubernatorial or US Senate contests. In the 2012 San Diego mayoral contest, the candidates spent a combined $10 million. In Chicago, Richard M. Daley spent $6 million in 2007, and Rahm Emmanuel spent $13 million in 2011. Antonio Villaraigosa's campaign spent $4.3 million in the 2005 Los Angeles mayoral contest, and, against a weak opponent, he spent $3 million in 2009. In the District of Columbia, which has a smaller voting population than any US congressional district, Adrian Fenty won in 2006 spending $3.8 million, but he lost four years later while spending $5.0 million.[12]

Nothing compares, however, with the extraordinary sums of money Michael Bloomberg invested in his three successful bids for mayor of New York City, about $268 million in total. In 2001 Bloomberg spent $74 million; in 2005 he spent $85 million; and in 2009 he spent $109 million—all his own money. (By contrast, the combined spending for all New York City mayoral candidates in 2013, when Bill de Blasio won, was "just" $45 million).[13] Bloomberg's total investment in his own campaigns is simply off the charts: no other candidate, not presidential candidates Ross Perot, Steve Forbes, nor statewide candidates Jon Corzine or Linda McMahon (about $100 million in two unsuccessful US Senate races in Connecticut) come close to what Bloomberg has spent. His nearest self-funding rival would be Meg Whitman, spending some $144 million of her own money in a much more populous jurisdiction. The amount of personal funds spent by billionaire Donald Trump in 2016 awaits to be tallied.

Judicial Elections and Consultants

... Something's afoot with our judicial system. Across the country, large sums of money—much of it secret—are pouring into the races for high court judges. And in several states, partisan groups with funds from undisclosed sources are out to punish justices for rulings the partisans don't like.

—Journalist Bill Moyers (2012)[14]

As seen in the profile of Joseph Cerrell in chapter 4, candidates for judicial office had long turned to political consultants for assistance. But what became a major juncture was the US Supreme Court 2002 decision in *Republican Party of Minnesota v. White*,[15] stating that judicial candidates, including incumbent judges, had the free speech right to make policy statements during their campaigns. Many court watchers decried the decision, arguing that allowing judges to make policy statements, just like any other candidate seeking elected office, could compromise their independence and integrity.[16] Political scientist James L. Gibson argued, however, that thus far there is little rigorous evidence, one way or another, on whether policy statements have any impact on the perceived impartiality of judges.[17]

Thirty-eight states conduct elections for their highest courts in the form of nonpartisan and partisan elections, and in up-or-down judicial retention votes. In a recent report, the National Institute on Money in State Politics observed that during the 2011–2012 election cycle, "many of these judicial races seemed alarmingly indistinguishable from ordinary political campaigns—featuring everything from Super PACs and mudslinging attacks to millions of dollars of candidate fundraising and independent spending."[18] Two dominant trends were emerging for judicial elections from 2000 to the 2011–2012 cycle: they were becoming more expensive and nastier. Misleading characterizations of sitting judges and judicial candidates appeared in ads. Candidates themselves may not stray too far and try to maintain a sense of judicial propriety, but for third-party groups—political parties, independent expenditure committees, and other outside interests—the gloves have come off.

The Ohio Republican Party sponsored an ad against former appeals court judge Bill O'Neill, who in an earlier decision had reversed a rape conviction: the ad, called "When Crime Occurs," had the tag line "When crime occurs, victims deserve justice. But as a judge, Bill O'Neill expressed sympathy for rapists."[19] The Judicial Crisis Network (JCN), a conservative Washington, DC–based 501(c)(4) organization, created an ad featuring the mother of a soldier killed in Afghanistan. University of Michigan law school dean and professor Bridget McCormack, running for a judgeship in Michigan, had once served as a volunteer co-counsel for a Guantanamo detainee. The ad, which ran 416 times during the last week of the election, had this tag line: "My son is a hero and fought to protect us. Bridget McCormack volunteered to free a terrorist. How could you?"[20] Andrew Rosenthal, in a scathing op-ed in the *New York Times*, charged that the ad "shamelessly exploits" the death of the soldier, and that McCormack, part of a team of American lawyers, was there to assure proper legal representation, not to "free" the terrorist. (McCormack, who won the contest, had her own resources, including a four-minute video featuring the stars of the television hit show "West Wing," urging voters to not forget the nonpartisan section of the ballot where judicial contests appear in Michigan, but also to vote for McCormack).[21] The JCN, once called the Judicial Confirmation Network (during friendlier Bush administration times), has become a "pipeline for secret money to other, better-known dark money groups," such as the Wisconsin Club for Growth and the America Future Fund. JCN is part of a network of nondisclosing groups associated with the Koch brothers. Another big player in the conservative judicial election business is Wellspring Committee, a dark money conduit, headed by Ann Corkery, who previously had served as finance chair for Mitt Romney's 2008 presidential campaign. [22]

A final example harkens back to Willie Horton and the 1988 presidential campaign. In Kentucky, former judge Janet Stumbo, trying for a 2012 comeback against state supreme court justice Will T. Scott, was hit with a commercial from the Scott camp, airing 71 times during the week before the election. The screen showed flashing images of black murderers and pregnant white women, then referred to the murder convictions that Stumbo had reversed: "Lee Parrish and Roger Wheeler were sentenced to death for ruthlessly murdering pregnant women. But former justice Janet Stumbo voted to reverse both convictions."[23] Scott was accused by Stumbo's allies of using racist tactics; Scott begged to differ. Stumbo lost the election to Scott, gaining less than 42 percent of the vote.

Judicial races in 2011–2012 cost approximately $56.4 million, with $15.4 million coming from independent expenditures, such as the Law Enforcement Alliance of America (linked to the National Rifle Association), the progressive America Votes, and conservative Americans for Prosperity, supported by the Koch brothers. This was more than a 50 percent increase in the amount of money spent for judicial contests by independent groups in 2003–2004, which had been the previous record.[24]

Congressional Elections

> *The most striking feature of modern congressional elections has been the ascendant importance of individual candidates and campaigns.*
>
> —Gary C. Jacobson (1997)[25]

During the 1970s and 1980s, more and more congressional races began using the services of political consultants. Senate races, in particular, many with multimillion-dollar budgets, were able to use a full range of political consultants, who engaged in general consulting, fundraising, research (polling, focus groups, opposition and candidate research), communication (direct mail, telephone banks, radio and television advertising), and voter appeal efforts (get-out-the vote, phone banks).

House candidates were slower in using consulting services. Political scientist Paul Herrnson noted that during the early 1990s, about 19 percent of congressional campaigns that responded to a survey had hired a campaign manager, 22 percent had used an opposition or candidate research consultant, 24 percent had employed a fundraiser, 60 percent had hired a polling firm, and 61 percent had used a media firm.[26] Typically, an incumbent member, with a 1990 campaign budget of $500,000 or so would be able to invest in most of these specialty services, while challengers, often underfunded and with less experience in running for office, would be able to afford far fewer professional services. Political scientist Stephen K. Medvic also looked at the congressional elections in the early 1990s, and found that during the 1990 cycle some 45.6 percent of House candidates had hired at least one political consultant, while in 1992, 62.6 percent of the candidates did so. He also found that Democrats tended to use consultants more than Republicans, and that the most common consultant hired was a pollster.[27]

Most often, the focus of journalists and researchers is on where money in a campaign comes from. However, journalists Sara Fritz and Dwight Morris decided to look at FEC finance records to see where money was spent. In their groundbreaking book *Gold-Plated Politics*, Fritz and Morris reveal how much consultants have earned from various candidates and what services the money was spent on, as well as providing an insight into the strategies of candidates. In 1990 elections, consultants took in 45 percent of all spending in congressional races, a total of $188 million. Of this, $116.7 million went for media work, $38 million for fundraising, and $12 million for polling. Squier/Eskew Communications billed nearly $8.2 million in business for US Senate candidates—Tom Harkin (Iowa), Howell Heflin (Alabama), Joseph Biden (Delaware), Daniel Akaka (Hawaii), Claiborne Pell (Rhode Island), Al Gore (Tennessee), and John D. Rockefeller IV (West Virginia). Sawyer/Miller Group took in $4.7 million, all of it in helping Harvey B. Gantt in his race against Jesse Helms in North Carolina. Ten pollsters earned more than $500,000 during the 1990 congressional races; Bill Bradley, running for re-election in the New Jersey Senate race, paid pollsters Joe Peritz & Associates $900,000.[28]

There was also an upsurge in direct mail fundraising at the congressional election level. Coyle, McConnell & O'Brien, a firm that didn't exist in 1985, grossed $3 million during the 1990 cycle for Harkin, John Kerry (Massachusetts), and Paul Simon (Illinois).[29] Cooper & Secrest specialized in congressional candidate polling and was considered "the pollster of choice" for many moderate and conservative Democratic congressional candidates during the 1980s and 1990s.[30]

Running against an incumbent House member can be daunting. From 1992 through 2012, the re-election rate of incumbents has been well into the 90 percent level, with only the 2010 Tea Party-backed Republican victory (85 percent), the 1994 Republican takeover of the House (90 percent), and the 1992 election (88 percent) falling below the 90 percent level.[31] Invariably, incumbents load up their campaigns with campaign funds from individuals, political action committees, and others who want the legislator to return. Not included in these equations are the millions of dollars spent by super PACs and other independent expenditures, as congressional campaigns have become nationalized.[32] Yet there can be surprises. House Majority Leader Eric Cantor (Virginia) had an enormous campaign war chest ($5.4 million), but was defeated in a June 2014 Republican primary by underfunded ($200,000 and with few consultants and no help from PACs) political neophyte David Brat. One study found that Cantor spent more money on food for his campaign ($168,000 on steakhouses alone) than Brat spent on his entire campaign.[33]

Ballot Measures

With ballot issues, you build your own campaign.
—consultant Rick Claussen (1998)[34]

Proposition 13 spawned a new era of direct democracy.
—Daniel A. Smith (1998)[35]

Direct democracy is big business in the United States. Voters in twenty-eight states and the District of Columbia, and in many local jurisdictions, are given the opportunity to participate in initiatives (ballot measures created by citizens, groups, and corporate interests voted on directly by the people), referendums (measures passed by the legislature that must be ratified by voters to become law), or recalls (citizens voting directly to remove an elected official). In eighteen states, citizens can directly amend the state's constitution; in twenty-two states, citizens can vote on statutory amendments; and sixteen states allow both constitutional and statutory amendments.[36]

As Table 11.3 indicates, well over $3 billion was spent on advertising, campaign expenditures, and political consultants for ballot measures from 2004 through 2010. Much of it was spent in the expensive California market, but it was also spent in twenty-seven other states and the District of Columbia. In addition, in a survey of American cities, over 90 percent that responded noted that they had some form of ballot initiative.[37]

TABLE 11.3 Ballot Measures throughout the United States, 2004–2010

Year	Number of Measures	Expenditures
2004	111	$505,126,122
2005	25	$466,154,298
2006	219	$649,402,094
2007	33	$55,405,084
2008	172	$813,668,200
2009	32	$131,415,086
2010	184	$395,114,853

Source: National Institute on Money in State Politics.

Issues vary over the years, but some of the more popular ballot initiatives deal with taxation, abortion, minimum wage, gambling and gaming, immigration, and, more recently, marijuana usage and same-sex marriage.[38] During the early years of the twentieth century, states in the West and the Great Plains, together with several eastern states, amended their constitutions to permit direct citizen involvement, through initiatives, referendums, and recall measures. By 1915, twenty-two states had adopted some form of direct democracy mechanism. No state comes close to California in the number of, dollars spent on, and contentiousness of its ballot issues.[39]

As seen in chapter 1, Clem Whitaker and Leone Baxter were able to launch their highly successful political consulting career by opposing a corporate sponsored ballot initiative in 1932. For the most part, direct democray was seldom used in California from 1922 through the mid-1970s, but that all changed when Howard Jarvis and Paul Gann submitted Proposition 13, an initiative to limit California property taxes. At the time, Jarvis was a seventy-five-year-old semiretired businessman living in Los Angeles, and Paul Gann was a retired car dealer and insurance salesman in Sacramento. Jarvis became a professional gadfly at age fifty-nine, and described himself in a cover story in *Time* magazine as a "pain the ass," and "a rugged bastard who's had his head kicked in a thousand times by the government."[40] This was Jarvis's fourth attempt at getting a tax-cutting proposition on the California ballot.

Jarvis and Gann were assisted by Orange County, California, political consultants William Butcher and Arnold Forde. Just 100 days before Proposition 13 was to appear on the June 1978 ballot, Butcher and Forde heard that no professional consultants were involved in the campaign. They made it a point to meet with Jarvis and Gann, were asked to help, and guided the effort to obtain a "Yes" for the ballot initiative. At the beginning, only one-third of voters supported Proposition 13, and hardly any elected officials endorsed it. To drum up support, Butcher and Forde used direct mail to warn voters of the dangers of a property tax hike.[41] Voters received an official-looking envelope, with the words "Your 1978 Property Tax Increase Statement Enclosed" and the words in red letters, 'RESPONSE REQUIRED." On the inside was a letter to the taxpayers, indicating how much their property taxes would go up, and requesting a donation to the "Yes on 13" campaign. The letter, of course, was not an official notice from the state, but was created by the consultants. It was a smashing success, raising $1.8 million for the initiative's campaign, and helping to establish Proposition 13 as the initiative securing the most number of individual donors in a California direct democracy battle.

Nearly 70 percent of registered adults voted on the measure, and it passed with 62.5 percent of the vote. Property taxes were capped at 1 percent of the cash value. The political impact of Proposition 13 was dramatic not only in California, but also nationwide, becoming the spark plug for other attempts to cut taxes or limit their increases through the ballot initiative process. In the 1978 general election, voters in five states approved tax-limit ballot initiatives, while in 1979, twenty-two states passed laws limiting property taxes, eighteen reduced income taxes, fifteen reduced sales taxes, and twelve cut or repealed other taxes.[42] From their efforts, Butcher and Forde received a nineteen-year contract from Jarvis and Gans.

By the mid-1980s, Butcher and Forde had managed a half-dozen post–Proposition 13 initiatives. Even two years after Jarvis's death in 1986, Butcher and Forde sent out an 800,000-piece mailing, using Jarvis's name and photo, soliciting funds to help pass a "new Proposition 13." In 2016 Jarvis lives on through a website called the Howard Jarvis Taxpayers Association, which bills itself as "dedicated to the protection of Proposition 13 and the advancement of taxpayers' rights."[43]

Doug Guetzloe, a Florida-based political consultant, parlayed the anti-tax movement into a successful business, helping to start a group in 1982 called Ax the Tax. He claims to have to saved taxpayers some $11 billion over the years by helping mobilize anti-tax drives. Guetzloe, a founder of the Florida Tea Party, also has had several run-ins with the law, the most recent landing him with a 15-month prison term for failing to pay his own federal income taxes.[44]

It is relatively easy to announce that a group or citizen will submit a ballot initiative before the voters, but it takes money and expertise to make it past the initial press release. Costs begin to mount up: the filing fee, the attorney fees for creating the proper language, and then the costs of getting the minimum number of signatures needed for a valid petition. Particularly in California, it is almost impossible to gather enough signatures using only volunteers. For an initiative to qualify in California, it must obtain 5 percent of the total votes cast during the previous gubernatorial election, or about 504,000 votes. If it is a constitutional amendment, then it is 8 percent, or around 807,000 votes. Petitioners are given 150 days to circulate a petition, and the initiative must be certified valid at least 131 days before the election. Other states have their own deadlines and petition signature requirements, some more difficult to obtain, like 15 percent for a constitutional amendment in Arizona, and some easier, like a 3 percent for statutory issues in Massachusetts or Ohio.[45] Depending on how much time a professional signature gathering firm has to assemble its subcontractors and their personnel, each valid signature may cost between $1 and $3.

While ballot initiatives were supposed to be a way for citizens to have their voice heard directly, through direct democracy, most ballot initiatives, particularly in California, are financed by business or commercial interests. Political consultants have considerable leeway in developing communication strategies to promote or defeat ballot initiatives. The most important is that there is no candidate involved: no individual who has to be coached and prepared, who is prone to fits of anger or tires easily, no spouse making demands, no personal skeletons in the closet, and no political party trying to wedge itself into the fray. Consultants are called in to help write the ballot initiative, gather the required signatures to make it to the election, frame the issue, and define the opponents. Denver-based consultant Rick Ridder has turned his business more toward ballot initiatives, which he says are "far more interesting and far more profitable" than candidate campaigns.[46]

"No" often trumps "yes," however. It is more difficult to pass a ballot proposal, while it is usually much easier to defeat one. Consultants are brought in to point out the foibles or unattractiveness of a ballot idea, and to show how it would harm society (and a group larger than those who have paid for the consultants in the first place).

Another early example was Proposition 5, a 1978 measure in California that would have virtually prohibited smoking anywhere except in one's home. This struck close to home for tobacco companies and those who sell tobacco products, such as convenience stores and newsstands, but the opponents of the ban knew they had to widen the circle and show that the proposed ban would hurt most Californians. Edward A. Grefe, in charge of grassroots efforts at tobacco giant Philip Morris, first heard about the effort to draft an anti-tobacco initiative in March 1977. Grefe worked on a plan to oppose the proposed initiative, and the Tobacco Institute hired the best-known Republican initiative and referendum firm in Califonia, Woodward & McDowell. Grefe recommended two themes: make the anti-smoking initiative a question of civil liberties and stress the negative economic impact of such a ban. Early polls, conducted by V. Lance Tarrance, showed that for the average Californian, this was a nonissue, ranking 100th among their concerns. But the polls also showed that tobacco interests would lose, 3 to 1.

To fight the proposition, an ad-hoc group, Californians for Common Sense (CCS), was created. The group had 12,000 volunteers, with 60 percent of them being smokers. In numbers reminiscent of the grassroots activities of Whitaker & Baxter some forty years earlier, Woodward & McDowell sent out 3 million pieces of direct mail under the banner of the CCS, dropped over 1 million pieces of literature at individual doorsteps, and framed the issue as a matter of infringement of civil liberties and a threat to small businesses. Of the 109 newspapers in the state giving editorial opinions, 97 urged defeat of the measure. The tobacco industry spent some $6 million, but won a resounding victory with 55 percent of voters rejecting the proposal.[47]

Ballot Issues and Professional Services

> *In terms of size, complexity and sophistication*
> *California's political consulting industry is . . . a world leader*
> *and has been since the days when it was the home*
> *of the first of these firms.*
> —Shaun Bowler, Todd Donovan, and Ken Fernandez (1996)[48]

The sequence of steps involved in preparing, presenting, and selling a ballot initiative all involve professional campaign assistance. Political scientists Todd Donovan, Shaun Bowler, and David McCuan laid out the steps needed: First, the petition has to be drafted by a law firm; next it must be tested through focus groups and polling to determine the right language and message; then coalitions have to be assembled during the drafting stage. Then, lawyers have to negotiate with state election officials the title and the summary of the language that will be made public. Next, the initiative campaign needs to obtain endorsements—from celebrities, from civic organizations, or from business groups. Consultants will also help in the timing, giving their judgment as to which election cycle, primary, or general election would be most advantageous. The next step is the critical circulation phase. It even may be desirable to create a counter petition.[49] Once these steps have been taken, then comes the hard part: convincing voters to support or reject the ballot initiative.

The battle to enact/or defeat California's Proposition 211 in 1996 illustrates the range of political consulting firms that were deployed. San Diego trial lawyer and securities specialist William Lerach, long active in Democratic politics, created Proposition 211, designed to expand lawsuits against publicly traded corporations over stock fraud. If enacted, the measure would have permitted shareholders to file suits for fraud, but only in California, if a corporation's stock prices dropped precipitously. Proposition 211 was one of the most expensive initiative to date: an estimated $52 million was spent, with the opponents spending about $37 million, while the proponents spent $15 million. The initiative was soundly defeated, 74.4 percent against to just 25.6 percent in favor.

Here are some of the firms that worked on the initiative:

- *Petition signing.* Kimball Petitions received $1.04 million to circulate the petitions and gather enough signatures to qualify for the November 1996 ballot.
- *Television ads.* Bill Carrick, who also was a senior strategist for the Clinton-Gore re-election bid of that year, and his firm were paid $9 million to produce and place ads supporting the proposition. Typically, the firm would receive up to 15 percent commission on the ads it placed, along with production fees.
- *Coalition building.* Stoorza, Zieghaus, Metzger, and Hunt was paid $299,932 to line up celebrities, public officials, and coalition groups to oppose the measure.
- *Door-to-door campaigning.* Voter Revolt was paid $205,000 to have workers go door-to-door in opposition to the measure.
- *Polling and focus groups.* Holm Group and Charlton Research received $325,000 and $246,404, respectively, to conduct focus group and survey research.
- *Public relations.* Edelman Associations was paid $257,022 to generate stories in newspapers and television and be the public representative for the campaign.
- *Opposition research.* The Dolphin Group was paid $15,000 to investigate lawyers and others who were backing the proposition.
- *Direct mail.* Forde and Mollrich received $585,524 for their direct mail services.
- *Fundraising.* Ann Hyde was paid $314,900 to raise funds against the proposition.
- *General consulting.* Goddard/Claussen First Tuesday, working against the proposition, collected at least $24.2 million (along with $4.6 million for several other ballot issues the firm was working on at the same time). Goddard/Claussen kept roughly $3 to $5 million in profits, with the rest going to subcontractors and television stations to purchase airtime.[50]

California is the land of gold for political consultants because it is so populous (38.8 million people in 2014), has so many media markets (fourteen), and has several distinct political cultures.[51] In recent years, several ballot issues have reached well over the $100 million mark. The Native American casino ballot initiatives in California in 2008 (Propositions 95, 96, and 97) combined were the most expensive ballot issues to date, with $108.3 million spent by several tribes favoring the proposals, while opponents (Hollywood Park Race Track, Bay Meadows Race Track, and several other Native American casinos) spent approximately $64.3 million, and altogether over $172.6 million was spent.[52]

Five other California propositions in recent years have cost between $100 million and $165 million. Proposition 79 (2005) would have provided low-income California residents with prescription drug discounts; it was readily defeated and $163 million was spent to fight for and against the measure. Proposition 87 (2006), which would have established a $4 billion fund to reduce petroleum consumption, was defeated, with a total of $155 million spent. Proposition 32 (2012) would have prohibited unions from deducting funds from worker paychecks for political purposes. It failed by a 12-point margin, and $149 million was spent. During the same year, Californians passed Proposition 30, creating a temporary tax on high-income earners to fund education; $148 million was spent by the proponents and opponents.

California voters passed Proposition 8 (2008), which restricted marriage to the union of a man and a woman; $106 million was spent on this initiative, with considerable help from members of the Mormon Church.[53] When Proposition 8 was challenged in the US Supreme Court, eighty prominent Republicans (but only one in the House of Representatives and none in the Senate) signed on to an *amicus curiae* brief in support of striking down the measure. Along with former presidential candidate Jon Huntsman and former New Jersey governor Christine Todd Whitman were a number of political consultants, including Ken Mehlman, Alex Castellanos, Mark McKinnon, Mike Murphy, Steve Schmidt, and Bob Wickers.[54]

The most expensive ballot initiative not coming from California was Question 7 (2012) in Maryland, asking whether gambling should be expanded in the state. A total of $95 million was spent, with two large casino gambling corporations, MGM (for) and Penn National Gaming (against) on opposing sides and providing the lion's share of funds.[55] After the dust settled, the ballot initiative passed, and new gambling venues were allowed. As seen here in Maryland and in California, casino gambling is a high stakes business, not just for the participants, but also for the consulting industry.

Recall of Elected Officials

Nineteen states permit the recall of elected officials; most do not require a specific reason for recall. Unlike the impeachment of an elected official, which is a legal matter, recall is a political matter, directly in the hands of the voters.[56] Two recent recall efforts, one successful, the other not, brought much attention, money, and the use of political consultants. During the summer of 2003, California governor Gray Davis was in deep political trouble, and opponents were mounting a recall effort. California congressman Darrell E. Issa bankrolled much of the early recall effort. Some Davis supporters spent $2.1 million, giving money to signature-gathering consulting firms so that they would not gather signatures against the governor. But once that was found out, millions of dollars flowed in to oust Davis, from Indian casinos, labor unions, state contractors, and others who were upset with the governor. Davis was recalled by over 55 percent of the voters. A total of $70 million was spent on the recall effort and on the subsequent new gubernatorial election, with movie actor Arnold Schwarzenegger elected to office.[57]

Wisconsin governor Scott Walker also faced a recall in 2012, chiefly because of his aggressive stance against state employee unions. In a highly contentious recall, Walker came up against Wisconsin organized labor and other organizations, but he was able to survive the recall. Some $63 million was spent, with Walker raising over $30 million and his Democratic opponent, Milwaukee mayor Tom Barrett, raising just $4 million. Two years later, in June 2014, state prosecutors charged that Walker was involved in a "criminal scheme" to coordinate the activities of conservative groups, like the Wisconsin Club for Growth, Citizens for a Strong America, and Wisconsin Manufacturers and Commerce. Walker characterized the charges of collusion with super PACs in the recall effort as "categorically false."[58] Walker survived that law suit, and in 2015 for about six months was a candidate for the Republican nomination for president.

For these two recalls alone, over $130 million was raised to win over voters. They were good paydays for the political consulting firms involved.

Political Consultants and Ballot Initiatives

In addition to William Butcher and Arnold Forde, several political consultants have been prominent in the business of ballot initiatives.

Jack McDowell (1916–1998) had journalism in his blood. His father was founder and publisher of the *Alameda Times-Star*, and McDowell became a journalist in 1942. He won a Pulitzer Prize in 1945 for a series in the *San Francisco Call-Bulletin* about whole blood donors from San Francisco (including McDowell) for GI casualties in the Marianna Islands. He became political editor of the *Call-Bulletin* in 1956 and covered Sacramento politics during the Pat Brown and Ronald Reagan years. In 1969 he left journalism to join the consulting firm of Spencer-Roberts; then, in 1971, he joined Richard and Mary Woodward who had created their own firm.[59]

Richard Woodward joined Spencer-Roberts in 1964 and served as an advance man and campus coordinator for the Rockefeller for President campaign. In 1966 he was the Northern California campaign director for Ronald Reagan's gubernatorial bid, and later manager of the Spencer-Roberts San Francisco office.

Based in San Francisco, Woodward & McDowell's first big win was the upset victory of S. I. Hayakawa over incumbent John Tunney in the 1976 US Senate contest in California. They also helped Gordon Humphrey defeat veteran Democratic senator Thomas McIntyre in New Hampshire in 1978.[60] Over the years, Woodward & McDowell has represented hundreds of clients.

One of Woodward & McDowell's biggest victories came with the 1990 defeat of Proposition 128, "Big Green," a measure that sought widespread authority to clean up cancer-causing chemicals and pesticides. Tom Hayden, a longtime activist and California assemblyman, was one the sponsors of the proposition. But Big Green went too far and cost too much, alienating many business interests and many voters. Agribusiness, chemical manufacturers, and others poured in $16 million to defeat the initiative. The lead consulting firm was Woodward & McDowell, who labeled Prop. 128 the "Hayden Initiative," creating a liberal bogeyman, and gave clarity (their clients' spin) to the cumbersome initiative. Big Green was a 16,000-word, complicated, and confusing laundry list of programs. Voters were faced with twenty-eight ballot issues that year, and were in no mood to approve anything. As a result, this mega-initiative went down to a resounding two-to-one defeat. "We've won a lot of big ones in the past," said Woodward, "but this one may be the biggest.[61]

Other California-based public affairs firms have been active in ballot initiative contests.

Charles (Chuck) Winner and Paul Mandabach's firm, Winner & Mandabach Campaigns (W&M), founded in 1986, boasts of having won more ballot initiative contests, 190, than any other firm, and has worked since 1990 in twenty-eight states, maintaining a 90 percent winning percentage. A related firm, Winner & Associates, founded in 1975 (as Winner-Wagner Associates, with co-founder Ethan Wagner) concentrates on strategic communications for corporations, trade associations, law firms, and other clients, and has assisted over 400 clients. Winner was active in California politics and established a firm in 1966 with Joseph Cerrell; he left politics for a while, and then became active in the 1972 Muskie presidential campaign. Paul Mandabach began his career as a research analyst for Opinion Research of California and early in his career was a freelance consultant on over twenty election campaigns. In 2000 the international public affairs firm Publicis purchased 60 percent of W&M.[62]

Wayne C. Johnson, of Sacramento, and his firm, The Wayne Johnson Agency, has been involved in more than 250 candidate races and a dozen statewide ballot initiatives in its thirty years of business. The firm has won more than 100 national awards for its campaign advertising. Johnson is the recent past president of the American Association of Political Consultants and has served as the American director on the International Association of Political Consultants.

Specializing in helping ballot committees write their proposals is Nielsen Merksamer, a Sacramento-based law firm, that from 1979 through 2012 assisted 327 ballot measure clients get the proper wording for their measures.[63] In 2010, Nielsen Merksamer assisted eight campaigns, receiving nearly $3.8 million in legal fees.[64] In addition, the law firms of Olson, Hagel & Fishburn (Sacramento) and Remcho, Johansen & Purcell (San Leandro) have provided extensive ballot initiative expertise.

Signature collection specialist Fred Kimball Sr. began a petition gathering business in the late 1960s, and by 1984 his sons Fred and Kelly had turned Kimball Petition Management (KPM) into the leading signature gathering firm in California. Journalist David Broder noted that the Kimball firm became the "favorites of teachers and unions, trial lawyers and gaming interests."[65]

Michael Arno, who earlier had worked for Kimball, founded Arno Political Consultants (APC) in 1979, specializing in signature collection for ballot initiatives. Over the years APC, based in Carlsbad, California, has collected more than 120 million signatures on 500 ballot initiatives in twenty states, mostly for conservative or libertarian causes.[66] National Voter Outreach, a Carson City, Nevada direct democracy firm, headed by Richard L. (Rick) Arnold, was created in 1988 and boasts 450 successful signature drives in forty-one states and the District of Columbia, as well as the collection of 36 million signatures.[67] In his early years, Arnold also worked for Kimball Petition Management.

CHAPTER 12

Consultants and Presidential Campaigns, 1984 and 1988

Something's terribly out of whack with the way
we ask our leaders to compete for democracy's highest prize.
—Journalist Paul Taylor (1989)

T HE 1984 AND 1988 presidential elections illustrate two important underlying elements of contemporary presidential politics. In 1984, no matter how disciplined or inventive political advisers and consultants happened to be, they could not overcome the power of incumbency, an improving economy, a nation at peace, and a president who was hard for voters not to like. While there were glimmers of hope for the campaign of former vice president Walter F. Mondale, little could be done to alter the reality of an overwhelming victory for Ronald Reagan. For those scholars who argue that campaigns don't matter, this would be Exhibit A. By contrast, 1988 was the election year when campaign operatives were critical, with experienced Republican operatives taking off the gloves, defining the contest on their terms, refocusing the debate, and boosting the vulnerable George H. W. Bush to victory. Michael Dukakis's campaign was riddled with conflicting advice, poor coordination, and a candidate unwilling to listen to veteran advisers. Up to this point in modern presidential campaigning, this is the best Exhibit A for those who say that campaign operatives, and their strategy and tactics, do indeed matter.

The 1984 Presidential Election: Ronald Reagan v. Walter Mondale

I understand you guys are selling soap and
I thought you'd like to see the bar.
—Ronald Reagan upon meeting media specialists
Phil Dusenberry and the Tuesday Team (1984)[1]

I'm no good at television.

—Walter Mondale to campaign manager Bob Beckel[2]

Political scientist Austin Ranney noted that the 1984 election, "depending on the measure used, it was either the second, fifth, or seventh greatest landslide in an American presidential election since the Civil War."[3] Like Johnson's victory in 1964 and Nixon's in 1972, the 1984 election results were hardly in doubt, and voters were emphatic. One popular book chronicling the election was aptly titled, "Wake Us When It's Over."[4]

No matter the odds, campaigns are about hope, aspirations, and perhaps catching the brass ring. Long-shot George McGovern was able to use the new Democratic Party reform measures to his advantage in the 1972 primaries (before getting crushed in the general election), while the unknown Jimmy Carter brilliantly weaved through the primaries in 1976 (and hung on to win the general). Perhaps in 1984, a Democratic candidate would catch fire in the primaries and give Reagan a run for his money. Whether it was the former vice president Walter Mondale or a newcomer, they would all need the help of professional consultants to guide them through the primary battles.

We also have to be wary of reading history backwards. Two years into his presidency, Reagan was in trouble with the American voters. During the 1992 midterm elections, the Republicans lost twenty-six seats. In addition, unemployment was sky-high, at levels never seen since the Great Depression. A January 1983 Gallup poll of registered voters preferred Walter Mondale 51–33 percent over Reagan.[5] Furthermore, recent electoral history had not been kind to presidents seeking re-election: Ford was defeated by Carter, and Carter was toppled by Reagan. Perhaps Reagan would be toppled by Mondale or some other Democratic hopeful. The Reagan landslide was months, years away when Democratic challengers began stirring.

Democrats and the Nomination

Eight Democrats vied for Democratic nomination, with three—former vice president Walter Mondale, Colorado senator Gary Hart, and civil rights activist Jesse Jackson—claiming front-runner status at different stages. It turned out to be a long, bitter, and costly primary fight, with Hart claiming twenty-five states, Mondale winning twenty-two, and Jackson taking two states plus the District of Columbia.

Mondale was the candidate of the established Democratic Party, a Humphrey protégé and supporter of big labor and entrenched liberal interest groups. John Reilly, Mondale's law partner, served as senior campaign adviser. Robert Beckel, who worked briefly for Robert Kennedy in his 1968 campaign for president and then joined the Carter administration in the State Department working on the Panama Canal treaty, served as campaign manager. Mondale's pollster was the highly respected Peter D. Hart (see profile in chapter 7). Mike Ford was in charge of field operations, joined by veteran operative Paul Tully. In the general election,

Patrick Caddell joined the campaign. Mondale's media was handled by Roy Spence, David Sawyer (after working for John Glenn and Gary Hart), and Frank Greer.

The most formidable rival to Mondale was thought to be Ohio senator John Glenn. The Reagan campaign took notice. As Dick Wirthlin laid out in his 180-page campaign plan, Glenn had three very positive things going for him: as a former astronaut and veteran of World War II and the Korean War, he was a genuine national hero; he was well known and well liked throughout the land; and, while being a Democrat, he was quite nonpartisan.[6] Wirthlin could have added another factor: Glenn was the popular US senator from the key swing state of Ohio. Assisting Glenn were campaign manager Bill White, who had been manager of Glenn's Senate staff; Robert Keefe, a longtime Capitol Hill presence, and, for a time, Joe Grandmaison served as political director. Bill Hamilton and former Carter aide Greg Schneiders conducted polls and gave strategic advice, and David Sawyer provided media assistance.[7]

Gary Hart was the new face in the crowd. He was elected senator from Colorado in November 1974, on the wave of the Watergate scandal; he announced his presidential candidacy in February 1983. Few of the pundits and wise men in Washington gave him much of a chance going up against Mondale or Glenn, or even California senator Alan Cranston. His media adviser, Ray Strother, wrote that Hart "was a joke to everyone except me and a small group of fellow true believers."[8] Hart's campaign manager was Oliver (Pudge) Henkel, a "straight-backed and somewhat garrulous tax lawyer with no big-league political experience."[9] Henkel's most significant qualification for the job was being Hart's Yale Law School classmate and best friend. That's the way Hart wanted it: friendship and loyalty over experience. In 1972 Hart was the fresh new consultant for McGovern, but now, in his own run, he didn't want any Washington-type consultants, old boys who had been running campaign after campaign. But Hart's 1984 campaign was "mass utter confusion," in Ray Strother's assessment: "It was the damnest campaign I've ever been involved with in my life.... We were trying to do too many things with too few people and no money."[10]

Hart's pollster was Dotty Lynch (1945–2014). In 1983 Lynch formed her own polling business and became the first woman pollster for a presidential candidate. She began her career in 1972 with Cambridge Survey Research, Pat Caddell's firm, and had worked on the McGovern campaign, the Carter campaign in 1976, and was in-house pollster for Edward Kennedy during the 1980 primary.[11] Lynch was also the first pollster-strategist to devise a national "women's strategy." She recognized a growing gender gap, and advised Hart to focus on issues important to women, have women in his commercials, and acknowledge in his speeches the importance and growing power of women.[12] "She's the person who raised the consciousness of the party leaders on the voter gap between men and women," observed media consultant Bob Squier in 1984, "She translated it and made people aware of it."[13] (Lynch later had a long and successful career as a political analyst at CBS News and as a professor at American University).

Pat Caddell, at age thirty-three was now the grand old man of modern presidential polling, having been involved in three presidential general election campaigns. While he had worked with Hart in 1972, Caddell hadn't immediately signed up with any candidate in 1984. Mondale's John Reilly initially thought of hiring Caddell, "though he was nothing but trouble in a campaign—an asshole with a big ego who managed to grab the credit for what worked and redirect the blame for what didn't."[14] Now Caddell was shopping around for the next Democratic candidate. As Bob Shrum put it, Caddell "was on his own relentless search for Mr. Right, with a memo arguing that a combination of experience and freshness—a mythical Senator Smith—could prevail in the primaries and against Reagan."[15] Neither his close friend Delaware senator Joe Biden (who eventually ran in 1988, then in 2008), nor Connecticut senator Chris Dodd (who ran in 2008), nor Missouri congressman Richard Gephardt (who ran in 1988 and 2004) took the bait. Finally, Caddell turned to Gary Hart. "Pat, on his own," wrote Strother, "began taking polls and bill the campaign for them, completely ignoring the data brought in by Dotty." Lynch remained the official pollster, but she and her "women's strategy" were pushed aside while Caddell "ranted and raved to gain complete control of the message."[16]

Mondale claimed the first victory in the Iowa caucuses, garnering a respectable 49 percent of the vote. But Hart pulled off a major upset in New Hampshire, trouncing Mondale and the rest of the field. From that point on, second-tier candidates—California senator Alan Cranston, former Florida governor Reubin Askew, South Carolina senator Ernest (Fritz) Hollings—quickly dropped out. Glenn, getting only 4 percent in Iowa and coming in third in New Hampshire, was soon out. For George McGovern, 1984 was his last hurrah (although he was tempted to run in 1992). He limped along through eight primaries, and came in third in Massachusetts, the only state where he was victorious in his 1972 race against Nixon. Rather than endorsing his former campaign manager, Gary Hart, McGovern endorsed Mondale: "I really feel more at home listening to Mondale than I do listening to someone who says this is a contest between the past and the future."[17] Jesse Jackson won only the District of Columbia and the primaries in South Carolina and Louisiana, but he stayed through the duration of the primaries. Jackson's campaign was managed by Arnold R. Pinkney, a veteran campaign aide who had helped Hubert Humphrey and Jimmy Carter in their bids for the presidency.[18]

The Hart campaign was packaged to be all about new ideas, fresh approaches, a newer generation. Handsome, athletic, and a youthful forty-six, Hart could lead the party and a new generation into the 1990s. Mondale, nearly twenty years older, was the establishment candidate, with solid liberal credentials and strong backing in Congress and state capitols. The Hart media team, led by Strother, used cutting-edge graphics, with computer technology to make a television ad look like a book turning pages. Also, the ads had a grid that faded into the background, a "geometric image that suggested something more like Star Wars than the old politics of Walter Mondale." The techniques are a little hokey today, but in 1984 they were futuristic—reinforcing the theme of Hart as the candidate with new ideas.[19]

Mondale fought back: Sure, you claim to have new ideas, Mr. Hart, but what are they, what are you trying to sell us? At a debate practice session, campaign manager Bob Beckel suggested Mondale challenge Hart's so-called "new ideas." Mondale reluctantly agreed, lifting the words from a popular hamburger commercial. Mondale demanded to know: "Where's the beef?"; that is, where is the substance to the so-called ideas platform of Hart? [20] Peter Hart, Mondale's pollster, also tried to understand Gary Hart's weaknesses and Mondale's strengths through a series of focus groups. Hart assembled a group of fifteen likely Democratic voters in Atlanta, voters who would either chose Gary Hart or were undecided. During a two-hour session, the pollster probed the participants' attitudes, and he showed them a thirty-second Mondale ad, which they all criticized. Toward the end of the focus group session, Peter Hart asked, Which of the two, Mondale or Hart, do you prefer to handle the economy? The answer was unanimous, Gary Hart. Then the pollster asked, Which of the two do you prefer to handle a serious international incident? The answer was again unanimous, Mondale.[21]

There was the opening: Mondale will keep us safe, he knows the dangers of an unsafe world. Three days later, the Mondale team began running an ad featuring a red telephone, the "hotline" between Washington and Moscow.[22] The phone was ringing. Who do you want to answer that phone? Then came the deep-voiced male narrator:

> The most awesome, powerful responsibility in the world lies in the hand that picks up this phone. The idea of an unsure, unsteady, untested hand is something to really think about. This is the issue of our times. . . . Vote as if the future of the world is at stake, because it is. Mondale. This president will know what he is doing. And that's the difference.

This Mondale ad ran from March 6 through June 14, in most of the primary states. Twenty-four years later, in 2008, the red phone ringing in the middle of the night also popped up in Hillary Clinton's 2008 primary campaign:[23]

"Three A.M."

[Visual: Darkness outside of a large, comfortable house. Kids are sleeping upstairs; telephone ringing in background.]

Male Narrator: It's 3 a.m., and your children are safe and asleep. But there's a phone in the White House and it's ringing. Something's happening in the world. Your vote will decide who answers that call. Whether it's someone who already knows the world's leaders, knows the military. Someone tested and ready to lead in a dangerous world.

[Visual: Mom peaks her head into one of the bedrooms. Phone still ringing.]

Narrator: It's 3 a.m., and your children are safe and asleep. Who do you
   want answering the phone?
Hillary Clinton: I'm Hillary Clinton and I approve this message [with a
   short flourish of military music].

The primary battle between Hart and Mondale, much like the 2008 battle
between Barack Obama and Hillary Clinton, did not end until the final weeks of
the primary season, on June 11, dubbed Super Tuesday III. Hart won more states,
but Mondale won more delegates, especially super delegates.

It would never be easy for a challenger to defeat a popular incumbent president; it would be even more difficult when the challenger goes through a long,
costly battle to get his or her party's nomination. Adding to Mondale's difficulties was his choice for vice president, Representative Geraldine A. Ferraro from
New York, the first woman nominated for vice president by a major party (the
second was Alaska governor Sarah Palin in 2008). Peter Hart thought choosing Ferraro was a "brilliant stroke," with "the potential of changing the equa-
tion."[24] Despite the euphoria of Mondale's pollster and many Democrats, the
choice of a New York liberal running mate, and a woman to boot, was music to
Republican ears. "It's over, folks," wrote a jubilant Lee Atwater wrote right after
the Democratic convention. "By choosing a Northern liberal as a running mate,
Mondale has sealed his own electoral inferiority." Atwater did the math: the
South had 155 electoral votes, while the West had 111—totaling 266, just 4 shy
of victory. Reagan might not get all of the South and the West, but certainly the
odds were in his favor. Then came the embarrassment of Ferraro's husband, John
Zaccaro, and his financial irregularities.[25]

The Reagan Re-election Campaign

Many of the Reagan campaign operatives from 1980 had moved on, but Mike
Deaver, James Baker, and Stuart Spencer sat down to determine who would
be the day-to-day administrator for the campaign. Spencer wanted either Paul
J. Manafort or Charlie Black; Spencer remembered that Deaver and Baker wanted
Ed Rollins, but at the same time they "were mad as hell at Rollins. Ed has a propen-
sity for dumping on everybody that he works with or works for."[26] Nevertheless,
Rollins got the job, but Spencer insisted that Lee Atwater, then serving in the
political shop of the White House, be chosen as Rollins's deputy. Rollins, in his
memoirs, takes credit for bringing Atwater onto the campaign team and bringing back his old boss, Lyn Nofziger: "I trusted Lyn absolutely. Counsellor, consigliere, father confessor, enforcer, you name it—Lyn wore all those hats for me."
Then there was Atwater: "Lee, on the other hand, was like my mischievous kid
brother, a guy I needed but couldn't trust."[27] Also on the campaign team was
Ken Khachigian, who had been close to Richard Nixon, and would now run the
opposition research team.

As in past Reagan presidential campaigns, there was tension and mistrust
among the senior advisers. Ed Rollins characterized the relationship between the

campaign and the White House as a "den of vipers." Nancy Reagan and Deaver didn't like Rollins; Khachigian "despised, and was despised by" Dick Darman; campaign treasurer Bay Buchanan "terrified" Lee Atwater "by the ferocity with which she nailed his expense account extravagances." James Baker and Paul Laxalt were vying for campaign leadership role. Nofziger loathed Spencer; and the feeling was mutual.[28] Rollins felt threatened by Wirthlin's oversized role as pollster and strategist, and Rollins successfully cut back on the polling operation.

In late 1983, the team of Ed Rollins, Lee Atwater, Jim Lake, Richard Wirthlin, Drew Lewis, Stu Spencer, Lyn Nofziger, Charlie Black, and Bob Teeter began putting together the re-election strategy. If the re-election strategy could be boiled down to one sentence, Teeter later remarked, it was this: "If there was a good economic recovery under way and no American troops anywhere and we were at peace, Ronald Reagan would be re-elected." This would be, Teeter believed, "one of those campaigns when good government and good politics do mix."[29]

The General Election

The detailed campaign script put together by Jim Johnson had Mondale winning the primaries with an early knockout, giving him time to prepare for Reagan in the general election. But Gary Hart spoiled the plans, causing Mondale to run through millions of campaign dollars much sooner than planned, and Hart's tenacity (and popularity) meant that Mondale could not concentrate on Reagan until Hart was finally whipped during the early summer. As Peter Goldman and Tony Fuller chronicled, the Mondale team "had been traumatized by Gary Hart's commando campaign and had never really recovered."[30]

Like Ford in 1976 after surviving a brutal primary challenge from Reagan, the Mondale forces were exhausted and unfocused: there was no plan, no defining message, and no way to chip away at Reagan's seemingly insurmountable lead. Peter Hart put on a brave face, urging Mondale in an August 1984 memo to fight with everything he had. "My advice is simple: Let 'er rip. Reach inside your soul and tell the voters why you are running and what this election is all about . . . you must reach the intensity you had when you were fighting back from political extinction this spring."[31]

Over the Labor Day weekend, the Mondale team sought out David Sawyer and Scott Miller to help turn its television campaign around. At this point, Mondale was some 20 points behind Reagan in national preference polls. Sawyer and Miller had been working for John Glenn for nearly a year, trying to make sure that Mondale was not the party's choice. After Glenn dropped out, they went to work for Gary Hart. Now they answered their party's call and tried to help Mondale during the general election. But they knew that they had little to work with, and little time to make their case.[32]

For months within the Mondale camp, there had been secret talks with Patrick Caddell, Gary Hart's pollster. Even before Hart dropped out, Caddell was approached, through the back channel of New York governor Mario Cuomo, to prepare a strategy memo for the eventual, as yet unnamed, Democratic nominee. The memo was "long, heated and bleakly visionary, a doomsday book of Democratic politics," but curiously flattering to Walter Mondale.[33] Should Mondale now bring Caddell into his campaign team? John Reilly knew that "Pat was a brilliant son of a bitch," but "he was nothing but trouble in a campaign." Caddell had been rejected before by the Mondale forces, and during the primaries, he tore Mondale apart both in public and private. But now he was back, ready to do battle for Mondale. During the month of August, Caddell holed up at his retreat at Martha's Vineyard, where he composed a 106-page battle plan for Mondale's revival. "Defeat his ideas and you will defeat Reagan," Caddell urged.[34] Peter Hart, Mondale's long-standing pollster, and Caddell were bumping heads with competing strategies and differing visions; it was the cerebral and quiet Hart against the mercurial Caddell.

There was one glimmer of optimism for the Mondale team: the first debate, held in Louisville, Kentucky, on October 7.[35] During the debate, Reagan was clearly off stride and soon commentators and Monday morning quarterbacks were wondering whether Reagan was just too old for the job. Stuart Spencer felt that Reagan just didn't do his homework. Richard Darman had prepared the briefing books, and the weekend before the debates, Spencer was with the Reagans at Camp David. Reagan had the debate preparation books, but he never opened them up. "We went in the cottage where he stayed," Spencer remembered, "the books went on the credenza. We spent the next eight hours watching old movies. Most of them were his movies. The next day I came over, the books were still sitting there. I look at them. I said something off the cuff to him. He didn't react. He was supposed to do his homework at Camp David. He didn't do his homework. He came back and he got killed. He knows it."[36] Reagan, however, later told journalist Jim Lehrer that he wasn't tired, but that he was "overtrained."[37]

In a memo written after the first debate, Caddell was ecstatic and hyperbolic. "Ten days ago in Louisville, Walter Mondale scored the greatest victory in the history of presidential debates. Within twenty-four hours, Mondale was 'winning' by 62 percent to 20 percent—an absolute reversal of debate expectations."[38] Ed Rollins put the best face on Reagan's poor performance, saying, "it made us look very, very hard at our organization."[39]

But the Democrats' bubble would soon burst. Roger Ailes was asked to come to Washington to listen to the Reagan prep sessions for the second debate. Ailes pried the president away from his handlers—Deaver, Baker, and Darman—and held private sessions with the president, urging him to not worry about minute details, but to go with his gut instincts. Reagan wanted to use an old line that had drawn some laughs before, and Ailes agreed, "That's perfect."[40] During the second debate, when reporter Henry Trewhitt asked Reagan if age was a factor in this election, the president responded, "Not at all. And Mr. Trewhitt, I want you to know also I will not make age an issue of this campaign. I am not going to exploit for political purposes my opponent's youth and inexperience." The audience laughed, Mondale smiled, but later confessed to newscaster Jim Lehrer, "Well, I'll tell you, if TV can tell the truth, as you say it can, you'll see that I was smiling. But I think if you come in close, you'll see some tears coming down because I knew he had gotten me there. That was really the end of my campaign that night, I think."[41]

Reagan's Media Team. The ads that Peter Dailey's team produced in 1980 for Reagan were "consciously unslick," as he attempted to portray Reagan as a statesman, rather than as a former actor.[42] But both Nancy Reagan and Mike Deaver found the 1980 ads boring, and Deaver began searching for someone to replace Dailey. In early 1984, Deaver called Phil Dusenberry, senior executive of BBDO, to the White House. Deaver wanted BBDO to handle the ad campaign. Dusenberry, the driving force behind some of BBDO's best-known slogans and campaigns, including General Electric's "We bring good things to life," was responsible for producing the well-received eighteen-minute Reagan bio, which was introduced at the Republican nominating convention, and later was the centerpiece of a thirty-minute telecast on all three television networks. Part of the tribute to Reagan was "a three-hankie sequence" of the president eulogizing the fallen Allied soldiers who fought on D-Day.

But BBDO, according to Dusenberry, had a "long-standing policy against taking sides in politics" (although it also had a long history of working for Republicans), and the Reagan re-election campaign would be too big of a project for Dusenberry to handle alone. Dusenberry's friend and fellow adman Jerry Della Femina suggested the creation of an ad hoc agency, similar to what Peter Dailey had assembled in 1972 and 1980. One of Della Femina's partners, James Travis, assembled an "all-star squad" of New York agency people, writers, art directors, and other creative people.[43] Thus was born the Tuesday Team. "As advertising professionals we knew the proper campaign for a candidate with these positives was to take the high road," wrote Dusenberry. The admen also knew that Mondale would necessarily run a negative campaign. "And positive beats negative every time in the ad effectiveness book," Dusenberry remarked.[44] (This is in contrast to Wirthlin's assessment of negative ads, in which he found that "a negative ad has about four-times the hitting power of a positive ad.")[45]

Sigmund (Sig) Rogich, a Las Vegas ad executive and ally of close Reagan friend Nevada senator Paul Laxalt, was brought on board to manage the enterprise. Veteran ad maker Hal Riney, a senior executive in the San Francisco office of Ogilvy & Mather, received a telephone call in June 1984 from New York copywriter Jim Weller, who was part of the Tuesday Team. Could Riney help? Riney flew out to Washington to be briefed by Richard Wirthlin and other Reagan aides, and was then given the task of coming up with something better than found in the 1980 Reagan commercials. Over a two-and-a-half-hour session, sitting at a bar on the first floor of his San Francisco office building, Riney created "Prouder, Stronger, Better" (often called "Morning in America"), "Bear in the Woods," and a third iconic commercial "America's Back." In final production he also did the voice-overs. The commercials were low-key and soft sell, fitting in perfectly with Reagan's own philosophy of communication.[46]

For the Tuesday Team, political advertising was new. Instead of trying to cram everything into a commercial, as political strategists tended to do, the Tuesday Team's approach was different. As Dusenberry explained, "we believed just the opposite, that less was more, and that something simple and engaging and heartfelt was really the way to go."[47]

The signature campaign ad, "Prouder, Stronger, Better" first aired on September 17, 1984.

"Prouder, Stronger, Better"

Male Narrator: It's morning again in America. Today, more men and women will go to work than ever before in our country's history. With interest rates at about half the record highs of 1980, nearly 2,000 families today will buy new homes, more than at any time in the past four years. This afternoon, 6,500 young men and women will be married. And with inflation at less than half of what it was just four years ago, they can look forward with confidence to the future.

It's morning again in America. And, under the leadership of President Reagan, our country is prouder and stronger and better. Why would we ever want to return to where we were less than four short years ago?

[Text: PRESIDENT REAGAN][48]

Media critic Bob Garfield said that this ad "is probably the greatest political ad of modern times." "It wasn't just the copy. It was also the peaceful, reassuring piano-and-woodwind serenade and the super-slow-mo images: tractors, white-picket fences, a bride hugging her gramma, a paper boy on his bike, Americans young and old raising the flag—every one of them contented and, incredibly, every one of them white."[49] The *Newsweek* team chronicling the election characterized this and other Reagan campaign visuals as coming "from a sunlit land in which no one was sick, sad, fat, infirm, or afflicted by ring around the collar, and everybody always smiled."[50]

The second ad, which first aired on October 1, 1984, was totally unlike the first.

"Bear in the Woods"

[*Visual: A close up of a bear, who saunters through the woods, then is partially hidden behind the trees, then goes through a stream.*]

[*Audio: Anxious, mysterious background music, with a thumping sound, like a heart beating.*]

Male Narrator: There is a bear in the woods. For some people, the bear is easy to see. Others don't see it at all. Some people say the bear is tame. Others say it's vicious and dangerous. Since no one can really be sure who's right, isn't it smart to be as strong as the bear?

[*Visual: The bear is on the top of a hill and approaches a man several feet away.*]

Male Narrator: If there is a bear.

[Text: President Reagan: Prepared for Peace] [51]

The message here is clear: Who better to deal with the bear—the wily and threatening Soviet Union—than a strong, determined leader. "Bear in the Woods" vividly lets us know that President Reagan, like you and I, knows that the bear is real, and it is both vicious and dangerous. In spare language, in simple but absorbing images, this political haiku presents the viewer with a powerful choice: those who see the danger (Reagan), and those who don't (Mondale).

Dick Wirthlin had created a Hierarchical Values Map (HVM) showing that voters were most concerned about securing world peace and worried about the economy (and Mondale's convention proclamation that he would increase taxes). Basing his work on a theoretical model developed by marketing professor Thomas J. Reynolds, Wirthlin determined which issues and values were "owned" by either Reagan or Mondale, and sought to understand the linkages between those values, policies, and the candidates. Wirthlin explained that the campaign would have three tasks to perform: "First, our television ads would need to challenge the fairness of Mondale's proposed tax increase. Second, we would need to connect the need to strengthen national defense with the preservation of world peace. And finally, the HVM suggested we must continue reinforcing the president's image as a strong, effective leader."[52] "Bear in the Woods" and "Prouder, Stronger, Better" fed directly into the hopes and fears of voters. Altogether, the Reagan team spent approximately $25 million on advertising spots, about the same amount spent by the Mondale team.[53]

So unusual and presumably effective was the "Bear in the Woods" ad, that, like the ad for the hotline phone ringing in the middle of night, it would have its imitators. Republican media consultant Mark McKinnon would reprise the menacing wild animal theme in his campaign commercial "Wolves" for George W. Bush in 2004.

In addition, the Reagan campaign used country singer Lee Greenwood's anthem "I'm Proud to be an American" as background for several of its feel-good ads. The song was reintroduced in George H. W. Bush's ads in 1988.[54] Reporter Sam Donaldson complained: "The essence of the Ronald Reagan campaign is a never-ending string of spectacular picture stories created for television and designed to place the president in the midst of wildly cheering, patriotic Americans. . . . God, patriotism, and Ronald Reagan, that's the essence this campaign is trying hard to project."[55] The overall theme of the Reagan campaign, in Stuart Spencer's way of thinking, was Reagan's leadership, and voters were given the choice between the old "Carter-Mondale past" and Reagan's "celebration of the present."[56]

The country was at peace, the economy was improving, and the incumbent president, asking voters for another term, enjoyed strong public support. Reagan, far more than Mondale, was comfortable with television, and far more adept at using this medium to convey his hopes and aspirations to the voting public. Under those circumstances, it is almost impossible to defeat Ronald Reagan. No amount of savvy political consulting, no slick advertising, and no clever polling results could have rescued Walter Mondale.

The central job of a private pollster is to tell the truth, often the harsh truth, as reflected in the survey results from likely voters. After the second debate, where Reagan joked about Mondale's inexperience, the margin went from a 12-point Mondale deficit to a 20-point deficit. It was time for pollster Peter Hart to inform the campaign of what the candidate already knew: the game was over.[57] In the final days of the election, last-minute money and resources were poured into Minnesota, to save the double embarrassment of Mondale losing his home state and the prospects of Reagan sweeping every state, losing only the Democratic stronghold of the District of Columbia. Mondale won Minnesota by less than 0.2 percent (3,761 votes),[58] and Reagan won 525 Electoral College votes to 13 for Mondale.

Defeat exacts its toll; defeat of historic proportions can be almost unbearable. Nearly a quarter-century later, Walter Mondale reflected on 1984 and the totality of his public career: "It's not just this defeat. It's the whole twenty-five years—of giving up your family life; of coming to meetings where no one showed up; of receiving pledges of campaign contributions which never were made; of just giving everything."[59] Nothing is worse than being crushed by a landslide—except to win the popular vote and lose the electoral count by an eyelash and judicial legerdemain, as Al Gore would discover in 2000.

The 1988 Presidential Campaign: George H. W. Bush v. Michael S. Dukakis

> *[Roger Ailes and Lee Atwater] choreographed a schizophrenic fall campaign in which Bush alternated between George the Ripper and George the Kind and Gentle; between red-meat pronouncements about the death penalty and haunted musings on the plight of the deserving poor.*
>
> —Journalist Paul Taylor (1990)[60]

> *People learned the wrong lesson from the 1988 campaign.*
> *The wrong lesson is that negative ads work. The right lesson is that if you stand up and fight back, you can beat them. If you don't, you'll lose.*
> —Frank Greer, Democratic media consultant (1990)[61]

During the 1970s and 1980s, voters were getting accustomed to slashing negative television advertisements, character assassination, and partial truths that were unleashed against rival candidates for governor, US senator, or other high-profile contests. Many candidates for statewide and local office tolerated such tactics. Winning, above all, was the goal. In 1988, some of that viciousness, irrelevancy, and character assassination spilled over into the presidential contest. "Morning in America," that gentle, feel-good idealized America of the 1984 campaign was replace in 1988 with "Willie Horton," the scowling African American rapist, striking fear in the hearts of decent Americans. The haiku of "Bear in the Woods" was replaced by a clownish image of Michael Dukakis riding in an Army tank, grinning under his battle helmet, as the text misled voters about his defense record. Issues that should have mattered, such as America's place in the world, the environment, and economic growth, were shunted aside for trivial and irrelevant themes. It was, as veteran reporter Walter R. Mears commented, "a campaign enthroned in irrelevance."[62] More caustically, journalist and campaign chronicler Jules Witcover observed that the 1988 campaign "marked the greatest triumph yet of negative television advertising concocted by hired guns."[63]

Several veteran political consultants decided to sit out the presidential elections. Working in a presidential primary can be all-consuming for a consulting firm, and with several candidates competing, there is never a guarantee of success. Democratic media consultants David Sawyer, Scott Miller, and David Garth in New York, and Robert Squier and Ray Strother in Washington, decided to stay out of the presidential primaries. Robert Goodman, from Baltimore, also decided against working on the Republican side. "I don't think you can do a presidential campaign and anything else as well," Goodman said.[64] Even newer firms, like Democratic media firm Frank Greer and Associates, which had enjoyed a string of congressional victories in 1986, were careful in weighing the chances of the three campaigns that approached them for help.

Bush and the Primaries

Vice President George H. W. Bush was the obvious candidate for the presidential nomination, but he was not the only Republican to run. By the end of 1987, former Delaware governor Pierre (Pete) DuPont, former secretary of state Al Haig, New York congressman Jack Kemp, televangelist and president of Christian Broadcasting Network Marion G. (Pat) Robertson, and Kansas senator Bob Dole also sought the nomination.

Bush was trying to live down the "wimp factor," the widespread notion that, unlike the virile and decisive Reagan, he was shallow and indecisive. Bush, who distinguished himself during World War II in the Pacific theater, flying fifty-eight missions and earning the Navy Distinguished Flying Cross, nevertheless was faced with a front page story in *Newsweek* in October 1987, on the day that he would announce his bid for the presidency. The cover, showing a jut-jawed Bush at the wheel of a family powerboat, had the words, "Fighting the 'Wimp Factor.'" Bush was livid. To dispel this lingering image, Roger Ailes helped prepare Bush for an interview with CBS anchor Dan Rather, just two weeks before the Iowa caucus. Ailes insisted on a live interview (so CBS couldn't edit the material unfavorably), a mole inside CBS informed the Bush camp of what Rather's questions would be, and Bush came out blasting. Rather hammered away on Bush's role in the Iran-Contra affair, then Bush rejoined, "It's not fair to judge my whole career by a rehash of Iran. . . . How would you like it if I judged your career by those seven minutes when you walked off the set in New York? Would you like that?" Minutes later, CBS was flooded with telephone calls protesting Rather's treatment of the vice president. The calls were allegedly orchestrated by Ailes as well.[65] Ailes later remarked, "CBS was trying [Bush] and convicting him and trying to execute him on national television. They had made up their minds. CBS made the fatal error of trying to become the political opposition to George Bush. And, when they did that, they put themselves in an arena where they can get knocked on their fanny."[66] Ailes later headed Fox News, the self-described "Fair and Balanced" network, which has repeatedly been criticized for being politically biased.

Dole was a surprise winner in the Iowa caucus, and Bush shocked everyone when he came in third, behind Robertson. Dole's advisers were brimming with confidence, and just a week before the New Hampshire primary, his pollster, Richard Wirthlin, walked into the candidate's hotel room, whistling "Hail to the Chief" and predicting that Dole would be the next president. In his memoirs, Dole commented "years later, I joked that I haven't seen that pollster since—and I haven't paid him either."[67] But New Hampshire was a different story: Governor John H. Sununu emphatically backed Bush, and Bush won decisively. For Wirthlin, Dole's pollster, the campaign was a "nightmare." In New Hampshire, Dole spotted a student holding a small sign in a crowd that said "I Support DuPont." With blood vessels bulging in his neck, and with his microphone still attached, Dole blurted out, "Why don't you crawl back underneath the rock that you came from." That outburst was played over and over, probably 120 times on various media, according to Wirthlin.[68] A few days later, when asked by NBC anchor Tom Brokaw if he had anything to say about George Bush, who was also seen on the split television screen, an angry Dole growled, "Stop lying about my record."[69] The dark, snarling Dole, first seen in the national election arena in 1976 as Gerald Ford's running mate, then as a candidate for the 1980 Republican nomination, surfaced once more, and it wasn't pretty.

The Dole campaign "seemed to go from bad to ridiculous," wrote veteran political reporters Jack Germond and Jules Witcover.[70] Dole won two other farm states, South Dakota and Minnesota, but then lost heavily in the Super Tuesday contests. Campaign manager Bill Brock abruptly fired two senior strategists, David Keene and Donald Devine, and Dole withdrew in late March. Jack Kemp, whose campaign manager was Ed Rollins, won no states and withdrew in early March, while Pat Robertson suspended his campaign in mid-May.

Election analyst Rhodes Cook argued that Bush primary and caucus successes may have been "too effective" in quickly dispatching his Republican opponents. Once locking up the nomination in March, the Bush re-election campaign fell off the radar of national news, with attention moving over to the Democrats, and particularly Dukakis's string of victories over Jesse Jackson, his last remaining challenger.[71]

The Bush campaign team was a seasoned one—many were veterans from the 1980 and 1984 Reagan campaigns. James Baker served as campaign chair, Lee Atwater as campaign manager, and Bob Teeter was the pollster. The media team was headed by Roger Ailes, and is discussed in more detail below. Robert Strauss, former chair of the Democratic National Committee, complained about the difference between the Republican campaign resources and the Democrats: "They [Republicans] press a button and all the best talent pops up. Our nominee presses a button and we get a bunch of very bright, very intelligent young people who have to reinvent the wheel."[72] Indeed, Lee Atwater counted at least twenty-five campaign and political operatives who had now worked three presidential contests in a row on the Republican side.

The one hiccup during the primary season was the selection of Indiana senator J. Danforth Quayle as Bush's running mate. Quayle had the enthusiastic backing of Roger Ailes, Bob Teeter, and Nicholas Brady. But Ed Rollins, now in the doghouse with Bush because he was working for Jack Kemp's campaign, thought Quayle was a big mistake: "It was a sign of ineptitude on the part of Bush's handlers."[73] James Baker was opposed to Quayle as well, and presumably leaked a story to the *New York Times*, hoping that the public reaction would be negative, and Bush would reconsider.[74] The Bush campaign staff was "caught off guard and unprepared," according to Bush campaign aide Mary Matalin.[75] No briefing material had been prepared on Quayle, no talking points, no explanation of his National Guard service, nothing about his personality or character. The press went beserk. With no other story to cover at the convention, the Quayle selection produced a feeding frenzy. It was like "dropping a hot dog into a tank of sharks," Roger Ailes remembered.[76] The new vice presidential candidate was introduced at an outdoor rally in downtown New Orleans. Quayle was like an overly enthusiastic teenager, pumping his fists, frenetically hugging George Bush, ready to attack the Democrats.

But soon came questions about his National Guard service during Vietnam and possible favoritism exerted by his politically powerful and wealthy family. During the convention, rumors were flying around the state delegations that he'd be dumped. Quayle, like Thomas Eagleton, Geraldine Ferraro, and, later, Sarah Palin, had been thrust into the harsh glare of national exposure and media scrutiny with little preparation. Veteran consultant Stuart Spencer was brought in to be Quayle's "mother hen," in Atwater's description: stay side-by-side with Quayle for two weeks on the road and avoid any press inquiries that would interfere with the campaign's overall message.[77]

Democrats and the Primaries

Gary Hart was the presumptive front-runner for the Democratic nomination; he had fought vigorously against Walter Mondale during the 1984 primaries, and seemed to the best candidate to try again. He was joined by civil rights activist Jesse Jackson, Illinois senator Paul Simon, Missouri representative Richard Gephardt, former Arizona governor Bruce Babbitt, Delaware senator Joseph Biden, Tennessee senator Al Gore Jr., and Massachusetts governor Michael Dukakis.

Still undecided was the most popular governor in the history of New York, Mario M. Cuomo, who in 1986 had won re-election by 65–30 percent over his Republican rival, Andrew P. O'Rourke. Cuomo called in two respected professionals to talk about the prospects of a primary campaign. Media consultant Bob Shrum and Kirk O'Donnell, senior aide to House Speaker Thomas P. (Tip)

O'Neill Jr., spent several hours talking with Cuomo about the demands and challenges of running for president. In the end, Cuomo declined to run, deciding he couldn't fulfill his duties as governor, nor was he about to put his family through the grinder of presidential primaries.[78] His principal adviser, son and future governor of New York, Andrew Cuomo, summed it up: "This was not the pitch to swing at."[79] Not now; perhaps in 1992. Cuomo's decision not to run was an important factor in Dukakis's decision to join the fray. Also deciding not to run were Edward Kennedy and Georgia senator Sam Nunn.

Gary Hart was the first to topple. He still owed millions from his 1984 campaign, and frustrated creditors (including an angry Pat Caddell) were complaining that they were not being reimbursed, while Hart plowed ahead with his 1988 campaign. But even more damaging were revelations of what had long been known to insiders: Hart was cheating on his wife, and had been doing so for years. He was, in the words of journalists Germond and Witcover, a "galloping womanizer."[80] Senior campaign staffers worried about the womanizing rumors in 1984, and before they joined the 1988 campaign, Paul Tully, political director, and Charles Manatt, national campaign co-chair, sought assurances that there was no "character" issue. They were promised that nothing was amiss.[81]

But the rumors would not go away; finally, Hart challenged *New York Times* reporter E. J. Dionne Jr.: "Follow me around. I don't care. I'm serious. If anybody wants to put a tail on me, go ahead. They'll be very bored."[82] *Miami Herald* reporters did just that. But soon a stakeout at Hart's Washington apartment, revelations about girlfriend Donna Rice, and a picture of Rice sitting on Hart's lap on the good ship *Monkey Business* meant that the Hart campaign was in serious trouble even before the first caucus vote in Iowa. Hart was soon the butt of late night comedian jokes, pursued by journalists looking for more dirt, and, most devastating for a politician, the object of ridicule. Even before the damaging photo appeared, he dropped out of the race on May 8, 1987. He reemerged in December, however, entering the New Hampshire primary. But after receiving only 4 percent of the New Hampshire vote, he quietly withdrew in March 1988.[83]

The second candidate to withdraw was Joe Biden. Just before the August 1987 primary debate at the Iowa State Fair, political analyst Bill Schneider showed the Biden campaign a videotape of British Labour Party leader Neil Kinnock. On the tape, Kinnock was telling voters what the Labour Party meant to working-class people. Biden began using Kinnock's speech, word-for-word, without giving proper attribution. The Delaware senator had appropriated material earlier from John Kennedy, and stories had surfaced about Biden not being completely forthcoming about his academic credentials.[84] The Kinnock videotape/Biden plagiarism was a front-page story in the *New York Times*, the *Des Moines Register*, and other news outlets. Who had leaked this story? Fingers were immediately pointed at the Dick Gephardt campaign, in particular media advisers David Doak and Robert Shrum. There was a lingering blood feud between Shrum and his former partner, Pat Caddell, who was heavily engaged in the Biden campaign. In fact, the leak came from the Dukakis camp. "The Dukakis operatives, the real culprits," wrote Bob Shrum in his memoirs, "went for a 'twofer': having fed the press the tape, they now fueled the reports that Doak and I had done it." The controversy "would almost destroy the Gephardt candidacy—as well as Doak and me."[85]

Journalist Paul Taylor argued that even without the Kinnock/plagiarism uproar, it was questionable that Biden would have survived. His campaign was in turmoil, with too many senior staffers fighting each other, pushing different visions and strategies. Tim Ridley, Biden's campaign manager, decried the situation: "I have never been in charge of anything so weird."[86] Caddell was the loud, determined, and disruptive voice. On the night that Biden decided to withdraw from the campaign, his senior advisers took the Amtrak train up to Biden's home in Wilmington, Delaware, to make preparations; Caddell was left behind in Washington, and he frantically tried to persuade the team to hold off. "You people have formed a vigilante group to get my candidate out of the race," Caddell said to press spokesperson Larry Rasky.[87] But no, the decision was irreversible; Biden would withdraw.

Paul Tully, now working for Dukakis, issued a blanket denial: no one on the Dukakis staff had been involved in the Kinnock tape leak. Then *Time* magazine fingered the Dukakis campaign. Dukakis self-righteously denounced negative campaigning saying he'd be "very, very angry" if anyone from his campaign had done this. Finally, campaign manager John Sasso confessed that he was behind the caper; indeed, Dukakis was angry, but he was also reluctant to fire his campaign manager. But the pressure was intense, and soon both Sasso and Tully resigned.[88]

It did not take long for candidates to concede defeat. Bruce Babbitt, whose pollster was Bill Hamilton, left early. The last candidate to get into the race, Paul Simon, whose campaign was managed by Brian Lunde and media consultant David M. Axelrod, was able to secure just his home state of Illinois. Richard Gephardt spent 148 days in Iowa, wooing Democratic voters, and he won this first, critical caucus. But in the end, he won only three states, including his own, Missouri. Working for Gephardt were campaign manager Bill Carrick and media advisers David Doak and Bob Shrum and Joe Trippi. Jesse Jackson, whose campaign was managed by Gerald Austin, won nine states, including most of the Deep South, Michigan, and the District of Columbia. Tennessee senator Al Gore Jr., won seven states, including a swath of Middle South states. His advisers included ad maker Ray Strother and pollsters Mark Mellman and Ed Lazarus.[89]

The Sasso resignation hurt the Dukakis campaign. In his place, deputy campaign manager Susan Estrich, thirty-four, a Harvard law professor and former Ted Kennedy staffer with a wide variety of policy experience, became the campaign manager. Estrich had no prior experience managing a major campaign, but she was now in charge. She was bright, and capable in her own ways, but to some she was out of her league. Journalist Joe Klein dubbed her "utterly incompetent."[90] On the other hand, journalist Howard Fineman concluded that Estrich had "brilliantly steered Dukakis to the nomination."[91] Replacing Paul Tully was Tom Kiley, a Boston pollster, who had no previous connections with Dukakis.

Gephardt spent much of his political capital in winning the Iowa caucus, and, as expected, Dukakis won in New Hampshire. Soon Babbitt and Simon were gone, with the four remaining—Dukakis, Gore, Gephardt, and Jackson—hoping that Super Tuesday, with its rich bounty of states and delegates, would carry them forward. Dukakis won eight primaries, Jackson won the Deep South, and Gore won the Middle South, leaving Gephardt with only a win in his home state of Missouri. Jackson continued with surprise wins in Illinois and Michigan. Dukakis regained his footing, winning eleven of the last twelve primaries, and then collected a raft of super delegates to cushion his win.

In the end, Dukakis won thirty of the primaries, and with the selection of Texas senator Lloyd Bentsen as his running mate, it looked like his campaign, despite its internal difficulties, might be on its way to victory. Unlike Quayle, Bentsen was a heavyweight, with solid political and public policy credentials. The main difficulty during the vice presidential selection process was placating Jesse Jackson, who had come in second to Dukakis, and for a variety of reasons felt slighted for not being chosen or even taken seriously as a vice-presidential choice. The Dukakis campaign was buoyant in the days after the rousing nominating convention, with a 17-point lead over Bush, 51 to 34 percent.[92] But the euphoria was short-lived.

The General Election

> *You have become the issue. . . . You have done two things*
> *in August, you have disappeared, and when you have*
> *reappeared you have looked unhappy and miserable.*
> —Susan Estrich to Michael Dukakis (1988)[93]

> *Never in recent memory has a campaign been so*
> *widely criticized for being overly bitter and*
> *devoid of substantive issues.*
> —Martin P. Wattenberg (1994)[94]

On August 17, Secretary of the Treasury James Baker resigned his office and took up a familiar role, as campaign chair for the Bush-Quayle campaign. Baker, the veteran of presidential campaigns since 1976, was the steady, disciplined, and decisive voice for the final stretch of the campaign. Bush, with a forceful acceptance speech ("read my lips, no new taxes"), was ready for the challenge. Lee Atwater was convinced that Dukakis's early success in the Democratic primaries was what doomed him in the general election. Dukakis had been too passive, Atwater asserted, and he just wasn't ready for the general election fight from the Bush camp.[95] Behind in the polls, it was time for Bush to come out swinging.

The Bush campaign's director of research, James Pinkerton, had been given a $1.2 million budget and a staff of "thirty-five excellent nerds," plus about sixty more assistants to comb through the record and life of Michael and Kitty Dukakis. In the end, Pinkerton's staff, under the direction of chief opposition researcher Don Todd, produced a 312-page opposition research report, called *The Hazards of Duke*.[96] In one of their findings, the researchers discovered that Dukakis had vetoed a bill that would ban weekend furloughs from prison for Massachusetts murders.

The furlough issue first came up in April 1988 during a Democratic candidate debate, when Al Gore accused Michael Dukakis of giving "weekend passes to convicted criminals."[97] Irwin (Tubby) Harrison, one of Dukakis's pollsters, had identified crime issues as a vulnerability. Susan Estrich wanted to run some early commercials where Dukakis basically said he was sorry and remind viewers that even Ronald Reagan's California had such a weekend pass program.[98] But such ads never materialized. Democrats, attacking each other, had handed the Republicans an explosive issue, so long as it could be exploited adeptly. A few weeks later, Republican strategist Lee Atwater said, "If I can make Willie Horton a household name, we'll win the election."[99]

Willie Horton had been sentenced to life in prison, without parole, for the 1974 murder of a teenage gas station attendant. In 1986 he was granted an unsupervised forty-eight-hour furlough from the Northeastern Correctional Center. He had also received nine previous furloughs. Even though Horton was a lifer, without chance for parole, the state of Massachusetts (along with a handful of states) permitted furloughs. This was part of a prison reform program instituted by Dukakis's predecessor, Republican governor Francis W. Sargent.[100] During the fateful 1986 furlough, Willie Horton disappeared, then was apprehended in Maryland ten months later. He was caught following a high-speed chase, after he had stolen a car, stabbed and pistol-whipped a man, and raped and beaten his fiancée over the course of eleven hours of captivity.

The Lawrence (Massachusetts) *Eagle-Tribune* took up the Horton case, publishing 175 articles on it (and later won a Pulitzer Prize for its efforts); the sister of the seventeen-year-old victim started a petition drive; and 57,000 signatures were collected demanding an anti-furlough referendum be placed on the November 1988 ballot. However, the state legislature preempted the referendum move by passing anti-furlough legislation in the spring of 1988.[101] The July 1988 issue of *Reader's Digest* published a piece called "Getting Away with Murder," by Robert James Bidinotto, on the Horton episode.

Two focus group sessions conducted by the Bush campaign in the spring of 1988 are probably the most famous in presidential campaign history. During a Paramus, New Jersey, focus group session, the entire Bush high command—Nicholas Brady, chief of staff Craig Fuller, Teeter, Ailes, and Atwater—watched the proceedings through a one-way mirror. The two sets of participants, fifteen in each group, were Democrats who had voted for Reagan but were inclined toward Dukakis. But then the moderator asked a number of questions: Would you support Dukakis if you knew he opposed capital punishment for murders? Vetoed legislation requiring teachers to lead schoolchildren in the Pledge of Allegiance? Permitted weekend passes for murderers? Support for Dukakis quickly melted away, turning into voter anger and frustration.[102] The Republican strategists knew they were on to something.

On Memorial Day weekend, 1988, Bush met with his senior staff and consultants at his home in Kennebunkport, Maine. All agreed that it was time to go on the offensive, redefine Dukakis, and give voters a red-meat look at the real Michael Dukakis: a tax-and-spend liberal, an ACLU member, a man who was weak on defense, for gun control, soft on crime, responsible for polluting Boston Harbor, and against the Pledge of Allegiance. And the governor who let Willie Horton go free to rape and kill. Lee Atwater, Roger Ailes, and their team were ready to go. Atwater vowed to "strip the bark off the little bastard [Dukakis]" and "make Willie Horton his running mate." [103]

Roger Ailes had filmed two of Willie Horton's victims, and was prepared to shoot a spot based on their story; but that commercial never materialized.[104] What the Bush team, headed by Roger Ailes and Dennis Frankenberry,[105] did produce, using a Utah prison as a prop, was "Revolving Door." The spot does not mention Willie Horton, and in the string of twenty or so prisoners walking through the "revolving prison door," only one appeared to be African American.

"Revolving Door"

[*Audio and visual: Black and white, ominous music, with a prison guard climbing a watch tower.*]

[*Text:* THE DUKAKIS FURLOUGH PROGRAM]
Male Narrator (VOICE-OVER): As Governor Michael Dukakis vetoed mandatory sentences for drug dealers, he vetoed the death penalty. His revolving door prison policy gave weekend furloughs to first-degree murderers not eligible for parole.

[*Visual: Revolving door, with prisoners going through a turnstile, then out again.*]
[*Text:* 268 Escaped.]

Male Narrator: While out, many committed other crimes like kidnapping and rape, and . . .
Male Narrator [AND TEXT]: many are still at large.
Male Narrator: Now Michael Dukakis says he wants to do for America what he's done for Massachusetts. America can't afford that risk. [106]

In the meantime, a supposedly independent group, the National Security PAC and its affiliate Americans for Bush, produced its own commercial, "Weekend Passes," which aired from September 21 through October 4. The group was headed by a former member of the Joint Chiefs of Staff, Admiral Thomas Moorer, and the ad was produced by Larry McCarthy, Floyd Brown, and Jesse Raiford, all of whom were former employees of Ailes Communications.[107] Pollster Tony Fabrizio, a protégé of Arthur Finkelstein, was also involved in the creative process. The commercial contrasted a handsome George Bush (who supports the death penalty for first-degree murderers) versus a scowling Michael Dukakis (who opposes the death penalty). But the main figure in the ad was Willie Horton, whose mug shot showed him with a threatening scowl and an unruly

Afro haircut. While cutting back and forth between Dukakis and Horton, the narrative says: "Dukakis not only opposes the death penalty, he allowed first-degree murderers to have weekend passes from prison. One was Willie Horton, who murdered a boy in a robbery, stabbing him nineteen times. Despite a life sentence, Horton received ten weekend passes. Horton fled, kidnapped a young couple, stabbing the man and repeatedly raping his girlfriend." The ad concludes with this vicious punch line: "Weekend prison passes. Dukakis on crime."[108]

Not until Jesse Jackson raised the issue late in the campaign were Republicans publicly charged with making racist appeals. Bush, Baker, Atwater, Ailes, Teeter, and other campaign officials stoutly denied any racial motive. "There's not a racist bone in my body," Bush told reporters. In the post-election wrap-up at Harvard University, campaign principals and reporters discussed the strategy and tactics used by the Dukakis and Bush operatives. There was a heated discussion of the Willie Horton issue, with Atwater, in particular, first claiming that he didn't know Horton was black, then that his comment about making Horton Dukakis's "running mate" was a "mistake, and "we are very sorry if anyone took it racially, because we had a concerted effort in our campaign to make sure that race was not used in any way, shape, or form." Roger Ailes agreed with Atwater: "If Willie Horton were white, we would have used the furlough program."[109] The Willie Horton and furlough ads offered a low point in presidential campaign communications. Republican consultant Roger Stone, no stranger to hardball politics, summed it up: "It's a racist ad. You [Lee Atwater] and George Bush will wear that to your graves."[110]

In addition, Dukakis was pounded for his veto of a Massachusetts bill that required teachers to lead students in the Pledge of Allegiance each day. Dukakis considered this a constitutional matter, not a political one. "Why would people take this seriously?" he wondered. The Bush campaign did: every swing voter in the state of Texas was sent a four-page brochure: "HERE ARE THE WORDS DUKAKIS DOESN'T WANT YOUR CHILDREN TO HAVE TO SAY . . ." Inside was a picture of two children with hands over their hearts, and the caption read: "I pledge allegiance . . ."[111]

When Dukakis visited a General Dynamics facility in Sterling Heights, Michigan, and took a ride on a 68-ton M1A1 Abrams Battle Tank, it was to demonstrate his push for conventional weaponry. But reporters covering the event doubled over in laughter, and the next day Bush deputy campaign manager Rich Bond called the silly visual a "huge gift" for the Republicans. In a thirty-second ad, "Tank," Dukakis was made to look ridiculous and was portrayed as soft on national defense. Produced by Greg Stevens for the Bush campaign, it showed Dukakis riding around in a tank, wearing an oversized helmet, grinning, and on the screen, with ominous voice-over cataloging all of the weapons programs that he opposed.[112] There was some stretching of the truth, but the message was clear: He's no General Patton, and he certainly doesn't want to protect the military. Stevens's firm, Stevens Reed Curcio & Potholm, later created the "Swift Boat Veterans" ad against John Kerry in 2004.

Donna Brazile, onetime protégé of Jesse Jackson, worked for the Dick Gephardt campaign, and once Gephardt bowed out in March, she was brought into the Dukakis campaign as deputy field director. Brazile, worn out and frustrated with what she saw as "the most horrific personal attacks" by Republicans against Dukakis, on a campaign bus blurted out, "You know, they talk about family values, but no one is going to report that George Bush has a mistress and her initials are J.F." Brazile, who is African American, recalled, "I was sick and tired of the reporters asking me about Dukakis and Black people, so I threw them something that I thought would change the subject."[113] For two and a half hours, Brazile gave her version of the "sermon on the mount' and reporters wrote down my every word." In hindsight, she wrote, "I should have shut up. But I was too angry to stop." She admitted in her memoirs that "I called the vice president of the United States a racist, a liar and a whore."[114] The Dukakis campaign fired her, but Brazile rebounded, and later became Al Gore's 2000 presidential campaign manager.

There were significant national issues, beyond the campaign-defined Pledge of Allegiance, furloughs, and Willie Horton, and in heated contests in Ohio and New Jersey, liberal Democratic senators Howard Metzenbaum and Frank Lautenberg were able to define their races on their own policy terms, and not be bogged down defending themselves as unpatriotic, soft on crime, or weak on national defense.[115] But not Michael Dukakis.

The Dukakis campaign was getting increasingly dysfunctional. There were two competing camps: the old Sasso people, and the Estrich people. According to consultant Mark McKinnon, who was then a Democratic consultant at the Sawyer/Miller Group, "the factions hated and mistrusted each other. The campaign had two pollsters, and they wouldn't share their information. We couldn't get any data from either of them." Many of the Sasso people were working on the assumption that Estrich was only temporary, and that Sasso would return.[116]

On August 26, campaign manager Susan Estrich brought together some veteran Democratic campaign operatives to assess the damage being done by the continued Bush attacks. Estrich, pollster Tubby Harrison, and strategists Tad Devine and Kirk O'Donnell were joined by Thomas Donilon (Biden's senior strategist), William Carrick (Gephardt's campaign manager), and Bob Beckel (Mondale's 1984 campaign manager). It was not pretty. As journalist Christine M. Black and Tom Oliphant described it, the meeting was "filled with profanity, table thumping, and raised voices." Why was Dukakis conducting gubernatorial business in Massachusetts instead of going on the offensive. "Get ahead of the Willie Horton story. It's killing you." Go after Bush: "Cut his head off, garrote the SOB."[117] But Dukakis would do none of it.

The Bush and Dukakis Media Teams

> When the 1988 presidential campaign came down to a choice
> between Willie Horton and the Pledge of Allegiance,
> the only people enriched were the campaign consultants.
>
> —Marjorie Randon Hershey (1988)[118]

Heading the Republican media team was Roger Ailes and his firm, Ailes Communications. He was joined by veterans from the Reagan 1984 Tuesday Team, Jim Weller, creative director, and Sig Rogich, executive producer, with Tom Messner and Barry Vetere as producers. New to the 1988 team were Dennis Frankenberry and Mike Murphy; Catherine Farrell was the time buyer, and Janet Mullins coordinated the ads for the Bush campaign.[119] It was Ailes who was clearly running the media show. He had been with Bush throughout the primary season, coaching him on his speech delivery and communication style, and overseeing the production of the media campaign.

In June 1988, it seemed like the Dukakis campaign had pulled together a dream team of Madison Avenue advertising superstars. *New York Times* reporter Randall Rothenberg wrote that the heads of the nation's "largest and most creatively distinguished" advertising agencies agreed to supervise the advertising. There were three dozen executives in all, including Marvin Sloves, the chairman of Scali, McCabe, Sloves; William Tragos, the chairman of TBWA Advertising; and Henry Bernhard, former vice chairman of Ogilvy & Mather.[120] With this expertise and advertising heft, surely they could go up against Bush and his man Ailes. On paper, yes; in reality, no.

In his penetrating analysis of the Dukakis advertising effort, communications scholar L. Patrick Devlin concluded, "The Dukakis media team was in trouble from day one."[121] Following the Republican campaign model, the Dukakis campaign tried to blend political media consultants with New York ad agency professionals. Republicans had proved successful in coordinating commercial advertising talent, like the November Group or the Tuesday Group in past presidential elections, but the Democrats had stopped using New York–based ad agencies after the 1964 Johnson campaign used Doyle Dane Bernbach (DDB). The Dukakis campaign enlisted Scott Miller of the Sawyer/Miller Group and Gary Susnjara, president of Saatchi and Saatchi DFS, as advertising directors. David Sawyer and Scott Miller "had done everything they could to block Mondale" from running; they had worked for Glenn and then Hart, then, in the end, they worked for Mondale during the disastrous election four years earlier. Scott Miller's first 1988 candidate, Joe Biden, had dropped out; so did his next client, Dick Gephardt. Dukakis would be Sawyer-Miller's last foray into domestic American political campaigns.[122]

But, as then-Democratic media consultant Mark McKinnon pointed out, commercial people just don't know how to put together political ads: "They think style, not substance; form, not content. Political media consultants are used to producing ads in 24 hours for $5,000. These folks couldn't imagine producing anything for less than $200,000, and if it had been left to them, most of the ads would have been ready just in time for Christmas." What was worse, "at one point I counted 92 ads that had been produced for the campaign. There was no strategy. No message. No focus."[123]

Another basic problem was that both Dukakis and Susan Estrich wanted to be in charge of the media, not the media consultants and campaign experts. It was also the problem of big egos bumping up against each other, with no firm direction, no media strategy, and even no campaign strategy. Should there be two-minute-long commercials with Dukakis addressing voters, or should the focus be on thirty-second spots? There was a "group shoot-on," where the best ads would be chosen. But then there were hurt feelings and fights about who should judge each other's work. There were twelve or fifteen agencies all trying to produce the same work. More than a thousand scripts were written but, astoundingly, only twenty or so were actually produced.[124]

When John Sasso returned to the campaign, out went the old media team, and in came a new one, headed by David D'Alesandro from the John Hancock Insurance company. D'Alesandro sized up the media campaign: "I walked in and say 'Show me the overall campaign strategy.' They say, 'There isn't one.' I say, 'OK, then show me the message strategies or show me the advertising strategy' and they tell me 'There isn't one.'" There was a strategy, countered Scott Miller—the squeeze on the middle class and Dukakis as the fighter standing up for their values and needs. "There was a strategy—the ads just never got shot," Miller said.[125]

There were other problems for the Dukakis campaign as well: Dukakis spent campaign ad money foolishly, Bush spent it far more strategically. DNC strategist Paul Tully had done a study of where the Republicans and Democrats had placed their ad money in 1988. Bush spent 76 percent of his advertising dollars in battleground states, in states where he won by less than 4 percent. Only 1 percent of the ad money went into states that Bush would easily win, and just 2 percent went into states where he would not be able to win. But Tully, who spent a year trying to disassemble the Dukakis media buying plans, found that the Dukakis campaign had spent nearly all of its money on national network television—spreading the money and the ads around equally to states he'd easily win, was guaranteed to lose, and the precious battleground states where the contest would be decided.[126]

L. Patrick Devlin argues that the Bush ads were "vastly superior" to the Dukakis ads.[127] The Bush campaign spent only 10 percent of its budget on producing the ads, while the Dukakis campaign spent an almost unheard of 20 percent. The Dukakis campaign aired forty-seven spots, but didn't keep any of them up long enough for them to sink in; Bush's campaign kept showing the same potent ads over and over, giving them enough repeat viewership to be absorbed by still undecided voters. Furthermore, some of the Dukakis ads simply made no sense. During mid-September, when the Dukakis campaign was undergoing a change in its advertising team (never a good sign), a series of Dukakis ads tried to portray Bush handlers as fat old white guys sitting around a table, plotting to remake the image of Bush. Dukakis liked the ads, but they were never tested before focus groups. But Ailes Communications did test them, and after the election, Ailes vice president Kathy Ardleigh commented that in their own focus groups, "nobody knew what the hell anybody was talking about." Many of the participants thought the ads were coming from the Bush camp, not the Dukakis camp.[128]

The Bush ads were relentless and deadly, and they drew deserved criticism. Media scholar Kathleen Hall Jamieson sharply criticized the Republican ad makers: "Never before in a presidential campaign have television ads sponsored by a major party candidate lied so blatantly as in the Campaign of '88."[129] Journalist Paul Taylor described Ailes and Atwater as the "junkyard dogs of the most experienced team of political consultants ever assembled to run a presidential campaign."[130] Yet media scholar Lynda Lee Kaid noted that the number of negative spots during the 1988 campaign were about the same as the average from 1952 through 1988.[131] Perhaps it was the intensity of the attacks that made them so memorable.

Democratic media consultant Frank Greer began the discussion of the 1988 campaign with a battle-tested maxim: let no attack go unanswered. But Dukakis didn't want to respond; and when his campaign did, it was too late. Dukakis, commenting in 2010 reflected on his reluctance: "There had been a lot of polarization under Reagan—I thought people were tired of that stuff. I said, 'I'm not going to respond.' It turned out to be a huge mistake."[132]

The 1988 campaign featured two different candidates and two different strategies. George Bush, trying to live down the "wimp factor," his living in the shadows of Ronald Reagan, and without a discernible grand plan for the presidency, was a pliable candidate, willing to listen to and to approve the plans of his veteran consultants. Pressing national issues of the day were swept off the table, replaced by relentless and effective attacks on Dukakis: attacking his patriotism, his "card carrying" membership in the ACLU, his environmental record, his softness on the military, and, above all, his failure to halt Willie Horton from committing heinous crimes. In the end, John Sasso said, Dukakis had failed to make a "convincing case for change. . . . Looking back, our own lack of a central and sustained theme created the vacuum—a playing field . . . that allowed flag and furloughs to dominate."[133] Dukakis, wanting to stay above the fray, failed to counter the attacks launched against him; he did not understand that he could not continue being governor with all its duties and at the same time be a viable presidential candidate. His campaign was riddled with tension and dissent; his constantly changing media team produced startlingly little good campaign material; and only in the last few weeks, when the conclusion was all but forgone, did Dukakis focus on a consistent theme. It was too late, and for the Democrats and Dukakis, a major opportunity to capture the White House was gone.

PART III

The Transformation of Consulting and Challenges Ahead, 1990–Present

CHAPTER 13

A New Generation of Consultants

In the trenches, I was a necessary evil.

—Dick Morris (1999)

*Candidates place their trust in their consultants and
expect these highly paid geniuses to deliver. . . .
If your lose, they look for the next genius.*

—David Axelrod (2015)

General Consulting

In the 1980s and into the 2000s, several general political consultants emerged, who were instrumental in developing the strategy and tactics for presidential and other campaigns from 1992 through 2012.

Richard S. (Dick) Morris (b. 1948) grew up in New York City, graduated from Columbia University, and got into politics by helping reform candidates in Manhattan. In 1977 Morris was reaching out to Democratic candidates throughout the country, pitching the argument that polls could be used to shape candidates' messages. Early in the fall of that year, Arkansas attorney general Bill Clinton's chief of staff, Steve Smith, called Morris, asking him to come to Little Rock to meet with Clinton.[1] Clinton was trying to figure out whether to run for the US Senate, which he preferred, or, as a fall back, the Arkansas governorship. Morris conducted the polling, showing that Clinton could easily beat lesser-known rivals in the gubernatorial race, but would have a more difficult time in the crowded Senate race. This was Morris's first candidate outside of New York; he was thirty years old, Clinton was thirty-one.[2]

The relationship between Clinton and Morris was on-again, off-again. Hired for the 1978 gubernatorial campaign, Morris was fired by Clinton in 1979. The

reason? Morris wrote that Clinton found his consultant's style, with its emphasis on negative, cutthroat campaigning, "undignified."[3] In her 2003 memoir,
Hillary Clinton wrote that the "young, abrasive" Morris rubbed people the
wrong way: "no one on [Bill Clinton's] staff or in his office could stand working
with Morris,"[4] so he was given the door. But Clinton's re-election campaign in
1980, run by what biographer David Maraniss called "well-meaning but inexperienced friends from the Little Rock country club,"[5] turned out to be a disaster, and
Hillary Clinton made a frantic call to Morris during the last days of the campaign
to enlist his help. Morris was in the thick of a campaign in Florida, working for
Republican senatorial candidate Paula Hawkins, but he came back to Arkansas
for a final poll and final attack ad against Clinton's opponent, Frank White. But it
was too late; the thirty-three-year-old fresh-faced governor of Arkansas had been
booted from office.

Clinton approached his old friend Betsey Wright, political director of the
Arkansas chapter of AFSCME, asking her to be the campaign director for his
1982 gubernatorial comeback. Hillary Clinton reached out to Morris, who was
rehired as an adviser, and he remained so throughout the 1980s. But in 1988
Wright was displaced, sent to be head of the state Democratic Party, and Gloria
Cabe took her place. In 1990 Clinton was agonizing over another run for governor, his fifth term in office. Clinton and Morris got into a heated shouting match,
with Clinton losing control and punching Morris. Despite the fisticuffs, Morris
stayed on through the end of this, the last of Clinton's gubernatorial contests.[6]

When Clinton decided to run for president in 1992, he asked Morris to handle
his race. But, according to Morris, "our late-night encounter in the governor's
mansion was still very raw in my mind. I had built up important relationships
with Republicans, and frankly, I didn't think much of his chances of winning.
So I turned him down." Morris recommended that Clinton hire James Carville
instead.[7] (Georgia governor Zell Miller, a recent Carville client, probably was
more influential in his endorsement of Carville).

In 1988 Morris had drafted a presidential announcement speech for Clinton,
but the Arkansas governor decided not to run that year. Morris was then faced
with what he called a "dismal array of traditional Democrats" as potential clients.
But, "in frustration," he crossed over to the Republican side again—something
rarely done by consultants before, and rarely done since—to work for Mississippi
congressman Trent Lott's Senate campaign, Jesse Helms's re-election campaign
in 1990, and with Republican consultant Lee Atwater.

Morris's abrasiveness and his movement back and forth between Democrats
and Republicans won him few friends. In his 2009 memoir, pollster Stanley
Greenberg, who first worked with Morris in one of Clinton's gubernatorial re-
election bids, wrote that "Morris is the kind of slimy character that keeps me
from calling myself a consultant," and his switching sides makes him "a pariah
among Democrats."[8]

Morris made his comeback when Clinton dumped his 1992 campaign team
(including Greenberg and Carville) and sought re-election in 1996 (See chapter
14). Immediately after the campaign, Morris wrote a best-selling account

of the campaign and the Clinton White House.[9] After his fall from grace in a 1996 prostitution scandal, Morris continued quietly to advise Clinton. But after the 1998 Monica Lewinsky scandal, Morris became a sharp and bitter enemy of Bill Clinton, turning on his former boss "with a vengeance."[10] He later also leveled vicious accusations against Hillary Clinton through books and commentary. David Maraniss wrote of the earliest relationship between Hillary Clinton and Morris: "Morris . . . established a special bond with Hillary, who shared his dark, untrusting perspective on politics."[11] This was a far cry from his condemnation of her in the trailer for the 2008 screed *Hillary: The Movie*: "She's deceitful. She'll make up any story, lie about anything, as long as it serves her purpose at the moment."[12] Morris for a time became of Fox News commentator and a columnist for the *New York Post*.

Morris teamed up with Richard Dresner, who for thirty years had been a political consultant. Dresner's clients included New York Democratic senator Daniel P. Moynihan, California Republican governor Pete Wilson, and Arnold Schwarzenegger in his first campaign for governor of California. Dresner is probably best remembered for his role in the campaign of Boris Yeltsin, running for president of Russia, in 1996 (see chapter 18).

C. James Carville Jr. (b. 1944) did not become active in politics until relatively late in life, and as a political consultant, it was very late. He came from a large and nonpolitical family residing in Carville, Louisiana. He graduated from Louisiana State University, both undergraduate and law school, spent a short stint in the US Marine Corps, was a high school teacher, and a sometime lawyer. In 1980, Louisiana media consultant Gus Weill helped Carville get his start in political consulting, and after several valiant tries (but no victories), Carville began to be noticed by some of the major consultants nationwide.[13] His first win came in 1988 with Robert P. Casey Sr., who was trying for the fourth time to become governor of Pennsylvania. Carville had several other successes in statewide contests, including Senator Frank Lautenberg's re-election in New Jersey in 1988; Zell Miller's bid for governor in Georgia in 1990, and Wallace Wilkinson's bid for governor of Kentucky in 1987. Carville became one of the hottest Democratic consultants when he helped former Kennedy administration aide Harris Wofford pull an upset victory in a special senatorial election in Pennsylvania in 1991 against former governor and US attorney general Richard L. Thornburgh.

As described in the next chapter, Carville's most important battle was the 1992 Clinton campaign for the presidency. Hillary Clinton, in her 2003 memoir, called Carville, "our friend, adviser and one of the most brilliant tactical minds in American politics."[14] On election night, as the eyes of the world focused on Bill Clinton and the celebration in Little Rock, network cameras honed in on Carville, standing close to the outdoor stage. Vice-president-elect Al Gore reached out from the platform, gave Carville a bear hug, and network newscasters noted that Carville was one of the main reasons for Clinton's victory. Carville and his girlfriend (and soon-to-be wife), Republican strategist Mary Matalin, were the hot couple of politics—fierce partisans locked in presidential combat, but lovebirds in private life. Following the 1992 campaign, Matalin and Carville wrote a best-selling memoir, *All's Fair: Love, War, and Running for President*,[15] appeared on endless rounds of talk shows and in television commercials, and were featured in hundreds of print stories. Carville was the star of a documentary, *The War Room*, which followed the Clinton campaign's inner workings.[16] Like Lee Atwater before him, Carville became a genuine celebrity, recognized by the casual voter and respected by seasoned professionals.

After Clinton, Carville did some domestic consulting, but soon gave that up. He was so well known that his presence on a campaign could have been disruptive. The cardinal rule in campaigns is that there is only one star, and that is the candidate; and Carville knew that his presence would overshadow the candidate and turn the attention toward him. What he perhaps didn't recognize was that he was now an international celebrity, recognized wherever he went (see, for example, chapter 18, on the 1994 Greek or 1999 Israeli elections). Carville became an informal adviser to President Clinton, staunchly defending him during the Whitewater investigation, and attacking special prosecutor Kenneth Starr.[17] Carville joined with British consultant Phillip Gould and Stanley Greenberg to form an international consulting firm, Gould Greenberg Carville NOP. He then teamed up with his business partner Paul Begala, Robert Novak, and Tucker Carlson to present a current political affairs show called *Crossfire* on Cable Network News (CNN). Carville has been a frequent commentator on elections and public affairs, and has written several spirited books on politics.

Right out of the University of Texas, Paul Begala (b. 1961) joined James Carville in 1985 working for Lloyd Doggett against Phil Graham in the US Senate race in Texas. They then teamed up to work on several important statewide races. While Carville got most of the attention for the Thornburgh victory in 1991, Begala deserved much of the credit for the organization and strategy behind the come-from-behind victory.[18] Begala is known as one of the Democratic Party's best wordsmiths, in the tradition of Robert Shrum and Ted Sorensen. Begala has authored or coauthored five books (some with Carville), has been a frequent television commentator, and a university law professor. Carville and Begala, along with Karl Rove, were inducted into the AAPC Hall of Fame in 2012.

Today, one of the best known political consultants is Karl Rove (b. 1950). Rove is not remembered for his successful direct marketing career, but for his larger role in getting George W. Bush elected and re-elected to the presidency, his role as political-policy adviser in the White House, and his post–White House role in super PAC politics. Rove grew up in a nonpolitical family, but became active in College Republicans at the University of Utah. His organizational skills caught the attention of party leaders, and by 1971 he was hired as executive director of that organization. In a nasty 1973 succession fight involving dirty tricks and a full-time campaign for five months, Rove (with the help of his chief assistant Lee Atwater) became College Republicans chairman. The contest had to be settled by the new Republican National Committee chairman, George H. W. Bush, who, impressed by Rove, offered him a full-time job at the RNC.[19] Shortly thereafter, Rove met Bush's son, George W.

In 1977 Rove moved to Houston, Texas, and while looking for work, called his old boss, Bush Sr., who had left his post as the CIA director and was back in private business. "I'm thinking of running for president, Karl, and I'd like your help," Bush said to Rove.[20] Karl Rove was to head the Fund for Limited Government, a political action committee created by James Baker to boost Bush's 1980 presidential chances. Rove soon left that position to work in the 1978 Texas gubernatorial campaign for Bill Clements, and when Clements won, Rove became his chief of staff.

Rove left the governor's office in 1981, setting up Karl Rove + Company, a direct mail firm in Austin. His business would soon expand from the narrow specialty of direct mail fundraising solicitations to general consultancy. In 1982 the Democratic Party was at its greatest strength in Texas, with Clements defeated and Democrats taking every major state elective office. But Clements made a comeback, with Rove as his adviser, and soon Democratic office holders were being toppled. Starting in 1984, Rove branched out and became a general consultant for Texas candidates, and he began doing direct mail consulting for candidates outside of Texas, including John Ashcroft in Missouri and Orrin Hatch of Utah. He aided one-time Democrat Rick Perry with his first political win as a Republican, then Kay Bailey Hutchison, and he then helped George W. Bush defeat the Democrat's remaining statewide office holder, Governor Ann Richards.

By the mid-1990s, journalist Nicholas Lemann observed, Rove was in a "highly unusual position for a political consultant—functioning more as in the manner of an old-fashioned political boss than of a for-hire member of the service sector."[21] Tom Cole, a one-time political consultant and later a member of Congress from Oklahoma, remarked that Rove "planned from the start to be the dominant guy in the emerging Republican Party in the second biggest state in the country. That's the political equivalent of deciding to be Microsoft."[22]

His consulting firm, becoming more and more the political power center in Texas, helped seventy-five US Senate, congressional, and gubernatorial candidates in twenty-four states.[23] His most important client, however, was George W. Bush, both in his successful gubernatorial bids in 1994 and 1998, and particularly in his presidential bids in 2000 and 2004 (see chapter 17 for these presidential races). In his 2010 memoirs, Rove wrote that George W.'s victory over incumbent governor Ann Richards "changed my relationship" with Bush. "I went from being a longtime friend to being a political partner."[24]

More than any other political consultant, with the exception of James Baker (who, while key to presidential campaigns, would not consider himself a political consultant), Rove has been instrumental in White House policymaking and politics, and, after his career in the White House, he has been influential in the days of super PAC politics. Joshua Green, writing in the *Atlantic*, commented that "Rove has no antecedent in modern American politics, because no president before Bush thought it wise to give a political adviser so much influence."[25]

Rove became not only the campaign chief but also the policy chief within the White House. He had mapped out five key policy goals that would have helped realign the political parties: establish educational standards, pass a "faith-based initiative" directing government funds to religious organizations, partially privatizing Social Security, create private health-savings accounts as alternatives to Medicare, and enact immigration reform to appeal to Hispanics.[26]

He also has attracted much controversy, from liberal Democratic critics as well as conservative Republicans. In an editorial in 2005, the *Boston Globe*, no friend of Rove's, characterized him this way: "Rove's record has been consistent. Over thirty-five years, he has been a master of dirty tricks, divisiveness, innuendo, manipulation, character assassination, and roiling partisanship."[27]

David Plouffe (b. 1967), a native of Wilmington, Delaware, attended the University of Delaware, and began his political career with the re-election campaign of Iowa senator Tom Harkin, and in his 1992 presidential quest. He ran several other campaigns, including the successful 1996 US Senate campaign for Robert Torricelli in New Jersey. He was the campaign director of the Democratic Senatorial Campaign Committee (DSCC) in 1995, and became deputy chief of staff for House leader Richard Gephardt in 1997. Plouffe was executive director of the Democratic Congressional Campaign Committee (DCCC) from 1999 to 2000. He then joined David Axelrod as a senior strategist and managed the Washington office of Axelrod and Associates (now AKPD Message and Media). In 2003–2004 he was senior adviser to the Gephardt for President campaign. His most important role was that of chief strategist for the Obama 2008 presidential campaign. Quiet and low-keyed, Plouffe was hardly known to the general public during this campaign, but afterward he wrote a best-selling account of the Obama victory, *Audacity to Win* (2009).[28]

Plouffe served as a senior adviser in the Obama White House from 2011 to 2013, replacing David Axelrod, who returned to Chicago to concentrate on the Obama re-election campaign. After the White House, Plouffe became a contributor to Bloomberg TV and ABC News, and in 2014 he became senior vice president at Uber, the alternative urban taxi service. In 2013 he and David Axelrod were inducted into the AAPC Hall of Fame.

When he was still a senior at the University of Montana, Jim Messina (b. 1969) managed a re-election campaign for the mayor of Missoula. He was later hired by US senator Max Baucus and joined his staff in Washington. Messina was chief of staff to New York representative Carolyn McCarthy, then chief of staff for Baucus and North Dakota senator Byron Dorgan. He spent a good deal of time on the campaign trail with various candidates, and eventually landed as deputy campaign manager for the Obama presidential campaign in 2008. Once Obama was in office, Messina joined the White House staff, becoming a valuable broker for presidential policymaking.[29] In 2012 he became the campaign manager for the Obama re-election bid. According to a *Politico* profile, Messina "has been building a political fiefdom through his deep ties to rich Democrats and a nexus of big money operations including the Obama nonprofit Organizing for Action."[30] Unlike Axelrod, Plouffe, or, before them, Karl Rove, Messina did not join the White House after Obama's re-election; rather, he chaired Organizing for Action, the Obama grassroots advocacy program. In January 2014, he became co-chair (along with former Michigan governor Jennifer Granholm) of Priorities USA, the super PAC and 501(c)(4) nonprofit that raised $85 million for Obama's re-election in 2012. Since then, Priorities USA has formally switched its assistance to Hillary Clinton. His business firm, Messina Group, has expanded its corporate, nonprofit, and political portfolios, advising gubernatorial candidates Charlie Crist in Florida and Anthony Brown in Maryland, British prime minister David Cameron, and representing the American Gaming Association.

Polling Consultants

Joel Benenson (b. 1952), a graduate of Queens College, began his career as a journalist for the *New York Daily News*, serving as the paper's Albany bureau chief, and he later worked for Mario Cuomo during the 1994 New York gubernatorial election. During the 1996 presidential campaign, Benenson worked with Mark Penn on the Clinton polling team, then founded his own firm, the Benenson Strategy Group (BSG) in 2000.[31] BSG has worked for a variety of national and international clients, including corporate and advocacy organizations, such as the National Football League, Planned Parenthood, Toyota, and the DSCC, as well as US senator Jeff Merkley (Oregon) and San Francisco mayor Ed Lee. One of his clients, New Jersey senator Robert Menendez, praised Benenson's analytical skills, saying he "uses the polling and demographic information in such a way that he becomes a powerful force in the strategic process."[32] Benenson is best known as chief polling strategist for the 2008 and 2012 Obama campaigns, and for his work as pollster during the Obama administration. He has become a senior strategist to Hillary Clinton in her 2016 presidential bid.

John Anzalone began his political career as an aide to David Wilhelm, who later became chair of the DNC. He worked with James Carville and Paul Begala in the closely watched Frank Lautenberg re-election in 1988. In 1994 Anzalone opened his polling firm, which is now called Anzalone Liszt Grove Research. The firm, based in Montgomery, Alabama, has polled for US senators Sheldon Whitehouse (Rhode Island), Ron Wyden (Oregon), and Kay Hagan (North Carolina), for Florida governor Charlie Crist, and for a long list of members of Congress, party committees, legislative caucuses, and other Democratic organizations and causes. His firm made news in 2006 by helping four of his House clients defeat incumbent Republicans. Chris Cillizza of the *Washington Post* dubbed his firm "one of the hottest," calling Anzalone "the best pollster you've never heard of."[33] Anzalone served on the polling team for Obama 2008 and 2012, polling in nine states, and with Benenson and David Binder he served on the Hillary Clinton 2016 campaign.[34]

David Binder, a San Francisco-based pollster, has worked for a variety of ballot issues and candidates, including San Francisco mayoral candidates Gavin Newsome and Willie Brown, and Los Angeles mayoral candidate Antonio Villaraigosa. Binder was also part of the polling team for Obama in 2008 and 2012, for Clinton in 2016, and he continues to conduct survey research work for the Democratic National Committee, among many other clients.[35]

Also working for Obama in 2008 and 2012 was Paul Harstad, a veteran pollster with nearly forty years of experience. His firm, based in Denver, has worked
for six current US senators, and Harstad was literally on the ground floor with
Obama, working for him when he was a little-known Illinois state senator.[36]

On the Republican side, Anthony (Tony) Fabrizio, Jr. (b. 1960) was the chief
pollster for Bob Dole's 1996 presidential campaign, and in May 2016 was hired by
Donald Trump's presidential campaign. He has served as a key political adviser
for more than a dozen US senators, including Connie Mack (Florida), Alphonse
D'Amato (New York), and Bob Bennett (Utah). He is a native of Brooklyn, and
attended Long Island University. In 1990 he formed a consulting firm with partner John McLaughlin, which lasted until 1996; Jim McLaughlin, John's brother,
continued working with Fabrizio for another decade before the two brothers created their own firm. Fabrizio was a senior counselor with Mercury Public Affairs
and recently opened a new polling business with David Lee, called Fabrizio, Lee &
Associates. Journalist Marc Caputo described Fabrizio as a "political assassin"
and one of the "masterminds behind the infamous Willie Horton ad" from the
1988 presidential campaign.[37] Fabrizio was influential in helping elect wealthy
political novice Rick Scott as governor of Florida and developing his message
and strategy for governing. Fabrizio's firm has a long list of corporate clients in
agriculture, energy, media, pharmaceuticals, hospitality, consumer goods, transportation, real estate, and the chemical and technology industries.[38]

Linda DiVall was the first Republican woman pollster to strike out on her
own, establishing American Viewpoint in 1985. Raised in suburban Chicago,
DiVall graduated with honors from Arizona State University. Over her long
career, DiVall has conducted survey research for the Republican Governors
Association; the RNC, NRCC, and NRSC, over fifty members of Congress; and
a number of US Senate candidates, including Roy Blunt (Missouri), Johnny
Isakson (Georgia), Jim Talent (Missouri), Fred Thompson (Tennessee), and
Richard Lugar (Indiana). She has been on the polling team of every Republican
presidential candidate since 1988. She was also pollster for Speaker of the House
Newt Gingrich, and for a wide variety of corporate and association clients. She
has frequently appeared as a guest analyst on election-night television. DiVall is
also an accomplished and avid amateur golfer.[39]

Q. Whitfield (Whit) Ayres, as an assistant professor of political science at the
University of South Carolina, began polling as a sideline to make extra money.
He first polled for Congressman Floyd Spence (South Carolina) in 1982.[40] Ayres
was an American Political Science Association (APSA) congressional fellow, and
while in Washington, he met Representative Carroll A. Campbell Jr. Campbell
later became South Carolina governor, and Ayres became his senior aide for
public policy. Ayres opened his own polling firm in the basement of his Atlanta
home in 1991, and began specializing in southern Republican clients. His clients have included US senators Bill Frist, Lamar Alexander, and Bob Corker (all
from Tennessee), Marco Rubio (Florida), and Lindsay Graham (South Carolina).
In 2003 Ayres moved his firm, now called North Star Opinion Research, to
Washington, DC, and has broadened his client base. Ayres has purposely kept

his client list relatively small, and has focused on individual attention: he "never intended to be a polling factory."

Ayres is the cofounder of Resurgent Republic, an independent, not-for-profit 501(c)(4), modeled on the Democracy Corps, which was founded by James Carville and Stanley Greenberg. Its purpose is to gauge public opinion about policy proposals being considered by the White House and Congress. The national survey advisory board has Glen Bolger, cofounder and partner at Public Opinion Strategies; Linda DiVall; John McLaughlin, CEO and partner of McLaughlin and Associates; and Jan van Lohuizen, president of Voter Consumer Research. He has also written a prescient book on what the Republican Party and its candidate need to do to win the 2016 presidential election.[41]

In 1986, Jan van Lohuizen, who earned his PhD in political science from Rice University, was director of polling at the National Republican Senatorial Committee, and had worked for two of the major early pollsters, Bob Teeter and Lance Tarrance. He has long been the principal pollster for Senate majority leader Mitch McConnell. Van Lohuizen began working for George W. Bush in 1991, when Karl Rove hired him to work on a local Texas sales tax issue that would help finance a new stadium for Bush's Texas Rangers. He became the principal pollster for the Bush 2000 and 2004 presidential campaigns, and served as a pollster for the Romney primary campaign in 2008. Commenting on the Romney experience three years later, van Lohuizen wrote that "it was one of the worst if not the worst campaign experiences I've had."[42] His firm, Voter Consumer Research, also has worked for corporate clients, including Wal-Mart, Anheuser-Busch, and Microsoft.

Polling for Presidents: Clinton through Obama

*The conventional wisdom that politicians habitually respond
to public opinion when making major policy decisions is wrong.*
—Lawrence R. Jacobs and Robert Y. Shapiro (2000)[43]

In their book on politicians and public opinion, written during the last year of the Clinton administration, political scientists Lawrence Jacobs and Robert Shapiro examine the connections between politicians and public opinion. They argue that there has been a "declining responsiveness" on the part of elected leaders to the policy preferences of the public. The Republican attempt to impeach Bill Clinton in 1998; the 1994 "Contract for America" policies on the environment, Medicare, and education; Clinton's health-care policy proposals; and his North American Free Trade Agreement (NAFTA) proposals—all of these failed to line up with public opinion.

Jacobs and Shapiro also observe that politicians "pursue a strategy of *crafted talk*"—that is, of trying to change public opinion so as to offset the costs of not following what the public actually wants.[44] Presidents try to understand the mood and wishes of the public, how to change the public's mind, and how to navigate through contentious times. Every president in the modern era has relied on pollsters and survey research. The Clinton White House turned to polling consultants Stan Greenberg, Dick Morris, Mark Penn, and Doug Schoen; the Bush II White House turned to Jan van Lohuizen and Fred Steeper; and the Obama White House relied on Joel Benenson.

Polling for Clinton

> [*Clinton*] *consults polls as if they were giant wind socks that tell him which way the wind is blowing.*
>
> —Dick Morris (1999)[45]

As seen in chapter 14, Bill Clinton relied primarily on Stan Greenberg and his firm for polling during the 1992 presidential election, and on Dick Morris and the polling firm of Penn and Schoen for survey analysis during the 1996 election. Greenberg worked as presidential pollster during the first two years of the first Clinton administration, while Penn and Schoen and Morris assisted the president during his remaining six years in office.

When he first appeared on the national stage, Clinton was not a voracious consumer of polls. According to Greenberg, Clinton didn't conduct a single poll during his year as head of the Democratic Leadership Council, before his announcement of running for president in 1992, nor before his New Covenant speeches that defined his position as a candidate. There was just one set of focus group analysis before the 1992 New Hampshire primary, and he did not poll on his free trade position, which was a crucial part of his "New Democrat" platform.

The policy centerpiece of the first term, national health-care reform, received a good deal of attention from public pollsters. In a *New York Times*/CBS poll, an overwhelming majority of those polled said they favored a complete overhaul of the health-care system, favored a health plan that would involve all Americans, and 61 percent were willing to pay higher taxes to achieve that goal. But the same poll showed a deep skepticism about the government's, and particularly the president's, ability to successfully overhaul the health-care system.[46]

But after the collapse of health-care reform and the stunning Democratic defeats in the 1994 congressional elections, Clinton began using public opinion research much more often to gauge policy options. This led some observers to conclude, Greenberg noted, "that his appetite for polls had no limits."[47]

From the vantage point of a dozen years after Bill Clinton's presidency ended, pollster Mark Penn emphasized that the president had to consider several "desks" when making decisions: he must consider the policy desk, the congressional desk, the special interest desk, the press desk, and the public opinion desk. From this perspective, public opinion is important, but it also becomes "just one spoke in the wheel of presidential decision making."[48]

Nevertheless, Clinton, probably the most campaign-astute president we have ever had, became consumed with polls. Dick Morris once told Clinton that he "was better at reading polls than any pollster I know."[49] Where should the president go on vacation? The answer came in part from the responses in a public opinion poll. Nantucket? No, voters considered it too elitist. A massive poll of 10,000 individuals conducted by Mark Penn looked at the lifestyle preferences of individuals—movies they enjoyed, sports they participated in, their religion, their marital status, and many other questions. From this came "lifestyle clusters," a categorization scheme similar to the old Claritas system created in the 1970s. A cluster of swing voters showed that they liked hiking, the outdoors, and technology. The Clintons settled on Jackson Hole, Wyoming (elitist without the reputation), where the president could be photographed wearing blue jeans and a cowboy hat. But even with the careful planning and apparent appeasement of the outdoor/hiking set, Clinton wasn't happy. "That's the first vacation I've taken that didn't help me in the polls," an irritated president scoffed to Dick Morris. "The first one. After all my *other* vacations, I've always risen a point or two. *This* vacation I didn't go up at all." Morris later admitted, "Sometimes I carried polling too far."[50]

During the Monica Lewinsky scandal, which broke on January 21, 1998, Clinton used poll results to assess the damage and to craft his response to the public. During the heat of the revelations, former Clinton aide (and later ABC News correspondent) George Stephanopoulos, chief of staff Erskine Bowles, former chief of staff Leon Panetta, and his former deputy chief of staff Harold Ickes all encouraged the president to come clean, tell the truth, and get the story out in the open. "But at this moment of maximum peril," wrote Stephanopoulos in his 1999 memoir, "the president chose to follow the pattern of his past. He called Dick Morris. Dick took a poll. The poll said lie. It was out of Clinton's hands."[51] The polling results showed that voters were concerned about a cover-up and obstruction of justice, rather than whether or not Clinton in fact had sexual relations. Morris was called before a federal grand jury to tell about the use of his polls during the scandal.[52]

Clinton polled and sought advice until the very end of his second term. On January 19, 2001, the last full day of the Clinton presidency, pollster Mark Penn was on a commercial flight headed to California. His cell phone rang. It was President Clinton, wanting Penn's advice on the soon-to-be-made public, and controversial, choices for presidential pardons.[53]

Polling for George W. Bush

> In terms of the modern presidency, [Jan] van Lohuizen
> is the lowest-profile pollster we've ever had.
> —Ron Faucheux, editor, *Campaigns & Elections* (2002)[54]

While he was on the campaign trail, George W. Bush endlessly proclaimed that he would govern "based on principle and not polls and focus groups."[55] Barry Jackson, a senior adviser to Bush and later chief of staff to John Boehner, observed that when the new team came into the White House in 2001, "there was a really clear sense that decisions were made first, then polling was used as a tool to help the president with whatever decision he had made."[56] In writing about the Bush White House polling, reporter Joshua Green observed that Fred Steeper, who conducted focus groups for the White House and was chief pollster for the president's father in 1992, and Jan van Lohuizen, who had worked with Karl Rove and for George W. Bush since 1991, were "the best kept secrets in Washington."[57] Despite Bush's protestations of not relying on survey research or qualitative analysis, many of his policy announcements were couched in words that were carefully tested through focus groups and polls. Bush reportedly kept his distance from van Lohuizen, but he relied on Karl Rove to ensure that polling was conducted on a wide variety of issues. Matthew Dowd, then a senior adviser at the RNC, coordinated the pollsters and worked with Steeper and van Lohuizen.

The observations made by Jacobson and Shapiro about the Clinton administration could also apply to the Bush II years. Several of Bush's policies were not all that popular with the public. His pollster and focus group specialist would discover words and phrases that would be palatable to the public, helping to sell his policies. Polling was used to test the language and message of a Social Security overhaul and possible privatization, Bush's energy plan, and a national service initiative. Polling was even used to determine the favorability ratings of Bush's two visible communications staffers, Karen Hughes and Ari Fleischer.[58]

Social scientist Kathryn Dunn Tenpas observed that Bush's use of polling was "by no means pathbreaking, nor is the amount of polling particularly astounding." But what was unusual was the chasm between words and actions. "Never before has a White House engaged in such anti-polling rhetoric or built up such a buffer between the pollsters and the president."[59]

Polling for Obama

> My job as the pollster is to tell [office holders]
> how to persuade the greatest number of people to their side
> of the argument.
>
> —Democratic pollster Joel Benenson[60]

Joel Benenson, chief pollster and senior strategist for the 2008 and 2012 Obama presidential campaigns, also was the pollster for the White House during the Obama years. He explained the difference between polling for a campaign and polling to achieve public policy. In campaigns, the objective is simple, though the process can be extraordinarily complex: reach 50 percent of the voters, plus one. In helping the president develop his message, Benenson noted that his job is to "make sure that the president is using his most persuasive argument." The president might have a variety of reasons for supporting a particular piece of policy, and he needs to know which policy option is the strongest. "Knowing that is valuable."[61]

For Benenson, the goal is not to focus on specific speeches or issues debated at the moment in Washington, but to look at the long view. The pollster doesn't just do snapshots and conclude what people think. "The key is understanding the attitudes that people are bringing to the table," observed Obama's pollster.[62] Benenson made nearly weekly trips to the White House meeting with senior political and policy advisers, *Time* reported.[63]

Benenson continued working for the Democratic National Committee on behalf of the Obama White House. Then in 2015, he moved over to the Hillary Clinton campaign as pollster and senior strategist, while David Simas, who was director of opinion research for the 2012 Obama re-election campaign, came on board in charge of the newly created White House Office of Political Strategy and Outreach.

Media

> *A good television ad has the same elements today as in years*
> *before: grab voters' attention, tap their emotions, and persuade them.*
> —Republican media consultant Jim Innocenzi (2014)[64]

Fred N. Davis III (b. 1942) took over his deceased father's three-employee commercial advertising firm in Tulsa, Oklahoma, when he was just nineteen. By the time he was in his mid-twenties, the firm had grown to over fifty employees and was handling corporate clients like Citibank, the Famous Amos Chocolate Chip Cookie Company, and 7-Eleven. In 1994, after moving his company to Los Angeles and renaming it Strategic Perceptions, he got a call from his uncle, Oklahoma congressman James Inhofe, asking for help in his race for the Senate against Congressman Dave McCurdy. Inhofe was behind by fifteen points in the polls, but after Davis stepped in to help, the race turned around and Inhofe won by fifteen points.[65]

Davis jumped into the rough and tumble of political advertising, working for California governor Arnold Schwarzenegger, Georgia governor Sonny Perdue, and Tennessee Senate candidate Bob Corker, while still maintaining a raft of corporate clients. As seen in chapter 19, Davis was the creative director for the McCain presidential campaign, and he produced the much-discussed "Celebrity" ad, belittling Barack Obama's worldwide popularity. He also proposed a sharp media attack on Obama, linking him to the inflammatory preacher Jeremiah Wright, but the client, conservative billionaire Joe Ricketts, backed off once the proposal became public.

Mark McKinnon (b. 1955), a graduate of the University of Texas, spent several years in Nashville working as a songwriter with Kris Kristofferson. In 1984 he joined Paul Begala and James Carville in the unsuccessful US Senate race for Lloyd Doggett in Texas.[66] McKinnon worked solely for Democratic candidates, including Texas governor Mark White, Louisiana congressman Buddy Roemer's gubernatorial campaign, and Texas treasurer Ann Richard's gubernatorial campaign. In 1988, he worked for the Dukakis for President campaign. But in 1996, McKinnon announced his retirement and his disgust with elective politics. But one year later, McKinnon met George W. Bush, struck up a personal friendship, and decided to work for his 2000 presidential campaign and then for his 2004 re-election campaign. McKinnon advised John McCain during the 2007 presidential primaries, leaving the campaign in May 2008. McKinnon, a one-time Democrat, and then a Republican, soured on Mitt Romney and admitted that he voted for Libertarian Gary Johnson during the 2012 presidential election.[67]

Stuart Stevens, born in Mississippi, was first involved in campaigns when he made ads for Jon Hinson, running for a congressional seat in Mississippi. He was a longtime collaborator of Karl Rove, who introduced him to George W. Bush. Stevens became senior media consultant for the 2000 and 2004 Bush presidential campaigns, and he wrote about the adventures of the candidate and consulting team during the 2000 election.[68] Stevens, with a wide variety of interests beyond political consulting, is probably the only political consultant who has skied the last 100 miles to the North Pole and, during the span of one month, dined at each of the twenty-nine European restaurants awarded three Michelin stars. He has also written three travel books based on his explorations in Europe and Africa and was a screenwriter for two popular television shows.[69] Russ Schriefer graduated from Manhattan College and worked for five years with Maverick Media and the Bush 2000 presidential campaign. He was program director for the 2004 Republican National Convention, and was responsible for the anti-Kerry "Windsurfing" ad, claiming to show Kerry's policies and votes were changing with the wind. Schriefer worked in six of the seven presidential elections up until 2012, and, like Stevens, he was a senior strategist for the Romney 2012 presidential campaign. Their firm, Stevens & Schriefer Group, and its most recent venture, Strategic Partners & Media, has served as media and campaign strategy advisers to governors Mary Fallin (Oklahoma) and Chris Christie (New Jersey), and to senators Johnny Isakson (Georgia), Roy Blunt (Missouri), Mel Martinez (Florida), and Rob Portman (Ohio), among many others.

Greg Stevens (1948–2007), a graduate of the University of Maine, first became involved in politics working for Gerald Ford's presidential campaign, and then for Thomas Kean in his gubernatorial bids in New Jersey. Stevens learned his craft from veteran consultants Charles Black, Lee Atwater, and Roger Ailes. He was hired by Ailes during the 1988 presidential campaign, and was responsible for editing the infamous tank commercial, showing Michael Dukakis, looking silly, driving an Abrams tank. In 1993 Stevens created his consulting firm, and was joined by Rick Reed, Paul Curcio, and, in 2003, Erik Potholm. The firm is now known as SRCP Media, and it boasts of having assisted twenty-six US senators, eight governors, and three presidential candidates. Stevens's firm was also responsible for the Swift Boat Veterans for Truth advocacy ads in 2004, which harshly questioned the legitimacy of John Kerry's Vietnam War record. The firm also came in for strong criticism in 1996 when it doctored the image of a Democratic opponent. Stevens's client, Virginia senator John Warner, fired the firm. Another doctoring episode occurred in a 2006 ad for US senator Mike DeWine of Ohio, where smoke was digitally added to the image of the Twin Towers taken during the September 11, 2001, terrorist attacks.[70]

Scott Howell, originally from South Carolina, but now based in Dallas, Texas, founded his firm, Scott Howell & Company (SHC), in 1993, after working with Lee Atwater and, later, Karl Rove. Howell has worked for a variety of Republican Party organizations and senators, including Lindsay Graham (South Carolina), Tom Coburn (Oklahoma), Norman Coleman (Minnesota), and John Thune, who in 2004 defeated US senator and majority leader Tom Daschle in South Dakota. In the bitter US Senate race in Tennessee between Bob Corker and Harold Ford Jr., Howell and consultant Terry Nelson were responsible for producing the controversial "Harold, Call Me" ad, which shows a white woman claiming to have met Ford, an African American, at a Playboy party at the Super Bowl. The RNC-sponsored ad concludes with the woman winking and saying to Ford, "Call me." The ad was harshly criticized as having a thinly veiled racist message. Political scientist John Geer of Vanderbilt University, who has written a major work on negative advertising, commented that the RNC ad was "breaking new ground and, frankly, breaking new lows," making the 1988 "Willie Horton" ad look tame by comparison.[71]

Bob Wickers started in the media consulting business in the early 1990s, working with veteran Dick Dresner. Wickers had been a media consultant and senior adviser for the Mitt Romney for President campaign in 2012 and the Mike Huckabee bid for the Republican presidential nomination in 2008. Along with a working for a number of US senators, Wickers also was on the team of American consultants who assisted Boris Yeltsin in his presidential bid in Russia in 1996, as seen in chapter 18.

On the Democratic side, several important media consultants began their craft. Each of them worked with well-established media consultants—Bob Squier, Bob Shrum, and Frank Greer, respectively.

Bill Knapp was raised in New York and was a researcher at NBC News. He was hired by media pioneer Bob Squier and, along with Carter Eskew, became a major Democratic consultant. He was particularly instrumental in the 1996 Clinton-Gore re-election campaign and in Barack Obama's 2008 campaign. Altogether, he has been a senior media strategist in five presidential campaigns, and in dozens of gubernatorial, senatorial, and congressional races, along with major nonprofits and Fortune 500 corporations. After Squier died in 2000, his firm went through several personnel changes, and ultimately the firm of Squier Knapp Dunn Communications merged in 2004 with an Albany, New York, public affairs firm to create SKDKnickerbocker. Knapp is a managing director of its Washington Office. In October 2015, SKDKnickerbocker was bought out by Stagwell Group, a private equity firm headed by longtime consultant and public relations executive Mark Penn.

Thomas A. (Tad) Devine has a long history of working in Democratic politics, beginning with Jimmy Carter's 1980 presidential campaign. He was campaign manager for vice-presidential nominee Lloyd Bentsen in 1988, and manager of Bob Kerrey's presidential campaign in 1992. Devine was senior strategist in the 2000 Gore presidential campaign, and he served in the same capacity for the 2004 Kerry campaign. He has a wide range of experience of campaigns for US senators, including Sheldon Whitehouse (Rhode Island), Bill Nelson (Florida), and Edward Kennedy (Massachusetts), and has extensive experience assisting international candidates in Israel, Ireland, Peru, Ukraine, and elsewhere. For many years, Devine was a partner with Bob Shrum, and in 2007 he created a media consulting firm with Julian Mulvey, and later with Mark Longabaugh.[72] During the 2016 Democratic presidential primary season, Devine and Longabaugh worked as senior advisers to Vermont senator Bernie Sanders.

Immediately after graduating from Oberlin College, Jim Margolis (b. 1955) worked as campaign manager for long-shot Michigan congressional candidate Howard Wolpe, a college professor who won in 1978. Margolis was hired as his chief of staff at the tender age of twenty-two. He worked for the presidential campaign of Walter Mondale in 1984, and the following year joined the relatively new Democratic media firm Greer & Associates, headed by Frank Greer. For a year, Margolis worked as chief of staff for the newly elected US senator Kent Conrad (North Dakota), but then returned to Greer's firm, now GMMB, where he is a senior partner of the firm. He was the senior media adviser for Obama's 2008 and 2012 presidential campaigns, and then worked for the 2016 presidential campaign of Hillary Clinton.[73]

For many years, Sal Russo, a Sacramento-based Republican political consultant and Tea Party entrepreneur, worked as an aide to California governor Ronald Reagan, and he later teamed up with consultant Ed Rollins. Russo served as deputy chief of staff to Governor George Deukmejian, and he assisted California Republicans as well as New York gubernatorial candidate George Pataki and New York senator Alphonse D'Amato. In 2001 Russo founded the Recall Gray Davis Committee, pushing for the recall of the governor of California. Russo created the Tea Party Express political action committee in 2009, and during its first year of operation the PAC raised more than $5.2 million. By 2011-2012, it had raised $10.1 million. Russo's group sent out fundraising e-mails attacking President Obama, "establishment" Republicans, and the media, warning that the Tea Party couldn't be pushed around "just because we make them feel uncomfortable."[74]

But much of the money raised on behalf of the Tea Part Express PAC was paid to Russo's consulting firm or King Media Group, a firm controlled by his wife. According to journalists Janie Lorber and Eric Lipton, "while most of that money passed through the firms to cover advertising and other expenses, that kind of self-dealing raises red flags about possible lax oversight and excessive fees for the firms, campaign finance experts said."[75] The reporters noted that Joe Wierzbicki, a senior associate of Russo's firm, proposed latching on to the Tea Party movement, hoping to resuscitate the firm's own faltering political action committee, Our Country Deserves Better, which was established in 2008 to battle against the Obama campaign.

Women and Minority Political Consultants

In reading this history, one could quickly and correctly conclude that political consulting is dominated by men, specifically white men. The irony is that one of the first political consultants was a woman, Leone Baxter. It would be many years before other woman joined the ranks, however, and when they did, it generally was in the specialties of survey research and fundraising. There have been exceptions, of course. In general consulting, one of the first women was Jill Buckley, profiled in chapter 6, and in more recent years, Rose Kapolczynski, a prominent California-based consultant. Stephanie Schriock, who was national finance director for Howard Dean in 2004, earned a reputation as a savvy campaign manager for US senators Jon Tester (Montana) and Al Franken (Minnesota), and currently heads EMILY's List, the powerhouse advocacy organization that aids women candidates for office.

As seen in the chapters on presidential elections, there have been three women who have been campaign managers: Susan Estrich for Dukakis in 1988, Donna Brazile for Gore in 2000, and Mary Beth Cahill for Kerry in 2004. Anita Dunn, who had worked in the Carter White House, joined Robert Squier's media firm in 1993, and was chief strategist for former New Jersey senator Bill Bradley's 2000 presidential campaign. Dunn held a senior communications role during the 2008 Obama campaign, and subsequently served as a White House communications director, after which she returned to her consulting firm, now called SKDKnickerbocker. In addition, Valerie Biden Owens was campaign manager for the presidential bids of her brother, US Senator Joe Biden.

Two other prominent veterans of presidential politics are Stephanie Cutter and Beth Myers. Cutter served as communications director for Senator Ted Kennedy in 2001, then as communications director for the Kerry presidential bid in 2004. In 2008 she served as chief of staff for Michelle Obama, and was deputy campaign manager for the Obama re-election campaign in 2012. Beth Myers cut her teeth in politics with the Reagan 1980 presidential campaign, was a protégé of Karl Rove, and became chief of staff to Massachusetts governor Mitt Romney. During Romney's 2008 bid for his party's nomination, Myers was his campaign manager, and she played a significant role in his 2012 campaign, including heading up the vice-presidential selection process. She recently formed a political consulting firm, The Shawmut Group, with Romney associates Eric Fehrnstrom and Peter Flaherty.[76] Katie Packer, who served as deputy campaign manager for Romney in 2012, has formed her own firm, Burning Glass Consulting, specializing in women and campaigns. Teresa Vilmain has had a prominent career in presidential primary politics, especially in the crucial caucus state of Iowa. Jill Alper, media and electoral strategist, and a principal at Dewey Square Group, based in Michigan, has broad experience in presidential campaigning, has worked in senior positions at the Democratic National Committee, and was recognized as "best Democratic campaign manager of the year" by the AAPC.

Democratic pollsters have included Dotty Lynch for Gary Hart's presidential bid in 1984; Celinda Lake, principal of the firm Lake Research; Anna Bennett, who founded Bennett, Petts & Associates in 1992; Diane Feldman, principal of the Feldman Group; and Anna Greenberg, principal of Greenberg Quinlan Rosner Research. Republican pollsters have included Linda DiVall, president of American Viewpoint, and Kellyanne Conway, head of The Polling Company.

Fundraisers have included Republicans Becki Donatelli, president and founder of Campaign Solutions/Connell Donatelli, the pioneer in online fundraising. Until 2004, Linda Davis specialized in campaign planning and fundraising for Democratic members of Congress and candidates for the House and

Senate. Her political fundraising also specialized in assisting political action committees. Republican Nancy Bocskor, who came to Washington working with Newt Gingrich, for many years was a Republican fundraising specialist; in recent years she has branched out to international consulting, particularly assisting women candidates and groups. Liz Chadderdon has won numerous awards for her tough and effective direct mail campaigns. Originally from Texas and beginning as a volunteer for Anne Richards, Chadderdon, who opened the Chadderdon Group in 1999, has assisted a broad range of Democratic clients in thirty-five states. Nancy Todd, a native of Louisiana, began her consulting career working for Matt Reese in 1979. Since the early 1990s, she has specialized in gambling issues. She was instrumental in the campaign to legalize casinos in Mississippi in 1990, which led to successful casino fights in Indiana, Missouri, Pennsylvania, and New York. She has worked in 196 campaigns in 42 states and 6 countries, and her clients have won 98 percent of the time. In recent years, Todd has emerged as a top-flight player in high-stakes poker tournaments. She was the first woman inducted into the AAPC Hall of Fame, in 2009; she was later joined by Ellen Malcolm, the founder and head of EMILY's List.

Kim Alfano began her media career in 1990. She has worked for Republican governors Terry Branstad (Iowa), Mitch Daniels (Indiana), and Bob Riley (Alabama); US senator Lamar Alexander (Tennessee); House majority leader Eric Cantor (Virginia); and a variety of corporate and issue advocacy clients. Mandy Grunwald worked for the Democratic media firm Sawyer/Miller, through her own firm she assisted Bill Clinton's 1992 presidential race, and in 2008 she was media adviser for Hillary Clinton's presidential bid. She also has assisted several US Senate candidates, including Daniel Patrick Moynihan (New York, 1982, 1988, 1994), Ken Salazar (Colorado, 2004), Elizabeth Warren (Massachusetts 2012), and Tammy Baldwin (Wisconsin, 2012). Sally Hunter, based in New York, specialized in international campaigns, and produced video material for eleven heads of state, as well as voter information, infomercials, and other persuasion pieces throughout Latin America and Europe.

While still predominantly a business for men, there has been a growth in the number of women who have become political consultants. In 2014, for example, 27 percent of the membership of the AAPC were women, up from just 9 percent a decade before.[77]

Writing in 2004, political scientist David Dulio noted that "the most striking feature of the consulting business is its racial makeup."[78] Over 95 percent of the principals in political consulting firms are white, just 1.6 percent are African American, 0.8 percent Hispanic, and 1.2 percent Asian Americans. Among African American consultants, Donna Brazile is probably the best known. Minyon Moore, a former White House aide and senior campaign strategist for Hillary Clinton, now heads up the state, local and multicultural practice of the Boston-based consulting firm Dewey Square Group. Twenty-year veteran Democratic pollster Ron Lester of Lester & Associates has assisted twenty-two members of Congress and the DCCC.[79] Pollster Cornell Belcher had earlier worked for Stan Greenberg, Ron Lester, and the Feldman Group, and he worked with the Democratic National Committee under the chairmanship of Howard Dean. Belcher founded the Brilliant Corners consulting firm and worked on the Obama 2008 and 2012 campaigns.

In 2014, the Congressional Black Caucus, the liberal donor organization Democracy Alliance, and others criticized the Democratic Party for not using more minority-owned consulting firms. "There is a racket," said Donna Brazile, "Everybody inside the Beltway is already connected, so it's always been difficult to expand opportunities for women and minorities to have a seat at the table." San Francisco lawyer and activist Steve Phillips, who has given millions to Democratic and liberal causes, announced that Democracy Alliance would launch an audit of the top Democratic committees to determine what funds were going to minority- and women-owned consulting businesses.[80]

Two prominent Asian American consultants, both working for Democratic candidates and progressive causes, stand out. Kam Kuwata (1953–2011), a Japanese–American consultant from California, started his political career in the Washington office of Senator Alan Cranston, and then became a campaign strategist for Cranston's re-election campaign and a spokesman for his 1984 presidential nomination bid. Kuwata, helped Dianne Feinstein win her US Senate seat, and also assisted Senator Daniel Akaka (Hawaii), Los Angeles mayor James K. Hahn, and US representative Jane Harman (California). Kuwata also helped the Obama 2008 presidential campaign, managing the Democratic National Convention in Denver.[81] Fred Yang, a Phi Beta Kappa graduate of Stanford University, got his start in politics at age fourteen, and later interned in Washington, DC. He is name partner in the influential Democratic polling firm of Garin-Hart-Yang. Yang has also provided public opinion surveys for NBC New and the *Wall Street Journal*, and he has written a column for *Campaigns & Elections* magazine.[82]

Along with Alex Castellanos, four other Hispanic consultants stand out: Sergio Bendixen, Lionel Sosa, Roger Salazar, and Mike Madrid. Bendixen, a native of Peru, is a major Hispanic pollster in the United States, and he holds the distinction of being the only Hispanic to have run a presidential campaign, that of California senator Alan Cranston in 1983. Bendixen opened his own consulting business in 1984, specializing in Hispanic constituents. He served as political analyst for Telemundo and Univision, continued working for Democratic clients in the United States and in Latin America, and pioneered the use of multilingual polls. Bendixen worked for the Hillary Clinton presidential bid in 2008, and he then worked for the Obama campaign during the general election. He is now partner with Fernand Amandi in the firm Bendixen & Amandi International.[83]

Lionel Sosa (b. 1939) founded Sosa, Bromley, Aguilar & Associates (now Bromley Communications), which became the largest Hispanic advertising agency in the United States. As a young man, Sosa was inspired by Dwight Eisenhower and became a Republican. A quarter-century later, as an aspiring advertiser but a novice in politics, he helped Texas senator John Tower win re-election, gathering a remarkable 37 percent of the Hispanic vote in Texas, far more than ever attained by a Republican statewide candidate. Sosa recalled this career breakthrough: "We didn't know doodly about politics and we didn't know doodly about Hispanic advertising." In 1980 the Reagan presidential campaign hired Sosa to help provide feel-good soft pieces, focusing on Reagan's personal charms. Altogether, he has been involved on the media teams of eight Republican presidential campaigns. Sosa is also an accomplished portrait painter, and was inducted into the AAPC Hall of Fame in 2015.[84]

Roger Salazar (b. 1970), whose parents were farmworkers, understands the complexity of reaching out to the diverse and growing Hispanic population not only in California, but also in Texas, New Mexico, Florida, New York, Chicago, the Dakotas, and other regions. He has worked on Capitol Hill, in the press operation at the Clinton White House, on the Gore (2000) and Edwards (2004) presidential campaigns, for California governor Gray Davis, and then served as a senior vice president at Porter-Novelli. He worked for Mercury Public Affairs and in 2014 opened his own firm, Alza Strategies ("Alza" is Spanish for "Rise") in Sacramento, California. Salazar observed that in California, in particular, "the Latino market is not a specialty, it is mainstream. It's not just a subgroup, but a diverse main group."[85] Some are newly arrived, some are fifth generation. But, Salazar noted, candidates and campaigns must understand that, despite this diversity, there is an underlying sense of solidarity: attack one segment, and you threaten all.

Mike Madrid, a partner in the California-based public affairs firm GrassrootsLab, has been involved in political campaigns for over twenty years. He graduated from Georgetown University in 1997, writing his senior thesis on Latino politics, and from there he became an expert in Latino communications and outreach strategies. His work has taken him across the nation, to Texas, Florida, and especially to California. In 2011 he developed the Leadership California Institute, an organization dedicated to educating future legislative leaders, and he has served as the political director of the California Republican Party.[86]

Leone Baxter and Clem Whitaker. *Courtesy: LIFE Picture Collection/Corbis; George Skadden, photographer*

Joseph Napolitan, Democratic general consultant.
Courtesy: Springfield, Mass., Republican

Louis Harris, Democratic pollster.
Courtesy: Lou Harris

Stuart Spencer, Republican media consultant. *Courtesy: C-SPAN*

Raymond Strother, Democratic media consultant. *Courtesy: Museum of the Gulf Coast, Port Arthur, Texas*

Matthew Reese, Democratic field operations consultant. *Courtesy: The West Virginia Encyclopedia*

Tony Schwartz, Democratic media consultant. *Courtesy: Joe Slade White Company*

Walter De Vries, Republican general consultant. *Courtesy: North Carolina Progress*

Charles Guggenheim, Democratic media consultant.
Courtesy: CGP, Inc., Steve Barrett, photographer

Joe Slade White, Democratic media consultant. *Courtesy: Joe Slade White*

Richard Wirthlin, Republican pollster. *Courtesy:*
Intellectual Reserve, Inc.

Bill Hamilton, Democratic pollster. *Courtesy:*
Hamilton Campaigns

Patrick Caddell, Democratic pollster, with Jimmy Carter.
Courtesy: White House photo

Peter Hart, Democratic pollster. *Courtesy: Hart*
Research Associates

Geoff Garin, Democratic pollster. *Courtesy: Hart Research Associates*

Lee Atwater, Republican general consultant, with George H.W. Bush. *Courtesy: White House photo*

Richard Viguerie, conservative direct mail consultant. *Courtesy: American Target Advertising, Wiki Commons*

Robert Squier, Democratic media consultant. *Courtesy: SKDKnickerbocker*

Roger Ailes, Republican consultant. *Courtesy: Wiki Commons; photographer, Christopher Tobey.*

Karl Rove, Republican general consultant. *Courtesy: White House photo*

James Carville, Democratic general consultant. *Courtesy: Office of James Carville, Wiki Commons*

Thomas Edmonds, Republican media consultant. *Courtesy: Edmonds Associates, Schuyler Richardson, photographer*

David Axelrod, Democratic media consultant. *Courtesy: White House photo*

David Plouffe, Democratic general consultant. *Courtesy: White House photo*

Donna Brazile, Democratic general consultant. *Courtesy: Donna Brazile & Associates; Ron Aira, photo; Wiki Commons*

Jim Messina, Democratic general consultant. *Courtesy: White House photo; Pete Souza, photographer*

CHAPTER 14

Consultants and Presidential Campaigns, 1992 and 1996

*I am nowhere near as in love with victory
as I am fearful of defeat.*

—James Carville (1994)

*It was painful to watch. The [1992] Bush campaign
was not worthy of the forty-first president.*

—Karl Rove (2010)

B OTH THE 1992 and 1996 presidential elections saw weakened presidents, Bush and Clinton, seeking re-election. Several veteran consultants from both parties sat out these contests and new players came in to assist the presidential candidates. The 1988 Bush campaign came on strong with a coherent, ruthless, and effective charge against Dukakis, but the 1992 Bush re-election campaign was unfocused, poorly managed, and riddled with problems. After the Republican congressional landslide in 1994, the successful Clinton 1992 campaign team was swept aside, and for a time, it looked like any Republican could beat a punch-weary Clinton. But Republican primary voters chose Bob Dole, the candidate most unlikely to beat Clinton, and Dole's campaign, riddled with dissension, misdirection, and turnover simply could not compete against a strong Democratic team and a natural campaigner in Bill Clinton. In those two defeats—1992 and 1996—the candidates themselves, Bush and Dole, were as much to blame as their consultants and strategist in their defeat.

The 1992 Presidential Election: George H. W. Bush v. Bill Clinton v. Ross Perot

Clinton Wins the Carville Primary

—*Washington Post* headline (December 3, 1991)[1]

George Bush was the beneficiary of the greatest baton
pass in presidential history in 1988, and he and his people tossed it away. . . .
Without a doubt, the 1992 Bush campaign was the worst performance
by an incumbent president in modern political history.

—Ed Rollins (1996)[2]

At the 1988 Republican presidential nominating convention in New Orleans, Vice President George H. W. Bush drew a line in the sand: there would be no new taxes when he became president, ending with the memorable cry: "Read my lips: no new taxes."[3] Some White House officials worried that "read my lips" went too far and foreclosed important fiscal options; but senior media adviser Roger Ailes approved the phrase, written by veteran speechwriter Peggy Noonan, and it went into Bush's acceptance speech.

But early in the Bush administration, with the economy growing sour and deficits ballooning, it looked like a tax hike might have to be considered as an unwanted but necessary option. Senior Bush political advisers wondered about the political fallout of breaking that very visible pledge. Richard Darman, director of the Office of Management and Budget, and pollster Bob Teeter had dinner with Ed Rollins, Reagan's 1984 re-election manager, when the topic of breaking the tax pledge came up. Rollins recalled, "I said, 'You guys are nuts, you can't break it." Many Republican legislators had already signed a pledge never to raise taxes, and to have their leader renege would be tantamount to political suicide.[4]

But Bush did break the pledge. The impact within the Republican Party was momentous. For Mary Matalin, political director of Bush/Quayle, the breaking of the pledge was "hurtful on many, many levels." It wasn't just a budget deal and a tax deal: "while that was bad enough," Matalin later observed, "it was credibility."[5] In Congress, conservative Republicans began peeling away from Bush and his ally, minority leader Robert Michel of Illinois, and lined up with Georgia congressman Newt Gingrich, the rising star on the Republican Right. Bush's broken tax pledge also led to a challenge from within his own party for the 1992 Republican nomination.

Buchanan and Perot

Patrick J. Buchanan, a one-time Nixon speechwriter, cable television pundit, and certifiably conservative talking head, decided to challenge Bush in the primaries. It was an audacious move, challenging the president from within his own party. George Wallace tried it in 1964, Ronald Reagan in 1976, and Ted Kennedy in 1980; all had failed. But Bush was just too much for the hard-right Buchanan: in Buchanan's view, Bush dashed the dreams of the Reagan revolution, he'd gone along with social engineers, and he broke his promise about raising taxes. "George Bush," Buchanan told a gathering of like-minded conservatives in November 1991, "if you'll pardon the expression, has come out of the closet as an Eastern Establishment liberal Republican" who has "sold us down the river again and again."[6]

Egged on by his even more aggressive sister, Angela (Bay) Buchanan, the former senior adviser to Presidents Nixon, Ford, and Reagan declared his candidacy. Buchanan was tempted to run for president in 1987, and would later run in 1996. The only senior political consultant who joined his campaign was pollster Tony Fabrizio, who lasted just a short time; Bay Buchanan served as campaign manager. Sister Bay wanted an old-fashioned campaign, not one contaminated by political consultants. She thought Washington consultants were, in the words of the *Newsweek* reporting team, a "worthless lot, a crowd of charlatans who brought nothing but high prices and inflated egos to the table."[7] Eventually, she signed on a young pollster, Frank I. Luntz, who had just opened up his own firm.

Buchanan's message was a combination of bitterness, resentment of the Washington ruling class (of which he was a part for many years), xenophobia (calling for a "Buchanan fence," a 200-mile barrier on the Texas-Mexican border and pleas for "America First"), and anti-Semitism.[8] Incredibly, Buchanan's campaign, underfunded and understaffed, pulled off a stunning moral victory, capturing 37 percent of the votes in the New Hampshire primary (to Bush's 53 percent). He spent ten weeks in the state and used up most of his campaign funds, $2 million, but he made his point. In no other state did he come close to that percentage, but he nevertheless hung on to the bitter end, gaining 23 percent of all the votes cast in the Republican primaries, rattling the Bush campaign, and causing immeasurable harm. Bush gained the nomination, but the president would also constantly be reminded of the disappointment from his own right wing by the aggressive, sharp-tongued Buchanan.

Pat Buchanan and the eventual Democratic candidate were not the only persons George Bush had to worry about. Texas billionaire and entrepreneur Ross Perot had decided to enter the race. At first he was coy about running, but during a February 20, 1992, interview with CNN's Larry King, Perot in effect said that he would run as an independent if supporters would rally and put him on the ballot in fifty states. Thanks to the John Anderson independent campaign in 1980, it would now be easier to qualify in each of the fifty states. But Perot's wasn't going to be the typical race: no handlers allowed, no political consultants needed or wanted.

The Perot populist revolt was catching fire, and in mid-May 1992 he was leading both George Bush and Bill Clinton in popularity polls. But there was no way Perot could conduct a nationwide campaign by himself, even with his dedicated core of volunteers, Perot employees, and seemingly unlimited funds from his own pocket. His point man was Tom Luce, Perot's lawyer, who had once run for governor of Texas as a Republican, but a man decidedly out of his league in big-time presidential politics. It quickly became evident that Perot needed professional help. Patrick Caddell, now in California assisting Jerry Brown's ragtag presidential campaign, gave Perot encouragement, but couldn't come on board. However, two veterans of presidential campaigns did: Hamilton Jordan, campaign manager for Jimmy Carter's outsider campaign in 1976 and his unsuccessful re-election in 1980, and Ed Rollins, campaign manager for Ronald Reagan's romp in 1984. Rollins was a Republican, and Jordan a Democrat, but both were upset with the direction in which traditional party politics were headed. Joining Rollins was his California-based consulting partner, Sal Russo. Rollins, pugnacious and scrappy, had had his fights with Reagan insiders, particularly with Nancy Reagan, and with Bush operatives. He had been tempted to join Perot, but held off because his wife, Sherrie, was working in a high-profile position in the Bush White House. But on June 4, 1992, he took the Perot job; his wife thought he was crazy. On the day her husband signed on with Perot, Sherrie Rollins resigned from her White House job, and in a written statement called for Bush's re-election as "crucial for the future of the country."[9]

The signing of the two experienced campaign managers, particularly Rollins, was a move "that further rattled an already demoralized White House and Republican establishment," observed journalists Ann Devroy and Michael Isikoff.[10] Perot called Jordan and Rollins his "Dream Team;" later, in his memoirs, Rollins characterized the Perot experience as "The Campaign from Hell."[11]

Perot had his eccentricities: Rollins would have to shave his beard to work with him. Country singer legend Willie Nelson, one of Perot's biggest supporters, wouldn't be invited to a fundraiser: "He's a dope smoker and doesn't pay his taxes," Rollins remembered Perot saying. The candidate also didn't want to spend money on any of the fundamental communication tools of politics— direct mail, issues research, polling, or television advertising, but he'd spend hundreds of thousands of dollars on electronic gadgets.[12] Frank Luntz, who first worked for Pat Buchanan, but then signed on with Perot, was to conduct polls. But Perot didn't want to spend money on private polls: "Why should I pay good money when I pick up a newspaper and read the polls there for free?"[13] Direct mail? "I'm not going to spend any money on junk mail," Perot insisted. Four million Perot enthusiasts had called a toll-free number, clambering to help the campaign; their names were entered into the computer files, but none of them was ever contacted.[14]

Veteran ad maker Hal Riney joined the team, but his vision of a campaign ad was far from what Perot wanted. Riney, who produced and did the voice-over for what *Advertising Age* called the best presidential spot ever created (Reagan's 1984 "Prouder, Stronger, Better," or "Morning in America") was frustrated by Perot, the businessman-candidate who had no concept of public relations and communications. Riney couldn't give Perot a direct answer on how much a television spot would cost to produce. That was enough for Perot, who was increasingly reluctant to spend his own money. While assuring Rollins that everything was all right, Perot went behind his back to Tom Luce and said, "Tom, get rid of this guy [Riney]. How outrageous. His prices are absurd."[15] Perot thought that all he needed to do was to let Larry King give him another hour or so on his cable show to get his message across. Why pay, when you can get it for free?

Yet, by mid-June, the quixotic Perot was ahead in California and Texas, and was a strong second in Ohio and Michigan. He was polling around 31 to 34 percent, and his campaign had not been spending any money. But by mid-July, the honeymoon was over: voters were getting tired of Perot; he sank in the polls; and his campaign began to disintegrate. Rollins quit; Hamilton Jordan, who had been in the doghouse with Perot for a month, limped along as campaign manager.

Then, in mid-July, the day of Clinton's acceptance speech at the Democratic nominating convention, Perot abruptly dropped out of the race. It had nothing to do with Clinton; in fact, according to Luce, Perot "didn't have the foggiest notion that Bill Clinton was making his acceptance speech that night."[16] Perot's withdrawal was more personal than political. Perot later explained on the television show *60 Minutes* that he quit because he'd learned that the Bush campaign was plotting to smear his daughter with a computer-altered photo and disrupt her July wedding. "I can't prove any of it today," Perot said in the interview, "but it was a risk I did not have to take." A Bush spokesperson said Perot's assertions were "all loony."[17]

Bush Runs for Re-election

Probably the most important factor in the Bush preparation for re-election was the absence of Lee Atwater and Roger Ailes. The master tactician of the 1988 Bush presidential campaign, then the chair of the Republican National Committee, Atwater had been incapacitated for much of 1990, and died of a brain tumor in March 1991. Ailes, coming off the stunning 1991 defeat of his client Richard Thornburgh in Pennsylvania, had moved away from private consulting to concentrate on commercial television, producing a syndicated show for Rush Limbaugh.[18] Ailes had expected to be the Bush campaign manager, but his involvement might also have been a liability for the campaign.[19]

Following the start of the "Desert Storm" invasion of Iraq in January 1991, a record-setting 89 percent of Americans approved the way George Bush was handling his job. Americans were rallying around the flag and their president. Bush's popularity was already high, at 64 percent, before Desert Shield, the military preparation staging that began in August 1990, then peaked with the invasion itself.[20]

Time is often the cruel enemy, and facing re-election, Bush squandered that precious commodity. By mid-summer 1991, there still had been no effort to gear up for the 1992 re-election.[21] Bush's political operatives and allies were getting worried. Fred Malek, Bush's as yet unannounced campaign manager, in early August 1991 warned the president that he would have to turn more toward economic issues than foreign affairs (where he was more comfortable), and to "prepare for the worst" by taking steps to reinvigorate the economy.[22]

Mary Matalin observed that there was a simple reason why the president put off campaigning: "President Bush liked to govern. The longer he delayed the beginning of his campaign, the longer he delayed being viewed—and having to view everything—through a political prism. He had a job to do and he liked doing it. He was president; he wanted to *be* president."[23]

Then came the wholly unexpected defeat of Richard Thornburgh, the former Bush attorney general and two-term governor, in a special Senate election in Pennsylvania. Harris Wofford, some 44 points down in the polls, had made an extraordinary comeback, engineered by Democratic consultants James Carville and Paul Begala. Yes, the Thornburgh campaign, with chief media adviser Roger Ailes and direct mail consultant Karl Rove, had collapsed, and Wofford's campaign, run by Carville and Begala, was aggressive and invigorated. But there was more. This should have been a clear signal to the White House that the mood of the country was changing, not just on Wofford's signature appeal for national health care, but also for larger issues of the security of the middle class.

Still, there was no preparation by Bush. The growing impatience of Bush's political advisers was directed chiefly at Bush's imperious, hardheaded chief of staff, former New Hampshire governor John Sununu. In 1984, when James Baker was chief of staff, he ran the Reagan White House and navigated the campaign at the same time. Baker made the decisions on where to go and what to say, and those decisions were passed along to the campaign team under Ed Rollins. But in 1992, according to Matalin, "everybody in the Republican interplanetary system knew that was a model doomed to failure were Sununu to remain as chief of staff."[24] Sununu had, in Matalin's blunt words, "the political sensitivity of a doorknob."[25] Something had to be done about Sununu. It was finally left to the president's son, George W., who quietly canvassed senior White House and campaign operatives, to come to the conclusion: Sununu was too much of a liability; he had to go.

On December 5, 1991, the Bush White House announced the names of senior staffers for the re-election campaign. Sununu had been replaced in the White House as chief of staff with Samuel Skinner, who had been Bush's secretary of transportation. Veteran pollster Bob Teeter became the chief strategist; Bob Mosbacher, the general chairman; Fred Malek, the campaign manager; Bobby Holt, the finance chairman; Charlie Black and Rich Bond were senior consultants. Mary Matalin, the only woman in the top echelons, served as political director. As Matalin was gently shoved to the front of the group for a photo op, it soon became a standard joke among the press to refer to them as "Mary and the White Boys."[26] (In most other presidential campaigns, the press would probably just say "the white boys," with no women at the upper echelons of campaign strategy).

But the joking stopped six weeks later when Skinner brought in new aides and shunted others aside. Things were getting worse. Soon the internal grumbling spilled over into the press: Skinner and his deputy chief, former Louisiana congressman W. Henson Moore, were developing a top-heavy mini-bureaucracy, creating "functional gridlock" and "operational constipation." One White House official complained that "we have 60,000 meetings and 20,000 proposals and endless sessions and it just doesn't get done." Veteran White House press secretary Marlin Fitzwater, disgusted with it all, nearly quit, but decided instead to take a vacation in Bermuda.[27]

The economy was in a funk, and the euphoria over the American victory in Iraq had faded long ago. By the end of 1991, Bush's approval ratings were slipping below 50 percent, soon headed below 40 percent.[28] Moreover, the Center for Media and Public Affairs, which monitored press coverage, observed that

76 percent of the stories about the Bush campaign were negative during the first three months of 1992. The director of the center, S. Robert Lichter, noted that Bush's coverage during this time had been "the worst of his entire presidency, and not only is it getting worse, because of the campaign, the volume of the bad coverage is so much greater."[29]

One continuing problem was the image and performance of Vice President Dan Quayle. There had been "Dump Quayle" rumors during much of the spring of 1992. Just as there had been stirrings to get Vice President Richard Nixon off the re-election ticket in 1956, and Vice President Spiro Agnew off the ticket in 1972, Bush was faced with growing internal efforts to remove Quayle. A March 1990 Gallup poll showed that 54 percent of respondents thought Quayle wasn't qualified to be president, and that 49 percent thought Bush should replace him in 1992. There had been embarrassments and verbal gaffes, and when Bush was hospitalized in May 1991 for an irregular heartbeat, news stories kept appearing: Is Quayle ready? Can he do the job? Is he a liability? Then Quayle, on his own, started carving out his own campaign theme of "family values," taking on the popular television character Murphy Brown (portrayed by actress Candice Bergen), who was raising a child on her own. He attacked "cultural elites" and "radical liberals." Then, at an elementary school in Trenton, New Jersey, trying to be the helpful grown-up, he corrected a twelve-year-old boy by putting an "-e" at the end of the word "potato" (the boy had correctly spelled it in the first place).

Elected officials can ward off criticism and shake off attacks against their policies, but when they become the subject of ridicule, they are at their most vulnerable. Late night comedians, cartoonists, and others were never happier than to have Dan Quayle as the butt of their frequent jokes. Most of the Bush campaign high command—Teeter, Malek, Black, and Bond—wanted to get rid of Quayle.[30] Secretary of State James A. Baker stayed in the background and kept quiet, but wrote in his 2006 memoir that "the biggest favor [Quayle] could have done for the president—and the country, in my opinion—would have been to graciously take himself off the ticket."[31] However, like Eisenhower and Nixon before him when facing the issue of an unpopular running mate, Bush publicly embraced his vice president.

For Republican pollster Fred Steeper, the situation in early 1992 couldn't have been any bleaker. "In my mind," wrote Steeper, "this is our worst political nightmare."[32] Bush's approval rating was only 40 percent, the country was in a twenty-month long recession, and 78 percent of voters thought that the country was on the "wrong track." From focus groups in Van Nuys, California, and Charlotte, North Carolina, in April 1992, Steeper found that "voters are disgusted. They are disgusted with politicians, partisan politics, and government gridlock," and they felt that Bush had been an "absent president" on domestic issues. Voters were intrigued by Perot, and the feisty outsider posed a major threat to Bush, while Clinton, with his own serious character flaws, did not appear to be a threat.[33]

Bush captured the Republican nomination. But the pesky Buchanan challenge showed that in state after state, 15, 20, even 30 percent of Republican voters preferred the red-meat, take-no-prisoners Buchanan approach to the moderate, accommodating version offered by Bush. Buchanan's last stand was his speech before the Republican nominating convention in Houston. He insisted on being heard. To a raucous, cheering convention, Buchanan declared that there was a "cultural war" taking place, fighting for the soul of America. "The agenda Clinton and Clinton would impose on America—abortion on demand, a litmus test for the Supreme Court, homosexual rights, discrimination against religious schools, women in combat—that's change, all right. But it is not the kind of change America wants."[34] Dan Quayle, in his 1994 memoir, remarked, "It still seems unbelievable that nobody insisted on clearing Buchanan's text in advance."[35] Bay Buchanan remarked that her brother was not going to submit his speech to the RNC or others for approval, but in the end he substituted another speech, which was read by both Craig Fuller, Bush's senior aide, and Bob Teeter, in charge of the Bush campaign.[36] In placating Buchanan, Bush had to bear the cost: his party was being perceived by nationwide television audiences as the party of mean-spiritness and bigotry. Writing in 2012, journalist Adam Nagourney remarked about how the Republican Party had changed over the past twenty years: "What many viewed as the fringes of the Republican Party twenty years ago have moved closer to the mainstream."[37]

Media consultant Tom Edmonds suggested to the Bush campaign that there be a tribute to Barry Goldwater, a six-minute video prepared by Edmonds and approved by the president himself. Clifton White, who had done so much to encourage Goldwater to run in 1964, but was then unceremoniously pushed aside by Goldwater's "Arizona mafia" during the general election, would introduce the Goldwater tribute. It also would have been a belated thank you from the party faithful to White, now in his last months of life. Unfortunately, scheduling pressures brought on by an increasing need to use the convention to more aggressively promote the president's re-election, forced the tribute, and acknowledgement of White, to be scrapped.[38]

Clinton and the Democratic Primaries

With George Bush's popularity at stratospheric levels right after Desert Storm, several high-profile Democrats thought twice about challenging him. Eventually, however, seven did. Two were clearly long shots: former Minnesota senator and 1968 contender Eugene McCarthy, and Virginia governor L. Douglas Wilder, the second African American (after Shirley Chisholm) to run for the presidency. The more likely contenders were former California governor Jerry Brown, who was trying again, Nebraska senator Bob Kerrey, Iowa senator Tom Harkin, former Massachusetts senator Paul Tsongas, and Arkansas governor Bill Clinton.

Harkin easily won his home state, with nearly 76 percent of the vote; but in doing so, he spent an extraordinary amount of his small campaign war chest. By the time he got to New Hampshire, he was nearly running on empty, gaining just 10 percent of the vote, and his only other win was the nonbinding Montana caucus in March. Jerry Brown had an erratic history of running for public office. He won the statewide office of secretary of state in California, and was twice elected governor; he ran for, and lost, the presidential nominations in 1976 and 1980; and he lost a Senate campaign in California in 1978.[39] Now, in 1992, he declared his candidacy at Independence Hall in Philadelphia. Brown attacked the "unholy alliance of private greed and corrupt politics" found in Washington, both from the Democrats and Republicans. He was inspired by his unpaid political adviser, Patrick Caddell, who had now settled in California, still looking for his mythical "Senator Smith." His campaign manager was Kathi Rogers, an experienced political operative from New Hampshire campaigns.[40] Altogether, Brown was able to pick up six states, but he could not even win his home state of California.

Paul Tsongas, a former Massachusetts senator, battled back from cancer and was able to win seven caucuses and primaries, including the crucial New Hampshire primary. His advisers included campaign manager Dennis Kanin, pollster Irwin (Tubby) Harris, and media advisers Michael Shea and Scott Miller. Bob Kerrey, a senator from Nebraska and Vietnam War hero, had assembled a strong consultant team of Bob Shrum and David Doak, as well as pollster Harrison Hickman. Kerrey tried, but failed, to convince James Carville to join him. Tennessee senator Al Gore Jr., who ran in 1988 for the Democratic nomination, decided not to run, and New York governor Mario Cuomo, again the looming presence in the Democratic Party, finally, in December 1991, announced that he would not run. According to Kerrey's campaign manager Tad Devine, Cuomo had received more network television coverage than any other candidate, and before he announced his decision not to run, Cuomo was in the top tier of candidates, all by himself. Stan Greenberg, Clinton's media consultant, said there was a "universal sigh of relief" when Cuomo announced his decision.[41]

Bill Clinton was a veteran of many political campaigns before he became a candidate for president. He ran unsuccessfully for Congress in 1974, losing to incumbent John Paul Hammerschmidt; he then won the Arkansas attorney general contest two years later, and then, in 1978, he became, at thirty-two years old, the youngest governor in the nation. He stumbled in his re-election drive in 1980, but came back in 1982, winning five successive two-year terms. In the fall of 1987, as he was pondering a run for the US Senate or the Arkansas governorship, Clinton brought in Dick Morris, a young political consultant from New York, who had been soliciting new clients around the country. Soon Morris, the pollster, would become a key part of Clinton's election team for this and subsequent elections.[42] After his impressive media campaign for Gary Hart in 1984, consultant Ray Strother was a hot property. Later that year, Morris brought Strother into the governor's mansion in Little Rock, and introduced him to the governor: "This is the genius who created Gary Hart."[43] Strother then worked for Clinton during the late 1980s as he prepared for re-election as governor. After Gary Hart's 1988 presidential bid collapsed, Clinton briefly, but seriously, considered jumping in; but, with excitement building and advisers ready, including Morris and Strother, Clinton decided against it.

By 1990 Clinton had grown tired of Dick Morris, and after a blowup with Strother, he decided to dump his media adviser as well.[44] Writing bluntly in his 2003 memoir, Raymond Strother assessed his relationship with Clinton: "I'm sorry I ever met Bill Clinton. He was a dream killer who ended our relationship by damaging my business and adding my body to those he climbed over to reach the White House."[45]

For his 1990 final run for Arkansas governor, Clinton brought in media consultant Frank Greer and pollster Stanley Greenberg. They would be an integral part of his team when he announced his run for the presidency in late 1991. As for his former pollster and adviser Dick Morris, Clinton later said that he "hated to give up" Morris, but "by then he had become so involved with Republican candidates and office holders that he was compromised in the eyes of virtually all Democrats."[46] Clinton's presidential campaign manager would be David Wilhelm, but the hottest general consultant on the Democratic firmament at the moment was James Carville, who had just help secure a near-impossible victory for Harris Wofford in the Pennsylvania special election for US Senate. Carville had helped Zell Miller win the gubernatorial race in Georgia in 1990, and Miller, who was an earlier endorser of Clinton, helped connect Clinton with Carville. Clinton and Carville (and his business partner Paul Begala) met several times before agreeing to work together. Carville's selection was greeted with newspaper headlines, and the *Washington Post* said that the "Clinton camp treated it as the December equivalent of winning the New Hampshire primary."[47] Clinton later wrote in his 2004 memoir that Begala and Carville brought "energy, focus, and credibility" to the campaign efforts.[48]

Clinton performed miserably in Iowa, gathering less than 3 percent of the vote. There was more trouble to come: before the New Hampshire primary, rumors of Clinton's alleged extramarital dalliances with Gennifer Flowers popped up in the tabloid *Star*, and there were also stories of Clinton trying to avoid the draft during the Vietnam War. Despite these obstacles, Clinton came in second to Paul Tsongas in the New Hampshire primary, managing to spin this into a moral victory, and claiming to be the "comeback kid." James Carville recalled, "I have never seen a human being perform like he performed that week in New Hampshire. It was stunning. It was more like an athlete than it was a political candidate. I mean, event after event, every interview, every town hall meeting."[49]

While Tsongas won the first primary, his candidacy soon collapsed. His senior adviser, Scott Miller, was ready to jump ship, not to the front-runner Clinton, whom he despised, but to Ross Perot. Miller was "disgusted" and "disillusioned" with the Democratic Party, contemptuous of Clinton, and openly pleaded to work with Perot's campaign, even if it meant "licking envelopes and handing out leaflets."[50] Miller never got the chance to work with Perot, but, as seen above, Hamilton Jordan, Ed Rollins, and other consultants made that jump.

In the first twelve primaries, Clinton was able to win just once, in Georgia, but soon Clinton would take command, winning big throughout the South and doing well in other regions of the country. Altogether, Jerry Brown would win six states, Tsongas would win seven, and Clinton would eventually win thirty-five primaries and caucuses. After the April 7 New York primary, James Carville and Stan Greenberg went to Clinton senior adviser Mickey Kantor with a plan: with the nomination now wrapped up, it was time for a small group of advisers to pull out from the day-to-day campaign and focus on Clinton's weakness—his character. During the previous presidential campaign, Democrats, thinking they were ahead, were stung by Republican counterattacks; and Democrats had been hit hard in 1984 and 1988. It could happen again, but the consultants were determined to stop it; thus was born the secret "Manhattan Project." The consultants were worried about Clinton's image. Greenberg, Carville, Frank Greer, and Mandy Grunwald decided to test Clinton's character issue before undecided voters. They first assembled a group of ten middle-aged white women in Allentown, Pennsylvania, who were independents or "weak" Democrats; a second focus group was composed only of men. The results were clear: Clinton had a definite character problem, but there was also good news coming from the focus group research. According to Greenberg, "in focus groups we discovered that simply knowing he was a poor kid from Arkansas would change everything, which is why Hope became so central to the campaign."[51] Or as Paul Begala put it: "This is what people knew: Yale, Georgetown, Oxford, dodged the draft, smoked pot, cheated on his wife. And because we reason by inference, they stitched all those things together and they came up with: rich, spoiled, never had a hard day in his life, driving his father's Alfa Romeo around the Ivy League campus. That's where the 'Man from Hope' came from."[52]

Coming out of the findings of this qualitative research was a seventeen-minute biographical film, which refocused the narrative of Clinton's character. Years earlier, Joe Napolitan had commented that a biographical film "is the best way to give a complete portrait of a candidate . . . [It] puts flesh and muscle on a candidate."[53] Produced by friends and successful television producers, Harry Thomason and Linda Bloodworth-Thomason, *A Man from Hope* tells of Clinton's impoverished background and his protecting his mother from an attack by Bill's stepfather. The film became a centerpiece of the Democratic nomination convention.

The General Election

> In terms of message, in terms of substance,
> in terms of a real plan for dealing with the economy,
> one of the failings of the Bush campaign was that they
> never offered a plan for the country.
> —Clinton/Gore media consultant Frank Greer (1992)[54]

James Baker acknowledged that his remarks of August 13, 1992, before assembled foreign service offices and State Department officials, was "one of the most difficult" speeches of his life.[55] Baker resigned as secretary of state to move back to the White House to again become chief of staff. His return, wrote *Washington Post* columnist David Broder, will "improve morale in the administration and the Republican Party." But Broder warned that Baker "can read the polls, but I wonder if he can feel the fear and frustration that Bush so far has failed to address."[56] The Bush campaign was listless, and Baker's experienced hand was needed. Baker had worked on the 1976 Ford campaign, the 1980 Reagan campaign, and had been Reagan's chief of staff, directing the 1984 re-election campaign along with his aide Richard Darman, while Ed Rollins and Lee Atwater executed it.

The campaign had bogged down, and during the past eight months there had been repeated complaints from Bush supporters that the decision making and execution of campaign plans bogged down between White House chief of staff Samuel K. Skinner and campaign chairman Robert Teeter.[57] Baker should have been there from the start, nearly everyone was saying.[58]

Republican opposition research, under David Tell, was in high gear, with plenty of ammunition against Clinton. Operatives were dispatched to Little Rock, where they collected thirty file drawers of official papers, bought twenty years' worth of microfilm copies of the major Arkansas newspapers, and collected hundreds of hours of Clinton on C-SPAN. The researchers found plenty, but the flip-flopping, the waffling on issues, the fibs, big and small, the womanizing, and his draft record were not damning enough. "Clinton is a pathological liar," a Bush campaign staffer said. "Unfortunately, George Bush is the only politician in America who can immunize him against that tag."[59] So much for "read my lips."

During the summer months, the Bush advisers took reams of survey research data, fed them into computers, and through multiple regression analysis, came up with a "satisfaction index" for Clinton and Bush.[60] What they discovered was that Bush could win the election, but only if they could convince the electorate to like Bush more. In the end, attacking Clinton (or Perot) wouldn't be the key. "Everything else was irrelevant, but the president," said a Bush media adviser. "Clinton was irrelevant. Quayle was irrelevant."[61] But the Bush team couldn't figure out how to move the numbers in Bush's favor. James Baker, writing in his 2006 memoir, thought that Bush was doomed by three factors: first, the Republicans had occupied the White House for twelve consecutive years, and voters were ready for a change; second, the failure of the Bush administration to follow Desert Storm with "Domestic Storm, an economic revitalization program." Baker's third reason was the re-energized Ross Perot.[62]

None of the twenty-five ads prepared by the Republican media team, which included Alex Castellanos and Mike Murphy, seemed to be working, and now they were being pushed aside in favor of Madison Avenue talent. In May, Martin Puris, the head of the New York-based advertising firm of Ammirati and Puris, was hired to oversee the media campaign, which was now called the November Company. Based in Manhattan rather than Washington, the November Company was mostly New York ad people; from the beginning, it clashed with Bush's political people. Memos were written, ads were made but never used, and suggestions were ignored. Thoroughly frustrated, Puris in early summer blurted out to a colleague, "Who do I have to sleep with to get *off* this campaign?"[63] By the time Labor Day rolled around, the Bush media campaign had gone nowhere. Baker dismissed those in charge, and promptly put Mitch Daniels, a former Reagan-Bush aide, in charge. But Daniels had to back out because of prior commitments in Japan. The election was just nine weeks away, and the Bush media plan, let alone its execution, was in disarray.[64]

New Bush ads were produced, but through technical problems and lack of creative skill, they fell through, failing to connect with voters. Frustrated, Baker called in veteran ad maker Sig Rogich and brought back Alex Castellanos. With just six weeks to go, they developed a "Man on the Street" theme, going around the country with hand-held cameras, interviewing ordinary voters—all of whom helped hammer home the theme that Clinton could not be trusted.[65] There was plenty of internal dissension in the campaign about whether to focus on Bush's positives or go negative against Clinton.

The Bush campaign made around 100 spots, but used just a small fraction of them. Focus groups, for one reason or another, objected to most of the spots, and the media consultants bowed to their wishes. Randomly selected voters had become television critics; they were listened to, and, as a consequence, the Bush advertising lost its creative punch. The biggest problem was that the advertising team wasn't able to turn the narrative to the future, to show convincingly what a second Bush term would be for the American people.[66] In his polls, Fred Steeper found that voters just resisted hearing about a Bush second-term agenda. Voters didn't think Bush cared about domestic issues.[67] In a word, voters were simply tired of Bush and there was little the campaign consultants could do to turn that impression around. Veteran presidential advertising consultant Geoff Kelly said, "It was just the worst [campaign] I've ever been involved in.... [Roger] Ailes or [Lee] Atwater should have been [there]."[68]

During the general election, when Perot reemerged, his campaign was run by Orson Swindle III, a former Marine Corps pilot and prisoner of war in Vietnam, who once shared prison space with John McCain. Swindle had run unsuccessfully for Congress, and had worked in the Reagan administration in the Department of Agriculture, but he had no experience in national presidential politics. Perot jumped back into the presidential race during the first week of October, connecting with voters through a series of thirty-minute broadcasts, then thirty-second and sixty-second spots. The first thirty-minute broadcast was produced by the 270 Group, a Dallas-based agency created specifically for the Perot campaign.[69] What was unusual, perhaps unprecedented, was that Perot spoke from behind a desk for thirty minutes, with the one camera focused on him alone and the charts that he held up to explain the maladies of current economic policies. As he flipped the charts, Perot sneered in disgust, "We used to have the world's greatest economic engine. We let it slip away and with it went millions of jobs and taxpayers."[70] Later, excerpts from his debate performances were aired as thirty-second commercials. The twenty-second spots, the eleven half-hour advertisements, and the four hour-long segments were produced for only $1 million, a paltry sum, leaving about $39 million left for airtime.[71] Through his television advertising blitz and his straight-talking, homespun performance in the televised presidential debates, Perot bounced back.[72]

The Clinton ad team was headed by Frank Greer and his firm, Greer, Margolis, Mitchell, and Grunwald (GMMG), with partner Mandy Grunwald as the media coordinator. Also included were veteran ad makers Carter Eskew, Mike Donilon, and Roy M. Spence Jr. Altogether, the media team had over 100 media creators, buyers, and coordinators.[73] The Clinton team, learning from past mistakes of Dukakis and other Democrats, put together a rapid response team to immediately respond to negative ads that came from the Bush camp or its allies.[74]

Also, learning from the successful Reagan campaign of 1984, the Clinton team used political radio as an effective communication tool. Jeff Eller and George Stephanopoulos put together a local radio media campaign, using an 800 number, with 1,100 incoming phone lines and a computerized voice mail system. Every day, the campaign and its surrogates would record a new message, which would then be available to the 7,500 radio stations throughout the country. Press one, and a message comes from Bill Clinton; press two, and it's Al Gore; press other numbers and surrogates like Mario Cuomo would supply a quote; or there would be a special message for African American or Hispanic radio audiences. Further, the Clinton campaign had radio equipment in forty-five states that were pumping out "actualities" from local personalities and political figures in support of the campaign.[75]

One of the key insights to the Clinton/Gore media efforts was its decision to place ads locally, targeting twenty states, rather than employing a national media strategy. Internal polls showed that Clinton was ahead in many states by September, and this meant that the media team could concentrate on battleground states. Altogether, 75 percent of the total television expenditures of Clinton/Gore went to local advertising. By contrast, the Bush and Perot campaigns had much more of a national focus. Strategically, it was a smart decision for the Clinton forces to concentrate on twenty battleground states, as they managed to win nineteen of them.[76]

It finally looked like victory for Democrats. And for one veteran operative, in particular, this would be the end of a long, agonizing draught. Paul Tully, a fixture in liberal Democratic politics, had labored for Robert Kennedy in the 1968 Democratic primaries, George McGovern in 1972, Morris Udall in the 1976 primaries, Edward Kennedy in the 1980 primaries, Walter Mondale in 1984, Gary Hart in 1987, and briefly for Michael Dukakis.

Electoral politics was Tully's passion and life's work. He had gone through more than two decades of fighting the good fight for liberal causes, only to have his candidates come up short. As political director of the Democratic National Committee, he had worked tirelessly for four years to defeat George Bush, but now just six weeks before Clinton defeated Bush, Paul Tully collapsed and died of a heart attack. For twenty-four of his forty-eight years, he breathed and lived politics. Heavy-set, chain smoking, caffeine addicted, staying up to all hours into the morning, he was, in journalist Dan Balz's words, "a man of prodigious appetites, but none larger than his passion for politics."[77]

Ross Perot, who quit the race in July, bounced back during the general election, received 19 million votes, or 18.9 percent of the vote. While he received no electoral votes, no third-party candidate had done as well as Perot in capturing the popular vote since former president Theodore Roosevelt's campaign under the Bull Moose Party in 1912. The incumbent president received just 37.5 percent of the popular vote, winning eighteen states and 168 electoral votes. Charlie Black, Bush's senior consultant, observed, "Look, in the end, the lack of performance on the economy was more important to the voters than whether you could trust Bill Clinton. That's the whole race, if you want to summarize it in one sentence."[78] Bill Clinton won 370 electoral votes from thirty-two states and the District of Columbia, but received just 43 percent of the popular vote.

The 1992 presidential race became the year that political consultants were on display. Documentary filmmakers D. A. Pennebaker and Chris Hegedus followed campaign manager James Carville and senior advisers George Stephanopoulos and Paul Begala as they plotted strategy and reacted to campaign events. Their documentary, *The War Room*, made the quirky Carville a celebrity. Throughout this 96-minute film, candidate Bill Clinton appeared in less than 30 seconds.[79] On election night, television cameras focused on Carville, who was appropriately in the crowd, while the Clintons and Gores enjoyed the spotlight on the makeshift stage. James Carville and Paul Begala tried to deflect any notion that consultants were critical to Clinton's success. In an op-ed piece in the *New York Times*, "It's the Candidate, Stupid!," the two consultants agreed that Clinton had put together "as good a staff as anyone" had ever assembled for a presidential race. "But the dirty little secret is that they would have won with the staffs assembled by Michael Dukakis or Walter Mondale. It has always been our belief that consultants don't win elections; candidates do."[80]

The 1996 Presidential Election: Bill Clinton v. Bob Dole

> *Bob Dole . . . ran one of the most hapless campaigns*
> *in modern political history.*
> —*Newsweek* reporting team (1997)[81]

> *Clinton is the first president we've had who is totally conversant*
> *with all the tactics and models that political consultants use,*
> *and could be a very successful political consultant himself.*
> —Republican consultant Mike Murphy (2001)[82]

Republicans, touting their "Contract with America," overwhelmed Democrats in the 1994 congressional elections, leading to serious questions as to whether Bill Clinton would survive in a second election. The failed national health-care legislation, the Whitewater scandal, continuing character issues, and political infighting among Democrats meant that Clinton indeed was in trouble, and certainly vulnerable if the right Republican, with the right message, would challenge him in 1996. But Clinton, ever the political survivor, surreptitiously changed political consultants and senior advisers, and the Republicans managed to come up with the poorest of choices to go against Clinton. Truly, as one of the journalistic chronicles labeled it, the 1996 presidential elections saw Clinton coming "Back from the Dead."[83]

The Clinton re-election team could look back at two recent examples of presidents running for re-election: the highly successful Reagan 1984 re-election and the dismal failure of George H. W. Bush in his 1992 re-election bid. To avoid the Bush example, Clinton would have to avoid the interparty battles that led to the Buchanan insurgency, start early, assemble a team of seasoned campaign consultants, raise money—lots of money—early, and weaken his Republican challenger with a television ad campaign that blanketed the airwaves during the primaries.[84] Clinton was successful in all of this, and he was helped immeasurably when the Republicans, through their primaries and caucuses, chose the least competitive candidate possible. Voters were not inspired, by either Clinton or Dole. Election Day saw the lowest turnout of eligible voters since 1924, with less than half of all adults participating.[85]

The Republican Primaries

On paper, the list of ten Republicans seeking the nomination had several experienced elected officials—former Tennessee governor and secretary of education Lamar Alexander, Texas senator Phil Gramm, Indiana senator Richard Lugar, Pennsylvania senator Arlen Specter, California governor and former US senator Pete Wilson, and Senate majority leader Bob Dole. In addition, conservative activist Pat Buchanan was running again, and the equally conservative California congressman Robert Dornan, businessmen Steve Forbes and Morry Taylor, and former ambassador Alan Keyes were also in the mix. Ross Perot, who ran his quixotic race in 1992, was back under the guise of the newly formed United We Stand America (UWSA) Party, but the novelty and enthusiasm were no longer there. Only Buchanan and Forbes, two outsiders, won any states and posed any kind of challenge to Dole.

Several Republicans sat this race out, including House speaker Newt Gingrich, former Senate majority leader Howard Baker, Arizona senator John McCain, and former New Jersey governor Tom Kean. Also sitting out were former vice president Dan Quayle and former chairman of the Joint Chiefs of Staff Colin Powell. Quayle had been running second in public opinion polls to Bob Dole, and in early 1995, about one year before the first primaries, he pondered a run for the nomination. Mark Goodin, a Republican communications specialist, prepared a six-page memo outlining an "Alternative Campaign," a roadmap for Quayle, something, Goodin wrote, "the nation desperately needs." But Quayle's heart was not in it: he couldn't ask people for money, even the big contributors from his home state of Indiana. There was a skeleton of an exploratory committee, but nothing more. On February 6, 1995, Quayle had made up his mind: he would not run; later, perhaps in 2000, but not now.[86]

Just like the Democrats in 1988 were waiting to see what Mario Cuomo would do, Republicans in 1996 were waiting for Colin Powell, the enormously popular and well-respected former chairman of the Joint Chiefs of Staff. Fifty-seven years old, his popularity was evident by the long lines of supporters and fans at bookstores and shopping centers who bought his autobiography, *My American*

Journey. As a military professional, he foreswore partisan politics and had never declared his political party preference. Powell struggled with the decision to put his name forward as a candidate, as a Republican; his family was dead set against it, particularly his wife, Alma, and in the end, on November 8, 1995, Powell said no.[87]

Malcolm G. (Steve) Forbes Jr. joined the race as the conservative antidote to the moderate Dole. His campaign manager was William Dal Col, a protégé of Arthur Finkelstein and a former aide to Jack Kemp. Also joining the team were pollster John McLaughlin, also out of the Finkelstein firm, and Carter Wrenn, veteran of nasty battles to elect and re-elect Jesse Helms in North Carolina.

Pat Buchanan, characterized as "the roaring wind" of the Republican Party by journalist Bob Woodward, gave a scare to George Bush in the 1992 primaries, badgering him throughout the primary process. Now he was back, declaring in March 1995 in New Hampshire that he would again be a candidate: "We may have lost that nomination [in 1992], my friends, but you and I won the battle for the heart and soul of the Republican Party."[88]

Bob Dole had been seeking high office now for two decades. He was Gerald Ford's vice-presidential running mate in 1976, ran for the presidential nomination in 1980, then again in 1988, and now in 1996. In the crucial first battles, Iowa and New Hampshire, battle lines were drawn, particularly between Forbes, Alexander, and Dole. It quickly got nasty. Before the Iowa caucuses, Dole hired Steve Goldberg and his firm, Campaign Tel, a telemarketing firm, to call some 10,000 to 30,000 Iowa Republicans to alert them to the horrors of Steve Forbes signature policy issue, the flat tax. Rather than attack over the airwaves, Campaign Tel reached Iowa Republicans in their homes through the telephone:

> My name is _____ and I'm calling with a special message for Iowa's farm families. Iowa's Farm Bureau has adopted a resolution that opposes the flat tax like the one offered by candidate Steve Forbes. Under the Forbes flat tax, Iowa farmers would pay an average of $5,000 more in taxes.[89]

These anti-Forbes calls were also made to prospective voters in South Carolina, South Dakota, North Dakota, Georgia, Connecticut, and New York, all states with upcoming Republican primaries. Trouble was, the Iowa Farm Bureau had never passed such a resolution, and some of the telemarketers were told to tell listeners that they worked for a bogus organization called Iowa Farm Families rather than working on behalf of Dole.

The night before the New Hampshire primary, voters were getting calls from the "National Research Council," again a phony group, castigating Pat Buchanan and Steve Forbes, and telling voters that "Lamar Alexander had raised taxes forty-nine times" when he was governor of Tennessee. The language in these attacks was almost identical to speeches and television commercials launched by Dole.[90] This is the same Bob Dole who bleated out to George Bush in the 1992 New Hampshire primary, "quit lying about my record!"

Dole eked out a victory in Iowa, a state he easily won in the 1988 primaries, but fell short in New Hampshire, which was again won by Pat Buchanan. Fed up with his staff for the loss, Dole fired three of his senior advisers, deputy chairman William B. Lacy and senior pollsters William D. McInturff and Neil Newhouse.[91] In a sense, Dole was killing the messenger: the polls that McInturff and Newhouse conducted were both professionally competent and accurate.[92] Next came consecutive Forbes victories in Delaware and Arizona. The South Carolina primary was considered a make-or-break situation for Dole: win, or get out. The Dole campaign was in turmoil when Mike Murphy and Don Sipple arrived to take over the media operation, and Tony Fabrizio and Fred Steeper were brought in to conduct polling. Sipple had just come off the failed Pete Wilson presidential bid, and earlier had helped George W. Bush in his 1994 upset victory over Texas governor Ann Richards. Sipple scrapped the negative attack ads and created a sixty-second spot about Dole the war hero and steadfast leader. The last line went: "Tested in war, proved in peace. He embodies the strength that is America. And a man that all of us can be proud to call president."[93]

Dole won decisively in South Carolina, and kept winning. He secured the nomination quickly, but his shortcomings as a campaigner were all too evident. "On Bob Dole's bad days," smirked journalist Roger Simon, "he looked like Grandpa Munster. On his really bad days, he sounded like him."[94] When he was around other World War II veterans, he looked relatively spry, despite his debilitating injuries. Nevertheless, he was seventy-two years old, two years older than Ronald Reagan was when he took office as president. Dole was a poor speaker, wouldn't stick to staff-prepared scripts, wandered off, and winged it. His handlers "lived in mortal fear that anyone will see too much of [Bob Dole], learn too much about [him], or talk too much."[95] Let Bob Dole be Bob Dole? No, that was too risky. "Even if you don't like me you ought to vote for me," Dole told a mystified cluster of voters in Medford, Oregon.[96] Campaign consultants could only cringe.

Furthermore, Dole didn't believe in the modern stage crafting of presidential campaigns. How helpful were the political consultants to Dole? What did he learn? "Virtually nothing," responded Don Sipple. "The cosmetics of modern campaigning are something Dole thinks should not make a difference. The appreciation for the picture, the aesthetics of the road show, the lighting, the sound. He didn't think it should *count*."[97]

By March 2, 1996, Dole had effectively sewed up the Republican nomination, and he could have begun hammering away at Clinton months before the general election. But with hardly any money in the bank, consultant and staff turmoil, and no consistent message, Dole all but disappeared from the public eye. He had a big chance to make a splash when he resigned from the Senate on June 11, but he failed to make a convincing case for why he was challenging Clinton. While Bill Clinton publicly congratulated Dole on his Senate service, Democrats poured it on with a tough campaign ad, playing in key states. In "Empty," the Democratic ad accused Dole of "quitting, giving up, leaving behind the gridlock he helped create."[98]

Dole ran through a gaggle of senior political consultants. New York senator Alphonse D'Amato tried to bully Dole into using Arthur Finkelstein, but Dole said no. But Finkelstein's protégés were in the thick of the campaign for Dole: Alex Castellanos, Chris Mottola, John Buckley, and Tony Fabrizio.[99] Republican consultant Doug Bailey, who had once employed Sipple, observed, "Dole has got every consultant known to man tied in some way to his campaign, and it's not clear how it's set up. They may have conflicting views and egos, but no one person gets close to Dole. From time to time, someone appears to be in charge, then something happens and another one pops up. It looks like all of them will get their fifteen minutes of fame."[100]

Dole's campaign manager was Scott Reed, formerly with the RNC, but with no ties to Dole or his staff; Reed stayed on until the bitter end. During the primaries, Dole's first set of senior consultants, McInturff and Lacy, were replaced by Murphy and Sipple. Then during the general election, Murphy and Sipple were replaced by Greg Stevens, Alex Castellanos, and Chris Mottola, who in turn were dumped during the last desperate weeks of the campaign.[101] Hurt and mystified, Murphy even wrote an open letter to his old boss, giving him campaign advice.[102]

During the Republican nominating convention, on the eve of Dole's acceptance speech, the "feuding among staff members was so fierce" that the campaign manager was forced to step in, fearful that the press and the outside world would catch wind of the bitter infighting.[103]

Clinton and Triangulation

Dick Morris's first client was the ambitious, thirty-year-old, long-haired attorney general of Arkansas, Bill Clinton, hoping to move up the political ladder. (See profile of Morris in chapter 13.) He had at times a tempestuous relationship with the Clintons, was fired by the governor in 1979, and stayed away from his presidential campaign in 1992; now, in October 1994, seventeen years after their first meeting, Morris, living in Connecticut, received a White House telephone call, with the president asking how he should handle the ongoing Haiti political crisis. Morris knew nothing about Haiti, but then realized: the call wasn't about Haiti, it was "about American politics a month before the 1994 election. And you do elections, so go for it."[104]

Hillary Clinton was instrumental in getting Morris back in the good graces of the president and into the White House. She was hoping to return the president "to his political senses" with his old, sometimes trusted political consigliere.[105] She called Morris in October 1994, right before the Republican congressional landslide. "Dick," she recalled in her 2003 memoir, "this election doesn't seem right to me. If I can get Bill to call you, will you help?"[106] Soon there were faxes and private late-night telephone conversations between Clinton and Morris, and secret meetings. Morris was simply and mysteriously known as "Charlie," and speeches written outside the White House speech shop, or policy phrases written by Morris, would seem to appear out of nowhere. Only the Clintons and Al Gore knew initially of Morris's behind-the-scenes work.

Morris didn't like the advice that Clinton's White House and campaign advisers were giving him, and he thought that the traditional liberal wing of the party was overwhelming the president with its own agenda. Morris wanted something else: he wanted Clinton to accept the most popular parts of the Republican agenda, get ahead of them, and claim them as his own. This meant deficit reduction, welfare reform, and cutting the bloat out of government. It also meant that the president could blunt Republican threats on programs that most people held dear, like the environment, education, and health care.[107] "Triangulate, create a third position," Morris urged the president, "not just in between the old positions of the two parties but above them as well. Identify a new course that accommodates the needs the Republicans address but does it in a way that is uniquely yours."[108] Hillary Clinton remarked that "Bill and I had learned to take Morris's opinions with a pound of salt and overlook his histrionics and self-aggrandizing. He was a good antidote to conventional wisdom and a spur to Washington bureaucratic inertia."[109]

Harold Ickes, nominally in charge of the re-election campaign, couldn't stand Morris. Their grudge went all the way back to the byzantine world of New York politics, where they both cut their teeth. Soon, however, Ickes, Stanley Greenberg, Mandy Grunwald, Frank Greer, George Stephanopoulos, Paul Begala, and James Carville—all veterans of the 1992 campaign—were shunted aside or their influence was greatly diminished.[110]

The team assembled by Morris was made of old allies and old antagonists. Morris called his high school friend pollster Douglas E. Schoen during the winter of 1994 and asked, "Did you want the Clinton campaign? I can get you the whole thing—polling, strategy, media."[111] Was he serious? Indeed he was, but Morris would have to stay in the background because of his work with Republican candidates in previous elections. Schoen surreptitiously began conducting polls for Clinton in December 1994. The first person that Schoen wanted to join in this still secret campaign team was his partner, Mark Penn. Morris agreed, but, according to Schoen, he wanted Penn on a tight leash. Penn, described by *Time* magazine as a "large and rumpled man with an absent-minded brilliance and a disheveled charm,"[112] would eventually become a rival to Morris, as Penn got his footing in the campaign team.

Then Schoen called his old colleague, Bob Squier. In April 1995, meeting in Bob Squier's Capitol Hill townhouse, was the team that would put Clinton over the top in 1996. Veteran ad maker Squier (who was barely on speaking terms with Morris) and two of his partners, Bill Knapp and Tom Ochs, were joined by New Yorker Hank Sheinkopf and Marius Penczner, a video producer from Nashville. The new Clinton message team called itself the November 5 Group. It wasn't until June 1995, six months after first being hired, that the news leaked that Morris, Schoen, and the others had been assembled.[113]

That month, Penn, worried that there was no defined campaign strategy, argued for conducting a super benchmark poll to "define the keys to re-establishing the president's image."[114] Two secret polling sites were set up, in Manhattan and in Denver, and respondents were asked a wide variety of questions, trying to establish a psychological profile of major voting blocs. The toughest groups to crack—and the most important for the outcome of the election—were the swing voters. In order to win over both Republican-leaning and Democratic-leaning swing voters, the Clinton message could not be totally negative or tough (like that of Dole) or soft and pliable (typical Democratic image), but some combination. And it all had to be about values: not religious pieties, only secular ones—protecting kids, promoting education, keeping cigarette advertising from kids.[115] Penn identified what he called an "under-the-radar group" that became known as "Soccer Moms." "These Moms did not want more government in their lives, but they were quite happy to have a little more government in their kids' lives to keep them on the straight and narrow."[116]

Media scholar L. Patrick Devlin observed that Clinton had a "seamless advertising campaign that linked his primary, postprimary/preconvention, and general election ads."[117] The advertising strategy, according to lead ad maker Bill Knapp, was to be optimistic, talk about values rather than programs, and talk about unity rather than class.[118] As Morris observed, "Week after week, month after month, from early July 1995 more or less continually until election day in '96, sixteen months later, we bombarded the public with ads."[119] One of the maddening things about the Clinton ad campaign, admitted Republican media consultant Alex Castellanos, was that the sixteen different comparison ads the Democrats produced seemed reasonable, not like old-fashion attack ads. The ads put the spotlight on Dole, defining him in a negative light, but in a way that their tone "killed you with kindness."[120]

The negative ads invariably carried the tag line about Dole: "Wrong in the Past; Wrong for Our Future." For the Clinton campaign, it was the perfect summation of Bob Dole. In negative ads, Dole often appeared in the foreground, and Speaker of the House Newt Gingrich in the background. This, of course, was no accident, as the Clinton team wanted to tie Dole to the increasingly unpopular Gingrich whenever it could. In the Squier/Knapp–produced ads, Gingrich and Dole were shot in black and white and "looked like villains from a silent-picture show."[121]

In December 1995, the Democrats launched a major advertising campaign, targeted at key electoral states. The Clinton advisers wanted to spend $55 million, but federal campaign law limited their budget to $37 million. The solution? Let the Democratic National Committee raise the soft money to pay for issue advocacy ads. The ads wouldn't say "vote for Clinton," but they might tell of the sins of the Republican Party and say as a tagline, "Vote Democratic." Another problem, however, was that federal law required that if the DNC was going to spend the funds, then two-thirds of the money had to come from hard money, or money that was legally reportable. But the Democrats wanted to spent soft money, which was more plentiful and unreportable. The solution: take the soft money, donate it to selected state Democratic parties, and let them spend it on the advertising (which was not regulated by federal law), rather than have the national party spend it.[122]

Dick Morris noted that the Democratic Party spent upwards of $85 million on television ads, which was comparable to the roughly $80 million spent altogether by Clinton and Bush during the 1992 primary and general election.[123] The compare/contrast ads ran in strategic media markets throughout the country, but not in New York, Washington, DC, or Los Angeles. Because the Democratic ads were not seen in the major media markets, they were essentially under the radar from national political commentators. Through these ads, Clinton was able to accomplish one of the fundamentals of political communication: define himself and define his opponent.

To help assure that Clinton and other Democrats would win in the fall, DNC chair Don Fowler pushed to have the state parties build reliable voter files. It was becoming evident in 1996 that success or failure could hinge on having an accurate and comprehensive understanding of how to effectively contact Democratic voters. The DNC turned to veteran consultant Bob Blaemire, whose firm built more voter files for Democratic state parties than any other firm.[124]

Democratic media consultant David Axelrod listened to Bob Dole's acceptance speech, and what particularly resonated was Dole's central point: "Let me be a bridge to a time of tranquility." No, Axelrod immediately knew, this was the wrong image, going back, not forward, and he suggested to the campaign that Clinton emphasize that "we must build bridges to the future, not the past." Axelrod also suggested that Clinton change the tone of the rancorous election season by concentrating on "ideas, not insults." Both suggestions were adopted by the Clinton team, and a new campaign slogan was unveiled: "Building a Bridge to the 21st Century."[125]

A few days before the opening of the Democratic National Convention, *Time* magazine ran a cover story about Dick Morris. On the magazine's cover was a picture of a confident Bill Clinton, and pasted onto his shoulder was a cutout photo of Morris, "the most influential private citizen in America," said *Time*.[126] Earlier, Bill Clinton had complained to his new 1996 political consultants, "I don't want to read about you in the press. I'm sick and tired of consultants getting famous at my expense. Any story that comes out during the campaign undermines my candidacy."[127] Now, here was Dick Morris, touted as the most influential private citizen in the country.

On the day before Bill Clinton was to accept his party's nomination for a second term in office, the story broke in the tabloid *Star* that Morris had a year-long, ongoing affair with a prostitute at his $400-a-night suite in the Jefferson Hotel, and that at times he let her listen in to telephone conversations between Morris and the president. Morris was forced to resign, and he and his wife were escorted away from campaign headquarters. Instant polling, however, showed that there was no discernible damage done to the president. Now Morris was free to work the confessional television talk show circuit, to join a twelve-step sex addiction program, and pocket the $2.5 million advance he had received from a publisher for an insider's view of the Clinton White House.

Taking over as senior campaign consultant was Mark Penn, whose stature and authority in the White House had been steadily gaining ground. But in reality, Clinton's top strategist and consultant was himself. "I have a theory," said Republican media strategist Mike Murphy, "that Clinton is the first political consultant who's actually president."[128] His political instincts, his understanding of the game of politics, and his ability to communicate were crucial to his success.

The General Election

In early September, Don Sipple quit, frustrated after learning that the Dole-Kemp campaign was bringing in yet another media consultant, this time Alex Castellanos. Castellanos then produced a hard-hitting attack ad against Clinton on drug use, with footage of Clinton admitting to an MTV audience of kids that he'd inhale if he had to do it all over again. It could have been a devastating ad, but just as soon as the ad went up and started to gain an audience, Dole pulled it off the airwaves, and substituted a "spend-and-tax liberal" ad instead.[129]

No matter what Dole tried, changing advisers, changing the message, retooling where he went and how he attacked Clinton, nothing was working. In fact, he had lost ground during September and into October. The Clinton team relentlessly pounded home its principal negative themes: Dole was too tied to Gingrich, he'd been in office far too long, and he was wrong on too many issues. As Bill Knapp put it, Dole was "too old and too out of it."[130] The debates just made things worse, with Clinton well prepared and credible, while Dole was unprepared and tired.

However, a small gesture by Bob Dole marked a turning point in campaign history. On Thursday evening, October 6, the first presidential debate, hosted at the Bushnell Theater in Hartford, Connecticut, was fairly unremarkable, and not very newsworthy. But in his closing remarks, Bob Dole did something no other presidential candidate had done: he invited listeners to find out more about the Dole-Kemp campaign by logging onto the campaign website: "I ask for your support. I ask for your help. And if you really want to get involved, just tap into my home page, www.DoleKemp96org. Thank you. God bless America." Dole didn't quite get the URL right—he forgot the "dot" before "org." But there were well over 2 million hits on the campaign website the next day. Thus began a new age in presidential communications. Certainly by today's standards the Dole website was hopelessly unsophisticated, but at the time, it was a remarkable achievement.[131]

Dole's last political adviser was Madison Avenue adman Norman Cohen, who suggested that in its last weeks the campaign hold its rallies in smaller venues so the crowds wouldn't seem so sparse.[132] But the final idea of the campaign came from Dole himself: an all-out nationwide barnstorm. On the last desperate days of the campaign, Dole subjected himself and his traveling reporters to a ninety-six hour marathon of campaigning. "If I'm gonna lose this, I'm gonna lose this my way," Dole declared to his campaign manager, Scott Reed.[133] The campaign plane touched down in twenty states, some at the oddest of hours, like the 4:30 a.m. arrival in Newark, New Jersey, with no one there to cheer on the candidate. Dole was exhausted, unfocused, and looked like death warmed over, but still he battled on.

If only men had voted, Dole would have won. But women voters made the difference for Clinton, preferring him by substantial numbers over Dole. Clinton pounded against "DoleGingrich," laid claim to the ideological, cultural, and political center, and won. In the end, Clinton won thirty-one states and the District of Columbia, and 379 electoral votes, but still less than half of the popular vote, with 49.2 percent. Dole won nineteen states, 159 electoral votes, and 40.7 percent of the popular vote. Ross Perot, winning no states and receiving no electoral votes, still captured 8.4 percent of the popular vote.

To the winner, went the spoils. Reporter John F. Harris noted the irony that some in the Clinton White House, chiefly Harold Ickes, the de facto campaign manager, tried to curtail early campaign commercials, but when he lost that fight, he was given the job of raising soft money through the DNC to pay for the ads. Ickes became the target of congressional and federal probes into his role in raising money. But the campaign consultants, who reaped the commissions and the fat monthly fees, were not under any investigation.[134]

Up to this point, the 1996 presidential election was the most expensive on record. A large portion of the money, $100 million, was spent by the November 5 Group, which produced and coordinated the ad expenditures. A political ad agency typically charges 15 percent of the total ad buys. Some of the early DNC ads had the 15 percent charge, but as the campaign went on and more and more money was spent, the percentage was lowered. Altogether, the November 5 Group was able to collect about $7 million in fees, or about 7 percent. The ad firm of Squier, Knapp, and Ochs, which actually produced the ads, was given 50 percent of the $7 million, while Dick Morris kept 25 percent, Penn and Schoen retained 10 percent, Hank Scheinkopf got a little under 10 percent, and Marius Penczner, a little under 5 percent. In addition, Dick Morris received a $15,000 monthly retainer; had he finished the last ten weeks of the campaign, he would have received another $700,000. Altogether, according to his own accounting, Morris made $500,000 in 1995, and about a million dollars in 1996. Penn and Schoen gathered in about $4.3 million for their polling work for the DNC and the Clinton-Gore team.[135] Presidential campaign consulting was becoming, for some, a very lucrative practice.

CHAPTER 15

Technological Advances

The 2012 technology race combined a tough interior of smart data with a glossy exterior of sophisticated messaging, advertising, and social outreach.
—Julie Germany on the 2012 presidential campaign (2013)[1]

A S TECHNOLOGY HAS advanced, political campaigns have taken advantage of their changes and efficiencies. But campaigns have usually followed the lead of the commercial world, rather than being at the forefront of innovation.

Computer Technology

During the 1952 presidential election, computer technology was first used to predict who would win. Given the widespread failure of political insiders to accurately predict the 1948 returns, a computer-based analysis seemed like an interesting proposition. The Remington Rand Univac Corporation made predictions for CBS television, but its findings turned out to be no better or worse than the predictions of reporters and political observers.[2] As seen in chapter 3, Democrats had experimented with computer analysis during the 1960 presidential campaign, working with the Simulmatics Corporation. Professors Ithiel de Sola Pool, Robert Abelson, and their colleagues examined the data stored on old IBM punch cards housed in the Roper Center survey research archives. These data came from sixty-six surveys conducted during the 1952, 1954, 1956, and 1958 congressional and presidential races, and the analyses of over 100,000 personal interviews. The researchers divided the voters into 480 distinct types, combined them with 50 pre-selected issues, and fed the information into an IBM 704 computer. The bulky computer spit out a million individual bits of information—incredible calculations at the time.

One of the most important questions for the Kennedy campaign was "What would happen on Election Day if the anti-Catholic criticism of Kennedy became significantly stronger?"[3] The computer simulation did not present a clear answer, but the bottom line was that Kennedy would not lose ground if the race focused on religion; in fact, he might gain support. Kennedy faced the issue squarely with his speech to a group of ministers assembled in Houston. Whether or not the computer simulation was a factor in his decision to speak, or whether he spoke simply out of political instinct, we do not know.

During the 1965 New York City mayoral race, Republican congressman John V. Lindsay's campaign was, in Barbara A. Carter's assessment, "the nation's first computerized campaign, a double-barreled caper that combined the use of storefront headquarters and computers."[4] Under the management of thirty-two-year-old Robert Price, the Lindsay campaign had 122 storefront offices spread throughout the city's seventy-six assembly districts. Each office had twenty-five volunteers, handing out literature, making phone calls, and knocking on doors. Lindsay's team analyzed more than 5,000 election districts (precincts in other cities), looking particularly at the 1,200 districts that had changed boundaries since the recent redistricting. They then held computer-based mock elections for the 1,200 new districts, to determine how citizens would have voted during the 1964 presidential and 1962 gubernatorial and Senate races.

By the 1970s, organizations, and even some political campaigns, were seeing the benefits of computer technology. Using computer analysis, the AFL-CIO attempted to compile a master list of 10 million union members that could be used as an accurate precinct-walking list. By midsummer 1973, the Committee on Political Education (COPE, the political arm of the AFL-CIO) had reached 8.9 million of its 10-million-member goal.[5]

Yet, it was difficult to convince some individual candidates that spending money on a campaign computer was worth it. Political consultant Joe Trippi remembered working for Los Angeles mayor Tom Bradley, who was running for governor of California in 1982. Trippi told campaign staffers that they needed a computer to organize names of supporters and potential Bradley voters. "They just stared at me. It was like I'd suggested we buy a submarine." It would cost $16,000, an enormous expenditure. The campaign wouldn't budge, so Trippi opened his own wallet and leased the top-of-the-line DEC PDP-11 for $500 a month. "It looked like a washing machine, only bigger, with a plastic, Star Trek-looking one-piece monitor/keyboard on top. It had a whopping 1.5 megabytes of memory."[6]

Polling firms, for years reliant on computer time on expensive mainframe computers, were, by the late 1980s, able to use personal computers and software developed particularly for survey research analysis. Eventually, as computer prices dropped and they became more efficient and portable, computer technology became essential for a well-oiled campaign.

During the late 1990s, some forwarding-thinking political consultants were predicting that computer technology and online communication would transform electioneering. One of the first to champion online communication was Phil Noble (b. 1951). A graduate of Birmingham-Southern College, who has also done graduate work at the University of Stockholm and was a resident fellow at the Kennedy School of Government at Harvard University, Noble began his political consulting career in 1979, specializing in candidate and opposition research, as noted in chapter 6. In 1996 he founded PoliticsOnline, an international company that provided assistance to clients throughout the world. Noble was the first political consultant to have his own business website, was a pioneer in online fundraising, and was the first to have an electronic newsletter, online courses for politics, e-mail petitions, and other innovations in the sphere of politics.[7] PoliticsOnline products and services were used by over 900 clients in more than fifty countries. Noble has developed major new media, technology, and e-democracy projects for the European Union and European Parliament, Council of Europe, the BBC, Bertelsmann Foundation, Amnesty International, among other organizations.

Online Fundraising

For decades, candidates and causes used direct mail and telephone solicitation for contacting potential donors. During the 1990s, nine out of ten congressional candidates and nearly every US Senate candidate used direct mail to solicit funds. But direct mail proved to be expensive. One example comes from the 1994 campaign by former lieutenant colonel and conservative talk show host Oliver North to unseat incumbent US senator Charles S. Robb in Virginia. North raised $17 million through direct mail, but could only keep $6 million for the campaign; the rest went to pay for the expenses of renting mailing lists, postage (13 million letters were sent out), and other associated costs.[8]

Then came online contributing, a far less expensive method of seeking campaign funds. Just as consumers became accustomed to purchasing goods over the Internet through secure sites, they became used to giving money to candidates and causes through websites and mobile phone apps. The online fundraising revolution has been particularly important in attracting new donors and small-amount donations.

During the 1996 presidential campaign, Bob Dole was able to raise almost $100,000 online, exceeding what Clinton could raise online. Then came the 2000 presidential primaries and a breakthrough in online fundraising. Political consultant R. Rebecca (Becki) Donatelli has been a pioneer in online fundraising, and her company, Campaign Solutions, along with affiliated companies eSolutions.com and Connell Donatelli, has helped Republican candidates and causes break into the world of online fundraising. During the 2000 presidential campaign, Donatelli helped Arizona senator John McCain collect $6 million online, including over $1 million the day after he won the New Hampshire primary. For the McCain-Palin presidential ticket in 2008, Donatelli's Campaign Solutions raised over $100 million online. On its website, Campaign Solutions touts that it has raised an average of $100,000 each day, every day, for the past decade for its wide-ranging set of clients. Connell Donatelli specializes in placing political and advocacy ads on the Internet and social media, using banner advertising, social advertising, and blog advertising.

McCain was just the start. During the 2004 presidential primary campaign, Howard Dean reached out to accept funds online. His campaign raised $15 million, a record amount, during the third quarter of 2003, when his candidacy looked almost assured. In 2005, Joe Rospars, Jascha Franklin-Hodge, and other staffers who worked on the Dean campaign formed an online fundraising and strategy consulting firm, Blue State Digital (BSD). Since its creation, BSD has served over 200 clients, including Obama for America, former British prime minister Tony Blair, Wal-Mart Watch, and the Communications Workers of America. Rospars became the director of new media for the Obama 2008 campaign and served as chief digital strategist for the Obama re-election campaign in 2011–2012.

On December 16, 2007, the 234th anniversary of the Boston Tea Party, Republican presidential hopeful Ron Paul, a congressman from Texas, collected $6 million from 24,940 supporters. A music promoter, Trevor Lyman, with no prior fundraising experience and no ties to the Paul campaign, created the website that called for Paul supporters to contribute. This was the largest one-day online contribution in presidential history, soon called a "money bomb," and would not be surpassed until the Obama campaign geared up.[9]

By 2008, Barack Obama's campaign had taken online fundraising to historic levels, tapping into a vast pool of small-amount donations through online contributions. The campaign used fundraising strategies often employed by nonprofits: asking for monthly donations or during short, defined periods of time, encouraging donors to reach out to their families and friends. The campaign sent out e-mail reminders, had "donate" buttons prominently displayed on web pages, used social networking sites, web videos, gaming sites, and other platforms to solicit funds. Altogether, more than 3 million donors made 6.5 million donations to Obama, totaling more than $500 million.[10]

One more convenience was added: donating by text message. In 2012 the Federal Election Commission permitted campaigns to accept donations by text message, provided that the carriers, like AT&T and Sprint, reduce their charges. Donors could text GOMITT (or 466488) or GIVE to 62262 (spelling out OBAMA). During the 2016 presidential primary season, Vermont senator Bernie Sanders has collected record amounts of donations online—$44.7 million alone in March 2016. By April 2016, his campaign had receive 6.5 million contributions from two million donors[11]

Along with candidates or political parties, a new platform emerged to make online contributions simple and convenient. ActBlue, an organization that called itself an "online clearinghouse for Democratic action," was founded in 2004 by Matt DeBergalis and Benjamin Rahn, to assist Democratic and progressive candidates, political parties, and organizations through online fundraising. By early June 2014, ActBlue had raised over $513 million, supported 10,000 organizations, and received funds from 8.4 million donors.[12]

Geotargeting and Microtargeting

Virtually every citizen has been sliced, diced, and categorized
into some demographic category, or an overlap of various categories.
—Steven Hill (2002)[13]

If television advertising is painting with broad brush strokes,
microtargeting is political pointillism.
—Chris Cillizza (2007)[14]

Starting in 1948, liberal and progressive political candidates for Congress have been assisted by the National Committee for an Effective Congress (NCEC), an organization established by Eleanor Roosevelt, West Virginia senator Harley M. Kilgore, and newspaperman Maurice Rosenblatt.[15] The organization, funded by a variety of private donors, including General Motors heir Stewart Mott, helped candidates with radio and television spots, get-out-the-vote drives, and targeting. NCEC used the skills of a growing number of Democratic political consultants. In 1974, in the first post-Watergate congressional elections, NCEC boasted that thirty-five out of the forty-nine candidates it supported won, and forty-three incumbent Republicans were defeated.

Among the surprise winners that year was lawyer and former congressional aide Tom Harkin, running for an Iowa congressional seat. Harkin defeated the incumbent, William J. Scherle, by 3,500 votes. Consultant Joe Rothstein designed a communications plan for Harkin, and Bob Squier filmed a series of "work days" (similar to what Squier had done for Bob Graham in Florida). For Maryland representative Gladys N. Spellman, NCEC discharged consultants Bob Beckel and Mike McClister to manage her campaign and had Squier produce radio spots. Spellman was able to defeat Republican John B. Burcham Jr. by 4,000 votes.[16]

Also significant in 1974, NCEC decided to provide geomapping information to Democratic candidates. It was a laborious, expensive, and time-consuming effort for NCEC researchers to contact individual county election boards to obtain information on who had voted. Most of the states had information on voters, including their name, age, and gender, but hardly any of the material was available in computer files. All this information had to be collected from paper copies, and then inputted manually by NCEC researchers. They coded voters by using ethnic name dictionaries to determine who might by Asian, Jewish, or Hispanic. NCEC also obtained voter information by race from southern states covered by the 1965 Voting Rights Act that were required to tabulate race in their files.[17]

Journalist Sasha Issenberg noted that NCEC researchers came up with three key formulas that could be applied to any precinct in the United States: a Democratic performance index; a persuasion index, indicating how much the precinct would swing from one party to another; and a GOTV percent, measuring the volatility of the get-out-the-vote turnout effort. By the 1980s, these analyses were considered crucial to determine the odds of Democratic candidates throughout the nation.[18]

Campaign consultants were trying to discover keys to understanding what groups of individuals should be targeted for fundraising and persuasion. For example, Republican campaign researcher Vincent Barabba in the 1970s discovered that families that had daughters who were in the Brownies were very good targets for Republican candidates.[19] Along with others in the business, Karl Rove, who opened his direct mail shop in 1981, started taking advantage of enhanced targeting information. For his first client, Texas governor Bill Clements, he mailed out nearly a million fundraising letters, in twenty-six different versions, depending on the demographics about the donors: where they lived, how much they had previously given, how long they had supported the governor. "I was counting on cutting-edge technology to carve out my niche in the direct mail business," Rove later wrote.[20]

Spurred on by the National Voter Registration Act of 1993 (the "Motor-Voter" law), states automated their voter files and integrated their databases. Altogether, there are now some 4,000 election boards, county clerk offices, and state boards of registrars. While the information collected varies by jurisdiction, it usually contains the voter's first and last name, residence and mailing address, birth date, telephone number, political party affiliation, e-mail address, date last voted, and more. Data mining firms augment these data with information about lifestyle and consumer habits. By 2000, campaigns were using voter and consumer databases and mapping technology. Aristotle, Inc., a data mining firm created in 1983 by brothers John and Dean Phillips, began collecting voter information from state and county election boards, and putting it into electronic format available for clients. If a client, for example, wanted to target voters who have hunting or fishing licenses, Aristotle could reach into its list of 5.4 million such voters. Today, Aristotle, which serves clients from all political parties, has over 190 million voter records containing voter histories, demographics, hobbies, donor histories—in all, over 500 fields of data.[21]

In 2011, Labels & Lists, a Bellingham, Washington–based data company founded in 1975, acquired one of its chief competitors, Voter Contact Services (VCS), the firm founded by Bill Daly.[22] The acquisition gave Labels & Lists, headed by Bruce Willsie, a national voter file to supplement its state-based data. Working with Moonshadow Mobile, Labels & Lists introduced VoterMapping.com in late 2011, an online subscription service that provides an extraordinary range of voter, political, and demographic information, on readily viewable maps, nationally, by states, or any of their local political jurisdictions.[23] Moonshadow and Labels & Lists further created "Ground Game," a cell phone and tablet application giving political data in map form, giving instant access to geotargeting information.[24]

Democratic consultant Hal Malchow used some of the first microtargeting techniques in 1995 for his client Oregon congressman Ron Wyden, who was running in a special US Senate election held in 1996. Malchow developed a statistical package, CHAID (Chi-Square Automatic Interaction Detection), that analyzed how different variables would affect voter behavior. Instead of in-depth interviews from random lists of telephone numbers, Malchow used shorter "minipolls" of 10,000 people. He used voter lists, census data, and consumer information to determine messages and demographics. When Wyden ran for a full Senate term in 1998, for example, Malchow found that young independents in high-education neighborhoods with high Asian populations would favor Wyden. In a typical poll, the number of such samples would be too small to be useful.[25]

Harold (Hal) Malchow began his campaigning career as a nine-year-old in his native Gulfport, Mississippi, hanging Nixon for President signs on his school bus and later nailing Goldwater signs onto telephone poles.[26] But then came the civil rights revolution, and Malchow embraced the insurgent Mississippi Freedom Party and progressive Democratic politics. In 2003, Malchow authored *The New Political Targeting*, a technical book describing how modern campaigns could do a better job in targeting voter contact. It was dedicated to targeting pioneer Matt Reese. Malchow wrote that many Americans were "astounded" at how close the 2000 presidential election was. But "what most Americans and many political observers fail to understand is that almost every competitive election is decided by a small percentage of voters." In most elections, more than half of the eligible voters turn up at the polling stations, and, Malchow contended, in most races for governor or senator, less than 20 percent of the voting electorate is truly undecided. But how to reach those undecided voters, and with what message? Malchow contended that modern campaigns were doing a "poor job of targeting."[27]

There may be some 500 fields of political, demographic, lifestyle, and consumer behavior available on voters today, but, according to Malchow, there are five characteristics that are most helpful in ascertaining political support: ethnicity and race, church attendance, marital status and gender, geography, and gun ownership.[28]

After the 2010 election cycle, Malchow's firm, MSHC Partners, disbanded, with the partners forming two successor firms. Malchow decided to quit politics. "Politics has gotten too negative for me. Every year it gets worse, and I really just need to take a step back from it at this point," said Malchow in late October 2010.[29] Malchow was inducted into the AAPC Hall of Fame in 2016.

On the Republican side, one of the most prominent microtargeters is Alexander P. (Alex) Gage. Gage graduated from the University of Michigan and served for fifteen years as vice president for the Detroit-based polling firm Market Opinion Research (MOR), working with Bob Teeter and Fred Steeper. In 1989, after MOR was sold, Gage, Steeper, and several others formed Market Strategies.[30] The firm did much of its work with corporate clients, and Gage learned of the massive amounts of data such firms kept on consumers—far more than kept by political campaigns. In 2002, Gage convinced Matthew Dowd, Karl Rove, and Ken Mehlman that microtargeting could prove critical for the re-election of Republican candidates, and particularly for George Bush in 2004. To test-market his ideas, the Michigan Republican Party hired Gage and media consultant Fred Wszolek to analyze the 5-million-person voter file for the state. They matched the files with commercial data collected by the marketing and technology company Axciom, with hundreds of fields, and found an 80 percent correlation between consumer data and voting preference.

In 2001 the Republican National Committee established the 72-Hour Task Force, to find the most effective way to identify Republican voters and get them to the polls on Election Day. Nearly a million dollars was spent experimenting in a number of states to come up with a better understanding of where the voters were and how to reach them. Under the direction of Blaise Hazelwood, the effort showed substantial increases in get-out-the-vote participation, particularly in Florida, Georgia, and Missouri in the 2002 congressional races.[31] Republican strategists deployed their get-out-the-vote (GOTV) plan three days before Election Day, hoping to match the GOTV efforts of the Democrats. While the 72-hour program received considerable attention and plaudits, there was a critical flaw in the Republican operation. Republicans couldn't, with any precision, locate their voters. They had, according to Gage, "bad customer files."[32]

This led Gage to create TargetPoint Consulting in 2003, and he became chief microtargeter for the Bush-Cheney re-election in 2004. Gage also held that role for the Mitt Romney 2008 bid for the Republican nomination. In 2012 Gage reflected on the advances in microtargeting, compared to 2004 and 2008: "We thought we were pretty smart—but today? It's mind-boggling. Someone handed us a magnifying glass and we said, 'Oh, We can see some people.' Then someone said, 'Try a microscope.' And now we're using electronic microscopes."[33]

Robert Blaemire, who had worked for Below, Tobe & Associates, opened up his own computer services consulting business, Blaemire Communications, in 1991, specializing in providing voter files for Democratic state parties and candidates. Previously, he had worked for Indiana senator Birch Bayh, and developed for the senator a mailing list of 2.8 million Indiana voters with 250 identification codes. He later assisted the National Education Association and helped launch a progressive political action committee, the Committee for American Principles. Blaemire Communications focused on assisting Democratic state parties, and in its last year of independent operation, Blaemire's firm had twenty-six state party clients. Blaemire Communications was absorbed by Catalist, the voter data firm created in 2006. Harold Ickes, a veteran political operative and former Bill Clinton adviser, and Laura Quinn, who headed the DNC data management unit, created Catalist, which provided Barack Obama and Hillary Clinton with data for the 2008 Democratic primaries. Catalist, which is privately supported and not a part of the DNC, provides voter bank data for progressive and Democratic organizations, and maintains voter data information on 185 million registered voters and 95 million unregistered voters.[34]

During the 2008 presidential election, Obama's national targeting director was Ken Strasma and his firm Strategic Telemetry. They, along with Catalist, provided voter data and analysis for the campaign. This resulted in a quicker turnaround time for voter file updates and higher quality databases. Strasma, a longtime veteran consultant and formerly with the NCEC, noted that the two years devoted to research and development of the microtargeting effort had "the most aggressive testing of microtargeting models that I had ever seen."[35]

From 2004 to 2012, the amount of available data has tripled, thanks to online communication, cookies, Twitter, Amazon and other online firms, résumé uploads, and Facebook and other social media sites. Ninety-one percent of Americans are digitally active, according to a study by Pew Internet Research, and leaving digital information with every transaction and download. Earlier, companies could sell 300 distinct bits of information; by 2012 they could offer up to 900 bits of information.[36] What have they learned? Among other things, someone who drinks Diet Dr. Pepper is more than likely to be a Republican who votes; 7UP drinkers tend to be apathetic Democrats; relatively uninterested Republicans drink Busch Light beer; Subaru owners are highly motivated Democrats; and Jaguar owners are highly motivated Republican voters.[37]

Even musical tastes can be analyzed. In January 2014, Pandora Media, an Internet radio service, began posting political ads tailored to the musical tastes of its 73.4 million monthly users. Pandora has built an enormous database with 450 points of data about every song ever recorded. It is now taking that information and cross-referencing it with the voting trends and ZIP codes of its members. Republicans tend to lean toward country, gospel, and New Age; Democrats lean toward jazz, electronic, and reggae music. There's a strong chance that this listener is a Democrat: ZIP code 94112 (San Francisco) + "Wake Me Up!" (Avicii) + "Blue Train" (John Coltrane). Likewise, this person is probably a Republican: ZIP code 77024 (Houston) + "Chillin' It" (Cole Swindell) + "Beautiful Day" (Jamie Grace).[38] Much of this kind of information is more hype and gee-whiz than useful, but it shows how granular the world of microtargeting can be. As seen in chapter 19, the two Obama campaigns (2008 and especially 2012) took microtargeting, big data, and analytics to a whole new level of sophistication.

Now emerging in the United States and international world of political consulting are the big daddies of big data, Google, Microsoft, and Facebook. They are able to amass all these data about individuals, and capitalize on the efforts done in the early 2000s by data pioneers. They have aggressively been selling their data files to political consulting clients and campaigns.

Data mining for political campaigning raises all sorts of privacy questions, and the ramifications have been widely debated. But Wally Clinton, typifying an attitude found among many political consultants, takes a pragmatic approach: "I'll leave [the privacy debate] to the intellectuals. It's my job to win elections, and [database technology] is an indispensable tool for winning elections."[39]

Websites and Online Communication

> *Authenticity is key to building relationship [with voters]*
> *because digital tools are just tools.*
>
> —Joe Rospars (2010)[40]

Long before there were political websites, there was *The Hotline*, a political news aggregation service created by Republican consultant Doug Bailey and Democratic consultant Roger Craver. When it started in 1987, it was first distributed by fax machine and carried a subscription rate of $4,000 per year. For political reporters, campaign staffers and consultants, *The Hotline* became required reading. In 1994 *The Hotline* went online and became the training ground for a number of prominent journalists, including CBS chief White House correspondent Chuck Todd, CBS morning show host Norah O'Donnell, *Congressional Quarterly*'s Craig Crawford, the *Weekly Standard*'s Stephen F. Hayes, and National Public Radio's Ken Rudin.[41]

Another aggregating service, but much different from *The Hotline*, is the *Drudge Report*. Matt Drudge was described by reporters Mark Halperin and John F. Harris in 2008 as "salacious, reckless, superficial, and unfair—an eccentric man perfectly in tune with the eccentricity that now pervades politics and journalism."[42] Drudge was one of the first to recognize the power of the Internet to relay news, gossip, and innuendo. He first came to prominence when he posted breaking gossip about the Monica Lewinsky scandal in 1998. His site soon attracted millions of viewers, and in mid-July 2015 there were over 8.8 billion clicks on the *Drudge Report* during the previous twelve months. Much of what is featured on the plain, simple home page becomes news or amplifies the news of the day because it is viewed by so many people. Drudge occupied the aggregating news site territory long before Google News and others appeared.

While *The Hotline* was emerging online and the *Drudge Report* was just beginning, campaigns were just discovering online communication. In a previous chapter, it was suggested that Bob Dole achieved a milestone in October 1996 when he announced his campaign website URL during a debate with Bill Clinton. Dole flubbed the URL address, but there were over 2 million hits on the website by the next day. But experiments with online communication came even earlier: Clinton's 1992 presidential election was the first to use the Internet, and in 1994 Edward Kennedy was the first US senator to have a website. In 1995 Lamar Alexander of Tennessee was the first presidential candidate to announce his candidacy over the Internet, and in 1997 Ted Mondale, a candidate for governor of Minnesota, was the first candidate to buy political advertising on a political website.[43] Thus a new era in political consulting had dawned: politics was about to go online.

Much of the early focus was on campaign websites and e-mail as weapons of choice for communicating with voters. Scholars examined campaign websites to determine their effectiveness as communication tools. Bruce Bimber and Richard Davis, for example, in looking at the 2000 and 2002 political campaigns, argued that the Internet was a niche communication tool, which helped reinforce political attachments and helped activists donate money more easily, but that it wasn't the great mobilization tool that enthusiasts thought it might be.[44] Many of the campaign websites were simply electronic bulletin boards, giving biographical information on the candidate, contact information, policy positions, and upcoming campaign events. Some didn't even have "donate" buttons. It would take several years before many campaign websites became interactive, permitting viewers to respond, post a blog, or other forms of interactivity.

New media scholar Michael Cornfield, writing in 2004, observed that while much attention had been given to campaign websites, the familiar, old technology of e-mail was often a superior means of communication. "Where politics is concerned, a flimsy e-mail list will outperform a sterling website ninety-nine days out of one hundred." The benefits of e-mail are evident: "e-mail is delivered;

websites must be found. E-mail is easy to read; websites must be navigated. E-mail is easy to respond to; website responses engender frame within frames . . . finally, e-mail is harder than a website for the press and opposition to monitor."[45] By 2000 the Republican National Committee was the first political organization to have amassed 1 million e-mail addresses, and by 2004 the Bush-Cheney presidential campaign had collected 6 million e-mail addresses. Then, in 2008, the Obama campaign accumulated over 13 million e-mail addresses, and aggressively used them for fundraising and calls for volunteers, often accompanied by a video and call to action.

In the 2004 Democratic primaries, Howard Dean made news by being the first presidential candidate to post a blog, have his own social network site, and a personalized page for fundraising. During the general election, the Bush re-election campaign quietly embraced digital activism and captured millions of e-mail addresses. In the 2008 Democratic primaries, Hillary Clinton announced her candidacy, "I'm in it to win it," through an Internet video. Receiving the most attention and traffic in 2008 was the MyBarackObama (MyBO) section of the Obama for America website.

Created in 2005 by three former employees of PayPal, YouTube was an instant success: a platform for anyone with a camera (or soon a smartphone) to post silly, entertaining, even informative videos. Google purchased YouTube in 2006, and by 2008 candidates were posting hundreds of videos on their own YouTube channel. Again, Obama led the way with 1,839 separate videos posted on his YouTube site, with 132.8 million viewers. His thirty-seven-minute speech on race relations was watched on YouTube by 4 million people, and a music video by hip-hop artist Will.i.am, "Yes, We Can," was viewed by over 10 million.[46] Andrew Rasiej and Micah L. Sifry estimate that if the YouTube videos posted by Obama in 2008 were thirty-second television ads, they would have cost about $47 million to air.[47]

Twitter was launched in March 2006, and by the 2008 elections it had become another useful device for communicating with volunteers and likely voters. Several candidates, especially John Edwards, Joe Biden, and Barack Obama, used Twitter to communicate. In order to be effective, Twitter, e-mail, and any other online communication device has to be different from the old media and communication tools. Joe Rospars, founder of Blue State Digital, argued that in order to be effective "you must use these channels to speak to people in a two-way conversation and really engage at a human level."[48]

Since the mid-2000s, politically oriented blogs have proliferated, both from traditional news sources (such as The Caucus [*New York Times*], The Fix [*Washington Post*], and Political Hotsheet [CBS News]) and new players (Redstate.com, *Huffington Post*, MyDD, Daily KOS).[49] The Howard Dean campaign in 2004 was the first to use a political blog, and both John Kerry and George W. Bush used blogging extensively during the general election. In 2006 Ned Lamont pulled an upset primary victory over incumbent senator Joe Lieberman in Connecticut, and much of the discontent against Lieberman was fueled by liberal blogs, like Daily KOS, FireDogLake.com, and MoveOn.org. (Lieberman, however, running as an independent, ultimately won the contest.)

Social networking sites have also become vehicles for political communication. The 2003–2004 Dean campaign first experimented with social media using MeetUp.com to attract supporters and volunteers. By 2008, social media sites were commonplace in campaigns. John Edwards signed up on at least twenty-three social media sites in 2008, more than any other candidate. The Obama campaign made extensive use of social media, blog postings, YouTube videos, and other online communication devices, even video games on X-Box and PlayStation. Obama had 2.2 million supporters on various Facebook sites, 800,000 on MySpace, and large followings on LinkedIn and other social network sites. Through MyBO, there were 400,000 blog postings, announcements for 200,000 offline events, and 35,000 volunteers were recruited. Altogether, Obama had been "friended" by over 7 million people. Nothing like this had ever been seen before in political campaigning.

Republicans seemed to be caught flatfooted, unwilling to reach out with the same degree as Democrats to new audiences and trusted constituents through the new tools of online communication. This was captured in a February 2013 *New York Times* magazine piece by Robert Draper, who wrote about "The Late Adopters," the Republican "disconnected old guard" that was being challenged by young, tech-savvy dissidents within its own party.[50] The cover illustration showed a "GOP Smartphone," which was a 1950s black rotary telephone, inside the magazine was a "GOP Laptop," illustrated as a 1950s manual typewriter, and a "GOP Hard Drive": a four-drawer file cabinet. It was harsh criticism and an unfair characterization, but it contained much truth in its underlying message.

By the 2016 presidential campaign, Republicans, Democrats, and outside organizations alike were scrambling to use advanced technologies to more efficiently use voter data for fundraising, organizing, compliance, get-out-the-vote drives, and other uses. Voter data information is guarded quite closely, for good reason: it can contain a goldmine of information on probable voters. That is why it was a stunning story to learn in mid-December 2015 that the Bernie Sanders campaign had momentarily breached the proprietary data files of the Clinton campaign that were held by NGP-VAN, the technology vendor used by Sanders, Clinton, and nearly all Democratic and progressive candidates for a wide variety of offices throughout the country. NGP-VAN is headed by Stu Trevelyan, a veteran of the 1992 Bill Clinton presidential campaign and the Clinton White House legislative team.[51]

Mobile Phone and Tablet Apps

The first Apple iPhone was introduced in June 2007, and with it came the introduction of applications (apps) designed to entertain, inform, and assist smartphone users. Hundreds, then thousands, of apps were soon available, many of them free for the iPhone and the iPod touch. During the last months of the 2008 general election, the Obama campaign released a free app, which allowed supporters and volunteers to have some of the campaign at their fingertips: a "Call

Friends" section helped volunteers call their friends to support Obama; a "Call Stats" section let viewers see how they were comparing in their phone calls to the leading callers in their state or region; and a "Get Involved" section helped supporters find local Obama offices that needed their assistance. Users could also browse through national news, Obama and Biden policy issues, and other information.

As noted above, mobile apps are particularly useful for volunteers and workers in the field, trying to contact individual voters. In past years, users have become accustomed to finding restaurants, gas stations, and grocery stores using Google or Bing maps, and now they can do the same with sophisticated mobile apps. Once a canvasser has met with a potential voter, she or he can then relay the information back to campaign headquarters and have the voter database network updated.

By the 2012 presidential election, mobile apps had become commonplace for candidates and causes. What was new, however, was the broader reach of these apps, to Amazon Kindles, android phones, iPads, and other tablets.[52]

Online Advertising

Political advertising on websites first appeared in 1998, when Peter Vallone was running against George Pataki in the New York gubernatorial race.[53] But online advertising was slow to catch on. In fact, during the 2004 presidential election, online advertising amounted to less than 1 percent of the total amount of television advertising spent in the biggest 100 markets.[54] During the 2008 elections, the amount of money spent on online advertising was still a tiny fraction of the overall media buys.

A marketing theory called Long Tail marketing focuses on communication to niche markets rather than broadcasting.[55] It was brought into the political communication space during the last few election cycles. US Senate candidate Al Franken was one of the first to use Long Tail techniques in his online advertising. For about $100,000, the Franken campaign in 2008 targeted 125 Minnesota groups, using more than 1,000 different pieces of advertising. For example, when a farmer went to his computer and looked up "farm supplies," "feed stores," or a variety of terms, up popped a Franken link on the Google search. The Franken campaign had purchased hundreds of keywords and phrases from Google AdWorks. Similarly, during the 2009 Virginia gubernatorial contest, when an individual typed in "Virginia jobs" on a Google search, the link for an ad would appear for Robert F. McDonnell, the Republican candidate and ultimate winner. Political online advertising has grown considerably since 2008. While online advertising was a "mere footnote" during the 2008 presidential campaign, it grew seven-fold during the 2012 campaign. As digital expert Julie Germany points out, "in 2012 winning the digital advertising war was just as important—if not more so—than winning the broadcast media war."[56]

Polling and New Technology

During recent presidential elections, there seemed to be a public opinion poll published every day. In 2008, at least forty organizations, some affiliated with universities, newspapers, or television networks, and commercial entities published surveys. Polling aggregate sites, like RealClearPolitics.com, FiveThirtyEight.com, Pollster.com, and *Huffington Post*'s HuffPost Pollster, published the results found in the various polls. However, while there has been an increased use of both public and private polling, it has become more difficult to reach persons willing to respond to pollsters' questions. In past decades, there would be response rates of 60 to 70 percent; recently, however, rates have dipped down to 20 percent, particularly in metropolitan areas.[57] This means that in order to complete 1,000 interviews, 5,000 persons have to be contacted, driving up the cost of a completed survey.

Since the 1970s, random digit dialing (RDD) had been the standard way of reaching individual phone numbers. However, with the growing number of cell phones, call block features, voicemail, and respondents' refusal to answer the phone, RDD has been called into question as the most efficient way to reach potential voters. At a 2002 conference on improving the accuracy of polling, political scientists Donald P. Green and Alan S. Gerber presented a paper titled "Enough Already with Random Digit Dialing," suggesting instead that pollsters use clustered random sampling from voter registration lists instead.[58] Why waste time and money dialing everyone (through RDD), rather than pinpointing those who are most likely to vote (voter registration files)? The benefits of going to a voter file rather than RDD became evident to pollsters, other political consultants, and candidates.

As of April 2015, some 92 percent of American adults owned cellphones, with 68 percent owning smartphones.[59] At least 25 percent of adults use cell phones only, with young, single adults having a much higher percentage of cell phone only. The standard method of conducting political surveys over the past forty years has been to use landlines, connected to households. The great benefit of cell phones is that they can be carried anywhere—to the grocery store, classroom, coffee shop, or in the car. This also poses a major problem: survey questions might be too intrusive for a public space; respondents might be more distracted, unwilling to answer candidly; and questions might take too much time. Who wants to have their cell phone minutes gobbled up by a fifteen- or twenty-minute survey?

Further, federal law prohibits automated dialing of cell phones, and calls must be dialed manually. This adds greatly to the cost of conducting the survey, up to four or five times the cost of a landline call.[60] As a further problem, cell phone only adults skew young, and if young voters are not accurately represented in political surveys, will there be significant sampling biases? Academics, professional survey research organizations, and pollsters are well aware of the potential problem.

Online surveys were first conducted during the late 1990s, when Harris International did preliminary testing of the 1998 congressional elections.

Then, during the 2000 presidential election, Harris International came in with very accurate survey results in seventy-two races using online surveys. By 2004, Zogby Interactive, the online polling firm of pollster John Zogby, was accurate in 85 percent of the state-by-state races it polled, and in 17 out of 18 US Senate races in 2006. However, while Zogby had a commendable won-loss record, his numbers were off by 8.6 percent, more than twice what other online polls were showing.[61]

Internet polling has several advantages: once the original start-up costs have been covered, Internet polling is less expensive than traditional telephone surveying; there can be interactivity and multimedia functions in online polling; and response rates can be much higher than traditional telephone calls. Furthermore, surveys results can be compiled in real time, and, finally, a panel could include 10,000 persons rather than the 1,000 found in a telephone survey.[62]

While online survey research has grown to become a $2 billion business, just 2 percent is related to politics and elections.[63] Political pollsters are generally wary of online polling, principally because of issues of bias in the sample and issues of self-selection. For example, Joel Benenson, commenting in 2007 when he was Obama's senior pollster, doesn't use online polling for campaigns because it is the least reliable method of identifying likely voters.[64]

Some surveys are also done automatically. Like automated telephone calls (robocalls), these automated surveys are called robo-polling. Some media polling firms, particularly the Rasmussen Report, SurveyUSA, and PPP (Public Policy Polling) conduct robo-polls. Telephone numbers are dialed automatically, and when someone answers the phone (doesn't matter who), an automatic message, not a live interviewer, will ask the questions. Usually, the questions are few in number. A number of media firms, such as ABC News, NBC News, CBS News, the Associated Press, *Wall Street Journal, New York Times,* and *Washington Post,* do not support or publish robo-polls. Just how accurate are such automated polls? The National Council on Public Polls, American Association of Public Opinion Research (AAPOR), and the Pew Research Center have noted that robo-polls have been as accurate as conventional polls in determining election outcomes.[65] Political scientist Gary C. Jacobson analyzed SurveyUSA's polls and found that when the polling firm conducted 600-person surveys through robo-polls it "pass[ed] all tests satisfactorily" for quality and accuracy.[66] Nevertheless, private pollsters are generally wary of automatic calls that probe the public's attitudes and beliefs.

There have been dramatic changes in survey research in recent years, with substantial increases in cell phones, the breakdown of RDD, the high refusal rate, the rise of online polling, automated surveys, and even quickie polls that ask just a handful of questions and come in at bargain-basement prices. Traditional polling is time-consuming and expensive, and private political pollsters, faced with cheaper alternative resources, will have to scramble to adjust and compete.

CHAPTER 16

Consulting, Issue Campaigns, and Government Affairs

The golden age of grassroots has arrived.

—Jack Bonner (1993)

Louise: *Having choices we don't like is having
no choices at all.*
Harry: *When they choose . . .*
Louise: *We lose.*

—from Health Insurance Industry of America issue ad (1993–1994)

PRESIDENTIAL, STATEWIDE, AND local candidate campaigns and ballot initiatives have been the stock in trade for the political consulting business. As seen in earlier chapters, more money is being poured into contests, attracting professional consultants who apply a wide range of services and specialties. Business interests and trade associations have backed ballot initiatives or have had to defend their interests against ballot challenges, and frequently the money spent on such noncandidate campaigns has been staggering. Another lucrative market for political consultants in recent decades has been corporate and trade issue advocacy and government relations.

Political Consultants and Issue Advocacy

*Issue advocacy can be defined as conducting a campaign
in order to influence the course of public policy.*

—Douglas A. Lathrop (2009)[1]

*If you can sell candidates as products,
why not products as candidates?*

—Barry Siegel (1991)[2]

As seen in chapter 1, during the 1930s and 1940s, Clem Whitaker and Leone Baxter were pioneers in employing public relations techniques in issue campaigns, ballot initiatives, and in battles against state and federal government policy proposals. Likewise, several of the consultants who were just getting started in candidate campaigns in the 1950s and 1960s began moving away from candidates to corporate political consulting and issue advocacy.

Following the 1982 election cycle, Matt Reese became one of the first political consultants to steer away from the roller coaster schedule of political campaigns toward the steadier (and more lucrative) work of corporate consulting. In 1983 his firm was approached by the Natural Gas Supply Association and was paid $1 million to help defeat a Missouri initiative calling for the re-regulation of natural gas. After that victory, Reese Communications began focusing on corporate clients, including AT&T, Blue Cross Blue Shield, Chevron, Citicorp, Georgia Power, McDonnell Douglas, and United Airlines. Smith & Harroff, the Republican firm founded by Jay Smith and Mark Harroff, was also one of the early political consulting firms to move to corporate clients and issue advocacy, where the bulk of its work now resides. Smith & Harroff clients have included the Nuclear Energy Institute, Westinghouse, and the Campaign for Tobacco-Free Kids.

The polling firm of Penn Schoen Berland (PSB) began working for corporate clients around the same time. Writing in 2007, Doug Schoen noted that "as we moved deeper into the business world, we were increasingly struck by the similarities between political campaigns and corporate marketing."[3] PSB helped a variety of blue chip companies, beginning with Texaco in 1985. The oil company had been hit with a $10 billion jury fine for violating a binding oral agreement with Pennzoil. The fine compelled Texaco to file for bankruptcy. Texaco sought help from PSB, hoping that a firm experienced in political campaigns might better represent them than a Madison Avenue commercial firm. PSB advised Texaco to "present the company's bankruptcy as a story about a blue chip firm with high-quality products and good ethics brought low by a ridiculously large jury award and fight the counter-story that this was the cautionary tale of an oil giant damaged by its own unethical behavior."[4] Later, PSB helped Eli Lilly expand its sales of the anti-depression drug Prozac. It helped inoculate Procter & Gamble against attacks made by a public interest group that its fat substitute product, Olestra, was dangerous. Procter & Gamble recognized that the experience PSB had with countering negative advertising in political campaigns would come in handy in this public relations battle.

PSB began using a new technique, called "mall testing," to help its client AT&T in its fight against upstart MCI. PSB tested MCI's "Friends and Family" advertising in shopping malls and discovered the best way to counter it was to point out its flaws and ridicule them. "We had a new game plan for AT&T," Schoen later wrote, "make fun of MCI."[5] A $200 million AT&T advertising campaign was launched in 1993, based largely on the survey research conducted by PSB. The mall testing, done for a corporate client, later became a tool, albeit an expensive one, for candidate campaigns. For example, during the 1996 presidential campaign, PSB would use mall testing to help refine and craft the message for the Clinton-Gore re-election campaign.

Why would a commercial company go negative against a competitor? Media consultant Alex Castellanos argued in 1992 that it was growing competition and hard times: "Hard times produce tough advertising and, like it or not, those hard times have brought Madison Avenue some of the toughest political-style advertising yet." Castellanos would urge commercial clients to think something like political clients, to "think in terms of two separate advertising campaigns and budgets, one to define themselves, another to define their rivals."[6]

Many other top-tier polling and media firms have had a steady list of corporate, nonprofit, and advocacy clients as well as candidates for office.

Grassroots and Astroturf

Not many grassroots movements begin
outside of Washington, DC

—David Rehr, president, National Beer Wholesalers (1991)[7]

Grassroots for hire.

—Edward Walker (2014)[8]

Speaker of the House William B. Bankhead, a Democrat from Alabama, spoke to newly elected members of Congress in November 1938, and gave them advice on how they could hold on to their jobs in Washington. "Your votes and speeches may make you well known and give you a reputation," said Bankhead, "but it's the way you handle the mail that determines your re-election."[9]

Elected officials, particularly those in Washington, are well-attuned to the needs and demands of the people who elected them to office. Over the years, interest groups have learned that if they want something from elected officials, they cannot simply rely on lobbyists and lawyers to get the job done. Direct lobbying of members of Congress is often stereotyped by the well-fed, smooth-talking, Washington-based lobbyist, who seeks out legislators in their personal offices, committee rooms, and after-hours receptions. Washington is filled with this particular species, but they often are not enough. Just as important in many cases is the voice of the people back home. That is where grassroots lobbying comes in.

The term "grassroots lobbying" embraces a variety of actions by employees, union members, shareholders, local citizens, and opinion leaders. Sometimes it comes in the form of letter writing and telephone campaigns, letters to the editor, e-mail and Twitter blasts, or visits to Washington or state capitols, all to put pressure on elected officials. Grassroots campaigns have to be timed and orchestrated, and invariably they are planned and funded by lobbying and law firms, labor unions, corporations, and advocacy groups.

Organized grassroots efforts have been around for decades. In 1948, Whitaker and Baxter, working for the American Medical Association, distributed some 40 to 50 million pieces of literature in doctors' waiting rooms and hospitals warning against "socialized medicine," and orchestrating over 8,000 endorsements from patriotic groups, women's organizations, and service and business groups in opposition to the president.

The oil and refinery company Atlantic Richfield Company (ARCO) was considered the "granddaddy of corporate grassroots organizations."[10] Begun in 1975, the grassroots program was an extension of the company's corporate culture, which encouraged employees to be deeply engaged in community activities, including the political process. ARCO's advocacy program came from an idea of Bill Duke, who had been a journalist and executive assistant to US senator Jacob Javits (New York). Duke "believed that ARCO was, in some ways, like a candidate for political office, always in need of conversation with constituents, communicating its views, winning public support, and reestablishing contact with its key community groups."[11] ARCO turned to its employees, retirees, royalty owners, and to opinion leaders. By 1985, ARCO had a pool of some 20,000 individuals and 12,000 organizations in its constituency relations system.[12]

The second corporation to establish a grassroots network was the tobacco giant Philip Morris, which launched its Civic Involvement Program in 1977, then Nationwide Insurance Company followed along with its own civic action program in 1978. The model for the civic action programs was educational, learning about issues that might affect the company, its employees, and their communities. Other aspects were more overtly political: encouraging participants to become involved in voter registration drives, speaker training, and exercises in how to communicate with legislators. Nationwide Insurance in 1995 boasted of having half of its 15,000 employees active in its civic action program. Other insurance companies also began gearing up employee action committees. Many had been caught flatfooted when California voters passed a ballot issue in 1988 that cut automobile insurance rates by 20 percent and established far-reaching regulatory standards.[13]

In the early 1980s, one study found that grassroots techniques were firmly established in Washington and throughout state capitals as tools to persuade and educate lawmakers. Of 175 Washington lobbying firms queried in 1983, some 84 percent had developed letter-writing campaigns, and 80 percent had used grassroots lobbying for their clients.[14] A number of corporations and trade associations began putting together their own grassroots activism programs. The AFL-CIO, the nation's largest union federation, has an entire unit devoted to grassroots support. In 2009 the US Chamber of Commerce boasted that its members sent more than one million letters to members of Congress urging they support a "pro-jobs" agenda.[15]

Several public relations and political consulting firms tout their ability to create grassroots support for clients. The more prominent groups are Beckel Cowan, Bivings Group, Bonner & Associates, Burson-Marsteller, Davies Communications, DCI Group, Direct Impact, Hill & Knowlton, Issue Dynamics, Inc., and National Grassroots & Communication.[16]

What lobbyist David Rehr wrote at the opening of this section is correct: many of the orchestrated grassroots campaigns are generated from Washington. The trick for grassroots mobilization companies is to make the deluge of telephone calls, or e-mails, or regular mail look spontaneous, from ordinary but concerned citizens, and above all genuine. One of best-known grassroots consultants, Jack Bonner, helps corporate clients figure out how much pressure they want to put on lawmakers. "We sit down with the lobbyists and ask: How much heat do you want on these guys? Do you want ten local groups or two hundred groups? Do you want one hundred phone calls from constituents or a thousand phone calls?"[17]

Sometimes, the outburst from citizens is genuine, only needing an outlet to show its anger. This was the case when Wes Boyd and Joan Blades founded MoveOn.org in 1988, building a political forum for like-minded citizens who were fed up with the Republican attempt to impeach President Clinton. More than a half-million persons signed an online petition stating that Clinton should be censured, not impeached, and that the country should "move on" to more important issues. MoveOn.org had staying power, and by 2002 some $2.5 million had been donated to the opponents of the Clinton impeachment, and created a virtual phone bank to get out the vote for antiwar candidates for office. By 2013, MoveOn.org claimed to have over 8 million members.[18]

Various groups aligned with the Tea Party movement have also sprung to life, some with the help of professional consultants. As noted in chapter 13, the Tea Party Express political action committee, for example, was created by longtime Republican political consultant Sal Russo, based in Sacramento. Investigations into the fundraising and spending of the Tea Party Express found that a large portion of the money collected had been pocketed by Russo and his related firms. A *Washington Post* investigation into several other Tea Party–related groups found that just a small fraction of the money raised went to 2014 Tea Party–backed candidates. Of six major Tea Party organizations, some $37.5 million had been raised for the 2014 congressional campaigns, but only $7 million was devoted to helping the candidates. About half of the money raised, roughly $18 million, went to pay for direct mail and fundraising, and Tea Party leaders and their families were paid hundreds of thousands of dollars. "The lavish spending underscores how the protest movement has gone professional," wrote journalist Matea Gold, "with national groups transforming themselves into multimillion-dollar organizations run by activists collecting six-figure salaries."[19]

When the Houston Astros baseball team moved into the first major league indoor stadium in 1966, it soon became evident that there was a problem. Natural grass wouldn't grow in the Astrodome, and a solution had to be found. Team owner Roy Hofheinz called on Monsanto, whose scientists at its Chemstrand division had recently invented a plastic, synthetic product—a fake grass. It was installed at the Astrodome and soon dubbed AstroTurf. Grassroots lobbying, the practice of engaging real citizens in lobbying efforts, has its fake form as well. It's called astroturf lobbying and it has been flourishing in Washington and throughout state capitals. Reporter Ben Smith observed during the summer of 2009 that Washington was a town "paved in Astroturf."[20]

Astroturf takes the spontaneity and legitimacy out of grassroots lobbying. Astroturfing comes in a variety of forms, but in general, a fake organization, often with a benign-sounding name, is created, masking the true identity of the organization; dummy websites and fake blogs are created; and persons are paid to respond, giving multiple responses. All this to create the illusion of a spontaneous plea from real citizens back home.

It takes the most junior congressional staffer, opening the mail or downloading e-mails, about three minutes to figure out that a grassroots campaign has been launched. No one on Capitol Hill is fooled by an orchestrated campaign, and within minutes they can readily figure out who is behind it. While it happens infrequently, some legitimate grassroots shops take that extra step into lying and deception and get caught.

In 1995, Beckel Cowan, the grassroots firm headed by consultant Bob Beckel, worked for the Competitive Long Distance Coalition, sending some 600,000 telegrams to members of Congress in support of the long-distance telephone companies. But about half of those telegrams were sent without proper authorization, causing a major embarrassment to the telephone coalition.[21]

In 2009, when Congress was considering climate change legislation, more than a dozen forged letters were sent to three members of Congress. The letters were from local senior advocates and civil rights leaders, all opposing provisions in the legislation. Virginia congressman Tom Perriello, for example, received letters, complete with letterhead stationery and logos, from two organizations in his district, the Albemarle-Charlottesville NAACP and Creciendo Junto, a nonprofit network serving the Hispanic community in Charlottesville. The two Charlottesville nonprofits, understandably, were outraged that their names and identities had been used falsely. The letters had been prepared by Bonner and Associates. The firm was investigated for alleged deceptive practices. Jack Bonner vehemently denied that this was intentional, and blamed a "rogue temporary employee."[22]

There have been attempts in Congress to bring transparency to grassroots lobbying. When the Lobbying Disclosure Act of 1995 was being considered, earlier versions had measures that required political consulting and public relations firms to register and report their expenditures. But these provisions were not adopted into law.[23] In 2007, the Legislative Transparency and Accountability Act originally had grassroots lobbying disclosure requirements, but they were stripped away in its final version.[24]

Political Consultants

One of the pioneers in corporate grassroots activities was Edward A. Grefe (b. 1937), a Republican political consultant who worked with Roy Pfautch in several campaigns during the 1970s. Working at Johns Hopkins University and in political circles, Grefe gained a reputation as a successful fundraiser for Republican candidates. In 1972 he established his own fundraising firm. James Kiss, working for the public relations firm of Hill and Knowlton, and Martin Ryan Haley, who was consulting with the Tobacco Institute, wrote in the *Harvard Business Review* one of the first articles urging corporations to use local employees as lobbyists.

The tobacco conglomerate Philip Morris responded to this, and in 1975 Grefe was invited to create a legislative support system for the company. At the time, only the oil company ARCO had a similar grassroots support system.[25] Grefe worked for Philip Morris for three years, then in 1978 created International Civics, a consulting firm to assist corporate clients on grassroots and corporate advocacy. Grefe's grassroots work expanded beyond the United States, with clients such as the Australian Soft Drink Association and Philip Morris in Canada, France, and Costa Rica. He is the author of two books on corporate grassroots activity.[26]

Another political consultant who specialized in direct mail and grassroots communication is Jack Bonner. Bonner graduated from the University of Arizona and became the public relations director for the city of Tucson from 1972 through 1977. From 1979 through 1982, he was press secretary, then political director, for Pennsylvania senator John Heinz III. In 1984 he opened Bonner and Associates, and since then has been at the forefront of aiding corporate and business-related clients with grassroots support. His long list of clients includes the American Sugar Alliance, Pharmaceuticals Research and Manufacturers Association (PhRMA), Edison Electric Institute, Philip Morris, Westinghouse, and the big three automobile manufacturers. One of Bonner's specialties is finding "white hat" organizations—local groups, such as the Boy Scouts, seniors, groups representing people with disabilities, and others who have broad local support. For example, when auto makers were trying to defeat congressional proposals for more fuel-efficient cars, Bonner's firm enlisted groups of seniors and persons with disabilities (who were having a hard time getting in and out of small cars) and police officers (who were afraid their big cruisers would be replaced by small imported cars).[27] Bonner was employing some of the same tactics that Whitaker and Baxter had refined decades earlier. In recent years, Bonner and Associates was rebranded as Advocacy to Win (A2W).

In his early years, Ben Goddard (b. 1943) worked on the presidential campaigns of Jimmy Carter, Gary Hart, Morris K. Udall, Bruce Babbitt, and Jesse Jackson. His political advertising firm was also the first to assist Russia president Boris Yeltsin in developing free-market reforms. Goddard is best remembered for his "Harry and Louise" commercials, created for the Health Insurance Association of America (HIAA). Goddard and his business partner, Rick Claussen, sold their business, Goddard Claussen/First Tuesday, which specialized in public affairs and ballot initiatives, to Porter Novelli, part of the Omnicom Group conglomerate in 1999, but after a while the partners negotiated an early release from their contracts, and started their own firm, Goddard Claussen Strategic Advocacy. More recently, Goddard joined with Gerry Gunster to form GoddardGunster, a media advocacy firm. In 2013, Rick Claussen joined Josh Ginsberg to form a new California-based public relations firm, Redwood Pacific.

Defeating Clinton's Health-Care Proposal

When the American Medical Association waged its lobbying and media war against Truman's proposed national health-care plan in 1948–1950, it was the most expensive effort to date, with the AMA spending approximately $2–3 million. As seen in chapter 1, behind much of the AMA's strategy and tactics was the California-based firm of Whitaker & Baxter. Forty-five years later, health care became the central policy goal of the Clinton administration; it, too, came up against fierce opposition. The fight for and against the Clinton health-care proposal amounted to lobbying and advocacy expenditures of between $100 million and $300 million.[28] What journalists Haynes B. Johnson and David S. Broder found was that, for the first time (or perhaps the second time, if you count Whitaker & Baxter) the players, or at least the opposition, "learned to use all the tools of modern politics and political communications for their special-interest objectives."[29]

The Health Insurance Association of America (HIAA), under its new leadership of A. Willis (Bill) Gradison Jr., a former Republican congressman from Ohio, set out to challenge the Clinton health-care initiative. HIAA was composed of 270 private insurance firms, which represented about one-third of America's health insurance industry. It was a trade association under a great deal of stress. Five of the largest insurers—Prudential, Cigna, Travelers, Metropolitan Life, and Aetna—had all left HIAA before Gradison took over.[30] HIAA had supported parts of the Clinton initiative, speaking publicly in favor of universal coverage, an employee mandate to pay for the coverage, and a federal package of defined benefits. According to Gradison, HIAA wanted to sit down with Hillary Clinton and work out some issues, but the White House wouldn't set up a meeting. As time went by, and with no word from the White House, HIAA's original tentative support turned into determined opposition.

HIAA enlisted Republican media consultant Jay Smith in 1989, then hired Republican pollster Bill McInturff; another pollster, Democrat Bill Hamilton, was hired to join McInturff in measuring public opinion. California-based media consultants Ben Goddard and Rick Claussen were retained to help with the public relations and television advertising.

In focus groups held in St. Louis, Charlotte, and Atlanta, McInturff and Hamilton found that several phrases well summed up voters doubts about the Clinton plan, and particularly about the ability of the federal government to deliver on health care: "They choose, you lose" and "There's got to be a better way." Gradison, in speaking about the subject around the country, concluded that "this issue will be settled at the kitchen tables in homes across America."[31]

According to Johnson and Broder, Bill Gradison was in a quandary: he wanted to criticize the president's plan but didn't want to be too negative, fearing that HIAA would be pushed away from the important congressional bargaining that would inevitably have to ensue.[32]

Many campaign-like weapons went into the HIAA-backed opposition to the health-care proposal, but the one most remembered was a series of television ads, featuring a comfortable middle-income husband and wife sitting at their kitchen table, discussing the Clinton proposal. The Goddard Claussen /First Tuesday–produced "Harry and Louise" ads started running in September 1993. These ads were modeled on a successful campaign run by HIAA, featuring Goddard

Claussen ads, against a 1992 California health-care reform initiative, Proposition 166 (recall the path taken by Whitaker & Baxter and its health-care fights).[33]

"Harry and Louise"

> *Harry and Louise, a middle-aged white couple, are sitting at their kitchen*
> > *table. Harry is scanning a newspaper, Louise is reading a printed ver-*
> > *sion of the president's health-care plan.*
>
> *Harry*: I'm glad the president's doing something about health-care reform.
> *Louise*: He's right. We need it.
> *Harry*: Some of the details.
> *Louise*: Like a national limit on health care?
> *Harry*: Really?
> *Louise*: The government caps how much the country can spend on all
> > health care and says, "That's it!"
> *Harry*: So, what if your health plan runs out of money?
> *Louise*: There's got to be a better way.

HIAA spent roughly $14 million on its television campaign against the Clinton health-care initiative. The ads were targeted mostly to Washington, New York, CNN, and the home media markets of key members of Congress; this was to ensure that lawmakers, their staffs, the national media, and key constituents would see them. Did the ads have a significant impact on the public? No, according to research conducted by communications scholar Kathleen Hall Jamieson.[34] But the ad campaign was significant enough to spook the White House and add to the mounting doubt of members of Congress.

There was far more to the anti-health-care campaign than "Harry and Louise." Goddard, who made the famous commercials (and later married the actress who portrayed Louise), observed: "The television was the tip of the iceberg. That was the big thing everybody saw, but we had a day-to-day operation communicating with those people who signed on board with us. We had outreach campaigns to friends and family, if you will, in the insurance industry and in other industries that were supportive. We reached out to a wide range of other public interest groups who for one reason or another had problems with the White House proposal. So we focused a lot of attention and a lot of energy specifically on the grassroots activities."[35]

While the HIAA was hitting the airwaves with "Harry and Louise" ads and its grassroots operation, the National Federation of Independent Business (NFIB), which was adamantly opposed to the Clinton plan, mobilized an extensive grassroots campaign, using telephone banks, direct mail, letters to members of Congress, and paid political ads. The Alliance for Managed Competition, composed of large insurance companies, retained grassroots specialist Jack Bonner, who salivated over the thought of going up against the Clinton health-care proposal: "What a great thing to go up against. Mandatory health care alliances, I have to join it? It's horrible! In America you don't use the word 'mandatory.' It's pejorative. If they [Clinton] hadn't used it, we would have. So that one was truly a walk in the park."[36]

Ultimately, the Clinton health-care package faded away, with Senate majority leader George Mitchell pulling the plug on a compromise package in early September 1994. Two months later, the Republicans overwhelmed the Democrats in congressional elections, taking charge of both the House of Representatives and the Senate.

Pollster Bill McInturff, in a television interview in 2000, stated that he felt the Clinton health-care proposal was flawed, and he was "proud of the work we did" in opposing it. He continued, "I am though very disappointed that Congress misread those results and has not moved forward with *substantial* private market based health care reforms, which clearly are needed."[37] The "Harry and Louise" campaign launched, in journalist Jeffrey Birnbaum's words, a "lobbying-by-television wave."[38] It was a turning point in political consulting: business and trade associations saw clearly that campaign techniques and tools could be used effectively to blunt unwanted legislation.

Two other examples demonstrate the use of campaign techniques and political pros working for, or against, corporate interests.

Wal-Mart Wars

> *This will be an effort by the entire labor movement.*
> —AFL-CIO Secretary-Treasurer Richard L. Trumka (2005)[39]

After the 2004 presidential election, Andrew Stern, president of the Service Employees International Union (SEIU), launched a campaign aimed at America's biggest retailer, Wal-Mart Stores. Wal-Mart Watch was created, under the direction of Stern and several Democratic operatives. Hired to work on the campaign was Jim Jordan, who for a short time was the campaign manager for John Kerry's primary run in 2004, and before that was with the Democratic Senatorial Committee. In two years' time, Wal-Mart Watch had "built a full scale campaign war room" with a field director, publications staff, and former Democratic campaign veterans waiting for the 2008 election cycle to unfold.[40] Wal-Mart Watch then became a part of the United Food and Commercial Workers International Union's Making Change at Wal-Mart program.

Wal-Mart countered by building up its Washington presence, particularly its political action committee, but also by hiring Leslie Dach, a public relations specialist who had handled the Wal-Mart account at the Edelman public-relations firm. Other prominent Republican operatives were also brought in, including Jan van Lohuizen, the pollster who assisted the 2000 and 2004 Bush presidential campaigns, and Terry Nelson, the Bush 2004 political director. Nelson, and his consulting firm, Crosslink Strategy Group, was charged with creating Working Families for Wal-Mart, to help spread the word about Wal-Mart's contributions.[41]

However, Wal-Mart stumbled several times. Former Atlanta mayor and congressman Andrew Young was hired to give Wal-Mart credibility in urban markets, but he made some very impolitic comments about local urban merchants who were not treating African American customers fairly: "I think they've ripped off our communities. First it was Jews, then it was Koreans, and now it's Arabs." Then Wal-Mart hired Terry Nelson, who was simultaneously working with the RNC, trying to get Bob Corker elected to the US Senate from Tennessee in 2006. Corker's opponent was Harold Ford Jr., a four-term member of Congress, and the first African American candidate to be elected to the Senate from the South since Reconstruction. One of the RNC ads was "Call Me Harold," featuring a young blond white woman, shoulders bare, giving Ford the come-hither look, saying they had met at a Playboy party. (Ford, indeed, had once attended a large *Playboy* magazine party before a Super Bowl game.) This ad became a matter of guilt-by-association, and became a problem for Wal-Mart. Rather than be associated with a possibly race-inflaming advertisement, and bowing to external pressure, Terry Nelson resigned from Wal-Mart. He then moved over to be campaign manager for John McCain until the campaign nearly imploded in 2007 and he was fired.[42]

For some, there seemed to be a growing public disdain for Wal-Mart, primarily because of the way it treats its employees. Lake Research Partners, the progressive Democratic polling firm, found that 28 percent of consumers surveyed had an unfavorable view of Wal-Mart, nearly five times the negative sentiment of rival retailer Costco.[43] The six heirs to the Walton family fortune are worth approximately $150 billion. Wal-Mart made $17 billion in profits in 2013, and its average "associate" makes somewhere between $8.81 and $11 an hour. "No matter the exact figure," wrote Timothy Egan in the *New York Times*, "there's no dispute that Wal-Mart's business model forces thousands of hard-working people to look for outside help just to get by."[44] Continued criticism, little movement in its stock performance, and the ongoing negative news about minimum wages and inequality most likely means that Wal-Mart and its critics will continue bring their case to the public and policy leaders through campaign-style techniques and methods.

Denying Climate Change

In a 2002 memo, Frank Luntz, a Republican pollster and wordsmith, wrote that so long as "voters believe there is no consensus about global warming within the scientific community," the status quo would prevail. Helping to spread doubt and uncertainty, corporate interests have invested millions in foundations, studies, and individual scientists who argue that the scientific evidence is not persuasive.

For years, it was ExxonMobil that pumped in large sums to spread doubt. *New Yorker* staff writer Steve Coll investigated the efforts by ExxonMobil and its chairman, Lee Raymond, to sow seeds of doubt on the science of climate change. In his book *Private Empire*, Coll noted that Raymond, with a doctoral degree in chemical engineering, believed that climate change was a hoax, and he saw to it that nonscientific groups and think tanks were funded to raise doubts and drive a wedge into the debate about the impact of climate change. In the meantime,

ExxonMobil scientists were trying to determine how the oil and gas company could benefit from the impact of climate change.[45]

In a 2012 interview with PBS *Frontline*, Coll remarked, "I can't think of an area of science that is relevant to public policy where the gap between what most people believe and what 97 percent of qualified scientists—however you want to define that phrase—believe is as wide as in the case of climate science."[46]

But recently, the Koch brothers have spent far more money than ExxonMobil supporting climate doubters and skeptics, from the Heritage Foundation to the Independent Women's Forum (which opposes presenting climate change as a scientific fact in American public schools).[47] A 2013 study by the University of Massachusetts, Amherst, Political Economy Research Institute named Koch Industries one of the top ten air polluters in the United States.[48] Greenpeace, an environmental advocacy group, issued a study showing that the Koch brothers had given $67 million from 1997 to 2011 to organizations that supported their climate-denying advocacy.[49]

In a 2013 study, environmental sociologist Robert J. Brulle of Drexel University studied the tax records of 91 "climate change counter-movement" (CCCM) groups that were funded by 140 various foundations.[50] In all, the foundations gave at least $558 million during this time to climate-denying organizations. Receiving funds were familiar conservative organizations, such as the Hoover Institute, the American Enterprise Institute, Heritage Foundation, Cato Institute, and Americans for Prosperity Foundation. Along with the Koch Industries and ExxonMobil were Scaife Affiliated Foundations, Lynde and Harry Bradley Foundation, Howard Charitable Foundation, John William Pope Foundation, the Searle Freedom Trust, and others. Brulle noted that "it is without question that conservative foundations play a major role in the creation and maintenance of the CCCM." And between 2000 and 2016, the number of foundations like Donors Trust and Donors Capital, where donations cannot be traced, have dramatically increased. With CCCM money pouring in, both reported and unreported, organizations, public relations firms, and political consultants have been able to continue sow doubt about the scientific validity of climate science.

However, beginning in 2013, Republican leaders in Congress have been shifting their objections to Obama climate policies from science-denying to the loss of jobs and a possible spike in the cost of energy. This jobs-centric emphasis "is no accident," said Republican political consultant Mike McKenna. "This is a strategy that leadership wants to take, especially in the House." At the same time, the rank and file Republicans in Congress "are perfectly willing to talk about the underlying science."[51]

Political Shops Go Corporate

> *Consulting firms are a deck of cards constantly*
> *being reshuffled, usually over disputes about money and egomania.*
> —Joe Klein (2006)[52]

Matt Reese, tired of the hectic life of a political consultant, decided to sell his firm, Reese Communications, and its subsidiary, Targeting Systems, Inc., in 1987. Martin Sorrell, who was leading a diversification strategy for the British public relations firm of Saatchi & Saatchi, acquired Wire and Plastic Products, Limited, a Kent, England–based company that manufactured grocery baskets and aluminum cookware. Wire and Plastic Products (WPP) became the unlikely vehicle to launch a worldwide public relations empire, but it did so aggressively. Reese Communications and Targeting Systems, Inc.—with a total of seventy employees—were purchased for $14 million up front and another $21 million for meeting five-year targets, astonishing sums for a political consulting shop. "I was amazed I got anything like I got for the company. I mean, I'd have sold it for half that, gladly," Reese recalled a decade later.[53] This acquisition was small potatoes for WPP Group, which by 2013 was a multibillion-dollar conglomerate with 170,000 employees, in 3,000 offices and 353 separate companies. Among the companies in the WPP Group are old-line public relations firms Ogilvy and Mather, JWT (J. Walter Thompson), Y&R (Young & Rubicam), and Burson-Marsteller, and newer firms like Blue State Digital, a technology firm begun in 2004, which played a key role in the Obama 2008 and 2012 campaigns.

Under WPP Group, Reese Communications, which once considered itself a family, began to disintegrate, with buyouts of senior Reese staffers, and an 80 percent turnover of staffers in the next two years. Reese recalled, "I worked for them [WWP] for a year and hated it, and we had some problems. . . . I don't know anything much about the company. . . . It's Reese Targeting Systems, RTS, or whatever it's called."[54]

Similarly, many other political consulting firms were either bought out by public relations conglomerates, or shifted their business away from candidate campaigns to issue advocacy, ballot initiatives, and corporate work. One compelling reason to shift from strictly candidate work is the need to smooth out the feast-or-famine cycle of elections. Republican pollster Whit Ayres observed, "My family has a curious desire to eat in odd-numbered years."[55] Ayres established his firm in 1991 in Atlanta, and did about 80 percent of his business conducting polls for Republican office seekers; by 2004, that number reversed, with 80 percent of revenue coming from noncandidate work. The Republican polling firm Public Opinion Strategies (POS) went into noncandidate work during the Clinton health-care fight of 1993. This issue-advocacy battle helped create a whole new business component for Bill McInturff and his POS colleagues. In 1996 almost all of POS's $6 million revenue came from candidate polling; in 2004, its total revenue was $21 million, split evenly between candidates and noncandidate business. For another Republican pollster, Tony Fabrizio (Fabrizio, McLaughlin & Associates, Inc.), only 15 percent of his business came from noncandidates in 1996; by 2004, some 90 percent of business was noncandidates.

The Democratic firm of Penn Schoen Berland, which was bought out in 2001 by WPP Group PLC, and became part of Burson-Marsteller, had the "vast majority" of its work done for corporate clients, such as AT&T, Coca-Cola, American Express, BP, Novartis, and Microsoft.[56] Mark Penn became the chief executive officer of Burson-Marsteller, and later moved to Microsoft, where in 2014 he became executive vice president and chief strategy officer. He left the following year to form a private equity firm, The Stagwell Group, which in late 2015 purchased the long-time media firm headed by Bob Squier, and now called SKDKnickerbocker. Doug Schoen became a news analyst at Fox News and the author of several books, including a 2010 book coauthored with pollster Scott Rasmussen on the Tea Party.[57]

In 1975, Gordon S. Black, a professor of political science at the University of Rochester, created Gordon S. Black Corporation, a market research and consulting firm. In 1996 Black acquired Louis Harris & Associates (LHA) from the Gannett Corporation, and the next year formed Harris Black International Ltd. (HBI). In 1999 Harris Interactive, building on Internet panels and creating the structure for online surveys, went public and soon created the Harris Online Panel. From 2001 through 2007, Harris Interactive has acquired two dozen affiliated market research firms in the United States, Canada, the United Kingdom, and Europe, including Richard Wirthlin's firm, Wirthlin Worldwide, Inc., in 2004.[58]

Jody Powell (1943–2009), a former campaign strategist and then press secretary for Jimmy Carter, became a syndicated columnist, a news commentator for ABC, and then an executive in the public relations firm Ogilvy & Mather. In 1991, he teamed up with Sheila Tate, a former press secretary to First Lady Nancy Reagan, to form Powell-Tate, a bipartisan lobbying and government relations firm, and a division of Gerald S. J. Cassidy's government relations organization, Cassidy and Associates. Later, Powell-Tate, which had tobacco firms, airlines, and other corporations as clients, became part of the international public relations firm Weber Shandwick. Powell-Tate, now headed by Pam Jenkins, has offices in Washington and Beijing.[59]

Bob Squier's media firm merged into SKDKnickerbocker, a New York, Washington, and Albany public relations firm, with former Squier partners Anita Dunn and Bill Knapp as principals in the Washington office, and as noted above, became part of The Stagwell Group in 2015. Frank Greer's media firm, GMMB, was acquired by Fleishman-Hillard in 1997, and is part of the worldwide public relations conglomerate Omnicom. Likewise, Murphy Pintak Gautier Hudome Agency was bought by Cassidy and Associates, and, as noted above, Goddard Claussen at one time was acquired by Porter Novelli.[60]

Other consulting firms have also moved into larger public relations or public affairs organizations, becoming the campaign, polling, microtargeting specialists for nationwide, even worldwide, conglomerates.

CHAPTER 17

Consultants and Presidential Campaigns, 2000 and 2004

2000 was about values. 1996 was about values.
1992 was about values. Presidential elections are always about values.
　　　　　　　　—Republican consultant Matthew Dowd (2004)

Working day-to-day on a presidential campaign is unlike any
other job on the planet. It's a thankless, outrageously difficult job,
the most emotionally draining, physically taxing, stress-creating job you can
imagine, and when it's done, it almost always ends in total, abject failure.
　　　　　　　　—Joe Trippi, campaign adviser to Howard Dean (2004)

IN 1988, MICHAEL Dukakis and his campaign stumbled and were outfoxed by a veteran team of Republican operatives. In 1992, the Bush re-election campaign was poorly managed and outsmarted by Bill Clinton, a natural campaigner, and an aggressive campaign staff. In 1996, Bob Dole and his ever-changing campaign team couldn't defeat a weakened Clinton and his team. Maybe nothing could have saved Dole, but Dukakis and Bush should have been able to prevail. Their defeats came about because of a combination of poor performances by the candidates themselves and poor, unfocused, and uncoordinated campaigns run by their operatives. The 2000 presidential election gave us a fourth example: Vice President Al Gore had the wind at his back, but he squandered his advantages and lost to George W. Bush and a disciplined team of advisers. By contrast, in 2004, the Bush re-election team, working for a weakened incumbent, outhustled and outmaneuvered a strong opponent, John Kerry.

The 2000 Presidential Election: George W. Bush v. Al Gore Jr.

> *Karl laid it all out on a napkin.*
>
> —Stuart Stevens (2001)[1]

> *The Gore campaign was dysfunctional, incoherent, and low on esprit de corps or unity.*
>
> —Samuel L. Popkin (2012)[2]

Gore and the Democratic Primaries

In 2000, Al Gore Jr. was in the same position as George H. W. Bush in 1988—ready to step up from eight years of service as vice president to the presidency. It should have been a coronation. Several politicians were interested in challenging Gore, but they dropped out quickly: Missouri congressman Dick Gephardt, Nebraska senator Bob Kerrey, Minnesota senator Paul Wellstone, and civil rights activist Jesse Jackson. Only former New Jersey senator Bill Bradley stepped forward to challenge Gore for the Democratic nomination. For a time, Bradley was gathering in more money and receiving good press, and Gore was understandably nervous. But it turned out to be no contest: Gore defeated Bradley in every early caucus and primary, and after a resounding loss on Super Tuesday, Bradley withdrew on March 9, 2000.

During his second term as vice president, most of the polling done for Gore was conducted by Douglas Schoen and Mark Penn. Schoen observed that "Gore's core political principles . . . seemed oddly unsettled. He was constantly looking for new approaches, new answers to the question of what he should espouse."[3] But, according to Schoen, Gore would rarely take the suggestions of his pollsters. Meanwhile, Mark Penn began working for Hillary Clinton as she prepared for her 2000 US Senate race in New York, while Gore began drawing away from the "Clinton people" following the January 1998 Monica Lewinsky episode. Schoen noted that the Gore camp saw Hillary Clinton as a potential rival, distrusted her, and by extension, "Mark and I became suspect."[4]

Gore was worried that voters might have "Clinton fatigue": tired of eight years of Bill Clinton, tired of the scandals and embarrassments, tired of the drama. But in front of Gore, Penn piped up: "I'm not tired of him. Are you?" As reporter Anne E. Kornblut remarked, "It was a flippant response—and the final straw for Gore, who had long been wary of Penn and concerned that his real loyalty was to Clinton and first lady Hillary Rodham Clinton." The arrogant and abrasive Penn was soon fired.[5] Penn retaliated by being the not-so-anonymous source of a number of unflattering articles in the national press about Gore's political troubles.[6]

Gore's first day-to-day campaign manager was Craig Smith, recommended by Bill Clinton, and a longtime political operative associated with Clinton both in Arkansas and in the White House. Donna Brazile was hired to be deputy campaign manager and national political director. Brazile had previously worked for Jesse Jackson, the Michael Dukakis 1988 presidential campaign, and Washington,

DC, delegate Eleanor Holmes Norton, and she held senior positions within the Democratic National Committee. Brazile had also run a highly successful 1998 program to boost African American voter participation, which was credited with helping Democrats win in several states.[7] The senior media consultants were Bob Squier and Bill Knapp, who were in charge of media during the 1996 Clinton-Gore re-election campaign.

Veteran pollsters Harrison Hickman and Paul Maslin were responsible for all state polling; the national polling was based on models created by political scientist and campaign specialist Samuel Popkin, and it incorporated data going back to the 1972 presidential election.[8] Stan Greenberg, who had helped get Bill Clinton elected in 1992 and was White House pollster until 1994, was brought into the campaign in July 2000, after the primaries were over.[9]

The campaign headquarters was in downtown Washington on K Street, the epicenter of national politics, with all of its distractions and free advice from self-appointed insiders. Trouble was brewing: Bill Bradley was raising a lot of money, making headway, and was looking like a serious threat. A bigger problem was that the Gore campaign staff was bloated, with too many consultants, too many staff, and competing groups giving advice—the vice-presidential staff, the operatives from Gore's 1988 presidential run, and his network of Tennessee advisers and operatives. Further, the campaign was hemorrhaging money. Al Gore complained to Brazile that the campaign, in her paraphrase, was "too big, too bloated, too busy hurting each other."[10]

It was time to shake up the campaign. Gore brought in Tony Coelho, a Democratic moneyman and former congressman from California who had resigned his seat under an ethical cloud, to be the campaign's general manager. Coelho displaced the old political team surrounding Gore, which included the removal of Gore's chief of staff, Ron Klain.[11] Gore and Coelho wanted to bring in Carter Eskew, a longtime friend and former colleague of Gore's at the *Nashville Tennessean*. Eskew was a brilliant media consultant who for years worked with Bob Squier, but in the early 1990s the two had a bitter falling out and hadn't spoken since. In July 1999, in a front-page interview with the *New York Times*, Squier disparaged Eskew's "deeply unprofessional behavior" in abruptly leaving Squier's firm.[12] That front-page story prompted Gore to remove Squier from the campaign team and put Eskew in charge. (Six months later, in early 2000, Bob Squier would be dead, succumbing to colon cancer.) Eskew then brought in veteran media consultants Bob Shrum and Tad Devine to work on the campaign.

Craig Smith was replaced by Donna Brazile as campaign manager, making her the second female (and first African American) to head up the campaign team for a presidential nominee. Brazile was charged with getting the campaign in order, including trimming the budget, firing staffers and consultants, and closing field offices. Tad Devine recommended that the campaign leave the political hotbed of downtown Washington and move to Nashville.[13] Gore implemented that suggestion and then announced that Brazile would be just one of three staffers to make the move.

While the staff shake-up was an obvious distraction, Gore fared better with the Democratic voters. In the key Iowa caucus, Gore relied on Paul Tewes and his business partner Steve Hildebrand to run the get-out-the-vote effort. Gore bested Bradley, 63 percent to 36 percent in Iowa, and he defeated Bradley in New Hampshire by 4 percentage points. Then came the fifteen primaries and caucuses on March 7, Super Tuesday. Gore won them all. In fact, Gore won every caucus and every primary, although Bradley did manage to pull some delegates. This is the only time in modern history of presidential primaries that a candidate in a contested race won every primary and caucus.

But after Super Tuesday, the Gore campaign appeared to lose its momentum. It was suffering from internal bickering and dissension, personality clashes, and a drift in the polls when compared to the Republican candidate, George W. Bush. All this bad news was splashed in the headlines of the *New York Times*, noting that the campaign had "drifted and lost focus" since the primaries.[14]

Coelho suffered some debilitating epileptic seizures (an affliction he had endured for years), and had to leave the campaign. In his place came William (Bill) Daley, the former Clinton commerce secretary and son of Chicago mayor Richard Daley.

In her 2004 memoir, Donna Brazile wrote about the frustrations of being an African American woman in a profession dominated by white men. She also wrote about the tug of war between her and the campaign's political consultants over the control of the campaign finances, and where precious money would ultimately be spent. "This was a campaign dominated by highly paid consultants and strategists who were either media gurus or pollsters," Brazile observed.[15] There were plenty of rumors circulating in the press and through the usual political gossip that she would be replaced once Coelho was gone and Daley took his place. Twelve years earlier, Brazile made some intemperate remarks about Bush Senior during the 1988 presidential campaign and was fired, and this time around, she got into trouble saying that Republicans would "rather take pictures with black children than feed them."[16] Republicans were incensed and Brazile was punished: she was able to keep her job title, but day-to-day campaign management was given over to media consultant and strategist Tad Devine.

George W. and the Republican Primaries

The Democrats in 1972 should have learned a valuable lesson: early and easy primary victories can lead to disaster in the general election. Swept to victory in the Democratic primaries by the antiwar, liberal coalition, George McGovern became the perfect foil for Richard Nixon in the general election. This was a lesson that Republicans also needed to learn. In 1996, Republican primary voters selected Bob Dole, perhaps out of sentiment, perhaps because he had lasted so long as a party stalwart: *good old Bob, we owe it to him after all he's done, carrying the torch of the Republican Party all those years.* But Bob Dole, the party's choice and a candidate even older than Ronald Reagan when he ran in 1980, was a big political gift to the Clinton re-election effort.

Republicans were determined not to repeat the error of choosing a Dole or a Republican version of McGovern. Thanks in large measure to political consultant Karl Rove, Republican leaders quickly lined up behind Texas governor George W. Bush. Rove was instrumental in helping Bush twice win the Texas governorship, and he plotted the strategy for the 2000 Republican presidential nomination. While he was still Texas governor, Bush demanded that Rove sell his direct mail business to eliminate any question of conflict of interest and so that he could devote all his time to helping Bush secure the nomination and the presidency.[17] Joining the Bush team were Joe Allbaugh as campaign manager, Karen Hughes as communications director, Mark McKinnon of Maverick Media as head of the media team, along with Stuart Stevens and his partner Russ Schriefer, and others. Allbaugh, who began his political consulting career in 1968, had served as Bush's campaign manager in 1994, and as his chief of staff in the governor's office. Hughes, a one-time executive director of the Texas Republican Party, was part of the tight circle, the "iron triangle" of Bush advisers: Allbaugh, Hughes, and Rove.[18]

But others wanted their crack at the nomination as well. As usual, there were long shots who couldn't even survive the pre-primary process. Declaring their candidacy, but then withdrawing before the first primary, were New Hampshire senator Robert C. Smith, former vice president Dan Quayle (trying again), Ohio congressman John Kasich, former Tennessee governor and US secretary of education Lamar Alexander, conservative commentator Pat Buchanan (his third attempt), and former US secretary of labor Elizabeth Dole. (Bob Dole and Elizabeth Dole made history, becoming the first married couple to run in separate years for the presidency; the Clintons were the second).

With little chance to win, conservative activists Gary Bauer and Alan Keyes participated in the primaries but won no delegates. With almost no preparation and planning, Utah senator Orrin Hatch declared his candidacy, but he also went nowhere. The wild card, following in the Pete DuPont and Ross Perot tradition, was Malcolm (Steve) Forbes Jr., a wealthy businessman ready to throw his family's money into a bid for the nomination, just as he did in 1996. Forbes came in second in the Iowa caucus, but from then on was a negligible force.

From the beginning, it looked like George W. Bush's nomination for the asking. "We planned a general election strategy from day one," wrote Bush's consultant Matthew Dowd. "The primary was really a part of that general election strategy.... This campaign was planned from the start as if we were going to be in a general election."[19] But the Bush campaign had to reconfigure after running into the "straight talk express" of John McCain.

Indeed, Arizona senator John S. McCain III presented the biggest challenge to Bush. McCain's campaign manager was Rick Davis; the chief strategist was media consultant Mike Murphy. John Weaver, a Texas consultant who had a long-standing personal and professional feud with Karl Rove, also assisted the campaign. Louisiana-based veteran political consultant Roy Fletcher was deputy national campaign manager, Dan Schnur was communications director, and the firm of Stevens Reed Curcio & Company was the media consultant.

McCain did not compete in Iowa, but held all his firepower for New Hampshire, where he overwhelmed Bush by eighteen points. This surprise victory interrupted the grand scheme of George W. Bush waltzing to victory. Next came South Carolina, Bush's "firewall." If he couldn't blunt McCain there, the well-laid Bush anointment plans might crumble. Earlier Bush had a 50-point advantage over McCain; now that was evaporating. It was time to fight back, and campaigning in South Carolina, a state schooled in Lee Atwater roughhouse tactics and aggressiveness, became ugly. Rumors flew (aided by anonymous fliers, e-mails, and push-polling) that McCain had been brainwashed while captive for five years in a Vietnam prison, that he had betrayed his country, that he had become crazy. A retired South Carolina Democratic politician said it was "the dirtiest, nastiest campaign I've ever seen."[20] But the most egregious attack, particularly in this race-conscious state, was the charge that John McCain had fathered an illegitimate black child. The McCains indeed had adopted a daughter from Bangladesh, taking her from an orphanage under the auspices of Mother Theresa. Who would spread such salacious rumors? "This whole thing, it was orchestrated by Rove, it was all Bush's deal," said Roy Fletcher, McCain's deputy campaign manager. "It was pretty rank, and they had an institution that was peddling all that shit, and it was a university, Bob Jones University."[21] Various press accounts also charged that Karl Rove was behind the rumormongering, but Rove flatly denied it, saying that it was a professor at the Christian fundamentalist Bob Jones University who was behind it.[22] Fliers appeared on the windshields of churchgoers' automobiles the Sunday before the election, luridly depicting "the Negro child." An anonymous push-polling operation was set up spread the rumor. It went something like this:

> *Telemarketer*: "Who are you planning to vote for, McCain or Bush?"
> *Voter*: "Bush."
> *Telemarketer*: "Great. I just want to remind you to vote on Tuesday."

But when a voter said "McCain," the tactic shifted:

> *Telemarketer*: "Oh, before you vote for McCain, did you know that. . . ."
> [Then the telemarketer would fill in the blanks "he fathered a black
> child out of wedlock," "he broke down and told his Vietnam captors
> what they wanted to know," or "he was a traitor to his country."][23]

Bush defeated McCain in South Carolina, 53 percent to 42 percent, and with it, McCain's chance at the nomination. Rick Davis, McCain's campaign manager, correctly called the whisper tactics and push-polls a "smear campaign": "the deeply personal, usually anonymous allegations that make up a smear campaign are aimed at a candidate's most precious asset: his reputation."[24] In his 2002 memoir, McCain wrote this about the South Carolina ugliness: "There wasn't a damn thing I could do about the subterranean assaults on my reputation except to act in a way that contradicted their libel."[25] Reporter Joe Klein observed that this "was one of the most disgraceful campaigns I've ever witnessed." Klein noted that there were no fingerprints left on the smear campaign, "but it was funny how these sorts of rumors always seemed to float about in campaigns run by Bush's chief strategist, Karl Rove. (In the 1994 Texas gubernatorial campaign, for example, there were rumors that the incumbent governor Ann Richards was a lesbian.)[26]

There was no comment from the Bush campaign: no apology, no protest at how third parties had soiled the good name of an opponent, just silence. Political commentator and former Democratic consultant Mark Shields, who had seen smear campaigns before in South Carolina and elsewhere, was blunt: "There's no doubt to me that it was a below-the-radar hate campaign against John McCain. Whether it was encouraged, orchestrated, condoned, whatever, it was not criticized or condemned by the Bush campaign or the candidate."[27]

While McCain's campaign faltered, his campaign was adept at using the new tools of the Internet and online communication. During the primaries, with the assistance of webmaster Max Fose, the campaign developed a customized e-mail system. Working with a company called Virtual Sprockets, the campaign was able to send different e-mail messages to specific audiences, reaching out to hundreds of thousands of e-mail recipients. From his 2000 e-mail list, McCain was able to organize 140,000 volunteers. His online fundraising, through consultant R. Rebecca (Becki) Donatelli, was equally surprising, allowing him to raise $6.4 million over the Internet in small donations.[28] While online communication was still in its infancy in political campaigns, the McCain nomination paved the way for far greater and more powerful use of online communications in later contests.

The Conventions and the General Election

The Democratic nominating convention turned out to be an extraordinary lift for the sagging Gore campaign. The well-crafted speech, delivered by an energized Gore, coupled with the selection of Joe Lieberman as his running mate, helped Gore immeasurably. So too, apparently, did a long, impassioned kiss between Gore and his wife, Tipper, caught on camera. Unlike most of the Gore campaign, this was unscripted, unplanned, and unanticipated. Stan Greenberg, and other pollsters, were taking the immediate pulse of the country, and showed a "bounce" of between 16 and 22 percent. Kathleen Frankovic, director of surveys at CBS News, observed that "Gore emerged with the highest bounce ever for a Democratic candidate." The only candidate who did better was George H. W. Bush in 1988, when he went from 17 points behind to 6 points ahead.[29] Bob Shrum enthused: "Al Gore's acceptance speech [helped greatly by Shrum's pen] may be one of the most successful convention speeches in political history, at least for the voters."[30] Bush's Karl Rove had a simpler reason for Gore's political recovery during the month of August: "I was surprised at how he did it: by picking a Jew and kissing his wife."[31]

Once again, both campaigns, through their respective political parties and allies, poured in millions of dollars of television campaign advertising. Communications scholar L. Patrick Devlin, who has been writing on presidential campaign commercials since 1972, noted that several important factors stood out in the 2000 presidential contest.[32] First, there was a massive amount of money spent—$240 million in total. Second, for the first time in presidential campaign history, spending by the national political parties exceeded the amount spent by the candidates. Third, Bush outspent Gore, and critically, he did so in key states like Florida. Finally, there were differences in the kinds of commercials produced: for Bush, they were mostly positive; for Gore, they were primarily contrast and negative ads.

The Gore-Lieberman media team. The consulting firms of Shrum, Devine & Donilon and Squier, Knapp had overall responsibility for the campaign's media. Bill Knapp, senior media adviser, was responsible for overseeing the production and media placement of all television and radio advertising for the Gore-Lieberman campaign. In a post-election review, Knapp focused on the four-part media strategy: first was to raise questions about Bush's record as Texas governor. McCain had already roughed up Bush during the primaries, and it was the Gore media team's responsibility to raise further questions about Bush's record as governor and to create doubts about his character. The media team tested spots showing Bush's screw-ups, along with spot advertising on Bush's failure to serve during Vietnam. These kinds of personal character techniques worked quite well against Bob Dole in 1996, observed Knapp, but they weren't working against Bush, according to the focus group results.[33] The second part of the media strategy was to introduce Al Gore, through biographical spots. The third and fourth parts of the strategy were to draw contrasts on key issues that divided Bush from Gore. But this turned out to be frustrating: "The Bush campaign was very, very effective at taking the sting out of some of those contrasts," noted Knapp. "It was a constant frustration to us that [the Bush campaign] would make progress on education. Bush spoke about education from the heart, it seemed sincere, it seemed real. That was a problem for us. Those ads in general tested well. We did not have a good attack line on education."[34] Most of the Gore ads were negative or contrast ads, but without a coherent theme or message, and the campaign produced far more ads than were produced by the Bush team.[35]

An example of the Gore ads attacking Bush was aired in Ohio. Called "Morph," the ad superimposed a map of Texas over Ohio, showing how Ohio would lose out if Bush got his way. Up in the corner of the ad is a picture of Bush looking peevish:

Male Narrator: George W. Bush wants to bring his Texas ideas to Ohio.
[*Text*: Texas: 8th worse paid]

Male Narrator: Manufacturing workers in Texas are the 8th worst paid
　　in the nation.
[*Text*: Ohio: 4th best paid]

Male Narrator: In Ohio, we're the 4th best paid.
[*Text*: Texas minimum wage is $3.35/hour]

Male Narrator: In Texas, the minimum wage is $3.35/hour. Six times,
    Bush's inaction killed increases. $3.35 an hour.
[*Text*: Texas under Bush: 29th to 48th worst place to raise a child]

Male Narrator: Under Bush, Texas went from the 29th to the 48th worst
    place to raise a child.
[*Text*: Bush opposed healthcare for 220,000 MORE CHILDREN]

Male Narrator: Bush even opposed providing health care for 220,000
    more Texas children. On November 7, is that the change we really
    want for Ohio?[36]

One of the policy areas that Gore was most proud of was his leadership in
environmental issues and climate change. But he rarely spoke about the subject
on the trail. Reporter Joe Klein asked several of Al Gore's campaign consultants
why Gore talked so little about it. Tad Devine replied, "He wanted to talk about
the environment, and I said to him, 'Look, you can do that, but you're not going to
win a single electoral vote more than you now have. If you want to win Michigan
and western Pennsylvania, here are the issues that really matter—this is what
you should talk about."[37] Gore was determined to make a strong speech on global
warming, and he wanted to do it in Michigan. All the advisers said no, and finally
they recruited Gore's chief environmental adviser, Kathleen A. (Katie) McGinty,
who finally persuaded Gore to back off. The reason was purely pragmatic: when
he's president he can revisit the issue, but if a strong environmental stand cost
him key Midwestern states, he will go nowhere. Finally, Gore relented.[38]

The Bush-Cheney media team. Mark McKinnon, who had worked for Bush
since his 1994 gubernatorial bid, headed the media team for Bush and Cheney.
His firm Maverick Media created all the commercials during the 2000 primaries.
Stuart Stevens and Russ Schriefer, who had worked on the 1996 Bob Dole campaign, were also part of the media team. Republican National Committee (RNC)
ads were created by Alex Castellanos and his firm Cold Harbor Films.[39]

Most of the Bush ads were positive, and most featured the candidate either
narrating or shown in the ads talking with or surrounded by others. The most
frequently shown Bush ad was called "Trust."[40] Bush himself narrated the thirty-
two-second ad, speaking directly to the audience in most shots, with soft music
accompanying it. The most compelling lines were these: "There's a big difference
in philosophy between my opponent and me. He trusts government; I trust you."

Bush (FACING THE CAMERA, IN CASUAL CLOTHES): I believe we need to
    encourage personal responsibility, so people are responsible for their
    actions.
[*Text*: Governor George W. Bush]

Bush: And I believe in government that is responsible to the people.

There's a big difference in philosophy between my opponent and me. He
    trusts government; I trust you.

I trust you to invest some of your social security money for higher returns.

I trust local people to run their own schools.

I trust you with some of the budget surplus.

We should help people live their lives, but not run them.

I'm askin' for your vote."

Probably the commercial that caused the most ruckus was the ad produced by
Alex Castellanos for the RNC, called "Priority."[41] Opponents and the press cried
foul, calling it an example of subliminal advertising. The ad derided Gore's prescription drug plan, and on the screen the words appeared: "The Gore prescription plan: the bureaucrats decide." For less than one-thirtieth of a second (almost
impossible to see), the letters RATS in "bureaucrats" appears in huge white letters.
Castellanos denied any wrongdoing, commenting that it was "purely accidental,"
saying "We don't play ball that way. I'm not that clever." But fellow Republican
media consultant Greg Stevens (along with a number of Democrats) commented
that "there is no way anything Alex Castellanos does is an accident." The commercial was shown approximately 4,000 times at a cost of $2.5 million.[42]

Where was the television campaign? Voters who lived in Alabama, Arizona,
Connecticut, the District of Columbia, Nebraska, or nineteen other states, and
watched television during the general election might have wondered if there was
a presidential campaign at all.[43] In none of those states did the Gore or Bush
campaigns, the DNC or the RNC, or Democratic or Republican special interests
spend money on television advertising. These twenty-five states and the District
of Columbia were safe electoral states—solidly in either the Republican or
Democratic camp. So there was no need to waste precious campaign resources
trying to win over these states, and conversely, no need to waste money on a
victory already won in those states. One exception was California: the Bush
campaign spent $10 million in ads, while the Gore campaign, in a disciplined,
strategic move, spent no dollars. Predictably, Gore won the state, 53.5 percent
to 41.7 percent, and all of its fifty-four electoral votes. Why would Bush spend
precious dollars there? Apparently Bush had promised California donors that
their money wouldn't be siphoned off to Bush campaign commercials in other
states.[44]

By contrast, residents of Florida, Ohio, or any one of the fifteen or so battleground states were inundated with television commercials. In Florida, the Bush
campaign and the Republican Party had a key advantage, outspending the Gore
and the DNC by 40 percent.[45] Week after week, the Republicans pounded Gore
on Florida television.

Furthermore, the Republicans brought out their other communications
weapons. Karl Rove noted that it was the campaign's goal "to place 70 million
phone calls in the last week of the campaign and we beat that by about 15 million."
In the final week, the campaign sent our 111.5 million pieces of mail; 16.5 million

pieces of literature, dropped door-to-door; 1.2 million yard signs; and 1.5 million bumper stickers.[46]

The contest was incredibly close in many states. Gore won four states—New Mexico, Wisconsin, Iowa, Oregon—by less than 1 percentage point; Bush won the highly contested and controversial Florida vote by just 537 votes out of 5,825,043 cast. Gore, the "Prince of Tennessee," son of the respected senator Albert Gore Sr., lost his home state, 51–47 percent, something a presidential candidate should never do. He lost Bill Clinton's home base of Arkansas as well, and he lost the reliably Democratic West Virginia.

Since 1960, West Virginia had voted Democratic in the presidential race every time, except in 1972 (Nixon) and 1984 (Reagan), two of the biggest blowouts in presidential history. In 1988, 1992, and 1996, the state had gone Democratic. But in 2000, Rove and other strategists thought Republicans had a chance here. Looking at the numbers, they tilted Republican: the number of gun owners, outdoor hunters, and those affected by Clinton administration mountaintop mining decision. The winning issues in the state were wedge issues—guns, abortions, and coal. Republicans paid attention to West Virginia: Cheney dropped in twice, Bush Senior and Barbara Bush went there, some of the first television ads were aired there, and the campaign built a grassroots organization. Political reporters James Moore and Wayne Slater observed that "no decision made in the 2000 general election more clearly illustrated [Rove's] political genius than the decision to compete in West Virginia."[47]

But credit for the Republican win in West Virginia also belongs to veteran political consultant Tom Edmonds and the National Rifle Association and its Political Victory Fund. Following Edmonds's urging, the NRA poured millions into grassroots efforts in West Virginia, convincing wavering voters, especially union workers, that Al Gore was not to be trusted on Second Amendment rights. The NRA effort—through a weekly coordination of all vendors, from mail, rallies, press, media, and fly-in visits from the NRA president, actor Charlton Heston—helped push Bush over the top in West Virginia, winning 52 percent of the vote.[48] Forty years earlier, James Roosevelt captured the hearts of West Virginia voters when he stumped for John Kennedy; now it was a legendary actor who would boost George Bush. Heston electrified the huge crowds: "You must forget all else and remember only freedom," Heston boomed, "Just freedom. Not what some shop steward or news anchor says. Just freedom."[49] Similar successful efforts targeted Gore's Tennessee and Clinton's Arkansas. Wayne LaPierre, chief executive officer of the NRA, characterized this as "the most important election in the history of the Second Amendment."[50] In a way, this was payback for what the NRA felt was raw treatment from the Clinton administration and Attorney General Janet Reno.

The Gore campaign was caught flatfooted. Jamie Sperling, media time buyer for the Gore campaign, noted that polling around Labor Day in early September found Gore leading in West Virginia by 12 or 13 points. It looked like a lock for Democrats, but in early October, support for Gore was plummeting, and even though the campaign tried to push Gore commercials during the last three weeks, it was too late.[51]

This was, indeed, the closest race in American history. Bush won 271 electoral votes, one more than needed; Gore won 266.[52] Gore received 544,000 more popular votes than Bush. The vote-count drama played out in Florida, with campaign lawyers taking center stage. Hanging and dimpled chads, butterfly ballots, lost absentee ballots, slipshod county election practices, sharp partisan bickering and posturing—all dominated the news during the weeks following the election. Leading the Republican charge was the venerable James Baker, whose main strategy was to halt any recounts. Analysis by the media after the Supreme Court decision that gave the election to Bush found that if there were a statewide recount, Gore would have won, and the more selected counties chosen for recount, the better Gore's chances were.[53] Reporter Jeffrey Toobin summed it up: "James Baker had it right all along. From election night forward, Bush was always ahead; any recounts jeopardized his lead. Baker's cynical war on the recounts—which he fought in courtrooms, in television studios, and in the streets—was the best way to make sure that George W. Bush became president."[54]

In December, the Supreme Court declared, in a 5-4 vote, reversed the judgment of the Florida high court ordering the recount to proceed. There would be no recount, and Bush was declared the winner of Florida's twenty-five electoral votes, and with them the presidency.

The 2004 Presidential Election: George W. Bush v. John F. Kerry

I knew how I would be portrayed, now more than ever—as the black cat of American politics, someone who had connived, confused, consulted, and condemned no fewer than eight Democratic presidential candidates to defeat. Now that's quite a record.

Bob Shrum on the "Shrum curse" (2007)[55]

Sometimes the truth hurts, and it pains me to say this, but Karl Rove is the pre-eminent political strategist in the U.S. today.

—James Carville (2005)[56]

The Democrats were hoping to defeat an increasingly unpopular president, who had lost the popular vote and barely won the electoral vote in 2000. They were hoping that George W. Bush would suffer the same fate as two weak incumbent presidents, Jimmy Carter in 1980 and Bush senior in 1992, rather than the strong victories of incumbents Richard Nixon (1972), Ronald Reagan (1984), and once-weakened Bill Clinton (1996). But with his re-election numbers at dangerously low levels, George W. Bush was able to fight back, stay on the message of national defense and protection against terrorism, and reach out to conservative Christian voters incensed by the possibility of same-sex marriages. Much of the success belongs to political consultant Karl Rove, campaign manager Ken Mehlman, and the campaign team.

The Democratic Candidates

The ten candidates for the Democratic nomination included those who barely got off the ground (Illinois senator Carol Moseley Braun, former NATO commander Wesley Clark, civil rights activist Al Sharpton, Ohio representative Dennis Kucinich, and Florida senator Bob Graham); those who, on paper, looked like strong contenders (Connecticut senator and 2000 vice-presidential candidate Joseph Lieberman, House majority leader Richard Gephardt of Missouri); and those who were serious contenders (former Vermont governor Howard Dean, North Carolina senator John Edwards, and Massachusetts senator John F. Kerry). A common thread that connected Gephardt, Edwards, and Kerry was media consultant Bob Shrum, who previously worked on presidential campaigns for each.

Gephardt, who also ran for his party's nomination in 1988, and had toyed with running in 2000, placed all his bets on a solid performance in the Iowa caucuses. His campaign was run by Steve Elmendorf, described by the *New York Times* as Gephardt's "political alter ego," and a close adviser for twelve years.[57] Gephardt came in a disappointing fourth place in Iowa and promptly ended his quest for the presidency. Elmendorf was quickly hired by the Kerry campaign as deputy campaign manager, working with his friend Mary Beth Cahill.

North Carolina senator John Edwards retained former Gore operative Nick Baldick and Chicago-based media consultant David Axelrod. In late 2001, Edwards had created New American Optimists, a political action committee designed to prepare for his 2004 presidential campaign. Working for this PAC were media consultant Robert Shrum and veteran campaign manager Steve Jarding.

Howard Dean presented the most interesting campaign, principally because of his aggressive use of online communication tools. Dean, a physician by profession and then governor of Vermont, was not particularly adept at online communication. But through his campaign manager, Joe Trippi, his campaign experimented with several online and interactive communication tools. Trippi, a long-time political operative, first worked for the Edward Kennedy presidential campaign in 1979, worked for David Doak and Robert Shrum, and during the 2004 cycle was lead partner of the Democratic media firm Trippi, McMahon and Squier.[58]

Dean was the first presidential candidate to create a blog (Blog for America), and the first campaign to hire a blogmaster. Dean encouraged supporters to suggest ideas, and to give advice and criticism, and he promised to listen and incorporate the best ideas into his campaign. This sounded like a revolutionary idea. Instead of being top-down, the campaign would be bottom-up: give the people what they want, rather than force on them a top-down candidacy, with a message disciplined by political professionals. In another way, this was not revolutionary at all: campaigns for decades had been using survey research, dial-meter sessions, focus groups, mall testing, and other instruments to determine what voters wanted. But the Dean approach certainly sounded new and exciting.

Further, the Dean campaign was able to use online communication for fundraising purposes. While McCain's 2000 campaign pioneered the use of online fundraising, the Dean campaign astounded the political world by raising $41 million, mostly from donors who gave between $25 and $100 each. Dean's online effort showed that the pool of potential presidential campaign contributors could be greatly expanded. During the 2000 presidential election, only 777,000 individuals (out of a total adult population of 185 million) gave money to candidates; now hundreds of thousands more were being added by Dean.[59]

The Dean campaign was also an early user of social media. Myspace had just been launched, in August 2003, and Facebook debuted in February 2004, but neither these nor other social media sites had moved into the mix of communication platforms useful to presidential elections. The social media vehicle that Dean used was Meetup.com, a site where people of like interests can communicate with one another. For example, in February 2004 there were 2,800 Chihuahua lovers on the Meetup.com site, along with 8,800 fans of Insane Clown Posse. Scott Heiferman of Meetup.com and Dean campaign manager Joe Trippi had conducted an experiment in 2003 to see if there was any interest in Dean on this website, and almost immediately 400 individuals signed up. By early February 2004, right in the thick of the primaries there were over 1,100 sites registered on Meetup.com as supporting Dean, along with 186,000 Dean enthusiasts.[60] Coming into the Democratic primaries, it certainly looked like the Dean campaign had tapped into a new, and unexpected, source of enthusiastic volunteers.

In the months before the Iowa caucus, Howard Dean was the clear frontrunner in media polls and media coverage. By the summer of 2003, the Democratic primaries appeared to be all but locked up for Dean, even six months before anyone would cast a vote. Thousands of enthusiasts showed up at his rallies. His memorable rallying cry was that he "represented the Democratic wing of the Democratic Party"—that he was the true antiwar liberal voice of the party, not some warmed over moderate. Even Al Gore quickly endorsed Dean. Four years earlier, at a low point in the early 2000 primaries, John Kerry came to Gore's side with a much-welcomed endorsement, but then irritated Gore with caustic comments about why he was losing in New Hampshire. There would be no Gore endorsement of Kerry in the 2004 primaries.[61]

Leading up to the Iowa caucus, hundreds of Dean volunteers, wearing distinctive orange wool caps, fanned out through Iowa to spread the message to Democratic caucus goers. But savvy Iowa Democrats, who had seen candidates come and go for decades, were not impressed. The race boiled down to the insurgent, flashy Howard Dean, the familiar, next-door neighbor Dick Gephardt, and John Kerry. The three candidates worked hard on their grassroots efforts, but also turned to an old, familiar means of communication, television, to get their message across. They poured in millions of dollars in advertising, much of it negative and hard-hitting.

The Kerry campaign ran a spot ad, "Courage," produced by media consultant Jim Margolis, which portrayed the young John Kerry testifying before the Senate Foreign Relations Committee in 1971:[62]

[*On screen*: Senate Foreign Relations Committee, 1971; Lt. John Kerry (ret.)]

Kerry (testifying before the committee): How do you ask a man to be the last man to die in Vietnam? How do you ask a man to be the last man to die for a mistake?

Voice-over: John Kerry. The 25-year-old swift boat commander who won three Purple Hearts and a Silver Star for bravery, then came home and helped rally the nation against that war.

Ever since, he's been on the front lines of the fights that matter . . .

In the four-way fight between Gephardt, Dean, Edwards, and Kerry in Iowa, with massive amounts of television advertising by the candidates and third parties, and by vigorous ground activities, Kerry won with 38 percent, Edwards came in second with 32 percent, Dean had 18 percent, and Gephardt garnered 11 percent. The most memorable point for Dean was his impassioned yell when he met admirers after the defeat; it went viral on YouTube. Dean promised to carry on, yelling out the names of the next primary states, but his enthusiasm fell short of the cold reality.

The television advertising didn't come just from the candidates. David W. Jones, a longtime Democratic operative, created a 527 organization in early November 2003; the 527 then folded in mid-February 2004. The organization, Americans for Jobs, Healthcare and Progressive Values, had but one purpose: to defeat Howard Dean in the primaries. "What we did," Jones recalled, "was very, very specific, very targeted." Only about twenty or twenty-two anonymous donors funded the whole operation. It produced several ads attacking Dean and pushing the idea that he was unelectable. One ad in particular, "Cannot," caught the attention of a wider public, particularly through the *New York Times*, and gave the group and its cause a big publicity boost. The thirty-second ad started with a picture of Osama bin Laden on the cover of *Time* magazine.

Voice-over: We live in a very dangerous world. And there are those who wake up every morning determined to destroy Western civilization. . . . Americans want a president who can face the dangers ahead. But Howard Dean has no military or foreign policy experience. And Howard Dean just cannot compete with George Bush on foreign policy. It's time for Democrats to think about that . . . and think about it now.

The ads were placed in New Hampshire and South Carolina, but on December 20, 2003, the group stopped all advertising because, beginning on December 21, it would have to comply with a new disclosure rule and release the names of all its donors.[63]

Dean would win only his home state of Vermont and the District of Columbia; he folded his campaign in mid-February. For Michael Whouley, Kerry's chief Iowa organizer, "the Iowa caucuses won us the nomination."[64] Six weeks later, the nomination was his. Gephardt dropped out in mid-January, winning no states; Wesley Clark won the Oklahoma primary; and John Edwards won the Carolinas. Every other primary and caucus quickly went to John Kerry.

The Kerry campaign leadership. A year earlier, the Kerry campaign was headed up by Jim Jordan, who had worked for Kerry for nearly five years. Early on, the Kerry campaign looked like the model of efficiency. But then Howard Dean started surging in the polls and it looked like Kerry would be outhustled. Jordan was based in Washington, and Kerry's other close advisers and staff were based in Boston. As Kerry sank, the infighting and finger-pointing intensified, to the point where the Washington group (Jordan and communications director Chris Lehane) and the Boston group (Bob Shrum and close Kerry advisers) each prepared Kerry's official announcement. In November 2003, two-and-a-half months before the Iowa caucus, Kerry fired Jordan, replacing him with Mary Beth Cahill, the chief of staff for Senator Edward Kennedy.[65] Along with Cahill were senior advisers Jim Margolis, a senior partner in GMMB, the firm headed by Frank Greer, and Shrum, now working in his eighth presidential campaign. But soon, Shrum and Margolis were fighting over consultants' fees and their pieces of the overall budget. By March 2004, Margolis had left the campaign, leaving Shrum's firm completely in charge. Shrum, according to reporter Evan Thomas of *Newsweek*, had a special relationship with the candidate: "He was Kerry's friend, his peer; everyone else was Kerry's employee."[66] Reporter Ken Auletta was less charitable: "There have been tensions within the Kerry campaign almost from the start, the sort of complaints that have followed Shrum throughout his career: of pushing rivals out of the way, of isolating the candidate, of blurring the message."[67]

Mark Mellman of the Mellman Group was the senior pollster; Diane Feldman was brought in to conduct focus group sessions. Journalist Joe Klein observed that Mellman was "frustrated" about having little access to Kerry and having his polling data reinterpreted by Shrum, and noted how much the campaign relied on focus group analysis: the campaign's "devotion to focus groups was slavish, historic, and ridiculous in the extreme."[68] Stephanie Cutter headed the communications group, and grassroots specialist Michael Whouley was brought in for the crucial primaries. Whouley, who worked for the 1992 Clinton and 2000 Gore campaigns, was one of the founding partners of the Boston-based political consulting firm Dewey Square Group.

When Cahill took the reins, the infighting stopped, and Kerry had a weight taken off his shoulders. "It just liberated me," Kerry said of Cahill's arrival. "It completely liberated me to focus on my message and focus on the energy I needed to put into day-to-day campaigning and on the people I was meeting. . . . It helped to make me a better candidate."[69] Cahill had been campaign manager for Vermont senator Patrick Leahy and Rhode Island senator Claiborne Pell, and had worked for Massachusetts representatives Robert F. Drinan, Barney Frank, and most recently was chief of staff for Edward Kennedy. Cahill became the third woman campaign manager for a major party presidential nominee, following Susan Estrich (Dukakis, 1988) and Donna Brazile (Gore, 2000).

The Bush Re-election Team

George Bush turned again to the experienced team that had brought him to the White House in 2000. Foremost was Karl Rove. In preparation for the 2004 re-election campaign, Rove sought advice from Republican veteran campaigners, among them James Baker, Michael Deaver, and Bob Teeter, who had been in the same position he now found himself in. Their advice: don't let the White House staff and the campaign get in each other's way and work at cross-purposes. To minimize the infighting, White House chief of staff Andrew Card appointed Rove as the one person in the White House through whom all campaign matters would flow. Rove suggested Ken Mehlman as campaign manager, and by February 2003, senior White House and campaign operatives were meeting at Rove's house for strategy meetings, known as the Breakfast Club. Joining in from the campaign were media consultant Mark McKinnon and Matthew Dowd.

Rove also noted that he called in a group of political scientists, led by University of Texas professor Daron Shaw, to review the campaign's priorities of targeted states. "We called this group of academic propeller heads 'Team B,'" Rove wrote in his memoirs.[70]

Defining Kerry. Republican strategists saw good news in the quick Kerry victories. With the primaries and caucuses wrapped up so quickly, there was little time for Kerry to enjoy free media coverage and little time for the general voting population to get to know the Democratic candidate. Kerry was a relative unknown: he had not yet presented himself or his narrative to voters.[71] This gave Republican strategists and their outside 527 allies the chance to fill in the blanks and to define Kerry themselves. It was hard for Kerry's camp to do this, because it did not have enough campaign funds after the primaries to run biographical commercials. After Kerry won the nomination on March 2, 2004, with his victories on Super Tuesday, the Bush campaign took advantage of its opponent's lack of funds and the next day "started hammering us," observed Kerry senior strategist Michael Donilon.[72] Bush campaign manager Ken Mehlman explained the tactic: "We had to . . . remind people why we went to war, remind people about the War on Terror, and remind people about Senator Kerry's, should we put it, complicated record on discussing these questions."[73]

Whenever there have been inconsistencies in voting or in public statements, opponents are quick to charge a candidate with "flip-flopping." This has been a standard arrow in the quiver of political ad makers for decades. Kerry became the perfect foil when he tried to explain a change in a vote to an audience of West Virginia military veterans. "I actually did vote for the 87 billion dollars before I voted against it." An audience of congressional staffers might have caught, and understood, the nuances of that statement; but in the hands of the Bush ad team it was admission of inconsistency, of flip-flopping, by Kerry himself. This fed right into the Bush media team's narrative of Kerry, the decorated Vietnam veteran, being wrong on military spending and waffling on his commitments.

"Troops"

> *Bush*: I'm George W. Bush and I approve this message.
> *Male Narrator*: Few votes in Congress are as important as funding our troops at war. Though John Kerry voted in October 2002 for military action in Iraq, he later voted against funding our soldiers.
> *Senate Clerk*: Mr. Kerry?
> *Male Narrator*: No. Body armor and higher combat pay for troops?
> *Senate Clerk*: Mr. Kerry?
> *Male Narrator*: No. Better health care for reservists?
> *Senate Clerk*: Mr. Kerry?
> *Male Narrator*: No. And what does Kerry say now?
> *Kerry* (SPEAKING TO VETERANS IN WEST VIRGINIA): I actually did vote for the $87 billion before I voted against it.
> [*Text*: John Kerry: Wrong on defense.]
> *Male Narrator*: Wrong on defense.[74]

The flip-flopper theme was reinforced by "Surfer," which showed actual footage of John Kerry windsurfing in Nantucket Sound. Windsurfing conjured up images of elitism and privilege, reinforced by silly-sounding music from the "Blue Danube Waltz." The narrator reels off how Kerry voted for, then against the Iraq war; for, then against $87 billion for troops; for, then against education reform; for, then against Medicare funding. For each "for" or "against," Kerry is seen tacking and surfing in another direction. Then the punch line: "John Kerry, whichever way the wind blows."[75]

Online Media Joining the Fray

In July 2004, right before the presidential nominating conventions, a digital entertainment studio called JibJab Media launched on its website a political parody, featuring cut-out cartoon figures of Bush and Kerry singing a version of

Woody Guthrie's "This Land Is Your Land." This clever three-minute animation reinforced crude political stereotypes:

> Bush singing: "I'm a Texas tiger; you're [Kerry] a liberal wiener."
> Kerry singing: "I'm an intellectual; you're [Bush] a stupid dumb-ass."
> Bush singing: "You're a U.N. pussy."
> Kerry singing: "You're a right-wing nut job."[76]

Soon the cartoon was shown on national television and immediately went viral, with 65 million hits on the JibJab website. This was just the first of many animations, parodies, and amateur videos that appeared on the Internet. Some were stupid, some clever, others made little sense at all.[77] The overall message, however, was clear: the Internet had opened up a whole new avenue for communication. Suddenly, political communication was becoming much more vocal and visceral, trying to grab the attention of voters.

During the 2004 nominating conventions, the television networks shrugged off the speeches during the first two days. The one bright spot was the keynote speech by a US Senate candidate from Illinois, Barack Obama, at the Democratic convention. Long gone were the days of 1960s when there was gavel-to-gavel coverage of the conventions, from the opening on Monday through the Thursday night presidential acceptance speech. If voters wanted to see more of the conventions in 2004, they had to resort to cable television (C-SPAN, MSNBC, Fox News, even Comedy Central, MTV, and BET). Political bloggers were, for the first time, given credentials to appear at the conventions. The bloggers, like Daily Kos, Instapundit, New Donkey, RedState.com, Blogs for Bush, Buzzmachine, and many others, were getting their message out. Yahoo.com had counted forty-eight separate political blogs covering the presidential election, with the biggest blogs belonging to the large metropolitan newspapers. Two years later, TownHall.com, a conservative website, managed to combine the new and the old: links to conservative talk radio and links to conservative blogs.[78]

Outside Voices

The 2004 campaign was unusual because of the television ads aired by two independent expenditure groups, both supporting Bush. The one series of ads, produced by an organization called the Swift Boat Veterans for Truth, directly attacked the credibility and character of John Kerry. The other source, a single ad pushed by the Progress for America Voter Fund, embraced George Bush as the protector of the country after 9/11.

Swift Boat Veterans. Journalist Paul Fahri wrote about the similarities between two political ads, the Willie Horton ad of 1998 and the Swift Boat Veterans ads in 2004: "Separated by 16 years, two of the most famous and controversial TV ads in presidential campaign history share a remarkable set of traits. Both were launched by nominally independent groups, not by the candidates themselves. Both aired in just a few small markets, gaining widespread exposure only through news media coverage. Both were denounced as inaccurate and unfair."[79] Both ads, it might be added, slammed Democratic presidential candidates from Massachusetts.

The Swift Boat Veterans for Truth, a 527 organization, sponsored a series of independent issue ads aimed directly at John Kerry's Vietnam war record and his integrity.[80] At the Democratic National Convention, Kerry introduced himself to the world: "I'm John Kerry, and I'm reporting for duty." Many veterans were still angry at Kerry for his 1971 appearance before a congressional committee, where he blasted the American war effort in Vietnam.

Swift Boat Veterans had little financial backing at first, but soon wealthy Bush supporters began opening their checkbooks. Bob J. Perry, a friend of both Bush and Karl Rove, contributed $4.5 million; Harold Simmons's Contran Corporation gave $3 million; and T. Boone Pickens chipped in $2 million. The Swift Boaters went to Republican media consultants Rick Reed and Chris LaCivita of the media firm of Stevens Reed Curcio & Potholm. The first ad they made was called "Any Questions?"

John Edwards: If you have any questions about what John Kerry is made of, just spend three minutes with the men who served with him.

[*On screen, appearing one after another are thirteen Vietnam vets; each stands before a backdrop showing his picture when he served in Vietnam; each picture has the man's name, with rank and service medals. The first is Al French*].

Al French: I served with John Kerry.

Bob Elder: John Kerry has not been honest about what happened in Vietnam.

Al French: He is lying about his record.

Louis Letson: I know John Kerry is lying about his first Purple Heart because I treated him for that injury.

Van O'Dell: John Kerry lied to get his bronze star. I know, I was there, I saw what happened.

Jack Chenoweth: His account of what happened and what actually happened are the difference between night and day. . . .

Bob Elder: He is no war hero.

Grant Hibbard: He betrayed all his shipmates . . . he lied before the Senate. . . .

Bob Hildreth: I served with John Kerry . . .

Bob Hildreth (OFF CAMERA): John Kerry cannot be trusted.

Media consultant Greg Stevens, lead partner in the firm, was no stranger to controversial presidential advertising. He was also the creator of the 1988 "Tank" ad that showed Michael Dukakis looking ridiculous in an Army tank. For the Swift Boaters, his partner Rick Reed produced the ads.

This first ad was placed in media markets in just three battleground states—Wisconsin, Ohio, and West Virginia—at the cost of $546,000 in airtime. The media consultants were paid just $300,000 for the ads, a mere drop in the bucket for what they earned during the 2003–2004 election cycle. But the important thing about the ads was how quickly they were boosted by free media, especially conservative talk radio, the Internet, cable and network television, and newspapers editorials. A second ad, "Sellout" was even more critical, using Kerry's own 1971 congressional testimony; altogether there were nine Swift Boat ads. Within three weeks of the first ad, airing in August 2004, the Gallup poll found that 80 percent of the country knew about the Swift Boat ads.[81] Patrick Devlin correctly observed that Kerry's "reporting for duty" quip at the nominating convention "now came back to haunt him."[82]

The Kerry team was slow to respond to this attack. Stephanie Cutter wanted to hit back, but both Shrum and Cahill decided that doing so would only give the Swift Boaters more attention.[83] Chris LaCivita speculated on their lack of response: "They knew we were going to hit them on April '71, his testimony before the Senate Foreign Relations Committee. They knew we were going to hit him on his meetings with the Viet Cong. . . . But they never imagined that we would actually go after him for specific actions he claimed he did while he was in Vietnam."[84] At a conference at the University of Virginia Center for Politics a month after the 2004 election, Mike McCurry, a Kerry adviser and former Clinton White House spokesman, said the Swift Boat ads were "one of the most dishonorable things I've ever seen happen in politics."[85] And perhaps more telling was the ability of an outside group to shift the attention to Vietnam, rather than Bush's difficulties with Iraq. Hamilton Jordan, former senior strategist for Carter (and later Perot) observed: "The fact that we're talking about Vietnam, not Iraq, is an indication" of Kerry's failure to define the presidential race on his own terms.[86] In his memoir, Bob Shrum recalled two crucial mistakes in 2004. Over his heated objections, Kerry decided to accept federal campaign funds during the general election: "We should never have accepted federal funding in the general election; but then I and others should have ignored the consequences of that and spent the money to hit back early and hard at the Swift Boat attacks."[87]

Who was responsible for the Swift Boat ads? Karl Rove wrote in 2010, "Of course, I was blamed for the Swift Boat ads, accused of helping to organize the group, orchestrating its activities, and creating its messages. I had no role in any of it, though the Swifties did a damned good job."[88]

A chance encounter between Bush and a widower and his daughter became probably the most successful sixty-second video of the 2004 campaign. It showed George Bush, the compassionate, protective father figure, embracing a teenage girl, Ashley, in Lebanon, Ohio.

"Ashley's Story."

> *Lynn Faulkner*: My wife Wendy was murdered by terrorists on September 11th.

Announcer: The Faulkner's daughter, Ashley, closed up emotionally. But when President George W. Bush came to Lebanon, Ohio, she went to see him, as she had with her mother four years earlier.

Linda Prince [FAMILY FRIEND]: He walked toward me and I said, "Mr. President, this young lady lost her mother in the World Trade Center."

Ashley Faulkner: And he turned around and he came back and he said, "I know that's hard. Are you all right?"

Linda Prince: Our president took Ashley in his arms and just embraced her. And it was at that moment that we saw Ashley's eyes fill up with tears.

Ashley Faulkner: He's the most powerful man in the world and all he wants to do is make sure I'm safe. That I'm okay.

Lynn Faulkner: What I saw was what I want to see in the heart and the soul of the man who sits in the highest elected office in our country.

Announcer: Progress for America Voter Fund is responsible for the content of this message.

Brian McCabe, a partner in the Washington-based public affairs firm DCI Group, and president of the American Voter Fund and Progress for America, Inc., noted that in a post-election survey conducted by Public Opinion Strategies, "Ashley's Story" was the most successful ad of the year on open-ended questions. It was produced by Larry McCarthy's media firm, MHW, Inc.[89] It was shown in October, just weeks before the election, backed by the most expensive television buy of the entire campaign. Two California executives, Alex Spanos and Dawn Arnall, each chipped in $5 million to the Progress for America efforts. It was particularly effective in Ohio and Wisconsin, and Progress for America Voter Fund pumped in $18.8 million for this ad, the largest spent for a single message during 2004.[90] The Kerry campaign's Shrum agreed that this was the "most powerful spot" of the entire campaign. The Bush team had managed to change the conversation back to 9/11, defense, and terrorism. "We had fought for months to keep the contest from simply being a 9/11 election," wrote Shrum. "Now that's what it would become."[91]

The General Election

It was a particularly difficult time for the Kerry campaign. It was losing steam, hit by the Swift Boaters, and becoming overly cautious. Kerry was not happy over the work being done by Shrum and Devine, but he wasn't about to fire them. For months, reporters had been complaining about the sharp-tongued communications director Stephanie Cutter, and insiders complained that she was too controlling and too slow.[92] Mary Beth Cahill was also in trouble, not trusted by Teresa Heinz Kerry, the candidate's wife, and not seeming to possess the skills needed to run a presidential campaign. There was plenty of second-guessing and kibitzing: Bill Clinton, Ted Kennedy, old campaign friends—they all weighed in. But the loudest by far was James Carville. He urged Kerry to bring Paul Begala in to help with strategy and communications; but Begala lasted just a few weeks.

Former Clinton spokesperson Joe Lockhart was brought in to help. Carville, thoroughly agitated to the point of crying, told Cahill that she should resign and have Lockhart come in to rescue the campaign. Such was the state of the besieged Kerry campaign prior to the debates. Fortunately for Kerry, he was able to gain ground through the debates and through Lockhart's communication and message skills.[93]

The media campaign. The Bush and Kerry teams, the parties, and the 527 groups supporting them spent a total of $620 million, which was a 235 percent increase over television advertising in the 2000 campaign.[94] Communications scholar L. Patrick Devlin considered the Bush ad campaign against Kerry as the "most negative campaign in presidential history."[95] Devlin found that of the eighty ads produced for Bush, a full 72 percent were negative, an all-time high. The emphasis of the ads was on Bush's strength and leadership versus the waffling and unsteadiness of Kerry.

The Bush-Cheney media team consisted of Mark McKinnon of Maverick Media, together with Stuart Stevens and Russ Schriefer. Also on the team were Matthew Dowd, Alex Castellanos, Chris Mottola, Fred Davis, Frank Guerra and Lionel Sosa, Scott Howell, and Sara Taylor.[96] The Kerry-Edwards media team began with Jim Margolis of GMMB along with Shrum, Devine & Donilon during the primaries. During the general election, GMMB was retained, but only for time-buying purposes. The firms of Squier, Knapp Dunn and Shrum, Devine & Donilon created and produced the ads. Bill Knapp and Mike Donilon were the chief creators and coordinators of the ads.[97]

The Kerry strategy was to localize ads, tailoring them from one state to another, and in the end producing a total of 160 separate ads. This was nearly twice the number produced by the Bush campaign. Shrum had a reputation of creating more ads than were needed, and of spending more on television commercials than necessary, all the while collecting a percentage on the advertising bill. In the old days, when his firm was Doak and Shrum, behind their backs, their critics called them "Soak and Run."[98]

But quantity was not equated with quality. In his analysis of the entire 2004 ad campaigns, Patrick Devlin concluded that "Bush had more creative, better produced, and more consistent ads."[99] The problem was that Kerry's ads lacked a coherent national theme. Bush's ad strategy pushed values and character, and, in Devlin's words, "values and character topped issues" in this contest.[100]

The ground game. One of the most important strategic decisions came from research gathered by Matthew Dowd in 2001. Dowd came to Rove with the interesting statistic that the percentage of voters who were truly independent had shrunk from 25 percent in 1984 to just 7 percent during the 2000 campaigns. The implications for 2004 were clear: "Forget independents. Find the Republicans hidden among the Democrats."[101] This meant digging for Bush-leaning supporters, using newly developed microtargeting techniques to find them and energize them to vote.

Republicans spent three years and several millions of dollars in creating their microtargeting tools. The Bush forces were able to draw upon up to 225 pieces of information about a prospective voter, to determine if he or she would likely vote for them, including the liquor they drank, whether they owned guns, the magazines they subscribed to, and the kind of car they owned.[102] As microtargeting pioneer Alex Gage remarked, "We wanted to be able to find out things like 'who are the 10,000 people in the city of Detroit whose top priority is to stop abortions.'"[103] In Florida, for example, the Bush campaign was able to locate churchgoers who were not Republicans (but could be persuaded to vote for Bush) and Hispanic mothers who supported No Child Left Behind.[104] All this added up. As journalist Thomas B. Edsall observed, "The ability of the Republican Party to target their voters—not only in such large areas as exurbia and in sprawling suburbs but also within black and Hispanic churches, in unions, and in overwhelmingly Democratic college towns—stunned Democratic Party leaders." In simple terms, it was targeting the guy who was a member of the United Auto Workers, but was also a gun owner or member of the NRA.[105]

Chuck DeFeo was in charge of the Bush's e-campaign. His unit built a massive e-mail list of 8.5 million names, and the campaign was the first to use online organizing tools, such as maps and directions to polling locations, door-to-door organizing, virtual precinct to contact other voters, public disclosure of donors, and instant rebuttal capability after debates.[106] While much of the attention was paid to Howard Dean and his online operation, the more effective and impressive during the 2004 campaign was that of the Bush operatives, quietly running under the radar of press scrutiny.

A major target and opportunity for the Bush campaign was the Christian Right. Karl Rove argued that there were some 4 million evangelical voters who failed to vote in 2000, and many had declined because of the last-minute news that George W. Bush had been arrested for drunk driving in 1976.[107] In 2004, Republicans returned to their 2000 strategy of building an "army of persuasion"—a massive, direct outreach program. Ken Mehlman had developed the key concept: the "Bush team leader" program. Volunteers would recruit five other leaders, sign up ten friends, participate in voter registration, write letters, post blogs, host parties at their homes, and distribute materials. There would be goals for Bush leaders in every county of every state. The leaders would receive thank you notes and small gifts; they would even have the chance to meet the president.[108]

Bush's Christian Right army was energized by a landmark state court decision. In November 2003, the Massachusetts Supreme Judicial Court legalized gay marriage in that state. For Karl Rove, it was an opportunity: "We saw it in polling, where Bush did better among Catholics, evangelicals, African-American churchgoers, and older working-class voters than we expected. We saw it in our campaign activities, with many African-American and Latino evangelical churchgoers and faithful Catholic communicants citing marriage as a major reason why, as Democrats, they crossed party lines to support Bush."[109] This worked to Bush's advantage, according to Rove: "Gay rights activists bent on defeating

George W. Bush helped re-elect him by overreaching on same-sex marriage. Bush's views were shared by most Americans. All he had to do was make his position clear and keep the tone civil."[110]

Key to the Bush strategy was the work of Ken Mehlman, the chair of the Republican National Committee and later the Bush-Cheney campaign manager. Mehlman had a major role in encouraging the anti–gay marriage amendments in eleven states. At the time, Mehlman, a "confirmed bachelor," was dogged by critics for being a closeted homosexual. (In August 2010, Mehlman publicly acknowledged that he was gay, and he has become active in supporting the expansion of rights for homosexuals.)[111] Dan Gurley worked for Mehlman overseeing the party's anti-gay activities; he later acknowledged publicly that he was gay, and by 2009 he was working for Equality North Carolina, a group dedicated to securing equal rights for LGBT individuals.[112] Karl Rove was particularly involved in the campaign to rouse conservative Christians to rally against the anti-gay amendments and to vote for Bush's re-election. Rove's adoptive father, Louis, whom Rove biographers had said was homosexual, died in July 2004, just as the anti-gay ballot effort was being directed by his son.[113]

According to James Moore and Wayne Slater, "Rove and company built the most successful confederation of religious voters in history during that summer of 2004. Not just white Protestants, but African Americans moved by opposition to gay marriage. And Catholics, which meant more Hispanics, a dream demographic in Rove's political calculus."[114]

In the end, it would be another nail-biter, and another victory for George Bush. But the early exit polls looked promising for Kerry. Some Democratic consultants, particularly Bob Shrum, were ready to call for a Kerry victory. "Can I be the first to call you Mr. President?" was the memorable kiss of death question Shrum asked Kerry when early exit polls showed him beating Bush.[115]

The focus in 2004 would be on the key battleground state of Ohio, which Bush won by 118,000 votes. There were persistent rumors of wrongdoing, of technical delays, of not enough voting machines to accommodate the long lines of voters, especially Democrats, in Ohio. Communications professor Mark Crispin Miller argued in a book aptly titled *Fooled Again* that there was voter intimidation and fraud in many states, and particularly in Ohio. A year after the election, Miller met Kerry, handed him a copy of his book, and Kerry made a remark about the election; according to Miller, "he said he believes it was stolen."[116] Journalist Mark Hertsgaard, in an article in *Mother Jones*, argues that the facts do not support such a claim.[117]

Removing an incumbent president is difficult. Mark Mellman later observed that 75 percent of incumbent presidents get re-elected: "There's a reason for that. You have to have a certain level of pain to un-elect an incumbent president. But the reality is the country was not feeling the level of pain that was required to oust an incumbent president."[118] Kerry and his team of consultants simply didn't make the case, and in the end they were outhustled and outmaneuvered by their Republican opponents.

CHAPTER 18

Consulting Internationally

*Is there a difference between making media spots in Venezuela
and the United States? "Sure," said Joseph Napolitan,
taking a puff on his third cigar of the day. "In Venezuela,
we make them in Spanish." (1985)*

*There is not an election that's seriously contested around the
world where Americans are not present as advisers on one side, or both.*
—Douglas E. Schoen (2000)

*In the Cold War, the CIA was all over the world teaching armies
how to fight and intelligence services how to spy. Now, instead of
teaching dictators how to be dictators, we're teaching people
how to win elections. That's a positive thing. It's the American influence.*
—Dick Morris (2000)

SINCE THE 1970s, international political consulting has been a growth industry for enterprising American campaign specialists. In 1981 there were
approximately thirty countries in which presidential and other candidates
had hired American consultants.[1] In the 1980s and 1990s, there was a steady
growth in American consulting throughout the world. American political consultants and the techniques they have developed are now staples in campaigns
in Latin American, Eastern Europe, throughout the English-speaking world, in
many African countries, and in virtually every country with democratic elections. When the Iron Curtain fell, and democracy began to flourish in Eastern
Europe in 1990, American consultants were at the ready. As journalist Walter
Shapiro noted, "Budapest, at its glorious dawn of democracy, seemed to boast
more Democratic and Republican strategists, pollsters, and media mavens than
all the steakhouses in Washington."[2] And when Boris Yeltsin needed help during
the 1996 Russian elections, he secretly turned to American consultants.

Why do Americans consultants go abroad? Democratic pollster Stanley
Greenberg, who worked for Bill Clinton, Nelson Mandela (South Africa), Tony

Blair (United Kingdom), Ehud Barak (Israel), and Gonzalo Sánchez de Lozada (Bolivia), gave three reasons: to foster democracy, to advance a particular political philosophy, or to get rich.[3]

From the Philippines election of Marcos, to the Russian election of Yeltsin, to current campaigns, American political consultants have been involved in hundreds of elections throughout the world. American consultants have brought technical knowledge and experience, as well as the most recent techniques in communication, polling, and market research. For better or worse, they have changed the nature of campaigns.

The Growth of Consulting Business Abroad

The emergence of international political consulting provides another chapter in the professionalization of elections and campaigns.[4] What candidates and parties abroad seem to need the most from American consultants are assistance in message development, general strategic advice, polling and focus group research, new media techniques, and new technologies like microtargeting. Sometimes the need is very rudimentary, such as identifying potential voters or designing basic campaign themes and messages; at other times, particularly in advanced electoral systems, American consultants are asked for more sophisticated assistance, such as integrating focus group research analysis into an overall theme development.

More American consultants are working in the international arena than ever before, and there is no indication that these opportunities will fade. The growth of international consulting results, first, from the emergence of democratic institutions throughout the world. In halting but persistent steps, democracy has become a central political norm throughout much of the world.[5] Freedom House, a New York-based organization that monitors political development worldwide, noted in a 1996 survey that 117 of 191 nations (67 percent) are democracies, up from 42 percent a decade earlier; by 2013, that number had risen to 122.[6] In Latin America during the 1970s, many of the military-controlled or one-party governments were replaced by two-party or multiparty systems, permitting genuinely contested elections for the first time. In Africa during the 1970s and 1980s, democratic elections were held, although in many countries, democracy in the late 1990s was a fragile, battered institution. In Eastern Europe, democracy has made some strides, despite the troubles in Ukraine. Both historically and symbolically, the 1994 South African all-race election, discussed below, was a centerpiece of this democratic phenomenon. In each of these regions, sometimes with little impact and at other times with splash and controversy, American political consultants have been on the front lines of democratic revolution.

The second reason is the emergence of the candidate-centered election and the corresponding decline of the political party in many countries as the primary vehicle for election victory. In the United States, the political party long ago ceased to fulfill that central function. While the party remains central in many countries with parliamentary systems, many ambitious candidates have found it wanting. Rather than trusting the party apparatus for campaign funds and election strategy, candidates are hiring their own independent political advisers, many of them Americans.

The third reason is the pervasiveness of television as an election tool.[7] Television viewership and ownership have increased dramatically throughout much of the world. Even in the poorest of countries, television antennae sprout from rooftops and satellite dishes dot the countryside. As democratic institutions have become more open, tight restrictions and bans have been lifted on the use of television for elections and campaigns.

Political scientist Margaret Scammell noted that until the 1980s, paid political advertising was basically confined to the Americas and Australia, but by the late 1980s and early 1990s, television commercials were permitted in Germany, Sweden, and Italy.[8] There were dramatic changes during the next fifteen to twenty years. In 2008, political scientist Fritz Plasser found there were at least sixty countries, mostly outside of Europe, where paid television campaigning had replaced traditional forms of campaigning, like posters, print advertising, and mass rallies.[9]

With increased freedom for candidates and parties to use television as a campaign vehicle, there has been a greater emphasis on American-style political commercials. Campaigns are becoming increasingly contested between individuals candidates, and fought over the airwaves with American-style tactics, strategies, and images.

The fourth reason is the growing technological sophistication and use of applied social science research in elections. Over the past twenty years, American campaigns have seen the rapid growth of technology, such as predictive dialing, computerized voting files, microtargeting, online communication, and social media. Particularly in developing countries, local campaign operatives generally do not have the skills or the experience to use these increasingly sophisticated election tools. The 2008 Obama presidential campaign's online presence and technology made a big impression on candidates and political parties in other countries.

Fifth, in some elections, American consultants are hired because of the prestige factor. A high-profile political consultant who helped elect the president of the United States can expect many other presidential campaigns throughout the world to come looking for similar assistance. Following Clinton's 1992 presidential victory, Clinton consultants Stanley Greenberg and Frank Greer went to South Africa to assist Nelson Mandela. Greek prime minister Constantine Mitsotakis hired Clinton advisers James Carville and Paul Begala, and Bush adviser Mary Matalin, for his re-election bid in 1994. Bush II political consultants also have worked abroad, and following the 2012 re-election victory of Barack Obama, his chief consultant, Jim Messina, was in high demand internationally.

These veterans of the most sophisticated political campaign marketplace, from Joseph Napolitan, Richard Wirthlin, Robert Shrum, to Jim Messina could immediately earn respect and command high consulting fees from presidents and presidential aspirants throughout much of the world. But, as seen below,

American consultants also can be a detriment to a campaign. Old suspicions and resentments against American power and influence surface as new-styled American campaign commercials, messages, and techniques seep into another country's electoral battles.

Finally, enterprising American consultants saw the opportunities of working abroad and actively sought out presidential candidates and political parties to offer their services. One of the most important strategies for American consulting firms is to have a mix of clients, political and nonpolitical, so that the vagaries of the American election cycle won't imperil their finances and operations from year to year. Some American consultants saw their bank accounts swell during off-cycles, when international clients came calling. Those Americans who went abroad usually had considerable experience in the US market. Democratic pollster Bill Hamilton stated, "We're in a position to export because we have the experience. We have more than 400,000 elections in the U.S. every two years. This allows us to hone our skills to see what works and doesn't work in persuading and motivating voters."[10]

American political consulting firms have branched out their business abroad, not only by forming relations with local campaign operatives and party officials, but also by establishing their own satellite offices overseas. The Wirthlin Group, for example, had offices in London, Brussels, and Hong Kong, and has done polling for the Conservative Party in Britain, the Likud in Israel, and the Liberal Party in Australia.[11] Other consulting firms, like Penn Schoen Berland (PSB), merged into networks of global public relations giants.

Just as in American campaigns, competition breeds more business for consultants. When a presidential candidate for one major party brings in acclaimed, high-profile American consultants, can the other major presidential candidates be left behind without their own American consultants? As Walter Shapiro caustically pointed out, bringing in a campaign adviser to a foreign country might be "a boon for democracy, but bring in a rival and you create that lucrative state known as consultant gridlock."[12]

American campaign consultants have worked for candidates and parties in nearby Canada and Mexico and in campaigns as far off as the island of Mauritius. Campaign consultants, for example, have helped craft survey research data in Russia, train candidates in image building in Austria, design effective thirty-second television spots in Colombia, conduct focus group research in Italy, build party organizations in Hungary, create party messages and slogans in South Africa, and develop computerized voter files in Ireland.

American political consultants have been most successful in developing business in countries where (1) candidate-centered presidential elections dominate, (2) television is a pervasive form of campaign communication, (3) local expertise in campaign techniques is unavailable or not of the highest caliber, (4) campaign funds are plentiful, (5) there are no severe time constraints on election activity, and (6) there are no insurmountable cultural barriers to American participation.

American consultants have been less successful in penetrating markets that have very short election periods, such as those typically found in parliamentary election systems, in countries with strong political parties in which professional party staff members have developed expertise in election techniques, in elections where the personal risk factor might be too great, and in countries where the cultural barriers to American manipulation of elections might be too high.

American Consultants in Latin America, Britain, Israel, and Russia

> *I have been a consultant in the last four presidential elections in Venezuela, a country often so crowded with American advisers that we could have had a quorum of the American Association of Political Consultants during some elections.*
>
> —Joseph Napolitan (1989)[13]

> *Latin American and European and every other international market are following roughly the same pattern that happened in the U.S. with campaign consultants, and the similarities are so great it's frightening.*
>
> —American consultant Phil Noble (1999)[14]

Starting in the early 1970s, American consultants have had increased opportunities in the Latin American and Caribbean election market, with Venezuelan presidential elections as the most important first ventures.[15] Venezuelan elections during the 1970s–1990s were tailor-made for American consultants: media access was extensive; there was no overt government interference with the press; election expenditures were wide open, with no imposed spending or contribution limits; there were ambitious candidates seeking the best election talent available; and there generally was sufficient time to develop a relation between candidate and American consultant. Venezuela was the breakthrough consulting experience for many American firms.

"We have had all the major consultants here," said a Venezuelan political adviser in 1988. "There's been David Garth, Pat Caddell, Robert Squier, Joe Napolitan, and David Sawyer."[16] Over the years, these and many other American consultants have worked in the lucrative Venezuelan political market. In a 1978 upset victory, American media consultant David Garth helped Luis Herrera Campins, the Christian Democratic (COPEI) candidate, defeat Democratic Action candidate Luis Pinerua Ordaz. Garth's name was splashed across Venezuelan newspapers, he was verbally attacked by the opposition, and he became an issue in the election.[17] In 1983, Napolitan advised Jaime Lusinchi, the leader of the leftist Democratic Action party and eventual winner, while Garth advised former president Rafael Caldera, the Christian Democrat candidate. In this bitter presidential election, which cost the two main parties an estimated $20 million, the use of American media advisors led to a chorus of complaints about foreign, especially American, meddling in Venezuelan affairs.[18]

In 1988, both major parties in Venezuela's presidential elections had hired big-name American consultants, many of whom had just finished the Dukakis-Bush presidential campaign or other elections in the United States. "After

November 8, if you were looking to interview American political consultants, the best place to find them would have been in the lobby of the Tamanaco Hotel" in Caracas, quipped Robert Squier, an adviser to winning presidential candidate Carlos Andrés Pérez in the December 4 election.[19] Squier's involvement with the Pérez campaign began two years earlier when he helped shape television advertisements used in the candidate's campaign for his party's nomination.[20]

American political consultants have become familiar with Latin American markets over the past twenty-five years, often working with local advertising firms, seasoned party professionals, and others who have a solid understanding of the nuances of past campaigns, a party's history, and the desires and whims of the electorate. Some American firms, like Squier Knapp Ochs, established satellite offices in Latin America.[21] One of the most prominent American consultants has been Ralph Murphine, who has worked for over 500 candidates for public office, and has advised candidates in sixteen Latin American presidential elections. Murphine, who began his career with pioneer consultant Matt Reese, was recognized as the International Consultant of the Year in 1997 by the AAPC.[22]

The 2000 Mexican Presidential Election

> It is the end of the old tradition of anti-Yanquismo. Who is
> going to shout, "Americans go home," when they are shouting "Americans, please
> come manage my campaign"?
>
> —Mexican writer Carlos Monsivais[23]

> Foreigners may not, in any manner, involve themselves
> in the political affairs of the country.
>
> —Article 33, Constitution of Mexico

In the 1990s, Mexico had endured several political upheavals, especially with the 1994 devaluation of the peso, the Zapatista uprising in Chiapas, persistent allegations of voter fraud and abuse, and the assassination of the ruling Institutional Revolutionary Party's (Partido Revolucionario Institucional, or PRI) original candidate for president, Luis Donaldo Colosio, and three months later, the assassination of PRI party secretary José Francisco Ruiz Massieu. In his 1994 inaugural address, President Ernesto Zedillo acknowledged that there were deeply ingrained political and economic problems, chief among them was electoral fraud. Mexico approved electoral reforms in 1997, and shortly thereafter held federal congressional and Mexico City mayoral elections, described as the "cleanest in Mexico's history."[24] That year, PRI lost the majority in the Chamber of Deputies, for the first time in seventy years. Following the 1997 elections, PAN (Partido Acción Nacional) controlled six governorships and the majorities in six state legislatures, while the PRD (Partido de la Revolución Democrática) elected Cuauhtémoc Cárdenas as governor of the Federal District, but no other governorship. PAN mayors governed nearly all of Mexico's largest cities, while the PRD governed Mexico City.[25]

By the time of the 2000 presidential contest, Mexican election law and atmosphere had been profoundly transformed. The election reform process brought about the establishment of a genuinely independent election authority, the Federal Electoral Institute (Instituto Federal Electoral, or IFE), which strengthened citizen participation through nonpartisan election monitoring, and there was a growing impartiality of the news media, establishment of substantial, direct public funding for political parties, free broadcast time for political parties, and open debates for presidential candidates.[26]

The 2000 presidential race in Mexico was like none seen before. PRI had dominated Mexican politics for over seventy years, and for decades, the president would choose his party's candidate in a time-honored tradition known as *el dedazo*—the "big finger" of the president pointing to the anointed candidate. With the opposition parties having little influence, the anointed successor was invariably elected. This time, however, Zedillo renounced the tradition of the big finger, making it possible for a wide-open, democratic primary for this first time in Mexican history.

As political analyst Michael Barone has noted, ever since 1929, with the founding of PRI, campaign posters would trumpet the name of the PRI presidential candidate in big block letters, framed by the red and green of the Mexican flag. Often, opposition posters were nowhere to be seen. But in 1999, it was a different climate: in the months leading up to the first-ever PRI primary, the posters read *Tú eliges al candidato* (You choose the candidate).[27]

For the primaries, all of the major PRI candidates turned to American political consultants to help develop their strategy and message and to assist local Mexican consultants. Favored candidate Francisco Labastida Ochoa, a former interior minister, brought in Stanley Greenberg, Jeremy Rosner, and James Carville. Greenberg and Carville, who until this time generally worked for challengers in international contests, were now working with the seemingly entrenched establishment party. Governor of the state of Tabasco, Roberto Madrazo hired consultants Tom O'Donnell, Doug Schoen, and Zev Furst; and Manuel Bartlett chose Gary Nordlinger. The principal opposition candidate, Vicente Fox of PAN, brought in Dick Morris. Few of these American consultants had ever worked in Mexico before, and few spoke Spanish. Nordlinger, both fluent in Spanish and with a long history of working in Latin America campaigns, was the exception.

Radio and print media in Mexico were mostly owned and operated by private individuals, and represented a wide variety of political points of view. Television, however, was dominated by two large networks–Televisa and TV Azteca–both of which traditionally had supported the ruling PRI. Mexico has had a long and unfortunate history of media bias and manipulation.[28]

The candidates mounted an aggressive television and radio campaign against their opponents. Up until this contest, television coverage of presidential elections was generally limited to news shows, usually with subtle or not so subtle biases favoring the ruling PRI. Challengers didn't have the funds for paid television commercials. Now, massive amounts of money were poured into commercials. In 2000, only in Russia and Brazil did voters rely so heavily on television as the vehicle for receiving information about politics and candidates.[29] The

Labastida campaign hired producers from some of Mexico's best-known soap operas to polish his image, giving him a softer, more "human" image. Labastida kissed babies, hugged grandmothers, and was swarmed by children. In an image reminiscent of Boris Yeltsin's "get'n down and boogying," Mexican viewers were amazed to see Labastida do a funky dance with the hosts of a morning talk show.[30] Veteran PRI politician Roberto Madrazo, long accused of local election rigging and connections with drug dealers, also received a television makeover, recasting himself as a maverick reformer who would shake up the old system.[31] Madrazo perked up the primary campaign with a daring television spot, "*Dale un Madrazo al Dedazo*," (Strike a Blow at the Big Finger) a pun and clever reference to the old style of picking a president.

In the United States, television viewers were long accustomed to seeing presidential candidates on popular shows. Mexican media in the 1990s was still a little uptight about jokes and making fun of the president. In the late 1990s, police commandos raided a factory that made rubber caricature masks of President Zedillo. The official reason was that the factory had violated copyright laws, but everyone knew that the seizure came because rubber masks violated an unwritten Mexican rule: do not mock the president. Going into the 1999 primaries, however, everything had changed. Candidate Manuel Bartlett confessed on television of cheating on his French exam so he could get a scholarship to college; Vicente Fox took off his trademark belt buckle, with screams of delight from the studio audience. Presidential candidates, especially Fox, appeared on comic Adal Ramones's freewheeling talk show, *Otro Rollo* (A Different Thing), which reached tens of millions of viewers. A couple of hours after Zedillo gave his state of the union speech, watched by 6.5 percent of the public, Fox appeared on slapstick comic Eugenio Dervez's show, attracting 40 percent of all television viewers. This was the election where politicians learned, as Americans had a decade earlier, that they had to play to the audience, guffaw at the off-color jokes, participate in silly games, and let talk show hosts ridicule them. In a version of the old Hollywood line "say whatever you will, just spell my name right," Vicente Fox summed it up: "All interviews are valuable."[32]

Rather than allowing PRI to set the political calendar, Fox jumped into the race in 1997, over two years before the presidential contest. He brought a new style: irreverent, sometimes raunchy, sporting a trademark belt buckle spelling out FOX, and wearing crazy hats. Vicente Fox had marketing in his veins. To many, he was the embodiment of the Marlboro Man—tall, rugged, plainspoken, decked out in cowboy boots and a black hat. He was a top Mexican executive of Coca-Cola, a manufacturer of cowboy boots, and former governor of the central state of Guanajuato. While governor, Fox spent millions—much from the state treasury—on television ads promoting his accomplishments to a national audience. He set up a "Friends of Fox" political action committee, independent of his own party, PAN, and used market-testing direct sales methods to attract 3.4 million members. Fox, while still governor, hired Dick Morris to create several campaign ads, portraying Fox as "the education governor."[33] Of all the candidates, Fox was probably the most natural as a television persona.

With his gravelly voice and plain-spokenness, Fox poked fun at his relatively colorless main rival, Francisco Labastida. Six-foot-five-inch Fox ridiculed five-foot-ten-inch Labastida as "shorty," or "wimp." Fox chided his opponent for helping his wife with shopping, calling Labastida a "queer," "chicken," and, more seriously, accused him of having links to narcotics trafficking. (Labastida struck back, challenging Fox's machismo by noting that all four of his children were adopted—"he couldn't even sire his own son," accused a Labastida pamphlet.) Fox gained in the polls against Labastida by being blunt and simplistic in his assessment of the problems facing Mexico, but probably hurt himself by using foul and rough language.[34]

Personality mattered, not issues. "Just like in the United States, now elections are about character and personality, and less about issues," noted Vicente Licona, chief pollster in Mexico for Louis Harris polls. "He who runs on the issues in Mexico's next election will lose."[35]

During the PRI primary, Labastida, advised by Carville and Greenberg, ran a winning campaign. But on the night of that primary victory, Labastida abruptly changed tactics, stating that he would run as a reformer, and began attacking PRI, proclaiming that, henceforth, he was the leader of the "new PRI." Carville strongly urged Labastida to take this outsider position, and dragged up the successful catch phrases of the Clinton 1992 victory—"It's the economy, stupid" and "It's change vs. more of the same"—and grafted them onto this campaign for president. Soon Labastida-backed billboards and bumper stickers throughout Mexico read: "It's the right kind of change, stupid." But there was a definite cultural snag. Journalist John Maggs observed, "Mexicans—unaware of the famous 1992 Clinton campaign tag line—couldn't understand why Labastida was calling them stupid," and more fundamentally, they weren't buying Labastida's attempt to wrap himself in the reformer mold and distance himself from the PRI. It just struck many as being insincere. At this time, in November 1999, Labastida led by nearly 20 points.[36]

Although the outcome was unclear until the last few days, Fox defeated the PRI and Labastida by a solid 7 percent.[37] For the first time, the election was overseen by an independent electoral commission. There were isolated instances of voter intimidation, ballot shortages, and other problems, but nothing compared to the old days of PRI vote-buying, ballot stuffing, and other forms of outright fraud.[38] Adolfo Aguilar Zinser, a Fox campaign adviser and independent Mexican senator, observed, "We have never transferred power from one group to another by peaceful means. Either you killed your enemy or organized a revolution; you didn't just win in a fair game."[39]

In 2000, Mexico crossed a threshold, with open primaries, democratic choice, and the importation of many America-styled campaign techniques. Presidential contenders turned a blind eye to Article 33 of the Mexican Constitution, which explicitly forbids foreign involvement in elections. Each of the principal candidates used American consultants to help shape strategy, campaign message, and slogans. The Americans set up campaign war rooms in Mexico City, conducted countless polls, did opposition research, and targeted their opponents with negative advertising.

Britain's Love-Hate Relationship with American Campaigning

There has been a full migration of American political packaging techniques to Britain.

—Nicholas J. O'Shaughnessy (1990)[40]

For many years in Britain, American-style campaigning was seen as almost a necessary evil. The political parties didn't like admitting that they use Americans, the British press bemoaned the negative-style tactics brought over by Americans, and for a long time British politicians snubbed what they considered the shabby practice of merchandising and packaging candidates and issues. Joseph Napolitan, who had opened an office in London in 1964, wrote in 1973 that the reluctance to retain professional consultants in British elections is "paranoiac."[41] But he predicted that "some day one of the British political parties is going to crack out of its chauvinistic shell, assemble from a number of countries the best political skills available in the world, and whip the bejesus out of the opposition."[42]

It didn't take long. In 1979, during Margaret Thatcher's first campaign as Conservative leader, British electioneering was "fundamentally altered" when British advertising agency Saatchi & Saatchi was given overall responsibility for political communications. The Labour Party was not far behind, with a highly praised television spot for Neil Kinnock.[43] American packaging techniques, indeed, had arrived, along with American consultants, with Napolitan and media consultant Sally Hunter, behind the scenes. By the 1990s, the British had turned the corner and began regularly hiring American consultants, adopting US strategies and techniques, such as focus groups and "pulse groups" to test commercials and campaign themes. Labour strategists were drawing on the advice of media consultants Bob Shrum and David Doak, pollster Mark Mellman, and the resources of the Democratic National Committee. The Conservatives drew on the advice of Republican pollster Richard Wirthlin.

"We're all going American," lamented one British Conservative; but it was a love-hate relationship.[44] John Rentoul, a BBC producer who made a documentary on this subject, said, "To be seen to have all these pollsters and strategy advisers is regarded somehow as taking away from a politician's integrity and beliefs. And it's even worse if the consultants are Americans."[45]

But senior campaign officials from both the Conservative and Labour parties conceded, off the record, that there was much need for media coaching, sophisticated polling analysis, and strategic positioning of candidates. For example, focus groups, a standard technique in American elections for over a decade, were a novelty to the April 1992 British elections.[46] After television or radio debates, the British public would listen to party spin doctors, who did their best to cast the debates in the most favorable terms for their candidates. The phenomenon was nothing new in Britain, but the term "spin doctor" still had an unpleasant American ring to it.[47]

In an unusual twist, British campaigns and themes crossed the Atlantic and landed in the 1992 American presidential race. The Bush-Quayle campaign shamelessly borrowed media ideas and footage from the Conservative Party and John Major's re-election campaign. Two Major campaign aides were invited to the Bush-Quayle campaign to show how they had propped up their own weak incumbent. As a *Newsweek* reporting team found, Bush attack ads showing Clinton as a big-time tax and spender were borrowed "almost frame for frame" from the Major campaign.[48] Republican operative Mary Matalin wrote that the Bush campaign borrowed "quite copiously" from Conservative Party advertising that emphasized the impact of taxes on individual taxpayers. Instead of the crane operator, salesman, engineer, and personnel director found in the Conservative Party's television spot, the Bush campaign substituted a steamfitter, a scientist, two sales representatives, and a house painter.[49] The message was the same: under the Labour [Democratic] Party, taxes for these individuals would go up by so many pounds [dollars]. This is not the first time that the Republican Party in the United States has borrowed from the Conservative Party of England. Themes from the first Reagan presidential campaign in 1980 were eerily similar to those of Margaret Thatcher a year earlier.

The Clinton campaign also compared notes with British consultants. Labour Party consultant Philip Gould contacted Clinton pollster Stan Greenberg during the 1992 campaign, and stayed several weeks in Little Rock, Arkansas, the Clinton campaign headquarters. Senior Clinton consultants talked strategy with Gould, seeing the campaign similarities in the Republican and Conservative Party tactics and message, and in the responses of the Democrats and Labour.[50] When Prime Minister John Major announced in March 1997 that general elections were to be held on May 1, the upcoming election was already being touted as the "most Americanized" in British history—"longer, more expensive, and more personality-oriented than ever."[51] For the first time in British elections, the Labour and Conservative Parties agreed to hold televised debates between Major and Labour Party leader Tony Blair, further emphasizing a central component of American-style elections, the focus on the individual and less attention to the party. "I think that is almost the final act of confirmation that British politics is adopting all those American features" previously deplored, stated Patrick Seyd of the University of Sheffield.[52]

In 2005, with Prime Minister Tony Blair running for re-election, American consultants were there. As *Washington Post* reporter Dan Balz observed, "American consultants are involved in virtually every aspect of the campaign" for Blair and the Labour Party.[53] Zack Exley, who was John Kerry's 2004 online director, worked to send out massive numbers of e-mails for Labour; Karen Hicks, from the DNC, directed get-out-the-vote activities; Stanley Greenberg, Bob Shrum, Joe Trippi, and Mark Penn all lent their advice and expertise. In the end, however, these consultants assisted but did not supplant the British Labour Party operatives and political advisers of Blair.

American and other consultants were hired for the May 2015 national elections. Jim Messina, Obama's campaign manager in 2012, was hired by the Conservative Party as it prepared for 2015 elections; Australian consultant Lynton Crosby became the party's senior election strategist. David Axelrod, Obama's 2008 and 2012 senior consultant, was hired by Ed Miliband and the Labour Party, and the Labour Party also retained Stanley Greenberg's polling firm. South African Ryan Coetzee was selected as the director of strategy for Nick Clegg and the Liberal Democrat Party. Veteran journalist Dan Balz and his colleagues noted that the winning Conservative Party drew heavily from Obama 2012 campaign, using analytics, social media, and microtargeting in its most competitive districts.[54]

Israel and American Consultants

[Arthur Finkelstein] has risen to the level of myth in Israel. The name Finkelstein is close to becoming an adjective, meaning devious, shrewd, negative.
                                    —Jerusalem-based journalist Sharon Moshavi (1999)[55]

Israelis take political consultants more seriously than any other country in which I have worked.
                                    —Stanley Greenberg (2009)[56]

American political consultants had regularly been involved in Israeli elections since David Garth assisted Prime Minister Menachem Begin in 1981.[57] During those early years, the advice was quite low-keyed and certainly not the centerpiece of the campaigns. This all changed in 1996, when American pollster and general strategist Arthur Finkelstein masterminded the upset victory of Benjamin Netanyahu over Prime Minister Shimon Peres. In earlier campaigns, Peres had used American consultants, but in 1996 he initially decided to do without them. Finkelstein engineered Netanyahu's long-shot campaign and overcame a 25-point deficit with tough, aggressive commercials. One showed the image of a blackened hulk of a burned-out bus, along with Peres shaking hands with Palestinian leader Yasser Arafat. The voice-over, in ominous tones, warned: "A dangerous combination for Israel." Finkelstein used many of the tricks of American politics, particularly framing the campaign as a contest of "us" versus "them." For the outsiders, a coalition of Sephardic Jews, Russian immigrants, ultranationalist West Bank settlers, and ultra-Orthodox Jews, it was a campaign of resentment and division—a campaign against the secular European Jews, the "pork eaters."

Peres, whose leadership was rocked by issues of terrorism, cried foul, but the Netanyahu message was effective. Not only did the television commercials convey the hard bite of American campaign nastiness, but they were also brutally relentless—hammering home, night after night, the simple but effective message that Israel was not secure under Peres. The Peres campaign failed to respond to the negative charges, and could not find its footing. Further, Netanyahu followed Finkelstein's advice and used an American-style debate trick: no matter what question you are asked, be sure to respond with the sure-fire sound bite: "Peres has brought neither peace to Israel nor real security." Netanyahu squeaked through to victory, and overnight Arthur Finkelstein became a celebrity, even a cult figure. "People in focus groups will talk about Finkelstein," said pollster Greenberg. "This is the only country in the world I've been to where they talk about the consultants by name."[58] His status was boosted even further by his attempts to remain unavailable, even invisible. Finkelstein insisted that his 1996 contract with the Likud Party included a provision that forbade any one to disclose his position with the campaign. To the Israeli media, Finkelstein was a modern day Rasputin, who not only engineered Netanyahu's victory, but was a rarely-seen *éminence grise* who whispered advice and policy schemes in the new prime minister's ear.[59]

One of the reasons for the influx of American advisers and American-style electioneering was the "direct election" reform measure passed in 1992. Since the enactment of these reforms, Israeli citizens have continued to vote for a party list of candidates for parliament, but also vote separately for prime minister. Netanyahu versus Peres in 1996 was the first test of this reform system of voting.

Reporter Adam Nagourney described the old way of doing political advertising, before Arthur Finkelstein and American slash-and-burn techniques.[60] Television commercials were permitted only in the final three weeks of a campaign; once the three-week period set in, the political parties would show "unhurried, literate" advertisements, which were generally shown once, with a new issue aired in the political advertising the next evening. It was, in effect, a "rolling, nightly debate" watched eagerly by Israeli voters. Finkelstein changed all that. His ads bore down on hard-hitting themes, and were 15-, perhaps 30-seconds long. One ad produced by Finkelstein for Netanyahu in the 1996 race, just 25-seconds long, depicted the smoky aftermath of the bombing of the No. 18 bus in Jerusalem, one of a series of Palestinian terrorist attacks. While the police sirens wailed in the background, the voice-over intoned: "No security. No peace. No reason to vote for Peres." Americans were used to seeing this kind of scorched-earth ad; after all, Finkelstein was one of the masters of this craft. But Israelis had never seen anything like it.

Ever since 1996, the Labor Party had ridiculed Netanyahu for hiring a high-profile American political consultant, but in 1999, Labor had its own answer: it hired veteran media consultant Robert Shrum, pollster Stanley Greenberg, and strategist James Carville to guide the campaign of Ehud Barak.[61] Here were top-flight American consultants, giving credibility to Barak's efforts. Carville probably received the most attention from the press—he usually does—appearing on the cover of the *New York Times Magazine*, peering over his half-rimmed glasses, holding an Israeli newspaper, scowling.[62] Adam Nagourney observed that the first time Ehud Barak met with his American political advisers, he was "reduced to the role of onlooker at his own press conference by reporters clamoring for a word with the famous and funny friend [Carville] of Bill Clinton.[63] But Clinton's 1999 pollsters and strategists, as well as the president himself, were also helping Barak. Mark Penn and Doug Schoen, professional rivals of Greenberg, were joined by Zev Furst. Schoen wrote that "Furst and I were working behind the scenes, polling continuously, and funneling our own advice and that of President

Bill Clinton."[64] With the help of Shrum, Carville, and Greenberg, Ehud Barak was able to defeat Netanyahu and Finkelstein. William Schneider, a longtime student of American politics, asked why Netanyahu lost. The answer was that "Netanyahu lost because voters rejected his U.S.-inspired politics of division." Israeli voters wanted unity; "One Israel," was the Labor Party's and Barak's slogan. Netanyahu and Finkelstein chose another, divisive path. For years after this 1999 election, Finkelstein, Greenberg, Penn, and other American consultants remained active in helping Israeli candidates and causes. In 2009, veteran Democratic media consultant Bill Knapp assisted Netanyahu, and in 2015, Jeremy Bird, who was national field director for the 2012 Obama campaign, headed a team of five consultants, working to keep Netanyahu from winning another term as prime minister. Veteran Democratic pollster Mark Mellman was credited with greatly assisting the Yesh Atid party in the January 2013 Knesset elections, and with assisting its leader, Yair Lapid.[65]

Making Russia Safe for Democracy

> The plum of American consulting contracts.
> —Political scientist Gerald Sussman on the 1996 Russian election[66]

The first American consultant to work in the Russian Federation was veteran Ralph Murphine, who helped in the successful 1991 All-Union Treaty Referendum, which advanced reforms put forward by Mikhail Gorbachev. That year, Boris Yeltsin was chosen as the president of the Russian Federation. Five years later, when he ran for re-election, Yeltsin faced stiff competition from Communist Party leader Gennadi A. Zyuganov. What better time to call in Americans for help? Two former aides to California governor Pete Wilson, George Gorton and Joseph Shumate, were contacted by a Russia émigré living in California. They, along with public relations specialist Steven Moore and Dick Dresner, an adviser for Wilson's failed presidential bid, were hired by Yeltsin's campaign several months before the July 1996 election. None of the American consultants spoke Russian, and none had experience working in Russia.[67] Their task was a daunting one: when hired, Yeltsin's approval rating was just 6 percent, and he was mired in fourth or fifth place in the crowded election field. During the election, their work was conducted in utmost secrecy, fearing the predictable negative response that Yeltsin was "serving his masters in the West."[68] But once the final round of the elections was over, the American role leaped to the front page. Featured as the cover story of *Time* magazine[69] and on ABC's *Nightline*, the American consultants boasted of their consulting acumen and significant contributions to the election of Yeltsin. Russian campaign aides insist that the Americans, who worked with Yeltsin's daughter, made only marginal contributions.

As *New York Times* reporter Alessandra Stanley wrote from Moscow, "there is no doubt that the Americans pulled off a masterly public relations coup back home."[70] Consultant Gorton retorted that Stanley was just "quoting the Kremlin line," quoting people "who, a week ago, were vociferously denying our very existence."[71]

Gorton explained in a Washington press conference what the American campaign team found to be the most important factors for Yeltsin's success: (1) convincing Yeltsin to get out of Moscow and run a western-style campaign, (2) developing and staying with an anti-Communist message, and (3) warning voters of the threat of civil unrest and even civil war if the Communists again took over.[72]

The California consulting team used a variety of well-honed American campaign techniques, including polling, focus groups, and dial-meter groups to test campaign commercials and speeches, along with negative advertising. The Americans tried to burnish Yeltsin's image, replacing a poster of a scowling Yeltsin with a smiling version.[73] One of the American consultants' achievements was finally convincing Yeltsin to appear in his own commercials. Consultant Dick Dresner had been a business partner with President Clinton's senior consultant Dick Morris. Nearly every other week during March, April, and May, and each week in June, Dresner passed on Russian polling results to Morris, who then passed them on to Clinton. Clinton was on his way to Russia, and, according to Morris, "he wanted to campaign, American-style, with Yeltsin," but Yeltsin backed away at the last minute.[74] The American consultants wanted Clinton to call Yeltsin and convince him to appear in his own television ads. The consultants were coy about whether Clinton actually made the call, but days later, Yeltsin finally appeared on television.[75] For their efforts, the American consultants were reportedly paid $250,000, plus expenses and production costs. George Gorton remarked that, for the first time since the 1972 Nixon race, he worked on a campaign with "essentially an unlimited budget."[76]

Like the Philippine election twenty-seven years earlier, the money paid to American consultants and their influence on the election told just a portion of the story. The Yeltsin campaign and its financial backers reportedly spent hundreds of thousands of dollars to bribe and influence Russian journalists to report favorably on Yeltsin and to denounce the Communist Party.[77] The official spending limit was a little over $3 million, yet there was a "massive injection" of cash, with estimates as high as $500 million. There was also a last-minute secret alliance with presidential candidate and former general Alexander Lebed, who had finished third during the first round of voting; Lebed later became Yeltsin's chief of national security. *Washington Post* reporters Lee Hockstader and David Hoffman surmised that Yeltsin also benefitted from opponents "so technically inept, so mired in ideological confusion and burdened with political pariahs that they became their own worst enemy."[78] The Yeltsin campaign was later popularized in a 2003 American comedy, *Spinning Boris*, starring Jeff Goldblum, Anthony LaPaglia, and Liev Schreiber.[79] Dresner was honored by the American Association of Political Consultants in 1996 as the "International Consultant of the Year."

Challenges of Consulting Abroad

In emerging democracies, where political institutions are often fragile and free elections are still something of a novelty, homegrown political consultants, if they can be found, are often inexperienced in handling the complete range of modern campaign techniques. When American consultants are brought in, they are usually asked to go far beyond the range of their specialty. For example, an American media consultant may become a campaign manager, a pollster may become an overnight expert on media strategy, or an opposition researcher may become a general strategist. Further, the American consultant may have to do far more improvising, work with vastly fewer campaign resources, and be forced to draw upon tactics and strategies honed in American elections that don't have much bearing on the campaign at hand. The consultant may be faced with state-imposed election laws that do not permit thirty-second television spots or do not permit candidates to purchase television ads at all, a pollster may find it impossible to conduct accurate telephone surveys because telephone service is so spotty and unreliable, or it may be difficult to conduct accurate door-to-door surveys when the citizenry still feels the cold chill of state censorship and repression.

In general, Western Europe has been a difficult market to crack for many American consultants. French and German parties and candidates, in particular, have been reluctant to bring in American consultants. If American campaign consultants were known to work in either of these countries, they would almost immediately become an election issue, another example of Yankee imperialism trying to interfere with a country's most cherished exercise, the choosing of its own leaders through the democratic process. But American consultant Phil Noble, who has a long history of working in Western Europe, has seen a "sea change" in attitudes toward the use of American techniques in Europe since 1990. While the door is still not fully open to American consultants, the techniques and strategies they have honed are increasingly being borrowed, copied, and mimicked throughout Western Europe.[80]

American consultants have found it almost impossible to break into the seemingly lucrative Japanese election market, and they have been slow to penetrate into Korea, Taiwan, or Southeast Asian countries, primarily for cultural and political reasons. However, there is some movement in the larger Southeast Asian market. Chang-Hwan Kim of Alliance Research Consultants, based in Seoul, sees Southeast Asia as "the largest market for American consultants in two or three years' time." Elections are becoming more competitive in Southeast Asia, and the demand for the whole range of campaign services has increased.[81] Eventually, American political consultants will move into this market, but they will still have a difficult time of it.[82]

Keeping quiet on American participation. Sometimes American involvement in elections is so sensitive that candidates and parties demand strict secrecy. In the 1974 French presidential election, Valery Giscard d'Estaing won by the narrowest of margins, eight-tenths of one percent. The election was an intense two-week contest, with American consultant Joe Napolitan playing a significant role in developing message and strategy. But his role was kept secret, with only six people in France knowing of his activities, and no stories breaking in the press. "I suspect had the [opposition] Socialists known about it," Napolitan observed, "it could have changed the outcome of the election." Napolitan later worked for Giscard d'Estaing's party for twenty-two months.[83]

Media consultant Robert Squier kept his work for Spanish prime minister Adolfo Suárez secret during the late 1970s. Spain had just broken away from forty years of dictatorship under the fist of Generalissimo Franco, and probably the last thing the Spanish public wanted to hear was that foreigners, particularly Americans, were now interfering with their first democratic elections. Squier was treated like a secret agent—he was picked up at the airport and whisked away to a hotel by campaign operatives. Later, he was picked up at the hotel, dropped off at a sealed, windowless room somewhere, given the daily newspaper clips, and told to make campaign and media recommendations; then he was dropped back at the hotel. There was no direct interaction with the campaign, totally unlike anything in an American election.[84]

Many other consultants are secretive about their participation, especially during the election season. Working for international clients is "one of the best kept secrets" in the political consulting business, stated consultant Robert Beckel in 1989. Confidentiality clauses in consulting contracts often keep consultants from identifying themselves as advisers for foreign parties or individuals.[85]

From 1991 through 1995, British Columbia premier Mike Harcourt retained Washington-based consultant Karl Struble for communications and political assistance. The $210,000 retainer was funneled through a British Columbia advertising firm, NOW Communications, which was linked with Harcourt's New Democratic Party. When this arrangement was revealed in early 1995, it caused a fury, with accusations that taxpayer money was secretly going to an American advisor. Adding to the complaints was the revelation that some 1,800 telephone calls and faxes were sent from the premier's advisers to their Washington consultants.[86] "It's incredible," pronounced Reform Party leader Jack Weisgerber, "major policy speeches have been crafted in the United States."[87] The British Columbia conflict-of-interest minister cleared the premier of wrongdoing, but concluded this arrangement was meant to disguise the use of a "foreign spin doctor." Liberal leader Gordon Campbell was not so charitable: "This was a secret, sweetheart deal put together by the premier's office which they tried to hide from the people of British Columbia."[88]

Understanding the nuances of language and communication. American campaigns are peppered with words and phrases that sometimes catch even English-speaking cousins off-guard. "What's a 'double whammy?'" a reporter asked when Britain's Conservative Party unveiled a new election poster bearing the legend "Labour's Double Whammy." The poster, designed by American consultants, displayed a boxer sporting red gloves, one glove labeled "more taxes" and the other labeled "higher prices?" The Conservative Party spokesman hesitated, looked at a sheaf of papers, then said: "it's an American slang, meaning something like a 'crippling curse.'"[89] "Double whammy" made no sense to the British press and voters, nor, at the time, did the phrase "spin doctor," one of the newer political phrases spawned in America, which was introduced to British, Canadian, and

Australian campaigns in the early 1990s. Former IAPC president Rick Ridder, an American consultant based in Denver, Colorado, wryly noted, "Never assume that your English is their English, even in an English-speaking country." Ridder, while working for the UK's Liberal Democrats, wrote a pamphlet about door-to-door canvassing. To his surprise, the final printed version was entitled "A Guide to Knocking Up." It made sense to the British, but had a much different meaning for Americans.[90]

When the country's language is not English, the translation to a smooth and convincing political message can be even more difficult. In the Caribbean island of Aruba, which became an independent nation in 1986, one of the biggest challenges for American consultants was the language, Papiamento, a mixture of Spanish, Portuguese, Dutch, English, French, Creole, and some African dialects.[91] Whatever the language difficulty, the US consultants managed to capture what they hoped to be the winning, universal appeal. In one of their jingles, "Don't worry, *ban sigui* [let's continue]," the strategy for the American Democratic advisers for the Aruban Peoples Party (Arubaanse Volkspartij, or AVP), Harrison Hickman and Rob Engel, was a "direct steal" from the Reagan-Bush feel-good campaigns of "Morning in America" and "don't worry, be happy." But it didn't work. The opposing People's Electoral Movement (the MEP Party) ridiculed the feel-good commercial and defeated the AVP.[92]

California consultants Sal Russo and Tony Marsh also found out how difficult it was to work in an unfamiliar language. Russo and Marsh were tapped by Ukrainian independence movement leaders to develop television commercials for their campaign. The call came unexpectedly through another Republican operative who had gone to Ukraine at the request of the National Endowment for Democracy. Russo and Marsh had never been to Ukraine or Russia. Their sound and video equipment would not work right, and they were under pressure to produce commercials quickly. Eventually, they produced five Ukrainian television commercials, mostly man-on-the-street interviews, but found the most difficult thing was in editing film in Ukrainian. "We couldn't pick up the nuances," Russo said.[93]

Avoiding a cultural tin ear. At times, American strategies or symbols just do not work in another country. Having an American candidate roll up his sleeves is a trite but familiar symbol: I'll get down to business and get things done for the people. But that straightforward message did not translate well in the 1978 Venezuelan presidential elections. David Garth made a television spot for Luis Herrera Campins, showing him rolling up his sleeves. In Venezuela, however, rolling up one's sleeves means "going out behind the bar and slugging someone." Some local officials were offended, but Garth's candidate nonetheless won the election.[94]

In the 1990 Peruvian presidential election, the New York-based media consulting firm Sawyer/Miller, which had considerable international experience, proved inept in working for Mario Vargas Llosa, one of Latin America's most important authors and literary scion of Peru's upper class. Running against Alberto Fujimoro, Vargas Llosa and his American consultants "failed to understand the intensity" of anger that divided the privileged, affluent, and light-skinned European stock (embodied by Vargas Llosa) and the great majority of poor Peruvians, who were uneducated, alienated, and of dark-skinned Indian heritage.[95] American consultants completely misunderstood the dynamics of the race, misread the rapid rise in popularity of their obscure opponent, failed to connect their candidate with the aspirations of the voters, produced offensive and inappropriate television commercials, charged inordinate consulting fees, and poisoned the political consulting market in that country. American consultant Ralph Murphine, who speaks Spanish fluently, has an apartment in Quito, Ecuador, and has spent much of his long career in Latin America, stated that Sawyer/Miller had violated Peruvian cultural norms and had ruined the Peruvian political market for American consultants. American consultants, Murphine asserts, cannot pick up the nuances of another culture in a month or even a year, no matter how hard they may try.[96] The debacle in Peru, wrote journalist James Harding, "made a laughingstock of Sawyer Miller."[97]

In 2014, American consultant Sam Patten wanted his client, Iraq's deputy prime minister Saleh al-Mutlaq to take a swipe at his opponent, former prime minister Ayad Allawi, for not participating in a televised debate in the Iraq parliamentary election. Bill Clinton's 1992 campaign had a staffer dressed in a chicken outfit, called "Chicken George." George Bush wouldn't debate Clinton, so he was followed around by Chicken George, just to get his goat. Why not try the same thing in Iraq? Patten suggested calling the local television stations, rounding up some chickens, and letting them loose in front of Allawi's political headquarters. But it made no sense: a chicken in Iraqi culture doesn't denote cowardice; that's left to female sheep. Well, round up the sheep, said Patten. But al-Mutlaq wasn't willing to go negative: stick with the issues, he told his consultant.[98]

Working against state-controlled media. One of the great difficulties faced by American consultants is working for candidates in countries with state-controlled television, radio, and newspapers. They also often work in a political atmosphere where all officials are suspect by the voting population.

When Corazon Aquino challenged Ferdinand Marcos in 1986, the Marcos-controlled media would not broadcast Aquino commercials or give her campaign favorable press coverage. The presidential election had wide international interest, particularly in the United States. The famed golf course architect Robert Trent Jones, a longtime family friend of Corazon and Benigno Aquino, recommended that American media consultant David Sawyer be brought into the campaign. Marcos was represented this time by Black, Manafort, Stone & Kelly. Because the Aquino campaign was shut out of media outlets in the Philippines, it was critical to win the support of American opinion leaders and the public. Both the Marcos and Aquino campaigns focused their efforts on US television network news, political talk shows, and guest shots on *Nightline*.[99] Walter Shapiro noted the "bizarre situation" that arose, with the Reagan administration overtly supporting the Aquino candidacy, while Black, Manafort, which had worked for Reagan in the past, was representing Marcos.[100]

During the 1990s, pollsters in the United States would not think of going door-to-door to conduct interviews. Such a technique was prohibitively expensive, time-consuming, and unnecessary, given the high percentage of households that own telephones. In many impoverished countries, however, it was often necessary to conduct door-to-door interviews because of the lack of telephones. However, door-to-door interviews also had their drawbacks, because potential respondents could feel threatened by the presence of strangers asking serious questions about an upcoming election. This was particularly evident in the Ortega-Chamorro 1990 presidential race in Nicaragua. Pollsters underestimated the support of challenger Violeta Chamorro, particularly among women, who were reluctant to state their support for her, especially when interviewed by men and if no one else was at home. Most Nicaraguan women stated that they supported Daniel Ortega, but in fact voted for Chamorro. American political consultants on both sides underestimated the impact that repression and cultural constraints had on the Nicaraguan vote.[101]

In Hungary in 1989, a coalition of reformers had forced a referendum after collecting the signatures of 220,000 citizens. In any American race, a newly developed list of 220,000 highly motivated reformists would be extremely valuable for direct mail, get-out-the-vote, voter contract, and fund-raising purposes. But as American consultant William R. Sweeney Jr. discovered, in Hungary this list was viewed with suspicion and seen as a potential weapon in the hands of a government with a long history of repression. After the election, the reformers burned the list in public to assure signers that their courage in signing the petition would not make them targets of government reprisal.[102]

In 2004, Aristotle International, the Washington, DC–based public affairs technology firm, played a key, behind-the-scenes role in Ukraine, during the so-called Orange Revolution, working for the pro-reform Our Ukraine (Nasha Ukraina) movement and its candidate Viktor Yushchenko. Neither Yushchenko nor his opponent, Viktor Yanukovych, who was backed by outgoing Ukrainian president Leonid Kuchma, reached the 50 percent level required during the first round of elections in October. The run-off election in November 2004 saw widespread corruption, absentee ballot stuffing, election fraud, and voter intimidation. Aristotle International's responsibility was to get reports out to the rest of the world, highlighting the voter fraud and intimidation, so that the international community would reject the results of the run-off. The firm set up a war room in Kiev (backed up by technical support from its Washington headquarters), hired 235 temporary poll watchers, tracked "ghost voters," hired a camera crew to document voter intimidation and ballot destruction, and launched an Internet site for fundraising for Our Ukraine. Through the efforts of Aristotle International and other pro-democracy organizations in exposing the fraudulent actions, and international pressure from the European Union and the United States, the Ukrainian Central Election Commission finally, in late December, declared Yuschenko the winner of the run-off election, together with Yulia Tymoshenko, who was chosen as prime minister.

Six years later, American consultants were in full force during the 2010 Ukrainian presidential election. Mark Penn, Hillary Clinton's chief strategist in 2008, aided Yuschenko in his re-election bid, Paul Manafort assisted chief opposition leader Viktor Yanukovych, and AKPD, David Axelrod's former firm, assisted Prime Minister Yulia Tymoshenko. Yanukovych easily won the election, and Tymoshenko, whose campaign harshly pointed out the shortcomings of her opponents, was soon thrown into jail on dubious grounds.[103] She was finally released in early 2014, and Yanukovych was ousted from power.

The unspoken rules of international consulting. Successful international campaign consulting requires that certain rules be followed. The first rule is getting into an election early. It is extremely important in any campaign, but especially in another country, for an American political consultant to be on the ground early, developing solid relationships between the candidate and advisers and learning the lay of the political landscape. Very often, American consultants will team up with local political consultants or campaign operatives, who know the political players, the issues, and the dynamics of the election.

The second rule is understanding the culture, history, language, and rituals in the country. Several examples above illustrate the difficulties that American consultants can run up against in another country. American campaign consultants need to have a thorough and sensitive understanding of the ethnic, religious, and political divisions; the history and dynamics of the elections; and a gifted ear for listening to the demands and aspirations of voters. Bill Hamilton observed that "American consultants, with all their experience, know too much about their own craft, and just don't know enough about the countries they are working in."[104]

Finally, the political consultant needs to play a subordinate role. Any campaign can get into serious trouble when the focus is on the consultants and not on the candidate, party, or message. This is much more pronounced when the American political consultant becomes a visible symbol of cultural imperialism, suggesting foreign, especially American, intervention into the affairs and choices of the people. In the earlier days in Venezuela and other Latin American countries, American consultants were getting more attention that the candidates they represented.

A campaign that violated all three of these principles was the Greek presidential race in 1993 between Prime Minister Constantine Mitsotakis and his challenger, the former prime minister Andreas Papandreou. In an election described as "short and nasty," American consultant James Carville became the target of death threats. Journalist Leonard Doyle reported that both sides of the presidential contest used American consultants to conduct television-based advertising, "combining vicious character assassination and innuendo to damage their opponents."[105] Coming into Greece only weeks before the election, Carville met with his client Mitsotakis, then seventy-five, at the latter's summer home outside of Athens and gave this cool assessment: "The Greek people don't understand all you've got to say and there's no time to explain it to them. You've got to talk about how Papandreou bankrupted the system." With Papandreou in ill health and rumored to be capable of working only two hours a day, Carville reportedly pushed the Mitsotakis camp to make his opponent's health a key issue.[106] Carville aide David Humphreville, who just three weeks earlier had resigned a position on Wall Street, told reporters, "We are going to tell the voters these are dangerous and unstable times: can you trust a guy like Papandreou?"[107]

The centerpiece of the Mitsotakis media campaign was a vintage Carville-inspired television commercial showing a frail and stooped Andreas Papandreou, seventy-four, kissing Libya's Colonel Muammar Gaddafi and Iraq's Saddam Hussein, followed by images of Mitsotakis greeting British prime minister John Major, German chancellor Helmut Kohl, and French president François Mitterrand. The voice-over intoned: "Which Greece do you want?"[108]

The opposition was horrified by the tactics of the "American spin doctor," and Carville became an issue in the campaign. One of the Greek newspapers printed a photograph of Carville's campaign headquarters with the caption, "This is where the Americans do their dirty tricks." Angry letters and faxes poured in, including a death threat from a mysterious group called the Cobras. Carville was forbidden to stroll onto his third-floor balcony and needed armed guards to stand sentry at campaign headquarters.[109]

Papandreou scored a convincing victory over incumbent Mitsotakis. The Mitsotakis campaign was criticized for failing to reassure Greek voters on his handling of difficult economic and foreign policy issues, and for "badly mishandling" the question of Macedonia and the Balkan threat. For the ailing Papandreou, who survived imprisonment, political scandal, and a widely publicized liaison with a much younger woman, this was a dramatic comeback victory.[110]

Negative campaigning and attack ads. Slash-and-burn negative advertising, a staple of some American campaigns, rarely works in other cultures and languages, as seen in Mexico (2000), Greece (1993), and several Israel elections. Another example where American tactics backfired is Australia in 1992. There was a flurry of protest when American consultants launched a Willie Horton–inspired campaign commercial that attacked the Labor Party. Australian voters had been subjected to the local version of hardball politics for years, but the Willie Horton approach carried negative advertising well beyond the sense of campaign propriety. The advertisements were prepared by American consultants Larry Cirignano and Bruce Blakeman for the Liberal Party in Queensland. The television ads disgusted and appalled viewers and led to a huge drop in support for the Liberals. What viewers saw was a smashed portrait of an attractive young white woman, followed by a shot of Bevan Meninga, an aboriginal man who had killed her. The woman's parents were shown grieving their loss, and finally a voice-over warned that the responsibility for her death lay with the ruling Labor Party.[111] Meninga, brother of a star rugby player, had left prison on an early-release program before committing this crime.

As one Labor official said, it was a "direct rip-off from the Willie Horton episode."[112] In an attempt to oust the Labor Party and Prime Minister Paul Keating, the Liberal Party also prepared pamphlets and full-page newspaper ads that charged the Queensland Labor government with having "blood on its hands" for murders committed by Meninga. Labor leaders returned the fire, accusing the Liberal Party of bringing "sleazy, American-style" campaigning to Australia.[113]

Attack ads are staples of American elections. Voters and editorialists are disgusted by them, but media consultants continue using them as effective tools in the campaign arsenal. What Americans may take for granted, however, viewers in other nations may find appalling. When such tactics are employed—including the hard-hitting ads in the Greek presidential election or the Willie Horton–inspired ads in Australia—the American consultants responsible for the attack ads demonstrate not only their lack of understanding of cultural sensitivities, but also their inability to serve their clients effectively.

Institutional Assistance

The US government has a long and checkered history of involvement in the elections of other countries. The CIA and other federal agencies manipulated elections in Italy right after World War II, propped up dictators like Mobutu Sese Seko in Zaire, and intervened in elections in Panama, Guatemala, and other Latin American countries. Sometimes the interference has led to protest and condemnation, such as the Iran-Contra episode in the mid-1980s; at other times, the manipulation goes unseen and unheard by the mass public. As democracy and democratic institutions become more prevalent throughout the world, US government attention has shifted focus from clandestine intervention to more open, effective forms of democracy-building.

On June 8, 1982, Ronald Reagan delivered one of his most important addresses, remembered in history as the Westminster Speech, before the British parliament. Reagan predicted that the "march of freedom and democracy" would leave Marxism-Leninism "on the ash heap of history as it has left other tyrannies which stifle the freedom and muzzle the self-expression of the people."[114] Reagan's speech was the impetus for Congress in 1983 to create the National Endowment for Democracy (NED), together with the National Democratic Institute (NDI), which is loosely affiliated with the national Democratic Party; the International Republican Institute (IRI), affiliated with the national Republican Party; and the Center for International Private Enterprise, affiliated with the US Chamber of Commerce. Earlier, organized labor's Free Trade Union Institute was created, conducting business abroad with labor union funds and grants from the US Agency for International Development (USAID).[115] A central purpose of these taxpayer-funded and independent organizations is to strengthen the election processes in newly democratic countries. In addition, a private, nonprofit organization, the International Foundation for Electoral Systems (IFES), has provided assistance in 135 countries, helping them to develop credible election systems and foster access to the ballot for women and ethnic minorities. IFES, headquartered in Washington, DC, was cofounded in 1987 by political consultants F. Clifton White and Joe Napolitan. Former consultant William Sweeney became the president of IFES in 2009.

What the CIA had done covertly for decades, the National Endowment for Democracy could now do in the open, supporting democracy and democratic movements throughout the world. The NED has worked through specific projects, such as training sessions for legislators and staffs, civic education associations, monitoring of elections, and creating an informal network of organizations promoting democracy.[116] The NED has financed unions in France, Paraguay, the Philippines, and Panama. It provided funds for Polish emigrés to keep the Solidarity movement alive and underwrote moderate political parties in Portugal, Costa Rica, Bolivia, and Northern Ireland. The NED gave more than $3 million in "technical assistance" for the Nicaraguan elections of 1990 and the candidacy of Violeta Chamorro.[117]

Among the most important achievements of the NDI was its assistance in the 1988 Chilean presidential plebiscite. A fifty-five-member international delegation, organized by the NDI, monitored the October 1988 plebiscite, which gave Chileans the opportunity to vote "yes" or "no" on an additional eight-year presidential term for General Augusto Pinochet, who was selected by the commanders-in-chief of the armed forces. The NDI provided technical assistance, and a special $1 million appropriation from Congress was used to acquire computers for voter registration and independent vote counting, to commission a national public opinion survey, and to produce civic education materials to compete with the government media campaign. The plebiscite, with a turnout of 97 percent of the registered voters, revealed the strong desire of Chileans for free elections. Joshua Muravchik credited the team of international observers and the well-publicized and accurate vote tallies from tempting Pinochet to overthrow the election results. Despite opposition and foot dragging from General Pinochet, ultimately those elections were held. Political consultants Annie Burns, David Collenette, Glenn Cowan, Frank Greer, Peter Hart, Fred Hartwig, and Jack Walsh worked with NDI to provide technical advice in polling, media, computerization and campaign organization.[118]

The International Republican Institute (IRI) first offered assistance to democratic reformers in Grenada in 1984. For its first ten years, the IRI worked to develop political parties and movements, train candidates and managers, and assist in campaign techniques—in short, to "instill the techniques and institutions of multi-party democracies."[119] In 1993, IRI had conducted programs in forty-five nations. However, since then it has had a "dramatic reappraisal and change" in its program focus. In 1994, IRI conducted programs in only thirty-two countries, and in 1995, nearly one-third of the IRI's budget was spent in the Commonwealth of Independent States, with Eastern and Central European countries next in priority of efforts.[120] By 2014, IRI had worked in over 100 countries, with two-thirds of the IRI's programs involving training political parties in campaign and organizational techniques, and in increasing participation of disenfranchised groups, such as women, youth, and indigenous peoples.[121]

Many American political consultants have assisted in NDI, IRI, and NED projects. The consultants engage in this work in much the same way as a lawyer who offers pro bono services. American consultants working under the auspices of these organizations are generally given only expense and travel money and must pledge not to work later in that country as a hired consultant for a party or candidate. One of the most important campaign assistance programs came during the historic all-race South African election of 1994.

The 1994 South Africa Election

> *The images of South Africans going to the polls that day*
> *are burned in my memory.*
>
> —Nelson Mandela (1994)[122]

The emergence of democracy in the last decades of the twentieth century has had a no more poignant or symbolically important event than the April 1994 South African all-race elections. Just four years before, in February 1990, South African President F. W. de Klerk acknowledged that the system of apartheid would end, that Nelson Mandela would be released from prison after twenty-seven years, and that the long-standing ban against the African National Congress (ANC), the South African Communist Party (SACP), the Pan Africanist Congress of Azania (PAC), the Azanian People's Organization (AZAPO) and other anti-apartheid parties and groups would be lifted.[123] With a worldwide television audience as witness, Nelson Mandela was released from prison on February 11, 1990.

What followed were four years of upheaval, uncertainty, and political tumult. Violence was unleashed at an unprecedented scale. Supporters of the ANC and the Inkatha Freedom Party (IFP) fought among themselves and right-wing Afrikaaners called for a separate, whites-only *volkstaat*, or independent state. During the next two years, the government and the ANC held protracted "talks about talks" to iron out long-standing issues of violence, armed struggle, and political freedom. From 1991 to 1993, the multiparty phase of discussions set the stage for an orderly transition of power from the white minority to the majority population.

Formal negotiations were to follow, through a forum called the Convention for a Democratic South Africa (CODESA I), attended by most of the political parties in December 1991, but boycotted by the Conservative Party and Herstigte Nasionale Party (which later called for a whites-only election), and by the AZAPO and PAC. Mangosuthu Buthelezi, the KwaZulu chief minister and leader of the Inkatha Freedom Party, also refused to attend. The conference ended with a Declaration of Intent, which committed the parties to an undivided South Africa and general democratic principles. The second round of negotiations broke down in May over disputes concerning percentages of voters needed to approve the constitution and the timing of its implementation.

The ANC called for nationwide strikes and rolling mass actions to put pressure on the government. Violence flared with the killing of forty-three people in the township of Boipatong and later significant bloodshed at Bisho, the capital of

Ciskei, following an ANC rolling mass action. The 200 wounded and 29 killed at Bisho refocused the attention of the parties to the difficult process of negotiations. When discussions ended in November 1993, South Africa had a new Interim Constitution, stipulating a five-year power-sharing arrangement among the winners of the first nonracial election.

Symbolically, one of the most important moments came just two weeks before the April 1994 election, when Mandela and de Klerk participated in presidential debates on CNN television. Five days later, and just a week before the election, Buthelezi, de Klerk, and Mandela announced that they had reached an agreement concerning the future role of the Zulu king and that the constitutional differences between the three parties would be resubmitted to international mediation after the election. Buthelezi then announced that the Inkatha Freedom Party would participate in the national elections.

A total of twenty-seven political parties registered to participate in the election, nineteen running at the national level and eight running at the provincial level. Two parties, AZAPO and the Conservative Party (CP) decided not to participate.[124]

"Some of the best and brightest in campaign management worldwide helped the ANC to wage a sophisticated campaign, capitalizing on the charisma and unquestionable integrity of Nelson Mandela," wrote the authors of the IRI report on the South African election.[125] The National Democratic Institute and the South Africa–based Center for Development Studies conducted Project Vote, a three-year voter education program that started in 1991. Project Vote was started so that millions of first-time voters could be given rudimentary knowledge of voting and democratic elections. In 1993, NDI, together with the Joint Center for Political and Economic Studies and the International Republican Institute (IRI), undertook the South African Election Support Project, a comprehensive program of electoral assistance and technical support to political organizations. The bipartisan teams gave advice on survey research, voter contact, communications, and organization.[126]

Pat Keefer, of the NDI's South Africa Project, noted that the primary goals were to build confidence among first-time voters, to demystify the process, and to show new voters what a ballot looked like and how to mark an "X." Of the 22.5 million people who were expected to vote, 17 million (including Nelson Mandela) had never voted before.[127] Several American activists, including actor Danny Glover and Spellman College president Johnnetta Cole, raised funds for an ANC voter education effort through the Fund for Democratic Elections in South Africa. The Fund, not missing a beat, set up a toll-free line (1-800-MANDELA), on which Mandela, in a recorded message, asked for financial support for voter education.[128]

About 500 American civil rights activists, labor leaders, academics, students, lawyers, church workers, and consultants descended upon South Africa in the weeks before the election to provide voter education and help mobilize the vote. The Southern Africa Project of the Lawyers' Committee for Civil Rights Under Law, headed by Gay J. McDougall, coordinated the logistics and training for the

American nongovernmental groups. They were to assist the 10,000 official South African election monitors in overseeing the balloting. In addition, the United Nations sent a 1,300-member observer mission.[129]

The computer technology demands for this election were enormously complex. BateTech Software, Inc., the American unit of Workgroup Systems, South Africa's largest distributor of software for personal computers, had the daunting task of installing a network system of more than 1,200 personal computers and training hundreds of people. What normally would have taken six or eight months was accomplished in just two. The computer system was driven by forty high-speed file servers linking forty-one separate sites throughout South Africa into a wide-area network. Kevin Smith of BateTech Software said the biggest challenge was to train the 600 workers to staff the sites. Some were skilled, others had never turned on a computer before. "One lady told the trainer she loved the screen and keyboard but wondered where the foot-pedal (as on a sewing machine) was," Smith said.[130]

About a year before the election, the ANC commissioned an extensive series of focus groups and survey research. The surveys told them that victory was not a foregone conclusion and that, even among black residents, there were large proportions of uncommitted voters as well as "significant inclinations" among Indian and colored citizens to abstain from voting.[131]

Shortly after President Clinton's inaugural in 1993, American political consultants Frank Greer and Stanley Greenberg were selected by Mandela to help turn the ANC into a grassroots political organization. As a professor at Yale University, Greenberg helped create the Southern African Research Program, had worked on poverty and race relations, and worked in South Africa as a Guggenheim Fellow. All that would have been ample background, but Greenberg and Greer were chosen for one simple reason—they were part of the team that put Clinton in the White house.[132] Mandela, according to Greenberg, "knew about and talked about the [Clinton campaign's] War Room," and he wanted the "same kind of intense, controlled direction" for the ANC's campaign.[133] Learning about American-style elections was part of Mandela's "personal transition as a leader."[134] In April of that year, the two advisers were conducting deliberately low-profile training sessions in South Africa, helping the ANC with everything from organizational structure and strategy to polling, media relations, and message development.[135] Initially, Greer and Greenberg's expenses were paid by the NDI, and later they worked at their own expense.[136]

Journalist David Lauter noted that Greenberg's advice to the ANC would have sounded familiar to those who followed Clinton's 1992 campaign. Greenberg has had considerable experience conducting polls in countries emerging from civil strife. He argued that left-of-center parties often do poorly because they assume that voters will side with them because they have fought against the old regime. In such situations, more conservative parties often triumph because they are able to convince voters that they are more attuned to their practical, daily needs.[137]

Frank Greer, who helped elect the first African American governor, L. Douglas Wilder of Virginia, noted that the ANC instinctively wanted to make this first all-race election a referendum on apartheid. However, Greer and Greenberg gave the ANC a message that was similar to the Clinton message of 1992, adopted from the lyrics of a 1970s Fleetwood Mac song: "Don't Stop Thinking about Tomorrow."[138] Greenberg stated that Mandela and the other ANC leaders were remarkably receptive to Clinton campaign ad tips, which included everything from polling to softening Mandela's sometimes stiff bearing at campaign rallies.

The most important strategic decision was for the ANC to position itself not as a liberation movement, but as a Clinton-style agent of change.[139] Greer worked with the basic slogans, refining them to "ANC, A Better Life for All," and "Working Together for Jobs, Peace and Freedom." As tag lines on ANC radio commercials in English, Afrikaans, Hindi, and numerous African dialects, Greer stated that these slogans "translate well into every language."[140] Greenberg noted that if the campaign had centered on apartheid, "the mood of the election would have been very different." Instead, the ANC message was about the future and ended up being a hopeful election with "very, very focused promises."[141]

Despite the advice from the US consultants, tension remained within the ANC about the overall campaign theme. Greenberg noted that the principal slogan was "A Better Life for All," which appeared in all the paid media. But there was strong support within the ANC for "Now is the Time," which was a particularly good theme for campaign rallies. However, "Now is the Time" was somewhat intimidating to voters who were not ANC supporters. A close observer could tell if an advertisement had been produced nationally ("A Better Life for All") or locally ("Now is the Time").[142]

For the election, the NDI and ANC produced colorful posters, emphasizing why people should vote. In a country with multiple languages and a low literacy rate, party symbols and photographs of party leaders became very important. The ANC party voter education materials were driven by each symbol, making for a very colorful and "graphically rich educational package."[143] The ANC produced its own campaign literature, right down to bumper stickers, and almost everything produced bore the likeness of Nelson Mandela.[144]

A three-tiered advertising strategy for television, radio, and print ads was devised by the American advisers and ANC aides. In January, four months before the election, the Mandela campaign launched an advertising campaign, which Frank Greer described as showing "everyday people" talking about "working together for jobs, peace and freedom" under an ANC government. The second phase consisted of the "contrast campaign," showing how the ANC's promise of better jobs, housing, and education so starkly compared with the inequities found under apartheid. Finally, in the last weeks of the campaign, was the "reassurance" stage, which tried to reassure white South Africans that an ANC government would respect their rights.[145]

Greer took the slogans crafted for the ANC and made them "talking points" for candidates throughout the country. Whenever an ANC office-seeker was asked what the party would deliver, the reply was right on message: "jobs, peace and freedom."[146] Polling was particularly difficult in many communities. Many South Africans had no telephone, and door-to-door public opinion surveying drew considerable suspicion by many who remembered the tactics of South Africa's secret police.[147]

After four long days of balloting, and then a longer period of counting the votes, the ANC and Nelson Mandela came in first in the election, with 62.65 percent of the vote, and won 252 of the 400 seats in the National Assembly. The National Party of de Klerk won 20.39 percent of the vote and eighty-two seats, while the Inkatha Freedom Party of Buthelezi won 10.54 percent and forty-three seats.[148] Mandela was installed as president, with ANC's Thabo Mbeki selected as first deputy president and de Klerk chosen as second deputy president.

Reflecting on the election, Stan Greenberg noted, "if you look at the graciousness of the way this [election] ended, if you look at the sense of inclusiveness, you haven't seen many elections like this, not just in Africa, but you haven't seen many in the US."[149] Greenberg's deep admiration was evident as he considered this historic election: "I've seen this process through from full-blown apartheid to its collapse . . . and I've never experienced anything like working with Mandela." Working in this moment of history was for Greenberg the "rarest of privileges."[150]

The Growing Professionalization of International Consulting Firms

In many ways, American consultants bring much-needed skills and experience to elections abroad. But there is no American monopoly on talent and ability. In Latin America, many local firms have developed talented, imaginative staffs who are now on equal footing with anything done in American campaigns. Leading political consultants include pollsters Jaime Durán Barba (Ecuador), Felipe Noguera (Argentina), Antonio Lavareda (Brazil), and Luis Stuhlman (Argentina), and general campaign consultants João Santana (Brazil), Mercedes Elena Bello (Venezuela), Mauricio Jaitt (Argentina), Mario Elgarresta (Ecuador, working from Florida), and Roberto Izurieta (based in Washington, DC).

In Europe, there are many outstanding political consultants, some of whom work for their political parties or political institutions: Bo Krogvig and Sten Olsson (Sweden), Harry Walter and Volker Riegger (Germany), Michel Bongrand (France), Sepp Hartinger (Austria), Mehmet Ural (Turkey), Phillip Gould and Peter Mandelson (Great Britain), and José Luis Sanchis (Spain). Canadians Greg Lyle and Gordon Robson in Vancouver; Australians Malcolm McGregor, Lynton Crosby, Ian Kortlang, and John Utting, and South African Ryan Coetzee were also prominent consultants.

One indication of the growth and maturity of the political consulting profession is the effort in Latin America to develop a professional association. In 1995, a number of Latin American political consultants formed such an organization, with Felipe Noguera (Argentina) and Jaime Durán Barba (Ecuador) as its founders. Some of the best Latin American consultants are using their skills throughout the Spanish-speaking countries, sometimes to compete against and sometimes to work alongside American consultants. In Europe, there is a growth in political consultancy, as evident by the creation in 1996 of the European Association of Political Consultants (EAPC).

The prospects for American international political consulting seem to be bright, and American consultants feel there is no end in sight for ambitious American firms, particularly if they team up with talented local consultants. Seminars and workshops operated by the International Association of Political Consultants (IAPC), the American Association of Political Consultants (AAPC), and other entities are increasingly making the best of the political techniques known to consultants and parties throughout the world.

American-style campaigning and election techniques are being employed, copied, and replicated throughout the world. A small band of American political consultants, no more than perhaps several hundred, are joining forces with a few veteran European and Latin American political consultants. Together with a new generation of homegrown political consultants, they are shaping the way campaigns are planned and conducted, and how voters are presented with issues and choices.[151] For better or worse, people meters plumb the preferences and fears of voters in England, Willie Horton wears different clothes and appears in Australia, and Bill Clinton's "War Room" travels to South Africa. David Butler and Austin Ranney observe that "in the final analysis, those who deplore the changes in electioneering in established democracies should take note of the eagerness of the rest of the world to emulate their practices.... Electioneering, warts and all, is an integral part of the democratic electoral process."[152]

CHAPTER 19

Consultants and Presidential Campaigns, 2008 and 2012

The '08 Campaign: Sea Change for Politics as We Know It.
—Front-page headline, *New York Times* (November 4, 2008)

By a number of important measures—economy, deficit and debt,
health care—Obama should have been a one-term president. . . . Instead,
Obama won because he not only made the election a choice between two
candidates, but positioned himself as the candidate who cared about average
voters and the middle class.
—Republican consultant Thomas N. Edmonds (2013)

ALL PRESIDENTIAL CAMPAIGNS go through rough patches, either of their own making or caused by the aggressiveness of their opponents or outside circumstances. The 2008 contest was no exception. The Hillary Clinton campaign was fraught with internal bickering, personality clashes, and strategic miscues. John McCain rode a rollercoaster of political fortune, starting as the Republican Party's putative front-runner, to being written off months before the first primaries, to finally emerging as the nominee. While Sarah Palin ignited the Republican faithful and flummoxed her detractors, McCain was faced with a distinctly uphill battle, fighting off the legacy of an unpopular incumbent, a rapidly deteriorating economy, and a majority of voters clamoring for change. By contrast, the Obama 2008 campaign, while it also encountered some rough patches, was one of the smoothest, best-run efforts in modern American history. Further, it was strategically savvy and groundbreaking in its use of technology and online communications.

In 2012, a weakened and vulnerable Obama faced re-election under trying economic and political circumstances. In 2010, Republicans, fueled by the Tea Party movement, came roaring back, reclaiming the House of Representatives, and Obama was on the defensive trying to defend unpopular policies, particularly the Affordable Care Act (Obamacare). Yet Obama's campaign deftly outmaneuvered and outhustled the Romney campaign and the independent organizations bent on defeating him. Romney raised and spent more money than Obama, but his campaign was also two steps behind in using technology and online communication, and essentially waged the last presidential campaign of the twentieth century.

The 2008 Presidential Election: John McCain v. Barack Obama

[And to] my campaign manager, David Plouffe, the unsung hero of this campaign, who built the best political campaign, I think, in the history of the United States of America.

—Barack Obama, election night (2008)[1]

The 2008 presidential election was a media extravaganza unparalleled in American history.

—Diana Owen (2010)[2]

The 2008 election was the first truly wide-open contest since 1952, with no incumbent running for re-election and no vice president attempting to reach the Oval Office. This meant there were plenty of hopefuls, in both major parties: twenty in all, with nine Democrats and eleven Republicans formally declared.[3] There were a number of familiar faces—Arizona senator John McCain, seeking the presidency for a second time; New York senator and former first lady Hillary Clinton; and former New York mayor Rudolph Giuliani. As usual, there were candidates who registered little national recognition: former Iowa governor Tom Vilsack, congressmen Tom Tancredo and Dennis Kucinich and others. Former US senator Fred Thompson and former Massachusetts governor Mitt Romney were better known, but still were hampered by their own political liabilities and shortcomings. First-term senator Barack Obama of Illinois, who made a splash at the 2004 Democratic nominating convention, was little known to the wider public. Even more unknown was Alaska governor Sarah H. Palin, who during the final twelve weeks of the campaign became the object of both admiration and ridicule.

The Democratic Primaries

I'm in, and I'm in to win.

—Hillary Rodham Clinton (2007)[4]

We all had enormous respect for the Clinton political machine and assumed they were three steps ahead of us.

—David Plouffe (2007)[5]

Hillary Clinton created a campaign in which authority always seemed to rest with someone else.

—Dan Balz and Haynes Johnson (2009)[6]

Six of the nine Democrats seeking the nomination were sitting or former members of the US Senate (Joseph Biden, Hillary Clinton, Christopher Dodd, John Edwards, Mike Gravel, and Barack Obama), two had been governors (Bill Richardson and Tom Vilsack), while Dennis Kucinich was a member of Congress. Biden, who also tried in 1988, informally announced in March 2006. Tom Vilsack was first to formally announce, on November 30, 2006, and he was the first to withdraw, less than three months later (and nearly a year before the first Iowa caucus), citing lack of funds.

Richardson gained little traction. His achievement-filled résumé was compelling, but it wasn't enough. To underscore Richardson's accomplishments, media consultant Mark Putnam crafted a humorous thirty-second commercial, with Richardson gamely playing along. Richardson is at a job interview, sitting uncomfortably in a chair. On the other side of the desk sits a job counselor, grilling out-of-work Richardson.

"Job Interview"

> *HR guy* (interviewing Richardson): OK, fourteen years in Congress. UN Ambassador. Secretary of Energy. Governor of New Mexico. Negotiated with dictators in Iraq, North Korea, Cuba, Zaire, Nigeria, Yugoslavia, and Kenya. Got a ceasefire in Darfur. Nominated for the Nobel Peace Prize four times.
> So [*HR guy chomps at a sandwich*], what makes you think you can be President?[7]

On December 27, 2006, John Edwards, Kerry's running mate in 2004, announced his candidacy through a web video, "Tomorrow Begins Today." With the wind blowing through his hair, and the sleeves rolled up on his khaki-colored work shirt, Edwards was surrounded by children from one of the Hurricane Katrina–hit wards in New Orleans. Looking at the camera, Edwards said:

> I'm John Edwards, and I'm in the upper ninth ward of New Orleans, where we've been working this afternoon.... Tomorrow morning from this place, I will announce that I am a candidate for president of the United States ... I will ask millions of Americans to join me in taking action and responsibility ... I wanted you to hear it first what it is I plan to do.[8]

The web video didn't make much of a splash, but it was picked up by the network news stations. It was meant to look authentic, a cinéma vérité production of Edwards hard at work, but in the end, it simply looked contrived. (A 2006 YouTube segment, showing Edwards primping and combing his hair for nearly two minutes before a television appearance, set to the song "I Feel Pretty" from *West Side Story*, drew more than ten times the viewers.)[9]

The Edwards campaign senior strategist was veteran Joe Trippi, who had managed Howard Dean's 2004 primary campaign. Harrison Hickman, a longtime adviser to Edwards and veteran of the 2000 Gore primaries, conducted the polling and assisted in the strategy. The campaign, while spending a considerable amount of money, was never able to gather momentum, and Edwards dropped out after the Florida primary. Edwards would soon be engulfed in his own personal sex scandal with videographer Rielle Hunter while his wife Elizabeth was battling terminal cancer.

Well before the primaries began, New York senator Hillary Clinton was everyone's front-runner. She had near 100 percent name recognition and was considered by political pros, Washington insiders, and the public at large as the probable candidate. Further, she had amassed considerable financial resources and her husband continued to be very popular with the Democratic Party faithful.[10] But she also entered the race with very high negatives, in the mid-40s, far higher than any other probable candidate.[11] There was speculation that she would run for the presidency in 2004, and Mark Penn, her pollster during her 2000 Senate run, had been asking survey questions about a possible Clinton candidacy in 2003. At the time, Penn was working for Senator Joe Lieberman and his campaign for the 2004 Democratic nomination; nonetheless, Clinton dispatched him to do "a hush-hush" poll of voters in Iowa.[12] In the end, Clinton was determined to finish out her Senate term and run successfully for a second in 2006.

On January 20, 2007, exactly two years before the inauguration of the next president, Clinton announced over a webcast that she was "in it to win it." In her web video, Clinton sat in a living room, bathed in soft, flattering light. She faced the camera directly and said she wasn't just starting her campaign:

> I'm beginning a conversation. With you. With America. Because we all need to be part of the discussion if we're all going to be part of the solution. And all of us have to be part of the solution. . . . So let's talk. Let's chat. Let's start a dialogue about your ideas and mine.[13]

David Plouffe later wrote that the Obama campaign knew what "I'm in it to win it" meant: Clinton "presented herself as the inevitable nominee." She would win, and why would donors, activists, or potential delegates waste their time with anyone else? Plouffe continued: "We thought it was a terrible misreading of the electorate—inevitability doesn't speak to a hunger for change—and they certainly misread the electoral terrain of the primary."[14]

A number of seasoned political operatives signed up for the Clinton campaign. Remarkably, however, the campaign manager, Patti Solis Doyle, had no experience working in, to say nothing of running, a campaign of this magnitude. Above all, she was loyal, almost a member of the Clinton family. Solis Doyle was the first person Hillary Clinton hired in 1992, had been manager of her political action committee, HillPAC, and helped in the 2000 senate race, before being tapped to manage the presidential campaign. "I was so proud of Patti and the exceptional job she did for me," Clinton remarked in her 2003 memoir.[15] The pollster and lead strategist was Mark Penn, who had worked for the Clinton White House during its second term, and had assisted Hillary Clinton in her New York Senate races in 2000 and 2006. Since 2005, Penn had been CEO of the public relations firm Burson-Marsteller, and his campaign polling firm, Penn

Schoen Berland (PSB), was on retainer to the Clinton campaign. Reporter Anne E. Kornbluth described Penn as "famously rumpled and awkward in public," but more importantly, he was everything that Clinton would want in a senior consultant: "undisputed brilliance and experience, according to even his enemies; clear opinions, with data to back them up; unwavering loyalty; and a relentless focus on the endgame: winning the general election."[16]

Howard Wolfson was the communications director, Neera Tanden was in charge of policy, while Terry McAuliffe, a longtime moneyman for Bill Clinton (and later governor of Virginia) was in charge of fundraising. Harold Ickes, another veteran Clinton operative, worked part-time for the campaign and was in charge of securing delegates. Mandy Grunwald, who had worked for the Bill Clinton 1992 election campaign, managed the media advertising. The only new person in the senior group of advisers was deputy campaign manager Mike Henry, a veteran of several critical statewide contests for other Democrats.[17]

There was friction in the Clinton team from the start: Penn thought Solis Doyle wasn't qualified for the campaign manager job; Solis Doyle, a favorite of longtime Clinton advisers, despised Penn.[18] It was supposed to be a Team of Rivals, like Abraham Lincoln and his cabinet—but the chief characterization of the Clinton team was infighting, back-stabbing, dysfunction, and failure of the campaign manager or candidate to enforce discipline. Reporter Joshua Green, in a lengthy postmortem on the collapse of the Clinton campaign, observed that, when pressed, Hillary was "her own shrewdest strategist . . . But her advisers couldn't execute strategy; they routinely attacked and undermined each other, and Clinton never forced a resolution."[19] Solis Doyle was relieved of her duties (but not fired), replaced by another old Clinton hand, Maggie Williams; later, Solis Doyle was hired by the Obama team, and put in charge of assisting the eventual vice presidential nominee. An exasperated Hillary Clinton said to Mark Penn: "I think she [Solis Doyle] was a disaster, Mark, and I am so disappointed. She turned out not to be able to manage. . . . She just was incapable. I put her in a position; she was unable to do it."[20]

Equally problematic was the role of Bill Clinton. At times unwanted kibitzer, at other times trying to keep a safe distance from his wife's campaign, the Democrat's most gifted campaigner just couldn't keep away. It is impossible to ignore a former president, and everything he said in his wife's defense or against Obama made news, often to the detriment of her campaign.

By contrast, the Obama high command was steady and unflappable: "No-Drama Obama," as the staffers called it. Steve Elmendorf, a Democratic strategist not associated with the campaign, commented that "normalcy seems to weave through them."[21] The senior adviser for the campaign was the veteran media consultant David Axelrod. Since 2002, Axelrod's firm, Chicago-based AKPD Message and Media, had worked on forty-two primary or general elections around the country, winning thirty-three of them. Axelrod was media adviser for John Edward's 2004 presidential campaign and previously had worked for five of the candidates running for the 2008 nomination.[22] The campaign manager was David Plouffe, who joined Axelrod's firm in 2002, and served as a senior adviser to Missouri congressman Richard Gephardt in his 2004 presidential campaign. After Obama won the US Senate primary in 2004, Robert Gibbs joined his campaign, and in 2008 Gibbs served as the campaign's communications director. Previously, Gibbs had been spokesperson for Deborah A. (Debbie) Stabenow's successful 2000 US Senate race in Michigan, and for the successful Ernest F. Hollings 1998 re-election campaign for the US Senate in South Carolina.[23] Steve Hildebrand, a veteran of South Dakota politics and Iowa caucuses, headed up (along with business partner Paul Tewes) the all-important grassroots efforts in Iowa and served as Plouffe's deputy national campaign director. As seen below, the Obama campaign staff also invested heavily in technology and online communications, efforts that set this campaign apart from all previous endeavors. The polling team was headed up by Joel Benenson, who helped work on the Obama message and overall campaign strategy. In charge of focus groups was David Binder. Others were brought into the mix, including Paul Harstad (Iowa caucus and others), John Anzalone (southern focus), and Cornell Belcher.

Months before the Iowa caucus, it certainly looked like a quick Clinton victory. In the *National Journal*'s Democratic Insiders Poll, drawing on the smartest, most plugged-in Democratic operatives (including David Axelrod), Obama ranked last among ten potential candidates in May 2006, with a 1 percent chance; Clinton had a 72 percent chance of winning the nomination.[24] In September and October 2007, Obama trailed Clinton in the polls by 20 to 30 points. But the Obama strategy was to strike hard in Iowa, pull off an impressive win, and watch the other states topple. Team Obama certainly knew Iowa. Journalists Dan Balz and Haynes Johnson noted that all of Obama's top staff—Axelrod, Plouffe, Hildebrand, Tewes, Mitch Stewart (Iowa caucus director), Emily Parcell (Iowa political director), Iowa native Larry Grisolano (overseeing polling and media), and Pete Giangreco (direct mail)—had significant experience working on the ground game and in Iowa.[25]

A key part of the Obama strategy was to reach out to young voters who had never participated in the caucuses before. The Obama team set up twenty-seven field offices in Iowa, far more than any other candidate. By contrast, the Clinton team had far less experience and presence in Iowa, and Hillary Clinton had only visited Iowa a couple of times. After earlier miscues and stagnation, Clinton turned to one of Tom Vilsack's senior advisers, Teresa Vilmain, a hard-driving organizer who excelled at grassroots mobilization.[26] Mark Penn had figured that 90,000 Iowans would turn up for the Democratic caucus; he later revised the figure upward to 150,000; Obama's team thought perhaps 167,000 would participate. But a record-breaking 239,872 turned out, including about 53,000 voters twenty-five and under, who heavily favored Obama.[27] Obama easily topped Edwards, with Clinton coming in an embarrassing third. What must have been most astonishing to the Clinton forces was that Obama captured more female voters than did Clinton. So much for the inevitability of her campaign.

Obama had the momentum and a compelling victory under his belt, but he had not achieved a knockout. Iowa was impressive, but the independent-thinking New Hampshire voters would make up their own minds. Clinton, reeling from

Iowa, nearly out of money, and with her senior staff at each other's throats, managed to pull off a surprising victory in New Hampshire. Women came back to Clinton, by 12 percent over Obama. Perhaps it was the well-publicized vulnerable moment when she answered a reporter's question in Portsmouth, or Obama's and Edwards's snide debate remarks that pulled women to her side.

However, the Clinton staff, in the words of Balz and Johnson, was "on the verge of a calamitous breakdown."[28] Solis Doyle was removed as campaign manager. But it wasn't just campaign mismanagement. Another of the major problems was the Clinton campaign's relations with the press. Jonathan Alter, senior editor of *Newsweek*, summed it up: "With the exception of [press aide] Jay Carson, [the Clinton campaign] had the worst press operation—for their candidate as well as for the media—of any Democratic campaign I've covered in twenty-five years. Their job was to help reporters, not antagonize them with arrogant behavior and complaints to editors."[29]

Even before the first caucus vote was cast, the Clinton campaign was burning through its funds, and no one seemed to have a handle on the financial rudder. It threw $29 million into trying to win the Iowa caucus, but Hillary Clinton only received 70,000 caucus votes (at a ridiculous cost of $414 per vote).[30] Clinton had some of the best establishment Democratic fundraisers working for her, and they raised massive amounts of money. Altogether, nearly a quarter of a billion dollars ($247.9 million) was raised by the Clinton campaign, including a transfer of $10 million from her Senate campaign committee funds, and $13.2 million in personal loans. As astonishing as this total was, three indelicate facts stood out. First, the campaign spent an enormous amount, 42 percent, on administrative costs (such as salaries and office space); second, by the time the Iowa caucuses were completed, the campaign was almost dead broke; and third, no matter how much Clinton kept raising, Obama would match or even up the ante. And Obama's team spent the money much more wisely and strategically.

In April 2008, the *Wall Street Journal* reported that Mark Penn, who continued to serve as CEO of Burson-Marsteller, attended strategy meetings with the ambassador from Colombia, where the subject was how to win passage of a free trade deal with the United States. Such a pact was anathema to American labor unions and to candidate Clinton.[31] Penn was trying to serve two masters, a balancing act that was fraught with difficulties, particularly under the harsh glare of a presidential contest. The inevitable uproar in the Clinton campaign meant that Penn had to be demoted; yet he still served on the Clinton team. His senior strategist place was taken by Howard Wolfson and veteran pollster and strategist Geoff Garin, trying to steady the campaign team.

It was an unprecedented primary season for the Democrats. Both Obama and Clinton had hoped to achieve an early victory. But after Iowa and New Hampshire, both camps realized that it would be a long, expensive fight. The Obama strategists kept their attention focused on securing delegates; Clinton's strategists focused on capturing states and popular votes. Well before the 2008 primary season, the Democratic Party adopted proportional representation, rather than winner-take-all, as the means for states to apportion delegates.

That meant it was possible for Obama, for example, to receive just 40 percent of a state's primary vote, but still receive a hefty share of the delegates. The separate state Democratic Party rules were varied and often complicated, and the Obama campaign smartly took advantage of the quirks of delegate selection. Obama won the primaries and the all-important convention delegates in the Deep South, states that Democrats normally lose in general elections, but have a fairly large number of African American voters. He also won in the Midwest, the Great Plains, and the Mountain states. Obama, unlike Clinton, aggressively courted super delegates, giving him a further advantage in the hunt for a majority. Altogether, Obama won twenty-nine states and the District of Columbia, garnering 2,285 delegates, while Clinton won twenty-one states and 1,973 delegates. In all, Clinton received a greater popular vote total than Obama in the caucuses and primaries. But popular vote counts for little in the quest for the nomination. To paraphrase James Carville's famous 1992 slogan, it's the delegates, stupid! Clearly Obama strategists outmaneuvered and outhustled the Clinton team. She doggedly stayed in the race, even past the point where victory would have been possible.

The Republican Primaries

Before the 2006 congressional elections, early bets for the Republican nomination centered on three US senators: George Allen of Virginia, Rick Santorum of Pennsylvania, and Bill Frist of Tennessee. But Allen, running for re-election, stumbled with his impolitic "macaca" comment and lost what should have been an easy victory; Santorum was trounced in his re-election bid; and Frist, a favorite of Karl Rove, decided to take his name out of consideration and retired from the Senate at the end of 2006.[32]

Several of the Republican candidates turned out to be ill-prepared for the rigors of the primary process. Kansas senator Sam Brownback, former Virginia governor James Gilmore, Colorado representative Tom Tancredo, and former Wisconsin governor Tommy Thompson all withdrew before the first primary, unable to raise the needed money, convince party leaders, or energize enough party activists. California representative Duncan Hunter, another highly unlikely candidate, withdrew very early during the primary season.

The Giuliani campaign signed on several veteran campaign consultants, including Mike DuHaime as campaign manager and Ed Goeas and the Tarrance Group for polling. Giuliani had become a household name, thanks in part to his role in the aftermath of the 9/11 attacks in New York; he was even proclaimed as *Time* magazine's "Person of the Year" in 2001. He had led or was in the top tier of straw polls of likely Republican voters in several states during the year before the primaries and had raised $56 million, second only to Romney's $90 million.[33] But his campaign employed an unusual strategy: Giuliani would gloss over the earlier primaries and concentrate on winning big in Florida, the fifth contest. In doing so, however, he left other candidates, especially McCain, to gather momentum and gain precious national visibility, while the former mayor sat on the sidelines.

It was a risky, and inevitably bad, strategy: when Giuliani came in third place in Florida, his campaign quickly folded.

Former Tennessee senator and television actor Fred D. Thompson's presidential bid never got off the ground. His close friend and former Nixon operative Ken Rietz tried to help, but the people Rietz brought in were soon fired or quit in what journalist Michael D. Shear characterized as "a disastrous summer of conflict and chaos" within the campaign.[34] Political operative Bill Lacy came in to pick up the pieces, but the Thompson campaign never went anywhere. Thompson half-heartedly entered the fray, but withdrew on January 22, 2008, picking up but eleven delegates.

Former Arkansas governor Mike Huckabee, aided by campaign manager Chip Saltsman, Ed Rollins, and James Pinkerton, was the best hope of the conservative-religious element of the party. Huckabee, a former Baptist minister, and virtually unknown outside of his home state, was the surprise winner in the Iowa caucus, blunting Mitt Romney's expensive campaign in the state, and convincing John McCain that he had to concentration fully on the first primary, New Hampshire. Huckabee's victory was aided by a massive e-mail campaign targeting conservative Christian Iowa voters. Randy Brinson, a physician in Montgomery, Alabama, had created a voter registration organization called Redeem the Vote, and had compiled an e-mail list of some 71 million individuals. James Caviezel, the actor who portrayed Jesus in the Mel Gibson produced movie *The Passion of Christ*, made a video to assist the Redeem the Vote effort, and it was distributed via e-mail to more than 60 million people. The Huckabee campaign took that e-mail list, and with the help of a firm called Webcasting TV came up with 414,000 potential contacts in Iowa.[35] In the end, Huckabee received 40,954 caucus votes, representing 35 percent of the Republican vote, giving him first place and 17 of the 34 Iowa delegates. While winning eight primaries and caucuses altogether, Huckabee ran out of steam and dropped out in early March 2008.

Just days before he left office in January 2007 as governor of Massachusetts, Mitt Romney formed a presidential exploratory committee. He was able to spend some $35 million of his own money (along with $20 million from other contributors) to help gain traction in the pre-primary and primary phase. Romney was assisted by Beth Myers, his longtime confidante, gubernatorial chief of staff, and protégé of Karl Rove.[36] She was chosen to be the campaign manager, while Carl Forti served as political director, Matt Rhoades as communications director, and pollster Alex Castellanos as senior adviser. Romney finished second to Huckabee in the Iowa caucuses, second to McCain in the New Hampshire primary, and was strong enough to win delegates in several subsequent primaries, but when Super Tuesday sent John McCain on to the inevitable path of victory, Romney withdrew from the contest on February 7, 2008. Altogether, he won eleven states, 291 delegates, and 4.7 million votes, but not enough to stop McCain.

Right after the 2006 congressional midterm elections, which were disastrous for Republicans, John McCain met with his senior political advisers: John Weaver, who had been with McCain during his 2000 attempt for the nomination and remained his principal political adviser; Rick Davis, who managed the 2000 campaign, was now signed up for another try; Mark Salter, his longtime friend and speechwriter; and a new adviser, Terry Nelson, who had served as the Bush-Cheney 2004 campaign's political director. Also there was longtime aide and finance director Carla Eudy. The time was ripe for a McCain comeback.

The initial plan called for McCain to raise $48 million during the first quarter of 2007—numbers that incumbent president George W. Bush could raise in 2004, but quite ambitious for McCain. The campaign team began spending heavily in field offices around the country, securing the services of dozens of expensive political consulting firms and individuals, and the central staff ballooned to over 300, "a huge battleship of a campaign" wrote veteran political reporters Dan Balz and Haynes Johnson.[37] But the money did not come in anywhere near projections, and the campaign was soon in the red, even before McCain officially announced. When the quarterly contributions report became public, McCain embarrassingly came in third behind Romney and Giuliani; he quickly fired his finance director.[38]

Furthermore, key advisers Weaver and Davis weren't getting along, and the internal fighting led to gridlock, indecision, and mismanagement. By summer 2007, McCain's campaign seemed to collapse. Two of McCain's top advisers, Weaver and Nelson, were fired (or quit) for mismanaging the campaign and failing to bring in money. Rick Davis was installed as campaign manager, while Mark Salter remained as an unpaid adviser. Hundreds of campaign staffers were fired, along with Rob Jesmer, political director and Reed Galeen, deputy campaign manager. The loss of John Weaver was particularly telling. Weaver's departure, some Republican insiders were saying, would be as unthinkable as Karl Rove being fired by George W. Bush or James Carville by Bill Clinton.[39]

The summer and fall of 2007 looked like the final, whimpering moments of a once promising campaign. But McCain kept on, drawing on Davis, Salter, and old political hand Charlie Black for strategic advice. McCain's campaign seemed to have reached bottom just a month before the Iowa caucuses, but during December 2007, he was energized when he received the endorsements of three key newspapers, the *Des Moines Register*, the *Boston Globe*, and the *Manchester Union Leader*. He came in third in Iowa, but his strongest competitor, Mitt Romney, was held to a second-place finish behind Huckabee. New Hampshire had been good to McCain in 2000, and now, eight years later, he pulled out all the stops and won this all-important first primary. McCain won again in the South Carolina primary, erasing some of the pain of the vicious campaign waged against him by George W. Bush in that state in 2000. Significantly, McCain won the crucial Florida primary, edging out Romney, Giuliani, and Huckabee. In this campaign, he was aided by the political organization of Florida governor Charlie Crist. On Super Tuesday, with twenty-one states in play, McCain won enough, particularly the delegate-rich states of California, New York, and Illinois, to give him an insurmountable lead. By March 4, McCain, aided by the Republican winner-take-all method of selecting delegates, had secured a majority of the delegates to be nominated.

But the victory was not a satisfying one for many in the Republican Party. Republican pollster Tony Fabrizio reminded us: "At no point in the primary process did any of the candidates, including the ultimate winner, ever receive a majority of votes in a primary. These men had many virtues, but none had a full set of attributes that Republican voters were looking for. John McCain won by making his way through the baffle as others fell."[40]

Rock Stars

After the Democratic primaries, Obama embarked on a well-publicized international trip in late July. The high point was the scene of 200,000 people gathered in Berlin waving American flags, cheering, and shouting "Obama, Obama." What possibly could the McCain forces do to minimize this rock-star-like adulation? Their solution was to mock it, link Obama to airhead celebrities, and raise doubts about his ability to lead. McCain's media consultant Fred Davis produced a thirty-second video, called "Celebrity," showing Obama before rapturous crowds intermingled with shots of Brittany Spears and Paris Hilton.

> *Female Voice-Over*: He's the biggest celebrity in the world
>
> But is he ready to lead?
>
> With gas prices soaring, Barack Obama says no to offshore drilling.
>
> And says he'll raise taxes on electricity.
>
> Higher taxes, more foreign oil. That's the real Obama.

David Axelrod characterized the ad as a "preposterous contrivance of a campaign rendered powerless in the face of the torrent of positive coverage" of Obama. For a moment, this video tried to blunt the Obama love-fest.[41]

McCain knew that he had to make a bold move, a "game changer." And that would have to come in the only missing piece in the contest, his choice of vice-presidential running mate. Tim Pawlenty looked like a solid, safe choice, but he was certainly no game changer. McCain's favorite was former Democratic vice-presidential nominee Joe Lieberman. Karl Rove was staunchly opposed to such a deal and told both McCain and Lieberman: choose Lieberman and you will tear the Republican Party apart. Hardly on anyone's short list was Alaska governor Sarah Palin. But the more other options were foreclosed, the more consultants Rick Davis and Steve Schmidt thought that Palin could be that energizing, historic pick: a true conservative, an telegenic mother of five, a governor, and surely a pick that would cement McCain's reputation as a maverick.[42] They urged McCain to consider her.

With Palin's selection, news commentators, pundits, and average voters scrambled to find out more about her. Wikipedia's entry on Palin, furiously edited just minutes before the announcement, was widely consulted. Few in the press and few in Washington knew who she was or how she could handle herself under the harsh spotlight during the remaining twelve weeks of the campaign.

The McCain staff was not prepared: there was no in-depth background material on Palin; there were no talking points prepared; she hadn't been briefed on key national and international issues; and, most critically, the press was caught off guard. It sounded eerily similar to George H. W. Bush's surprise selection of Dan Quayle in 1988. Journalists Elisabeth Bumiller and Michael Cooper noted, "the last thing he [McCain] wanted was the kind of rush decision that President George Bush had made in 1988 in selecting his running mate, Dan Quayle."[43] But that is precisely what happened: a rush decision, encouraged by senior consultants, with little forethought and preparation.

The General Election

> *Don't control me. This is my campaign.*
>
> —John McCain (2008)[44]

Sarah Palin was the sensation at the Republican nominating convention, forcefully delivering her acceptance speech, which was crafted by veteran Republican speechwriter Matthew Scully. In her own account of the 2008 election, Palin wrote that "throughout the campaign, the speeches [Matthew] handed me were like poetry, so smooth, such amazing flow. But the convention speech he wrote was in a league of its own."[45] For about the first week, the Obama camp was thrown off guard by the Palin selection: enthusiasm on the Republican Right surged; overnight polls saw McCain gaining on, even surpassing, Obama; and the media were fixated on this newest star.

The general election period became the silly season. In a mid-September comment made in western Virginia, Barack Obama criticized McCain for following Bush's failed policies. "You can't put lipstick on a pig. It's still a pig. You can't wrap an old fish in a piece of paper and call it change. It's still going to stink after eight years." Righteous indignation was the immediate reaction from some Republicans: how dare the president make such sexist remarks and take a cheap shot at Sarah Palin. Obama shot back that McCain's campaign was wrapping itself in "phony outrage." Election chronicler Richard Wolffe reminds us how distorted our national debate became: "For two full days, the phrase [lipstick on a pig] was debated in the media—more than an entire election's worth of coverage of Social Security, China, or New Orleans."[46]

Rumor, innuendo, and falsehood. The Obama campaign was subject to numerous rumors: *Obama was a Muslim. Obama was a Kenyan, not an American. He was endorsed by the Black Panthers. He "palled around with terrorists." He was a socialist. Obama didn't get to Harvard Law School on his own merits.* None of these statements were true, but these and other even more vicious rumors circulated widely through talk radio, viral e-mails, and online communication. Every presidential campaign has its distortions, rumors, and falsehoods, but 2008 raised the level of noise and obfuscation to heights not seen before. Most of the rumormongering was directed at Barack Obama, and was coming chiefly from right-wing radio, bloggers, social media, e-mails, and word of mouth.

Sometimes it came directly from the other campaign. After the *New York Times* published a front-page story about Obama's relationship with William Ayers, the founder of the 1960s radical group the Weatherman, McCain's Nicolle Wallace fired off an e-mail to Palin with attack lines against Obama: "This is not a man who sees American as you and I do—as the greatest force for good in the world. This [Obama] is someone who sees America as imperfect enough to pal around with terrorists who targeted their own country." Palin eagerly jumped on the phrase and repeated it at a Colorado fundraiser.[47]

Attacks didn't come solely from right-wing media or the McCain camp. Just a month after Obama announced his campaign, in mid-March 2007, Clinton's senior strategist Mark Penn laid out what he considered a key Obama weakness, his "lack of American roots." "All of these articles about his boyhood in Indonesia and his life in Hawaii are geared towards showing his background is diverse, multi-cultural and putting that in a new light. Save it for 2050. It also exposes a very strong weakness for him—his roots to basic American values and culture are at best limited." Penn's advice: use the word "America" and the visual of the American flag as often as possible.[48] Just as Lee Atwater wrapped George H. W. Bush in the American flag during the 1988 campaign, so would Clinton's campaign pull out its own patriotic bunting, if Penn had his way. Hillary Clinton rejected Penn's advice.[49]

False information persisted and flourished, and by the end of the campaign a full 23 percent of Texans believed that Obama was a Muslim, while nationwide, 14 percent of Republicans, 5.5 percent of Democrats, and 4.8 percent of independents agreed.[50] In the last days of the campaign, there were ugly scenes of citizens lashing out against Obama at McCain gatherings.

Democratic Strategy. Al Gore would have won the presidency if he could have won Florida; John Kerry would have won the presidency if he could have won Ohio. The Obama team didn't want the race to come down to its fortunes in one state, forced to rely on such a razor-thin margin. "Nothing was more important to us strategically than having a wide playing field," wrote David Plouffe. "This was my goal from Day One."[51] Helping make the strategic decisions was the polling analysis from Benenson Strategy Group and Harstad Strategic Research, which worked in seven of the key battleground states, and several other polling firms. A goal for the campaign was to identify "up for grabs" voters, those undecided voters who would be critical in the battleground states. Joel Benenson noted that the "up for grabs" moved into the single digits during the last weeks of the campaign.[52]

Through its grassroots outreach, media coverage and campaign events, the Obama campaign widened the battleground playing field and forced McCain to defend a much broader range of states. The ground game, in particular, entered a new level of sophistication. The nationwide voter contact effort, headed by Steve Hildebrand and Jon Carson, was able to contact 8 million voters. In twelve key states, more than 4 million new voters were added, the great majority of them voting Democratic. The Obama campaign also took advantage of state laws in thirty-four states that permitted no-fault early voting, locking up his base supporters and many of those who were tentatively committed weeks before Election Day.[53]

The Obama team had many more resources in the field than McCain. In Florida, for example, Obama had fifty-six field offices, more than a hundred field organizers, and about 150,000 volunteers. McCain was compelled to hire part-time workers to help canvass voters.[54] In the end, Obama was able to capture nine states—New Mexico, Virginia, North Carolina, Colorado, Iowa, Nevada, Florida, Ohio, and (amazingly) Indiana—that had gone to Bush in 2004. Altogether, those states carried 103 electoral votes, a full 38 percent of those needed for election.

Triple-O. Since 2000, political consultants and observers have talked about the breakthrough in campaign electronic communications. They were surprised at John McCain's ability to raise $1 million overnight and online after his unexpected 2000 New Hampshire primary. They were amazed at the enthusiasm generated by blogging, social networking, and online fundraising found in the Howard Dean primary campaign in 2004. But all this paled in comparison to what came in 2008, and particularly from the Obama campaign.

Barack Obama was the candidate who wore two BlackBerry smartphones on his belt; John McCain had to have his e-mail printed out by a staffer before he would read it. In many ways, this epitomized the campaigns and their approach to online communication. While the McCain campaign utilized many of the tools of the Obama team, it was nevertheless always two or three steps behind.

The Obama effort was dubbed "Triple-O," the Obama Online Operation, a team of about thirty young tech-savvy operators, headed by chief technology adviser Julius Genachowski, Joe Rospars (founder of Blue State Digital), and Kevin Malover. Chris Hughes, one of the founders of Facebook, was also on the team. The goal was to reach both potential voters and committed activists through the way they communicate. Television, yes, for many voters, but for younger voters, the campaign innovatively reached out through social network sites (Facebook, MySpace, LinkedIn), the My.BarackObama (MBO) portal site, and YouTube. By Election Day, the Obama campaign "knew" more than 7 million supporters through his social network and campaign websites.[55]

The debates. The debates were not kind to John McCain. He appeared old and tired, he paced back and forth, and at times he looked angry. Democratic media consultant Peter Fenn observed that "McCain appeared in all three debates to be auditioning for a part in *Grumpy Old Men*, and after the final exchange, he was given the lead."[56] The network polls showed that the viewing audience thought that Obama had bested McCain in each of their debates, and Obama's approval rating climbed.

Most worrisome to the McCain campaign was the performance of Sarah Palin in her one debate against Joe Biden. With her shaky performances during national interviews and her thin grasp of national and international issue, the expectation level was low. Debate preparation was agonizing, not only for the candidate but for her handlers, Steve Schmidt and Nicolle Wallace, but Palin gave a better than expected performance. Biden acquitted himself simply by making no patronizing or off-the-wall, off-message remarks.

Television coverage. But for all the attention to new media and online communication, old reliable television ads played an important role throughout the campaign. Campaign Media Analysis Group tracked some 380 distinct television ads from April 3 to November 5, 2008, coming from the Obama and McCain teams, the national political parties, and a variety of outside interests.[57] For Obama, veteran consultant Larry Grisolano was in charge of coordinating all paid media, while longtime media consultant and senior strategists John Del Cecato and GMMB's Jim Margolis and his team crafted biting and aggressive ads. As expected, some media markets serving battleground states were inundated with advertisements: Philadelphia ($15.9 million from Obama and $11.5 million from McCain); Washington, DC, aiming for the competitive northern Virginia voters ($16.7 million-Obama, $5.2 million-McCain); Cleveland ($7.1 million-Obama, $4.7 million-McCain); Denver ($8.6 million-Obama, $6.8 million-McCain); and the Miami, Tampa Bay, Orlando, Jacksonville markets in Florida. But some major media markets had hardly any campaign advertising: Seattle ($3,458-Obama, $1,300-McCain); Los Angeles ($12,475-Obama, $900-McCain). During this period, the McCain team spent $125 million on campaign advertising, while Obama spent $236 million. The Republican National Committee spent heavily in the battleground states, where they spent $36.4 million, while energy entrepreneur T. Boone Pickens spent $21.7 million.[58]

The one unusual feature of the media advertising was the half-hour Obama infomercial. Almost as a throwback to the 1950s (or perhaps a slicker version of Ross Perot's 1992 and 1996 efforts), the Obama campaign decided to air a thirty-minute program on prime-time television on the network and leading cable channels. At a cost of between $4 million and $5 million, the program was seen by 33.5 million people; one in five homes in the top television markets had tuned in, making it the most watched political commercial in presidential history. As journalist Abdon H. Pallasch commented, the infomercial "sewed together the best footage of Obama's campaign travels around the country—hugging the ladies in the kitchen in hairnets, shaking hands on the assembly line, and delivering his best lines at speeches and debates with adorable footage of him playing with his photogenic daughters."[59] The footage was filmed by Davis Guggenheim, son of pioneer media consultant Charles Guggenheim; Davis was also well-known for producing Al Gore's 2006 documentary *An Inconvenient Truth*. Mark Putnam of the Obama media team firm of Murphy-Putnam wrote and produced the infomercial.[60]

It would have been difficult for any Republican candidate to win in 2008. Voters were ready for a change, confidence in George W. Bush had plummeted, and the country faced a serious economic crisis just weeks before the election. It was even harder for McCain. He had an enormous uphill battle just to win the Republican nomination; he was not fully trusted by many conservatives; he was fairly or unfairly portrayed as Bush's best buddy; and he was going up against a charismatic candidate with enormous appeal, buckets full of campaign money, a nearly flawlessly run campaign. What perhaps is surprising is how well John McCain did under these crippling circumstances.

The 2012 Presidential Election: Barack Obama v. Mitt Romney

> We knew that we could reach literally almost everyone in the United States. That was a totally new dynamic that didn't exist in 2008.
> —Teddy Goff, digital director, Obama for America (2012)[61]

> Romney for president: The last 20th century campaign
> —Republican consultant Thomas N. Edmonds (2013)[62]

The Republican Primaries

Who would take on a weakened, vulnerable Barack Obama? The Republican establishment was having difficulty finding a candidate not named Romney. For the Washington crowd, Mitt Romney, who had come in a strong second in the 2008 Republican primaries, was not their kind of guy. As journalists Mark Halperin and John Heilemann wrote, "Romney wasn't liked *or* disliked—he was a stranger."[63] Former Florida governor Jeb Bush, next in line in the Bush political dynasty, said no. Another potential candidate was Haley Barbour, a former Mississippi governor, RNC chair, lobbyist, and all-around rainmaker for the Republican Party. But Barbour had considerable baggage, personal and political, and wisely chose not to enter.[64] Mitch Daniels, the Indiana governor, was well liked by establishment Republicans and a favorite of George W. Bush. But despite intense pressure, he decided not to run. Mike Huckabee, winner of the Iowa caucus in 2008, also said no. Even entrepreneur and reality TV star Donald J. Trump Sr., who was convinced that Obama's Hawaiian birth certificate was phony, stood aside: it would cost too much money, he said, and too many business opportunities would be lost if he ran for the presidency in 2012.

Twelve Republicans declared as candidates for their party's nomination. While the candidates appeared to have a wide range of experience—one current governor, five former governors, three sitting members of Congress, a former US senator, and a former speaker of the House—in reality the field was quite weak. The members of Congress, Michele Bachmann of Minnesota, Thaddeus McCotter of Michigan, and Ron Paul of Texas, were on the fringes of the party; former Pennsylvania senator Rick Santorum had been roundly defeated in 2006 for re-election; former speaker of the House Newt Gingrich of Georgia had resigned in 1999 and was neither respected nor trusted by many Washington Republicans; and hardly anyone had remembered former Louisiana governor Buddy Roemer, who had been out of elective politics for twenty years. Former Minnesota governor Tim Pawlenty generated little excitement and was one of the first to drop out. Bush pollster Jan van Lohuizen observed that Pawlenty was "utterly lacking in charisma . . . and utterly boring."[65] Ironically, Mitt Romney's campaign viewed Pawlenty as the "strongest, most viable" alternative to Romney, according to Matt Rhoades, Romney's campaign manager.[66] Former New Mexico governor Gary Johnson's libertarian ideas were too quirky, and once Georgia business executive Herman Cain's extramarital activities became known, he, too, became a mere footnote.[67]

John Weaver, McCain's former senior consultant, was back, this time encouraging former Utah governor and US ambassador to China Jon Huntsman Jr. to join the race. Weaver thought the Republican field was weaker than it had been since 1940,[68] and Huntsman would appeal to the moderate broad spectrum of Republican, Democratic, and independent voters, presenting a solid alternative to fellow Mormon Mitt Romney and the other candidates. Like Patrick Caddell, wishing to find the ideal candidate, his "Mr. Smith," Weaver had been hoping to find that sensible, moderate alternative. With his good looks, state executive and international experience, and billionaire father behind him, Jon Huntsman looked like the answer to Weaver's dream. Huntsman became convinced, resigned his ambassadorial post in Beijing, and joined the fray. But this was not his father's Republican Party: voters in the primaries and caucuses were more conservative, more strident, and unwilling to listen to hints of moderation or cooperation across the aisle. Having been appointed by Obama certainly didn't help, and spilling out phrases in Mandarin at a Republican debate rubbed many of the faithful the wrong way.

On paper, Texas governor Rick Perry looked very promising: solid conservative credentials, a dynamic personality, and a mixture of Texas swagger, rugged good looks, and fundraising prowess. Once a Democrat and Texas chairman of Al Gore for President in 1988, Perry, at the urging of Karl Rove, switched parties and, with Rove's help, successfully ran for the post of Texas agricultural commissioner.[69] Texas governor since 2001, Perry announced late in the pre-primary months that he would compete for the Republican nomination.

In fact, Perry rained on the parade of Michele Bachmann. She had just won the highly visible Ames, Iowa, straw poll; and on the same day, Perry announced his candidacy, taking the spotlight away from her. Bachmann's campaign chair was longtime consultant Ed Rollins, while Keith Nahigian, also a veteran of many presidential campaigns, was the campaign manager.

But the Perry campaign was a disaster, not at all prepared for the rigors of a national contest. "There's never been a more ineptly orchestrated, just unbelievably subpar, campaign for president of the United States than this one," observed a senior adviser to Rick Perry.[70]

Right after the New Hampshire primary, where Perry came in dead last, he lit into the alternative investment firm Bain Capital, and, by extension its cofounder Mitt Romney: "They're just vultures sitting out there on the tree limb waiting for the company to get sick. And then they swoop in, they eat the carcass, they leave with that, and they leave the skeleton."[71] The charge of "vulture capitalist" had a familiar ring to it: Stuart Stevens, chief strategist and ad maker for Mitt Romney, had used it in an earlier race, when he was working for Steve

Poizner, battling against former eBay chief executive Meg Whitman during the Republican primary in the 2010 California gubernatorial race. Stevens had made a commercial for the Poizner campaign called "Vulture" that attacked Whitman and her alleged close ties with Wall Street financiers Goldman Sachs.[72]

There was infighting between the Washington consultants and the Texas consultants surrounding Perry. Perry brought in David Carney and Rob Johnson, two veteran operatives. Carney had helped Perry in defeating Texas senator Kay Bailey Hutchison in a heated Republican primary for governor in 2010. Carney and Johnson had worked for Newt Gingrich during the early stages of the 2012 primary season, but with Gingrich taking off on a two-week vacation in the Greek islands, his staff imploded. In June 2011, the Gingrich campaign, headed by campaign manager Rob Johnson, resigned en masse. Carney and Johnson then went over to Perry, urging him to climb into the race. Perry's wife insisted on having old Bush hand Joe Allbaugh brought in, and Carney and Johnson recruited veteran Washington consultants Tony Fabrizio and Nelson Warfield.[73]

Herman Cain was encouraged by the vigorous and enthusiastic rallies that greeted him, particularly with some 15,000 Tea Party enthusiasts who showed up at a Milwaukee rally. Cain made the decision to run during the 2010 Christmas holiday, when he thought that the Republican Party didn't have any candidate who could win. What was the campaign's strategy? Mark Block, Cain's campaign manager, said he gave credit to David Plouffe and his book on the 2008 Obama campaign, *Audacity to Win*. "That was standard reading for anybody who came onto the staff. And we followed their blueprint."[74] The campaign strategy, however, didn't account for repeated allegations of sexual harassment made public by Cain's trade association colleagues. Soon, Cain was out of the running.

From the beginning, Mitt Romney was the candidate to beat. He had run before, had methodically accumulated the most campaign money, had established a political action committee to boost his chances, and had assembled a veteran staff. Matthew (Matt) Rhoades, who had been director of opposition research for the Bush 2004 campaign and director of communications for the Romney 2008 campaign, was the campaign manager.[75] Katie Packer Gage served as deputy campaign manager. Joining the team were veteran media strategists Russ Schriefer and Stuart Stevens, longtime Republican operatives Ron Kaufman and Eric Fehrnstrom, communications director Gail Gitcho, and political director Rich Beeson.

The Republican candidates dropped off quickly: Bachmann immediately after the Iowa caucuses (January 4); Perry, a week after New Hampshire (January 19). The strategy for Huntsman was "New Hampshire or bust," said Matt David, his second campaign manager (Susan Wiles was his first),[76] and the campaign's focus was to go after Romney. But New Hampshire voters were not kind to Huntsman, giving him a third place finish, just 16.9 percent of the vote, and his only two delegates to the national convention. A week later, Huntsman withdrew, then endorsed Romney. The other candidates quickly dropped out or suspended their campaigns.

Santorum was the last to fall: after his surprise win in Iowa, he won another ten states and received over 20 percent of the popular vote, but ceased his campaign on

April 10, immediately before his home state primary in Pennsylvania. Santorum's chief strategist was John Brabender, veteran media consultant and longtime adviser to Santorum. BrabenderCox, the media firm assisting Santorum, lit into Romney with a commercial called "Rombo," featuring a Romney look-alike actor in an old warehouse, blasting away with an assault gun, filled with mud. There were pop-up figures of Rick Santorum, but none of the mud landed on him. "Mitt Romney's negative attack machine is back, on full throttle," warned the male voice-over. "This time, Romney is firing his mud at Rick Santorum. Romney and his Super PAC have spent a staggering $20 million brutally attacking fellow Republicans." Romney, the ad charged, was trying to hide his big-government plans, but in the end he is getting mud all over himself.[77] To show its ideological versatility and business acumen, BrabenderCox later produced positive radio ads for Romney during the general election.[78]

The pro-Romney super PAC Restore Our Future dumped $3 million of negative advertising during the Iowa caucuses and another $8.7 million in Florida, mostly targeting Newt Gingrich. The ads were produced by McCarthy Hennings Media, Larry McCarthy's firm. The most biting, called "Baggage," went after Gingrich.[79] "You know what makes Barack Obama happy?" asks the female voice-over. "Newt Gingrich's baggage. Newt has more baggage than the airlines." At an airport luggage carousel, travel bags are bursting open—with cash spilling out (from Gingrich's cozy and lucrative consulting contract with Freddie Mac; his reprimand as Speaker by Republicans, no less; his collaborating with, of all people, House speaker Nancy Pelosi). The tag line was memorable: "Newt Gingrich—too much baggage!"

Winning the Republican nomination was an expensive enterprise. Stuart Stevens of the Romney campaign estimated that the campaign spent $135 million just to win the nomination.[80] While Republicans fought each other, the Obama team quietly but efficiently was being reassembled.

The Obama Re-election Team

Jim Messina learned that he would be Obama's campaign manager while on a vacation trip with Obama in Hawaii. In December 2010, Messina was wading through waist-high surf with the president, and Obama called him over. "I've got a favor I want to ask," said Obama. "I'd like you to run the re-elect."[81] But this time, the race would be different, quite different. In what journalist Joshua Green dubbed "what may be the highest-wattage crash course in executive management ever undertaken," Messina prepared for his new job by having long, private conversations with high-power chief executives. He met with Steve Jobs, who explained how the campaign could exploit technology in news ways; he met with Steven Spielberg and sat down with the DreamWorks marketing team on how to motivate voters. Messina met with Anna Wintour, editor of *Vogue*, who convinced him that selling campaign-related merchandise could be a considerable source of income for the campaign. Probably his most important CEO mentor was Eric Schmidt, of Google, who got to know Messina during the 2008 Democratic primaries, when Messina was deputy to David Plouffe.[82]

Along with Messina were veterans from the 2008 campaign: David Axelrod and David Plouffe, Robert Gibbs and Jim Margolis. Stephanie Cutter was deputy campaign manager, David Simas oversaw the polling team, which again included the firms headed by Joel Benenson, David Binder, Paul Harstad, John Anzalone, and Cornell Belcher.[83] Harper Reed was chief technology officer, Joe Rospars was chief digital strategist, and veteran fundraiser Julianna Smoot headed the campaign finance efforts.[84] Larry Grisolano again headed up the media team and was assisted by Eric Smith, who coordinated the media on the campaign with the Democratic National Committee.[85]

Like Ronald Reagan in 1984, Bill Clinton in 1996, and George W. Bush in 2004, Barack Obama had the luxury of seeking re-election without any challenger from within his own party. The Democrats and Obama faced a reenergized congressional Republican Party, fueled by Tea Party activists, who swept into the majority in Congress following the November 2010 elections. The Obama team would have to prepare for a difficult re-election fight. In January 2011, the unemployment rate was a dispiriting 9.0 percent. Since May 2009, the monthly Bureau of Labor Statistics had posted an unemployment rate above 9 percent, and there was a total of twenty months of sluggish economic news, never good news for an incumbent seeking re-election. Since 1964, four presidents—Ford, Carter, Reagan, and Bush I—ran for re-election while the national unemployment rate was over 6 percent during their fourth year; only Reagan won. Obama's job approval rating, at 63.5 percent when he was sworn in, plummeted to 45.3 percent during the last days of December 2010. The costly, complex, and controversial Affordable Care Act, quickly dubbed "Obamacare" by his opponents, became a rallying cry against him.

Jeremy Bird, who became the Obama campaign's national field director, noted that the re-election team had to do several things. First, it had to expand the electorate beyond what had voted, and crushed the Democrats, during the 2010 congressional elections. "There are people who voted for us in 2008 that did not vote for us in 2010," Bird observed. Those voters had to be registered and convinced to select Obama. Those voters would be part of "our persuasion universe." Second, the campaign had to reach new voters, those first-time voters who had not reached eighteen during the 2008 election. Finally, the campaign had to build an organization—the grassroots neighborhood team program, the research program, the media team, and the analytics team. They had to assemble a coalition that looked like 2008, not 2010. "We had to take advantage of 2011 and use that time to build up something that's really hard to do in a presidential campaign."[86]

Bird acknowledged that "the most worrisome group was young people." When Bird worked for Obama in Ohio in 2008, the campaign had one or two campus representatives at Ohio State University; this time around, in 2012, there would be five to ten such representatives at OSU. Other college and university efforts would ramp up their efforts as well.

Going after Romney early. The campaign also made a crucial decision to go after Romney even before the dust had settled in the Republican primaries. The

Obama strategists were putting into place a fundamental principle of campaign management: define your opponent before he can define himself. In earlier years, Republicans aggressively went after Michael Dukakis during the 1988 election, and the Swift Boat Veterans had ripped into John Kerry during the 2004 election. They portrayed Dukakis and Kerry as unfit for the presidency, and were able to get that message out to the voting public before the two Democrats could get their own positive message out. The Obama team, under the direction of David Simas, would do the same against Romney, through a series of aggressive and caustic campaign commercials starting in June, pointing out Romney's shortcomings as governor of Massachusetts and the damage done to workers and factories thanks to Bain Capital. The Newt Gingrich campaign had already laid the groundwork with its brutal attacks against Romney and Bain. One of the important insights that David Axelrod contributed was that early negative ads, done right and done often, can sink an opponent. At the beginning of the summer, voters still did not have a good understanding of Romney; this was the opportunity for the Obama team to fill in the blanks. Axelrod told Obama, "Every impactful ad I can think of in presidential elections over the past thirty years aired before Labor Day."[87]

Digital Obama compared to 2008. Teddy Goff, who had worked on the 2008 campaign as well, was the director of digital campaign for Obama 2012. He noted that the 2008 campaign "was really groundbreaking and really a marvel. The fact is that Facebook was about a tenth the size it is now. Twitter was nowhere. I mean, we never talked about it once. Even the smart phone—now it's sort of hard to imagine or remember a time when you weren't checking your phone every five minutes—but the iPhone had been invented during that campaign, in the summer of 2007."[88]

The 2012 campaign ramped up the technology, investing over $100 million. One of the key differences in the Obama digital operation was that while the 2008 campaign had plenty of data on voters, it was not coordinated. The chief analytics officer, Dan Wagner, who earlier had been in charge of targeting for the Democratic National Committee, headed the fifty-four-person analytics staff in a windowless office, known as the Cave. He hired the Analyst Institute, a research consortium founded by the AFL-CIO in 2006 to coordinate field research. The ultimate task was simple, but also very complex: to get every voter—all 69.4 million—who had voted for Obama in 2008 to vote again for him in 2012, plus add all those new and young voters to the fold. As journalist Sasha Issenberg wrote, the plan was audacious: to reassemble the Obama coalition, one voter at a time, through personal contacts, and to persuade wavering voters. The Obama strategists were not just using marketing techniques, but also applying some of the methodologically innovative work of social scientist Donald Green and Alan Gerber, who, as seen in chapter 15, field-tested several methods of voter contact to determine what worked and what didn't.[89]

Under the direction of Carol Davidsen, the Obama team created Project Narwhal, a program that linked various pools of data into a coherent system, so that they could have a single political profile on the donors, volunteers, online activists, and offline voters. Under the leadership of Joe Rospars, the campaign created a sophisticated e-mail fundraising effort, with carefully tested and proven messages. Also under Davidsen was the innovative software platform called the "Optimizer," which gave the Obama media team a granular look at the television viewing habits of American voters and offered a much more efficient way to show campaign ads. The Optimizer broke the day into 96 quarter-hour segments, surveyed some sixty channels to determine the most effective time and place to air spots, and matched Obama's list of persuadable voters with their cable providers' billing information. The Obama campaign wanted to be as efficient as possible with its targeted advertising, spending its money as wisely as possible. It was, explained Larry Grisolano, who oversaw the advertising campaign, "all because of our pre-occupation with spending by the Koch brothers and other outside groups."[90]

In 2012, Obama had 33 million Facebook friends (globally and in the United States), and was "friends" with about 98 percent of the US-based Facebook users.[91] College student Alex E. cast his first presidential vote when he chose Obama in 2008, but now in 2012, he wasn't really sure. But over the course of the 2012 campaign, he was called, visited, e-mailed, tweeted, and, through his Facebook page, urged by several of his friends to vote once more for Obama. The Obama campaign was turning to some of the most potent and trusted forms of communication, word-of-mouth and friend-to-friend, to reach Alex and countless millions of other potential voters. All of this was backed up by millions of dollars invested in microtargeting and data analytics, with the ability to focus on individual voters and the hundreds of data points known about each of them.

The Romney campaign had its own digital wonder, a voter-turnout mobile app under the name of Project Orca. This super app, to be used on Election Day, would link 800 Romney volunteers in Boston's TD Garden to some 30,000 volunteers throughout the country, who would report in on who had voted and who still should be contracted. But the glitzy mobile app was never tested in TD Garden, and it crashed repeatedly and turned out to be of little use.[92]

Number one surrogate. Former president George W. Bush (or for that matter, John McCain) was of no use to the Romney campaign, but Obama adeptly used former president Bill Clinton. Clinton was one of the stars of the Democratic nominating convention and he appeared in Obama commercials urging voters to choose Obama. "It was in its truest sense," wrote Republican consultant Evan Tracey, "a transfer of popularity from the former president to help close the deal."[93] The bitterness of the 2008 campaign was behind them, and Hillary Clinton was now secretary of state and presumptive heir to the Democratic leadership. For the Clintons and Obama, the alliance was a "mutual non-aggression and trade pact with long-run reciprocities implied if not spelled out in the treaty," observed communications scholar Michael Cornfield.[94]

Outside Voices

> *Contract killers out there in super PAC land.*
> —Democratic consultant David Axelrod's description of
> Karl Rove (Crossroads GPS) and the
> Koch brothers (Americans for Prosperity) (2012)[95]

In past presidential elections, outside voices contributed to the conversation. Most notably in recent times was the 2004 Swift Boat Veterans ads aimed at the credibility of John Kerry. Both Obama and McCain in 2008 sought to keep outside voices at a minimum, and overall, the 527s and independent organizations were not as prominent in 2008 as they were in 2004. But all this changed in 2012. Super PACs and nonprofit groups, the 501(c)(4) organizations, ostensibly organizations dedicated to promoting "social welfare," played increased roles in shaping the presidential election debate. Many such groups broadly interpreted their mission and began pouring millions of dollars into the presidential and other campaigns. From April 10, when Mitt Romney officially won the Republican nomination, until early September, these outside groups accounted for 55 percent of all ads on the Republican side, while Romney and the RNC provided 45 percent. In all, nonprofits, set up by organizations as diverse as the National Rifle Association and Planned Parenthood, spent over $300 million in 2012 on campaign activity, compared to just $5.8 million in 2008.[96] Outside interests came roaring back in 2012, particularly because of the 2010 decision of the US Supreme Court in *Citizens United v. Federal Election Commission*.[97] The Court held that the free speech portion of the First Amendment to the Constitution prohibited federal restrictions on independent expenditures by corporations or (by extension) labor unions or associations.

What worried the Obama campaign was the impending attack ads launched by American Crossroads, Karl Rove's organization, and Americans for Prosperity, the super PAC of the Koch brothers. The Kochs, in particular, had spent millions during the 2010 congressional campaigns and were gearing up to spend unknown millions during the 2012 presidential contest. To counter the Koch brothers, the Obama campaign unleashed its first ads in mid-January 2012, against "secretive oil billionaires," as the ad labeled them. This was, as journalist Daniel Schulman noted, part of a "carefully calibrated strategy to defang the Kochs and neutralize the impact of their attack ads."[98]

Adman Fred Davis proposed in May 2012 to make an anti-Obama ad in time for the Democratic National Convention that would "do exactly what John McCain would not let us do," when Davis worked for him in 2008. The $10 million ad plan was to be for the super PAC Ending Spending Action Fund, funded by Joe Ricketts, founder of the brokerage firm TD Ameritrade and whose family owned the Chicago Cubs baseball team. The ad would tie Obama with the controversial Rev. Jeremiah Wright, with an "extremely literate conservative African-American" being the spokesperson. In the fifty-four-page proposal, obtained by the *New York Times*, Obama was characterized as "the metrosexual black Abraham Lincoln" who "has emerged as a hyper-partisan, hyper-liberal elitist politician."[99] But the subject was simply too hot to handle, particularly for the Ricketts family business connections in Chicago, and in the end it was not shown.

Veteran political reporter Dan Balz of the *Washington Post* labeled an ad prepared by Priorities USA, the pro-Obama super PAC as the "most egregious example of a campaign out of bounds" and the most dishonest campaign ad of the year.[100] Titled "Understands," the ad featured Joe Soptic, a GST Steel employee who had lost his job:

> *Joe Soptic* (facing the camera): 'I don't think Mitt Romney understands what he's done by closing the plant. I don't think he realized that peoples' lives completely changed.
>
> [*Text*: Mitt Romney and Bain Capital made millions for themselves and then closed this steel plant.]
>
> *Joe Soptic*: When Mitt Romney and Bain closed the plant, I lost my health care and my family lost their health care. [*Soptic then explained that his wife became ill, and that it was terminal cancer*]. I don't think Mitt Romney realizes what he's done to anyone, and furthermore, I do not think that Mitt Romney is concerned.

While the ad ran just twice, it caused a furor. Critics charged: How dare the Obama forces and its allies suggest that someone died of cancer because of the business transactions of Romney? Obama privately said the ad crossed the line and was irritated that his campaign had been drawn into the fight. Later, Bill Burton, senior strategist for Priorities USA, defended the ad: "We didn't say that Mitt Romney caused someone to get cancer, and I think you have to presuppose that voters are idiots to think that they would take that from that ad."[101]

Advertising

One of the best campaign commercials was produced by Mark Putnam for the Obama campaign. It was a thirty-second commercial called "47 Percent," which took the infamous words of Mitt Romney about "47 percent of American people," and contrasted them with a montage of veterans and working men and women, shot in black and white, facing the camera, not at all amused:

> There are 47 percent of the people who will vote for the president, no matter what, who are dependent on the government, who believe they are victims, who believe government has a responsibility to care for them, who believe they are entitled to heal care, to food, to housing—you name it. And they will vote for this president no matter what. And so my job is to not worry about those people—I'll never convince them that they should take personal responsibility and care for their lives.[102]

The *Los Angeles Times* and *Politico* both dubbed this the best ad of the entire presidential campaign.

Analysis done by the Campaign Media Analysis Group showed that Republicans outspent Democrats on television advertising during the general election. In all, over $1 billion was spent on the presidential ads, with Republicans spending about $580 million and Democrats spending $470 million.[103] Altogether, counting up ads from the Obama and Romney campaigns and from pro-Democratic and pro-Republican organizations, a total of 474 unique presidential campaign ads were aired, up by 40 percent from 2008. Altogether, the Obama campaign aired more than a half million of its own ads, while the Romney campaign aired just 190,000 ads. Of all the pro-Republican ads, just 36 percent were directly controlled by the Romney campaign, while 66 percent of the pro-Democratic ads were controlled by the Obama campaign. The Obama campaign was able to stretch its dollars better, because as a candidate campaign, it qualified for the lowest rate broadcasters offered. The outside ads from the various super PACs had to pay the prevailing, and more expensive, rate.[104]

Outside Republican ads came from groups like Restore our Future PAC (Romney PAC), American Crossroads and Crossroads GPS (Karl Rove), Americans for Prosperity (Koch brothers), National Rifle Association, and American Energy Alliance (Koch brothers, inter alia). Pro-Obama groups included Priorities USA Action, Service Employees International Union (SEIU), and the American Federation of State, County, and Municipal Employees (AFSCME). In analyzing the ads, political communications scholars John C. Tedesco and Scott W. Dunn conclude that "fear that the presidential election would be the most negative on record—due mostly to the influx of advertisements from super PACs following the *Citizen United* ruling—proved to be true."[105]

While "Hope and Change" were the slogans for the Obama 2008 campaign, "Forward" was the organizing message in 2012. Republican media consultant Evan Tracey noted that "Forward" was "effective on a number of levels: it was inclusive, inspirational, and formed a narrative." It became the pervasive theme of the campaign.[106]

The Results and Aftermath

Bold predictions, wishful thinking. Joel Benenson, one of Obama's senior strategists, thought that the 2012 campaign was some of the best work that his polling firm had ever done.[107] The benchmark analysis, the first polls taken, began in August 2011, testing voters' sense of the economy, whether or not the country was headed in the right direction, and Obama's performance. By not using outdated sets of polling questions in the benchmark or subsequent polls and focus groups, by taking into account new communication tools such as cell phones, and by deeply probing the impact of the 2008 recession, Benenson's group was able to unearth the "hidden architecture of opinion" of likely voters. For example, rather than probing the issue of "are you better off than you were four years ago?" (the old Reagan 1980 question), voters were asked "who will make your life better four years from now?" The Obama camp also was conservative in its screening of probable voters: if there is a 50/50 chance a person might vote and favored Obama, that prospect wouldn't count as a strong enough possibility. With cautious screening, imaginative probing, and seeking out voters who might not traditionally be questioned, the polling team was able to confidently predict that Obama would carry most of the battleground states.

But a number of conservative commentators and former consultants confidently predicted that Obama would crash and burn, making their predictions right up to Election Day. Part of that is pure political bluster: of course, you don't admit defeat, lest it become a self-fulfilling prophecy. Romney's senior pollster, Neil Newhouse, complained about some of the public pollsters showing a small Obama lead in the last few weeks, insisting that the race was much closer than they predicted. Many of the conservative talking heads amplified Newhouses's skepticism.[108] Arthur Finkelstein privately assured his Israeli clients that Obama would be defeated; Karl Rove, who predicted a Romney win, was embarrassed and flustered on election night television as the reality of Obama's win in Ohio (and hence the country) settled in. Dick Morris confidently predicted that Obama would be smothered by Romney. Peggy Noonan, Charles Krauthammer, George Will, and many other conservative commentators assured their listeners of Obama's demise. They dismissed Nate Silver, the most accurate of all prognosticators. Silver, working for the *New York Times*, had correctly predicted the outcome in all fifty states and the District of Columbia and came within one-tenth of a percentage point of Obama's popular vote, and he had consistently told readers that Obama would win.

After eighteen months of pre-primary and primary election jousting by Republican hopefuls, and finally the general election, little had changed from the election results of four years before. Two states that went for Obama in 2008—Indiana (the biggest anomaly) and North Carolina—returned to the Republicans and Romney in 2012. And that was it. Nearly $6 billion spent; over 1.5 million television ads aired; millions of phone calls made and e-mails sent; hundreds of consultants employed; and thousands of campaign workers, paid and unpaid, and untold number of volunteers labored for their candidates and their causes. Despite their efforts, just 57.5 percent of the eligible adult population voted; roughly 97 million adults sat out the election. Obama received 6.85 million votes fewer than in 2008; Romney received 808,000 fewer than McCain.[109]

It was never going to be easy to take on Obama: he was a gifted campaigner, with all the resources of an incumbent; he had a seasoned campaign staff, with no primary challenger. The economy was the albatross around Obama's neck, but, slowly and surely, the economy was getting better. In the primaries, Romney had to fend off challenger after challenger who was more conservative, more appealing to the any-body-but-Romney crowd. Demographics were increasingly hurting Republicans, with more Hispanic voters moving to the Democratic fold.

With expectations so high for a Romney win, disappointed Republican Party operatives, pundits, and strategists soon brought out the long knives. Some criticism was directed at Romney himself, but others looked at the strategy and tactics of the challenger's campaign. Republican consultant Thomas Edmonds observed that while the Romney campaign was a solid and professionally run effort, it made some critical mistakes: it underestimated the Obama team, particularly its ground game and technology; it didn't make the election a referendum on Obama; during the last days of the campaign, it shifted its limited resources from battleground states to marginal states; it wasn't cost-efficient in using both old and new media technology; and, finally, it failed to used Paul Ryan to reach out to younger voters.[110] Republican consultant Mike Murphy was less charitable: "It's time for the GOP to face the hard truth, no matter how painful. The Republican brand is dying, many of our strategists are incompetent, and we still design campaigns to prevail in the America of twenty-five years ago."[111]

Probably most surprised was Romney himself, who appeared flummoxed and confused at the news that he indeed had lost. He had not prepared a concession speech, but now he needed one. Then, a few days after the election, Romney was on a conference call to some major donors and explained why the president won re-election: Obama won because he offered gifts to targeted groups:

> You can imagine for somebody making $25,000 or $30,000 or $35,000 a year, being told you're now going to get free health care, particularly if you don't have it, getting free health care worth, what, $10,000 per family, in perpetuity—I mean, this is huge .... Likewise with Hispanic voters, free health care was a big plus. But in addition with regard to Hispanic voters, the amnesty for children of illegals, the so-called Dream Act kids, was a huge plus for that voting group.[112]

Almost immediately Republican leaders began disavowing Romney's "gifts" statement (which sounded a lot like his infamous "47 percent" comment a few months earlier), pledging to open the Republican Party to a broader swath of voters, and speculating on who would be the probable party candidate in 2016.

A more measured assessment came from political scientists John Sides and Lynn Vavreck. Obama won, they argued, because the environment favored him. The economy was growing enough, and the Obama campaign was adept at "rallying partisans and making the economy more salient to undecided voters."[113] An incumbent, historically, receives a three-point advantage simply for being the incumbent. For Romney to overcome the growing economy, to say nothing of the incumbency factor, his campaign would have needed "a massive investment in advertising and a field operation probably two to three times the size of the one he had."[114]

But the Romney campaign (as well as the McCain campaign four years earlier), while understanding basic campaign and marketing techniques, was never fully able to exploit the innovations of microtargeting, social media, and Big Data in the way that Obama's forces could. Political marketing scholar Bruce I. Newman, studying the Obama 2008 and 2012 campaigns, stated that the Obama model represented "one of the most successful start-ups in the history of marketing" and represented a "paradigm shift" in the way marketing tools were used in politics, establishing a new set of best practices that could be applied not only to politics but to the corporate and nonprofit world.[115]

However, Charles and David Koch, whose network of political action committees, super PACs, and nonprofits spent at least $407 million during the 2012 election cycle, were undeterred by the Obama victory. "We raised a lot of money and mobilized an awful lot of people, and we lost, plain and simple," said David Koch. "We're going to study what worked, what didn't work, and improve our efforts in the future. We're not going to roll over and play dead."[116]

CHAPTER 20

Outside Groups, Plutocrats, and Dark Money

Consultants and the 2016 Presidential Campaign

This Court now concludes that independent expenditures, including those made by corporations, do not give rise to corruption or the appearance of corruption. That speakers may have influence over or access to elected officials does not mean that those officials are corrupt. And the appearance of influence or access will not cause the electorate to lose faith in this democracy.

—Justice Anthony M. Kennedy,
Citizens United v. Federal Election Commission (2010)

TWO OF THE fundamental objectives of the 1971 federal campaign law and its 1974 amendments were to promote transparency and establish contribution limits. Donors would have to identify themselves and give their addresses and the names of their employers. They were permitted to give just $1,000 to candidate campaigns during a primary and general election, $5,000 to a political action committee (PAC), and $20,000 to a national political party, with a cap of $25,000 for all contributions during any political year. Deep-pocket donors often complained that they had "maxed out," that they had given as much as the federal law would allow. Candidates for office were allowed to spend as much as they wanted for their own campaigns, thanks to the Supreme Court decision in *Buckley v. Valeo* (1976), which considered such individual money as a form of free speech, protected by the First Amendment.

During the last decades of the twentieth century, a new form of campaign money sprang to life, called "soft money," which could be raised in unlimited amounts for party-building activities. The money spigot was turned on full blast, and soft money (as opposed to the regulated "hard money") became the weapon of choice. The Bipartisan Campaign Reform Act (BCRA) of 2002 increased the individual contribution limits and eliminated soft money. But within a nano-second, campaign lawyers and operatives had discovered ways to circumvent the law. They relied on other parts of the Internal Revenue code, rediscovering section 527, which was designed for tax-exempt political organizations (such as a political party, committees, or associations), 501(c)(4) social welfare organiza-tions, and 501(c)(6) business and chamber of commerce organizations.

These organizations were not under the jurisdiction of the federal campaign law and were particularly attractive to people and groups who wanted to give a lot of money but didn't want others to know about it. Both 527 groups and 501(c)(4) and (6) organizations could raise unlimited amounts of money. While 527 groups are now required to name their donors, the 501(c) donors can remain anonymous. Soon critics were calling these anonymous funds "dark money." These 501(c) organizations can support or advocate the defeat of candidates, but the primary mission of the organizations is supposed to be the promotion of the common good and the general welfare. In reality, the central purpose of many of these organizations soon became blatantly evident: "promoting the common good" meant defeating an opponent.

Journalist Thomas B. Edsall wrote that tax-exempt nonprofit organizations, such as 501(c) groups, had become the "weapon of choice for those who want to influence elections without leaving fingerprints."[1] During the 2003–2004 elec-tion cycle, there was $5.8 million in dark money; in 2011–2012 it ballooned to $310.8 million. Most of the money went through 501(c)(4) social welfare groups; but a considerable amount came through 501(c)(6) organizations, nonprofit trade associations (e.g., the US Chamber of Commerce). During the 2011–2012 election cycle, 85 percent of the nondisclosed money ($265.2 million) came from conser-vative groups, while 11.2 percent ($10.89 million) came from liberal groups.[2]

Not only can dark money organizations hide their donors, but they also can readily evade any scrutiny from the Internal Revenue Service. Journalism fellow Lee Aitken pointed out that 501(c)(4) groups are allowed to "self declare" as tax exempt organizations and can operate for nearly two full years before facing IRS scrutiny, such as to determine whether they are legitimately "social welfare" orga-nizations, or whether they should have registered as a 527 nonprofit organization engaged in political activity instead (and thus be required to disclose its donors). Thus an organization can come into existence, spend millions on independent expenditures, have Election Day come and go, and still not face the scrutiny of an overburdened IRS.[3] Aitken points out that some of the groups participating in the 2012 election cycle "remained completely unknown until late 2013, when they filed an initial tax return." One such group was Freedom Partners, which spent $250 million during the 2012 cycle.[4] The IRS will have a difficult time going after social welfare groups because Republicans in the late fall 2015 budget reconcili-ation bill slipped in a provision that would block the tax agency from creating rules to prevent such dark money abuse.

Except for the enormous size of today's dark money contributions, one could readily conclude we haven't progressed much from Lyndon Johnson's time as Senate majority leader in the 1950s, when bags of Texas oil money were secretly flown up to Washington and handed out to grateful politicians.

This rush of money was aided by the *Citizens United* decision, which opened the gates to unlimited amounts of corporate and labor union funds to be used as independent expenditures throughout candidate elections. In early 2010 the US Supreme Court, in a sharply divided opinion, ruled that the federal government could not curtail independent political spending by corporations in candidate elections. This decision overturned the BCRA ban on "electioneering communications" by corporations or labor unions thirty days before a presidential primary or sixty days before a general election. The Court, through Justice Anthony Kennedy, characterized that BCRA ban as "classic examples of censorship."[5] But many, including President Obama, cried foul. During his State of the Union address one week later, Obama stated that the Supreme Court had "reversed a century of law that I believe will open the floodgates for special interests."[6] Soon, however, Obama and Democrats would belatedly join Republicans in courting big money to invest in super PACs and dark money organizations.

Super PACs and Independent Expenditures

> *Well-funded groups like Americans for Prosperity and Senate Majority PAC have the ability to change the landscape. They can go on early when the candidates can't buy, they can be up over the summer, they're always on, and they can basically snap their fingers and go up on air.*
>
> Elizabeth Wilner, Kantar Media/CMAG (2014)[7]

> *If the Koch network ever decided to challenge the Republican establishment, it certainly had the trappings of a political party that might give the GOP a good run for its money.*
>
> —Kenneth P. Vogel (2014)[8]

Even before *Citizens United*, several labor organizations, ideological interest groups, trade groups, and corporations were building large traditional PACs that did more than simply give money to candidates. PAC management expert Steven E. Billet characterized these as "Monster PACs"—seventy-two PACs that had raised and spent at least $2 million each during the 2005–2006 election cycle.[9] Some of the Monster PACs were EMILY's list (the largest, at $34 million), MoveOn.org (second largest, at $27 million), down to the American Society of Anesthesiologists ($2 million). Billet observed that these Monster PACs had "fundamentally changed the calculus of campaign giving." They didn't simply write checks to candidates, they also recruited candidates, mobilized support, ran parallel campaigns, and trained campaign operatives. In many ways, he argued, the Monster PACs "have taken on the trappings of political parties."[10]

These Monster PACs were a precursor to new and richer independent expenditure committees, soon dubbed "super PACs." These new PACs owe their existence to another 2010 court decision, *SpeechNow.org v. Federal Election*

Commission.[11] In this case, a federal district court ruled that the $5,000 contribution limits imposed on PACs was unconstitutional and that independent organizations should be permitted to raise as much money as they want. SpeechNow. org, a 527 organization founded by conservative operatives, successfully argued that the $5,000 imposition was a suppression of free speech. The federal government argued that lifting the $5,000 limit could lead to "preferential access for donors and undue influence over office holders." But the district court ruled that whatever the merits of the government's arguments before *Citizens United,* "they plainly have no merit after *Citizens United.* . . . Contributions to groups that make only independent expenditures cannot corrupt or create the appearance of corruption."[12]

The federal courts in 2010, then, administered a one-two punch for freeing up federal campaign funds for outside interests. *Citizens United* provided for unlimited independent spending by corporations, labor unions, and organizations during any time in a campaign; *SpeechNow.org* permitted unlimited raising of money by such independent groups. Thanks to *SpeechNow.org,* hundreds of new organizations were created. By October 2015, there were a total of 1,212 registered super PACs; the great majority of these registered PACs, however, neither raised nor spent any money. (See below for the most active 2016 presidential super PACs).[13] These super PACs had to list the names and amounts of the contributions, but they could raise as much money as they were able. Yet unlike regular PACs, super PACs were prohibited from giving any funds directly to a candidate.

Candidates, political parties, and ordinary PACs were now competing for precious campaign funds with these new independent expenditure committees. For many consultants and candidates, this didn't sit well. Republican consultant Wayne C. Johnson voiced a common complaint: "It's a bad model. We have to make sure there isn't a super PAC out there spending $200 or $500 million dollars. The money needs to go to the candidates. It needs to go to the campaigns."[14]

In *McCutcheon v. Federal Election Commission* (2014), the Supreme Court, by a five-to-four vote, struck down the federal campaign law ban on the total amount of money a person could contribute over a two-year cycle to a candidate, party, or political action group. Only 646 contributors had spent the maximum of $117,000 for the 2012 election cycle; they had donated more than $93 million directly to federal candidates and national political parties. But now the ban was lifted, and big-time givers could write checks to their hearts content.[15] Justice Steven G. Breyer, writing for the four dissenters, captured the danger of this new, unbridled world of big money politics: "taken together with *Citizens United v. Federal Election Commission,* today's decision eviscerates our Nation's campaign finance laws, leaving a remnant incapable of dealing with the grave problems of democratic legitimacy that those laws were intended to resolve."[16]

The 1971-74 and 2002 campaign laws were indeed eviscerated and as Obama and many others predicted, special interest money, unlimited and often not disclosed, began flooding into US Senate, congressional, and presidential elections. Table 20.1 shows the total amount of campaign money that has flooded into presidential and congressional races during the past several cycles.

TABLE 20.1 Funds Spent in Federal
Elections by Presidential Candidates, Senate
and House Candidates, Political Parties,
and Independent Organizations, 1998–2014
(in billions)

Cycle	Total	House, Senate	Presidential
2014	$3.665	$3.665	—
2012	$6.285	$3.664	$2.621
2010	$3.643	$3.643	—
2008	$5.285	$2.485	$2.799
2006	$2.852	$2.852	—
2004	$4.147	$2.237	$1.910
2002	$2.181	$2.181	—
2000	$3.082	$1.669	$1.413
1998	$1.618	$1.618	—
Total	$32.758	$24.014	$8.743

Source: OpenSecrets.org website, www.opensecrets.
org/bigpicture (accessed January 24, 2015).

The Nationalization of Campaigns

At one time, campaign dynamics were relatively simple: the candidate of one party went up against the candidate from the other party. All politics, in Tip O'Neill's often-cited phrase, is local. Issues fought over in a North Carolina congressional district might be quite different from those in a New Hampshire or California congressional district. Around the mid-1980s, however, we began to see more and more national organizations trying to influence the outcome of heretofore local or regional races. Traditionally, outsiders would give funds through PACs or directly to the candidates. The US Chamber of Commerce or the national AFL-CIO would donate money and ground troops. But in 1985, a new dimension was added: independent expenditures by ideologically based organizations. The Jesse Helms–affiliated National Congressional Club (NCC) vowed to "spend as much as we can raise," said Carter Wrenn, the executive director. NCC targeted liberal Democratic senators Alan Cranston (California), Gary Hart (Colorado), and Christopher Dodd (Connecticut).[17] They were perhaps encouraged by the 1984 defeat of Illinois senator Charles Percy. A moderate Republican, Percy was a target of pro-Israeli interests in the United States, and Michael Goland, a member of the American Israel Public Affairs Council (AIPAC) who lived in California, spent over $1.1 million in independent expenditure money on mailings and television ads to help oust Percy.[18] Outside groups and individuals soon became important players in US Senate, congressional, and presidential primary and general elections.

With contribution limits stripped away in 2010, independent expenditures exploded in number and in the amount of money they spent. One of the first super PACs formed was American Crossroads, a conservative political organization, created by former White House operatives Karl Rove and Ed Gillespie.

During the 2010 cycle, the first year of its operation, American Crossroads led the field in spending more than $21 million in independent expenditures.[19] Soon, Rove created Crossroads GPS (Grassroots Policy Strategies), a 501(c)(4) organization, which had the advantage of being able to hide the names of donors (but not of recipients).

By 2012, independent expenditures had mushroomed, thanks to the loosening of campaign finance law, more aggressive and more ideologically driven activist groups, and the more assertive role played by wealthy private donors. During the 2011–2012 election cycle, a total of $305.3 million was spent by independent expenditure committees. The Sunlight Foundation, a nonpartisan, nonprofit organization based in San Francisco, found that 78 percent of the money was spent opposing candidates, while 20 percent was spent supporting candidates. Over $200 million was spent opposing Democrats, and $38.6 million was spent opposing Republicans. A little over $11 million was spent supporting Democrats, and $49.8 million helped support Republicans. Nearly all of the independent expenditure political ads were shown during the final, frenetic weeks of the presidential campaign.[20]

These groups are not registered with the Federal Election Commission (FEC) as political committees because they claim that their primary purpose is not political. The Sunlight Foundation noted that the amounts shown in Table 20.2 are for independent expenditures only, which have to be reported. Many of these groups also spent millions running issue ads, whose expenditures do not have to be reported. For example, Crossroads GPS, which is headed by Steven Law, redacted the names of all fifty-three contributors who gave more than $1 million each in 2012, and blanked out the names of the 291 donors who gave $5,000 or more.[21]

The Bipartisan Campaign Reform Act of 2002 required that federal candidates declare that they approve of campaign advertising, with the now familiar, "I'm [Candidate A] and I approve this message." In a way, this would be a shaming device: a candidate would think twice before putting up a scurrilous or untrue ad attacking an opponent. But no such message is attached to independent expenditure ads. After *Citizens United*, the House of Representatives passed the DISCLOSE Act, which would require noncandidate groups to "stand by their ad." But the Senate refused to go along, and the DISCLOSE Act never became law. However, it is often through independent expenditures that a campaign's dirty work is done. Super PACs, 501(c)(4) groups, and other outsiders can attack an opponent with stark and controversial messages, while their favored candidate can innocently claim no knowledge of the campaign ad, or even criticize its content. The Swift Boat ads of 2004 or the Willie Horton ads of 1988 are two of the most egregious examples. In recent cycles, attacks on Obamacare have been frequent themes. As the 2016 presidential campaign unfolded, voters had to brace themselves for more negative and caustic commercials coming from well-funded super PACs and dark money organizations aimed at tearing down opponents.

In 2012, House and Senate candidates, the political parties, and independent organizations raised and spent around $3.66 billion; another $2.62 billion was spent on the presidential election. For the 2014 congressional elections, the Center for Responsive Politics estimated that $3.67 billion of campaign dollars were spent, including about $900 million from outside sources.[22] These are historic sums, but they are also finite. Donors, particularly wealthy ones, feel pressed from all corners—from the political party, from the independent expenditure committee, from the candidates themselves. There is a growing concern, expressed above by consultant Wayne Johnson, that outside money, which can generate television and online ads, field organizations, get-out-the-vote campaigns, and other trappings of a campaign, deprives candidate campaigns of much-needed resources. Give the money directly to candidates and their campaigns, Johnson and others would argue, instead of investing in an outside organization.

2014 Senate Races and the Flood of Outside Money

> *The next Senate was just elected on the greatest wave*
> *of secret, special-interest money ever raised*
> *in a congressional election.*
>
> —*New York Times* editorial, on the 2014 Senate races (2014)[23]

> *The irony is that the more political ads air on TV,*
> *the more voters tune them out. It just became a white noise.*
> *The return on investment is absurd.*
>
> Mark McKinnon, Republican ad maker (2014)[24]

TABLE 20.2 Independent Expenditures of Noncommittee FEC Filers, 2011–2012

Organization	Independent Expenditures	Main Purpose and Amount Spent
Crossroads Grassroots Policy Strategies (GPS)	$70,586,641	Oppose Democrats ($62.4 million)
Americans for Prosperity	$33,539,772	Oppose Democrats ($33.5 million)
US Chamber of Commerce	$32,676,075	Oppose Democrats ($27.9 million)
American Future Fund	$23,959,072	Support Republicans ($12.4 million)
Americans for Job Security	$15,872,866	Oppose Democrats ($15.2 million)
Americans for Tax Reform	$15,794,582	Oppose Democrats ($14.4 million)
American Action Network	$11,786,129	Oppose Democrats ($10.4 million)
League of Conservation Voters	$10,897,016	Oppose Republicans ($8.6 million)
Americans for Responsible Leadership	$9,787,783	Support Republicans ($6.5 million)
Patriot Majority	$7,509,017	Oppose Republicans ($6.6 million)

Source: FEC filings and Sunlight Foundation.

During the 2014 congressional elections, an unprecedented amount of outside money flowed into critical US Senate contests, and those funds were crucial in defeating five Democratic incumbent senators and in aiding Majority Leader Mitch McConnell in keeping his hotly contested seat. In the ten most expensive US Senate contests in 2014, the outside money made an impact: Democrats Kay Hagan (North Carolina), Mark Udall (Colorado), David Pryor (Arkansas), Mary Landrieu (Louisiana), and Mark Begich (Alaska) all lost, and in all but the Louisiana campaign, outside groups spent more than the candidates combined.

The total sums spent on these races exceed the sums spent in previous cycles. Much of the money was wasted, as voters were saturated with television ads, telephone calls, get-out-the-vote drives, and so forth. It was campaigning on steroids, as outside groups, the political parties, and the candidates tried to woo voters. In Alaska, for example, just 264,876 citizens voted, and $62.3 million was spent trying to convince them; for every vote cast, $235 was spent in advertising and campaign services. It was not so long ago that spending $5 per vote cast seemed like an outrageous sum.

In the most expensive 2014 Senate contest, the Kentucky race between Senate Majority Leader Mitchell McConnell and Democratic challenger Allison Lundergan Grimes, McConnell benefitted from at least $23 million in spending from outside groups. Some were traditional players, like the National Rifle Association or the National Homebuilders Association, but the biggest outside group, called Kentucky Opportunity Coalition, spent $7.6 million on McConnell's behalf. The Kentucky Opportunity Coalition was a 501(c)(4) organization, a "social welfare" group. What was its social welfare purpose? Well, the re-election of McConnell. Who gave money? We don't know. As the *New York Times* editorial writers stated, "It could be anyone who wants to be a political player but lacks the courage to do so openly—possibly coal interests, retailers opposed to the minimum wage, defense contractors, but there's no way for the public to know. You can bet, however, that the senator knows exactly to whom he owes an enormous favor."[25]

The avalanche of outside money funneled through super PACs and dark money sources was just a foretaste of the funds that would pour into the presidential nominating campaigns of 2016.

Consultants, Big Money, and the 2016 Presidential Campaign

> *"Not since before Watergate have so few people and businesses provided so much early money in a campaign, most of it through channels legalized by the Supreme Court's* Citizens United *decision . ."*.
>
> —*New York Times* (October 10, 2015)[26]

As this book is completed, near the conclusion of the 2016 primary season, several features stand out that make this presidential contest different from previous campaigns. The first is the astounding amount of early money coming from multimillionaires that went to super PACs that were aligned with (but heaven forbid, not coordinated with) individual candidates. But the money was mostly for naught, as party insiders could not capture the support of primary voters. The flip side of the money game was the astounding number of individuals who gave small donations to Bernie Sanders, sustaining his campaign throughout. The second is the failure of professionals and insiders in both parties to read the mood of the country and understand that this would be the year of anger, disillusionment, and impatience with politics as usual. The third feature was how a supposedly strong field of Republican candidates gave way to outsiders, like Ben Carson, Ted Cruz, and Donald Trump, and how the seemingly unbeatable Hillary Clinton had trouble fending off the self-proclaimed outsider, Bernie Sanders. Finally, this was the year of the insult, the outrage, the finger pointing, and the year where facts and truth were supplanted by braggadocio and bluster. Much of that tone was set by Donald Trump, the master of media attention and manipulation, with the mainstream media and his fellow competitors as willful enablers.

Republican Candidates

> *The Republican Party must focus its efforts to earn new supporters*
> *and voters in the following demographic communities:*
> *Hispanic, Asian and Pacific Islanders, African Americans, Indian*
> *Americans, Native Americans, women, and youth.*
> *This priority needs to be a continual effort that*
> *affects every facet of our Party's activities,*
> *including our messaging, strategy, outreach, and budget.*
> —Republican Party Growth and Opportunity Project (December 2012)[27]

> *No one tells me what to say.*
> —Donald Trump, explaining why he doesn't
> hire private pollsters (2015)[28]

Like the 2008 campaign, the 2016 presidential election was a wide-open contest on the Republican side. Mitt Romney, after much hesitation and flat-out denials, signaled to big-money supporters that he was ready to try a third time for the White House, crafting a message based on empathy for and support of the middle class (perhaps trying to recast his 2012 image). Then, abruptly, Romney changed his mind; there would be no third run for the White House.

In all, the Republican lineup was bulging with seventeen seekers, and compared to the very thin lineup in 2012, it was sprinkled with seasoned elected officials. There were four governors—Chris Christie (New Jersey), Bobby Jindal (Louisiana), John Kasich (Ohio), and Scott Walker (Wisconsin); five former governors—Rick Perry (Texas), Jeb Bush (Florida), George Pataki (New York), Mike Huckabee (Arkansas), and Jim Gilmore (Virginia); four US senators—Ted Cruz (Texas), Rand Paul (Kentucky), Lindsey Graham (South Carolina), and Marco Rubio (Florida); and one former US senator—Rick Santorum (Pennsylvania). In addition, there were three who had never served in public office before—entrepreneur Donald Trump, business executive Carly Fiorina, and former neurosurgeon Ben Carson.

For each of these candidates, the task was difficult: start raising money early, begin setting up campaign structures in early primary states, and hope to get noticed by the press and the public. What was new this time around would be the emergence of super PACs, many of whom collected more campaign money than did the candidates' own campaigns.

The first Republican to formally announce was Texas senator Ted Cruz, and with him came four pro-Cruz super PACs (called Keep the Promise I through IV). They raised $31 million, from deep-pocket Texas admirers, in the week after Cruz announced.[29] The Cruz campaign was headed by Jason Johnson and Jeff Roe, and drew upon several of his Senate staffers. Veteran polling consultant Kellyanne Conway headed one of the four super PACs.

Former Florida governor Jeb Bush, for a longtime noncommittal, in late fall 2014 publicly acknowledged his serious interest in the presidency. Establishment money poured into his leadership PAC, Right to Rise, and it looked like Bush was the odds-on favorite of the old Republican guard and the extensive Bush family network. It took him, however, another seven months to formally declare his candidacy. His noncampaign suffered several missteps, and as the *Washington Post* wrote, dozens of Bush backers and well-placed Republicans characterized his effort as an "overly optimistic, even haughty" operation.[30] But his middle-of-the-road policy focus on immigration and education did not sit well with party conservatives, and as other Republican rivals jumped in, Bush slipped in the polls. His quiet demeanor sent the message that he didn't have the "fire in his belly" to be the nominee. Before even announcing his candidacy officially in June 2015, Bush was forced to shake up his campaign staff. Bush was aided by longtime political consultant Mike Murphy, who operated Right to Rise, and his veteran chief of staff Sally Bradshaw. David Kochel, who had worked for Romney in his two presidential bids, was to head the campaign, but he was replaced by Danny Diaz, a veteran of the Romney 2012, McCain 2008, and Bush 2004 presidential campaigns.[31]

Chris Christie, once the high-flying twice-elected governor of New Jersey and chair of the Republican Governors Association, stumbled with the "Bridgegate" scandal, but he eventually announced his candidacy in June 2015. Christie's chief strategist was Mike DuHaime of Mercury Public Affairs, who had previously been Rudy Giuliani's top presidential strategist in 2012, and had been the top strategist in Christie's 2009 and 2013 gubernatorial campaigns. Bill Stepien, Christie's former campaign manager, had severed ties with the governor. Running the pro-Christie super PAC, America Leads, was Phil Cox, a former executive director of the Republican Governors Association.[32]

Announcing in June 2015, Texas governor Rick Perry hired Austin-based consultant Jeff Miller as campaign manager, and retained former campaign manager Rob Johnson as chief strategist, but shed much of his 2012 presidential team. The pro-Perry super PAC, Opportunity and Freedom PAC, was headed by Mississippi-based consultant Austin Barbour and California-based consultant Tony Russo.[33] One of the last to announce, Perry was also the first to announce his campaign had folded, ceasing operations on September 10, 2015.

Florida senator Marco Rubio hired Terry Sullivan, who had previously run the pro-Rubio super PAC Reclaim America, to be his campaign manager. Joining Sullivan was Rich Beeson, a veteran operative who was Mitt Romney's

2012 political director. Longtime Republican pollster Whit Ayres, of North Star Opinion Research, also signed up for the race. The Rubio-affiliated super PAC, Reclaim America, was headed by Warren Tompkins, business partner of Terry Sullivan.[34]

Former Louisiana governor Bobby Jindal created two organizations, a federal PAC, Stand Up to Washington, and a policy group, America Next. His group of consultants included OnMessage, Inc., a Virginia-based media firm that had worked for Jindal for over a decade and employed his former campaign manager, Timmy Teepell.[35] Jindal, however, bowed out in mid-November 2015, after the fourth Republican debate.

Kentucky senator Rand Paul relied on Chip Englander as his campaign manager, and turned to veteran pollster Tony Fabrizio and operative Chris LaCivita, among others. The super PAC affiliated with his campaign, RAND PAC, was headed by former chief of staff Doug Stafford.[36] Wisconsin governor Scott Walker, who finally entered the race in July 2015, brought with him a veteran team of pollsters from the Tarrance Group (Ed Goeas, Brian Tringali, and B. J. Martino), which had previously aided him in his recall and re-election fights.[37] Walker showed early promise, especially in preliminary polling done in Iowa, but by September 2015, he suspended his campaign, effectively ending his bid for the nomination. The well-financed super PAC supporting Walker, the Unintimidated PAC, was left with the task of trying to figure out what to do with their $20 million war chest.

Carly Fiorina, former CEO of Hewlett-Packard, signed up consultants Frank Sadler, who once worked for Koch Industries, and Stephen DeMaura, who headed a pro-business advocacy group, Americans for Job Security. However, some of Fiorina's consultants and staffers from her failed 2010 US Senate race in California remained bitter, with Fiorina owing them around $500,000 in wages and costs.[38] Super PACs are not supposed to have the name of their favored candidate in their title, but through a little trickery, the CARLY PAC was created (coming from the acronym "Conservative, Authentic, Responsive Leadership for You").

The second-to-last Republican to jump in was John Kasich, governor of Ohio, who had sought the presidential nomination when he was a member of Congress in 2000. Working for Kasich were two longtime political consultants, strategist John Weaver and media specialist Fred Davis. The campaign manager was Beth Hansen, Kasich's former chief of staff and a veteran Ohio campaign operative.[39] Lindsey Graham, senator from South Carolina, chose Christian Ferry as his campaign manager; Ferry was deputy campaign manager for Graham's close friend John McCain's 2008 presidential campaign. Graham's former deputy chief of staff Andrew King headed the super PAC, Security Is Strength.[40]

Running for a second time for their party's nomination were former Arkansas governor and television talk show host Mike Huckabee (running in 2008), former Pennsylvania senator Rick Santorum (2012), former Virginia governor Jim Gilmore (2008), and Kasich (2000). Gilmore, along with George Pataki, caught the attention of the news media only on the days that they announced, were ignored by the press and public, and even shunted aside during the Republican debates.

Political neophyte and retired neurosurgeon Ben Carson, closely tied to the Republican Party's religious right, relied on Barry Bennett as his campaign manager. Bennett earlier had advised Ohio senator Rob Portman and had worked in the polling firm of Mary Cheney, the daughter of former vice president Dick Cheney. Also assisting Carson was longtime Republican consultant Ed Brookover, who headed the political practice section of the Republican consulting firm of Greener and Hook and conservative media personality Armstrong Williams. By the end of December 2015, however, Carson was down from his early polling lead and frustrated with his advisers: "They want me to be more bombastic, they want you to attack other people . . . They want me to act more like a politician."[41]

Making the biggest splash was entrepreneur Donald Trump, who announced his candidacy from his Trump Tower office building in Manhattan. To bolster the "crowd" at Trump's announcement event, actors were hired at $50 per person to "wear t-shirts and carry signs and help cheer" Trump, according to an e-mail solicitation from Extra Mile Casting.[42] Trump, probably the most recognizable Republican candidate thanks to his television show *The Apprentice*, and to decades of self-promotion, soon became the media's darling and drew considerable support from voters disenchanted with Republican mainstream politicians. Trashing Hispanics, vowing to build a formidable border fence, demanding that no Muslims be allowed to migrate to the United States., and belittling other candidates as "losers" or worse language, Trump quickly became the voice of the angry outsider, especially white, blue-collar voters with modest formal education. He became a social media star, composing many of his own Twitter statements (6,345 in all from June to December 2015) at all hours of the night, and ridiculing opponents, the media (liberal and otherwise), and all forms of political correctness. To give but two examples posted December 18, 2015: "@JebBush has embarrassed himself & his family with his incompetent campaign for President," and later, "The last thing our country needs is another BUSH! Dumb as a Rock!" "The dark power of his words," wrote reporters Patrick Healy and Maggie Haberman, "became the defining feature" of his campaign.[43]

Record numbers of viewers watched the Republican debates. Especially during the first debate, all eyes were on Trump, to see what he would say next, whom he would insult, and how the other candidates would react. The media fell right into this silliness, fawning over Trump, amplifying his insults of Fox moderator Megyn Kelly and fellow candidate Carly Fiorina. For much of the primary season, Trump dominated the news, getting an extraordinary amount of free media attention. He was outrageous, he was crude, he was bombastic—just the kind of performance needed to boost sagging cable news ratings and to feed the passions of a solid core of anti-establishment supporters.

Trump, sounding like Ross Perot twenty years earlier, was to be the candidate who eschewed media handlers, focus group sessions, and the other trappings of modern campaigns. Focus groups? Don't need them, Trump said, he would depend on his own instincts.

His campaign manager was Corey Lewandowski, a one-time operative for the Koch-funded Americans for Prosperity who had briefly worked for the RNC. Among Republican strategists and insiders, there was both shock and bitterness over Trump's continued appeal. As one disgruntled New Hampshire Republican operative said, "Any serious person in Washington could never work for [Trump], because it would just destroy your career and you'll never be respected by anyone around here."[44] Lewandowski would be joined later by seasoned Republican political operative Paul Manafort and several others.

At the beginning of 2016, just one month before the first caucus votes were cast in Iowa, four Republicans had dropped out—Perry, Walker, Jindal, and Graham. Other Republicans—particularly Pataki, Gilmore, Huckabee, Paul, and Santorum—barely registered any response in nationwide Republican approval ratings and were soon gone. Bush, especially, and Kasich failed to live up to earlier expectations, while Carson appeared to lose out to Cruz for the religious right vote. Increasingly, Rubio or Christie looked like the best choices for establishment Republicans, but still trailed the raucous and popular Trump.

In November, the policy issues shifted sharply away from Obamacare, balanced budgets, and other standard domestic policy issues. The mass shootings at a Planned Parenthood facility in Colorado reignited the decades-long debate on gun control. The November Paris terrorist attacks and the ISIS-inspired mass shooting in San Bernardino, California, turned the presidential debate to national security and the plight (or threat) of Syrian refugees. The language got ugly, with threats against American mosques, separating Christian from Muslim refugee seekers, and demands for tougher screening processes for asylum seekers. Through it all, Cruz, Christie, and Trump seemed to benefit, from their tough talk and demand for action.

While Trump relied on his own crowd appeal, Cruz and his campaign sought out and wooed likely state delegates and used some of the newer techniques of voter identification. Cruz used "psychographic targeting," a relatively new way of targeting voters in the United States, but used by commercial companies and by candidates in Mexico and elsewhere. This targeting is used to pinpoint those voters who should receive phone calls, e-mail or direct mail messages, or be visited by the field staff. Cruz paid at least $750,000 to Cambridge Analytica, a US affiliate of a behavioral research firm based in London. The firm surveyed 150,000 households nationwide looking for basic traits of openness, conscientiousness, extraversion, agreeableness, and neuroticism. To this, the Cruz campaign added information from Facebook and other social media. As the Washington Post reported, Cruz's big data operation doesn't just perform voter outreach, it helps make key decisions, like where Cruz should travel, what he should say, who his precinct captains should be (extraverts), and other crucial information.[45]

By mid-May, the Republican primary fight had been settled. Establishment favorite Jeb Bush had dropped out after the disappointing South Carolina primary; Fiorina, Christie, Rubio, and Carson also made their exits, announcing that they had suspended their campaigns. That left just three, Kasich (who had won just Ohio), Cruz (claiming his outsider status and champion of true conservatism), and Trump. Cruz had assiduously courted delegates, using the same canny attention to detail that aided Barack Obama during the 2008 delegate hunt. But the numbers simply weren't there for Cruz. When Trump decisively won New York, then five middle Atlantic and northeastern states, and then Indiana, it was over. Cruz conceded that there was no path forward for him, and after the Indiana primary results came in, he suspended his campaign; Kasich faced reality the next day and folded.

The rumblings and hand wringing over a contested convention abated, party officials swallowed hard, and most accepted the reality that Trump would be the Republican Party's nominee for president in 2016.

Democratic Candidates

> *Are we prepared to take on the enormous economic and*
> *political power of the billionaire class, or do we continue to slide*
> *into economic and political oligarchy?*
> —Democratic candidate Bernie Sanders (2015)[46]

For many agonizing months, Vice President Joe Biden would not rule out a run for the nomination. He had tried twice before, in 1988 and 2008, with no success. Finally, in October 2015, he announced that he would not seek the nomination. Still grieving over the loss of his son, Beau, and not sure if he could mount a credible campaign against Hillary Clinton, Biden abandoned his long-held dream of the Oval Office. Rumors swirled around Massachusetts senator Elizabeth Warren, but she forcefully swatted aside any suggestion that she might become a candidate. Like his father decades before him, New York governor Andrew Cuomo appeared ready to make a run for the nomination, but soon backed away.

In the end, five Democrats declared their candidacy: Hillary Clinton, Vermont senator Bernie Sanders, former Maryland governor Martin O'Malley, former Virginia senator Jim Webb, and former Rhode Island governor Lincoln Chafee.

The Hillary Clinton campaign was the first to organize. In January 2014, Obama's 2012 campaign manager, Jim Messina, signed on to co-chair (along with former Michigan governor Jennifer Granholm) Priorities USA, the super PAC and its 501(c)(4) nonprofit, which had raised $85 million for Obama's re-election. Priorities USA formally switched its allegiance from Obama to Clinton to actively assist her in 2016. Public opinion polls throughout the first half of 2014 showed Clinton leading all potential Democratic contenders by wide margins. But not until April 2015 did Clinton formally announce her candidacy. Her senior strategy team had few holdovers from her 2008 presidential bid. A list of senior advisers who participated in a daily morning conference call showed the difference from the 2008 campaign. As reporters Jennifer Epstein and Mark Halperin wrote, "No one who played a high-level strategic role in Clinton's previous campaign is routinely included in the daily conversation—a reflection of the campaign's insistence that it will not repeat the mistakes of 2008."[47]

A number of veterans from Obama's 2012 came on board. Joel Benenson, who had been Obama's pollster since 2007, was chosen as chief strategist, while pollsters John Anzalone and David Binder also joined the team. Jim Margolis, senior adviser on the 2012 Obama campaign, became media adviser. Jennifer Palmieri became communications director, and Teddy Goff became senior advisor for digital strategy. Longtime friend and media adviser Roy Spence also signed on. There were also two senior advisers who had worked for Clinton in 2008—longtime aide Huma Abedin and veteran media consultant Mandy Grunwald—along with 2008 research director Tony Carr and speechwriter Dan Schwerin. Robby Mook, who was a midlevel Clinton adviser in 2008, became the campaign manager for the 2016 campaign. Heading up the administrative management role of the campaign was longtime consultant Charlie Baker, of the Boston based firm Dewey Square Group.[48]

Soon thereafter, Bernie Sanders announced his presidential aspirations. His campaign manager was Jeff Weaver, who had worked on earlier Sanders campaigns. The consultant with the most presidential experience was Tad Devine, who had previously worked for Dukakis (1988), Gore (2000), and Kerry (2004), in addition to helping Sanders in previous races. Also working for Sanders as senior advisor was Mark Longabaugh, business partner of Devine, and pollster Ben Tulchin. Martin O'Malley, who was given a key speaking role at the 2012 Democratic convention but made little impression, hired veterans Dave Hamrick as campaign manager and Bill Hyers as chief strategist. Jim Webb, who had once served in the Reagan administration, was assisted by longtime Virginia operative David (Mudcat) Saunders.[49] Lincoln Chafee, once a Republican US senator, also sought the nomination. Neither Webb nor Chafee made any headway, and by September 2015 both had closed down their campaigns. Like Gilmore and Pataki, Webb and Chafee might someday end up in the bonus round of a political trivia contest about 2016 candidates.

By January 2016, a month before the Iowa caucus, the Democratic results looked much clearer than the Republican. Hillary Clinton, held a sizeable lead over Sanders and O'Malley, had the money, organization, and deep bench of political consultants to assist her.

Ballotpedia, an online encyclopedia of American politics, noted that of all the presidential aspirants, both Republican and Democratic, the Lindsey Graham campaign had the most senior advisers and political consultants with prior presidential experience, a total of twenty-one presidential campaigns in all, many of them coming from the McCain team. By contrast, the Pataki and Chafee teams had the least experienced advisers and consultants.[50] However, apart from the nose counting of prior presidential experience, the Clinton team had the most experienced (and successful) team of consultants and advisers, many of whom came from the Obama 2008 and 2012 campaigns.

Yet, Sanders held on, gained support from disaffected Democrats and independents. The seventy-four-year old had a strong following among young voters, particularly college students. Sanders was also able to reap millions of dollars in small amounts ($27 average, he liked to brag), noting that there were more than 6 million individual donations to his cause.

Clinton won primary states in the South and in other states that had traditional Democratic voters; Sanders won in states that held caucuses, and continued to dog Clinton throughout the latter stages of the primary season. He couldn't catch Clinton, who not only had more elected delegates but had the lion's share of Democratic super delegates. Sanders was hampered, too, by the proportional method of handing out delegates: he may have won a state by 10 percent over Clinton, but still only gain one or two more delegates than she.

Enter the Plutocrats

We're going to fight the battle as long as we breathe.
—David Koch, 2012[51]

These super PACs have changed the way presidential campaigns are run.
—Republican consultant Scott Reed (2011)[52]

Republican consultant Scott Reed was commenting on the 2012 presidential election and the possible impact of a $55 million super PAC created to help Rick Perry. The PAC, Make Us Great Again, was run by close friends and professional associates of Perry and his team, but the Perry campaign denied any kind of coordination or collaboration. Certainly no monkey business here. But Perry famously flamed out in 2012, and as a candidate in 2015 he again turned to deep-pocketed Texans to assist his new organization, Opportunity and Freedom PAC. That super PAC raised just $4.1 million before Perry once again exited early.[53] Years ago, fellow Texan John Connally had raised $11 million but was able to capture only one delegate during the 1980 Republican presidential nomination campaign, and was widely ridiculed for his one "eleven million dollar delegate." But Perry's two runs for the nomination both ended abruptly, in 2012 right after the New Hampshire primary and in 2016 well before any votes were cast. Perry provides a cautionary tale about the poor rate of return on investment that many eager super PAC contributors faced in recent years.

As seen above, the Koch brothers spent over $400 million to try to defeat Obama and Democrats in 2012; casino billionaire Sheldon Adelson spent some $150 million, first propping up Newt Gingrich, then supporting Mitt Romney through his super PAC. George Soros, once the powerhouse Democratic donor and poster boy for liberal super funders, gave $24 million to defeat George W. Bush in 2004, a sum that pales in comparison to the funds spent later by Adelson and the Kochs.[54]

For 2016, Adelson vowed to spend money on a Republican nominee, if that nominee had broad appeal within the party.[55] In what was soon dubbed the "Sheldon Primary," a gathering of probable Republican candidates—Bush, Christie, Walker, Kasich, and perhaps others—traveled to Las Vegas in late March 2014 to talk to Adelson. The meeting was officially for the Republican Jewish Coalition, but it really was to woo Adelson and, more importantly, his money. *Washington Post* reporter Dan Balz called this "an event emblematic of how warped the system of financing presidential elections has become."[56] For much of the 2016 Republican primaries, Adelson just sat on his money, unwilling to invest in any of the candidates. Once Donald Trump cinched the nomination, however, Adelson decided to open his wallet, possibly $100 million to help Trump's cause. Newt Gingrich, whose anemic 2012 campaign was kept afloat with $20 million of Adelson's money, decried such a system in which candidates bowed at the feet of an almighty billionaire. Gingrich's solution: give candidates more money—"We desperately need an election reform which allows candidates to receive the same amount of money as super PACs."[57]

The most well-known, but still secretive, outside players were the billionaire Koch brothers, David and Charles, who have aggressively spent their money to influence elections.[58] Their early venture was the founding of Citizens for a Sound Economy (CSE), created in 1984 by David Koch and Richard Fink. The Kochs invested $7.9 million in it between 1986 and 1993. In 1990, a spin-off of CSE, Citizens for the Environment (CFE), labeled acid rain and other environment matters as "myths." But as the *Pittsburgh Post-Gazette* reported, there was no citizen membership to CFE.[59] In 1997 a shell corporation, Triad Management, poured $3 million into attack ads against Democrats in twenty-six House and three Senate races. A Senate investigation found that more than half the advertising funds came from the Economic Education Trust, and that the trust was financed wholly or mostly by the Kochs. Charles Lewis of the Center for Public Integrity said this scandal was "historic." Triad was the "first time a major corporation used a cutout [a front operation] in a threatening way. Koch Industries was the poster child of a company run amok."[60]

Journalist Kenneth Vogel described the Koch political operation as "among the most dominant forces in American politics, rivaling even the official Republican Party in its ability to shape policy debates and elections."[61] In late 2013, *Politico* ran a story about another Koch-related organization that had been operating under the radar screens, Freedom Partners. This organization sent out $236 million in 2012 to a variety of conservative nonprofits.[62] Freedom Partners also counted on annual dues of $100,000 from 200 unnamed donors. The 60 Plus Association, American Energy Alliance, American Future Fund, Americans for Limited Government, and National Right to Life have all received funds through this Koch operation and other parts of their extensive network. The Koch brothers' longtime aide was Richard Fink, chairman of the Charles G. Koch Charitable Foundation.[63]

Since 2003 the Koch brothers have been holding summits twice a year for selected wealthy patrons and conservative elected officials and media types. Former House majority leader Eric Cantor (Virginia); governors Christie, Perry, and Robert McDonnell (Virginia); Supreme Court justices Antonin Scalia and Clarence Thomas; and commentators Rush Limbaugh and Glenn Beck have been among those invited. A 2012 winter conference in Indian Wells, California, raised $150 million; an earlier summit in Rancho Mirage, California, raised $49 million. The summit is secretive about its agenda and who is invited. But during their January 2015 annual meeting, the Kochs were not shy to announce their spending goal for the 2016 presidential election. The Kochs and their conservative allies planned to raise and spend some $889 million, more than doubling their 2012 efforts, and putting them on par with the 2016 spending planned by the national Republican Party and its congressional counterparts.[64]

The Koch brothers have invested heavily in grassroots advocacy, hoping to build a network of like-minded conservative ground forces and a massive database of prospective voters, just as Obama had built one for his successful re-election campaign. They are building, in the analysis of journalist Matea Gold, a "quasi-political party outside the traditional infrastructure, one made up of nonprofit groups financed by secret donations, free of campaign finance limits."[65]

As of mid-2015, some 1,000 full-time staffers were working for Koch-sponsored Americans for Progress, Concerned Veterans for America, and the Libre Initiative (to attract Latino voters). In addition, the Koch network has created a secretive operation, referred to by insiders as a competitive intelligence team of twenty-five. The purpose of this Arlington, Virginia–based operation is to provide intelligence on liberal- and progressive-leaning organizations, tracking their canvassing, phone-banking systems, and voter registration drives. Kenneth Vogel, who broke the story on the intelligence network, noted the "audaciousness" of the Koch's mission: "While the Republican Party focuses on winning elections, the Kochs want to realign American politics, government and society around free enterprise philosophies."[66]

This conservative funding momentum has overshadowed liberal and progressive deep-pocket donors. In early May 2014, a group of wealthy liberal donors met for a four-day session in Chicago, called the Democracy Alliance, to build a liberal equivalent to the funding done by the Koch brothers and others on the conservative side. To become a "partner" in the Democracy Alliance, the annual dues are $200,000. Over its nine years of existence, the Democracy Alliance has poured some $500 million into a number of left-leaning organizations.[67] Billionaire Tom Steyer pledged to put up $100 million for the 2014 elections to assist candidates who advocated climate change policy.[68]

Wealthy donors stepped in early to help their favorite candidate, donating generously to the super PACs affiliated with them. Table 20.3 shows the mega-donors who had given at least $5 million to super PACs during the 2016 primary season.

The Center for Responsive Politics noted that by May 2016, super PACs had raised $710 million, with the top one hundred donors giving 49 percent of the money, and just 1 percent of the donors giving 60 percent of that total.[69] And up to this point, the usual suspects—the Koch brothers and Adelson—had not been heard from. But many other rich donors weighed in, funneling millions into the super PACs. A *New York Times* investigation published in October 2015 found that just 158 families, along with the companies they controlled, had supplied $176 million during the first phase of the primary campaigns, accounting for nearly half of all money raised. Of those families, 138 had contributed at least $250,000 each to Republican candidates, while 20 such families contributed to Democratic candidates. Another 200 families had contributed at least $100,000 each. "Not since before Watergate have so few people and businesses provided so

TABLE 20.3　The $5 Million Club of Supporters

Name (state)	Amount Given in millions (Through May 2016)	Principal Support
Robert Mercer (New York)	$16.6	Keep the Promise PAC (Cruz)
Thomas Steyer (California)	$13.0	NextGen Climate Action (liberal)
Paul Singer (New York)	$10.5	variety of conservative PACs
Farris and Jo Ann Wilks (Texas)	$10.2	Keep the Promise PAC (Cruz)
Toby Neugebauer (Tennessee)	$10.0	Keep the Promise PAC (Cruz)
Richard Uihlein (Illinois)	$9.9	Walker PAC, anti-Trump PAC
James and Marilyn Simons (New York)	$9.3	Priorities USA (Clinton)
Ronnie and Marie Cameron (Arkansas)	$8.7	Conservative Solutions PAC (Rubio)
Kenneth Griffin, Anne Dias (Illinois)	$8.4	Conservative Solutions PAC (Rubio)
George Soros (New York)	$8.0	Priorities USA (Clinton)
John Joe Ricketts (Nebraska)	$7.5	Walker PAC, anti-Trump PAC
Norman Braman (Florida)	$7.2	Conservative Solutions PAC (Rubio)
Haim and Cheryl Saban (California)	$7.0	Priorities USA (Clinton)
Donald Sussman (Connecticut)	$6.0	Priorities USA (Clinton)
Steven Cohen (Connecticut)	$6.0	America Leads PAC (Christie)
James and Mary Pritzker (Illinois)	$5.6	Priorities USA (Clinton)
Michael Bloomberg (New York)	$5.6	Independence USA PAC
Daniel and Staci Wilks (Texas)	$5.1	Reigniting the Promise PAC (Cruz)
Warren and Harriet Stephens (Arkansas)	$5.0	variety of conservative PACs
Lawrence Ellison (California)	$5.0	Conservative Solutions PAC (Rubio)

Source: Center for Responsive Politics, "2016 Top Donors to Outside Spending Groups," updated May 2016, http://www.opensecrets.org/outsidespending/summ.php?disp=D (accessed May 17, 2016).

much early money in a campaign," concluded the authors of the report, Nicholas Confessore, Sarah Cohen, and Karen Yourish.[70]

Indeed, during the 1972 presidential campaign, two mega-donors directed eye-popping amounts of funds to Richard Nixon's re-election committee. Insurance magnate W. Clement Stone gave $2.1 million, or nearly $12 million in 2015 dollars, and Richard Mellon Scaife gave Nixon $1 million ($5.7 million in 2015 dollars). Soon Congress had passed the first effective campaign finance law, banning such huge donations. But the millions poured into super PACs during the 2012 and

TABLE 20.4 Top 2016 Super PACs, Their Affiliation, and Amount Raised and Spent (in millions)

Group	Supporting/Opposing	Raised	Spent
Right to Rise USA	Supports Bush	$121.1	$81.2
Conservative Solutions PAC	Supports Rubio	$60.6	$55.6
Priorities USA Action	Supports Clinton	$67.4	$5.7
Keep the Promise I	Supports Cruz	$14.2	$9.4
America Leads	Supports Christie	$20.3	$18.5
Our Principles PAC	Opposes Trump	$16.1	$18.3
The Unintimidated PAC	Supports Walker	$24.1	$2.2
Reigniting the Promise	Supports Cruz	$17.2	$1.5
Opportunity and Freedom	Supports Perry	$10.0	$0

Source: Center for Responsive Politics, "2016 Outside Spending, by Super PAC," May 16, 2016, https://www.opensecrets.org/outsidespending/summ.php?chrt=V&type=S (accessed May 17, 2016)

especially 2016 presidential contests came thanks to the carte blanche given to wealthy donors through the *Citizens United* and the *SpeechNow.org* decisions.

The Super PACs

> *The rules of affiliation are just about as porous as they can be, and it amounts to a joke that there's no coordination between these individual super PACs and the candidates.*
>
> —Rep. David E. Price (D-NC) (2015)[71]

Nearly every candidate in the 2016 election, both Republican and Democratic, had a super PAC (sometime several). Super PACs are supposed to be independent of the campaign, and not share money, strategy, or tactics. But this has been done with a wink and a nod. Many of the super PACs are staffed with former consultants, staffers, and friends of the candidate, and many of the finance types have worked previously for the candidate. Outside groups aren't supposed to coordinate with the campaigns, but just exactly what coordination might mean is open to wide interpretation. As journalist Matea Gold pointed out in July 2015, since 2010 the Federal Election Commission has yet to open an investigation into an alleged coordination between a super PAC and a campaign, although there have been twenty-nine complaints.[72]

By May 2016, some 142 single-candidate super PACs had been created, either to support a candidate or try to defeat a candidate. Table 20.4 shows several of the biggest super PACs and the candidates that they supported. .[73] In addition the Scott Walker super PAC, Unintimidated PAC, had raised $20 million; but Walker dropped out of the Republican nomination contest in September 2015.

Super PACs, especially those affiliated with Republican candidates, spent millions of dollars during the crucial first primaries. But bulging super PAC accounts didn't mean success, just ask Donald Trump who had no super PAC and no deep-pocket donors, except himself. The saddest case was Right to Rise, the Bush-aligned super PAC, which had burned through nearly half of its $103 million by the end of 2015, with no discernible bump in Bush's favorability ratings. Among the big winners are local television broadcast stations, which are able to charge the super PACs a much higher advertising rate than candidate campaigns. In Iowa, for example, Federal Communication Commission records showed that a thirty-second spot shown during the 10:00 p.m. evening news on Des Moines station KCCI cost candidate Marco Rubio's campaign $750; a thirty-second Right to Rise commercial during the same segment cost $5,000.[74] Broadcasters are required to charge the lowest unit rate to candidate campaigns.

Up through May early June 2016, at the conclusion of the primaries, the candidates, political parties, and outside interest groups raised and spent record amounts. The fall campaign promises to break the record established by the 2012 presidential campaign. The 2010 and 2014 Senate and House contests as well set records as the most expensive congressional contests in history. Through it all, political consultants, working for candidates, for national parties, and for super PACs and other outside groups, charging their fees and reaping their bonuses, will do just fine.

CHAPTER 21

Political Consulting Today

*There is nothing political consultants love more
than celebrating their own genius.*

—Barack Obama in a video tribute to
David Axelrod and David Plouffe (2013)

*The pressure you get from the consultant class to conform
to the norm and do these stock standard
things drives me nuts, personally.*

—Representative Paul Ryan (2014)

I T MAY COME as no surprise that the general public has little regard for political consultants. The public has a low opinion of members of Congress, presidential candidates, and other elected officials. It is little wonder, then, that
the public would have a low opinion of the operatives who help get candidates
elected to office or point out their warts and try to defeat them. In a September
1989 nationwide survey, the Democratic polling firm Mellman & Lazarus found
that among seven professions, political consultants had the worst reputation.
Only 34 percent of the public had a positive view of consultants, while 40 percent
had a negative view. Lawyers, often a maligned class, were viewed positively by
57 percent of the respondents, and negatively by 35 percent. Scientists and medical doctors were viewed positively by 86 and 85 percent, respectively.[1] There is
little to suggest that the reputation of political consultants has improved since
then. While the general public disparages the work of consultants, candidates for
office, who rely on their services and expertise, are just as conflicted.

Consultants and Candidates

No other business would put up with the crap we take from candidates.
—Democratic direct mail specialist Frank Tobe (1988)[2]

Well, it was really Karl Rove who gave us Obama. . . . The thing
that really bothers me, however, is he raised $400 million—spent $400 million
on fighting Democrats—didn't win a race.
Didn't do well in any races and just took $400 million
and threw it out the window.

—Donald Trump (2013)[3]

In many ways, there is a love-hate relationship between candidates and consultants. Candidates recognize that they cannot be elected or re-elected to office without the assistance of consultants. But, at times, the relationship can get testy, particularly when consultants are tempted to breach confidentiality, tell tales, and turn on their former clients. In 1996, Bill Clinton was irritated at his consultants Dick Morris and Doug Schoen: "I don't want to read about you in the press. I'm sick and tired of consultants getting famous at my expense. Any story that comes out during the campaign undermines my candidacy."[4] No sooner had the president voiced his objections than he and Morris appeared on the cover of *Time* magazine. Morris was a cutout figure, pasted on Clinton's shoulder, and was dubbed "the most influential private citizen in America."[5] Days later came the salacious revelation that Morris had been in the company of a prostitute, sharing confidential White House information with her over the course of months.

The Morris episode struck a raw nerve with others. Vermont senator Patrick Leahy remarked, "It's the people who elect the candidate, not the consultants . . . I don't think necessarily you should fire them [consultants]. Maybe just draw, quarter and behead them."[6] Former Republican consultant and political operative Lyn Nofziger weighed in, "You'd think that the nation had never gotten along without them. But I will tell you this: we'd still have elections, and someone would win and some would lose, if we assassinated every one of the consultants, and the country might be better off."[7]

Most consultants are discreet about their relationship with their clients, adopting something akin to the doctor-patient or lawyer-client relationship. But some consultants have not been shy in criticizing their former clients. For example, in his memoirs, Republican consultant Ed Rollins declared, "In three decades as a political junkie, I never worked a more miserable, depressing, or rotten race than the 1994 [Michael] Huffington [California] Senate campaign. Compared to Michael and Arianna Huffington—two of the most unprincipled political creatures I'd ever encountered—Ross Perot had to be St. Francis of Assisi."[8] Democratic media consultant Ray Strother, in his memoirs, confessed, "I'm sorry I ever met Bill Clinton. He was a dream killer who ended our relationship by damaging my business and adding my body to those he climbed over to reach the White House."[9]

Some consultants boasted about how they were responsible for the success of their candidates. "We are the pre-selectors," the precocious thirty-year-old Democratic pollster Patrick Caddell bragged in 1980. "We determine who shall run for office."[10] Republican media producer Robert Goodman remade the image of Malcolm Wallop, running for a US Senate seat from Wyoming in 1976. He took the bookish Wallop, who had a PhD in English, and cast him as a "political

Marlboro man."[11] The media consultant put a white hat on the balding Wallop, and placed him on a horse leading a caravan to Washington. Goodman bragged, "We dig up Wallop, he doesn't know where he is going. He was behind, 72 to 18. He was nowhere. I invented that candidacy.... We took him, a man of the landed gentry, and created the most spectacular, invigorating Wyoming campaign they had ever seen. We won by 12 to 15 points."[12] Ed Rollins bragged that George Nethercutt "could never have beaten [House majority leader] Tom Foley without me and the professionals I put around him."[13]

This braggadocio and tales out of school bothered veteran Joe Napolitan: "I've always felt the relationship between candidate and his advisor is like that between a doctor and his patient. All of us know things about our candidates that would be embarrassing. Our candidates know things about us that would be embarrassing, but to go out and write about this stuff afterwards and, you know, for money . . . I think that's a breach of confidence. I don't understand how these guys can do it."[14]

Sometimes political consultants have publicly disagreed with their former clients. First-generation consultant Herbert Baus wrote an open letter in February 1974 to his former client Richard Nixon, which was published in the *Los Angeles Times*: "As one who supported and rooted for you in every race you've run—and worked for and advised you in many—I suggest the time has come for you to bow out.... My advice—and I speak as an old ally—is that you should resign, for the good of yourself, your party and your country."[15]

Two former Democratic pollsters, Doug Schoen and Pat Caddell, writing in an opinion piece in the *Washington Post* right after the 2010 midterm election "shellacking" meted out by the GOP and Tea Party candidates, recommended that the best thing Obama could do was not seek re-election. If he decided to seek re-election, "we are guaranteed two years of political gridlock at a time when we can ill afford it. But by explicitly saying he will be a one-term president, Obama can deliver on his central campaign promise of 2008, draining the poison from our culture of polarization and ending the resentment and division that have eroded our national identity and common purpose."[16]

Walter De Vries did not criticize a former client, but he had a low opinion of the client's son. As noted in Chapter 4, De Vries was a longtime aide to Michigan governor George W. Romney. In an October 2012 letter sent to a selected group of newspaper reporters, De Vries blasted Mitt Romney for not living up to the record of his father. De Vries harshly criticized the younger Romney for his inconsistent policy positions during the 2012 campaign: "I've tried to track Mitt Romney's shifts—some 180 degrees others 360—on key issues during the campaign. I've stopped at thirty: abortion, stem-cell research; climate change and global warming; campaign finance; and equal pay for women are just a few." De Vries, who considered himself an Independent, announced he'd vote for Obama. In a comment to the *New York Times*, he added, "George [Romney] would never have been seen with the likes of Sheldon Adelson or Donald Trump."[17]

Baus, Caddell, Schoen, and De Vries were critical, but fair-minded in their criticisms of their former bosses. But nothing compares to the raw vengeance of Dick Morris, who has been openly hostile to both Bill and Hillary Clinton, attacking them through his books, television commentary, political action committee, and even a dedicated anti-Hillary website.

An Exciting but Difficult Life

I started off a true believer—a servant of democracy, determined to
change the system. By the time I quit, I'd learned how
to manipulate the system, and I use all the tricks of the trade
to help elect my candidates. There is one bottom line in
political consulting: winning. Nothing else matters.
—political consultant Mark McKinnon (1996)[18]

All of us who work in politics are sick in some way, shape or form.
But if you're a campaign manager, it's a special kind of sickness.
—Democratic political consultant Jeffrey Pollock (2013)[19]

Several prominent consultants, sometimes at the top of their game, decided they just couldn't continue. Democratic media consultant Charles Guggenheim had been involved in more than 100 campaigns, including four presidential campaigns. In 1982 he reflected on the business: "You become . . . so involved in winning that you no longer discuss issues and character on their merits. You are sparring, looking for ways to jab and get out. . . . They're not bad people. They're fundamentally in a bad business . . . I think the system is sick."[20]

For Democratic media consultant Carter Eskew, it meant realizing that losing a campaign wasn't the worst thing that could come his way. "It takes an incredible fear of losing" to be good at making political ads. "You have to think that, literally, you'll die if you lose." Eskew, who was responsible for some of the most pointed attack ads in modern campaign history, said that he "began to think there were worse things than losing. What's so bad about losing? Sometimes it's worth it, to do the right thing. That's why I got out."[21]

Media consultant Mark McKinnon explained why, in 1996, he got out of the business:

Maybe I got tired of juggling ten to twenty campaigns at once. Maybe I got tired of candidates asking me what their firmly held convictions should be. . . . Maybe I simply lost my political idealism. Maybe I got tired of being in a dingy campaign office a thousand miles from home missing yet another of my daughters' birthdays.[22]

At the time, McKinnon was a Democratic consultant, working with James Carville, Paul Begala, and later David Sawyer. But McKinnon's farewell to politics was short-lived; he was introduced to George W. Bush, signed up, and became a major Republican political consultant during the late 1990s and 2000s.

For some consultants who live out of a suitcase for long months at a time, a consulting business can exact a heavy toll. Joe Napolitan kept a log of his work in

1976, and it gives some indication of the peripatetic nature of the business. From his office in Springfield, Massachusetts, Napolitan wrote:

> Saturday, April 10, 1976
>
> A long, tough day in the office, but one I needed. . . . My schedule for the next five weeks reads like this:
>
> Week of April 12: New York and Alaska
> Week of April 19: West Virginia, Brussels and Paris
> Week of May 3: West Virginia and Caracas
> Week of May 10: New York and Puerto Rico
>
> Somehow I managed to get home every week so far this year, despite three trips to Puerto Rico, three to Venezuela, two to Europe, one to Hawaii, and eight or nine to West Virginia, and I'll be able to get home every weekend for the next five weeks. Hell of a way to live, though, and I must admit I'm getting tired, and the prospect of spending tomorrow in the office writing a questionnaire for Venezuela doesn't excite me very much either.[23]

Democratic consultant Gary Nordlinger, who spent much of his time working internationally, said, "You wake up in the middle of the night not knowing what city you are in. You look at the ash tray in the hotel room to figure out where you are. And you can go for weeks without eating off a plate."[24] Media consultant Hank Sheinkopf echoed the toll taken on normal life: "Anyone who wants to live in hotel rooms and travel up to 300,000 miles a year, be away from family, roots and home for extended periods, as I've done for most of the last 20 years, would understand that we earn money the hard way."[25]

Steve Hildebrand, Obama's deputy campaign manager in 2008, dropped out of the business to run his own coffee shop in Sioux Falls, South Dakota. He spoke about the stress and rigors of trying to run a fifty-state primary campaign:

> Everyone was fucked up. You're working eighty-to-ninety hours a week, you have no time with your family, you have no time to exercise, eat right; you're not sleeping at night. Your stress level is at the highest it's ever been. And so then you add depression to it.[26]

It takes a special kind of political animal—candidate and handler alike— to cope, let alone thrive, under the harsh glare of a presidential, or other high-pressure, campaign. As *Washington Post* reporter Lois Romano summarized: "Forget the perception of a well-greased campaign machine gliding the candidate from place to place where he smiles those smiles for 20-second spots on the evening news. That's not the half of it. With the glamor of the road comes the stuff that political addicts thrive on: a carnival of chaos and kooks, of misstatements and missed planes, and of time-honored wrangling that makes it a wonder anything gets done."[27]

Consultants can battle hard, lose days and weeks of sleep, but in the end, they can appreciate what the opponent's side has gone through. Even the most successful and celebrated consultants have been on the losing side; nearly all have seen heartbreaking losses and undeserved victories. At the end of each presidential election, since 1972, campaign managers and senior aides have gathered at Harvard's Kennedy School of Government or at the Annenberg School at the University of Pennsylvania to dissect the race; these sessions are conducted with civility and grudging respect for those who have won and those who have lost.

The principal professional association, the American Association of Political Consultants, is structured so that the board of directors has equal representation of the two political parties, and the officers rotate annually between Republican and Democrat. While some of its members are on the leading edge of politics and partisan debate, the annual meetings are remarkably free of rancor.

Veteran consultants, particularly, tend to respect their worthy consultant opponents. Republican consultant Stu Spencer remembered his rival and Democratic counterpart Joe Cerrell: "When the campaign was over, we talked to each other; we'd go out to dinner."[28] Republican media consultant John Deardourff and Democratic media consultant Bob Squier had done battle against each other in many campaigns. In late 1999, however, they were both facing a much tougher battle: both were diagnosed with untreatable colon cancer. Quietly, over a few months, they reached out to each other, talked on the phone for several hours a day, gossiped about politics, campaigns they'd waged, and candidates they worked for. It was a mutual respect from two of the best in the business.[29] Squier succumbed in early 2000, while Deardourff lived another four years. Roger Ailes, who squared off against Squier on NBC's *The Today Show* during the 1980s, wrote a moving eulogy and spoke at Squier's funeral.

What Do Consultants Think?

Throughout this study, consultants have expressed their opinions, shared their frustrations, and have given their judgments. But it wasn't until 1998 that the first major survey was taken of political consultants to determine what was on their minds. The Pew Research Center for the People & the Press, in conjunction with political scientists James Thurber, Candice Nelson, and David Dulio, summarized the views of the 200 political consultants who were surveyed:

> Political consultants have a clear conscience: Most do not think campaign practices that suppress turnout, use scare tactics and take facts out of context are unethical. They are nearly unanimous—97 percent—in the belief that negative advertising is not wrong, and few blame themselves for public disillusionment with the political process.[30]

According to the study, consultants believed that the news media were the leading cause of voter cynicism; most consultants (66 percent) felt voters were poorly informed; 48 percent said that the caliber of congressional candidates was only fair or poor; and 42 percent thought that with enough money they could sell voters on a weaker candidate. The consultants did condemn the practice of push polling (70 percent said it was "clearly unethical") and nearly all (98 percent) said that making statements that are factually untrue was "clearly unethical."

The sample of 200 consultants was overwhelming white (98 percent) and disproportionately male (82 percent). They were highly educated, with just 6 percent not having a college diploma, and more than half having a family income of at least $150,000. When asked what motivated them to be involved in political consulting, their answers focused on three factors: the thrill of competition, the money, and their own political beliefs.

Ethics and Political Campaigning

> *I will not indulge in any activity which would corrupt or degrade the practice of political campaigning.*
>
> —First article in the Code of Professional Ethics,
> American Association of Political Consultants (1994)

Campaigning is a rough and tumble business. Complex issues are oversimplified; soft slogans replace hard policy choices; and candidates tell people what they want to hear, not what they need to hear. Political communication too often stokes envy and resentment, opponents are belittled, voting records are distorted, and half-truths and misleading statements are wrapped in fifteen- or thirty-second sound bites. Much of this comes from the work of political consultants, with the tacit or direct approval of their candidates and clients. Blame the consultants, shame them for their underhanded practices, but, in the end, it is the candidates themselves who are responsible for whatever appears on their behalf. At times, however, candidates will turn a blind eye to campaign shenanigans, claim no responsibility, and wring their hands about how terrible campaign politics has become. This is particularly true when the salacious or irresponsible charges come from anonymous super PACs and other independent expenditure organizations.

The 1988 presidential election brought considerable criticism and press scrutiny of campaign tactics and messages, particularly following the infamous Willie Horton commercials. In reaction to this criticism, the AAPC scheduled a conference, held at the College of William and Mary, which brought together academics, ethicists, and consultants to discuss campaign ethics and behavior. Brad O'Leary, AAPC president, hoped to have case studies from previous elections published to show what went right or wrong, and develop fair practice guidelines.[31] If any AAPC members had violated those guidelines, then, O'Leary said, "we would say we don't want you in the umbrella of our organization."[32]

However, nothing further happened until finally, in 1994, the AAPC developed its own broadly worded code of ethics. But the code of ethics was rarely enforced, and most consultants (81 percent) when polled said that the code had "little or no" effect on their conduct or the conduct of other consultants.[33] Besides,

84 percent of political consultants in a 1994 survey said that they rated their own profession's ethics as "fairly high" or "high."[34] Thomas M. (Doc) Sweitzer typified the reaction of many consultants: hey, we're not as bad as those other guys: "We're certainly more honest than the legal profession. And we're definitely more honest than the advertising profession. I don't sell cigarettes to kids."[35] Consultant Gary Nordlinger, who served as chair of the ethics committee, noted in 1998 that the AAPC code wasn't enforced that much because "not very many people file complaints with us. I guess they tend to be very happy with the conduct of our members."[36] Political scientist James Thurber, who was instrumental in developing the first major poll of political consultants, argued that consultants needed to take "some of the blame, stop pointing the finger elsewhere and to try to improve the quality of campaigning so that we may have better governance and improve our democracy."[37]

The one decisive action the board of directors of the AAPC took came in 1996, when it deemed "push polling"—the persuasion telemarketing calls made under the guise of a legitimate survey—as a "clear violation of the AAPC's code of ethics and a degradation of the political process."[38] Private polling firms were alarmed that their reputations were being harmed by "push polling," and two leading Republican pollsters, Glenn Bolger and Bill McInturff condemned the "sleazy smear tactics often used in negative advocacy phone banks."[39] While the AAPC and pollsters rebuked the practice, they did not abolish it, and there was evidence that it still was being practiced.[40]

Can we believe what pollsters tell us? Legitimate survey research demands that pollsters adhere to strict guidelines, scientific norms, and professional standards. Specious, inaccurate, or incomplete polling rightfully has been condemned by professional public opinion societies. Probably the best-known examples of misrepresenting public opinion was the survey research conducted by Republican pollster and strategist Frank I. Luntz on behalf of the 1994 congressional campaign and its "Contract with America." Luntz claimed that at least 60 percent of Americans supported each of the ten reforms offered by the Contract, but this claim was, in the judgment of political scientist George F. Bishop, "misleading at best and specious at worst."[41] Social scientists Michael W. Traugott and Elizabeth C. Powers determined that with one exception, support for congressional term limits, the claims were without foundation or subject to different interpretation.[42] A survey by the Gallup Poll in October 1994 found that 75 percent of the American adults had not even heard of the Contract with America. In 1997 Luntz was censured by the American Association for Public Opinion Research (AAPOR) for failing to provide data to verify his claims of public support for the Contract. He was again censured in 2000 by the National Council on Public Polls for allegedly mischaracterizing 2000 Republican National Convention focus group results on MSNBC.[43]

One recent trend in questionable practice has been what might be called "faux TV"—campaign advertising disguised as legitimate, objective news reporting. Former Maryland governor Robert Ehrlich was trying to make a comeback in 2010 against incumbent Martin J. O'Malley. In a three-minute commercial, a friendly reporter (who actually had been a well-known television reporter, but was now working for Ehrlich), asked softball questions, and wrapped up by intoning the usual reporter's ending, "reporting live from Ocean City, this has been . . ." The commercial, fobbed off as a television interview, was posted on Facebook, YouTube, and other online sites.[44]

In 2014 the National Republican Congressional Committee was heavily criticized for creating fake look-alike Democratic websites, and several months later the NRCC was charged with creating faux news websites. Voters are lured to the sites through Google search ads. The one-page sites and videos have the look and feel of an impartial voice (one was called "North County Update" and another called "Central Valley Update"), they start with an impartial voice, but then take a more biting, partisan tone. More than twenty Democratic candidates for the 2014 midterm election were targeted. Democrats cried foul, but a spokesperson for the NRCC defended the practice, saying "this is a new and effective way to disseminate information to voters who are interested in learning the truth about these Democratic candidates."[45]

Today's voters find themselves in a perplexing situation. Whom can they believe, whom can they trust? Electronic media is a viral free-for-all; rumor, innuendo and false and misleading stories compete with legitimate news; talk show personalities pound away at elected officials; false websites and fake news accounts blossom; and instant polls, with little or no scientific validity, become news items. Candidates are coached on what to say, when to say it, and whom they should say it to. It is little wonder that voters are upset, frustrated, and distrustful.

The Changing Face of Political Consulting

> *There is one big difference [between the old school*
> *political consultants and the new ones]. These young ones*
> *don't drink like we used to drink.*
>
> —Stuart Spencer (2001)[46]

> *The old days, when our profession was a bunch of guys*
> *shooting the breeze in the back room and going with their gut,*
> *based on years of politics, is over.*
> *And the days when we are a true profession is here.*
>
> —Mark Mellman (2005)[47]

Niche categories and subspecialties have been carved out in the political consulting world, with website specialists, digital advertising strategists, microtargeting technicians, online fundraising, ethnic targeting, web-based polling, text-messaging and social media specialists, telephone town hall consultants, e-mail specialists, and more. None of these categories existed twenty or twenty-five years ago, but they have now become integral components of successful campaigns.

We can use the year 2000 as the dividing line between the older practice of campaigns and consulting (the late twentieth-century model, 1970s–2000), and the new practice (early twenty-first -century model, 2000–present).[48] While much has changed, there are many practices and dynamics that have remained the same. The fundamentals haven't changed: campaigns must find voters who are likely to vote, communicate with them, and get them out to the polls on Election Day. But achieving this mission has changed dramatically in some instances, and changed little at all in others. Here are some major developments going from the late twentieth-century model to the early twenty-first-century model.

First, the role of consultants. During the twentieth century, consultants dominated campaign strategy and tactics: they were relied on to develop the campaign message and theme, and have the discipline to maintain a consistent message. They were responsible for communicating the message to the public, broadcasting it through television, and narrowcasting it through radio, direct mail, and telemarketing. Consultants were responsible for getting voters out to the polls on Election Day. In all, the campaign was a top-down approach: the candidate would listen to the recommendations of consultants and campaign operatives, rather than rely on unfiltered information directly from voters.

In the early twenty-first century, consultants still dominate, but the online component has become much more integral to campaigns. Rather than a traditional top-down approach, decisions are more fluid, with ideas, direction, and support coming from the grassroots.

Second, the role of television and online communication. In the late twentieth century, for most statewide and presidential contests, television was the most important medium of communication. Today, television is still important, but with the explosion of the online access, new channels of free media, and the fundamental transformation of communications, media consultants have many more channels of communication, and consumers have many more choices.

Third, the 24/7 campaign. Twentieth-century consultants often had more time to craft messages, respond to attacks, and analyze the ups and downs of the campaign. Now, with 24/7 news and communication cycles, campaigns have sped up, response times have shortened, and the campaigns have little time to take stock and adjust. Twitter feeds, YouTube postings, smartphone candid shots, viral messaging all have made campaign communications an all-day, all-the-time blur of information.

Fourth, experience versus analytics. For twentieth-century consultants, much of their success came from instinct, past experience in campaigns, and guesswork. The early twenty-first-century consultants have a greater reliance on research, data, and metrics to guide them through campaigns. Guesswork is just that: if it can't be measured and analyzed, it isn't useful to the twenty-first-century consultant.

Fifth, fundraising changes. In the twentieth century, fundraising was focused on the relatively small group of big donors, those who could give as much as the federal or state law would permit. There were small-amount contributors, but given the expense of direct mail and telephone solicitation, it was not worth it to aggressively go after small-amount donors. (There were exceptions, of course, like Jesse Helms, who focused on the anger and resentment of such donors). Now, big-ticket fundraising is even more important. Unlimited funds are funneled into super PACs and 501(c)(4) organizations, dark money abounds, and rich contributors can open their wallets with abandon. What little was left of campaign finance laws has been gutted by federal court decisions. There is far greater potential of funds coming from small donors, thanks to online solicitation, but simple arithmetic tells us that it takes 200,000 online donors giving an average of $50 each to match a single plutocrat who writes a $10 million check.

Sixth, outsiders. The 2016 presidential race illustrates the emerging role of outside groups. Several super PACs and 501(c)(4) groups have raised more than the candidates they support; some have been left holding bags of big money when their candidates have exited the field; some candidates have been propped up by outside groups long after they had a chance to capture their party's nomination. And outside interests have shown the capacity to outmaneuver the national political parties in fundraising, analytics, get-out-the-vote efforts, and other functions usually associated with the political parties. Outside interests, some with vast sums of money, give political consultants and operatives another lucrative outlet for their talents and services.

Finally, citizen involvement. Except for presidential campaigns, during the late twentieth century, campaigns had limited citizen involvement. High-priced campaigns were run by professionals, and there was no place for amateurs. Now, thanks to social media and other forms of digital technology, citizens and activists can have much greater access to information, and possibly a greater sense that campaigns are including them. A central question, remains, however: Will citizens participate, will they become engaged actively in campaigning and voting, or will they become disillusioned, distrustful, or simply tune out of politics?

While the world of online communication and analytics is evolving rapidly, there are definitely vested interests who want to keep the old style of politicking. As seen throughout this book, millions of dollars are at stake in statewide elections, and multiple billions of dollars are spent in campaigns throughout America during presidential election cycles. Plenty of people, from media consultants to local television station owners, have a strong vested, and moneyed, interest in keeping the old model of campaigning. As consultant Brian Franklin argues, "Networks, advertisers, ratings companies, cable and broadcast companies, media buyers and TV consultants already successful within the current model have plenty of reason to resist these changes and treat them as potentially disruptive to their businesses."[49] He sees little pressure for firms to change the status quo, and not too many incentives to move away from it. There's a "dogmatic devotion" to buying 1,000 gross rating points, which Franklin believes is an "antiquated approach."

Franklin is a twenty-first-century consultant who came from the nonprofit and corporate creative side of marketing and communication. One thing that struck him in political campaigns was the lack of coordination and branding between online, television, and direct mail. This, he argued, was a waste of money, and would never happen in corporate advertising. He wanted to create a one-stop shop, but realized after talking to experienced professionals that that was not how political campaigns are run. Writing in 2014, Franklin argued that the industry of political consulting is "very muddled right now" because of the convergence of digital and traditional media.[50] Analytics are putting pressure on television. As online communication becomes more popular, television is becoming more like the online world and getting involved in digital space. The consulting world is muddled because campaigns themselves have been so transformed in recent years, and they will continue to undergo changes in years to come.

Campaigns and Our Future

There are three trends that will have a direct impact on the evolving way political campaigns are conducted. The first is the emergence of dark money and the unlimited funding of campaigns and outside interests. As seen in previous chapters, there seems to be no end in sight to the raising of funds for federal (and state) campaigns. Two of the pillars of federal campaign law—disclosure and limits—have been swept aside.

With the blessing of the Supreme Court, campaign spending becomes the expression of free speech, to be protected and promoted, without serious understanding of the consequences. It would be a monumental task to override the Court. Congress does not have the political will to do it, and reformers don't have the clout or votes to achieve it.

The second trend will be the continued influence of outside groups, who try to use their influence to elect presidents, statewide officials, even local school boards and judges. As seen in the earlier chapters, wealthy individuals have flexed their muscles, emptied their pockets, and signed on to independent expenditure groups hoping to bring about change. If they are not careful, the national political parties and their allies might be relegated to a secondary role as ideological-driven, private groups, and shell organizations, with allegiance only to themselves and their members, become more aggressive.

The third trend—the polarization and fragmentation of political discourse—bears a little more comment. In a 2014 report, the Pew Research Center noted that "political polarization is the defining feature of early 21st century American politics, both among the public and elected officials."[51] In a survey of over 10,000 adults from January through March 2014—the largest survey of its kind—the Pew Research Center found that Republicans and Democrats were "further apart ideologically than at any point in recent history."[52] Twenty years ago, the median Republican was more conservative than 70 percent of Democrats; in 2014, the spread was 94 percent. And twenty years ago, the median Democrat was more liberal than 64 percent of Republicans; in 2014, that jumped to 92 percent.

Republicans are much more unfavorable toward Democrats, and Democrats return the favor with their antipathy. Most striking is that those with the loudest, most strident voices (most liberal and most conservative) participate at greater rates throughout the political process.

Especially in conservative circles, there has been ideological turmoil. The stunning defeat of House majority leader Eric Cantor in the 2014 Virginia Republican primary was an indication of the bitterness and near civil war being fought within the Republican Party. Such turmoil was evident in John Boehner's painful decision to step down from the Speaker's role and resign from Congress in October 2015, and most telling in the raucous and unapologetic voice of Donald Trump in the 2016 presidential nomination spectacle. Liberals and progressives, too, have had their public feuding, as Bernie Sanders has proved to be a persuasive sparring opponent of Hillary Clinton.

Into this mix comes the Wild West of communication, where anyone with a Twitter account, a smartphone, or a web page can spout off. In a way, this is the robust, unfiltered, chaotic world of democratic politics that many throughout the world wish they could emulate; in another way, it is the unfortunate reality of modern campaigning—candidates drowned out by outside voices, hyperbole, and bluster overwhelming calm and deliberation; massive spending on negative ads by unknown persons and innocuous-sounding groups; fake websites and faux television; and anonymous pranksters and provocateurs determined to scuttle campaigns. Microtargeting messaging now infiltrates not only our snail mail, but telephone messages and television viewing as well. What can we make of candidates who have 7,000 variations of their basic message? Are they artfully spreading their multifaceted policy platforms, or are they trying to be all things to all people? Political fact-checking organizations and news commentary pointing out errors and exaggerations are rebutted as evidence of political correctness, mainstream media bias, or just plain wrong, the facts be damned.

Money, outside voices, partisan rancor, and unfiltered, raucous, even poisonous communication are all twenty-first-century campaign realities. Consultants will thrive under these circumstances, as they apply their skills and craft to capture voters' attention and get their candidates elected. Millions of dollars will pour in for political advertising, for polling, for microtargeting analyses, for opposition research, and for other niche services. Through it all, the business of political consulting will grow and prosper, and consultants will continue to play an essential part in the messy business of democratic politics and campaigning.

The rest of us should be cautious but vigilant, hoping that, out of all this, we will be able to select the best public officials, who will craft the best public policy, and ultimately give us the best form of representative democracy that can be achieved. This is a tall order, but as citizens, it is our responsibility, even duty, to see to it that we prevail.

Key Consultants and Senior Advisers for Presidential Candidates, 1952–2016

1952 Election: Dwight Eisenhower v. Adlai E. Stevenson II
Eisenhower-Nixon campaign:
Herbert Brownell, campaign manager
Batten, Barton, Durstine & Osborn (BBDO), media
Alfred Hollender, Grey Advertising, media
Rosser Reeves, Ted Bates & Company, media
Roy Disney, Citizens for Eisenhower, media
Kudner Agency, media
George Gallup, polling

Stevenson-Sparkman campaign:
Joseph Katz Company, media
Lou Cowan, media

1956 Election: Eisenhower v. Stevenson
Eisenhower-Nixon campaign:
BBDO, media
Young & Rubicam, Citizens for Eisenhower, media
Ted Bates, Citizens for Eisenhower, media

Stevenson-Kefauver campaign:
Charles Guggenheim, media
Chester Herzog, Norman, Craig & Kummel, media

1960 Election: John F. Kennedy v. Richard M. Nixon
Kennedy-Johnson campaign:
Robert F. Kennedy, senior adviser
Lawrence O'Brien, director of campaign
Jack Denove Productions, media
Guild, Bascom and Bonfigli, media
Louis Harris, pollster

Nixon-Lodge campaign:
H.R. Haldeman, senior advance man
Carroll Newton, BBDO, media
Campaign Associates, media team
Gene Wyckoff, media
Ted Rogers, media
Ruth Jones, J. Walter Thompson, media buyer
Herbert Klein, press
Opinion Research Corporation, polling

1964 Election: Lyndon B. Johnson v. Barry Goldwater

Johnson-Humphrey campaign:
Doyle, Dane Bernbach (DDB), media
Tony Schwartz, media
Oliver Quayle III, pollster

Goldwater-Miller campaign:
F. Clifton White, campaign adviser
Denison Kitchel, campaign manager
William Baroody, campaign adviser
Leo Burnett Advertising, media
Interpublic: Erwin Wasey, Ruthrauff and Ryan, media
Opinion Research Corporation, polling

1968 Election: Richard Nixon v. Hubert H. Humphrey v. George Wallace

Nixon-Agnew campaign:
John Mitchell, campaign manager
Peter Flanigan, strategist
Harry Treleaven, media
Maurice Stans, strategist
Leonard Garment, strategist
Frank Shakespeare, strategist
David Derge, polling analysis
Opinion Research Corporation, polling
Herb Klein, press
John Sears, strategist

Humphrey-Muskie campaign:
DDB, media
Lawrence O'Brien, campaign adviser
Joseph Napolitan, media and campaign adviser
Shelby Storck, media
Robert Short, finance adviser
Tony Schwartz, media
Gerald Hursh, polling

Wallace-LeMay campaign:
Seymour Trammel, campaign chair
Ed Ewing, campaign coordinator
Bill Jones, campaign coordinator

1972 Election: Richard Nixon v. George McGovern

Nixon-Agnew campaign:
John Mitchell, campaign manager
Jeb Stuart Magruder, campaign head
Peter Dailey, November Group, media
Robert Teeter, pollster

McGovern-(Eagleton) Shriver campaign:
Gary Hart, campaign manager
Frank Mankiewicz, campaign adviser
Charles Guggenheim, media
Patrick Caddell, pollster
Morris Dees, direct mail
Bob Shrum, speechwriter
Richard (Rick) Stearns, research director

Other prominent consultants:
William Hamilton, pollster, Edmund Muskie campaign
Robert Squier, media, Muskie
Bob Shrum, speechwriter, Muskie

1976 Election: Jimmy Carter v. Gerald Ford

Carter-Mondale campaign:
Benjamin Brown, deputy campaign director
Patrick Caddell, pollster
James A. Johnson, deputy campaign manager, Mondale
Hamilton Jordan, campaign manager
Richard Moe, campaign director, Mondale
Jody Powell Jr., press secretary
Gerald Rafshoon, media director
Tony Schwartz, media
Peter Bourne, campaign adviser

Ford-Dole campaign:
Richard B. Cheney, chief of staff, White House
Howard (Bo) Callaway, campaign manager

Rogers C. B. Morton, campaign manager

Doug Bailey and John Deardourff, media

Peter H. Dailey, November Group, media

Stuart Spencer, senior adviser

BBDO, media

Robert Teeter, director of research

Clifton White, senior adviser

Other prominent consultants:

John P. Sears, campaign director, Ronald Reagan campaign

Richard Wirthlin, pollster, Reagan

Bruce Eberle, direct mail specialist, Reagan

Lyn Nofziger, press secretary, Reagan

Arthur Finkelstein, strategist in North Carolina and Texas, Reagan

Charles Black, Midwest field director, Reagan

Carter Wrenn, North Carolina strategist, Reagan

Peter D. Hart, pollster, Morris K. Udall campaign

1980 Election: Ronald Reagan v. Jimmy Carter

Reagan-Bush campaign:

Paul Laxalt, general manager

John D. Sears, campaign manager

William Casey, campaign manager

Stuart Spencer, campaign adviser

Richard Wirthlin, pollster

Elliott Curson, media

Peter Dailey, Campaign '80 group, media

Michael Deaver, media relations

Carter-Mondale campaign:

Hamilton Jordan, campaign manager

Jody Powell, press secretary

Gerald Rafshoon, media

Patrick Caddell, pollster

Richard Moe, manager, Mondale

Other prominent consultants:

Roger Craver and Thomas Mathews, direct mail, John Anderson campaign

David Garth, media, Anderson

Jim Nowland, campaign manager, Anderson

Robert Goodman, media, George H. W. Bush campaign

David Keene, political organization, Bush

James Baker, campaign manager, Bush

Robert Teeter, pollster, Bush

Eddie Mahe Jr., campaign director, John Connally campaign

Doug Bailey and John Deardourff, media, Howard Baker

Richard Viguerie, direct mail, Phil Crane campaign and Connally campaign

Arthur Finkelstein, polling, Phil Crane campaign (then Reagan campaign)

Bob Shrum, media, Edward Kennedy campaign

Scott Miller, media, Kennedy

1984 Election: Ronald Reagan v. Walter Mondale

Reagan-Bush campaign:

Lee Atwater, deputy campaign director

James Baker, senior adviser

Michael Deaver, senior adviser

Ed Meese, strategist

Lyn Nofziger, strategist

Ed Rollins, strategist

Stuart Spencer, general adviser

Robert Teeter, senior consultant and marketing director

Richard Wirthlin, director of polling and planning

Mondale-Ferraro campaign:
Jim Johnson, campaign chair
Peter D. Hart, pollster
Pat Caddell, pollster
Robert Beckel, campaign manager
Roy Spence, media
David Sawyer, Scott Miller, media
Frank Greer, media
John Reilly, senior adviser
Tom Donilon, senior adviser
Mike Ford, senior adviser
Joe Trippi, field operations

Other prominent consultants:
Pat Caddell, unofficial pollster for
    Gary Hart campaign
Dotty Lynch, pollster, Hart
Oliver (Pudge) Henkel, campaign
    manager, Hart
William (Billy) Shore, political
    director, Hart
Raymond Strother, media, Hart
James Carville, southern field
    coordinator, Hart
Sergio Bendixen, campaign manager,
    Alan Cranston
William Hamilton, pollster, John
    Glenn campaign
David Sawyer, media, Glenn
J. Joseph Grandmaison, political
    director, Glenn
Greg Schneiders, strategist, Glenn
Bob Keefe, strategist, Glenn
Scott Miller, media, Glenn

1988 Election: George H. W. Bush v. Michael Dukakis
Bush-Quayle campaign:
Roger Ailes, media
Media team: Jim Weller, Sig Rogich,
    Tom Messner, Barry Vetere,
    Dennis Frankenberry,
    Mike Murphy
Greg Stevens, media
Robert Teeter, pollster

Fred Steeper, pollster
Lee Atwater, campaign manager
James A. Baker III, general manager
Stu Spencer, media, Dan Quayle

Dukakis-Bentsen campaign:
John Sasso, campaign manager
Susan Estrich, campaign manager
Scott Miller, media liaison
Gary Susnjara, advertising director
Dan Payne, media
Ken Swope, media
Michael Kaye, media
Ed McCabe, media
Malcolm MacDougall, media
David D'Alesandro, media
Jim Dale, media
Irwin (Tubby) Harrison and David
    Goldberg, pollsters
Tom Kiley, pollster and strategist
Thomas A. (Tad) Devine, campaign
    manager, Bentsen
George Stephanopoulos, deputy com-
    munications director

Other prominent consultants:
Murphy & Castellanos, media, Robert
    Dole campaign
William Brock, campaign
    manager, Dole
David Keene, adviser, Dole
Donald Devine, adviser, Dole
Don Ringe, Ringe Media, media,
    Dole
Richard Wirthlin, pollster, Dole
Phil Dusenberry, media, Jack Kemp
    campaign
Tarrance, Hill, Newport & Ryan,
    pollster, Kemp
Joe Trippi, deputy campaign man-
    ager, Gary Hart campaign (then
    Gephardt)
Bill Dixon, campaign manager, Hart
Paul Tully, political director, Hart;
    briefly for Dukakis

William (Billy) Shore, adviser,
Hart

Bill Carrick, political director,
Richard Gephardt campaign

David Doak and Bob Shrum, media,
Gephardt

Kennan Research Consultants, pollster, Gephardt

Campaign Group (Philadelphia),
media, Al Gore campaign

Raymond D. Strother, media, Gore

David Garth, media, Gore

Mark Mellman and Ed Lazarus,
pollsters, Gore

David Axelrod, media, Paul Simon
campaign

Brian Lunde, campaign
manager, Simon

Harrison Hickman and Paul Maslin,
pollster, Simon

Gerald Austin, media, Jesse Jackson
campaign

Tim Ridley, manager, Joe Biden
campaign

Valerie Biden Owens, Biden

Pat Caddell, pollster, Biden

Bill Hamilton, pollster, Bruce Babbitt
campaign

**1992 Election: George H. W. Bush
v. William Clinton**

Bush-Quayle campaign:
Fred V. Malek, campaign manager
Bob Teeter, pollster and chief political
strategist
James Baker, campaign manager
Jim Lake, deputy campaign manager
Fred Steeper, pollster
Charles Black, senior adviser
Mike Murphy, media
Sig Rogich, media
Alex Castellanos, media
Tom Edmonds, media
Mary Matalin, political director

David Tell, research director
David Carney, national field
director
Robert Heckman, deputy director

Clinton-Gore campaign:
James Carville, senior adviser
Paul Begala, senior adviser
George Stephanopoulos, communica-
tions director
David Wilhelm, first campaign
manager
Dee Dee Myers, press
Stan Greenberg, pollster
Celinda Lake, pollster
Frank Greer, media
Jim Margolis, media
Mandy Grunwald, media
Carter Eskew, media
Mike Donilon, media
Rahm Emanuel, fundraiser
Michael Whouley, national field
director
Jeff Eller, field operations

Other prominent consultants:
Tony Fabrizio, pollster, Patrick
Buchanan campaign
Frank Luntz, pollster, Buchanan
Hamilton Jordan, senior adviser, Ross
Perot campaign
Ed Rollins, senior adviser, Perot
Sal Russo, senior adviser, Perot
Frank Luntz, pollster, Perot
Hal Riney, media, Perot
Harrison Hickman, pollster, Bob
Kerrey campaign
Thomas A. (Tad) Devine, campaign
manager, Kerrey
David Doak and Robert Shrum,
media, Kerrey
Michael McCurry, press, Kerrey
Joe Rothstein, media, Kerrey
William (Billy) Shore,
consultant, Kerrey

Dennis Kanin, campaign manager, Paul Tsongas campaign

Tubby Harrison, pollster, Tsongas

Michael Shea, media, Tsongas

Paul Goldman, senior adviser, Douglas Wilder campaign

Joe Johnson, campaign manager, Wilder

Ron Lester, pollster, Wilder

Lorraine Voles, press secretary, Tom Harkin campaign

Tim Raftis, campaign director, Harkin

Patrick Caddell, unpaid senior adviser, Jerry Brown campaign

Joe Trippi, adviser, Brown

1996 Election: Bill Clinton v. Bob Dole

Clinton-Gore campaign:

Dick Morris, senior adviser

Doug Schoen and Mark Penn, pollsters

Stan Greenberg, pollster

Bob Squier, media

Bill Knapp, media

Marius Penczner, media

Hank Sheinkopf, media

Joe Lockhart, press secretary

Michael Whouley, campaign manager, Gore

Dole-Kemp campaign:

Scott Reed, campaign manager

Don Sipple, chief campaign strategist

Tony Fabrizio, pollster

Public Opinion Strategies, pollster

Nelson Warfield, press secretary

Bill Lacy, chief campaign strategist

Jill Hanson, political director

Mari Will, campaign communications director

Stevens, Reed and Curcio, media

Other prominent consultants:

William Dal Col, campaign manager, Steve Forbes campaign

John McLaughlin, pollster, Forbes

Carter Wrenn, strategist, Forbes

Craig Fuller, campaign chair, Pete Wilson campaign

George K. Gorton, campaign manager, Wilson

Don Sipple, campaign strategist, Wilson

2000 Election: George W. Bush v. Al Gore, Jr.

Gore-Lieberman campaign:

Tony Coehlo, campaign chair

Bill Daley, campaign chair

Craig Smith, campaign manager

Donna Brazile, campaign manager

Mark Penn, pollster

Harrison Hickman, pollster

Paul Maslin, pollster

Mark Mellman, pollster

Carter Eskew, media

Bill Knapp, media

Bob Squier, media

Bob Shrum, media

Tad Devine, media and senior strategist

Stanley Greenberg, pollster

Celinda Lake, pollster

Michael Whouley, adviser

Larry Grisolano, direct mail

Bush-Cheney campaign:

Karl Rove, senior adviser

Ken Mehlman, campaign manager

Matthew Dowd, pollster and director of media

Joe Allbaugh, senior strategist

Karen Hughes, senior strategist

Stuart Stevens, media

Russ Schriefer, media

Mark McKinnon, Maverick Media, media

Alex Castellanos, Cold Harbor Films, media for RNC

Jan van Lohuizen, pollster

Ari Fleischer, press

Other prominent consultants:

Rick Davis, national campaign manager, John McCain campaign

John Weaver, senior strategist, McCain

Roy Fletcher, deputy national campaign manager, McCain

Dan Schnur, communications director, McCain

Stevens Reed Curcio & Company, media, McCain

Gina Glantz, campaign manager, Bill Bradley campaign

Douglas C. Berman, campaign chair, Bradley

Anita Dunn, media, Bradley

Ed Turlington, deputy manager, Bradley

MacWilliams, Cosgrove, Smith and Robinson, media, Bradley

Kaplan Thaler Group, media, Bradley

Mo Elleithee, communications, Bradley

2004 Election: George W. Bush v. John F. Kerry

Bush-Cheney campaign:

Ken Mehlman, campaign manager

Mark Wallace, deputy campaign manager

Karl Rove, senior strategist

Karen Hughes, senior adviser

Nicolle Devenish, communications director

Steve Schmidt, deputy communications director

Matthew Dowd, chief strategist

Terry Nelson, political director

Chuck DeFeo, e-campaign director

Matt Rhoades, director of research

Mark McKinnon, chief media adviser

Stuart Stevens and Russ Schriefer, media

Alex Castellanos and Robin Roberts, media

Fred Davis, media

Lionel and Kathy Sosa, media

Chris Mottola, media

Scott Howell, media

Frank Guerra, media

Jan van Lohuizen, pollster

Mike DuHaime, Northeast field director

Kerry-Edwards campaign:

Jim Jordan, first campaign manager

Mary Beth Cahill, campaign manager

Bob Shrum, senior strategist

Mike Donilon, adviser

Tad Devine, media

Jim Margolis, media

Bill Knapp, media

Mark Mellman, pollster

Chris Lehane, communications director

Stephanie Cutter, communications director

Joe Lockhart, communications director

Andrei Cherny, speechwriter

Michael Whouley, senior adviser, field operations

John Sasso, senior adviser

Mike McCurry, senior adviser

Michael Sheehan, debate coach

Nick Baldick, campaign manager, Edwards

Harrison Hickman, pollster, Edwards

Other prominent consultants:

Jerry Rafshoon, media, Howard Dean campaign

Joe Trippi, campaign manager, Dean
 campaign
Steve McMahon, senior adviser, Dean
 campaign
Nick Baldick, campaign manager,
 John Edwards campaign
David Axelrod, media, Edwards
Harrison Hickman, pollster, Edwards
Steve Murphy, campaign manager,
 Dick Gephardt campaign

2008 Election: Barack Obama
v. John McCain
Obama-Biden campaign:
David Axelrod, senior strategist
David Plouffe, campaign manager
Steve Hildebrand, deputy campaign
 manager
Valerie Jarrett, senior adviser
Robert Gibbs, senior strategist for
 communications and message
Anita Dunn, senior strategist
Robert Bauer, counsel
Betsy Myers, chief operating officer
Jim Messina, chief of staff
Marianne Markowitz, chief financial
 officer
Julius Genachowski, chief technology
 adviser
AKPD Media and Message, media
Jim Margolis, Jason Ralston, GMMB,
 media production and media buy
Steve Murphy and Mark
 Putnam, media
David Dixon and Rich Davis,
 media
Bill Knapp, media
Meyer Associates Teleservices,
 telemarketing
Chuck Pruitt, direct mail
Larry Grisolano, direct mail and
 media coordination
Joel Benenson, pollster
Anna Bennett, pollster

Cornell Belcher, pollster
David Binder, pollster
John Anzalone, pollster
Julianna Smoot, fundraising

McCain-Palin campaign:
Steve Schmidt, campaign
 manager
Mike DuHaime, deputy campaign
 manager
Rick Davis, campaign manager
Christian Ferry, deputy campaign
 manager
John Weaver, senior strategist
Nicolle D.Wallace, senior adviser
Sarah Simmons, strategy director
Mark Salter, senior adviser
Charles Black, senior adviser
V. Lance Tarrance Jr., pollster
Greg Strimple, senior adviser, polling
 and media
Bill McInturff, pollster
Ed Goeas, pollster
Fred Davis, media
Mark McKinnon, media
Cesar Martinez, media
MH Media, media
Foxhole Productions, media
Chris Mottola, media
Justin Germany, media
McCain Ad Council: Sid Rogich,
 Lionel and Kathy Sosa, Jim Farwell,
 John Brabender, Paul Wilson,
 Jim Innocenzi, Bob Wickers,
 John Gautier, Alex Castellanos,
 Myra Adams, Harold Kaplan, and
 Richard Price

Other prominent consultants:
Stan Greenberg, pollster, Christopher
 Dodd campaign
Jim Jordan, senior adviser, Dodd
Mark Penn, senior strategist, Hillary
 Clinton campaign
Mandy Grunwald, media, Clinton

Penn, Schoen Berland, direct mail and
pollster, Clinton
Geoff Garin, senior strategist, Clinton
Diane Feldman, pollster, Clinton
Sergio Bendixen, pollster, Clinton
Joe Trippi, senior strategist, John
Edwards campaign
Harrison Hickman, pollster, Edwards

Beth Myers, campaign manager, Mitt
Romney campaign
Alex Gage, head of strategy, Romney
Carl Forti, political director, Romney
Stevens, Curcio, Reed, & Potholm,
media, Romney
Ed Goeas, pollster, Rudy Giuliani
campaign

2012 Election: Barack Obama
v. Mitt Romney

Romney-Ryan campaign:
Matt Rhoades, campaign manager
Kathryn (Katie) Packer Gage, deputy
campaign manager
Eric Fehrnstrom, senior adviser
Kevin Madden, senior adviser
Beth Myers, senior adviser
Peter G. Flaherty II, senior adviser
Ron Kaufman, senior adviser
Bob Wickers, senior adviser
Stuart Stevens, strategist
Russ Schriefer, strategist
Rich Beeson, political director
Gail Gitcho, communications
director
Zac Moffatt, digital director
Lanhee Chen, policy director
Spencer J. Zwick, fundraising
American Rambler Productions,
advertising and media buy-
ing Ferhnstrom, Stevens,
Schriefer, media
Alex Lundry, chief, data science unit
Robert White, campaign chair
Ed Gillespie, senior adviser

Neil Newhouse, director of poll-
ing Dan Senor, senior adviser,
Congressman Ryan
Carl Forti, senior adviser, Restore Our
Future Super PAC

Obama-Biden campaign:
Jim Messina, campaign manager
David Axelrod, campaign consultant
David Plouffe, campaign consultant
Jen Dillon O'Malley, deputy campaign
manager
Julianna Smoot, deputy campaign
manager
Stephanie Cutter, deputy campaign
manager
Robert Gibbs, senior adviser
Jim Margolis, senior adviser
Larry Grisolano, media coordinator
Eric Smith, media
Ann Liston, media consultant
Terry Walsh, media consultant
John Del Cecato, media consultant
Fernard Amandi, media consultant
Mike Donilon, media consultant
Ricki Fairley-Brown, media
consultant
Clifford Franklin, media consultant
James Aldrete, media consultant
Mark Putnam, media consultant
David Simas, director of opinion
research
Joel Benenson, lead pollster
Paul Harstad, pollster
David Binder, pollster
John Anzalone, pollster
Sergio Bendixen, pollster
Diane Feldman, pollster
Cornell Belcher, pollster
Pete Giangreco, direct mail
Katherine Archuleta, political director
Ben LaBolt, press secretary
James Kvaal, policy director
Elizabeth Jarvis-Shean, research
director

Harper Reed, chief technology officer

Joe Rospars, chief digital strategist

Michael Slaby, chief integration and innovation officer

Teddy Goff, digital director

Rayid Ghani, chief data scientist

Dan Wagner, chief analytics officer

Carol Davidsen, product manager, Narwhal, Optimizer

Matthew Barzun, finance chair

Bob Bauer, general counsel

Other campaigns:

Mark Block, chief of staff, Herman Cain campaign

Linda Hansen, deputy chief of staff, Cain

John Brabender, senior adviser, Rick Santorum campaign

Rob Johnson, campaign manager, Rick Perry campaign

Joe Allbaugh, campaign manager, Perry

David Carney, strategist, Perry

Tony Fabrizio, pollster, Perry

Nelson Warfield, strategist, Perry

Curt Anderson, strategist, Perry

Jim Innocenzi, media, Perry

David Weeks, media, Perry

Vince Haley, campaign manager, Newt Gingrich campaign

Phil Musser, senior adviser, Tim Pawlenty campaign

Keith Nahigian, campaign manager, Michele Bachmann campaign

Brett O'Donnell, senior policy adviser, Bachmann

Ana Navarro, senior strategist, Jon Huntsman campaign

Matt David, campaign manager, Huntsman

Trygve Olson, senior adviser, Ron Paul campaign

2016 presidential primaries

Republican candidates

Terry Sullivan, campaign manager, Marco Rubio campaign

Whit Ayres, pollster, Rubio

Rich Beeson, senior adviser, Rubio

Heath Thompson, Rubio

J. Warren Tompkins, Conservative Solutions PAC (Rubio)

Chip Englander, campaign manager, Rand Paul campaign, then senior advisor, Rubio

Doug Stafford, Paul

Mike Biundo, strategist, Paul

John Yob, strategist, Paul

Tony Fabrizio, pollster, Paul

America's Liberty PAC (Paul)

Jeff Roe, campaign manager, Ted Cruz campaign

Jason Johnson, Cruz

Kellyanne Conway, Keep the Promise PACs (Cruz)

Rick Wiley, Our American Revival (527) (Scott Walker campaign)

Ed Goeas, B.J. Martino, Brian Tringali, pollsters, Walker

Danny Diaz, campaign manager, Jeb Bush campaign

Sally Bradshaw, senior strategist, Bush

David Kochel, strategist, Bush

Mike Murphy, strategist, Right to Rise PAC (Bush)

Beth Hansen, campaign manager, John Kasich campaign

John Weaver, strategist, Kasich

Fred Davis, media, Kasich

Matt David, strategist, Kasich

Stuart Stevens, strategist, Chris Christie campaign

Terry Allen, campaign manager, Rick Santorum campaign

John Brabender, senior strategist, Santorum

Barry Bennett, campaign manager,
Ben Carson campaign
Ed Brookover, senior
strategist, Carson
Mike Murray, senior adviser, Carson
Corey Lewandowski, campaign manager, Donald Trump campaign
Michael Glassner, deputy campaign manager, Trump
Paul Manafort, senior adviser, Trump
Ed Brookover, senior adviser, Trump
Barry Bennett, strategist, Trump
Rick Wiley, national political
director, Trump
Roger Stone, adviser, Trump
Christian Ferry, campaign manager,
Lindsey Graham campaign

Democratic candidates
Robby Mook, campaign manager,
Hillary Clinton Campaign
Joel Benenson, senior strategist,
Clinton
David Binder, pollster, Clinton
John Anzalone, pollster, Clinton Jim
Margolis, media, Clinton
Teddy Goff, digital media, Clinton

Huma Abedin, vice chair, Clinton
John Podesta, campaign chair,Clinton
Mandy Grunwald, media, Clinton
Geoff Garin, pollster and strategy,
Priorities USA (Clinton)
Harold Ickes, Priorities USA (Clinton)
Jim Messina, Priorities USA (Clinton)
Guy Cecil, Priorities USA (Clinton)
David Hamrick, campaign manager,
Martin O'Malley campaign
Bill Hyers, strategist, O'Malley
Adam Goers, deputy campaign manager, O'Malley
Damian O'Doherty, Generation
Forward PAC (O'Malley)
Jeff Weaver, campaign manager,
Bernie Sanders campaign
Phil Fiermonte, field director, Sanders
Tad Devine, senior strategist, Sanders
Mark Longabaugh, senior strategist,
Sanders
Revolution Messaging, digital media,
Sanders
Michael Briggs, communications
director, Sanders
David (Mudcat) Saunders, strategist,
Jim Webb campaign

American Association of Political Consultants Hall of Fame Inductees

1991 Joseph Napolitan
F. Clifton White

1992 Matthew A. Reese
Stuart Spencer

1998 Robert Goodman
Robert Squier

1999 William Hamilton

2001 Tony Schwartz

2002 Peter D. Hart

2003 Walter D. Clinton

2005 Thomas N. Edmonds

2007 Dick Woodward
Joseph Cerrell

2008 Raymond Strother

2009 Nancy Todd
Richard B. Wirthlin

2010 Charles Black
Stanley B. Greenberg

2011 Roger M. Craver
Morris S. Dees
Edward J. Rollins

2012 Paul Begala
James Carville
Karl Rove

2013 David Axelrod
David Plouffe
Arthur Finkelstein
V. Lance Tarrance Jr.
Lee Atwater (posthumously)
Robert Teeter (posthumously)

2014 Ellen Malcolm
David Garth
Lyn Nofziger
George Gorton

2015 Lionel Sosa
Robert Shrum

2016 Eddie Mahe Jr.
Hal Malchow

NOTES

Preface and Acknowledgments

1. William Greider, *Who Will Tell the People: The Betrayal of American Democracy* (New York: Simon and Schuster, 1993), 1.

Introduction

Epigraph quote from Anthony King, *Running Scared: Why Politicians Spend More Time Campaigning Than Governing* (New York: The Free Press, 1997), 3; emphasis in the original.

1. For example, political scientist Stephen K. Medvic writes that a professional political consultant is "a person who is paid, or whose firm is paid, to provide services for one presidential/national or more than one non-presidential/ subnational campaign (whether candidate or issue) per election cycle for more than one such cycle, not including those whose salary is paid exclusively by a party committee or interest group." Medvic, "Professional Political Consultants: An Operational Definition," *Politics* 23, no. 2 (2003): 119–27, at 124. See also David A. Dulio, *For Better or Worse: How Political Consultants Are Changing Elections in the United States* (Albany: State University of New York Press, 2004).

2. Walter De Vries, "American Campaign Consulting: Trends and Concerns," *PS: Political Science and Politics* 22, no. 1 (March 1989): 21.

3. Dulio, *For Better or Worse*, 186.

4. Larry J. Sabato, *The Rise of Political Consultants: New Ways of Winning Elections* (New York: Basic Books, 1981), 3. Earlier works include Stanley Kelley, *Professional Public Relations and Political Power* (Baltimore: Johns Hopkins University Press, 1956).

5. Karen M. Kaufmann, John R. Petrocik, and Daron R. Shaw, *Unconventional Wisdom: Facts and Myths about American Voters* (New York: Oxford University Press, 2008), 13.

6. Ken Goldstein, Matthew Dallek, and Joel Rivlin, "Even the Geeks Are Polarized: The Dispute over the 'Real Driver' in American Elections," *The Forum* 12, no. 2 (2014): 211–22.

7. Kaufmann, Petrocik, and Shaw, *Unconventional Wisdom*, 167.

8. Daron R. Shaw, *The Race to 270: The Electoral College and the Campaign Strategies of 2000 and 2004* (Chicago: University of Chicago Press, 2006), 26ff.

9. Gary C. Jacobson, "How Do Campaigns Matter?" *Annual Review of Political Science* 18 (May 2015): 31–47.

10. Quintus Tullius Cicero and Philip Freeman, *How to Win an Election: An Ancient Guide to Modern Politicians* (Princeton: Princeton University Press, 2012). Drawing twenty-first-century lessons from Cicero, see Quintus Tullius Cicero and James Carville, "Campaign Tips from Cicero," *Foreign Affairs,* May/June 2012; Philip Freeman, "The Attack Ad, Pompeii-Style," *New York Times,* August 31, 2012, A23.

11. See Paul Boller, *Presidential Campaigns* (New York: Oxford University Press, 1984), John Sides, Daron Shaw, Matt Grossmann, and Keena Lipsitz, *Campaigns and Elections: Rules, Reality, Strategy, Choice* (New York: W. W. Norton, 2012), 52–81; and Robert J. Dinkin, *Campaigning in America: A History of Election Practices* (New York: Greenwood, 1989).

12. Robert V. Friedenberg, *Communication Consultants in Political Campaigns: Ballot Box Warriors* (Westport, CT: Praeger, 1997), 2–4; see also Robert V. Friedenberg, "A Prehistory of Media Consulting for Political Campaigns," in David D. Perlmutter, ed., *The Manship Guide to Political Communication* (Baton Rouge: Louisiana State University Press, 1999), 11–18.

13. Friedenberg, *Communication Consultants in Political Campaigns,* 4.

14. Quoted in Dinkin, *Campaigning in America,* 12.

15. Ibid., 20.

16. Friedenberg, *Communication Consultants in Political Campaigns,* 7–9.

17. Alexander Heard, *The Costs of Democracy* (Chapel Hill: University of North Carolina Press, 1960), 400.

18. Dan Nimmo, *Political Persuaders: The Techniques of Modern Election Campaigns* (1970; reprint, New Brunswick, NJ: Transaction Publishers, 2001), 11.

19. Friedenberg, *Communication Consultants in Political Campaigns,* ch. 4.

20. William C. Harris, *Lincoln's Rise to the Presidency* (Lawrence: University Press of Kansas, 2007), 225.

21. Jon Grinspan, "'Young Men for War': The Wide Awakes and Lincoln's 1860 Presidential Campaign," *Journal of American History* 96 (September 2009), 357–78, at 357.

22. Emerson D. Fite, *The Presidential Campaign of 1860* (New York: Macmillan, 1901), 232.

23. Dinkin, *Campaigning in America,* 67–68.

24. Ibid., 95–102.

25. William T. Horner, *Ohio's Kingmaker: Mark Hanna, Man and Myth* (Columbus: Ohio University Press, 2010); Lewis L. Gould, *The Presidency of William McKinley* (Lawrence: University Press of Kansas, 1980), 11; Robert V. Remini, *A Short History of the United States* (New York: HarperCollins, 2008), 186, sets the total amount of funds raised by industrialists and corporate interests at around $16 million.

26. Gilbert C. Fite, "Election of 1896," in Arthur M. Schlesinger Jr., ed., *History of American Presidential Elections, 1789–1968* (New York: Chelsea House, 1971), vol. 2, 1787–1873; Susan Herbst, *Numbered Voices: How Opinion Polling has Shaped American Politics* (Chicago: University of Chicago Press, 1993), 139.

27. Dawes became comptroller of the currency under McKinley, and later served as Warren G. Harding's first budget director. He won the Nobel Peace Prize for his plan for collecting German reparations following World War I, and later became vice president of the United States under Calvin Coolidge (1925–1929).

28. Sides, Shaw, Grossmann, and Lipsitz, *Campaigns and Elections,* 65–66.

29. Gould, *The Presidency of William McKinley,* 228. Dinkin, *Campaigning in America,* states that there were a total of 250 million pieces of campaign literature distributed; at 114.

30. Gould, *The Presidency of William McKinley,* 228.

31. Louise Overacker, *Money in Elections* (New York: Macmillan, 1932), 107.

32. On Sherman's appointment to the State Department and Hanna's appointment to the Senate, see Gould, *The Presidency of William McKinley,* 17–19.

33. Matthew Josephson, *The President Makers: The Culture of Politics and Leadership in an Age of Enlightenment, 1896–1919* (1940; reprint, New York: Frederick Ungar, 1964); Francis Russell, *The President Makers: From Mark Hanna to Joseph P. Kennedy* (Boston: Little, Brown, 1976). On Robert Woolley, see Dan Balz and John Maxwell Hamilton, "In 2016, We're Going to Campaign Like It's 1916," *Washington Post*, January 5, 2015.

34. Edward L. Bernays, *Propaganda* (1928; reprint, New York: Ig Publishers, 2005), 111.

35. Ida Tarbell, *The History of Standard Oil Company*, 2 vols. (Gloucester, MA: Peter Smith, 1904; reprint, New York: Harper & Row, 1966); John Spargo, *The Bitter Cry of Children* (New York: Johnson Reprint Company, 1969); Frank Norris, *The Octopus: A Story of California* (Garden City, NY: Doubleday, 1947).

36. On the Ludlow Massacre and Lee's role with the Rockefellers, see Kirk Hallahan, "Ivy Lee and the Rockefeller's Response to the 1913–1914 Colorado Coal Strike," *Journal of Public Relations* 14, no. 4 (2002): 265–315.

37. Sidney Blumenthal, *The Permanent Campaign: Inside the World of Elite Political Operatives* (Boston: Beacon, 1980), 15.

38. Industrial Relations Counselors, Inc., "The Rockefeller Road to Reform and Representation," from Industrial Relations Counselors website, http://www. ircounselors.org/history/history03.html (accessed June 23, 2013).

39. On Lee's career, see Ray Eldon Hiebert, *Courtier to the Crowd: The Story of Ivy Lee and the Development of Public Relations* (Ames: Iowa State University Press, 1966). See also, Scott M. Cutlip, *The Unseen Power: Public Relations: A History* (New York: Routledge, 2013).

40. Sig Mickelson, *The Electric Mirror: Politics in an Age of Television* (New York: Dodd, Mead, 1972), 108. On the transition from the older-style militaristic campaigns to image campaigns, see Dan Nimmo and Robert L. Savage, *Candidates and Their Images: Concepts, Methods, and Findings* (Pacific Palisades, CA: Goodyear Publishing Company, 1976), 6–9; Gene Wyckoff, *The Image Candidates* (New York: Macmillan, 1968); Stanley Kelley Jr., *Professional Public Relations and Political Power* (Baltimore: Johns Hopkins Press, 1956).

41. "Ad Age Advertising Century: Top 100 People," AdAge.com, March 29, 1999, http://adage.com/century/people.html (accessed June 29, 2013).

42. John A. Morello, *Selling the President, 1920: Albert D. Lasker, Advertising, and the Election of Warren G. Harding* (Westport, CT: Praeger, 2001) , 32.

43. Ibid., 39–40.

44. Ibid., 49.

45. Randolph C. Downes, *The Rise of Warren Gamaliel Harding, 1865–1920* (Columbus: Ohio State University Press, 1970), 428, cited in Morello, *Selling the President, 1920*, 51.

46. Morello, *Selling the President, 1920*, 67–69.

47. Richard M. Fried, *The Man Everybody Knew: Bruce Barton and the Making of Modern America* (Chicago: Ivan R. Dee, 2005), 120.

48. Morello, *Selling the President, 1920*, 184.

49. Kerry W. Buckley, "A President for the 'Great Silent Majority': Bruce Barton's Construction of Calvin Coolidge," *New England Quarterly* 76, no. 4 (December 2003): 593–626, at 598.

50. Ibid.

51. Bruce F. Barton, *The Man Nobody Knows* (1925; reprint, New York: Colliers Books, 1987).

52. Buckley, "A President for the 'Great Silent Majority,' " 600.

53. Bruce Barton, "Concerning Calvin Coolidge," *Collier's*, November 22, 1919, 8.

54. Edwin Diamond and Stephen Bates, *The Spot: The Rise of Political Advertising on Television*, 3rd ed. (Cambridge, MA: MIT Press, 1992), 42.

55. Buckley, "A President for the 'Great Silent Majority,' " 605.

56. Ibid., 610–11.

57. Fried, *The Man Everybody Knew*, 123.
58. Ibid.
59. Buckley, "A President for the 'Great Silent Majority,'" 612–14.
60. Fried, *The Man Everybody Knew*, 189–90.
61. Robert E. Sherwood, *Roosevelt and Hopkins: An Intimate History* (New York: Harper, 1950), 189–90.
62. Jules Abels, *Out of the Jaws of Victory* (New York: Henry Holt, 1989), 142. The group included Carl Byoir, Steve Hannagan, and John Flynn.
63. "Ad Age Advertising Century: Top 100 People."
64. Craig Allen, *Eisenhower and the Mass Media* (Chapel Hill: University of North Carolina Press, 1993), 79–82. In 1928, BDO merged with George Batten's Batten Company, forming Batten, Barton, Durstine & Osborn (BBDO).
65. Larry Tye, *The Father of Spin: Edward L. Bernays and the Birth of Public Relations* (New York: Henry Holt, 1998).
66. Ibid., 56.
67. See "Our Presidents," from the official White House website, http://www.whitehouse.gov/about/presidents/calvincoolidge (accessed June 12, 2013).
68. Quoted in *Washington Post*, October 21, 1924.
69. Ibid., 77–79; see also Edward L. Bernays, *Biography of an Idea: Memoirs of Public Relations Counsel Edward L. Bernays* (New York: Simon & Schuster, 1965), 339–42.
70. Tye, *The Father of Spin*, 79–80; see also Bernays, *Biography of an Idea*, 644–45.
71. Bernays, *Biography of an Idea*, 634.
72. Ibid.
73. Tye, *The Father of Spin*, 81–82.
74. Ibid., 82. See Frank Luntz, *Words That Work: It's Not What You Say, It's What People Hear* (New York: Hyperion, 2006).
75. Tye, *The Father of Spin*, 86–87; Bernays, *Biography of an Idea*, 640.
76. Dinkin, *Campaigning in America*, 129.

Chapter 1

Epigraph quote from Greg Mitchell, *The Campaign of the Century: Upton Sinclair's Race for Governor of California and the Birth of Media Politics* (New York: Random House, 1992), 84; Whitaker and Baxter in Carey McWilliams, "Government by Whitaker and Baxter: Part III, The Triumph of Chrome-Plated Publicity," *The Nation*, May 5, 1951, at 419; Robert J. Pitchell, "The Influence of Professional Campaign Management Firms in Partisan Elections in California," *Western Political Quarterly* 11, no. 2 (June 1958): 278–300, 280.

1. Pitchell, "The Influence of Professional Campaign Management Firms in Partisan Elections in California."
2. Alexander Heard, *The Cost of Democracy* (Chapel Hill: University of North Carolina Press, 1960), 420.
3. McWilliams, "Government by Whitaker and Baxter," 419.
4. Ibid.
5. Stanley Kelley Jr., *Professional Public Relations and Political Power* (Baltimore: Johns Hopkins University Press, 1956), 21.
6. Transcript of Clement Sherman Whitaker Jr. oral history interview, conducted by Gabrielle Morris, Regional Oral History Office, University of California at Berkeley (September 15, 1988), for the California State Archives State Government Oral History Program, 3.
7. McWilliams, "Government by Whitaker and Baxter," 347.
8. Ibid., 346.
9. Mitchell, *The Campaign of the Century*, 128.

10. However, they did not get around to incorporating Campaigns, Inc. until 1950.

11. Irwin Ross, *The Image Merchants: The Fabulous World of Public Relations* (Garden City, NY: Doubleday, 1959), 69.

12. McWilliams, "Government by Whitaker and Baxter," 347–48.

13. Quoted in Joe Klein, *Politics Lost: How American Democracy Was Trivialized by People Who Think You're Stupid* (New York: Doubleday, 2006), 96–97.

14. Curt Gentry, ". . . Right Back Where We Started From," *Columbia Journalism Review* 31 (September/October 1992), 60.

15. Mitchell, *The Campaign of the Century*, 83.

16. Ross, *The Image Merchants*, 69.

17. Walt Anderson, "California: Frank F. Merriam vs. Upton Sinclair," in *Campaigns: Cases in Political Conflict* (Pacific Palisades, CA: Goodyear Publishing Co., 1970), 122. Sinclair's books included *The Jungle*, *The Metropolis*, *The Industrial Republic*, and *The Machine*—all published before World War I. The *Profits of Religion*, "probably the single book which was most used against him," was published in 1920; also used were *The Brass Check*, *The Goose Step: A Study in American Education* (which criticized the ROTC), and *The Goslings: A Study of American Schools* (which criticized the Boy Scouts).

18. Ross, *The Image Merchants*, 69.

19. Mitchell, *The Campaign of the Century*, 128–29.

20. Ibid., 355–56. Also, Jill LePore, "The Lie Factory: How Politics Became a Business," *The New Yorker*, September 24, 2012.

21. Anderson, *Campaigns*, 125.

22. Ibid., 129.

23. Gentry, ". . . Right Back Where We Started From."

24. Sidney Blumenthal, *The Permanent Campaign: Inside the World of Elite Political Operatives* (Boston: Beacon Press, 1980), 144.

25. James N. Gregory, "Introduction" to Upton Sinclair, *I, Candidate for Governor, and How I Got Licked* (Berkeley: University of California Press, 1994, 1934), x–xi.

26. Anderson, *Campaigns*, 129.

27. Schlesinger quoted in book review of Mitchell's book, Nelson Lichtenstein, "California Scheming," *New York Times Book Review*, May 10, 1992, 1.

28. Mitchell, *The Campaign of the Century*, 84.

29. Pitchell, "The Influence of Professional Campaign Management Firms in Partisan Elections in California," 290.

30. Ibid.

31. McWilliams, "Government by Whitaker and Baxter," 420.

32. Kelley, *Professional Public Relations and Power*, 49–53.

33. Blumenthal, *The Permanent Campaign*, 146–47.

34. Ross, *The Image Merchants*, 81–82.

35. Ibid., 82.

36. Leo Katcher, *Earl Warren: A Political Biography* (New York: McGraw-Hill, 1967), 163–65, at 165.

37. Transcript of Carey McWilliams oral history interview, conducted by Amelia Fry, University of California-Berkeley, Earl Warren Oral History Project (November 1969), http://content.cdlib.org/view?docId=ft9f59p1z7;NAAN=13030&doc.view=frames&chunk.id=doe10144&toc.id=doe8478&brand=calisphere (accessed June 23, 2013).

38. Quoted in Mitchell, *The Campaign of the Century*, 570.

39. Katcher, *Earl Warren*, 164.

40. Perhaps he had confused the spelling with that for Supreme Court Justice Charles Evans Whittaker, who served as associate justice (1957–1962) during part of the Warren years on the Court.

41. G. Edward White, *Earl Warren: A Public Life* (New York: Oxford University Press, 1982), 80.

42. Daniel J. B. Mitchell, "Impeding Earl Warren: California's Health Insurance Plan that Wasn't and What Might Have Been," *Journal of Health Politics, Policy and Law* 27, no. 6 (December 2002): 947–76, at 957.

43. Earl Warren, *The Memoirs of Chief Justice Earl Warren* (1997; reprint, Lanham, MD: Madison Books, 2001), 161–63.

44. Mitchell, "Impeding Earl Warren," 952–57.

45. White, *Earl Warren*, 107.

46. Ibid., 957–60.

47. Ibid., 958–60.

48. Whitaker Jr. oral history interview, 48.

49. Herbert M. Baus and William B. Ross, *Politics Battle Plan* (New York: Macmillan, 1968), 44.

50. Warren, *The Memoirs of Chief Justice Earl Warren*, 188.

51. Katcher, *Earl Warren*, 187.

52. Carleton B. Chapman and John M. Talmadge, "Historical and Political Background of Federal Health Care Legislation," *Law and Contemporary Problems* 35, no. 2, Health Care: Part I (Spring 1970); Monte M. Poen, *Harry S. Truman versus the Medical Lobby* (Columbia: University of Missouri Press, 1979); Kelley, *Professional Public Relations and Power*, 67–106. See also Daniel S. Hirschfield, *The Lost Reform: The Campaign for Compulsory Health Insurance in the United States from 1932 to 1943* (Cambridge, MA: Harvard University Press, 1970) and Richard Harris, *A Sacred Trust* (Baltimore: Penguin Books, 1969).

53. Harry S. Truman, *Annual Message to Congress on the State of the Union*, January 5, 1949, in John Wooley and Gerhard Peters, The American Presidency Project (online), Santa Barbara: University of California (hosted), Gerhard Peters (database), http://www.presidency.ucsb.edu/?pid=13293 (accessed June 12, 2013).

54. "A Simplified Blueprint of the Campaign against Compulsory Health Insurance. Prepared by Clem Whitaker and Leone Baxter, directors of the National Education Campaign of the American Medical Association, for the information of State and County Medical Societies," February 21, 1949, in Robert Griffith and Paula Baker, ed., *Major Problems in American History since 1945* (Lexington, MA: DC Heath, 1992), chapter 4: "Truman, Eisenhower, and the Transformation of American Politics, 1945–1960." Emphasis in the original.

55. "Welfare State Hit as a Slave State," *New York Times*, November 12, 1949, 13.

56. For example, I. M. Rubinow, "In Defense of Socialized Medicine," *The Nation* (May 21, 1928), 508–10.

57. Transcript of Oscar Ewing oral history interview, conducted by J. R. Fuchs, Truman Presidential Library (May 1, 1969), http://www.trumanlibrary.org/oralhist/ewing3.htm (accessed June 13, 2013).

58. "Heads of AMA Rebuke Critics of Assessment," *Washington Post*, February 19, 1949.

59. See, for example, Michael F. Cannon, "Does Barack Obama Support Socialized Medicine?" *Cato Institute Briefing Papers*, No. 108 (October 7, 2008); http://www.cato.org/pub_display.php?pub_id=9679 (accessed July 13, 2013). Cannon writes, "Reasonable people can disagree over whether Obama's health plan would be good or bad. But to suggest that it is not a step toward socialized medicine is absurd."

60. Sam Zagoria, "AMA Levies Compulsory Dues to Fight Truman Health Plan," *Washington Post*, December 9, 1949, 1.

61. Ross, *The Image Merchants*, 66, 79.

62. Kelley, *Professional Public Relations and Power*, 74–75.

63. Poen, *Harry S. Truman versus the Medical Lobby*, 100; Kelley, *Professional Public Relations and Political Power*, 81. See also Dennis W. Johnson, "Medical Care for the Elderly and the Poor," in *The Laws That Shaped America* (New York: Routledge, 2009).

64. Pitchell, "The Influence of Professional Campaign Management Firms in Partisan Elections in California," 282.

65. David Lee Rosenbloom, *The Election Men: Professional Campaign Managers and American Democracy* (New York: Quadrangle Books, 1973), 47–48.

66. Whitaker Jr. oral history interview, 94.

67. Eugene C. Lee and William Buchanan, "The 1960 Election in California," *Western Political Quarterly* 14, no. 1 (March 1961), 316–17.

68. Genevieve Troka, "Inventory of the Whitaker & Baxter Campaigns, Inc. Records," California State Archives, http://www.oac.cdlib.org/findaid/ark:/13030/kt7p3036z9/.

69. Whitaker Jr. oral history interview, 94.

70. See Rodney G. Minott, *The Sinking of the Lollipop: Shirley Temple vs. Pete McCloskey* (San Francisco: Diablo Press, 1968).

71. Quoted in James M. Perry, *The New Politics: The Expanding Technology of Political Manipulation* (New York: Clarkson N. Potter, 1968), 15.

72. California Commission on Campaign Financing, *Democracy by Initiative: Shaping California's Fourth Branch of Government*, Los Angeles, 1992, cited in Shaun Bowler, Todd Donovan, and Ken Fernandez, "The Growth of the Political Marketing Industry and the California Initiative Process," *European Journal of Marketing* 30, no. 10–11 (1996), 175.

73. Pitchell, "The Influence of Professional Campaign Management Firms in Partisan Elections in California," 283.

74. Ross, *The Image Merchants*, 80.

75. Pitchell, "The Influence of Professional Campaign Management Firms in Partisan Elections in California," 283.

76. Kelley, *Professional Public Relations and Power,* 65 n. 43.

77. Rosenbloom, *The Election Men*, 69–70.

78. Myrna Oliver, "Herbert Baus: Obituary," *Los Angeles Times*, May 13, 1999.

79. Baus and Ross, *Politics Battle Plan*, 258.

80. Stephen E. Ambrose, *Nixon: The Education of a Politician, 1913–1962* (New York: Simon & Schuster, 1987), 237.

81. Greg Mitchell, *Tricky Dick and the Pink Lady: Richard Nixon vs. Helen Gahagan Douglas—Sexual Politics and the Red Scare, 1950* (New York: Random House, 1998), 47.

82. David Mark, *Going Dirty: The Art of Negative Campaigning* (Lanham, MD: Rowman & Littlefield, 2006), 31.

83. Richard M. Nixon, *Six Crises* (1960; reprint, New York: Touchstone Books, 1992), 85.

84. Chotiner quoted in Russell Baker, "Chotiner Advises GOP How to Win," *New York Times*, May 13, 1956, 65.

85. Totton J. Anderson, "The 1958 Election in California," *Western Political Quarterly* 13, no. 1 (March 1959): 276–300, at 292.

86. Bill Becker, "Nixon Campaign Called 'Dirtiest,'" *New York Times*, October 19, 1962.

87. Ibid.

88. Herbert S. Parmet, *Richard Nixon and His America* (Boston: Little, Brown, 1990), 426–27.

89. Kelley, *Professional Public Relations and Power*, 64 n. 38.

90. Carroll Kilpatrick, "Democratic 'Find' Helps Win 6 Senate Elections," *Washington Post,* September 17, 1957, A20; and Joseph S. Miller, *The Wicked Wine of Democracy: A Memoir of a Political Junkie, 1948–1995* (Seattle: University of Washington Press, 2008).

91. Heard, *The Cost of Democracy*, 413.

92. Ibid., 419.

93. Ibid., 418, n. 54. Rosenbloom, *The Election Men*, 52.

Chapter 2

Epigraph quotes from James A. Farley, *Behind the Ballots: The Personal History of a Politician* (New York: Harcourt, Brace, 1938), 323; George Gallup and Saul Forbes Rae, *The Pulse of Democracy: The Public-Opinion Poll and How It Works* (New York: Simon & Schuster, 1940), 8; and Louis Harris, "Polls and Politics in the United States," *Public Opinion Quarterly* 27, no. 1 (Spring 1963): 3–8, at 6.

1. Tom W. Smith, "The First Straw: A Study of the Origins of Election Polls," *Public Opinion Quarterly* 54, no. 1 (Spring 1990): 21–36.
2. Smith, "The First Straw," 28–29.
3. Lincoln quote from speech at Columbus, Ohio, September 16, 1859, in John G. Nicolay and John Hay, eds., *Complete Works of Abraham Lincoln* (New York: Francis D. Tandy Co., 1905), 5:188.
4. Susan Herbst, *Numbered Voices: How Opinion Polling Has Shaped American Politics* (Chicago: University of Chicago Press, 1993), 74–80.
5. David W. Moore, *The Superpollsters: How They Measure and Manipulate Public Opinion in America* (New York: Four Walls Eight Windows, 1995), 34.
6. Claude E. Robinson, *Straw Votes* (New York: Columbia University Press, 1932); Irving Crespi, "Polls as Journalism," *Public Opinion Quarterly* 44 (1980): 462–76, at 462.
7. Quoted in Richard Rockwell, "Roper Center for Public Opinion Research," in Samuel J. Best and Benjamin Radcliff, eds., *Polling America: An Encyclopedia of Public Opinion* (Westport, CT: Greenwood Press, 2005), 2:712.
8. Peverill Squire, "*Literary Digest* Poll of 1936," in Best and Radcliff, eds., *Polling America*, 1:428–32. See also Peverill Squire, "Why the 1936 *Literary Digest* Poll Failed," *Public Opinion Quarterly* 52 (Spring 1988): 125–33; and Maurice C. Bryson, "The *Literary Digest* Poll: Making of a Statistical Myth," *American Statistician* 30 (November 1976): 184–85.
9. Squire, "*Literary Digest* Poll of 1936," 428.
10. In 1972 Richard Nixon readily defeated George McGovern, winning 49 states, losing only Massachusetts and the District of Columbia, and receiving 520 electoral votes. In 1984 Ronald Reagan trounced Walter Mondale, winning 49 states, losing only Minnesota and the District of Columbia, and receiving 525 electoral votes. In the 1820 election, James Monroe received 231 electoral votes, while his main opponent, John Quincy Adams, received 1 vote. Historical election results: Electoral College Box Scores, 1789–1996, US National Archives and Records Administration, http://www.archives.gov/federal-register/electoral-college/scores.html#1820.
11. Gallup and Rae, *The Pulse of Democracy*, 44.
12. "Dr. Gallup Chided by *Digest* Editor," *New York Times*, July 19, 1936.
13. Jean M. Converse, *Survey Research in the United States: Roots and Emergence 1890–1960* (Berkeley: University of California Press, 1987), 118; Squire, "*Literary Digest* Poll of 1936," 428.
14. Squire, "*Literary Digest* Poll of 1936," 431.
15. Ibid.
16. David W. Moore, *The Opinion Makers: An Insider Exposes the Truth Behind the Polls* (Boston: Beacon Press, 2008), 42–43.
17. Converse, *Survey Research in the United States*, 118–19.
18. Katherine A. Bradshaw, "'America Speaks': George Gallup's First Syndicated Public Opinion Poll," *Journalism History* 31, no. 4 (Winter 2006): 198–206, at 201. On Gallup's early years, see Susan Ohmer, *George Gallup in Hollywood* (New York: Columbia University Press, 2006).
19. Gallup biographical sketch, Gallup.com, http://www.gallup.com/corporate/178136/george-gallup.aspx (accessed March 31, 2016).

20. Charles Roll, "Private Opinion Polls," *Proceedings of the Academy of Political Science* 34, no. 4, The Communications Revolution in Politics (1982): 67–68, at 61.
21. Bradshaw, "'America Speaks,'" 198.
22. Ibid., 202.
23. Ibid., 201.
24. Converse, *Survey Research in the United States*, 119.
25. Ibid., 119–20.
26. Elmo Roper biographical entry, The Roper Center, Cornell University, http://ropercenter.cornell.edu/elmo-roper/, (accessed March 31, 2016).
27. Samuel J. Best, "Sampling Process" in Best and Radcliff, eds., *Polling America*, 2:722–28. See also Leslie Kish, *Survey Sampling* (New York: John Wiley, 1995).
28. On the advantages and disadvantages of quota sampling, see Charles W. Roll and Albert H. Cantril, *Polls: Their Uses and Misuses in Politics* (Cabin John, MD: Seven Locks Press, 1980), 66–68.
29. Martin R. Frankel and Lester R. Frankel, "Fifty Years of Survey Sampling in the United States," *Public Opinion Quarterly* 51, no. 2: S127–38.
30. On probability sampling, see Best, "Sampling Process," 722–28.
31. Frankel and Frankel, "Fifty Years of Survey Sampling in the United States," S128.
32. Daniel Katz, "The Public Opinion Polls and the 1940 Election," *Public Opinion Quarterly* 5, no. 1 (March 1941): 52–78.
33. Robert E. Burke, "The Election of 1940," in Arthur M. Schlesinger Jr., ed., *History of American Presidential Elections, 1789–1968* (New York: Chelsea House, 1971), vol. 4, *1940–1968*, 3006.
34. Daniel Katz, "The Polls and the 1944 Election," *Public Opinion Quarterly* 8, no. 4 (Winter 1944–1945): 468–87, at 468.
35. Earl Latham, "Political Statistics," *Journal of Politics* 10, no. 4 (November 1948): 636–58, at 645–46.
36. Quoted in *New York Herald-Tribune*, September 1948, cited in Irwin Ross, *The Loneliest Campaign: The Truman Victory of 1948* (New York: New American Library, 1968), 2–3.
37. Daniel Katz, "An Analysis of the 1948 Polling Predictions," *Journal of Applied Psychology* 33, no. 1 (February 1949): 15–28, at 16.
38. Ibid., 15.
39. Richard Norton Smith, *Thomas E. Dewey and His Times* (New York: Simon & Schuster, 1982), 544.
40. Albert H. Cantril, *The Opinion Connection: Polling, Politics, and the Press* (Washington, DC: CQ Press, 1991), 13.
41. Quoted in Cabell Phillips, "And the Polls: What Went Wrong?" *New York Times*, November 7, 1948, E4.
42. Jules Abels, *Out of the Jaws of Victory* (New York: Henry Holt, 1959), 275.
43. Allen quoted in Tim Jones, "Dewey Defeats Truman: Well, Everyone Makes Mistakes," *Chicago Tribune*, n.d., http://www.chicagotribune.com/news/politics/chi-chicagodays-deweydefeats-story,0,6484067.story (accessed June 25, 2013).
44. Zachary Karabell, *The Last Campaign: How Harry Truman Won the 1948 Election* (New York: Knopf, 2000), 19.
45. Frederick Mosteller, Herbert Hyman, Philip J. McCarthy, Eli S. Marks, and David B. Truman, *The Pre-election Polls of 1948: A Report to the Committee on Analysis of Pre-election Polls and Forecasts* (New York: Social Science Research Council, 1949), 1. On further refinement of suggestions made by the Social Science Research Council, see Elizabeth A. Martin, Michael W. Traugott, and Courtney Kennedy, "A Review and Proposal for a New Measure of Poll Accuracy," *Public Opinion Quarterly* 69 (Autumn, 2005): 342–69.
46. Phillips, "And the Polls: What Went Wrong?"
47. George Gallup, "The Gallup Poll and the 1950 Election," *Public Opinion Quarterly* 15, no. 1 (Spring 1951): 16–22.

48. From The Field Pollwebsite, http://www.field.com/fieldpoll, and Jason Marsh, "At 82, State's Polling Dean Watches 'Cultural Explosion' Detonate," *North Gate News Online* (University of California-Berkeley Graduate School of Journalism), October 7, 2003, http://journalism.berkeley.edu/ngno/2003/10/07/at-82-states-polling-dean-watches-cultural-explosion-detonate/ (accessed June 24, 2013).

49. Mervin D. Field, "Political Opinion Polling in the USA," in Robert Worcester, ed., *Political Opinion Polling* (New York: St. Martin's Press, 1983), 198–208, at 203.

50. Louis Harris, "A Pollster Defends the Polls," *New York Times Magazine*, November 5, 1961.

51. Robert M. Eisinger and Jeremy Brown, "Polling as a Means toward Presidential Autonomy: Emil Hurja, Hadley Cantril and the Roosevelt Administration," *Journal of Public Opinion Research* 10, no. 3 (Fall 1998), 244.

52. Melvin G. Holli, *The Wizard of Washington: Emil J. Hurja, Franklin Roosevelt, and the Birth of Public Opinion Polling* (New York: Palgrave, 2002), 40. David Greenberg, "FDR's Nate Silver," *Politico*, January 16, 20016

53. Ibid., 40–41.

54. Ibid., 41–43.

55. Ibid., 71–72.

56. Robert M. Eisinger, *The Evolution of Presidential Polls* (New York: Cambridge University Press, 2003), 83.

57. Quoted in Eisinger and Brown, "Polling as a Means toward Presidential Autonomy," 242.

58. Alvin Johnson, "'Prof.' Hurja, The New Deal's Political Doctor," *Saturday Evening Post*, June 15, 1936, 8.

59. Holli, *The Wizard of Washington*, 72–73.

60. See Lawrence R. Jacobs and Robert Y. Shapiro, "Issues, Candidate Image, and Priming: The Use of Private Polls in Kennedy's 1960 Presidential Campaign," *American Political Science Review* 88, no. 3 (September 1994): 527–40; Lawrence R. Jacobs and Robert Y. Shapiro, "The Rise of Presidential Polling: The Nixon White House in Historical Perspective," *Public Opinion Quarterly* 59 (June 1995): 163–95.

61. Farley, *Behind the Ballots*, 323.

62. Hadley Cantril, "How Accurate Were the Polls?" *Public Opinion Quarterly* 1, no. 1 (January 1937): 97–101, at 100.

63. Richard W. Steele, "The Pulse of the People: Franklin D. Roosevelt and the Gauging of American Public Opinion," *Journal of Contemporary History* 9, no. 4 (October 1974): 195–216, at 208.

64. Ibid., 209.

65. Ibid.

66. Eisinger and Brown, "Polling as a Means toward Presidential Autonomy," 246.

67. John M. Crewdson and Joseph B. Treaster, "Worldwide Propaganda Network Built by the CIA," *New York Times*, December 1977, 1, cited in Timothy Richard Glander, *Origin of Mass Communications Research during the Cold War* (Mahwah, NJ: Lawrence Erlbaum, 2000), 89–90.

68. Roll, "Private Opinion Polls," 67–68.

69. Gerard B. Lambert, *All Out of Step: A Personal Chronicle* (Garden City, NY: Doubleday, 1956), 268.

70. Ibid., 68.

71. Hadley Cantril, *The Human Dimension: Experiences in Policy Research* (New Brunswick: Rutgers University Press, 1967); quote from Seymour Sudman, "The President and the Polls," *Public Opinion Quarterly* 46, no. 3 (Autumn 1982): 301–10, at 303.

72. Harry S. Truman, *Memoirs* (Garden City, NY: Doubleday, 1955), 177, quoted in John G. Geer, *From Tea Leaves to Opinion Polls: A Theory of Democratic Leadership* (New York: Columbia University Press, 1996), 177.

73. Sudman, "The President and the Polls," 303–4.

74. Eisinger and Brown, "Polling as a Means toward Presidential Autonomy," 253; Brandon Rottinghaus, "Reassessing Public Opinion in the Truman Administration," *Presidential Studies Quarterly* 33, no. 2 (June 2003): 325–32.

75. Craig Allen, *Eisenhower and the Mass Media: Peace, Prosperity, and Prime-Time TV* (Chapel Hill: University of North Carolina Press, 1993), 38, cited in Eisinger, *The Evolution of Presidential Polls*, 113.

76. Eisinger, *The Evolution of Presidential Polls*, 84–85.

77. Roll, "Private Opinion Polls," 73.

78. Winston Allard, "Congressional Attitudes toward Public Opinion Polls," *Journalism Quarterly* 18 (1941): 47–50, and Carl Hawver, "The Congressman and His Public Opinion Poll," *Public Opinion Quarterly* 18 (1954): 123–29, cited in Herbst, *Numbered Voices*, 91.

79. Roll, "Private Opinion Polls," 61–62; Jacob Javits, "How I Used a Poll in Campaigning for Congress," *Public Opinion Quarterly* 11, no. 2 (1947): 222–26; also, Jacob K. Javits with Rafael Steinberg, *Javits: The Autobiography of a Public Man* (Boston: Houghton Mifflin, 1981), 97.

80. Stanley J. Kelley, *Professional Public Relations and Political Power* (Baltimore: Johns Hopkins University Press, 1956), 189.

81. American Institute for Political Communication, *The New Methodology: A Study of Political Strategy and Tactics* (Washington, DC: American Institute for Political Communication, 1967), 20; Clayton Knowles, "Candidates Still Depend on Pros, Not Poll-Takers, to Map Tactics," *New York Times*, October 13, 1962, 23.

82. William R. Hamilton, "Political Polling: From the Beginning to the Center of American Election Campaigns," in James A. Thurber and Candice J. Nelson, eds., *Campaigns and Elections American Style* (Boulder, CO: Westview Press, 1995), 161–80.

83. Ibid., 163.

84. Louis Harris, *Is There a Republican Majority? Political Trends, 1952–1956* (New York: Harper, 1954).

85. Moore, *Superpollsters*, 74–75.

86. Ibid.

87. Transcript of Louis Harris oral history, interviewed by Vicki Daitch, April 12, 2005, John F. Kennedy Library, 4.

88. Theodore H. White, *The Making of the President 1960* (New York: Atheneum, 1961), 55–56.

89. Richard Nixon also used a private pollster, Claude Robinson of the Opinion Research Corporation, a former Columbia University scholar and partner of George Gallup.

90. Gary A. Donaldson, *The First Modern Campaign: Kennedy, Nixon, and the Election of 1960* (Lanham, MD: Rowman & Littlefield, 2007), 52.

91. Jacobs and Shapiro, "Issues, Candidate Image, and Priming," 528.

92. Shaun A. Casey, *The Making of a Catholic President: Kennedy v. Nixon 1960* (New York: Oxford University Press, 2009), 62–64; White, *The Making of the President 1960*, 101; Lawrence R. Jacobs and Melinda S. Jackson, "Presidential Leadership and the Threat to Popular Sovereignty," in Michael A. Genovese and Matthew J. Streb, *Polls and Politics: The Dilemmas of Democracy* (Albany: State University of New York Press, 2004), 33.

93. Casey, *The Making of a Catholic President*, 63.

94. Eisinger, *The Evolution of Presidential Polling*, 88.

95. Louis Harris, interviewed by Mark Blumenthal at AAPOR conference, Miami, Florida, May 14, 2009, http://www.pollster.com/blogs/aapor09_lou_harris.php?nr=1 (accessed July 25, 2014).

96. Quoted in Moore, *Superpollsters*, 78.

97. Jacobs and Shapiro, "Issues, Candidate Image, and Priming."

98. Ibid., 532.

99. Jacobs and Jackson, "Presidential Leadership and the Threat to Popular Sovereignty," 32.
100. Harris interview.
101. Casey, *The Making of a Catholic President*, 160–61; Eisinger, *The Evolution of Presidential Polling*, 88–89. See also Ithiel de Sola Pool and Robert Abelson, "The Simulmatics Project," *Public Opinion Quarterly* 25, no. 2 (Summer 1961): 167–83.
102. Harris oral history, 27.
103. Richard P. Hunt, "Poll Taker Gave Mayor His Cues," *New York Times*, September 10, 1961.
104. Clayton Knowles, "Harris Abandons Private Polling," *New York Times*, April 1, 1963.
105. Moore, *Superpollsters*, 122.
106. Douglas E. Schoen, *The Power of the Vote: Electing Presidents, Overthrowing Dictators, and Promoting Democracy around the World* (New York: William Morrow, 2007), 24.

Chapter 3

Epigraph quotes from Stevenson in David Halberstam, *The Fifties* (New York: Villard Press, 1993), 232; Gary A. Donaldson, *The First Modern Election: Kennedy, Nixon, and the Election of 1960* (Lanham, MD: Rowman & Littlefield, 2007), 157; and W. J. Rorabaugh, *The Real Making of the President: Kennedy, Nixon, and the 1960 Election* (Lawrence: University Press of Kansas, 2009), 201.

1. "Fine Oratory for All," *Washington Post*, June 13, 1900, 3; cited in Judy Chrichton, *America 1900: The Turning Point* (New York: Henry Holt, 1998), 155, 156; Louise Overacker, *Money in Elections* (New York: Macmillan, 1932), 23.
2. Edward McChesney Sait, *American Parties and Elections* (New York: Century Co., 1927), 504, quoted in Overacker, *Money in Elections*, 24.
3. Christopher H. Sterling and John M. Kitross, *Stay Tuned: A Concise History of American Broadcasting*, 2nd ed (Belmont, CA: Wadsworth Publishing, 1990), 69.
4. Edward W. Chester, *Radio, Television, and American Politics* (New York: Sheed and Ward, 1969), 16.
5. Ibid., 23.
6. Richard M. Fried, *The Man Everybody Knew: Bruce Barton and the Making of Modern America* (Chicago: Ivan R. Dee, 2005), 123.
7. Ithiel de Sola Pool, "What Will Be New in the New Politics?," in Ray Hiebert, Robert Jones, Ernest Lotito, and John Lorenz, eds., *The Political Image Merchants: Strategies in the New Politics* (Washington, DC: Acropolis Books, 1976), 255.
8. T. Harry Williams, *Huey Long* (New York: Knopf, 1969).
9. Donald Warren, *Radio Priest: Charles Coughlin, the Father of Hate Radio* (New York: Free Press, 1996), and Sheldon Marcus, *Father Coughlin: The Tumultuous Life of the Priest of the Little Flower* (Boston: Little, Brown, 1972).
10. Diana Mankowski and Raisa Jose, *Flashback: The Seventieth Anniversary of FDR's Fireside Chats* (Chicago: The Museum of Broadcase Communications, n.d.).
11. Joanne Morreale, *The Presidential Campaign Film: A Critical History* (Westport, CT: Praeger, 1993), 34.
12. Chester, *Radio, Television, and American Politics*, 34.
13. Ibid., 39.
14. Sig Mickelson, *From Whistle Stop to Sound Bite: Four Decades of Politics and Television* (New York: Praeger, 1989), 71.
15. Ibid., 48.

16. Kathleen Hall Jamieson, "The Evolution of Political Advertising in America," in Lynda Lee Kaid, Dan Nimmo, and Keith R. Sanders, eds., *New Perspectives on Political Advertising* (Carbondale: Southern Illinois University Press, 1986), 14.

17. Ibid.

18. Morreale, *The Presidential Campaign Film*, 32–33.

19. Louise Overacker, *Money in Elections* (New York: Macmillan, 1932), 30. Newberry was elected senator, but in 1921 he was tried and convicted of violating the Federal Corrupt Practices Act for election irregularities; he subsequently resigned. His conviction was overturned in *Newberry v. United States*, 256 US 232 (1921), when the Supreme Court held unconstitutional parts of the Federal Corrupt Practices Act.

20. Ibid., 34, and *President Coolidge, Taken on the White House Ground*, a film by Lee De Forest, Internet Archive, http://archive.org/details/coolidge_1924 (accessed July, 2013).

21. Kathleen Hall Jamieson, *Packaging the Presidency: A History and Criticism of Presidential Campaign Advertising* (New York: Oxford University Press, 1984), 30–32.

22. Jack Redding, *Inside the Democratic Party* (New York: Bobbs-Merrill, 1958), 254; Morreale, *The Presidential Campaign Film*, 35–37; and Jamieson, *Packaging the Presidency*, 29–33.

23. Stephen C. Wood, "Television's First Political Spot Ad Campaign: Eisenhower Answers America," *Presidential Studies Quarterly* 20, no. 2, Eisenhower Centennial Issue (Spring 1990): 265–83, at 265.

24. Mike Conway, "The Birth of CBS-TV: An Ambitious Experiment at the Advent of U.S. Commercial Television," *Journalism History* 32, no. 3 (Fall 2006): 128–38.

25. Sterling and Kitross, *Stay Tuned*, 258.

26. Roger Simon and Art Samuels, "Philadelphia Story: Politics Would Never Be the Same after Dewey, Truman and Television Came to Town," *U.S. News & World Report*, August 7, 2000.

27. Arthur Krock, "The Democrats Could Learn from Television," *New York Times*, July 4, 1948, E3; "Television Aid for Democrats," *New York Times*, July 8, 1948, 7.

28. David McCullough, *Truman* (New York: Simon & Schuster, 1992), 636–44.

29. Roger Simon, "The Killer and the Candidate: How Willie Horton and George Bush Rewrote the Rules on Political Advertising," *Regardie's*, October 1, 1990.

30. Morreale, *The Presidential Campaign Film*, 37.

31. David Ogilvy, *Ogilvy on Advertising* (New York: Vintage, 1985), 210.

32. Chester, *Radio, Television, and American Politics*, 75; "awe inspiring" quote from John Crosby writing in the *New York Herald Tribune*; Edwin Diamond and Stephen Bates, *The Spot: The Rise of Political Advertising on Television*, 3rd ed. (Cambridge, MA: MIT Press, 1992), 43.

33. Ogilvy, *Ogilvy on Advertising*, 210.

34. Ibid., 210–11.

35. Quoted in Vance Packard, *The Hidden Persuaders* (New York: Ig Publishers, 2007, 1957), 182.

36. "Connecticut GOP Hopeful Gains," *New York Times*, October 29, 1950, 52.

37. James A. Hagerty, "Connecticut Race Called Close; Edge Given to Lodge Over Bowles," *New York Times*, October 27, 1950, 22.

38. Mickelson, *From Whistle Stop to Sound Bite*, 76–7.

39. Chester, *Radio, Television, and American Politics*, 76.

40. Ibid., and William Howard, *The Kefauver Committee and the Politics of Crime, 1950–1952* (Columbia: University of Missouri Press, 1974).

41. Noel L. Griese, "Rosser Reeves and the 1952 Eisenhower TV Spot Blitz," *Journal of Advertising*, December 1, 1975, 34–38, at 35.

42. Chester, *Radio, Television, and American Politics*, 78.

43. William B. Pickett, *Eisenhower Decides to Run* (Chicago: Ivan R. Dee, 2000), xv–xvi. See also Blanche Wiesen Cook, *The Declassified Eisenhower: A Divided*

Legacy of Peace and Political Warfare (New York: Penguin, 1984); cf. Stephen E. Ambrose, *Eisenhower*, vol. 1, *Soldier, General of the Army, President-Elect, 1890–1952* (New York: Simon & Schuster, 1983).

44. Pickett, *Eisenhower Decides to Run*, 187–88.

45. Ibid., 200.

46. Kurt Lang and Gladys Engel Lang, *Politics and Television* (Chicago: Quadrangle Books, 1968), 78–79.

47. Chester, *Radio, Television, and American Politics*, 82–83.

48. Halberstam, *The Fifties*, 224.

49. Robert V. Friedenberg, *Communication Consultants in Political Campaigns: Ballot Box Warriors* (Westport, CT: Praeger, 1997), 154.

50. Ibid., citing Chester, *Radio, Television, and American Politics*, 79, 83.

51. Diamond and Bates, *The Spot*, 46.

52. Museum of the Moving Image, *The Living Room Candidate: Presidential Campaign Commercials 1952–2008*, www.livingroomcandidate.org/commercials/1952/ike-for-president (accessed June 15, 2013).

53. Diamond and Bates, *The Spot*, 58.

54. Mickelson, *From Whistle Stop to Sound Bite*, 71.

55. On the history of the Eisenhower spots, see Wood, "Television's First Political Spot Ad Campaign"; Diamond and Bates, *The Spot*; Jamieson, *Packaging the Presidency*, 83–86; and Darrell M. West, *Air Wars: Television Advertising in Election Campaigns 1952–2008*, 4th ed. (Washington, DC: CQ Press, 2009).

56. Griese, "Rosser Reeves and the 1952 Eisenhower TV Spot Blitz," 35

57. Rick Perlstein, *Before the Storm: Barry Goldwater and the Unmaking of the American Consensus* (New York: Hill and Wang, 2001), 386.

58. Jamieson, *Packaging the Presidency*, 84.

59. Halberstam, *The Fifties*, 230.

60. Wood, "Television's First Political Spot Ad Campaign," 275–79; Diamond and Bates, *The Spot*, 54–56.

61. Samuel Lubell, *The Future of American Politics* (New York: Harper & Row, 1952).

62. Stanley Kelley Jr., *Professional Public Relations and Political Power* (Baltimore: Johns Hopkins Press, 1956), 188; emphasis in the original.

63. Robert Spero, *The Duping of the American Voter: Dishonesty and Deception in Presidential Television Advertising* (New York: Lippincott & Crowell, 1980), 35.

64. Sig Mickelson, *The Electric Mirror: Politics in an Age of Television* (New York: Dodd, Mead, 1972), 58.

65. Quoted in Packard, *The Hidden Persuaders*, 193.

66. Mickelson, *The Electric Mirror*, 104. For Republican National Committee ten-minute film on the need to elect Wendell Willkie president in 1940, see "The Truth About Taxes," https://www.youtube.com/watch?v=eiJ3AS-CgRI (accessed September 15, 2015).

67. Stephen Fox, *The Image Makers: A History of American Advertising and its Creators* (New York: Vintage, 1985), 309, cited in Morreale, *The Presidential Campaign Film*, 32–33.

68. Wood, "Television's First Political Spot Ad Campaign," 279.

69. Diamond and Bates, *The Spot*, 48.

70. Kelley, *Public Relations and Political Power*, 191.

71. Alexander Heard, *The Cost of Democracy* (Chapel Hill: University of North Carolina Press, 1960), 415.

72. Diamond and Bates, *The Spot*, 46–49.

73. Ibid., 195.

74. *The New Methodology: A Study of Political Strategy and Tactics* (Washington, DC: The American Institute for Political Communication, 1967), 11.

75. Mickelson, *From Whistle Stop to Sound Bite*, 14–15.

76. Quoted in Halberstam, *The Fifties*, 237.

77. Herbert Parmet, *Richard Nixon and His America* (Boston: Little, Brown, 1990), 239–40.
78. Ibid., 244.
79. Halberstam, *The Fifties*, 239; Gladwin Hill, "Nixon Puts Fate up to GOP Chiefs," *New York Times*, September 23, 1952.
80. Speech transcript from PBS *American Experience*, "The Checkers Speech," September 23, 1952, http://www.pbs.org/wgbh/americanexperience/features/primary-resources/nixon-checkers (accessed June 25, 2013).
81. Parmet, *Richard Nixon and His America*, 250.
82. Diamond and Bates, *The Spot*, 340–41. They argue that Nixon's presentation "combined four rhetorical modes in one inspired act: Nixon identifies himself as hardworking and gives details of his family's financial life; he argues his case with specific facts and figures, using documents when necessary; he attacks the Communist-coddling, big-spending opposition; and he ends with an appeal for support so that Eisenhower can do the job of saving America." At 341.
83. Chester, *Radio, Television, and American Politics*, 96–98.
84. J. Leonard Reinsch, *Getting Elected: From Radio and Roosevelt to Television and Reagan* (New York: Hippocrene Press, 1990), 108.
85. Ibid., 101.
86. Chester, *Radio, Television, and American Politics*, 103.
87. Diamond and Bates, *The Spot*, 76–77; Jamieson, *Packaging the Presidency*, 92–94.
88. Mickelson, *The Electric Mirror*, 115; Diamond and Bates, *The Spot*, 76–78.
89. Reinsch, *Getting Elected*, 109.
90. Transcript of Charles Guggenheim oral history; interviewed by John Franzén, American Association of Political Consultants Interview Collection, 1997–1999, George Washington University Libraries, June 20, 1997, 6.
91. Guggenheim interview, KETC Living St. Louis, n.d., http://www.youtube.com/watch?v=PpsJjSo7NHM (accessed May 20, 2013); Jamieson, *Packaging the Presidency*, 62.
92. Mickelson, *From Whistle Stop to Sound Bite*, 74.
93. Robert Montgomery biographical sketch, from The Earl of Hollywood website, http://www.earlofhollywood.com/RMbio.html (accessed July 7, 2013).
94. "Platform Double-Talk," from Museum of the Moving Image, Living Room Candidate website, http://www.livingroomcandidate.org/commercials/1952/platform-double-talk (accessed July 7, 2013).
95. Mickelson, *From Whistle Stop to Sound Bite*, 76.
96. Museum of the Moving Image, Living Room Candidate website, http://www.livingroomcandidate.org/commercials/1956 (accessed August 29, 2013).
97. Chester Burger, "Telephone News on Television." Unpublished report prepared for the American Telephone and Telegraph Company, September 1955, 2, cited and quoted in Stuart Ewen, *PR! A Social History of Spin* (New York: Basic Books, 1996), 390–91.
98. Claude Robinson, "The Gentle Art of Persuasion," *Public Relations Journal* 12 (June 1956), 4, cited in Ewen, *PR!*, 392.
99. Marshall McLuhan, *Understanding the Media: The Extensions of Man* (New York: McGraw-Hill, 1964), 287; Kennedy quoted in Pierre Salinger, *With Kennedy* (New York: Doubleday, 1966), 54.
100. Diamond and Bates, *The Spot*, 90.
101. Packard, *The Hidden Persuaders*, 181.
102. Kelley, *Professional Public Relations and Political Power*.
103. Donaldson, *The First Modern Election*, 112.
104. Theodore H. White, *The Making of the President 1960* (New York: Atheneum Publishers, 1961), 322.
105. Donaldson, *The First Modern Election*, 49–50.
106. Rorabaugh, *The Real Making of the President*, 47.

107. White, *The Making of the President 1960*, 115–16. White noted that there was no tape recording, no transcript of the speech left for history, and that his recollection came from his memory and notes.

108. Jamieson, *Packaging the Presidency*, 130, 134–35.

109. White, *The Making of the President 1960*, 120–21.

110. Museum of the Moving Image, Living Room Candidate, http://www.livingroomcandidate.org/commercials/1960 (accessed August 15, 2013).

111. Robert MacNeil, *The People Machine: The Influence of Television on American Politics* (New York: Harper & Row, 1968), 196–97.

112. L. Patrick Devlin, "Campaign Commercials," *Political Persuasion* (May/June 1985): 45–50.

113. Gene Wyckoff, *The Image Candidates: American Politics in the Age of Television* (New York: Macmillan, 1968), 51.

114. Museum of the Moving Image, Living Room Candidate, http://www.livingroomcandidate.org/commercials/1960 (accessed August 15, 2013).

115. Ibid.

116. Wyckoff, *The Image Candidates*, 55–57; Diamond and Bates, *The Spot*, 102; Museum of the Moving Image, Living Room Candidate, http://www.livingroomcandidate.org/commercials/1960 (accessed August 15, 2013).

117. Theodore White, *The Making of the President: 1964* (New York: Atheneum, 1965), 294.

118. Reinsch, *Getting Elected*, 133–34.

119. Stephen E. Ambrose, *Nixon*, vol. 1, *The Education of a Politician, 1913–1962* (New York: Touchstone, 1987), 563–72; also an eyewitness account from Mickelson, *From Whistle Stop to Sound Bite*, 119–26.

120. Rorabaugh, *The Real Making of the President*, 154.

121. Dan Nimmo, *The Political Persuaders* (Englewood Cliffs, NJ: Prentice-Hall, 1970), 161–62; David L. Vancil and Sue D. Pendell, "The Myth of Viewer-Listener Disagreement in the First Kennedy-Nixon Debate," *Central States Speech Journal* 38, no. 1 (1987): 16–27; Vancil and Pendell argue that there is no solid evidence to conclude that there was disagreement in the assessment of viewers and listeners.

122. Diamond and Bates, *The Spot*, 107.

123. G. Scott Thomas, *A New World to Be Won: John Kennedy, Richard Nixon, and the Tumultuous Year of 1960* (Santa Barbara, CA: Praeger, 2011), 212.

124. Baker quoted in Thomas, *A New World to Be Won*, 213.

125. Friedenberg, *Communication Consultants in Political Campaigns*, 21.

Chapter 4

Epigraph quote from Roberts, Walt Anderson, "Spencer-Roberts: Dynamic Duo of California Politics," *Los Angeles Times*, December 11, 1966, W20; from Matt Reese, James Ledbetter, "Reese's Pieces," *Campaigns & Elections*, December 1989; Ithiel de Sola Pool, "What Will Be New in the New Politics," in Ray Hiebert, Robert Jones, Ernest Lotito, and John Lorenz, eds., *The Political Image Merchants: Strategies in the New Politics* (Washington, DC: Acropolis Books, 1976), 248.

1. Nimmo also identifies twelve early campaign management firms, including Whitaker and Baxter; Spencer-Roberts and Associates; Baus and Ross; Civic Service, Inc. (Roy Pfautch); and Matthew A. Reese and Associates. Dan D. Nimmo, *Political Persuaders: The Techniques of Modern Election Campaigns* (New Brunswick, NJ: Transaction, 2001, 1976), 231–32.

2. Penn Kimball, *Bobby Kennedy and the New Politics* (Englewood Cliffs, NJ: Prentice-Hall, 1968), 169.

3. Joseph Napolitan, *The Election Game and How to Win It* (Garden City, NY: Doubleday, 1972), 65.

4. Nelson Polsby and Aaron Wildavsky, *Presidential Elections: Contemporary Strategies of American Electoral Politics*, 8th ed. (New York: Free Press, 1991), 210.

5. Napolitan quoted in David Chagall, *The New Kingmakers* (New York: Harcourt Brace Jovanovich, 1981), 9.

6. Video of Stuart Spencer, "Life and Career of Stuart Spencer," C-SPAN (June 3, 1988), http://www.c-span.org/video/?2835-1/life-career-stuart-spencer (accessed April 5, 2016).

7. On Napolitan's background and early years, see Joseph Napolitan, "Present at the Creation (of Modern Political Consulting)," in David D. Perlmutter, ed., *The Manship School Guide to Political Communication* (Baton Rouge: Louisiana State University Press, 1999), 19–26; Joseph Napolitan, interview with author, June 19, 2003, New York City; Transcript of Joseph Napolitan oral history, interviewed by John Franzén, American Association of Political Consultants Interview Collection, The George Washington University Libraries, December 3, 1996; Chagall, *The New Kingmakers*, ch. 2; Sidney Blumenthal, *The Permanent Campaign: Inside the World of Elite Political Operatives* (Boston: Beacon Press, 1980), ch. 7.

8. Stanley Kelley Jr., *Professional Public Relations and Political Power* (Baltimore: Johns Hopkins University Press, 1956).

9. Napolitan, "Present at the Creation," 19.

10. Napolitan interview with author and "Newspapers Ban News," *Time* (October 13, 1958), 70–72.

11. Napolitan, "Present at the Creation," 19–20.

12. Lawrence F. O'Brien, *No Final Victories: A Life in Politics from John F. Kennedy to Watergate* (New York: Ballantine Books, 1976), 97.

13. Joseph Napolitan Associates, "Survey of Political Attitudes, Pennsylvania" April 25, 1963, John F. Kennedy Library, http://www.jfklibrary.org/Asset-Viewer/Archives/JFKPOF-105-006.aspx; and "Survey of Political Attitudes, Massachusetts," June 15, 1963, http://www.jfklibrary.org/Asset-Viewer/Archives/JFKPOF-105-005.aspx.

14. Schlackman and Strother quoted in "Joseph Napolitan, the Originator, Dead at 84," *Campaign & Elections*, December 4, 2013.

15. Lou Cannon, *Reagan* (New York: G.P. Putnam's Sons, 1982), 103–4; David S. Broder, "The Men Behind 'The Men Who—'" *New York Times*, January 5, 1964, SM15.

16. Transcript of Stuart K. Spencer oral history, interviewed by Whit Ayres, American Association of Political Consultants Oral History Project, George Washington University, February 2, 1999; transcript of Stuart Spencer Oral History, interviewed by Paul B. Freedman et al., Ronald Reagan Oral History Project, Miller Center of Public Affairs, University of Virginia, November 15–16, 2001. For background on the Reagan campaign, see Matthew Dallek, *The Right Moment: Ronald Reagan's First Victory and the Decisive Turning Point in American Politics* (New York: Oxford University Press, 2004).

17. Cannon, *Reagan*, 104.

18. See Walt Anderson, *Campaigns: Cases in Political Conflict* (Pacific Palisades, CA: Goodyear Publishing, 1970), 204.

19. Bill Boyarsky, *Ronald Reagan: His Life and Rise to the Presidency* (New York: Random House, 1981), 94.

20. Spencer oral history (Virginia), 23. See also Stuart K. Spencer oral history, interviewed by Richard Norton Smith, Gerald R. Ford Presidential Library Oral History Project, December 2, 2008, http://geraldrfordfoundation.org/centennial/oralhistory/stu-spencer (accessed April 15, 2015).

21. James A. Baker III with Steve Fiffer, *"Work Hard, Study . . . and Keep Out of Politics!" Adventures and Lessons from an Unexpected Public Life* (New York: G. P. Putnam's Sons, 2006), 131.

22. Walt Anderson, "Dynamic Duo of California Politics," *Los Angeles Times West Magazine*, December 11, 1966, 21.

23. James F. Kelleher, "TV's Perennial Star: The Political Candidate," *Public Relations Journal* 12 (April 1956), 18.

24. Stuart Ewen, *PR! A Social History of Spin* (New York: Basic Books, 1996), 395–97.

25. David Lee Rosenbloom, *The Election Men: Professional Campaign Managers and American Democracy* (New York: Quadrangle Books, 1973), 22.

26. Michael K. Deaver, *Nancy: A Portrait of My Years with Nancy Reagan* (New York: William Morrow, 2004), 37.

27. Totton J. Anderson and Eugene C. Lee, "The 1966 Election in California," *Western Political Quarterly* 20, no. 2.2 (June 1967): 535–54.

28. Ibid., 544, n. 8, from Anderson, "Spencer-Roberts."

29. From the Spencer-Roberts website, http://www.spencer-roberts.com.

30. F. Clifton White with Jerome Tuccille, *Politics as a Noble Calling: The Memoirs of F. Clifton White* (Ottawa, IL: Jameson Books, Inc., 1994), 1.

31. Ibid., 55.

32. Theodore H. White, *The Making of the President 1964* (New York: Atheneum, 1965), 91–92.

33. Bruce Lambert, "F. Clifton White, 74, Long a Republican Strategist," *New York Times*, January 10, 1993.

34. White, *Politics as a Noble Calling*, 223–25; IFES website, www.ifes.org.

35. Robert Meyers, "They Owe It All to Whatshisname," *Los Angeles Times*, April 2, 1972, M19.

36. Transcript of Joseph Cerrell oral history, interviewed by Dennis O'Brien, John F. Kennedy Library Oral History Program, June 13, 1969, 8.

37. Larry Sabato, *The Rise of Political Consultants: New Ways of Winning Elections* (New York: Basic Books, 1981), 13.

38. Data from Cerrell Associates website, http://www.cerrell.com/practice/campaigns-issues-management (accessed June 25, 2013).

39. Transcript of Joseph Cerrell oral history, interviewed by John Franzén, American Association of Political Consultants Oral History Project, George Washington University Libraries, October 24, 1997, 1.

40. Transcript of Walter De Vries oral history, interviewed by John Franzén, American Association of Political Consultants Oral History Project, George Washington University Libraries, November 7 1997, and Walter De Vries telephone interview with author, May 13, 2012.

41. Ibid.

42. Walter De Vries and V. Lance Tarrance Jr., *The Ticket-Splitter: A New Force in American Politics* (Grand Rapids, MI: Eerdmans, 1972). Tarrance and De Vries, with Donna L. Mosher, later wrote *Checked and Balanced: How Ticket-Splitters Are Shaping the New Balance of Power in American Politics* (Grand Rapids, MI: Eerdmans, 1998).

43. De Vries oral history.

44. On the role of De Vries and Currier in the 1966 Michigan gubernatorial campaign on Romney's behalf, see James M. Perry, *The New Politics: The Expanding Technology of Political Manipulation* (New York: Clarkson N. Potter, 1968), ch. 4.

45. De Vries oral history.

46. De Vries quoted in Perry, *The New Politics*, 71.

47. Ibid., 105.

48. De Vries oral history.

49. Walter DeVries, "Taking the Voter's Pulse," in Hiebert et al., eds., *The Political Image Merchants*, 63–64.

50. Ibid., 64.

51. Nimmo, *Political Persuaders*, 227–28.

52. Robert Wernick, "The Perfect Candidate," *Life*, June 3, 1966, 41ff.

53. Hal Evry, *The Selling of a Candidate: The Winning Formula* (Los Angeles: Western Opinion Research Center, 1971).

54. Rosenbloom, *The Election Men*, 84.

55. Sabato, *The Rise of Political Consultants*, 303.

56. Mabel Chesley, "Kirk Document Provides Light," *Daytona Beach (Florida) Morning Journal*, October 2, 1966, 5A.

57. Transcript of Peter D. Hart interview, conducted by Sara Fritz, The Center for Public Integrity: 2008 (March 12, 2007), http://www.buyingofthepresident.org/index.php/interviews/peter_hart1/(accessed June 25, 2013).

58. Nimmo, *Political Persuaders*, 232.

59. Louis Harris, "Polls and Politics in the United States," *Public Opinion Quarterly* 27, no. 1 (Spring 1963): 3–8, at 3.

60. Robert King and Martin Schnitzer, "Contemporary Use of Private Polling," *Public Opinion Quarterly* 32, no. 3 (Autumn 1968): 431–36.

61. Alden Whitman, "Oliver Quayle 3d Dies at 52; Public Opinion Poll Specialist," *New York Times*, April 16, 1974, 42.

62. Ibid., and "Oliver Quayle Dies, Opinion Poll Head," *Washington Post*, April 16, 1974, C4.

63. Transcript of Robert M. Teeter oral history, interviewed by Whit Ayres, American Association of Political Consultants Interview Collection, George Washington University Libraries, February 16, 2000.

64. David W. Moore, *The Superpollsters: How They Measure and Manipulate Public Opinion in America* (New York: Four Walls Eight Windows, 1995), 225.

65. Ibid., 221.

66. Transcript of Richard B. Wirthlin oral history, interviewed by Whit Ayres, American Association of Political Consultants Interview Collection, George Washington University Libraries, December 9, 1999.

67. Ibid.

68. Tarrance e-mail communication with the author, May 28, 2013. Merrill became professor emeritus of the Walter Cronkite School of Journalism and Mass Communications. He conducted surveys in twenty-seven states and several countries, and his clients included governors and members of Congress. Merrill was the founding director of the ASU Survey Research Center, the Public Opinion Research Center, and the Cronkite/Eight Poll. See profile of Merrill at http://morrisoninstitute.asu.edu/researchers-and-staff/bruce-merrill (accessed July 12, 2013).

69. Wirthlin wrote that Goldwater "gave me the endorsement of a lifetime," when he said to Reagan, "Ron, there are few people in politics you can trust absolutely, but Dick Wirthlin is one of those persons." Dick Wirthlin with Wynton C. Hall, *The Greatest Communicator: What Ronald Reagan Taught Me about Politics, Leadership, and Life* (Hoboken, NJ: John Wiley and Sons, 2004), 16.

70. Ibid., 9–12.

71. Ibid., 14.

72. Vincent P. Barabba (b. 1934) later became head of the US Census Bureau (1973–1976; 1979–1981), was director of market intelligence at Eastman Kodak (1981–1986), and general manager, corporate strategy and knowledge development, at General Motors Corporation (1986–2003); he then became founder and chairman of Market Insight Corporation. Biographical sketch from Market Insight Corporation website, http://www.marketinsightcorp.com/about-us.html. See also, Oral History—Vincent P. Barabba, US Census Bureau, interviewed by Barbara Milton and David Pemberton, August 7, 1989, http://www.census.gov/prod/2003pubs/oh-Barabba.pdf (accessed August 15, 2013).

73. David S. Broder, *Changing of the Guard: Power and Leadership in America* (New York: Simon & Schuster, 1980), 407.

74. Wirthlin oral history; Moore, *The Superpollsters,* 196.

75. Mark S. Mellman, "Wirthlin: The Passing of a Giant," *The Hill,* March 22, 2011.

76. Transcript of Bill Hamilton oral history, interviewed by John Franzén, American Association of Political Consultants Interview Collection, 1997–1999, George Washington University Libraries, December 12, 1996, 2.

77. Betty Glad, *Jimmy Carter: In Search of the Great White House* (New York: W. W. Norton, 1980), 124–25.

78. Lois Romano, "Hamilton: Telling It Like It Is," *Washington Post,* January 18, 1984, C11.

79. Margalit Fox, "Tony Schwartz, Father of 'Daisy Ad' for the Johnson Campaign, Dies at 84," *New York Times,* June 17, 2008.

80. Transcript of Charles Guggenheim oral history, interviewed by John Franzén, American Association of Political Consultants Interview Collection, The George Washington University Libraries, June 20, 1997, Part 1.

81. Transcript of video, "Charles Guggenheim on Candidate Biography Films," PBS Newshour, July 3, 2000, www.pbs.org/newshour/bb/media-july-deco0-guggenheim_7-03 (accessed May 11, 2016).

82. Ann Hornaday, "Forty Years On, RFK Ad Make Still Frames the Campaign," *Washington Post,* May 3, 2008, C1.

83. Ibid.

84. Guggenheim interview, PBS .

85. Ibid.

86. Jonathan Rowe, "Media Mogul Bows Out of the Political Ad Game," *Christian Science Monitor,* November 29, 1988, 3.

87. Guggenheim's son, P. Davis Guggenheim, is also a film director and producer, having produced, among other works, the Academy Award-winning *An Inconvenient Truth* (2006), a biographical film on Barack Obama (2008), and *Waiting for "Superman"* (2010), a documentary on the failure of US education. See chapter 19 on his role in the Obama 2008 presidential campaign.

88. Transcript of Raymond D. Strother oral history, interviewed by John Franzén, American Association of Political Consultants Interview Collection, 1997–1999, George Washington University Libraries, October 10, 1997, 2.

89. Raymond D. Strother, "The Louisiana Political Candidate and the Advertising Organization," MA thesis, Louisiana State University, 1965, later published by Kennedy Press in Baton Rouge. After consulting for Martha Layne Collins, a candidate for the Kentucky governorship, and Richard M. Daley, a candidate for the Chicago mayorship, those races put into perspective his original thesis: "I have come to believe that paid television plays only a minor part in two kinds of race: small ones, such as for city council, where personal contact is of utmost importance; and the largest of them all, presidential campaigns, where the press does a wonderful job of informing voters without interference from paid ads." Raymond D. Strother, *Falling Up: How a Redneck Helped Invent Political Consulting* (Baton Rouge: Louisiana State University Press, 2003), 156–57.

90. "Louisiana Legends," LPB Television, Baton Rouge, Louisiana website, http://www.lpb.org/programs/legends/weill.html (accessed August 15, 2013).

91. Strother, *Falling Up,* 55.

92. Ibid., 56.

93. Rudy Maxa, "GOP Guns Take Aim at '78 Elections," *Washington Post Magazine,* October 16, 1977.

94. Blumenthal, *The Permanent Campaign,* 188.

95. Myra McPherson, "The Winner . . . John Deardourff," *Washington Post*, November 9, 1978, D1; Patricia Sullivan, "Pioneering GOP Consultant John Deardourff Dies at 61," *Washington Post*, December 28, 2004, B6.

96. On the activities of Campaign Consultants, Inc., see James M. Perry, *The New Politics: The Expanding Technology of Political Manipulation* (New York: Clarkson N. Potter, 1968), 33–40.

97. Rosenbloom, *The Election Men*, 148–56.

98. Douglas L. Bailey, interview with author, Arlington, Virginia, February 6, 2013.

99. Blumenthal, *The Permanent Campaign,* 186; Sullivan, "Pioneering GOP Consultant John Deardourff Dies at 61," B6.

100. Ken Adelman, "What I've Learned: Doug Bailey," *Washingtonian*, November 2006, https://www.washingtonian.com/articles/print/2006/11/01/what-ive-learned-doug-bailey.php (accessed August 15, 2013).

101. His birth name was David Goldberg.

102. Blumenthal, *The Permanent Campaign*, 86–87.

103. John J. Goldman, "Garth Leads the Field as Campaign Consultant," *Los Angeles Times*, March 3, 1978.

104. Jim Mason, *No Holding Back: The 1980 John B. Anderson Presidential Campaign* (Lanham, MD: University Press of America, 2011), 238.

105. Sam Roberts, "Three Mayors Seek to Honor a Master of Campaigns," *New York Times*, June 1, 2010. See also Sam Roberts, "David Garth, 84, Dies; Consultant Was an Innovator of Political TV Ads," *New York Times*, December 15, 2014.

106. Joseph Lelyveld, "Rafshoon vs. Garth," *New York Times*, August 21, 1977, B06. See also "David Garth, Kingmaker" a two-part tribute to Garth, created in conjunction with the creation of a communications chair at CUNY in Garth's name. George Arzt Communications, produced and directed by Kay van de Linde, 2010, https://www.youtube.com/watch?v=QGCfpBoX6Io and https://www.youtube.com/watch?v=BidJ9yZ1Fbk (accessed January 15, 2014).

107. Transcript of Robert Goodman oral history, interviewed by Wayne C. Johnson, American Association of Political Consultants Interview Collection, George Washington University Libraries, October 25, 1999.

108. Ron Susskind, "The Power of Political Consultants," *New York Times*, August 12, 1984, A32.

109. "My Kind of Town," lyrics by Sammy Cahn, music by Jimmy Van Heusen, 1964. Special thanks to Ed Grefe for bringing this to my attention.

110. Bernard Weintraub, "Bush Gets Lessons in Performing on TV," *New York Times*, January 13, 1980, 23.

111. Rudy Maxa, "Robert Goodman: GOP's Jingle Man Prospers with TV," *Washington Post*, March 11, 1979.

112. Weintraub, "Bush Gets Lessons in Performing on TV."

113. Goodman oral history.

114. On Goodman Agency products, see Homer E. Dybvig, "Analysis of Political Communication through Selected Television Commercials Produced by Robert Goodman Agency," PhD diss., Southern Illinois University, 1970.

115. Joe McGinnis, *The Selling of the President 1968* (New York: Simon & Schuster, 1969).

116. Leonard Garment, *Crazy Rhythm: My Journey from Brooklyn, Jazz, and Wall Street to Nixon's White House, Watergate, and Beyond* (New York: Times Books, 1997), 139.

117. Gabriel Sherman, *The Loudest Voice in the Room: How the Brilliant, Bombastic Roger Ailes Built Fox News—and Divided the Country* (New York: Random House, 2014), 66.

118. Zev Chafets, *Roger Ailes: Off Camera* (New York: Sentinel, 2013), 57.

119. Ibid., 54.
120. Kerwin Swint, *Dark Genius: The Influential Career of Legendary Political Operative and Fox News Founder Roger Ailes* (New York: Union Square Press, 2008), 108–9.
121. Roger E. Ailes and Jon Kraushar, *You Are the Message: Secrets of the Master Communicators* (New York: Doubleday, 1989). On his television career, see Sherman, *The Loudest Voice in the Room.*
122. Dick Morris, *Behind the Oval Office: Getting Reelected Against All Odds* (Los Angeles: Renaissance Books, 1999), 53.
123. Thomas J. Fleming, "Selling the Product Named Hubert Humphrey," *New York Times Magazine*, October 13, 1968, 45.
124. For an early biographical sketch of Schwartz, see Rosenbloom, *The Permanent Campaign*, 116–31.
125. Patricia Sullivan, "Tony Schwartz: His Ads Targeted Viewer Emotions," *Washington Post*, June 17, 2008.
126. Tony Schwartz, *The Responsive Chord* (New York: Doubleday, 1974). He also wrote *Media: The Second God* (New York: Doubleday, 1983).
127. American Institute for Political Communication, *The New Methodology*, 11.
128. W. R. Rorabaugh, *The Real Making of the President: Kennedy, Nixon, and the 1960 Election* (Lawrence: University Press of Kansas, 2009), 157.
129. O'Brien, *No Final Victories*, 62.
130. Robert A. Caro, *The Years of Lyndon Johnson*, vol. 4, *The Passage of Power* (New York: Knopf, 2012), ch. 3.
131. Transcript of Matthew A. Reese Jr. oral history, interviewed by William L. Young, John F. Kennedy Library Oral History Program, October 24, 1964, 8–9.
132. Ibid. See also transcript of Matthew A. Reese Jr. oral history, interviewed by John Franzén, American Association of Political Consultants Interview Collection, the George Washington University Library, December 12, 1997; Ledbetter, "Reese's Pieces."
133. O'Brien, *No Final Victories*, 75.
134. Reese, oral history, JFK Library, 8–9.
135. Caro, *The Passage of Power*, 29
136. Sasha Issenberg, *The Victory Lab: The Secret Science of Winning Campaigns* (New York: Crown, 2010), 39.
137. Bart Barnes, "Matt Reese, Veteran Political Consultant, Dies at 71," *Washington Post*, December 3, 1998, B10.
138. Transcript of Lawrence F. O'Brien oral history interview XXII, June 19, 1987, interviewed by Michael L. Gillette, Lyndon B. Johnson Library.
139. Reese oral history, AAPC, 8.
140. Ledbetter, "Reese's Pieces."
141. David L. Rosenbloom, ed., *The Political Market Place* (New York: Quadrangle Books, 1972).
142. Nicholas Lemann, "Industry," in David Broder et al., *The Pursuit of the Presidency 1980* (New York: Berkley Books, 1980), 25.
143. Kathleen Teltsch, "Frenchman to Sell U.S. Election Methods Abroad," *New York Times*, March 19, 1967, 17. Even earlier was Andrew Mulligan, "Gaullist to Go American to Get Votes," *Los Angeles Times*, April 6, 1966, 19.
144. Napolitan interview, June 19, 2003; Joseph Napolitan, "Thoughts on IAPC Beginning its Fourth Decade," International Association of Political Consultants website, http://www.iapc.org/secondletter.asp; Lloyd Garrison, "Political Aides Form World Unit," *New York Times*, November 24, 1968, 40.
145. Andrea Spring, "AAPC: The First Twenty-five Years," *Campaigns & Elections* (December 1993/January 1994).
146. Napolitan, *The Election Game and How to Win It*, 5.
147. Quoted in Spring, "AAPC: The First Twenty-five Years."

Chapter 5

Epigraph quotes from Bernbach in Robert Mann, *Daisy Petals and Mushroom Clouds: LBJ, Barry Goldwater and the Ad that Changed American Politics* (Baton Rouge: Louisiana State University Press, 2011), 44; anonymous Republican campaign manager quoted in David Lee Rosenbloom, *The Election Men: Professional Campaign Managers and American Democracy* (New York: Quadrangle Books, 1973), 44.

1. Darrell M. West, *Making Campaigns Count: Leadership and Coalition-Building in 1980* (Westport, CT: Greenwood, 1984), 17.
2. Ibid., 20.
3. Tarrance quoted in Barry M. Goldwater with Jack Casserly, *Goldwater* (New York: Doubleday, 1988), 214–15.
4. Karl A. Lamb and Paul A. Smith, *Campaign Decision-Making: The Presidential Election of 1964* (Belmont, CA: Wadsworth, 1968), 105; also, Theodore H. White, *The Making of the President 1964* (New York: Atheneum Publishers, 1965), 90–96.
5. Robert D. Novak, *The Agony of the G.O.P. 1964* (New York: Macmillan, 1965), 467.
6. Grenier's role was captured in a twenty-five-minute documentary, *Campaign Manager*, by Richard Leacock and Noel E. Parmentel Jr. for Pennebaker Hegedus Films; Rick Perlstein, *Before the Storm: Barry Goldwater and the Unmaking of the American Consensus* (New York: Hill and Wang, 2001), 24.
7. F. Clifton White with Jerome Tuccille, *Politics as a Noble Calling: The Memoirs of F. Clifton White* (Ottawa, IL: Jameson Books, 1994) 155. See also White, *The Making of the President 1964*, 90–97. The draft movement was the subject of Clifton White's earlier book, F. Clifton White with William J. Gill, *Suite 3505: The Story of the Draft Goldwater Movement* (New Rochelle, NY: Arlington House, 1967).
8. Perlstein, *Before the Storm*, 255. For profiles of Goldwater's inner circle of campaign advisers, see "Senator's Staff Works Smoothly," *New York Times*, July 16, 1964, 16.
9. "Senator's Staff Works Smoothly."
10. Michael Kramer and Sam Roberts, *"I Never Wanted to be Vice-President of Anything!" An Investigative Biography of Nelson Rockefeller* (New York: Basic Books, 1976), 281.
11. White, *The Making of the President 1964*, 123–25; Charles A. H. Thomson, "Mass Media Performance," in Milton C. Cummings Jr., ed. *The National Election of 1964* (Washington, DC: Brookings Institution, 1966), 114–15.
12. Stephen Shadegg, *What Happened to Goldwater?* (New York: Holt, Rhinehart, and Winston, 1965), 167, cited in Kathleen Hall Jamieson, *Packaging the Presidency: A History and Criticism of Presidential Campaign Advertising* (New York: Oxford University Press, 1984), 181.
13. Theodore White observed that this ad "probably had greater penetration than any other paid political use of television except for Richard M. Nixon's Checkers broadcast in 1952." White, *Making of the President 1964*, 323.
14. "Social Security," for the Democratic National Committee. Produced by DDB, Aaron Ehrlich, Stan Lee, Sid Myers, and Tony Schwartz. Museum of the Moving Image, Living Room Candidate website, http://www.livingroomcandidate.org/commercials/1964 (accessed September 5, 2013).
15. "Eastern Seaboard," for the Democratic National Committee. Produced by DDB, Aaron Ehrlich, Stan Lee, Sid Myers, and Tony Schwartz. Museum of the Moving Image, Living Room Candidate website, http://www.livingroomcandidate.org/commercials/1964 (accessed September 5, 2013).
16. "Ad Age Advertising Century: Top 100 Campaigns," Advertising Age, March 29, 1999; http://adage.com/article/special-report-the-advertising-century/ad-age-advertising-top-100-advertising-campaigns/140150 (accessed May 10, 2016).

17. Lamb and Smith, *Campaign Decision-Making*, 159.

18. Perlstein, *Before the Storm*, 387.

19. Edwin Diamond and Stephen Bates, *The Spot: The Rise of Political Advertising on Television*, 3rd ed. (Cambridge, MA: MIT Press 1992), 122–28. Much has been written on the "Daisy" commercial. See Mann, *Daisy Petals and Mushroom Clouds*; "Daisy: The Complete History of an Infamous and Iconic Ad," Conelrad website, www.conelrad.com/daisy. Montague Kern, *30-Second Politics: Political Advertising in the Eighties* (New York: Praeger, 1989), 32–34; and Jamieson, *Packaging the Presidency*, 198–205.

20. Burch and Goldwater memoirs quoted in Diamond and Bates, *The Spot*, 125, 128.

21. Goldwater interview with Bob Costas, "Goldwater Comments on Daisy Ad," n.d., http://www.youtube.com/watch?v=v6_PGj3VQXI&feature=related (accessed September 6, 2013).

22. Randall Rothenberg, "The Media Business: Advertising: The Power of the Sound of Speech," *New York Times*, August 21, 1989.

23. Lamb and Smith, *Campaign Decision-Making*, 90.

24. Margalit Fox, "Tony Schwartz, Father of 'Daisy Ad' for the Johnson Campaign, Dies at 84." *New York Times*, June 17, 2008.

25. Quoted in Mann, *Daisy Petals and Mushroom Clouds*, 67.

26. Ibid., 115.

27. Ibid., 70; and Transcript from Living Room Candidate, http://www.livingroomcandidate.org/commercials/1964/ice-cream (September 3, 2013).

28. Advertising Age, "Erwin, Wasey & Co.," *AdAge Encyclopedia*, September 15, 2003, http://adage.com/article/adage-encyclopedia/erwin-wasey/98457/(accessed September 5, 2013).

29. F. Clifton White and William J. McGill, *Why Reagan Won: The Conservative Movement 1964–1981* (Chicago: Regnery Gateway, 1981), 122.

30. Lee Edwards, *Goldwater: The Man Who Made a Revolution* (Washington, DC: Regnery, 1995), 330.

31. Charles A. H. Thomson, "Mass Media Performance," in Cummings, *The National Election of 1964*, 124–26. Lee Edwards wrote that at a 1981 reunion of Draft Goldwater operatives, Clif White announced that he wanted to show "Choice." Goldwater agreed and said, "Okay, let's look at that dirty movie." Afterward, Goldwater said, "I still think we were right" not to show it. Edwards, *Goldwater*, 330.

32. Thomas W. Benham, "Polling for a Presidential Candidate: Some Observations on the 1964 Campaign," *Public Opinion Quarterly* 29, no. 2 (Summer 1965): 185–99, at 192, 195–6.

33. Lichenstein interview in Donald T. Critchlow, *The Conservative Ascendancy: How the GOP Right Made Political History* (Cambridge, MA: Harvard University Press, 2007), 75.

34. Bruce E. Altschuler, *LBJ and the Polls* (Gainesville: University of Florida Press, 1990), 7.

35. Lamb and Smith, *Campaign Decision-Making*, 204–5.

36. The Ripon Society, *From Disaster to Distinction: A Republican Rebirth* (New York: Pocket Books, 1966), 18.

37. Lewis Chester, Godfrey Hodgson, and Bruce Page, *An American Melodrama: The Presidential Campaign of 1968* (New York: Viking Press, 1969), 689.

38. Quoted in Richard Nixon, *RN: The Memoirs of Richard Nixon* (New York: Grosset & Dunlap, 1978), 303.

39. James R. Jones, "Behind L.B.J.'s Decision Not to Run in '68," *New York Times*, April 16, 1988. Jones was Johnson's administrative chief of staff. According to Jones, the president planned to announce his decision at the conclusion of his 1968 State of the Union address in January, but decided that would jeopardize his legislative agenda.

40. Transcript, Lawrence F. O'Brien oral history, Interview XXII, interviewed by Michael L. Gillette, Lyndon B. Johnson Library, June 19, 1987. On the Indiana primary, see Ray E. Boomhower, *Robert F. Kennedy and the 1968 Indiana Primary* (Bloomington: Indiana University Press, 2008).

41. Dan T. Carter, *The Politics of Rage: George Wallace, the Origins of the New Conservatism, and the Transformation of American Politics* (New York: Simon & Schuster, 1995), 327.

42. In the end, Nixon was able to win Florida, Virginia, South Carolina, Tennessee, and the border state of Kentucky; Wallace won five Deep South states: Arkansas, Mississippi, Louisiana, Alabama, and Georgia.

43. Bruce E. Altschuler, *Keeping a Finger on the Public Pulse: Private Polling and Presidential Elections* (Westport, CT: Greenwood, 1982), 22–24.

44. Ibid., 26–32.

45. Joseph Napolitan, *The Election Game and How to Win It* (Garden City, NY: Doubleday, 1972).

46. Altschuler, *Keeping a Finger on the Public Pulse*, 44–48.

47. Transcript, Lawrence F. O'Brien oral history, interview XXIV, interviewed by Michael L. Gillette, Lyndon B. Johnson Library, July 22, 1987.

48. Chester, Hodgson, and Page, *An American Melodrama*, 613–15.

49. Ibid., 617–18.

50. Ibid., 286–87, 659.

51. Ibid., 637–38, quote at 638.

52. Ibid., 638–39; Walter Pincus, "O'Brien and Aides Spark Party Hunt for Men, Funds," *Washington Post*, October 28, 1968.

53. Thomas J. Fleming, "Selling the Product Named Hubert Humphrey," *New York Times Magazine*, October 13, 1968, 45.

54. Jules Witcover, *The Year the Dream Died: Revisiting 1968 in America* (New York: Warner Books, 1997), 365–66.

55. Napolitan interview with author; also Napolitan, *The Election Game*, 41–42.

56. Chester, Hodgson, and Page, *An American Melodrama*, 640. Napolitan vehemently denied this: "Someone in the agency [DDB] said I was anti-black because of my criticism of these spots. 'Napolitan wanted no black faces at all,' the anonymous agency spokesman said. Bullshit! The first Humphrey television spot ever to go on after the convention had a black face on it. So did the second one. So did many of the others. So did the two thirty-minute films, the half-hour Q-and-A programs, the election eve telethons. But the two spots that DDB presented that day would have alienated both the Black Panthers and the Ku Klux Klan, one hell of an accomplishment in sixty seconds." Napolitan, *The Election Game*, 27.

57. Chester, Hodgson, and Page, *An American Melodrama*, 636; Napolitan interview with author. Also on the team, which Napolitan described as "perhaps the best media team ever assembled for a political campaign," was Harry Muheim, Bill Wilson, Sid Aronson, and Hal Tulchin. Napolitan, *The Election Game*, 43.

58. Maurice Carroll, "Nixon's Television Spots Emerging as Hard-Hitting, Humphrey's as Soft-Sell," *New York Times*, October 1, 1968, 32.

59. See Robert V. Friedenberg, *Communication Consultants in Political Campaigns: Ballot Box Warriors* (Westport, CT: Praeger, 1997), 165–66.

60. Joseph Napolitan, "Media Costs and Effects in Political Campaigns," *Annals of the American Academy of Political and Social Science* 427, *Role of the Mass Media in America Politics* (September. 1976): 114–24, at 117.

61. See, for example Milton L. Rakove, *Don't Make No Waves . . . Don't Back No Losers* (Bloomington: Indiana University Press, 1976).

62. Jamieson, *Packaging the Presidency*, 234.

63. Lawrence F. O'Brien, *No Final Victories: A Life in Politics—From John F. Kennedy to Watergate* (Garden City, NY: Doubleday, 1974), 258.

64. Ibid., 233–34.
65. O'Brien oral history, interview XXIV, LBJ Library, 7.
66. Dennis D. Wainstock, *Election Year 1968: The Turning Point* (New York: Enigma Books, 2012), 178; Jamieson, *Packaging the Presidency*, 271–72; Ted Van Dyk, *Heroes, Hacks, and Fools: Memoirs from the Political Inside* (Seattle: University of Washington Press, 2007), 92–93.
67. Edward W. Chester, *Radio, Television, and American Politics* (New York: Sheed and Ward, 1969), 279.
68. Jamieson, *Packaging the Presidency*, 236.
69. Chester, *Radio, Television, and American Politics*, 269–70.
70. Carroll, "Nixon's Television Spots Emerging as Hard-Hitting."
71. Leonard Garment, *Crazy Rhythm: My Journey from Brooklyn, Jazz, and Wall Street to Nixon's White House, Watergate, and Beyond* (New York: Times Books, 1997), 136–37.
72. Joe McGinniss, *The Selling of the President 1968* (New York: Trident Press, 1969).
73. Garment, *Crazy Rhythm*, 136.
74. Rick Perlstein, *Nixonland: The Rise of a President and the Fracturing of America* (New York: Scribner, 2008), 332. While focusing on racial politics and views of presidents, Kenneth O'Reilly, *Nixon's Piano: Presidents and Racial Politics from Washington to Clinton* (New York: Free Press, 1995) also informs us that Nixon, who couldn't read music, played everything in the key of C, trying to avoid all those nasty sharps and flats.
75. Perlstein, *Nixonland*, 332–33.
76. McGinniss, *The Selling of the President 1968*, 75.
77. Richard Nixon, *In the Arena: A Memoir of Victory, Defeat, and Renewal* (New York: Simon & Schuster, 1990), 265.
78. Ibid., 265–66.
79. For an analysis and criticism of the McGinniss book, see Jamieson, *Packaging the Presidency*, 262–69.
80. Perlstein, *Nixonland*, 333.
81. Museum of the Moving Image, Living Room Candidate, http://www.livingroomcandidate.org/commercials/1968 (accessed September 5, 2013).
82. Nixon, *RN*, 329.
83. *David Leip's Atlas of U.S. Presidential Elections*, 1968, http://uselectionatlas.org (accessed April 5, 2016).
84. J. Leonard Reinsch, *Getting Elected: From Radio and Roosevelt to Television and Reagan* (New York: Hippocrene, 1990), 238.
85. O'Brien oral history, interview XXIV, LBJ Library.
86. Napolitan, *The Election Game and How to Win It*, 250.
87. Steven Stark, "Serving TV Winners," *The Atlantic*, March 1985, 24.
88. Napolitan, *The Election Game*, 253.
89. Raymond Bonner, *Waltzing with a Dictator* (New York: Times Books, 1987), 76ff. Campaign manager Ernesto Maceda said, in an interview years afterward, "We were prepared to cheat all the way." Everett Martin of *Newsweek* wrote, "I have covered several Asian elections where dirty tactics were used. But never have I seen so much personally." Cited in Bonner, *Waltzing with a Dictator*, 77.
90. Napolitan cited Benjamin Romualdez, governor of Leyete, and Imelda Marcos's brother, as the campaign manager, calling him "one of the best I've worked with anywhere" (*The Election Game*, 252). Napolitan was apparently taken with Marcos: on first meeting him, Napolitan wrote, "He is bright, knowledgeable, handsome, charismatic—the kind of candidate you like to work with" (246), and calling him "one of the world's legitimate war heroes" (245). One of the issues that Napolitan hit hard was the fact that Osmeña had been convicted of collaboration with the Japanese during World War II. Bonner painted a strikingly different portrait of Marcos, destroying the myth of Marcos as a war hero. See Bonner, 319ff.

91. Napolitan and Squier were not the first Americans to help manipulate elections in the Philippines. Central Intelligence Agency operative Edward G. Lansdale basically ran the successful presidential campaign for Defense Minister Ramon Magsaysay in 1953. CIA chief Allen Dulles apparently offered Lansdale $5 million to direct the presidential campaign, but Lansdale cabled back to Dulles that only $1 million would be needed to win the election for Magsaysay. John M. Broder, "Political Meddling by Outsiders: Not New for U.S.," *New York Times*, March 31, 1997, 1.

92. Napolitan quoted in Robert Rizzuto, "Political Strategist and Springfield Native Joe Napolitan Remembered for His Strategic Vision and Global Impact," *The Republican* (Springfield, MA), December 3, 2013, http://www.masslive.com/politics/index.ssf/2013/12/political_strategist_and_sprin.html (accessed January 4, 2014).

93. Paul Vitello, "Joseph Napolitan, Pioneering Consultant Dies at 84," *New York Times*, December 9, 2013.

Chapter 6

Epigraph quotes from Unruh in Lou Cannon, *Ronnie and Jesse: A Political Odyssey* (New York: Doubleday, 1969), 99; Transcript of Matthew A. Reese Jr. oral history, interviewed by John Franzén, American Association of Political Consultants Interview Collection, George Washington University Libraries, December 12, 1997.

1. Transcript of Raymond Strother oral history, interviewed by John Franzén, American Association of Political Consultants Interview Collection, George Washington University Libraries, October 10, 1997, 22.

2. Howell Raines, "Age Issue Is Focus of Mississippi Race," *New York Times*, October 22, 1982, http://www.nytimes.com/1982/10/20/us/age-issue-is-focus-of-mississippi-race.html (accessed July 22, 2014).

3. Ibid.

4. Louise Overacker, *Money in Elections* (New York: Macmillan, 1932), 1, quoting *Congressional Record* 62 (67th Congress, 2d session, January 12, 1922), 1115.

5. Geoff Pender, "MS GOP Senate Race Spending at $17.4 M," *Clarion-Ledger* (Jackson, Mississippi), June 24, 2014, http://www.clarionledger.com/story/politicalledger/2014/06/24/cochran-mcdaniel-money-election-pacs/11327227/ (accessed July 22, 2014).

6. American Institute for Political Communication, *The New Methodology: A Study of Political Strategy and Tactics* (Washington, DC: American Institute for Political Communication, 1967), 63–80; Center for Responsive Politics, OpenSecrets.org, http://www.opensecrets.org/races/election.php?state=ME&cycle=2008 (accessed May 20, 2013).

7. Robert Caro, *The Years of Lyndon Johnson: Master of the Senate* (New York: Alfred A. Knopf, 2002), 403–13.

8. Dan T. Carter, *The Politics of Rage: George C. Wallace, the Origins of the New Conservatism, and the Transformation of American Politics* (New York: Simon & Schuster, 1995), 335.

9. Herbert E. Alexander, *Financing Politics: Money, Elections, and Political Reform*, 4th ed. (Washington, DC: CQ Press, 1992), 20.

10. Frank Sorauf, *Money in American Elections* (Glenview, IL: Scott, Foresman, 1998), 33.

11. *Buckley v. Valeo*, 424 U.S. 1 (1976). Online version is available at https://www.law.cornell.edu/supremecourt/text/424/1.

12. Lois Romano, "Horror Stories from the Campaign Front: When Something Can Go Wrong, It Will," *Washington Post*, February 26, 1984, C1.

13. Transcript of Peter Hannaford oral history, interviewed by Stephen F. Knott and Russell L. Riley, Ronald Reagan oral history Project, University of Virginia Presidential Oral History Program, January 10, 2003, 37.

14. Transcript of Stuart Spencer oral history, University of Virginia, 124.

15. Pollock quoted in Sandy Bergo, "A Wealth of Advice: Nearly \$2 Billion Flowed Through Consultants in 2003–2004 Federal Elections," The Center for Public Integrity (September 2006), http://www.publicintegrity.org/print/6632 (accessed September 16, 2013).

16. For an overview of the creation of soft money, see Anthony Corrado, "Giving, Spending and 'Soft Money,'" *Journal of Law and Society* 6, no. 1 (1997): 45–55.

17. See analysis and summary in Dennis W. Johnson, *No Place for Amateurs: How Political Consultants Are Reshaping American Democracy* (New York: Routledge, 2001), 177–93.

18. Ibid., 178–80. Center for Responsive Politics, "Leadership PACs, 2012," OpenSecrets.org, https://www.opensecrets.org/pacs/industry.php?txt=Q03&cycle=2012 (accessed July 18, 2014).

19. William A. Link, *Righteous Warrior: Jesse Helms and the Rise of Modern Conservatism* (New York: St. Martin's Press, 2008), 364.

20. Charles Babington, "Senator Alms," *The New Republic*, May 28, 1990, 15.

21. Ibid., 16.

22. Ibid.

23. William D. Snider, *Helms and Hunt: The North Carolina Senate Race, 1984* (Chapel Hill: University of North Carolina Press, 1985), 52.

24. Bart Barnes and Matt Schudel, "N.C. Senator's Hard-Line Conservatism Helped Craft Republican Social Agenda," *Washington Post*, July 5, 2008.

25. Snider, *Helms and Hunt*, 52. Also part of Jefferson Marketing was the Campaign Committee, with two dozen staffers to assist conservative candidates, mostly in North Carolina, and the Hardison Corporation, which handled accounting. Helms's conservative tax-exempt think tanks, located in Washington, DC, were the Institute for American Relations (IAR), the Centre for a Free Society, the Institute on Money and Inflation, and the American Family Institute. The IAR Foreign Affairs Council and the Congressional Club Foundation were tax-exempt lobbying organizations. At 53.

26. Johnson, *No Place for Amateurs*, 180.

27. Ibid., 182.

28. Center for Responsive Politics, "527s" Advocacy Group Spending, OpenSecrets.org, http://www.OpenSecrets.org/527s (accessed July 22, 2014).

29. Campaign Finance Institute, *Soft Money Political Spending by 501(c) Nonprofits Tripled in 2008 Election*, February 25, 2009.

30. Ed Rollins with Tom DeFrank, *Bare Knuckles and Back Rooms: My Life in American Politics* (New York: Broadway Books, 1996), 339.

31. Transcript of Jill Buckley oral history, interviewed by John Franzén, American Association of Political Consultants Interview Collection, the George Washington University Libraries, August 25, 1997, 1.

32. Transcript of Charles Black oral history, interviewed by Kim Alfano, American Association of Political Consultants Interview Collection, the George Washington University Libraries, October 25, 1999. Robin Toner, "The New Spokesman for the Republicans: A Tough Player in a Rough Arena," *New York Times*, July 31, 1990.

33. BKSH (Black, Kelly, Scruggs & Healy) was created out of the merger of BMSK and Gold and Liebengood.

34. Jacob Weisberg, "Meet Roger Stone, Washington's Slickest Operator: State-of-the-Art Sleazeball," *The New Republic*, December 1985, 20.

35. Stephanie Mansfield, "The Rise and Gall of Roger Stone; the Political Strategist, Playing Hardball," *Washington Post*, June 16, 1986, C1. Also, Matt Labash, "Roger

Stone, Political Animal," *The Weekly Standard*, November 5, 2007, 26–36; and Jeffrey Toobin, "The Dirty Trickster," *The New Yorker*, June 2, 2008.

36. John Brady, *Bad Boy: The Life and Politics of Lee Atwater* (Reading, MA: Addison Wesley, 1997), 38–39.

37. Ibid., 70–71.

38. Ibid., 116–17.

39. Ibid., 270–322; "Lee Atwater's Last Campaign," *Life*, February 1991.

40. Mary Matalin and James Carville, with Peter Knobler, *All's Fair: Love, War, and Running for President* (New York: Touchstone, 1994), 10.

41. *Boogie Man: The Lee Atwater Story*, directed by Stefan Forbes, 2008; Brady, *Bad Boy*.

42. Buckley oral history, 1.

43. Edmonds quoted in Adam Green, "The Pollies," *The New Yorker*, March 7, 2005.

44. Interview with Joseph Napolitan, June 19, 2003.

45. David Lee Rosenbloom, *The Election Men: Professional Campaign Managers and American Democracy* (New York: Quadrangle Books, 1973), 74–75.

46. Bill Peterson, "The Kingmaker of the 30-Second Spot: Robert Squier, Political Image-Maker on a Winning Streak," *Washington Post*, November 27, 1979, B1.

47. Bob Barnes, "Robert Squier, Leading Political Consultant, Dies at 65," *Washington Post*, January 25, 2000, B5.

48. Joe Slade White telephone interview with author, May 29, 2013.

49. Ibid.

50. James Harding, *Alpha Dogs: The Americans Who Turned Political Spin into a Global Business* (New York: Farrar, Straus and Giroux, 2008), 27–29.

51. Tom Long, "David H. Sawyer, Was a Consultant to Many Leading Politicians," *Boston Globe*, July 6, 1995, 47.

52. Biographical material, Scott Miller, at Core Strategy Group website, http://www. corestrategygroup.com/bios/miller_s.asp (accessed September 15, 2013).

53. Brett D. Fromson, "Two Major PR Firms Plan Merger," *Washington Post*, January 26, 1992, C1. The four Sawyer/Miller partners were Mark Malloch Brown, Harris Diamond, Jack Leslie, and Ed Reilly. Also working for the Sawyer/Miller group were consultants Mandy Grunwald, Mark McKinnon, and Ed Rollins.

54. William Welch, "Frank Greer: This Year's Hot Political Consultant," Associated Press, March 10, 1990.

55. J. Brian Smith, *John J. Rhodes: Man of the House* (Phoenix: Primer Publishers, 2005).

56. Lloyd Grove, "The 'Star Wars' Soft Sell: On TV, Pitching Space Defense with Doodles And a Smiling Sun," *Washington Post*, November 4, 1985.

57. Thomas N. Edmonds interview with author, March 13, 2014.

58. Castellanos website, http://www.alexcastellanos.com/about-alex/(accessed June 29, 2014).

59. Quoted in Gary W. Selnow, *High-Tech Campaigns: Computer Technology in Political Communication* (Westport, CT: Praeger, 1994), 51.

60. Terry Cooper, "Professionally OP-Researched Campaigns Are Better Campaigns," Complete Campaigns website, n.d., http://www. completecampaigns.com/article.asp?articleid=96 (accessed July 24, 2014).

61. See Greg Mitchell, *Tricky Dick and the Pink Lady: Richard Nixon versus Helen Gahagan Douglas: Sexual Politics and the Red Scare, 1950* (New York: Random House, 1998).

62. Reprinted in Karen S. Johnson-Cartree and Gary A. Copeland, *Negative Political Advertising* (Hillsdale, NJ: Lawrence Erlbaum, 1991), 87.

63. Ed Walsh, "Wes Cooley Told to Pay Investors in Fraud Case," *Oregonian*, February 4, 2005, B1; "Wes Cooley Resurfaces," *Oregonian*, February 5, 2005; AP, "Ex-Sergeant Accuses Congressman of Lying," *New Orleans Times-Picayune*,

June 16, 1996, A19; Leslie Philips, "Congressman's Past Questioned, Oregon Investigates Discrepancies," *USA Today,* May 1, 1996, 6A.

64. Brady, *Bad Boy,* 171.
65. James Carville, conversation with author, 1989.
66. Phil Noble telephone interview with author, July 26, 2014.
67. Carla Marinucci, "Clinton's Man in California a Pro at Digging Up Dirt," *San Francisco Chronicle,* May 12, 2007; Robin Abcarian, "He's the Man to Fear— Unless He's on Your Side," *Los Angeles Times,* May 3, 2008, A1; Christopher Haugh, "Ace Smith Campaigns against Teen Social Isolation," SFGate.com, April 19, 2012, http://www.sfgate.com/health/article/Ace-Smith-campaigns-against-teen-social-isolation-3492937.php (accessed July 24, 2014).
68. Cooper, "Professionally OP-Researched Campaigns Are Better Campaigns."
69. Alexander Burns, "Hey GOP, American Bridge Is Watching," *Politico,* July 28, 2013; Janie Lorber, "American Bridge 21st Century Super PAC is Hub of Left," *Roll Call,* February 13, 2012. American Bridge website, http://americanbridgepac.org (accessed December 8, 2014).

Chapter 7

Epigraph quotes: Kennedy quoted in William R. Hamilton, "Political Polling: From the Beginning to the Center," in James A. Thurber and Candice J. Nelson, eds., *Campaigns and Elections American Style* (Boulder, CO: Westview, 1995), 164, and Lois Romano, "Pollsters: The Figures Candidates Count On," *Washington Post,* January 15, 1984, C1. This might be an apocryphal quotation: Hamilton attributes the quote to Robert Kennedy, not John Kennedy. Hart quoted in Barbara Everitt Bryant, "In Memoriam: Robert M. Teeter, 1939– 2004," *Public Opinion Quarterly* 68, no. 4 (Winter 2004), 652. Caddell quoted in William J. Lanouette, "When a Presidential Candidate Moves, a Pollster May Be Pulling the Strings," *National Journal,* December 15, 1979, 2092. Harrison quote in Dennis Farney, "The Reagan-Bush Landslide: Pollsters' Predictions of Election Results Varied as Much as the Methods They Used," *Wall Street Journal,* November 8, 1948, 1.

1. Hamilton quoted in Larry R. Humes, "Polling the Pollster," University of Florida *Today,* September 1988, http://www.hamiltoncampaigns.com/articles/polling.htm (accessed May 20, 2013).
2. Douglas E. Schoen, *The Power of the Vote: Electing Presidents, Overthrowing Dictators, and Promoting Democracy Around the World* (New York: William Morrow, 2007), 24.
3. Leo Bogart, *Silent Politics: Polls and the Awareness of Public Opinion* (New York: Wiley-Interscience, 1972), 29.
4. Romano, "Pollsters."
5. Bruce E. Altschuler, *Keeping a Finger on the Public Pulse: Private Polling and Presidential Elections* (Westport, CT: Greenwood, 1982), 7–9.
6. Beth Bogart, "Pollsters Given Vote of Confidence," *Advertising Age,* November 2, 1987, S-1.
7. Transcript of Robert M. Teeter oral history, interviewed by Whit Ayres, American Association of Political Consultants Oral History Project, George Washington University Libraries, February 16, 2000.
8. Transcript of Peter D. Hart interview, conducted by Sara Fritz, "The Buying of the President 2008" Project, Center for Public Integrity, March 12, 2007.
9. Ibid.
10. Mark S. Mellman telephone interview with author, June 4, 2013.

11. Transcript of Peter D. Hart Oral History, interviewed by John Franzén, American Association of Political Consultants, George Washington University, December 22, 1997, 11.

12. Karlyn Bowman, "Knowing the Public Mind," *Wilson Quarterly* 25, no. 4 (Autumn 2001): 90–98.

13. Penn quoted in Jason Horowitz, "Rumpled Mark Penn, Clinton Pollster, Goes Back to Battle," Observer.com, August 1, 2002.

14. David Beattie, interview with author, May 14, 2012.

15. Lisa R. Carley-Baxter, "Computer Assisted Telephone Interviewing (CATI)," in Samuel J. Best and Benjamin Radcliff, *Polling in America: An Encyclopedia of Public Opinion*, vol. 1 (Westport, CT: Greenwood, 2005), 109.

16. Teeter oral history, AAPC.

17. Hart interview.

18. Humes, "Polling the Pollster."

19. David W. Stewart and Prem N. Shamdasani, *Focus Groups: Theory and Practice* (Newbury Park, CA: SAGE, 1990), 9. For a historical analysis of focus group usage, see David L. Morgan, *Focus Groups as Qualitative Research* (Beverly Hills, CA: SAGE, 1988), 11–14. See also Robert K. Merton and Patricia L. Kendall, "The Focused Interview," *American Journal of Sociology* 51 (1946): 541–57; Robert K. Merton, Marjorie Fiske, and Patricia L. Kendall, *The Focused Interview*, 2nd ed. (New York: Free Press, 1990) and Paul F. Lazarsfeld, *Qualitative Research: Historical and Critical Essays* (Boston: Allyn and Bacon, 1972); Michael X. Delli Carpini and Bruce Williams, "The Method is the Message: Focus Groups as a Method of Social, Psychological, and Political Inquiry," *Micropolitics* 4 (1994): 57–85.

20. Hamilton quoted in Romano, "Pollsters."

21. Hart oral history; David W. Moore, *The Superpollsters: How They Measure and Manipulate Public Opinion in America* (New York: Four Walls Eight Windows, 1995), 161–80.

22. Hart oral history.

23. Ibid.

24. Ibid.

25. Karen Tumulty, "Can Geoff Garin Save Clinton?" *Time*, April 7, 2008.

26. For background on Caddell, see Joe Klein, *Politics Lost: How American Democracy Was Trivialized by People Who Think You're Stupid* (New York: Doubleday, 2006), 28; and Moore, *The Superpollsters*, 129–61.

27. James Harding, *Alpha Dogs: The Americans Who Turned Political Spin into a Global Business* (New York: Farrar, Straus and Giroux, 2008), 64–65.

28. Klein, *Politics Lost*, 29–30.

29. Moore, *The Superpollsters*, 182.

30. Ibid., 183.

31. J. M. Lawrence, "Irwin "Tubby" Harrison, 81, Pollster, Oracle for Democrats," *Boston Globe*, January 3, 2012.

32. David M. Halbfinger, "As Campaign Picks Up, Kerry Turns to Old Circle," *New York Times*, June 5, 2004; and Marttila Strategies website, http:marttilastrategies.com (accessed October 1, 2013).

33. Tarrance profile and background from interview with author, March 13, 2013. One-man, one-vote decision, *Reynolds v. Sims*, 377 U.S. 533 (1964). Online version available at https://www.oyez.org/cases/1963/23.

34. Craig Shirley, *Reagan's Revolution: The Untold Story of the Campaign That Started It All* (Nashville: Nelson Current, 2005), 164.

35. Alicia Mundy, "King Arthur Tests Legend," *Mediaweek*, July 22, 1996, 21.

36. Quoted in Jonathan Karl, "Arthur Finkelstein: Out of Sight but in Control," CNN, October 14, 1996, http://www.cnn.com/ALLPOLITICS/1996/news/9610/10/karl.finkelstein/index.shtml (accessed October 1).

37. William M. Honan, "Johnson May Not Have Poll Fever, But He Has a Good Case of the Poll Sniffles," *New York Times*, August 21, 1966, 228.
38. Nixon quoted in Bogart, *Silent Politics*, 31.
39. Kathryn Dunn Tenpas, "Words vs. Deeds: President George W. Bush and Polling," *Brookings Review* (Summer 2003): 33–35.
40. Lawrence R. Jacobs and Robert Y. Shapiro, "The Rise of Presidential Polling: The Nixon White House in Historical Perspective," *Public Opinion Quarterly* 59, no. 2 (Summer 1995): 163–95, at 164.
41. Ibid., 167.
42. Honan, "Johnson May Not Have Poll Fever."
43. Joshua Green, "The Other War Room," *Washington Monthly*, April 2002.
44. Honan, "Johnson May Not Have Poll Fever."
45. Ibid.
46. Eric F. Goldman, *The Tragedy of Lyndon Johnson* (New York: Knopf, 1969), 196.
47. Jacobs and Shapiro, "The Rise of Presidential Polling," 167.
48. Ibid., 168, n. 12.
49. Ibid., 177.
50. Goldman, *The Tragedy of Lyndon Johnson*, 196–99.
51. Robert M. Eisinger, *The Evolution of Presidential Polling* (New York: Cambridge University Press, 2003), 58–60.
52. Lawrence R. Jacobs and Robert Y. Shapiro, "The Public Presidency, Private Polls, and Policy Making: Lyndon Johnson." Prepared for delivery at the annual meeting of the American Political Science Association, Washington, DC, September 2–5, 1993, 17.
53. Ibid., 94–95.
54. Ibid. Honan, "Johnson May Not Have Poll Fever."
55. Louis Harris, *The Anguish of Change* (New York: W. W. Norton, 1973), 23.
56. Bruce E. Altschuler, "Lyndon Johnson and the Public Polls," *Public Opinion Quarterly* 50 (Autumn 1986): 285–99.
57. Diane J. Heith, *Polling to Govern: Public Opinion and Presidential Leadership.* (Stanford, CA: Stanford University Press, 2004), 25.
58. Tenpas, "Words vs. Deeds," 33.
59. Jacobs and Shapiro, "The Rise of Presidential Polling," 178.
60. Eisinger, *The Evolution of Presidential Polling*, 100.
61. Ibid., 103.
62. Wynne Pomeroy Waller, "Presidential Leadership and Public Opinion: Polling in the Ford and Carter Administrations," Unpublished PhD dissertation, Columbia University, 2000, 49; Lawrence R. Jacobs and Robert Y. Shapiro, "Disorganized Democracy: The Institutionalization of Polling and Public Opinion Analysis during the Kennedy, Johnson, and Nixon Presidencies." Prepared for presentation at the annual meeting of the American Political Science Association, New York, September 1–4, 1994, 6.
63. Waller, "Presidential Leadership and Public Opinion," 67.
64. Ibid., 70–71.
65. Gerald R. Ford, *A Time to Heal* (New York: Harper & Row, 1979), 161–62; Waller, "Presidential Leadership and Public Opinion," 63.
66. Moore, *The Superpollsters*, 226.
67. Eisinger, *The Evolution of Presidential Polling*, 155.
68. Ibid., 156.
69. Klein, *Politics Lost*, 38–39.
70. Heith, *Polling to Govern*, 35.
71. Ibid.
72. Sidney Blumenthal, "Marketing the President," *New York Times*, September 13, 1981, 43, cited in Shoon Kathleen Murray and Peter Howard, "Variations in White House Polling Operations: Carter to Clinton," *Public Opinion Quarterly* 66 (2002), 532.

73. Edwin Meese III, *With Reagan: The Inside Story* (Washington, DC: Regnery Gateway, 1992), 74.

74. Murray and Howard, "Variations in White House Polling Operations," 538.

75. Richard S. Beal and Ronald H. Hinckley, "Presidential Decision Making and Opinion Polls," *Annals of the American Academy of Political and Social Science* 472, *Polling and the Democratic Consensus* (March 1984), 72.

76. Murray and Howard, "Variations in White House Polling Operations," 541.

77. Ibid., 538–39.

78. Ibid., 541.

79. Beal and Hinckley, "Presidential Decision Making and Opinion Polls," passim.

80. Murray and Howard, "Variations in White House Polling Operations," 543.

81. Wynton C. Hall, "'Reflections of Yesterday': George H. W. Bush's Instrumental Use of Public Opinion Research in Presidential Discourse," *Presidential Studies Quarterly* 32, no. 3 (September 2002), 542. Hall, who became, in his own words, a "celebrity ghostwriter," also assisted Richard Wirthlin in writing his book about Reagan, *The Greatest Communicator.*

82. Hall, "'Reflections of Yesterday.'"

83. Green, "The Other War Room."

84. Murray and Howard, "Variations in White House Polling Operations," 544–45.

85. The Tarrance Group website, http://www.tarrance.com/history/ (accessed July 30, 2014).

86. Moore Information website, http://www.moore-info.com/ (accessed July 31, 2014).

87. Democracy Corps website, http://www.democracycorps.com/about-us/ (accessed October 30, 2013).

88. GQR partners are Al Quinlan, Jeremy Rosner, and Anna Greenberg. From GQR website, http://gqrr.com/GQR/who-we-are/ (accessed May 7, 2014).

89. Douglas E. Schoen, *The Power of the Vote: Electing Presidents, Overthrowing Dictators, and Promoting Democracy around the World* (New York: William Morrow, 2007), 5.

90. John F. Harris and Jim VandeHei, "Penn, Like Rove, Wants Intellectual Cred," *Politico*, September 6, 2007, http://www.politico.com/story/2007/09/penn-like-rove-wants-intellectual-cred-005671.

91. Burson-Marsteller website, http://www.burson-marsteller.com/leaderships/donald-a-baer-worldwide-chair-and-ceo-chairman-penn-schoen-berland (accessed November 6, 2013).

92. Chris Cillizza, "Merger Mania: Democratic Polling Firms May Join Forces," *Roll Call,* September 4, 2003.

93. Hickman Analytics website, www.hickmananalytics.com (accessed September 18, 2013).

94. Mark S. Mellman, interview with author, June 4, 2013.

95. Lake biographical sketch, Lake Research Partners website, http://www.lakeresearch.com/index.php/the-lrp-team/celinda-lake, accessed November 6, 2013.

96. Celinda Lake and Kellyanne Conway, with Catherine Whitney, *What Women Really Want: How American Women Are Quietly Erasing Political, Racial, Class, and Religious Lines to Change the Way We Live* (New York: Free Press, 2005).

97. Fairbank, Maslin, Maullin, Metz & Associates (FM3) website, http://www.fm3research.com/about (accessed July 31, 2014).

Chapter 8

Epigraph quotes from Ailes in Joe McGinnis, *The Selling of the President 1968* (New York: Pocket Books, 1968), Thomas E. Patterson and Robert D. McClure, *The Unseeing Eye: The Myth of Television Power in National Politics* (New York: G. P. Putnam's Sons, 1976), 94–95.

1. L. Patrick Devlin, "An Analysis of Presidential Television Commercials, 1952–1984," in Lynda Lee Kaid, Dan Nimmo, and Keith R. Sanders, eds., *New Perspectives on Political Advertising* (Carbondale: Southern Illinois University, 1986), 25–33; see also L. Patrick Devlin, "Campaign Commercials," *Society* 22, no. 4 (May 1, 1985): 45–50.
2. Victor S. Navasky, "The Making of the Candidate," *New York Times Magazine*, May 7, 1972, 27.
3. Ibid.
4. Transcript of Stuart K. Spencer Oral History, interviewed by Whit Ayres, American Association of Political Consultants Oral History Project, George Washington University, February 2, 1999, 13.
5. Christopher Lydon, "Media Experts Doubt Value of TV Ads," *New York Times*, November 5, 1970, 28.
6. Ibid.
7. Gary R. Edgerton, *The Columbia History of American Television* (New York: Columbia University Press, 2007), 286.
8. Robert MacNeil, *The People Machine: The Influence of Television on American Politics* (New York: Harpers & Row, 1968), xiii.
9. Peter Fenn, "The New Media in Political Campaigns: What the Future Holds," in Dennis W. Johnson, ed., *Routledge Handbook of Political Management* (New York: Routledge, 2009), 127.
10. Lewis Chester, Godfrey Hodgson, and Bruce Page, *An American Melodrama: The Presidential Campaign of 1968* (New York: Viking, 1969), 640.
11. Shapp later became governor of Pennsylvania (1971–1979) and was an unsuccessful candidate for the Democratic nomination for president in 1976. See Garry Pierre-Pierre "Milton J. Shapp Is Dead at 82," *New York Times*, November 26, 1994.
12. Joseph Napolitan, *The Election Game and How to Win It* (New York: Doubleday, 1972), 66–67.
13. Jonathan Rowe, "Media Mogul Bows Out of the Political Ad Game," *Christian Science Monitor*, November 29, 1988.
14. For a sketch of the early history of cable television, see Thomas R. Eisenmann, "Cable TV: From Community Antennas to Wired Cities," *Business History Review*, July 10, 2000, http://hbswk.hbs.edu/item/1591.html (accessed August 1, 2014).
15. Ken Auletta, *Three Blind Mice: How the TV Networks Lost Their Way* (New York: Random House, 1991).
16. Fenn, "The New Media in Political Campaigns," 127.
17. "Americans Using TV and Internet Together 35% More Than a Year Ago," Nielsen Newswire, March 22, 2010, www.nielsen.com/us/en/insights/news/2010/three-screen-report-q409.html (accessed May 5, 2016).
18. Michael M. Franz, Paul B. Freeman, Kenneth M. Goldstein, and Travis N. Ridout, *Campaign Advertising and American Democracy* (Philadelphia: Temple University Press, 2008), 1, citing data from Nielsen Monitor-Plus.
19. Kantar Media, "Ten Years of Campaign Ads," http://mycmag.kantarmediana.com/misc/10YearsOfCampaignAds.html (accessed July 2, 2014); Elizabeth Wilner, "On Points: We've Classified 50,000 + Campaign Ads since 2004. Here They Are," *Cook Report*, April 8, 2014, http://cookpolitical.com/story/7061 (accessed July 2, 2014); "Unravel," YouTube, http://www.youtube.com/watch?v=9gZAMrWG_xo (accessed July 2, 2014).
20. "Over Half of Americans Say They Tend Not to Trust the Press," *Business Wire*, March 6, 2008.
21. Jennifer Waits, "FCC Reports That the Number of Radio Stations Increased in the U.S. Last Quarter," *Radio Survivor*, July 11, 2014, http://www.radiosurvivor.com/2014/07/11/fcc-reports-non-commercial-fm-stations-lpfm-stations-fm-translators-u-s-rise-last-quarter/(accessed August 1, 2014).

22. Sirius XM Holdings Inc. and Subsidiaries, 2014 Form 10-K, Annual Report, February 5, 2015, filed with the US Securities and Exchange Commission, www.annualreports.com/click/11128 (accessed May 5, 2016).

23. Fenn, "The New Media in Political Campaigns," 127–28.

24. Garry South, "The Mind's Eye: It Doesn't Matter What You Look Like on the Radio," *Campaigns & Elections*, June 1992.

25. John Franzén, "Consultants and Client," in David D. Perlmutter, ed., *The Manship School Guide to Political Communication* (Baton Rouge: Louisiana State University Press, 1999), 296.

26. Jim Innocenzi telephone interview with author, August 15, 2014; and Sandler Innocenzi website, http://www.sandler-innocenzi.com/(accessed June 13, 2014).

27. Adam Nagourney, "Onetime McCain Insider is Offering Advice (Unwanted) from the Outside," *New York Times*, October 2, 2008; Twitter @MikeMurphy.

28. Revolution Agency website, http://www.revolution-agency.com/people/mike-murphy/ (accessed August 5, 2014).

29. Dave Lesher, "Meet a Very Laid-Back Political Maniac," *Los Angeles Times*, August 11, 1996.

30. Pete Wilson ad on illegal immigration, YouTube.com, https://www.youtube.com/watch?v=lLIzzs2HHgY (accessed August 5, 2014).

31. Sipple promotional materials, https://www.visualcv.com/donaldsipple (accessed August 5, 2014).

32. Richard Blow, "The True Character of a Spin Doctor?," *Mother Jones*, September/October 1997, http://www.motherjones.com/politics/1997/09/true-character-spin-doctor (accessed August 5, 2014); "GOP Strategist Quits Over Beating Reports," *Los Angeles Times*, August 9, 1997, http://articles.latimes.com/1997/aug/09/news/mn-20767 (accessed August 5, 2014).

33. Brabender Cox Mihalke promotional material, http://www.cyclopaedia.info/wiki/Brabender-Cox-Mihalke (accessed August 5, 2014).

34. On Shrum's career, see Ken Auletta, "Kerry's Brain," *The New Yorker*, September 20, 2004.

35. In 2013, Tad Devine was a partner in the Washington-based media firm of Devine-Mulvey-Longabaugh, with Julian Mulvey and Mark P. Longabaugh; in 2013, Mike Donilon was partner in the Chicago-based media firm AKPD.

36. Robert Shrum, *No Excuses: Concessions of a Serial Campaigner* (New York: Simon & Schuster, 2007).

37. For background, see David Axelrod, *Believer: My Forty Years in Politics* (New York: Penguin, 2015), 25–85. For a biographical sketch of Axelrod, see Robert G. Kaiser, "The Player at Bat," *Washington Post*, May 2, 2008, C1.

38. "The Ax-Man Cometh," *The Economist*, August 21, 2008, http://www.economist.com/node/11965249/print; and Daniel Libit, "David Axelrod's Last Campaign," *Chicago Magazine*, September 2011, http://www.chicagomag.com/Chicago-Magazine/September-2011/David-Axelrods-Last-Campaign/ (accessed June 14, 2014).

39. Grant Pick, "Hatchet Man: The Rise of David Axelrod," *Chicago Magazine*, December 1987, http://www.chicagomag.com/Chicago-Magazine/December-1987/Hatchet-Man-The-Rise-of-David-Axelrod/ (accessed June 14, 2014).

40. Axelrod, *Believer*, 99.

41. Ben Wallace-Wells, "A Star Strategist Offers Democrats a New Vision," *New York Times*, March 30, 2007.

42. Quoted in Kaiser, "The Player at Bat"; David Mendell, *Obama: From Promise to Power* (New York: HarperCollins, 2007).

43. Axelrod, *Believer*, 182.

44. AKP&D Message and Media website, http://akpdmedia.com/newsroom/axelrods-firm/ (accessed June 18, 2014).

45. Struble Eichenbaum Communications website and promotional materials, http://www.strublemedia.com/ (accessed September 5, 2014).

46. Fenn Communications Group website and promotional materials, http://www. fenn-group.com/ (accessed August 15, 2014).

47. Gary Nordlinger interview with author, May 28, 2013. Biographical material on Nordlinger Consulting Group website, http://www.nordlinger.com/downloads/ gary_nordlinger.pdf (accessed July 1, 2014).

48. John Franzén promotional materials, http://www.franzenco.com/about.html (accessed August 4, 2014).

49. Jesse McKinley, "Parole Granted to Political Consultant in a Corruption Case," *New York Times,* April 23, 2013.

50. Biographical information, Fordham University, http://www.fordham.edu/ academics/programs_at_fordham_/elections__campaign_/faculty/henry_ sheinkopf_30988.asp (accessed August 5, 2014).

51. Fouhy quoted in Carmen Sirianna and Lewis Friedland, *Civic Innovation in America: Community Empowerment, Public Policy, and the Movement for Civic Renewal* (Berkeley: University of California Press, 2001), 225.

52. Brabender quoted in Todd Shields, "Politics as Usual: Spend, Spend, Spend," *Adweek,* December 15, 2003.

53. Susan B. Glasser, "Winning a Stake in a Losing Race: Ad Commissions Enriched Strategists," *Washington Post,* May 1, 2000, A1.

54. Cathleen Decker. "Checchi Says Voter Optimism Doomed His Bid for Governor," *Los Angeles Times,* June 11, 1998.

55. Fenn, "The New Media in Political Campaigns," 128.

56. Jim Margolis interviewed by Jules Witcover, Center for Public Integrity, "The Buying of the President 2008" Series, March 5, 2007. See also, Robin Kolodny and Michael G. Hagen, "What Drives the Cost of Political Advertising?" in Johnson, ed., *Routledge Handbook on Political Management,* 194–207.

57. Margolis interview.

58. Conversation with the author in 1988.

59. Wirthlin quoted in Leo Bogart, *Silent Politics: Polls and the Awareness of Public Opinion* (New York: John Wiley, 1972), 30.

60. Mark Penn and Doug Schoen, "Neuro-Personality Poll," October 1995, memo to the president, in Evan Thomas et al., *Back from the Dead: How Clinton Survived the Republican Revolution* (New York: Atlantic Monthly Press, 1997), 237.

61. DIRECTV Press Release, "DIRECTV and DISH Revolutionize Political TV Advertising Landscape with Combined Addressable Advertising Platform Reaching 20 + Million Households," January 27, 2014, http://investor.directv.com/ press-releases/press-release-details/2014/DIRECTV-and-DISH-Revolutionize- Political-TV-Advertising-Landscape-with-Combined-Addressable-Advertising- Platform-Reaching-20-Million-Households/default.aspx?print=1 (accessed June 9, 2014).

62. Quoted in Emily Schultheis and Alex Byers, "Political TV Ads' Latest Target: Individuals," *Politico,* February 12, 2014, http://www.politico.com/story/ 2014/02/political-ads-latest-target-individuals-103443.html (accessed June 10, 2014).

63. E. B. Boyd, "How Rep. Michele Bachmann Used Mobile Ads to Turn Beer and Corn Dogs into Votes from Fair Folk," *Fast Company,* October 27, 2010, http:// www.fastcompany.com/1698173/how-rep-michele-bachmann-used-mobile-ads- turn-beer-and-corn-dogs-votes-fair-folk (accessed June 8, 2014).

64. Transcript of Stuart Spencer Oral History, interviewed by Paul B. Freedman et al, Ronald Reagan Oral History Project, Miller Center of Public Affairs, University of Virginia, November 15–16, 2001, 24.

65. Lynda Lee Kaid, Mitchell S. McKinney, and John C. Tedesco, "Applied Political Communication Research," in Lawrence R. Frey and Kenneth N. Cissna, eds., *Routledge Handbook of Applied Communication Research* (New York: Routledge, 2009), 453–80. See the individual authors and papers in this bibliographic essay.

66. See, for example, John G. Geer, *In Defense of Negativity: Attack Ads in Presidential Campaigns* (Chicago: University of Chicago Press, 2006); Stephen Ansolabehere and Shanto Iyengar, *Going Negative: How Attack Ads Shrink and Polarize the Electorate* (New York: Free Press, 1995); Richard R. Lau, Lee Sigelman, Caroline Heldman, and Paul Babbitt, "The Effects of Negative Political Advertisements: A Meta-Analytic Assessment," *American Political Science Review* 93, no. 4 (December 1999): 851–75; Richard R. Lau and Gerald M. Pomper, "Effectiveness of Negative Campaigning in U.S. Senate Elections," *American Journal of Political Science* 46, no. 1 (January 2002): 47–66. Also, David Mark, *Going Dirty: The Art of Negative Campaigning* (Lanham, MD: Rowman and Littlefield, 2006); and Kerwin C. Swint, *Mudslinging: The Top 25 Negative Political Campaigns of All Time* (Westport, CT: Praeger, 2005).

67. Jack Germond and Jules Witcover, *Mad as Hell: Revolt at the Ballot Box, 1992* (New York: Warner Books, 1993), 73.

68. Strother quoted in Paul Taylor, "In Politics of Attack, First Shots Often Backfire," *Washington Post*, July 10, 1990, A10.

69. Rowe, "Media Mogul Bows Out of the Political Ad Game," 3.

70. "Bloodhounds," https://www.youtube.com/watch?v=bcpuhiIDx3Q (accessed May 10, 2014).

71. Jane Mayer, "Who Let the Attack-Ad Dogs Out?" *The New Yorker*, February 15, 2012; and Jane Mayer, "Attack Dog: The Creator of the Willie Horton Ad Is Going All Out for Mitt Romney," *The New Yorker*, February 13, 2012.

72. Helms quoted in Mary C. Curtis, "Jesse Helms is Still Stirring Up Controversy," *Washington Post*, December 6, 2012.

73. Mayer, "Attack Dog."

74. Kathleen Hall Jamieson, *Dirty Politics: Deception, Distraction, and Democracy* (New York: Oxford University Press, 1992), 93.

75. "White Hands," on YouTube, http://www.youtube.com/watch?v=3Lw8_f6_2XQ (accessed June 30, 2014).

76. Interview with Alex Castellanos, Wisconsin Public Television (1998).

77. David Mark, *Going Dirty*, 103.

78. "Laughter," https://www.youtube.com/watch?v=Qwk_epMblW4 (accessed May 10, 2014).

79. "Jesse—The Mind," https://www.youtube.com/watch?v=zSACk65D3pk (accessed May 10, 2014).

80. Appeared on North Woods website, http://www.northwoodsadv.com, but no longer posted. Hillsman is the author of *Run the Other Way: Fixing the Two-Party System, One Campaign at a Time* (New York: Free Press, 2004).

81. "Fast Paul," https://www.youtube.com/watch?v=NbmMlTsKo3o; "Looking for Rudy," https://www.youtube.com/watch?v=nfZuplTlu4M (accessed May 10, 2014).

82. "Meatballs," https://www.youtube.com/watch?v=pUgTDmD4vW4 (accessed May 10, 2014).

83. "Squeal," https://www.youtube.com/watch?v=pUgTDmD4vW4 (accessed May 12, 2014); Philip Rucker and Dan Balz, "Sharp Talk about Hogs Shakes Up a Senate Race," *Washington Post*, May 12, 2014, A1.

84. "Shot," from Something Else Strategies website, http://somethingelseworks.com/video/92769803 (accessed May 12, 2014).

85. Something Else Strategies website, http://www.somethingelsestrategies.com/ (accessed May 12, 2014).

86. "Roger Ailes on Political Media," *Campaign & Elections*, May/June 1988.

87. Steve Lilienthal, "Targeting the Individual Voter," *Campaigns & Elections*, April 2005, 39.

88. Justin Germany interview with author, June 18, 2010, in Dennis W. Johnson, *Campaigning in the Twenty-First Century: A Whole New Ballgame?* (New York: Routledge, 2011), 40.

89. Chris Good, "Video of the Day: Best Campaign Video This Year, Featuring MC Hammer," *The Atlantic*, October 25, 2011, http://www.theatlantic.com/politics/archive/2011/10/video-of-the-day-the-best-campaign-video-this-year-featuring-mc-ha (accessed June 15, 2014). "Ed Lee is 2 Legit 2 Quit," https://www.youtube.com/watch?v=fbdd_Faszok (accessed March 3, 2015).

Chapter 9

Epigraph quotes from Dees in David Chagall, *The New Kingmakers* (New York: Harcourt, Brace Jovanovich, 1981), 388; Walter D. Clinton and Anne E. Clinton, "Telephone and Direct Mail," in David D. Perlmutter, *The Manship School Guide to Political Communication* (Baton Rouge: Louisiana State University Press, 1999), 137.

1. Viguerie quoted in Todd Meredith, "Direct Mail: The Tactical Edge" in Ronald A. Faucheux, ed., *Winning Elections: Political Campaign Management, Strategy and Tactics* (New York: M. Evans, 2003), 340.
2. Craver quoted in Frank I. Luntz, *Candidates, Consultants, and Campaigns: The Style and Substance of American Electioneering* (New York: Basil Blackwell, 1988), 150.
3. Mark R. Wilson, "Mail Order," in *Encyclopedia of Chicago*, www.encyclopedia.chicagohistory.org/pages/779.html (accessed February 2, 2014).
4. Herbert Alexander, *Money in Politics* (Washington, DC: Public Affairs, 1972), 32–33.
5. See Walter H. Weintz, *The Solid Gold Mailbox: How to Create Winning Mail Order Campaigns by the Man Who's Done It All* (Hoboken, NJ: Wiley, 1987).
6. Richard A. Viguerie and David Franke, *America's Right Turn: How Conservatives Used New and Alternative Media to Take Power* (Chicago: Bonus Books, 2004), 91–92.
7. Richard A. Viguerie, *The New Right: We're Ready to Lead* (Falls Church, VA: The Viguerie Company, 1981), 45.
8. Richard Schlackman and Jamie Douglas, "Attack Mail: The Silent Killer," *Campaigns & Elections*, July 1995, 25; Karl A. Lamb and Paul A. Smith, *Campaign Decision-Making: The Presidential Election of 1964* (Belmont, CA: Wadsworth, 1968), 124.
9. Viguerie and Franke, *America's Right Turn*, 83–84.
10. Morris Dees with Steve Fiffer, *A Season for Justice: The Life and Times of Civil Rights Lawyer Morris Dees* (New York: Charles Scribner's Sons, 1991), 134.
11. Ibid.
12. Ibid., 138.
13. Richard Viguerie in "McGovern Campaign Marked the Beginning of Direct Mail," *All Things Considered*, National Public Radio, August 1, 2012, transcript.
14. Stephen Isaacs, "'76 Hopefuls Make Direct-Mail Appeal," *Washington Post*, July 27, 1975, A1.
15. Ibid.
16. David Mark, *Going Dirty: The Art of Negative Campaigning* (Lanham, MD: Rowman & Littlefield, 2006), 214.
17. "Direct Mail," *Campaigns & Elections*, May 1997, 22.
18. Schlackman and Douglas, "Attack Mail," 25.
19. Douglas E. Schoen, *The Power of the Vote: Electing Presidents, Overthrowing Dictators, and Promoting Democracy around the World* (New York: William Morrow, 2007), 39. On the latter, more muddied years, of Father G. and his family, see Jennifer Redfearn, "Sins of the Father," *Village Voice*, January 16, 2007, http://www.villagevoice.com/2007-01-16/news/sins-of-the-father/; accessed April 1, 2014.
20. Liebman was a cofounder of Young Americans for Freedom and the American Conservative Union, and supported a variety of conservative and anticommunist causes. Anguished over what he considered the increased homophobia of the conservative movement and the Republican Party, Liebman eventually wrote to

his friend and mentor, William F. Buckley Jr., announcing that he was gay. In 1992 Liebman wrote his memoir, *Coming Out Conservative: An Autobiography* (San Francisco: Chronicle Books, 1992).

21. Viguerie and Franke, *America's Right Turn*, 99.

22. Ibid., 102–3.

23. Rick Perlstein, *Nixonland: The Rise of a President and the Fracturing of America* (New York: Scribner, 2008), 639.

24. Luntz, *Candidates, Consultants, and Campaigns*, 51.

25. From ConservativeHQ.com website, http://www.conservativehq.com/about (accessed September 12, 2013).

26. Craver quoted in Denison Hatch, "Fighting Prejudice . . . and Winning," *Target Marketing* 16, no. 11 (November 1993), 21.

27. Denison Hatch, "Fundraiser Extraordinaire," *Target Marketing* 16, no. 11 (November 1993), 26.

28. Craver on his blogsite, "The Agitator," http://www.theagitator.net (accessed April 1, 2014).

29. Hatch, "Fundraiser Extraordinaire."

30. "Roger Craver on the Roots of CMS," Craver, Mathews, Smith & Company website, http://cravermathewssmith.com/about-cms/ (accessed January 1, 2003).

31. Ibid.

32. Profile of Craver in Sherri Kimmel, "Finding Common Cause," *Dickinson Magazine*, Fall 2008.

33. "Our Clients: Case Studies," Eberle Associates website, http://www.eberleassociates.com/case-studies.asp#JW (accessed April 1, 2014)

34. Ibid.

35. The Richard Norman Company website, http://www.richardnorman.com (accessed April 1, 2014).

36. Ralph Z. Hallow, "Big Player Profile: Brad O'Leary," *Campaigns & Elections*, September 1997, 18–26.

37. Ibid.

38. Bradley O'Leary, *The Audacity of Deceit* (Los Angeles: WND Books, 2008). On a point-by-point criticism of O'Leary's claims, see Terry Krepel, "Brad O'Leary and His Misleading Zogby Polls," *Huffington Post*, May 12, 2009, http://www.huffingtonpost.com/terry-krepel/brad-oleary-and-his-misle_b_201911.html (accessed April 16, 2014).

39. From the AAPC website, profile of board members, 2010, cited in Anthony Pignataro, "Watching the Schlackman," CalWatchdog.com, http://calwatchdog.com/2010/11/21/watching-the-schlackman (accessed April 25, 2014).

40. Winning Directions website, http://www.winningdirections.com/bios/fazio.htm (accessed April 13, 2014).

41. A.B. Data website, http://www.abddirect.com/profile/chuck-pruitt/(accessed April 24, 2014).

42. The Robot Report website, http://www.therobotreport.com/about (accessed October 1, 2013).

43. Rove quoted in Lou Dubose, Jan Reed, and Carl Cannon, *Boy Genius: Karl Rove, the Architect of George W. Bush's Remarkable Political Triumph* (New York: Public Affairs, 2005), 86.

44. Liz Chadderdon, president, The Chadderdon Group, Alexandria, Virginia, telephone interview with the author, June 18, 2010; see also Johnson, *Campaigning in the Twenty-First Century*, 41.

45. Daly quoted in David Beiler, "Precision Politics," *Campaigns & Elections*, February/March 1990.

46. Phillips quoted in PBS *Frontline*, "The Digital Campaign," WGBH/Boston, October 2012, http://www.pbs.org/wgbh/pages/frontline/digital-campaign/.

47. "Switch split": "Does this precinct tend to vote for one candidate of a certain type from election to election, or does this precinct tend to have a tendency to split the ballot in the same election?" Transcript of Walter D. Clinton oral history, interviewed by John Franzén. American Association of Political

Consultants Oral History Project, George Washington University Libraries, December 22, 1997, 5.

48. Ibid.

49. Transcript of Walter D. Clinton interview with author, Washington, DC, May 19, 2003.

50. Ibid.

51. Sasha Issenberg, *The Victory Lab: The Secret Science of Winning Campaigns* (New York: Crown Books, 2012), 124.

52. Beiler, "Precision Politics."

53. Communication from Bob Blaemire, October 2, 2014; from Jonathan Robbin biographical information, Ricercar website, http://ricercar.com/JRCV-D#1960s (accessed April 25, 2014); see also Michael Weiss, *The Clustering of America* (New York: Harper & Row, 1988). Claritas was later sold to The Nielsen Company; the original forty clusters became sixty-six behavioral and lifestyle segments.

54. Glenda A. Hughes, "Remembering Bill Daly, Voter Contact Pioneer," *Campaigns & Elections*, February 2011, 11. Hughes was president of Voter Contact Services.

55. Phillips tells the story in John Aristotle Phillips and David Michaelis, *Mushroom: The True Story of the A-Bomb Kid* (New York: Pocket Books, 1979); see also David Michaelis, "What's a Nice Kid Like John Phillips Doing with an A-Bomb? *New York*, July 18, 1977.

56. Eric Roston, "Elect Tech," *Time*, June 2004.

57. James Verini, "Big Brother, Inc.," *Vanity Fair*, December 13, 2007.

58. Wally Clinton, "Consumer-Driven Politics: Using Telephones and Direct Mail to Build New Relationships with Voters," *Campaigns & Elections*, April 2002, 44.

59. Clinton oral history, 5.

60. Ibid. Transcript of interview with Walter Clinton, National Public Radio, "Phone Banks: A Staple of Campaigning Since 1968" (July 31, 2012), http://www.npr.org/2012/07/31/157678602/phone-banks-a-staple-of-campaigning-since-1968.

61. Clinton interview, National Public Radio.

62. Ibid.

63. Alan S. Gerber and Donald P. Green, "Do Phone Calls Increase Voter Turnout? An Update," *Annals of the American Academy of Political and Social Science* 601 (September 2005), 152.

64. Alan S. Gerber and Donald P. Green, "Do Phone Calls Increase Voter Turnout? A Field Experiment," *Public Opinion Quarterly* 65, no. 1 (Spring 2001): 75–85, at 77.

65. American Association of Political Consultants, July 7, 2014, enews@theaapc.org (accessed July 7, 2014).

66. R. Sam Garrett, *Automated Political Telephone Calls ("Robo Calls") in Federal Campaigns: Overview and Policy Options*, Congressional Research Service, RL34361, February 7, 2008; updated by Garrett and Kathleen Ann Ruane, authors, March 22, 2010.

67. Voice Broadcasting Corporation website, www.voicebroadcasting.com (accessed November 27, 2013).

68. Dennis W. Johnson, "An Election Like No Other?," in Dennis W. Johnson, ed., *Campaigning for President 2008: Strategy and Tactics, New Voices and New Techniques* (New York: Routledge, 2009), 14–15.

69. Garrett, *Automated Political Telephone Calls ("Robo Calls") in Federal Campaigns*, 6.

70. Gerber and Green, "Do Phone Calls Increase Voter Turnout?," at 82. See also, Gerber and Green update, "Do Phone Calls Increase Voter Turnout? An Update," 192.

71. Donald P. Green and Alan S. Gerber, *Get Out the Vote! How to Increase Voter Turnout*, 2nd ed. (Washington, DC: Brookings Institution Press, 2006)/, 70–71.

72. Ibid., 94.

73. Quoted in Shane D'Aprile, "New GOTV Research Irks Some Consultants," *Politics*, April 28, 2008.

74. Clinton oral history, 1.
75. American Directions Group website, http://americandirections.com/site/index. php/about-us (accessed April 24, 2014).

Chapter 10

Epigraph quote from Spencer in Mark Z. Barabak, "Stuart Spencer has a Few Zingers Left," *Los Angeles Times,* October 20, 2002. A variation of Spencer's assessment of Ford is given in Moore, *The Superpollsters,* 225: "Mr. President, as a campaigner, you're no fucking good." Victor Gold, "Who's In Charge?" *Washingtonian,* October 1996, 49; F. Clifton White with Jerome Tuccille, *Politics as a Noble Calling: The Memoirs of F. Clifton White* (Ottawa, IL: Jameson Books, 1994), 11.

1. Hart quoted in Ernest R. May and Janet Fraser, *Campaign '72: The Managers Speak* (Cambridge, MA: Harvard University Press, 1973), 189. Hart later wrote about election night: "Then in mid-evening the first figures from Ohio were very troublesome. Within a few minutes, Connecticut, and then Ohio, were projected for Nixon. I knew it was all over." Gary Warren Hart, *Right from the Start: A Chronicle of the McGovern Campaign* (New York: Quadrangle/New York Times, 1973), 319.
2. Kevin B. Phillips, *The Emerging Republican Majority* (Garden City, NY: Anchor Books, 1970).
3. Ben J. Wattenberg and Richard M. Scammon, *The Real Majority* (New York: Coward McCann, 1970).
4. May and Fraser, *Campaign '72,* 32.
5. On the 1972 presidential election, see Theodore H. White, *The Making of the President, 1972* (New York: Atheneum, 1973); Bruce Miroff, *The Liberals Moment: The McGovern Insurgency and the Identity Crisis of the Democratic Party* (Lawrence: University Press of Kansas, 2007); Richard Dougherty, *Good-Bye, Mr. Christian: A Personal Account of McGovern's Rise and Fall* (New York: Doubleday, 1973); May and Fraser, *Campaign '72;* and Gordon L. Weil, *The Long Shot: George McGovern Runs for President* (New York: W. W. Norton, 1973).
6. Odle oral history in Gerald S. and Deborah H. Strober, *Nixon: An Oral History of His Presidency* (New York: Harper Perennial, 1994), 249.
7. Magruder oral history in Strober, *Nixon,* 249.
8. Transcript of Teeter oral history, AAPC, 13. Biographical Sketch, Robert M. Teeter, Gerald R. Ford Library, http://www.fordlibrarymuseum.gov/library/ guides/findingaid/Teeter,_Robert_-_Papers.htm (accessed November 8, 2013).
9. Rick Perlstein, *Nixonland: The Rise of a President and the Fracturing of America* (New York: Scribner, 2008), 648.
10. Jeb Stuart Magruder, *An American Life: One Man's Road to Watergate* (New York: Atheneum, 1974), 152–53; White, *The Making of the President, 1972,* 327.
11. Lawrence R. Jacobs and Melinda S. Jackson, "Presidential Leadership and the Threat to Popular Sovereignty," in Michael A. Genovese and Matthew J. Streb, eds., *Polls and Politics: The Dilemmas of Democracy* (Albany: State University of New York Press, 2004), 44.
12. Ibid., 33.
13. Magruder, *An American Life,* 154.
14. Ibid.
15. May and Fraser, *Campaign '72,* 81. Besides Haldeman, several other Nixon operatives had worked at J. Walter Thompson: Larry Higby, Dwight Chapin, Ken Cole, and Ronald Ziegler. Magruder, *An American Life,* 7
16. Edwin Diamond and Stephen Bates, *The Spot: The Rise of Political Advertising on Television,* 3rd ed. (Cambridge, MA: MIT Press, 1992), 181. See also, Robert Spero,

The Duping of the American Voter: Dishonesty and Deception in Presidential Television Advertising (New York: Lippincott & Crowell, 1980), 106–37.

17. Diamond and Bates, *The Spot*, 180.

18. May and Fraser, *Campaign '72*, 52.

19. Kathleen Hall Jamieson, *Packaging the Presidency: A History and Criticism of Presidential Campaign Advertising* (New York: Oxford University Press, 1984), 395–96.

20. Richard Nixon, *RN: The Memoirs of Richard Nixon* (New York: Grosset & Dunlap, 1978), 669.

21. Also running in this crowded Democratic field were Oklahoma senator Fred Harris, Los Angeles mayor Sam Yorty, former Hawaii representative Patsy Mink, Indiana senator Vance Hartke, former Minnesota senator Eugene McCarthy, New York City mayor John V. Lindsay, Arkansas representative Wilbur Mills, New York representative Shirley Chisholm, and Washington senator Henry M. Jackson.

22. See, for example, Paul A. Smith, *Electing a President: Information and Control* (New York: Praeger, 1980), 21–30; chairing the commission after McGovern was Minnesota congressman Don Fraser. Several other Democratic Party commissions worked for party reform during this period as well: the O'Hara Commission on Rules (1969–1972) (Michigan congressman James O'Hara); the Mikulski Commission (1973–1974) (Maryland congresswoman Barbara Mikulski); the Compliance Review Commission (1974–1976); the Sanford Charter Commission (1973–1974) (North Carolina governor Terry Sanford); and the Winograd Commission (1975–1978) (former Michigan state party chairman, Morley Winograd). See also William Cavala, "Changing the Rules of the Game: Party Reform and the 1972 California Delegation to the Democratic National Convention," *American Political Science Review* 68, no. 1 (March 1974): 27–42.

23. On Clinton's time in the McGovern campaign, see David Maraniss, *First in His Class: A Biography of Bill Clinton* (New York: Simon & Schuster, 1995), ch. 15. Also working for McGovern in Texas was Taylor Branch, later the biographer of Martin Luther King Jr.: *At Canaan's Edge: American in the King Years, 1965–68* (2006); *Pillar of Fire: America in the King Years, 1963–65* (1998); and *Parting the Waters: America in the King Years, 1954–63* (1989), all published by Simon & Schuster; and author of *The Clinton Tapes: Wrestling History with the President* (New York: Simon & Schuster, 2009).

24. White, *The Making of the President, 1972*, 105–7.

25. Weil, *The Long Shot*, 198.

26. Robert Sam Anson, *McGovern: A Biography* (New York: Holt, Rinehart and Winston, 1972), 266 fn.

27. Hart, *Right from the Start*, 90.

28. Robert Shrum, *No Excuses: Concessions of a Serial Campaigner* (New York: Simon & Schuster, 2007), 22–53.

29. Anson, *McGovern*, 266.

30. Weil, *The Longshot*, 38–39.

31. Ibid., 39.

32. May and Fraser, *Campaign '72*, 202.

33. R. W. Apple, "Democratic Governors Rebuke Consultant Who Suggests They 'Concede' 30 States in November," *New York Times*, February 22, 1972, 17.

34. Stephen E. Ambrose, *Nixon: The Triumph of a Politician, 1962–1972* (New York: Simon & Schuster, 1989), 620.

35. May and Fraser, *Campaign '72*, 217, 219.

36. Study cited in Diamond and Bates, *The Spot*, 200.

37. Ambrose, *Nixon*, 623.

38. Richard Reeves, *President Nixon: Alone in the White House* (New York: Simon & Schuster, 2001), 513.

39. White, *The Making of the President, 1972*, 213–15, and generally chapter 8. On the Eagleton candidacy, see Joshua M. Glasser, *The Eighteen-Day Running Mate: McGovern, Eagleton, and a Campaign in Crisis* (New Haven, CT: Yale University Press, 2012).

40. Edward A. Grefe, interview with the author, Washington, DC, March 20, 2013. In the late 1960s, Grefe was a political consultant working for Roy Pfautch of Civic Services, Inc., the St. Louis-based consulting firm working on Curtis's behalf.

41. Stanley Kelley Jr., *Interpreting Elections* (Princeton, NJ: Princeton University Press, 1983), 115–16.

42. Haynes Johnson, "Public Sees McGovern Image Slipping," *Washington Post*, October 2, 1972, cited in Glasser, *The Eighteen-Day Running Mate*, 283.

43. White, *The Making of the President, 1972*, 326.

44. Transcript from Living Room Candidate, http://www.livingroomcandidate.org/commercials/1972 (accessed June 23, 2013).

45. Perlstein, *Nixonland*, 738.

46. May and Fraser, *Campaign '72*, 79. Jeb Magruder commented that CREEP had the "most extensive political direct-mail campaign ever run, as well as the financial direct mail."

47. White, *The Making of the President, 1972*, 321–23.

48. Ibid., 324–25.

49. Ibid., 328.

50. Magruder, *An American Life*, 270.

51. Jack W. Germond and Jules Witcover, *Blue Smoke and Mirrors: How Reagan Won and Why Carter Lost the Election of 1980* (New York: Viking Press, 1981), xiii.

52. Lawrence F. O'Brien, *No Final Victories: A Life in Politics—From John F. Kennedy to Watergate* (Garden City, NY: Doubleday, 1974), 331.

53. Diamond and Bates, *The Spot*, 201.

54. Thomas E. Patterson and Robert D. McClure, *The Unseeing Eye: The Myth of Television Power in National Politics* (New York: G. P. Putnam's Sons, 1976), 135.

55. Ward Sinclair, "Stage Right and Stage Left, Consultants Setting Campaign Tones," *Washington Post*, May 11, 1982, A2.

56. Guggenheim interview, KETC.

57. Shrum, *No Excuses*, 52.

58. Victor Gold, "Who's In Charge?," *Washingtonian*, October 1996, 49.

59. Bill Boyarsky, *Ronald Reagan: His Life and Rise to the Presidency* (New York: Random House, 1981), 193

60. Eddie Mahe, "The Low-Water Mark for the Republicans," in Tony Payton, *Campaign War Stories* (Fairfax, VA: Allegiance Press, 2004), 146–47. Teeter quote comes from Mahe's recollection.

61. Mary Matalin and James Carville, with Peter Knobler, *All's Fair: Love, War, and Running for President* (New York: Random House, 1994), 42.

62. Gerald R. Ford, "Remarks on Taking the Oath of Office as President," Gerald R. Ford Presidential Library, August 9, 1974.

63. Joel Roberts, "Polls: Ford's Image Improved over Time," CBSNews.com, http://www.cbsnews.com/2100-500160_162-2301584.html (accessed April 4, 2013).

64. Teeter in Jonathan Moore and Janet Fraser, eds., *Campaign for President: The Managers Look at '76* (Cambridge: Ballinger, 1977), 38–39.

65. Richard Wirthlin, in Moore and Fraser, eds.,*Campaign for President*, 22–23.

66. Memorandum to Richard Cheney from Robert Teeter, November 12, 1975, Re: Analysis of Early Research, Box 63, Robert Teeter Papers, Gerald R. Ford Presidential Library, http://www.fordlibrarymuseum.gov/library/document/0027/002700157-001.pdf (accessed April 1, 2-13)

67. Transcript of Peter Hannaford oral history, interviewed by Stephen F. Knott and Russell L. Riley. Ronald Reagan Oral History Project, University of Virginia Presidential Oral History Program, January 10, 2003, 32–33.

68. Lara M. Brown, *Jockeying for the American Presidency: The Political Opportunism of Aspirants* (Amherst, NY: Cambria Press, 2010), 221.

69. Boyarsky, *Ronald Reagan*, 194.

70. On the beginning of the nomination quest, see Jules Witcover, *Marathon: The Pursuit of the Presidency, 1972–1976* (New York: Viking Press, 1977), 373–97, quote at 64–76.

71. Memorandum to Cheney from Teeter.
72. Ibid.
73. White, *Politics as a Noble Calling*, 203.
74. Victor Gold, "Who's In Charge?," *Washingtonian*, October 1996, 49.
75. Moore, *The Superpollsters*, 225–26.
76. Robert Teeter, in Moore and Fraser, eds., *Campaign for President*, 118–19.
77. Lyn Nofziger, *Nofziger* (Washington, DC: Regnery Gateway, 1992), 164.
78. Transcript of Stuart Spencer oral history, American Association of Political Consultants Interview Collection, The George Washington University Libraries, February 2, 1999, Part 2, 1.
79. Transcript of Stuart Spencer oral history, interviewed by Paul B. Freedman, Stephen F. Knott, Russell L. Riley, and James Sterling Young. Ronald Reagan Oral History Project, University of Virginia, November 15–16, 2001, 36.
80. Ibid., 37.
81. Lois Romano, "Stu Spencer, Quayle's Co-Pilot," *Washington Post*, September 13, 1988, C1.
82. Witcover, *Marathon*, 373–97, quote at 378.
83. Richard Wirthlin, in Moore and Fraser, eds, *Campaign for President*, 68.
84. Moore, *Superpollsters*, 198–99.
85. Michael K. Deaver, *A Different Drummer: My Thirty Years with Ronald Reagan* (New York: HarperCollins, 2001), 66.
86. Nancy Reagan, with William Novak, *My Turn: The Memoirs of Nancy Reagan* (New York: Random House, 1989), 191.
87. Nofziger, *Nofziger*, 164.
88. Transcript of Lyn Nofziger oral history, interviewed by Stephen F. Knott and Russell Riley. Ronald Reagan Oral History Project, University of Virginia, March 6, 2003, 16. Nofziger's first name is Franklyn; but Reagan always called him Lynwood.
89. William A. Link, *Righteous Warrior: Jesse Helms and the Rise of Modern Conservatism* (New York: St. Martin's, 2008), 152–56.
90. Joe Klein, *Politics Lost: How American Democracy Was Trivialized by People Who Think You're Stupid* (New York: Doubleday, 2006), 72.
91. Craig Shirley, *Reagan's Revolution: The Untold Story of the Campaign That Started It All* (Nashville: Nelson Current, 2005), 166–75.
92. Lou Cannon, *President Reagan: The Role of a Lifetime* (New York: Simon & Schuster, 1991), 342; Adam Clymer, "Richard Wirthlin, Pollster Who Advised Reagan, Dies at 80," *New York Times*, March 17, 2011.
93. Diamond and Bates, *The Spot*, 215–17.
94. Michael K. Deaver, *Nancy: A Portrait of My Years with Nancy Reagan* (New York: William Morrow, 2004), 104. See also Witcover, *Marathon*, 65–76.
95. Richard B. Wirthlin with Wynton C. Hall, *The Greatest Communicator: What Ronald Reagan Taught Me about Politics, Leadership, and Life* (Hoboken, NJ: John Wiley & Sons, 2004), 18, 19.
96. Peter Hannaford commented: "There was a lot of discomfort with Sears in the '76 campaign. His drinking was so bad that at one point we got one of Marty's [Martin Anderson's] colleagues, Darrell Trent—who was with Hoover at the time—to travel everywhere with Sears and be his keeper, make sure that he kept down his intake. No, it was pretty bad. We recognized Sears' brilliance when he was on target, but he was rather a controversial figure within the Reagan camp. A lot of Reagan's key supporters and friends who raised money didn't like him, didn't trust him. I don't know that any of us did, but I think we recognized his importance politically to us. But it was a real problem." Hannaford oral history, 68. Richard Wirthlin, in his memoirs, said this about Sears: "Sears is one of the most complex persons I've ever met. He is at once one of the most talented, undisciplined, manipulative, creative, and insecure people I've ever met." Wirthlin, *The Greatest Communicator*, 19.

97. Sidney Blumenthal, *The Permanent Campaign* (Boston: Beacon Press, 1980), 199–200. See also Rowland Evans and Robert Novak, *The Reagan Revolution* (New York: E. P. Dutton, 1981), 41–58.

98. John Deardourff, in Moore and Fraser, eds., *Campaign for President*, 69.

99. Carter quoted in Betty Glad, *Jimmy Carter: In Search of the Great White House* (New York: W. W. Norton, 1980), 209.

100. Burton I. Kaufman and Scott Kaufman, *The Presidency of James Earl Carter, Jr.*, 2nd rev. ed. (Lawrence: University Press of Kansas, 2006), 12. Dr. Peter Bourne, a psychiatrist and family friend, wrote up a ten-page memo on July 25, 1972, outlining how Carter could win the presidency in 1976. Glad, *Jimmy Carter*, 210.

101. Martin Schram, *Running for President, 1976: The Carter Campaign* (New York: Stein and Day, 1977), 64–65.

102. The Iowa caucus had been in use during the 1972 presidential election, but George McGovern's grassroots efforts there were mostly ignored by the press. See Hugh Winebrenner, *The Iowa Precinct Caucuses: The Making of a Media Event* (Ames: Iowa State University Press, 1987), 67–93.

103. Jeffrey M. Jones, "Iowa, New Hampshire Results Often Shift National Preferences," Gallup Politics, January 3, 2008, http://www.gallup.com/poll/103537/iowa-new-hampshire-results-often-shift-national-preferences.aspx (accessed June 14, 2014).

104. Congressional Quarterly, *Presidential Elections, 1789–1996* (Washington, DC: Congressional Quarterly Press, 1997), 1976 Presidential Primaries. On the Iowa caucus, see Schram, *Running for President 1976*, 6–18.

105. Rafshoon quoted in Moore and Fraser, eds., *Campaign for President*, 87.

106. Powell quoted in Ibid.

107. Jonathan Moore, "Introduction," in Ibid., 2. The twelve other candidates were California governor Jerry Brown, Georgia governor George C. Wallace, Arizona congressman Morris K. Udall, Washington senator Henry Jackson, Idaho senator Frank Church, Texas senator Lloyd Bentsen, Indiana senator Birch Bayh, former Peace Corps director Sergeant Shriver, Oklahoma senator Fred Harris, pro-choice advocate Ellen McCormack, Pennsylvania governor Milton Shapp, and West Virginia senator Robert Byrd.

108. "Jimmy Carter's Big Breakthrough," *Time*, May 10, 1976, http://cgi.cnn.com/ALLPOLITICS/1996/analysis/back.time/9605/10/(accessed June 23, 2013).

109. Transcript of Spencer oral history, Reagan Project, 57.

110. Herbert B. Asher, *Presidential Elections and American Politics: Voters, Candidates, and Campaigns since 1952*, 3rd ed. (Homewood, IL: Dorsey Press, 1984), 153.

111. Schram, *Running for President 1976*, 252, 253.

112. Ibid., 253.

113. Ibid., 253–68.

114. L. Patrick Devlin, "An Analysis of Presidential Television Commercials, 1952–1984," in Lynda Lee Kaid, Dan Nimmo, and Keith Sanders, eds., *New Perspectives on Political Advertising* (Carbondale: Southern Illinois University Press, 1986), 30–31.

115. Diamond and Bates, *The Spot*, 212, 219.

116. Joseph Lelyveld, "Ford Delays Ads on TV until after First Debate," *New York Times*, September 14, 1976, 28.

117. "Peace," Museum of the Moving Image, Living Room Candidate, produced by Bailey/Deardourff, http://www.livingroomcandidate.org/commercials/1976 (accessed April 3, 2013).

118. "Man on the Street—Democrats," Museum of the Moving Image, Living Room Candidate, produced by Bailey/Deardourff, http://www.livingroomcandidate.org/commercials/1976 (accessed April 3, 2013).

119. Kandy Stroud, *How Jimmy Won: The Victory Campaign from Plains to the White House* (New York: William Morrow, 1977), 179.

120. Ibid., 196–97.

121. On Carter and Ford advertising, see William L. Benoit, *Seeing Spots: A Functional Analysis of Presidential Television Advertisements, 1952–1996* (Westport, CT: Praeger, 1999), 69–85.

122. Lou Cannon, *Ronald Reagan: Role of a Lifetime* (New York: Public Affairs, 1991), 35.

123. White, *Politics as a Noble Calling*, 205.

124. Romano, "Stu Spencer, Quayle's Co-Pilot."

125. Quoted in William Schneider, "The Democrats in '88," *The Atlantic* (April 1987), 54; cited in John Kenneth White, *The New Politics of Old Values* (Hanover, NH: University Press of New England, 1988), 49.

126. Richard B. Wirthlin, "The Republican Strategy and Its Electoral Consequences," in Seymour Martin Lipset, ed., *Party Coalitions in the 1980s* (San Francisco: Institute for Contemporary Studies, 1981), 244.

127. Transcript of Nofziger oral history, 2–3.

128. Boyarsky, *Ronald Reagan*, 197.

129. Shirley, *Reagan's Revolution*, 335–36.

130. Reagan, *My Turn: The Memoirs of Nancy Reagan*, 205.

131. Cannon, *President Reagan*, 66–67.

132. Edwin Meese III, *With Reagan: The Inside Story* (Washington, DC: Regnery Gateway, 1992), 11.

133. Paul A. Smith, *Electing a President: Information and Control* (Westport, CT: Praeger, 1982), 127.

134. Timothy Naftali, *George H. W. Bush* (New York: Times Books, 2007), 35–36.

135. Bernard Weintraub, "Bush Gets Lessons in Performing on TV," *New York Times*, January 13, 1980, 23.

136. Herbert S. Parmet, *George Bush: The Life of a Lone Star Yankee* (New Brunswick, NJ: Transaction Books, 2001), 221.

137. Jonathan Moore, ed., *The Campaign for President: 1980 in Retrospect* (Cambridge, MA: Ballinger, 1981), 113.

138. Along with Sears, his two lieutenants, Jim Lake and Charles Black, were dismissed. Reagan, *My Turn*, 205.

139. Craig Shirley, *Rendezvous with Destiny: Ronald Reagan and the Campaign that Changed America* (Wilmington, DE: ISI Books, 2009), 181.

140. Ed Rollins, with Tom DeFrank, *Bare Knuckles and Back Rooms: My Life in American Politics* (New York: Broadway Books, 1996), 72.

141. Andrew E. Busch, *Reagan's Victory: The Presidential Election of 1980 and the Rise of the Right* (Lawrence: University Press of Kansas, 2005), 68.

142. Albert R. Hunt, "The Campaign and the Issues," in Austin Ranney, ed. *The American Elections of 1980* (Washington, DC: American Enterprise Institute for Public Policy Research, 1981), 162.

143. Moore, ed., *The Campaign for President: 1980*, 68–69.

144. Ibid., 69.

145. Cannon, *President Reagan*, 69.

146. Transcript of Michael Deaver oral history, interviewed by James Sterling Young, Stephen Knott, Russell L. Riley, Charles O. Jones, and Edwin Hargrove. Ronald Reagan Oral History Project, University of Virginia, September 12, 2002, 30.

147. Moore, ed., *The Campaign for President: 1980*, 69–70.

148. Cannon, *President Reagan*, 77.

149. Transcript of Spencer oral history, Reagan Project, 20.

150. Ibid.

151. Mark R. Levy, "Polling and the Presidential Elections," *Annals of the American Academy of Political and Social Science* 472 (March 1984): 85–96.

152. Wirthlin, "The Republican Strategy and Its Electoral Consequences," 241.

153. Ibid., 243–44.

154. Smith, *Electing a President*, 124.
155. Jamieson, *Packaging the Presidency*, 394.
156. Ibid., 396–97.
157. Shirley, *Rendezvous with Destiny*, 198.
158. Smith, *Electing a President*, 136–37.
159. Richard Ben Cramer, *Bob Dole* (New York: Vintage, 1995), xv.
160. On Garth and the Anderson campaign generally, see Jim Mason, *No Holding Back: The 1980 John B. Anderson Presidential Campaign* (Lanham, MD: University Press of America, 2011). See also Mark Bisnow, *Diary of a Dark Horse: The 1980 Anderson Presidential Campaign* (Carbondale: Southern Illinois University Press, 1983).
161. Jamieson, *Packaging the Presidency*, 398–99.
162. Jack W. Germond and Jules Witcover, *Blue Smoke and Mirrors: How Reagan Won and Why Carter Lost the Election of 1980* (New York: Viking Press, 1981), 236–37, quote at 237.
163. Ibid., 171. The flirtation with Ford is treated in depth in chapter 8.
164. Carl M. Cannon, "Reagan and Ford Flirt, But It's Bush," *National Journal* 32, no. 32 (August 5, 2000).
165. Bernard Weinraub, "Troubled Kennedy TV Effort Changes Direction Again," *New York Times*, May 18, 1980, 30.
166. Transcript of Jody Powell oral history, interviewed by Charles O. Jones et al., Carter Presidency Project, University of Virginia, December 17–18, 1981, 93. On the Kennedy campaign, see Shrum, *No Excuses*, chapter 4.
167. Historical Speeches, Edward Kennedy, "The Cause Endures," August 12, 1980, http://www.historyplace.com/speeches/tedkennedy.htm (accessed June 23, 2013).
168. George J. Church, "Carter Running Tough," *Time*, August 25, 1980.
169. Wirthlin, *The Greatest Communicator*, 70.
170. Ibid.
171. William J. Lanouette, "Candidates Turn to the Pollsters for Advice on Campaign Strategies," *National Journal* (October 18, 1980), 1742.
172. Patrick H. Caddell, "The Democratic Strategy and Its Electoral Consequences," in Lipset, ed., *Party Coalitions in the 1980s*, 279–81.
173. Shirley, *Rendezvous with Destiny*, 553.
174. "Nancy Reagan," Museum of the Moving Image, Living Room Candidate, produced by Campaign '80; http://www.livingroomcandidate.org/commercials/1980 (accessed April 3, 2013).
175. Mark R. Levy, "Polling and the Presidential Elections," *Annals of the American Academy of Political and Social Science* 472 (March 1984): 85–96.
176. Ibid., 86
177. Ibid., 87.
178. Ibid.
179. Richard Wirthlin, in Moore, *The Campaign for President: 1980*, 224
180. Germond and Witcover, *Blue Smoke and Mirrors*, 276.
181. Kaufman and Kaufman, *The Presidency of James Earl Carter, Jr.*, 243–45; Adam Clymer, "Richard Wirthlin, Pollster Who Advised Reagan, Dies at 80," *New York Times*, March 17, 2011.
182. Shirley, *Rendezvous with Destiny*, 565–67.
183. Ibid., 556.
184. Kaufman and Kaufman, *The Presidency of James Earl Carter, Jr.*, 245.
185. Caddell, "The Democratic Strategy and Its Electoral Consequences," in Lipset, ed., *Party Coalitions in the 1980s*, 274.
186. Cannon, *President Reagan*, 70–71; see also James A. Baker III, with Steve Fiffer, *"Work Hard, Study . . . And Keep Out of Politics!" Adventures and Lessons from an Unexpected Public Life* (New York: G. P. Putnam's Sons, 2006), 122–31.

Chapter 11

Epigraph quote of Bailey in Sara Fritz and Dwight Morris, *Gold-Plated Politics: Running for Congress in the 1990s* (Washington, DC: Congressional Quarterly , 1992), 107.

1. Ron Suskind, "The Power of Political Consultants," *New York Times*, August 12, 1984, A32.
2. Squier died in January 2000, but his firm, under Bill Knapp continued to work on the Gore campaign. See chapter 17.
3. Linda Casey et al., "An Overview of Campaign Finances, 2009–2010 Elections," National Institute on Money in State Politics, April 12, 2012, http://www. followthemoney.org/research/institute-reports/an-overview-of-campaign-finances-2009-2010-elections/ (accessed November 13, 2013), 14.
4. Ibid., 16.
5. Ibid.
6. Ibid.
7. Chris Meyer, "Ten Years in the Making," *Campaigns & Elections*, April/May 1990, 40.
8. Mike Allen, "Small Town, Va., to Determine Control of the State Senate," *Washington Post,* December 16, 1996, B1; Dennis W. Johnson, *No Place for Amateurs: How Political Consultants Are Reshaping American Democracy* (New York: Routledge, 2001), 222–23.
9. Rachel E. Stassen-Berger and Glenn Howatt, "Spending on Minnesota Legislative Races Has Doubled in 10 Years," *Minneapolis Star-Tribune*, September 1, 2013, http://www.startribune.com/politics/statelocal/221951951.html (accessed June 21, 2014).
10. Dale Emmons telephone interview with the author, November 7, 2013.
11. "The Ax-Man Cometh," *The Economist*, August 21, 2008, http://www.economist. com/node/11965249 (accessed June 20, 2014).
12. John Metcalfe, "The Skyrocketing Cost of Running for Mayor of a Major U.S. City," *CityLab*, November 6, 2012, http://www.citylab.com/politics/2012/ 11/skyrocketing-costs-running-mayor-major-us-city/3814/ (accessed June 26, 2014).
13. "Contributions to Local Elections, Candidates in Elections in New York," National Institute on Money in State Politics, http://beta.followthemoney.org/ show-me?s=NY&c-r-ot=C#[{1|gro=c-t-id{1|gro=c-%20t-p{1|gro=c-t-ico{1|gro=c-t-sts{1|gro=c-r-id (accessed August 6, 2014).
14. *Moyers & Company*, Bill Moyers, October 12, 2012, quoted in National Institute on Money in State Politics, *The New Politics of Judicial Elections*, 2012, http:// newpoliticsreport.org/report/2012-report/introduction (accessed August 6, 2014).
15. 536 U.S. 765 (2002).
16. James L. Gibson, *Electing Judges: The Surprising Effects of Campaigning on Judicial Legitimacy* (Chicago: University of Chicago Press, 2012).
17. Ibid., 3. On judicial elections, see also Matthew J. Streb, *Running for Judge: The Rising Political, Financial, and Legal Stakes of Judicial Elections* (New York: New York University Press, 2007).
18. The New Politics of Judicial Elections," 2011-12 Report, Introduction, www. newpoliticsreport.org/report/2012-report/ (accessed May 13, 2016). The report was also sponsored by Justice at Stake and the Brennan Center for Justice at the New York University School of Law.
19. http://www.youtube.com/watch?v=hfcxVscDx4s (accessed July 12, 2014)
20. http://www.youtube.com/watch?v=6twOgKpiXbs (accessed July 12, 2014).
21. Andrew Rosenthal, "Everyone Deserves Legal Representation," *New York Times*, November 1, 2012; "Walk and Talk the Vote—West Wing Reunion,"

video, http://www.youtube.com/watch?v=v52FLMOPSig (accessed July 14, 2014).

22. Viveca Novak and Peter Stone, "The JCN Story: Building a Secretive GOP Judicial Machine," Center for Responsive Politics, March 23, 2015, http://www.opensecrets.org/news/2015/03/the-jcn-story-building-a-secretive-gop-judicial-machine/ (accessed October 6, 2015).

23. Hall of Shame, *The New Politics of Judicial Elections*, 2011–12 Report, http://newpoliticsreport.org/report/2012-report/chapter-2/hall-of-shame/ (accessed July 11, 2014). On McCormack's assembling the *West Wing* cast, see "How Michigan Judicial Candidate Bridget Mary McCormack Got 'The West Wing' Cast for Her Video," *Washington Post*, September 20, 2012, http://www.washingtonpost.com/blogs/reliable-source/post/how-michigan-judicial-candidate-bridget-mary-mccormack-got-the-west-wing-cast-for-her-campaign-video/2012/09/20/a2d53326-0347-11e2-91e7-2962c74e7738_blog.html (accessed July 14, 2014).

24. Linda Casey, "Courting Donors: Money in Judicial Elections, 2011–2012," National Institute on Money in State Politics, March 18, 2014.

25. Gary C. Jacobson, *The Politics of Congressional Elections*, 4th ed. (New York: Longman, 1997), 5.

26. Paul S. Herrnson, *Congressional Elections: Campaigning at Home and in Washington* (Washington, DC: Congressional Quarterly Press, 1995).

27. Stephen K. Medvic, *Political Consultants in U.S. Congressional Elections* (Columbus: The Ohio State University Press, 2001), 144.

28. Joe Peritz & Associates was in business from 1981 through 1993.

29. Fritz and Morris, *Gold-Plated Politics*, 104–5.

30. Alan Secrest renamed the firm Secrest Strategic Services and in 2012 closed it down. In 1988, when Rahm Emanuel was national campaign director for the Democratic Congressional Campaign Committee, in *Godfather I* style, he and two of his staffers sent Secrest a rotting fish wrapped in newspaper; an accompanying note said, "It's been awful working with you. Love, Rahm." Carol Felsenthal, "The Definitive Rahm Dead Fish Tale, 'Barry Obama,' and More," *Chicago*, June 29, 20912; interview with Chris Sautter, http://www.chicagomag.com/Chicago-Magazine/Felsenthal-Files/June-2012/Chris-Sautter-and-the-Definitive-Dead-Fish-Tale-Plus-Barry-Obama-Bill-Daley-and-More/ (accessed June 20, 2014).

31. Center for Responsive Politics, "Re-election Rates over the Years," Open Secrets website, https://www.opensecrets.org/bigpicture/reelect.php (accessed April 9, 2014).

32. See, for example, the listing of 353 super PACs receiving funds from corporations and LLCs during the 2012, 2014, and 2016 election cycles. Center for Responsive Politics, "The Other Dark Money: Our Complete List of Corporate & LLC Contributions to Super PACs," May 9, 2016, www.opensecrets.org (accessed May 14, 2016).

33. Russ Choma, "Dave Versus Goliath, By the Numbers," https://www.opensecrets.org/news/2014/06/dave-versus-goliath-by-the-numbers/ (accessed May 14, 2016).

34. Claussen quoted in Dan Morain, "Making of a Ballot Initiative," *Los Angeles Times*, April 16, 1998, A1,

35. Daniel A. Smith, *Tax Crusaders and the Politics of Direct Democracy* (New York: Routledge, 1998), 157.

36. Tari Renner, "Local Initiative and Referendum in the United States," Initiative & Referendum Institute, University of Southern California [n.d.], http://www.iandrinstitute.org/Local%20I&R.htm (accessed June 30, 2014).

37. Ibid.

38. See ProjectVoteSmart database, http://votesmart.org/elections/ballot-measures/2014#.U6HQVi9AKDA (accessed June 17, 2014), and Ballotpedia.org website, http://ballotpedia.org/2014_ballot_measures (accessed June 18, 2014).

39. On ballot issues, see David B. Magleby, *Direct Legislation: Voting on Ballot Propositions in the United States* (Baltimore: Johns Hopkins University Press, 1984); Thomas E. Cronin, *Direct Democracy: The Politics of Initiative, Referendum, and Recall* (Cambridge: Harvard University Press, 1989); Larry J. Sabato, Howard R. Ernst, and Bruce A. Larson, eds. *Dangerous Democracy? The Battle over Ballot Initiatives in America* (Lanham, MD: Rowman & Littlefield, 2001); John Haskell, *Direct Democracy or Representative Government: Dispelling the Populist Myth* (Boulder, CO: Westview, 2001); David S. Broder, *Democracy Derailed: Initiative Campaigns and the Power of Money* (New York: Harcourt, 2000); Johnson, *No Place for Amateurs,* 2nd ed., ch. 9.

40. "Sound and Fury over Taxes," *Time,* June 19, 1978, 12–21, quoted in Smith, *Tax Crusaders and the Politics of Direct Democracy,* 28.

41. Nora B. Jacob, "Butcher and Forde, Wizards of the Computer Letter," *California Journal,* May 1979, 162–68 http://www.unz.org/Pub/CalJournal-1979may-00162 (accessed June 16, 2014).

42. Smith, *Tax Crusaders and the Politics of Direct Democracy,* 27–33.

43. Howard Jarvis Taxpayers Association, http://www.hjta.org/ (accessed June 19, 2014).

44. Mark Schleub, "Doug Guetzloe: A Man for All Political Seasons," *Orlando Sentinel,* October 15, 2006, http://www.orlandosentinel.com/community/orl-guetzloeprofile-012307,0,7564429.story (accessed June 19, 2014).

45. California Secretary of State, "Statewide Initiative Guide," rev. January 2015, http://www.sos.ca.gov/elections/ballot-measures/how-qualify-initiative/initiative-guide/ (accessed April 13, 2016); David S. Broder, "Collecting Signatures for a Price," *Washington Post,* April 12, 1998, A1.

46. Rick Ridder telephone interview with author, July 24, 2014.

47. Edward A. Grefe, *Fighting to Win: Business Political Power* (New York: Law & Business, Inc., 1981), 158–60.

48. Shaun Bowler, Todd Donovan, and Ken Fernandez, "The Growth of the Political Marketing Industry and the California Initiative Process," *European Journal of Marketing* 30, no. 10–11 (1996): 173–85, at 176.

49. Todd Donovan, Shaun Bowler, and David McCuan, "Political Consultants and the Initiative Industrial Complex," in Sabato, Ernst, and Larson, eds., *Dangerous Democracy?,* 105–22.

50. Dan Morain, "Consultants Win in Fights over State Initiatives," *Los Angeles Times,* November 3, 1996, A3; and Johnson, *No Place for Amateurs,* 2d ed., 205–6.

51. Polidata Regional Maps: California, http://www.polidata.org/pub/maps/rg2000/ca_reg.pdf (accessed August 5, 2014).

52. Reid Wilson, "The Most Expensive Ballot Initiatives," *Washington Post,* May 17, 2014; Ballotpedia, "California Proposition 94," http://ballotpedia.org/California_Proposition_94,_Pechanga_Band_of_Luiseno_Mission_Indians_Gaming_Compact_%282008%29 (accessed June 20, 2014).

53. Jesse McKinley and Kirk Johnson, "Mormons Tipped Scale in Ban on Gay Marriage," *New York Times,* November 14, 2008.

54. Geordy Boveroux, "Prominent GOP Consultants Join Gay Marriage Brief," *Campaigns & Elections,* February 26, 2013, http://www.campaignsandelections.com/campaign-insider/365132/prominent-gop-consultants-join-gay-marriage-brief.thtml (accessed June 29, 2014). The one elected Republican member of Congress supporting the brief was Ileana Ros-Lehtinen (Florida). Catalina Camia, "Top Republicans Urge Court to Support Gay Marriage," *USA Today,* February 26, 2013, http://www.usatoday.com/story/news/politics/2013/02/26/gay-marriage-supreme-court-republicans-prop-8/1949265/ (accessed June 29, 2014).

55. Joy Resmovits, "Maryland Question 7 Pits Casino against Casino in Debate on Education Dollars," *Huffington Post,* October 12, 20102, http://www.huffingtonpost.com/2012/10/12/maryland-question-7-ads_n_1961672.html (accessed June 20, 2014).

56. National Conference of State Legislatures website, http://www.ncsl.org/research/elections-and-campaigns/recall-of-state-officials.aspx (accessed June 20, 2014).

57. Thomas B. Edsall, "Recall Loopholes in Campaign Finance Law," *Washington Post*, September 25, 2003, A8; John Wildermuth, "Schwarzenegger's GOP Rivals Quitting," *San Francisco Chronicle*, August 8, 2013, A1. The only other governor to be recalled was Lynn Frazier of North Dakota in 1921.

58. Matea Gold and Tom Hamburger, "Wisconsin Gov. Scott Walker Suspected of Coordination with Outside Groups," *Washington Post*, June 19, 2014. The unsealed US Court of Appeals court order and supporting documents are available on the *New York Times* website, http://www.nytimes.com/interactive/2014/06/19/us/20walker-docs.html (accessed June 20, 2014).

59. Obituary, "Jack McDowell, Pulitzer Prize Winner, Political Consultant," *San Diego Source/Daily Transcript*, May 14, 1998; The Hon. George P. Radanovich, "Honoring Jack McDowell, Pulitzer Prize Winning Journalist, Political Consultant, Beloved Father and Husband," *Congressional Record*, May 14, 1998, E863, Extension of Remarks. http://www.gpo.gov/fdsys/pkg/CREC-1998-05-14/pdf/CREC-1998-05-14-pt1-PgE863-4.pdf

60. Bob Korda, "Woodward and McDowell: Keepers of the Treasure Chest," *California Journal*, May 1979, 159–61, http://www.unz.org/Pub/CalJournal-1979may-00159 (accessed June 19, 2014).

61. Tom Furlong, "Expensive Victory for Business," *Los Angeles Times*, November 8, 1990; Maura Dolan and Richard C. Paddock, "California Elections: Proposition 128 'Big Green' Reached Too Far, Backers Say," *Los Angeles Times*, November 8, 1990.

62. Winner and Mandabach website, http://www.wmcampaigns.com/;"Winner and Mandabach" entry in Ballotpedia, http://ballotpedia.org/Winner_%26_Mandabach_Campaigns, n.d. (accessed July 8, 2014).; Winner & Associates website, http://www.winnerandassociates.com/experiencedteam_bio.aspx?subpage=page3&bio=Charles+Winner (accessed August 8, 2014).

63. Nielsen Merksamer Parrinello Gross & Leoni, LLP, website, http://web.nmgovlaw.com/practice/summary-of-representative-ballot-measures/(accessed June 19, 2014).

64. Data from Ballotpedia, http://ballotpedia.org/Nielsen,_Merksamer,_Parrinello,_Mueller_%26_Naylor (accessed June 19, 2014).

65. Broder, "Collecting Signatures for a Price."

66. Arnold Political Consultants website, http://www.apcusa.com/ (accessed June 19, 2014).

67. National Voter Outreach website, http://www.directdemocracy.com/index.php?option=com_content&view=article&id=84&Itemid=41 (accessed June 19, 2014).

Chapter 12

Epigraph quote from Paul Taylor, *See How They Run: Electing the President in an Age of Mediaocracy* (New York: Alfred A. Knopf, 1990), 114.

1. Phil Dusenberry, *Then We Set His Hair on Fire: Insights and Accidents from a Hall of Fame Career in Advertising* (New York: Portfolio, 2005), 23.

2. Peter Goldman et al., "Making of a Landslide: A Month of Wandering in the Wilderness," *Newsweek*, November 1984, 91.

3. Austin Ranney, "Reagan's First Term," in Austin Ranney, ed., *The American Elections of 1984* (Durham, NC: Duke University Press, 1985), 1. On the nature and definition of "landslide elections," see Stanley Kelley Jr., *Interpreting Elections* (Princeton, NJ: Princeton University Press, 1983), 26–42.

4. Jack W. Germond and Jules Witcover, *Wake Us When It's Over* (New York: Macmillan, 1985).

5. John J. Brady, *Bad Boy: The Life and Politics of Lee Atwater* (Reading, MA: Addison-Wesley, 1997), 114–15.

6. Richard B. Wirthlin, with Wynton C. Hall. *The Greatest Communicator: What Ronald Reagan Taught Me about Politics, Leadership, and Life* (Hoboken, NJ: John Wiley & Sons, 2004), 136.

7. Peter Goldman, Tony Fuller, et al., *The Quest for the Presidency 1984* (New York: Bantam Books, 1985), 74–75.

8. Raymond D. Strother, *Falling Up: How a Redneck Helped Invent Political Consulting* (Baton Rouge: Louisiana State University Press, 2003), 174.

9. Goldman, Fuller, et al., *The Quest for the Presidency 1984*, 89.

10. Transcript of Strother oral history, AAPC, 10, 11.

11. Lynch biographical sketch, American University, http://www.american.edu/uploads/resume/Lynch%20Online%20Extended%20Bio.pdf (accessed August 15, 2014).

12. Paul Vitello, "Dotty Lynch, Pollster Who Saw the Gender Gap, Is Dead at 69," *New York Times*, August 13, 2014.

13. Squier quoted in Lois Romano, "Lynch: Breaking Into a 'Man's Business,'" *Washington Post*, January 14, 1984, C8.

14. Goldman, Fuller, et al., *The Quest for the Presidency 1984*, 295.

15. Robert Shrum, *No Excuses: Concessions of a Serial Campaigner* (New York: Simon & Schuster, 2007), 140.

16. Strother, *Falling Up*, 186.

17. Germond and Witcover, *Wake Us When It's Over*, 181, n. 25.

18. Douglas Martin, "Arnold R. Pinkney Dies at 83; Steered 1984 Jesse Jackson Run," *New York Times*, January 18, 2014.

19. Strother, *Falling Up*, 180–81.

20. Steven M. Gillon, *The Democrat's Dilemma: Walter F. Mondale and the Liberal Legacy* (New York: Columbia University Press, 1992), 343.

21. David W. Moore, *The Superpollsters: How They Measure and Manipulate Public Opinion in America* (New York: Four Walls Eight Windows, 1995), 172–74.

22. Ibid., 174.

23. "Red Phone," YouTube, http://www.youtube.com/watch?v=kddX7LqgCvc.

24. Hart quoted in Moore, *The Superpollsters*, 178–79.

25. Lee Atwater memorandum, July 1984, in Goldman, Fuller, et al., *The Quest for the Presidency 1984*, 414.

26. Transcript of Spencer oral history, Reagan Project, 87.

27. Ed Rollins, with Tom DeFrank, *Bare Knuckles and Back Rooms: My Life in American Politics* (New York: Broadway Books, 1996), 125.

28. Ibid., 128–30.

29. Teeter quoted in Jonathan Moore, ed., *Campaign for President: The Managers Look at '84* (Dover, MA: Auburn House, 1986), 103.

30. Goldman, Fuller, et al., *The Quest for the Presidency 1984*, 271.

31. Memorandum from Peter D. Hart to Walter F. Mondale, August 1984, in Goldman, Fuller, et al., *The Quest for the Presidency 1984*, 418.

32. James Harding, *Alpha Dogs: The Americans Who Turned Political Spin into a Global Business* (New York: Farrar, Straus and Giroux, 2008), 82–84.

33. Goldman et al., "Making of a Landslide."

34. Ibid.

35. The debate can be seen in its entirety on YouTube, http://www.youtube.com/watch?v=jj_xt5G1sFE (accessed August 15, 2014).

36. Spencer oral history, Reagan Project, 54.

37. Transcript of Reagan interview with Jim Lehrer, "Debating our Destiny: 1984 There Your Go Again . . . and Again," Public Broadcasting System, August 7, 1989, http://www.pbs.org/newshour/debatingourdestiny/interviews/reagan.html#1984.

38. Goldman, Fuller, et al., *The Quest for the Presidency 1984*, 440.

39. Rollins quoted in Moore, *Campaign for President* (1986), 205.

40. Kerwin Swint, *Dark Genius: The Influential Career of Legendary Political Operative and Fox News Founder Roger Ailes* (New York: Union Square Press, 2008), 21.

41. Transcript of Mondale interview with Jim Lehrer, "Debating Our Destiny," http://www.pbs.org/newshour/debatingourdestiny/dod/1984-broadcast.html.

42. Goldman, Fuller, et al., *The Quest for the Presidency 1984*, 264.

43. Ibid., 264.

44. Dusenberry, *Then We Set His Hair on Fire*, 21–22; Phil Dusenberry interview, *NewsHour with Jim Lehrer*, July 2000, http://www.pbs.org/newshour/media/biofilms/dusenberry.html (accessed February 2, 2014).

45. Wirthlin oral history, AAPC, 19.

46. George Raine, "Creating Reagan's Image," *San Francisco Chronicle*, June 9, 2004, C1. Bernie Vangrin of Hal Riney and Partners was the art director; filmed by John Pytka of Levine/Pytka Productions.

47. Ibid.

48. "Prouder, Stronger, Better," First Tuesday-Hal Riney productions, Living Room Candidate, http://www.livingroomcandidate.org/commercials/1984 (accessed June 24, 2013).

49. Bob Garfield, "Ronald Reagan, Myth of a Brilliant Ad Team: A Look Back at the 1984 Commercial," *Advertising Age*, June 14, 2004.

50. Goldman, Fuller, et al., *The Quest for the Presidency 1984*, 265.

51. "Bear," First Tuesday-Hal Riney productions, Living Room Candidate, 1984, http://www.livingroomcandidate.org/commercials/1984 (accessed June 14, 2013).

52. Wirthlin and Hall, *The Greatest Communicator*, 142–43.

53. L. Patrick Devlin, "Campaign Commercials," *Society* 22, no. 4 (May 1, 1985), 45.

54. Kathleen Hall Jamieson, *Dirty Politics: Deception, Distraction, and Democracy* (New York: Oxford University Press, 1992), 51.

55. Quoted in Michael J. Robinson, "Where's the Beef? Media and Media Elites in 1984," in Ranney, ed., *The American Elections of 1984*, 182.

56. Jane Mayer and Doyle McManus, *Landslide: The Unmaking of the President, 1984–1988* (Boston: Houghton Mifflin, 1989), 7.

57. Mark Shields, *On the Campaign Trail* (Chapel Hill, NC: Algonquin Books, 1985), 103.

58. Dave Leip, "Atlas of U.S. Presidential Elections," http://www.USelectionatlas.org.

59. Ted Van Dyk, *Heroes, Hacks and Fools: Memoirs from the Political Inside* (Seattle: University of Washington Press, 2007), 289.

60. Taylor, *See How They Run*, 206.

61. Greer quoted in Paul Taylor, "In Politics of Attack, First Shots Often Backfire," *Washington Post*, July 10, 1990.

62. Walter R. Mears, *Deadlines Past: Forty Years of Presidential Campaigning—A Reporter's Story* (Kansas City, MO: Andrews McMeel, 2003), 217.

63. Jules Witcover, *No Way to Pick a President* (New York: Farrar, Straus Giroux, 1999), 60

64. Andrew Rosenthal, "The Courtship of a Consultant," *New York Times*, August 24, 1987, A14.

65. Swint, *Dark Genius*, 46–49.

66. "Roger Ailes on Political Media," *Campaign & Elections*, May/June 1988.

67. Bob and Elizabeth Dole, *Unlimited Partners: Our American Story* (New York: Simon & Schuster, 1996), 269.

68. Wirthlin oral history, 17.

69. Jack W. Germond and Jules Witcover, *Whose Broad Stripes and Bright Stars?: The Trivial Pursuit of the Presidency 1988* (New York: Warner Books, 1989), 145. Later, Dole remarked, "I obviously didn't feel too good. I said what was on my mind. . . . There ought to be some virtue in telling the truth."

70. Ibid., 149.

71. Rhodes Cook, "The Nominating Press," in Michael Nelson, ed., *The Elections of 1988* (Washington, DC: CQ Press, 1989), 43.

72. Quoted in Robin Toner, "Dukakis Camp Insularity Bemoaned," *New York Times*, October 28, 1988, 10; cited in Marjorie Randon Hershey, "The Campaign and the Media," in Gerald M. Pomper et al., *The Election of 1988: Reports and Interpretations* (Chatham, NJ: Chatham House, 1989), 88.

73. Rollins, *Bare Knuckles and Back Rooms*, 189.

74. Taylor, *See How They Run*, 167.

75. Mary Matalin and James Carville, with Peter Knobler, *All's Fair: Love, War, and Running for President* (New York: Random House, 1994), 180.

76. Ibid., 160.

77. Lois Romano, "Stu Spencer, Quayle's Co-Pilot," *Washington Post*, September 13, 1988, C1.

78. On the Cuomo decision, see Taylor, *See How They Run*, ch. 5; Shrum, *No Excuses*, 174–76.

79. Jeffrey Schmalz, "The Mystery of Mario Cuomo," *New York Times*, May 15, 1988.

80. Germond and Witcover, *Whose Broad Stripes and Bright Stars?*, 169.

81. Taylor, *See How They Run*, 42.

82. E. J. Dionne Jr., "Gary Hart, the Elusive Front-Runner," *New York Times*, May 3, 1987.

83. Matt Bai, "How Gary Hart's Downfall Forever Changed American Politics," *New York Times Magazine*, September 21, 2014.

84. Shrum, *No Excuses*, 180.

85. Ibid., 181.

86. Taylor, *See How They Run*, 102.

87. Lois Romano, "The Rankling Puzzle of Pat Caddell," *Washington Post*, November 18, 1987, B1.

88. Taylor, *See How They Run*, 104–105.

89. On the Gore campaign see, David Maraniss and Ellen Nakashima, *The Prince of Tennessee: The Rise of Al Gore* (New York: Simon & Schuster, 2000), 205–38.

90. Klein, *Politics Lost*, 104.

91. Howard Fineman, "Campaign Organization," in David R. Runkel, ed., *Campaign for President: The Managers Look at '88* (Dover, MA: Auburn House, 1989), 83.

92. Germond and Witcover, *Whose Broad Stripes and Bright Stars?*, 359.

93. Quoted in Christine M. Black and Thomas Oliphant, *All by Myself: The Unmaking of a Presidential Campaign* (Chester, CT: The Globe Pequot Press, 1989), 192.

94. Martin P. Wattenberg, *The Decline of American Political Parties, 1952–1994* (Cambridge, MA: Harvard University Press, 1994), 132.

95. Roger Simon, *Road Show: In America, Anyone Can Become President; It's One of the Risks We Take* (New York: Farrar, Straus and Giroux, 1990), 329.

96. Klein, *Politics Lost*, 102–3; Brady, *Bad Boy*, 171.

97. Taylor, *See How They Run*, 190.

98. Germond and Witcover, *Whose Broad Stripes and Bright Stars?*, 357.

99. Runkel, ed., *Campaign for President*, 119. On the issues surrounding the Willie Horton ad, see Tali Mendelberg, *The Race Card: Campaign Strategy, Implicit Messages, and the Norm of Equality* (Princeton, NJ: Princeton University Press, 2001), ch. 5.

100. Taylor, *See How They Run*, 190–91.

101. Ibid., 191–92.

102. Brady, *Bad Boy*, 178–79.

103. Herbert S. Parmet: *George Bush: The Life of a Lone Star Yankee* (New Brunswick, NJ: Transaction, 2001), 334–36, quotes from 336.

104. Edwin Diamond and Stephen Bates, *The Spot: The Rise of Political Advertising on Television*, 3rd ed. (Cambridge, MA: MIT Press 1992), 277.

105. On Frankenberry's drunk driving conviction, the community service ads he was compelled to create, and the Republican Party paying attention to his handiwork, see Jamieson, *Dirty Politics*, 30

106. Museum of the Moving Image, Living Room Candidate, http://www. livingroomcandidate.org/commercials/1988 (accessed June 23, 2013).

107. J. H. Hatfield, *Fortunate Son: George W. Bush and the Making of an American President*, 3rd ed. (New York: Soft Skull Press, 2002), 84.

108. Museum of the Moving Image, Living Room Candidate, http://www. livingroomcandidate.org/commercials/1988 (accessed June 23, 2013).

109. Atwater quoted in Runkel, ed., *Campaign for President*, 116–17; Ailes, 120. Also Mendelberg, *The Race Card*, 139 n. 1.

110. Stone in the video trailer for *Boogie Man: The Lee Atwater Story*, http://www. youtube.com/watch?v=9UwJYfTC9Hw (accessed May 12, 2014).

111. Taylor, *See How They Run*, 204.

112. Museum of the Moving Image, Living Room Candidate, http://www. livingroomcandidate.org/commercials/1988 (accessed June 23, 2013); see also Josh King, "Dukakis and the Tank: The Inside Story of the Worst Campaign Photo Op Ever," *Politico*, November 17, 2013.

113. Donna Brazile, *Cooking with Grease: Stirring the Pots in American Politics* (New York: Simon & Schuster, 2004), 142–43.

114. Ibid., 143, 145.

115. Alan I. Abramowitz and Jeffrey A. Segal, "Beyond Willie Horton and the Pledge of Allegiance: National Issues in the 1988 Elections," *Legislative Studies Quarterly* 15, no. 4 (November 1990): 565–80. I worked on the Lautenberg re-election campaign in 1988.

116. Mark McKinnon, "The Spin Doctor Is Out," *Texas Monthly*, November 1996, 130. McKinnon later became a major Republican political consultant.

117. Black and Oliphant, *All by Myself*, 192.

118. Hershey, "The Campaign and the Media," 100.

119. L. Patrick Devlin, "Contrasts in Presidential Campaign Commercials of 1988," *American Behavioral Scientist*, March/April 1989, 391–92.

120. Randall Rothenberg, "Dukakis Getting Aid from Top Ad Agencies," *New York Times*, July 14, 1988.

121. Devlin, "Contrasts in Presidential Campaign Commercials of 1988," 398.

122. Harding, *Alpha Dogs*, 82, 204–5.

123. McKinnon, "The Spin Doctor Is Out."

124. Randall Rothenberg, "Disarray in Dukakis's Ad Team," *New York Times*, October 20, 1988.

125. Devlin, "Contrasts in Presidential Campaign Commercials of 1988," 398.

126. Tom Rosenstiel, *Strange Bedfellows: How Television and the Presidential Candidates Changed American Politics* (New York: Hyperion, 1993), 279.

127. Devlin, "Contrasts in Presidential Campaign Commercials of 1988."

128. Ibid., 400–401.

129. Kathleen Hall Jamieson, "For Televised Mendacity, This Year Is the Worst Ever," *Washington Post*, October 30, 1988, C1-C2.

130. Taylor, *See How They Run*, 193.

131. Lynda L. Kaid and A. Johnston, "Negative versus Positive Television Advertising in U.S. Presidential Campaigns, 1960–1988," *Journal of Communications* 41 (1991): 53–64.

132. Michael Takiff, *A Complicated Man: The Life of Bill Clinton as Told by Those Who Know Him* (New Haven, CT: Yale University Press, 2010), 92. In 2012, Dukakis reflecting on his experience in the 1988 campaign, wrote about his "failure to plan for and deal with the attacks that were leveled at" him. William G. Mayer and Jonathan Bernstein, eds., *The Making of the Presidential Candidates 2012* (Lanham, MD: Rowman and Littlefield, 2012), 105.

133. Quoted in Black and Oliphant, *All by Myself*, 10–11.

Chapter 13

Epigraph quotes from Dick Morris, *Behind the Oval Office: Getting Reelected against All Odds* (Los Angeles: Renaissance Books, 1999), 50; and David Axelrod, *Believer: My Forty Years in Politics* (New York: Penguin, 2015), 83.

1. David Maraniss, *First in His Class: A Biography of Bill Clinton* (New York: Simon & Schuster, 1995), 352–53.
2. Morris, *Behind the Oval Office*, 45.
3. Ibid., 50.
4. Hillary Rodham Clinton, *Living History* (New York: Simon & Schuster, 2003), 90.
5. Maraniss, *First in His Class*, 384.
6. Ibid., 455; Morris, *Behind the Oval Office*, 64–65.
7. Morris, *Behind the Oval Office*, 68.
8. Stanley B. Greenberg, *Dispatches from the War Room: In the Trenches with Five Extraordinary Leaders* (New York: Thomas Dunne, 2009), 12.
9. Morris, *Behind the Oval Office*.
10. Howard Kurtz, "Dick Morris, High on the Critical List," *Washington Post*, February 3, 1999, C1.
11. Maraniss, *First in His Class,* 407.
12. *Hillary: The Movie*, trailer, http://www.youtube.com/watch?v=BOYcM1z5fTs (accessed March 26, 2014). Directed by Alan Peterson.
13. I worked with Carville on the Richard Davis for Senate (Virginia, 1982) race, and later on the Frank Lautenberg re-election (New Jersey Senate, 1988) and the Zell Miller for governor (Georgia, 1990) contest. I also worked against Carville in other races.
14. Clinton, *Living History*, 149.
15. Mary Matalin and James Carville, with Peter Knobler, *All's Fair: Love, War, and Running for President* (New York: Simon & Schuster, 1994).
16. *The War Room* (1993), directed by Chris Hegedus and D. A. Pennebaker.
17. See Howard Kurz, *Spin Cycle: How the White House and the Media Manipulate the News* (New York: Simon & Schuster, 1998), 129–33.
18. Dale Russakoff, "The Bulldozer behind Wofford's Landslide: Consultant Carville Showed Candidate How to Marshal Middle-Class Discontent," *Washington Post*, November 7, 1991, A31.
19. On the fight to become chair of the College Republicans, see Nicholas Lemann, "The Controller," *New Yorker*, May 12, 2003, 68–83. Rove has been the subject of more biographies (and two documentaries) than any other political consultant. The works include James Moore and Wayne Slater, *Rove Exposed: How Bush's Brain Fooled America* (Hoboken, N J: Wiley, 2006); James Moore and Wayne Slater, *The Architect: Karl Rove and the Master Plan for Absolute Power* (New York: Crown, 2006); James Moore, *Bush's Brain: How Karl Rove Made George W. Bush Presidential* (Hoboken, NJ: Wiley, 2011); Lou Dubose, Jan Reed, and Carl Cannon, *Boy Genius: Karl Rove, the Architect of George W. Bush's Remarkable Political Triumph* (New York: Public Affairs, 2005); Craig Unger, *Boss Rove: Inside Karl Rove's Secret Kingdom of Power* (New York: Scribners, 2012); Bill Israel, *A National Seized: How Karl Rove and the Political Right Stole Reality, Beginning with the News* (Spokane, WA: Marquette Books, 2011); Paul Alexander, *Machiavelli's Shadow: The Rise and Fall of Karl Rove* (New York: Macmillan, 2008); *Bush's Brain*, directed and produced by Michael Paradies Shoob and Joseph Menley, Tartan Films, 2004; *Karl Rove: The Architect*, directed and produced by Michael Kirk, *Frontline* coproduction with the Washington Post and Kirk Documentary Group, WGBH Boston, 2005. Rove has also written his memoirs, *Courage and Consequence: My Life as a Conservative in the Fight* (New York: Threshold Editions, 2010).
20. Rove, *Courage and Consequence*, 48–49.
21. Lemann, "The Controller," 77.

22. Dubose, Reed, and Cannon, *Boy Genius*, 18.

23. Data from Karl Rove website, http://www.rove.com (accessed April 1, 2014).

24. Rove, *Courage and Consequence*, 99.

25. Joshua Green, "The Rove Presidency," *The Atlantic*, September 2007, 51–72.

26. Ibid., 56.

27. Editorial, "Rove's Role," *Boston Globe*, August 28, 2005, http://www.boston.com/news/globe/editorial_opinion/editorials/articles/2005/08/28/rove_role/?page=2 (accessed July 12, 2014).

28. David Plouffe, *The Audacity to Win: The Insider Story and Lessons of Barack Obama's Historic Victory* (New York: Viking, 2009).

29. Kenneth P. Vogel and Maggie Haberman, "Meet Jim Messina: The Democratic Karl Rove," *Politico*, February 24, 2014, 15.

30. Ibid.

31. Benenson Strategy Group website, http://www.bsgco.com (accessed August 12, 2014), and interview with author, August 15, 2014.

32. Jill P. Capuzzo, "Obama Seldom Asks His Pollster to Play the Role of an Oracle," *New York Times*, February 3, 2008, 16.

33. Chris Cillizza, "Winners and Losers: Of Mountains and Magnolias," *Washington Post*, May 14, 2008.

34. Anzalone Liszt Grove Research website, http://www.algpolling.com/#!our-firm/c3i4 (accessed August 13, 2014). Anzalone Liszt Grove Research also has offices in Washington, DC, New York, and Hawaii.

35. David Binder Research website, http://www.davidbinderresearch.com/about.htm (accessed August 13, 2014).

36. Harstad Strategic Research, Inc., website, http://www.harstadresearch.com/contact/paul-harstad/ (accessed August 13, 2014).

37. Marc Caputo, "Tony Fabrizio: Gov. Rick Scott's Unrelenting Engineer of Strategy," *Miami Herald*, July 16, 2011. Fabrizio wrote a chapter in my edited book on the 2008 presidential campaign, "John McCain: From Frontrunner to Dead-in-the-Water to Nominee," in Dennis W. Johnson, ed., *Campaigning for President 2008: Strategy and Tactics, New Voices and New Techniques* (New York: Routledge, 2009), 31–43.

38. Fabrizio, Lee & Associates website, http://www.fabriziolee.com/tony-fabrizio.html (accessed July 30, 2014).

39. Biographical material from American Viewpoint website, http://www.amview.com (accessed December 12, 2013).

40. Whit Ayres interview with author, June 6, 2013; North Star Opinion Research website, http://www.northstaropinion.com/ (accessed August 12, 2014). Whit Ayres, *2016 and Beyond: How Republicans Can Elect a President in the New Era* (Alexandria, VA: Resurgent Republic, 2015).

41. Resurgent Republic website, http://resurgentrepublic.com/about (accessed February 18, 2014).

42. Jan van Lohuizen quoted in John Ellis, "Bush Pollster Assesses GOP Presidential Campaign," *Business Insider*, July 12, 2011, http://www.businessinsider.com/bush-pollster-assesses-gop-presidential-campaign-2011-7#ixzz3AIT28dba (accessed August 13, 2014).

43. Lawrence R. Jacobs and Robert Y. Shapiro, *Politicians Don't Pander: Political Manipulation and the Loss of Democratic Responsiveness* (Chicago: University of Chicago Press, 2000), xi.

44. Ibid., xii.

45. Morris, *Behind the Oval Office*, 84.

46. Robin Toner, "Clinton's Health Plan: Poll on Changes Finds Support amid Skepticism," *New York Times*, September 22, 1993.

47. Greenberg, *Dispatches from the War Room*, 397.

48. Mark Penn remarks at the Society of Presidential Pollsters annual forum, Graduate School of Political Management, George Washington University,

Washington, DC, April 19, 2013, https://www.youtube.com/watch?v=_g2XWE-LUZA (accessed April 90, 2015).

49. Morris, *Behind the Oval Office*, 143.

50. Ibid., 235–40, Clinton quote at 238, Morris quote at 235.

51. George Stephanopoulos, *All Too Human: A Political Education* (Boston: Little, Brown, 1999), 436. For a detailed analysis of White House polling and the Lewinsky crisis, see Diane J. Heith, "Polling for a Defense: The White House Public Opinion Apparatus and the Clinton Impeachment," *Presidential Studies Quarterly* 30, no. 4 (December, 2000): 783–90.

52. Heith, "Polling for a Defense," 786.

53. Conversation with Mark Penn, November 17, 2013, Washington, DC.

54. Faucheux quoted in Joshua Green, "The Other War Room," *Washington Monthly*, April 2002.

55. Green, "The Other War Room," 1.

56. Jackson remarks at the Society of Presidential Pollsters forum.

57. Green, "The Other War Room," 1.

58. Ibid.

59. Kathryn Dunn Tenpas, "Words vs. Deed: President George W. Bush and Polling," *Brookings Review* (Summer 2003): 33–35.

60. Benenson interviewed by Matthew Smith, "Polling and Policy: Joel Benenson Discusses the Role of Polling in Setting Presidential Agendas," *Chicago Policy Review*, April 15, 2013.

61. Ibid.

62. Peter Goodspeed, "Pollster Fine-Tunes President's Message," *National Post*, June 19, 2009, A20

63. Michael Scherer, "What Obama Didn't Tell Barbara Walters," *Time*, August 16, 2010. Trips by Benenson based on Secret Service logs.

64. Jim Innocenzi interview with the author, August 14, 2014.

65. Davis promotional biography, Strategic Perception, Inc., website, http://www.strategicperceptioninc.com/fred.php (accessed March 20, 2014).

66. Chris Landers, "Mark McKinnon (Maverick Media)," Center for Public Integrity, http://www.publicintegrity.org/2006/09/26/6642/mark-mckinnon-maverick-media (accessed March 21, 2014).

67. "After Election Day Defeats, What's Next for the GOP," interview with Mark McKinnon, National Public Radio, November 8, 2012, http://www.npr.org/2012/11/08/164722734/after-election-day-defeats-whats-next-for-gop (accessed August 30, 2014).

68. Stuart Stevens, *The Big Enchilada: Campaign Adventures with the Cockeyed Optimists from Texas Who Won the Biggest Prize in Politics* (New York: Free Press, 2001).

69. Noam Scheiber, "The Square and the Flair," *New Republic*, August 2, 20123, http://www.newrepublic.com/article/magazine/politics/105738/stuart-stevens-romney-strategist-interesting (accessed August 30, 2014).

70. Adam Bernstein, "Political Operative and GOP Media Strategist Greg Stevens, 58," *Washington Post*, April 18, 2007. SRCP Website, http://www.srcpmedia.com/firm/about-us (accessed August 11, 2014).

71. Geer quoted in Sean Alfano, "Rove Protégé behind Racy Tennessee Ad," CBS News, October 26, 2006, http://www.cbsnews.com/news/rove-protege-behind-racy-tennessee-ad/ (accessed August 30, 2014). See John G. Geer, *In Defense of Negativity: Attack Ads in Presidential Campaigns* (Chicago: University of Chicago Press, 2008).

72. Devine Mulvey Longabaugh website, http://dmlmessage.com/ (accessed August 16, 2014).

73. For examples of Margolis's work, see "The Methods of Margolis," *New York Times* May 8, 2012, http://www.nytimes.com/interactive/2012/05/07/us/politics/201205007-margolis.html?_r=2&#/#link_o (accessed August 29, 2014).

On Margolis's role in the 2012 presidential campaign, see Jeremy W. Peters, "Aggressive Ads for Obama, at the Ready," *New York Times*, May 8, 2012.

74. Dan Morain, "Fracture within GOP Adds to Tea Party Coffers," *Sacramento Bee*, February 13, 2013.

75. Janie Lorber and Eric Lipton, "GOP Insider Fuels Tea Party and Suspicion," *New York Times*, September 18, 2010.

76. "50 Politicos to Watch: Players in a Romney Presidency," *Politico*, July 12, 2012, http://www.politico.com/news/stories/0712/78292.html (accessed August 13, 2014).

77. AAPC Board meeting, March 2014. The author is an academic adviser and board member of this organization.

78. David A. Dulio, *For Better or Worse? How Political Consultants are Changing Elections in the United States* (Albany: State University of New York Press, 2004), 45–46.

79. Ron Lester LinkedIn page, https://www.linkedin.com/profile/view?id=8608525&authType=NAME_SEARCH&authToken=rYuR&locale=en_US&srchid=128144421407956312668&srchindex=1&srchtotal=65&trk=vsrp_people_res_name&trkInfo=VSRPsearchId%3A128144421407956312668%2CVSRPtargetId%3A8608525%2CVSRPcmpt%3Aprimary (accessed August 13, 2014).

80. Kenneth P. Vogel, "'There Is a Racket'—Dems Pressed on Consultant Diversity," *Politico*, May 1, 2014.

81. Mark Z. Barabak, "Kam Kuwata Dies at Fifty-Seven," *Los Angeles Times*, April 12, 2011.

82. Hart Research Associates website, http://www.hartresearch.com/about/bios/yang.html (accessed August 15, 2013).

83. Real Clear Politics, "One of the Most Important Men in Politics You Haven't Heard Of," May 11, 2009, http://www.realclearpolitics.com/articles/2009/05/11/sergio_bendixen_the_man_you_should_but_dont_yet_know_96443.html (accessed August 29, 2014); Bendixen Amandi International website, http://bendixenandamandi.com/ (accessed August 29, 2014).

84. Cathy Booth Thomas, "Lionel Sosa," *Time*, August 22, 2005, 25 Most Influential Hispanics in America; Joe Patoski, "Lionel Sosa: In Spanish or English, He Knows the Meaning of Selling," *Texas Monthly*, September 1996, http://www.texasmonthly.com/content/advertising-%E2%80%A2-lionel-sosa (accessed April 8, 2015); Sosa biographic sketch, AAPC. http://theaapc.org/awards/hall-of-fame/lionel-sosa/ (accessed June 12, 2015)

85. Roger Salazar, telephone interview with author, April 16, 2014.

86. Biographical information from the GrassrootsLab website, http://grassrootslab.com/madrid (accessed July 15, 2015).

Chapter 14

Epigraph quotes from Carville in Mary Matalin and James Carville, *All's Fair: Love, War, and Running for President* (New York: Random House, 1994), 470; from Rove in Karl Rove, *Courage and Consequence: My Life as a Conservative in the Fight* (New York: Simon & Schuster, 2010), 58.

1. Eric Pianin, E. J. Dionne Jr., and Mark Stencel, "Clinton Wins the Carville Primary," *Washington Post*, December 3, 1991, A8.

2. Ed Rollins, with Tom DeFrank, *Bare Knuckles and Back Rooms: My Life in American Politics* (New York: Broadway Books, 1996), 264, 261.

3. The phrases, "read my lips," "kinder, gentler nation" and "thousand points of light" came from speechwriter Peggy Noonan. Peggy Noonan, *What I Saw at the Revolution* (New York: Ballantine Books, 1990), 321–28. Dick Darman, Bob Teeter, Bob Zoellick, and others added suggestions and pored over the text; Bush also made final edits.

4. Jack Germond and Jules Witcover, *Mad as Hell: Revolt at the Ballot Box, 1992* (New York: Warner Books, 1993), 26–27.

5. Charles T. Royer, ed., *Campaign for President: The Managers Look at '92* (Hollis, NH: Hollis Publishing, 1993), 109.

6. Peter Goldman et al., *Quest for the Presidency, 1992* (College Station: Texas A&M University Press, 1994), 318.

7. Ibid., 336.

8. See, for example, Anti-Defamation League, *From Columnist to Candidate: Patrick Buchanan's Religion War* (1992), http://archive.adl.org/special_reports/pb_archive/pb_92-94.pdf.

9. Ann Devroy and Michael Isikoff, "Rollins and Jordan Sign Up With Perot; GOP Shaken by Reagan Ex-Aides Decision," *Washington Post*, June 4, 1992, A1.

10. Ibid.

11. Ed Rollins, *Bare Knuckles and Back Rooms*, ch. 8 (or, as Rollins calls it, "Round 8"); "Dream Team" reference at 232.

12. Ibid., 234–35.

13. Jules Witcover, *No Way to Pick a President: How Money and Hired Guns Have Debased American Elections* (New York: Routledge, 2001), 63.

14. Rollins, *Bare Knuckles and Back Rooms*, 235.

15. Germond and Witcover, *Mad As Hell*, 366.

16. Luce quoted in Royer, *Campaign for President*, 165.

17. Richard L. Berke, "Perot Says He Quit in July to Thwart GOP 'Dirty Tricks,'" *New York Times*, October 26, 1992.

18. See David Brock, Ari Rabin-Havt, and Media Matters, *The Fox Effect: How Roger Ailes Turned a Network into a Propaganda Machine* (New York: Anchor Books, 2012), 34–38.

19. Kerwin Swint, *Dark Genius: The Influential Career of Legendary Political Operative and Fox News Founder Roger Ailes* (New York: Union Square Press, 2008), 109.

20. David W. Moore, "Bush Job Approval Reflects Record 'Rally' Effect," Gallup News Service, September 18, 2001, http://www.gallup.com/poll/4912/bush-job-approval-reflects-record-rally-effect.aspx (accessed July 2, 2014).

21. Matalin and Carville, *All's Fair*, 81.

22. Fred Malek, Memorandum for the President, August 8, 1991, in Goldman et al., *Quest for the Presidency, 1992*, 619.

23. Matalin and Carville, *All's Fair*, 263–64.

24. Ibid., 82.

25. Matalin quoted in Royer, *Campaign for President*, 114.

26. Matalin and Carville, *All's Fair*, 91–92.

27. Ann Devroy, "White House Said to be in Gridlock; Fitzwater Frustrated; Skinner Aide Moore Focus of Criticism," *Washington Post*, April 4, 1992, A1. Also, James Ceasar and Andrew Busch, *Upside Down and Inside Out: The 1992 Elections and American Politics* (Lanham, MD: Rowman & Littlefield, 1993), 36–37.

28. "Job Performance Ratings for President Bush (G.H.W.), 1989–1993" Roper Center, University of Connecticut, http://webapps.ropercenter.uconn.edu/CFIDE/roper/presidential/webroot/presidential_rating_detail.cfm?allRate=True&presidentName=Bush%20(G.H.W.)#.UdRELRzGonZ (accessed April 2, 2013).

29. Devroy, "White House Said to be in Gridlock."

30. Germond and Witcover, *Mad as Hell*, 395–402, at 399.

31. James A. Baker III, with Steve Fiffer, *"Work Hard, Study . . . and Keep Out of Politics:" Adventures and Lessons from an Unexpected Public Life* (New York: Putnam's Sons, 2006), 318.

32. Goldman et al., *Quest for the Presidency, 1992*, 356.

33. Memorandum, April 28, 1992, from Fred Steeper, "Implications of the April Focus Groups," in Goldman et al., *Quest for the Presidency, 1992*, 674–75.

34. Quoted in Adam Nagourney, "'Cultural War' of 1992 Moves in from the Fringe," *New York Times*, August 29, 2012.

35. Dan Quayle, *Standing Firm: A Vice-Presidential Memoir* (New York: HarperCollins/Zondervan, 1994), 346.

36. Bay Buchanan in Royer, *Campaign for President*, 208.

37. Nagourney, "'Cultural War' of 1992."

38. Conversation with Tom Edmonds, September 4, 2014.

39. Brown's pubic service career continued after the 1992 nomination: he was mayor of Oakland (1999–2007), attorney general of California (2007–2011), then the thirty-ninth governor of California (2011–). He had also been the thirty-fourth governor (1975–1983).

40. Germond and Witcover, *Mad as Hell*, 109–111.

41. Devine and Greenberg quoted in Royer, *Campaign for President*, 43.

42. David Maraniss, *First in His Class: A Biography of Bill Clinton* (New York: Simon & Schuster, 1995), 352.

43. Raymond D. Strother, *Falling Up: How a Redneck Helped Invent Political Consulting* (Baton Rouge: Louisiana State University Press, 2003), 207.

44. Ibid., 208–212.

45. Ibid., 206.

46. Bill Clinton, *My Life* (New York: Knopf, 2004), 370.

47. Pianin, Dionne, and Stencel, "Clinton Wins the Carville Primary."

48. Clinton, *My Life*, 383.

49. Michael Takiff, *A Complicated Man: The Life of Bill Clinton as Told by Those Who Know Him* (New Haven, CT: Yale University Press, 2010), 121. For political consultants' reaction to the Gennifer Flowers and the Vietnam draft episodes, see Royer, *Campaign for President*, 53–78.

50. Lloyd Grove, "The Really Disgusted Democrat; Ad Man Scott Miller Is Ready for Perot," *Washington Post*, May 26, 1992, D1.

51. Ibid.

52. Takiff, *A Complicated Man*, 129.

53. Napolitan quoted in Joanne Morreale, *The Presidential Campaign Film: A Critical History* (Westport, CT: Praeger, 1993), 3.

54. Greer quoted in Royer, *Campaign for President*, 267.

55. Baker, "*Work Hard, Study . . . and Keep Out of Politics,*" 319. Joining Baker from the State Department were his top lieutenants: communications director Margaret Tutwiler, deputy chief of staff Robert B. Zoellick, policy adviser Dennis Ross, and political aide Janet G. Mullins.

56. Quoted in Ibid., 320.

57. David Broder, "Baker Team Settles In at White House; Emphasis to Be Put on Swift Decisions," *Washington Post*, August 25, 1992, A5.

58. Herbert S. Parmet, *George Bush: The Life of a Lone Star Yankee* (New Brunswick, NJ: Transaction Books, 2001), 504.

59. Goldman et al., *Quest for the Presidency, 1992*, 526.

60. Tom Rosenstiel, *Strange Bedfellows: How Television and the Presidential Candidates Changed American Politics, 1992* (New York: Hyperion, 1993), 275.

61. Ibid.

62. Baker, "*Work Hard, Study . . . and Keep Out of Politics,*" 333.

63. Goldman et al., *Quest for the Presidency, 1992*, 519.

64. Devlin, "Contrasts in Presidential Campaign Commercials of 1992," 276–77; Goldman et al., *Quest for the Presidency, 1992*, 517–21.

65. Devlin, "Contrasts in Presidential Campaign Commercials of 1992," 290–93.

66. Ibid., 282.

67. Ibid., 276–77.

68. Ibid., 282.

69. Perot's 270 Group emerged from the Dallas-based advertising firm of Temerlin-McClain; the 270 Group was headed by Dennis McClain, the president and

creative director of the firm. Devlin, "Contrasts in Presidential Campaign Commercials of 1992," 282.

70. Kevin Sack, "Perot Charts Poor Economy in 30-Minute TV Talk," *New York Times*, October 7, 1992.

71. Devlin, "Contrasts in Presidential Campaign Commercials of 1992," 283.

72. On the 1992 presidential debates, see William L. Benoit and William T. Wells, *Candidates in Conflict: Persuasive Attack and Defense in the 1992 Presidential Debates* (Tuscaloosa: University of Alabama Press, 1996).

73. Devlin, "Contrasts in Presidential Campaign Commercials of 1992," 273.

74. Paul Fahri, "Two Political Ads Share More Than Fame and Controversy," *Washington Post*, September 2004, A2.

75. Rosenstiel, *Strange Bedfellows*, 316.

76. Devlin, "Contrasts in Presidential Campaign Commercials of 1992," 275.

77. Dan Balz, "The Voracious Democrat: Paul Tully's Hunger for Politics," *Washington Post*, September 26, 1992, D1; see also Chris Black, "Paul Tully: Key Strategist for Clinton, the Democratic Party," *Boston Globe*, September 25, 1992, 75; Robin Toner, "Paul Tully is Dead at 48; Top Democratic Strategist," *New York Times*, September 25, 1992, A21.

78. Black quoted in Royer, *Campaign for President*, 181.

79. Edwin Diamond and Robert A. Silverman, *White House to Your House: Media and Politics in Virtual America* (Cambridge, MA: MIT Press, 1997), 108–9. Chris Hegedus and D. A. Pennebaker, dirs., *The War Room* (1994).

80. James Carville and Paul Begala, "It's the Candidate, Stupid!" *New York Times*, December 4, 1992, A31.

81. Evan Thomas et al., *Back from the Dead: How Clinton Survived the Republican Revolution* (New York: Atlantic Monthly Press, 1997), xiii.

82. Witcover, *No Way to Pick a President*, 64.

83. Thomas, et al., *Back from the Dead*.

84. A good summary of this comes from Kathryn Dunn Tenpas, "The Clinton Re-election Machine: Placing the Party Organization in Peril," *Presidential Studies Quarterly* 28, no. 4: 761–67.

85. Robert E. Denton Jr., ed., *The 1996 Presidential Campaign: A Communication Perspective* (Westport, CT: Praeger, 1998), xiii.

86. Bob Woodward, *The Choice* (New York: Random House, 1996), 89–96

87. Ibid., ch. 19.

88. Ibid., 147.

89. Glenn R. Simpson, "Dole Campaign Has Paid over $1 Million to Firm That Uses Telemarketing to Criticize Opponents," *Wall Street Journal*, March 12, 1996. A20.

90. Thomas B. Edsall, "Calls from Phone Banks Echo Dole's Negative Television Ads," *Washington Post*, February 20, 1996, A4.

91. See Larry J. Sabato, "Presidential Nominations: The Front-Loaded Frenzy of '96," in Larry J. Sabato, ed. *Toward the Millennium: The Elections of 1996* (Boston: Allyn and Bacon, 1997), for Lacy's account of the firing, 76–77.

92. Stephen Glass, "Attack Dogs," *New Republic*, March 25, 1996, 18.

93. Dave Lesher, "Meet a Very Laid-Back Political Maniac," *Los Angeles Times*, August 11, 1996.

94. Roger Simon, *Showtime: The American Political Circus and the Race for the White House* (New York: Times Books, 1998), 28.

95. Ibid., 27.

96. Dole quoted in Tom Rosenstiel, "The Road to Here" in Sabato, ed. *Toward the Millennium*, 2.

97. Simon, *Showtime*, 310, emphasis in the original.

98. Erica J. Seifert, *The Politics of Authenticity in Presidential Campaigns 1976–2008* (Jefferson, NC: McFarland, 2012), 156–57; Kathleen Hall Jamieson and Paul A. Waldman, "Watching the Adwatches," in Larry M. Bartels and Lynn Vavreck,

Campaign Reform: Insights and Evidence (Ann Arbor: University of Michigan Press, 2000), 111.

99. Eric Pooley, "The Mystery Man Who Inspired Dole's Latest Strategy," *Time*, October 7, 1996, 54.

100. Bailey quoted in Charles S. Clark, "Political Consultants: Are Advisers and Handlers Harming Democracy? *CQ Researcher* 6, no. 37 (October 4, 1996).

101. Dennis W. Johnson, *No Place for Amateurs: How Political Consultants Are Reshaping American Democracy*, 2nd ed. (New York: Routledge, 2007), 223.

102. Mike Murphy, "How to Win," *Weekly Standard*, October 21, 1996, 18, in Johnson, *No Place for Amateurs*, 222.

103. Elizabeth Kolbert and Adam Nagourney, "Staff Turmoil Seems a Staple of Dole's Management Style," *New York Times*, September 15, 1996, 1.

104. Morris, *Behind the Oval Office*, 4.

105. Sidney Blumenthal, *The Clinton Wars* (New York: Farrar, Straus and Giroux, 2003), 138–39.

106. Clinton, *Living History*, 251.

107. Steven M. Gillon, *The Pact: Bill Clinton, Newt Gingrich, and the Rivalry That Defined a Generation* (New York: Oxford University Press, 2008), 143.

108. Morris, *Behind the Oval Office*, 80.

109. Clinton, *Living History*, 290.

110. The contempt for Morris among several of the Clinton 1992 consultants was palpable. George Stephanopoulos wrote of his first meeting Morris in 1994: "He was a small sausage of a man encased in a green suit with wide lapels, a wide floral tie, and a wide-collared shirt. His blow-dried pompadour and shiny leather briefcase gave him the look of a B-movie mob lawyer, circa 1975—the kind of guy who gets brained with a baseball bat for double-crossing his boss." *All Too Human: A Political Education* (Boston: Little, Brown, 1999), 331.

111. Douglas E. Schoen, *The Power of the Vote* (New York: William Morrow, 2007), 213.

112. Richard Stengel and Eric Pooley, "Masters of the Message," *Time*, Election Issue 148 (23).

113. Schoen, *The Power of the Vote*, 222.

114. Stengel and Pooley, "Masters of the Message."

115. Ibid.

116. Mark J. Penn, with E. Kinney Zalesne, *Microtrends: The Small Forces behind Tomorrow's Big Changes* (New York: Grand Central Publishing, 2007), xiii.

117. L. Patrick Devlin, "Contrasts in Presidential Campaign Commercials of 1996," *American Behavioral Scientist* 40, no. 8 (August 1997): 1058–84, at 1058.

118. Ibid., 1060.

119. Morris, *Behind the Oval Office*, 139.

120. Devlin, "Contrasts in Presidential Campaign Commercials of 1996," 1063.

121. Stengel and Pooley, "Masters of the Message."

122. Anthony Corrado, "Giving, Spend and 'Soft Money,'" *Journal of Law and Policy* 6, no. 1 (1997): 45–55.

123. Morris, *Behind the Oval Office*, 138.

124. Correspondence from Bob Blaemire, October 2, 2014.

125. Axelrod, *Believer*, 109.

126. *Time*, September 2, 1996.

127. Stengel and Pooley, "Masters of the Message," 18.

128. Witcover, *No Way to Pick a President*, 64.

129. Stengel and Pooley, "Masters of the Message," 24.

130. Thomas et al., *Back from the Dead*, 178.

131. "The First Clinton-Dole Presidential Debate," October 6, 1996, Debate Transcript, Commission on Presidential Debates website, http://www.debates.org/pages/trans96a.html (accessed August 15, 2009). Also, Johnson, *Campaigning in the Twenty-First Century*, ix.

132. Stengel and Pooley, "Masters of the Message."
133. Thomas, et al., *Back from the Dead*, 199.
134. John F. Harris, "Clinton's Campaign Consultants Reaped Millions from TV Ads," *Washington Post*, January 4, 1998, A4.
135. Ibid.

Chapter 15

1. Julie Germany, "Advances in Campaign Technology," in Dennis W. Johnson, *Campaigning for President 2012: Strategy and Tactics* (New York: Routledge, 2013), 80
2. James Coleman, Ernest Heau, Robert Peabody, and Leo Rigsby, "Computers and Election Analysis: The New York Times Project," *Public Opinion Quarterly* 28, no. 3 (Autumn, 1964): 418–46, at 418–19.
3. Ithiel de Sola Pool and Robert Abelson, "The Simulmatics Project," *Public Opinion Quarterly* 25, no. 2 (Summer, 1961): 167–83; James M. Perry, *The New Politics: The Expanding Technology of Political Manipulation* (New York: Clarkson N. Potter, 1968), 165–70. See also Sasha Issenberg, *The Victory Lab: The Secret Science of Winning Campaigns* (New York: Crown Books, 2012), 116–24.
4. Barbara A. Carter, *The Road to City Hall: How John V. Lindsay Became Mayor* (Englewood Cliffs, NJ: Prentice-Hall, 1967), 119.
5. Rex Hardesty, "The Computer's Role in Getting Out the Vote," in Robert Agranoff, ed., *The New Style of Elections Campaigns*, 2nd ed. (Boston: Holbrook Press, 1977), 189–90.
6. Joe Trippi, *The Revolution Will Not Be Televised: Democracy, the Internet, and the Overthrow of Everything* (New York: Regan Books, 2004), 23–24.
7. Phil Noble telephone interview with author, July 26, 2014.
8. Dennis W. Johnson, *No Place for Amateurs: How Political Consultants Are Reshaping American Democracy* (New York: Routledge, 2001), 161.
9. Kenneth P. Vogel, "'Money Bomb': Paul Raises $6 Million in 24-Hour Period," *USA Today*, December 17, 2007.
10. Garrett M. Graff, "Barack Obama: How Content Management and Web 2.0 Helped Win the White House," *Infonomics*, March–April 2009; Jose Antonio Vargas, "Obama Raised Half a Billion Online," *Washington Post*, August 20, 2008.
11. Julie Germany, "Advances in Campaign Technology," in Dennis W. Johnson, ed., *Campaigning for President 2012: Strategy and Tactics* (New York: Routledge, 2013), 89. Clare Foran, "Bernie Sanders's Big Money," *The Atlantic*, March 1, 2016 and Jordan Fabian, "Obama Praises Sanders's Small-Dollar Fundraising Operation," *The Hill*, April 28, 2016.
12. ActBlue website, https://secure.actblue.com/(accessed June 6, 2014).
13. Steven Hill, *Fixing Elections: The Failure of America's Winner Take All Politics* (New York: Routledge, 2002), 158.
14. Chris Cillizza, "Romney's Data Cruncher," *Washington Post*, July 5, 2007.
15. A detailed history of the NCEC is found in William T. Poole, "The National Committee for an Effective Congress," The Heritage Foundation, April 1978, http://thf_media.s3.amazonaws.com/1978/pdf/ia5.pdf (accessed January 7, 2014). From 1956 on, industrialist Sidney H. Scheuer was the president of NCEC.
16. Ibid.
17. Issenberg, *The Victory Lab*, 47.
18. Ibid., 47–49.
19. David Lee Rosenbloom, *The Election Men: Professional Campaign Managers and American Democracy* (New York: Quadrangle Books, 1973), 38–39.
20. Karl Rove, *Courage and Consequence: My Life as a Conservative in the Fight* (New York: Simon & Schuster, 2010), 56.
21. Aristotle website, http://aristotle.com/political-data/voter-lists-online/ (accessed June 6, 2014).

22. Shane D'Aprile, "Labels & Lists Buys VCS," *Campaigns & Elections*, December 2, 2011, http://www.campaignsandelections.com/print/278162/labels-and-lists-buys-vcs.thtml (accessed June 10, 2014).
23. See votermapping.com, http://www.votermapping.com/ (accessed June 10, 2014).
24. Moonshadow Mobile website, http://www.moonshadowmobile.com/category/ground-game/ (accessed June 13, 2014).
25. Dana Milbank, "Virtual Politics," *New Republic*, June 5, 1999.
26. Much of this profile comes from Issenberg, *The Victory Lab*, ch. 2, passim.
27. Hal Malchow, *The New Political Targeting* (Washington, DC: Campaign & Elections, 2003), 1, ii.
28. David Paul Kuhn, "DNC Blunts GOP Microtargeting," *Politico*, May 23, 2008.
29. "Democratic Mega-Firm MSHC Shutting Its Doors," *The Hill*, October 27, 2010.
30. For background on Gage, see Issenberg, *The Victory Lab*, 109–13.
31. Dan Balz, "Getting the Votes—and the Kudos," *Washington Post*, January 1, 2003, A17.
32. Issenberg, *The Victory Lab*, 114.
33. Terrence McCoy, "The Creepiness Factor: How Obama and Romney Are Getting to Know You," *The Atlantic*, April 2012.
34. Catalist website, http://www.catalist.us/news (accessed June 15, 2014). Robert Blaemire, "The Evolution of Microtargeting," in James A. Thurber and Candice J. Nelson, eds., *Campaigns and Elections American Style*, 4th ed. (Boulder, CO: Westview, 2014), 217–36.
35. Strasma quoted in Tom Schaller, "Obama's Top Targeter Bullish on Montana and Worried about Gingrich," FiveThirtyEight website, June 8, 2009, http://fivethirtyeight.com/2009/06/obamas-top-targeter-bullish-on-montana.html (accessed June 15, 2014).
36. McCoy, "The Creepiness Factor."
37. Ibid.
38. Benny Evangelista, "Pandora Tailors Political Ads Based on Music Tastes," *SFGate*, February 22, 2014, http://www.sfgate.com/technology/article/Pandora-tailors-political-ads-based-on-music-5258940.php (accessed August 21, 2014); Elizabeth Dwoskin, "Pandora Thinks It Knows If You Are a Republican," *Wall Street Journal*, February 13, 2014, http://online.wsj.com/news/articles/SB10001424052702304315004579381393567130078#printMode (accessed August 21, 2014).
39. Clinton quoted in Mitch Betts, "Candidates Use Databases, Mapping Technology to Target Voters," *Computerworld*, October 30, 2000.
40. Commentary: Joe Rospars, accompanying article, "Is the Key to Number 10 a High Social Standing?" *Marketing Week*, April 22, 2010, http://www.marketingweek.co.uk/analysis/essential-reads/is-the-key-to-number-10-a-high-social-standing/3011937.article (accessed June 12, 2014).
41. Matt Schudel, "Douglas L. Bailey, Founder of Political News Digest, Dies at 79," *Washington Post*, June 11, 2013.
42. Mark Halperin and John F. Harris, *The Way to Win: Taking the White House in 2008* (New York: Random House, 2006), 61.
43. Dennis W. Johnson, *Campaigning in the Twenty- First Century: A Whole New Ballgame?* (New York: Routledge, 2011), 12, 105.
44. Bruce Bimber and Richard Davis, *Campaigning Online: The Internet in U.S. Elections* (New York: Oxford University Press, 2003), ch. 2; see also Steven M. Schneider and Kristen A. Foot, "Web Campaigning by U.S. Presidential Primary Candidates in 2000 and 2004," in Andrew Paul Williams and John C. Tedesco, eds., *The Internet Election* (Lanham, MD: Rowman & Littlefield, 2006); Dennis W. Johnson, "Campaigning on the Internet," in Stephen C. Craig, ed., *The Electoral Challenge: Theory Meets Practice* (Washington, DC: CQ Books, 2006), ch. 7.
45. Michael Cornfield, *Politics Moves Online: Campaigning and the Internet* (New York: Century Foundation Press, 2004), 27.

46. Johnson, *Campaigning in the Twenty-first Century*, 12–16.
47. Andrew Rasiej and Micah L. Sifry, "The Web: 2008's Winning Ticket," *Politico*, November 12, 2008. Obviously, the comparison is a rough one, because it does not take into account the differentials in airing commercials, their placement, and other factors.
48. Rospars, commentary.
49. The Caucus, http://thecaucus.blogs.nytimes.com; The Fix, http://blog/ washingtonpost.com/thefix; Political Hotsheet, http://www.cbsnews.com/ politics; Redstate.com, http://www.redstate.com; *Huffington Post*, http://www. huffingtonpost.com/; MyDD, http://mydd.com; and Daily KOS, http://dailykos. com.
50. Robert Draper, "The Late Adopters," *New York Times Magazine*, February 17, 2013.
51. NGP-VAN website, http://www.ngpvan.com/ (accessed December 20, 2015); Rosalind S. Helderman, Anne Gearan, and John Wagner, "DNC Penalizes Sanders Campaign for Improper Access of Clinton Voter Data," *Washington Post*, December 18, 2015.
52. Germany, "Advances in Campaign Technology," 87–89.
53. Karen Jagoda and Nick Nyhan, *E-Voter 98: Measuring the Impact of Online Advertising for a Political Candidate: A Case Study*, 2nd ed. (Westhill Partners, January 1999), http://evoterinstitute.com/wp-content/uploads/2009/03/ evoter98report.pdf (accessed June 12, 2014).
54. Michael Cornfield and Kate Kaye, "Online Political Advertising: The Prehistoric Era Continues," 720 Strategies, http://www.720strategies.com/site/ page/online_political_advertising_the_prehistoric_era_continues (accessed June 10, 2014).
55. Chris Anderson, "The Long Tail," *Wired*, October 2004, http://archive. wired.com/wired/archive/12.10/tail.html (accessed June 10, 2014); Chris Anderson, *The Long Tail: Why The Future of Business is Selling Less of More* (New York: Hyperion, 2006); Josh Koster, "Long-Tail Nontargeting," *Politics*, February 2009, http://www.politicsmagazine.com/magazine-issues/february- 2009/long-tail-nanotargeting/ (accessed June 10, 2014).
56. Johnson, *Campaigning in the Twenty-First Century*, 20. Germany, "Advances in Campaign Technology," 85.
57. Pew Research Center for the People and the Press, "Methodology: Collecting Survey Data," n.d., Pew website, http://people-press.org/methodology/ collecting/#3 (accessed June 17, 2014); Scott Keeter, Courtney Kennedy, Michael Dimock, Jonathan Best, and Peyton Craighill, "Gauging the Impact of Growing Nonresponse on Estimates from a National RDD Telephone Survey," *Public Opinion Quarterly* 70, no. 5 (2006): 759–79.
58. Donald P. Green and Alan S. Gerber, "Enough Already with Random Digit Dialing: A Proposal to Use Registration-Based Sampling to Improve Pre-Election Polling," Gallup Conference on Improving the Accuracy of Polling, Washington, DC, May 2–4, 2002.
59. Monica Anderson, "Technology Device Ownership: 2015," Pew Research Center, October 29, 2015, www.pewinternet.org/2015/10/29/technology- device-ownership-2015/pi_2015-10-29_device-ownership_0-01/ (accessed May 19, 2016).
60. Scott Keeter, "How Serious Is Polling's Cell-Only Problem?" Pew Research Center Publications (June 20, 2007), http://pewresearch.org/pubs/515/polling- cell-only-problem (accessed June 17, 2014); see also Mark Mellman, "Pollsters' Cellphonobia," *The Hill*, May 23, 2007.
61. Carl Bialik, "Grading the Pollsters," *Wall Street Journal*, November 6, 2006.
62. Johnson, *Campaigning in the Twenty-First Century*, 73–74.
63. "U.S. Online MR Gains Drop," *Inside Research* 20, no. 1 (2009): 11–134.

64. Benenson quoted in Thomas Crampton, "About Online Surveys, Traditional Pollsters Are: (C) Somewhat Disappointed," *New York Times*, May 31, 2007.

65. Mark Blumenthal, "The Case for Robo-Pollsters," *National Journal Online*, September 14, 2009, http://www.nationaljournal.com/njonline/print_friendly. php?ID=mp_20090911_5838 (June 14, 2014).

66. Gary C. Jacobson, "The Polls: Polarized Opinion in the States: Partisan Differences in Approval Ratings of Governors, Senators, and George W. Bush," *Presidential Studies Quarterly* 36, no. 4 (December 2006): 732–57, at 733.

Chapter 16

Bonner epigraph quote from Stephen Engelberg, "A New Breed of Hired Hands Cultivates Grass-Roots Anger," *New York Times*, March 17, 1993, A1.

1. Douglas A. Lathrop, "Political Consultants, Interest Groups and Issue Advocacy Work: A Lasting Relationship," in Dennis W. Johnson, ed., *Routledge Handbook on Political Management* (New York: Routledge, 2008), 452.

2. Barry Siegel, "Spin Doctors to the World." *Los Angeles Times Magazine*, November 24, 1991.

3. Douglas E. Schoen, *The Power of the Vote: Electing Presidents, Overthrowing Dictators, and Promoting Democracy around the World* (New York: William Morrow, 2007), 195

4. Ibid., 197.

5. Ibid., 207

6. Alex Castellanos, "Subaru for President: Look Who's Running Negative Advertising!" *Advertising Age*, April 20, 1992, 24.

7. Quoted in Elizabeth Drew, "Bush's Weird Tax Cut," *New York Review of Books*, August 1991.

8. Edward T. Walker, *Grassroots for Hire: Public Affairs Consultants in American Democracy* (New York: Cambridge, 2014).

9. Bankhead quoted in C. Estes Kefauver and J. Levin, *A Twentieth-Century Congress* (New York: Duell, Sloan and Pearce, 1947), 171–72; Kefauver was one of the freshman members of Congress.

10. Edward A. Grefe and Martin Linsky, *The New Corporate Activism: Harnessing the Power of Grassroots Tactics for Your Organization* (New York: McGraw-Hill, 1995), 141.

11. Ibid., 151.

12. Ibid., 152.

13. See Dwight M. Jaffe and Thomas Russell, "The Regulation of Auto Insurance in California," Haas School of Business, University of California, Berkeley, faculty papers, 2001, http://faculty.haas.berkeley.edu/jaffee/papers/Auto2.pdf (accessed August 24, 2014).

14. Kay Lehman Schlozman and John T. Tierney, "More of the Same: Washington Pressure Group Activity in a Decade of Change," *Journal of Politics* 45, no. 2 (1983): 351–77. Also, Ken Kollman, *Outside Lobbying: Public Opinion and Interest Group Strategies* (Princeton, NJ: Princeton University Press, 1998).

15. US Chamber of Commerce, Press Release, "U.S. Chamber Grassroots Sets a Record," December 22, 2009, https://www.uschamber.com/press-release/us-chamber-grassroots-sets-new-record (accessed August 25, 2014).

16. "Astroturf," *SourceWatch Encyclopedia*, http://www.sourcewatch.org/index. php?title=AstroTurf (accessed September 22, 2009). SourceWatch is a project of the Center for Media and Democracy, a Madison, Wisconsin–based nonprofit, nonpartisan public interest organization.

17. Bonner quoted in William Greider, *Who Will Tell the People: The Betrayal of American Democracy* (New York: Simon and Schuster, 1993), 3.

18. MoveOn.org website, http://front.moveon.org/about (accessed December 6, 2013).

19. Janie Lorber and Eric Lipton, "GOP Insider Fuels Tea Party and Suspicion," *New York Times*, September 18, 2010. Matea Gold, "Tea Party PACs Reap Money for Midterms, but Spend Little on Candidates," *Washington Post*, April 26, 2014; Stephanie Mencimer, "Tea Party Patriots Investigated: 'They Use You and Abuse You,'" *Mother Jones*, February 14, 2011, http://www.motherjones.com/politics/2011/02/tea-party-patriots-investigated (accessed July 16, 2015).

20. Ben Smith, "The Summer of Astroturf," *Politico*, August 21, 2009.

21. David Segal, "PR Firm Retreats on Telegrams; Phone Companies' Lobbying Tarnished," *Washington Post*, September 16, 1995. A subcontractor, NTS Marketing, Inc., a telemarketing and fundraising firm, had responsibility for calling individuals and getting permission to send out telegrams to Congress on their behalf.

22. Eliza Newlin Carney, "A Grassroots Cautionary Tale," *National Journal*, October 19, 2009.

23. Thomas P. Lyon and John W. Maxwell, "Astroturf Lobbying," *Journal of Economics and Management Strategy* 13, no. 4 (Winter 2004): 561–97.

24. "Misinformation Campaign Defeats Grassroots Lobbying Disclosure in Senate," *OMB Watch*, January 23, 2007, http://www.ombwatch.org/node/3151 (accessed February 2, 2014).

25. Edward A. Grefe, interview with author, Washington, DC, March 20, 2013. James Kiss and Martin Ryan Haley, "Larger Stakes in Statehouse Lobbying," *Harvard Business Review* 52 no. 1 (January–February 1974): 125–35.

26. Edward A. Grefe, *Fighting to Win: Business Political Power* (New York: Law & Business, 1981); Edward A. Grefe and Martin Linsky, *The New Corporate Activism: Harnessing the Power of Grassroots Tactics for Your Organization* (New York: McGraw-Hill, 1995).

27. Ken Silverstein, "Hello. I'm Calling This Evening to Mislead You," *Mother Jones*, November/December 1997, http://www.motherjones.com/politics/1997/11/hello-im-calling-evening-mislead-you?page=2 (accessed August 26, 2014).

28. For a detailed analysis of the health-care debate and political advertising, see Darrell M. West, Diane Heith, and Chris Goodwin, "Harry and Louise Go to Washington: Political Advertising and Health Care Reform," *Journal of Health Politics, Policy and Law* 21, no. 1 (Spring 1996): 35–68.

29. Haynes Johnson and David S. Broder, *The System: The American Way of Politics at the Breaking Point* (Boston: Little, Brown, 1996), 195.

30. Ibid., 199.

31. Johnson and Broder, *The System*, 205.

32. Ibid.

33. West, Heith, and Goodwin, "Harry and Louise Go to Washington," 47.

34. Annenberg Public Policy Center, "The Role of Advertising in the Health Care Reform Debate, Part One: A Preliminary Report of Research Funded by the Robert Wood Johnson Foundation" (Philadelphia: Annenberg Public Policy Center, University of Pennsylvania, July 18, 1994). University of Pennsylvania release.

35. Interview with Ben Goddard, Hedrick Smith blog, n.d., http://www.hedricksmith.com/site_powergame/files/goddard.html (accessed April 15, 2016.

36. Quoted in Johnson and Broder, *The System*, 214.

37. Interview with Bill Plante, CBS Smoke-filled Room, May 30, 2000, http://www.cbsnews.com/news/archive-bill-mcinturff/ (accessed March 31, 2014).

38. Jeffrey Birnbaum, "Returning to the Genre He Started," *Washington Post*, November 29, 2004, E1.

39. "Declaring War on Wal-Mart," *Bloomberg Businessweek*, February 6, 2005, http://www.businessweek.com/stories/2005-02-06/declaring-war-on-wal-mart

40. John Harwood and Gerald F. Seib, *Pennsylvania Avenue: Profiles in Backroom Power* (New York: Random House, 2008), 176.

41. Michael Barbaro, "Wal-Mart Tires to Enlist Image Help," *New York Times*, May 12, 2006; see also Jeffrey Goldberg, "Selling Wal-Mart," *The New Yorker*, April 2, 2007.

42. Harwood and Seib, *Pennsylvania Avenue*, 180–81; Michael Barbaro, "Wal-Mart Dismisses Adviser Who Created GOP Ad," *New York Times*, October 28, 2006.

43. Timothy Egan, "The Corporate Daddy: Walmart, Starbucks, and the Fight against Inequality," *New York Times*, June 19, 2014.

44. Ibid.

45. Steve Coll, *Private Empire: ExxonMobil and American Power* (New York: Penguin, 2012). See also Naomi Oreskes and Erik M. Conway, *Merchants of Doubt: How a Handful of Scientists Obscured the Truth on Issues from Tobacco to Global Warming* (New York: Bloomsbury, 2010).

46. "Steve Coll: How Exxon Shaped the Climate Debate," PBS *Frontline, Climate of Doubt*, October 23, 2012, http://www.pbs.org/wgbh/pages/frontline/environment/climate-of-doubt/steve-coll-how-exxon-shaped-the-climate-debate/ (accessed August 12, 2014). See also, Oreskes and Conway, *Merchants of Doubt*.

47. Jane Mayer, "Covert Operations," *The New Yorker*, August 30, 2010.

48. Ibid. In 2013, Koch Industries was ranked 14th in the Political Economy Research Institute's annual listing.

49. "Koch Brothers: Funding $67,042,064 to Groups Denying Climate Change Science Since 1997," Greenpeace, n.d., http://www.greenpeace.org/usa/en/campaigns/global-warming-and-energy/polluterwatch/koch-industries/ (accessed August 12, 2104).

50. Robert J. Brulle, "Institutionalizing Delay: Foundation Funding and the Creation of U.S. Climate Change Counter-Movement Organizations," *Climatic Change* 122, no. 4 (February 2014): 681–94, http://drexel.edu/%7E/media/Files/now/pdfs/Institutionalizing%20Delay%20-%20Climatic%20Change.ashx (accessed August 24, 2014).

51. Darren Goode, "GOP Climate Tack: Talk Jobs, Not Science," *Politico*, June 27, 2013, http://www.politico.com/story/2013/06/gop-climate-tack-talk-jobs-not-science-93482.html (accessed August 26, 2014).

52. Joe Klein, *Politics Lost: How American Democracy Was Trivialized by People Who Think You're Stupid* (New York: Doubleday, 2006), 141 (see ch. 10, n. 90).

53. Transcript of Matthew Reese oral history, interviewed by John Franzén. American Association of Political Consultants Interview Collection; George Washington University Libraries, Part 1 of 2, December 12, 1996, 2.

54. Ibid., 3.

55. Jeffrey H. Birnbaum, "Political Pollsters Don't Live on Elections Alone," *Washington Post*, November 15, 2004, E1.

56. Ibid.

57. Doug Schoen and Scott Rasmussen, *Mad as Hell: How the Tea Party Movement Is Fundamentally Remaking Our Two-Party System* (New York: Harper, 2010).

58. "Our Heritage," from the Harris Interactive website, http://www.harrisinteractive.com/AboutUs/Heritage.aspx (accessed February 2, 2014).

59. Powell-Tate website, http://www.powelltate.com/about-us/our-people/ (accessed June 1, 2013); and Adam Bernstein, "Trusted Press Aide Helped Carter Reach White House," *Washington Post*, September 15, 1969.

60. Louis Jacobson, "Moving Beyond Attack Ads," *National Journal*, June 22, 2002, 1894.

Chapter 17

Epigraph quotes from Matthew Dowd in Kathleen Hall Jamieson, ed., *Electing the President 2004: The Insiders' View* (Philadelphia: University of Pennsylvania Press, 2006), 25; Joe Trippi, *The Revolution Will Not Be Televised: Democracy, the Internet, and the Overthrow of Everything* (New York: Regan Books, 2004), 16.

1. Stuart Stevens, *The Big Enchilada: Campaign Adventures with the Cockeyed Optimist from Texas Who Won the Biggest Prize in Politics* (New York: Free Press, 2001), 24.
2. Samuel L. Popkin, *The Candidate: What It Takes to Win—and Hold—the White House* (New York: Oxford University Press, 2012), 7.
3. Douglas E. Schoen, *The Power of the Vote: Electing Presidents, Overthrowing Dictators, and Promoting Democracy around the World* (New York: William Morrow, 2007), 342.
4. Ibid.
5. Anne E. Kornblut, "Clinton's PowerPointer," *Washington Post*, April 30, 2007, http://www.washingtonpost.com/wp-dyn/content/article/2007/04/29/AR2007042901661.html.
6. Joshua Marshall, "Coelho and Company," *American Prospect*, December 19, 2001, http://prospect.org/article/coelho-and-company (accessed May 2, 2014); for example, Richard L. Berke, "As Gore Slips, Advisers Second-Guess Early Moves," *New York Times*, October 9, 1999.
7. Marshall, "Coelho and Company."
8. Stanley Greenberg in Kathleen Hall Jamieson and Paul Waldman, eds., *Electing the President 2000: The Insider's View* (Philadelphia: University of Pennsylvania Press, 2001), 87.
9. Ibid., 80.
10. Donna Brazile, *Cooking with Grease: Stirring the Pots in American Politics* (New York: Simon & Schuster, 2004), 215
11. Marshall, "Coelho and Company."
12. Melinda Henneberger, "At the Helm of Gore's Campaign, 2 Old Friends Who Don't Speak," *New York Times*, July 9, 1999.
13. Robert Shrum, *No Excuses: Concessions of a Serial Campaigner* (New York: Simon & Schuster, 2007), 311 (see ch. 10, n. 28).
14. Richard L. Berke, "Gore's Campaign Struggling to Regain Primary Energy," *New York Times*, May 15, 2000.
15. Brazile, *Cooking with Grease*, 237.
16. Ceci Connelly, "Gore Aid Dealt from Bottom of Race Deck, Powell Says," *Washington Post*, January 7, 2000, A4.
17. Kornblut, "Clinton's PowerPointer."
18. Dan Balz, "Bush's 'Iron Triangle' Points Way to Washington," *Washington Post*, July 23, 1999, C1.
19. Matthew Dowd quoted in Jamieson and Waldman, eds., *Electing the President 2000*, 15.
20. Quoted in Elizabeth Drew, *Citizen McCain* (New York: Simon & Schuster, 2002), 5.
21. Fletcher quoted in Richard Gooding, "The Trashing of John McCain," *Vanity Fair*, November 2004, http://www.vanityfair.com/politics/features/2004/11/mccain200411.print (accessed May 9, 2014).
22. Andy Barr, "Karl Rove Denies Roll in John McCain Rumor in South Carolina," *Politico*, March 8, 2010.
23. Gooding, "The Trashing of John McCain." The telemarketer quotes are illustrative, and may not have been the exact words spoken.
24. Richard H. Davis, "The Anatomy of a Smear Campaign," *Boston Globe*, March 21, 2004.
25. John McCain, with Mark Salter, *Worth the Fighting For* (New York: Random House, 2002), quoted in Gooding, "The Trashing of John McCain."
26. Joe Klein, *Politics Lost: How American Democracy Was Trivialized by People Who Think You're Stupid* (New York: Doubleday, 2006), 149 (see ch. 10, n. 90).
27. Gooding, "The Trashing of John McCain."
28. Brandon C. Waite, "E-mail and Electoral Fortunes: Obama's Campaign Internet Insurgency," in John Allen Hendricks and Robert E. Denton Jr., *Communicator-in-Chief: How Barack Obama Used New Media Technology to Win the White House* (Lanham, MD: Lexington Books, 2010), 106.

29. Kathleen Frankovic in Jamieson and Waldman, eds., *Electing the President 2000*, 123.

30. Bob Shrum in ibid., 109–110.

31. Karl Rove, *Courage and Consequence: My Life as a Conservative in the Fight* (New York: Threshold Editions, 2010) 177.

32. L. Patrick Devlin, "Contrasts in Presidential Campaign Commercials of 2000," *American Behavioral Scientist* 44, no. 12 (August 2001): 2338–69, at 2338.

33. Bill Knapp in Jamieson and Waldman, eds., *Electing the President 2000*, 167.

34. Ibid., 167–68.

35. Devlin, "Contrasts in Presidential Campaign Commercials of 2000," 2342.

36. Museum of the Moving Image, "Living Room Candidate," http://www.livingroomcandidate.org/commercials/2000 (accessed May 13, 2014).

37. Klein, *Politics Lost*, 20–21.

38. Shrum, *No Excuses*, 362–63.

39. Devlin, "Contrasts in Presidential Campaign Commercials of 2000," 2342.

40. "Trust," https://www.youtube.com/watch?v=6FxL242-z6I (accessed May 10, 2010).

41. "Priority," https://www.youtube.com/watch?v=2NPKxhfFQMs (accessed May 12, 2014).

42. Richard L. Berke, "Democrats See, and Smell, Rats in G.O.P. Ad," *New York Times*, September 12, 2000.

43. Data compiled by Daron R. Shaw, *The Race to 270: The Electoral College and the Campaign Strategies of 2000 and 2004* (Chicago: University of Chicago Press, 2006), 79–80.

44. Devlin, "Contrasts in Presidential Campaign Commercials of 2000," 2341.

45. Ibid.

46. Karl Rove in Jamieson and Waldman, eds., *Electing the President 2000*, 219.

47. James Moore and Wayne Slater, *Bush's Brain: How Karl Rove Made George W. Bush Presidential* (Hoboken, NJ: John Wiley, 2003), 261–68, quote at 264.

48. Thomas N. Edmonds, interview with author, March 13, 2014.

49. Moore and Slater, *Bush's Brain*, 268.

50. John Micklethwait and Adrian Wooldridge, *The Right Nation: Conservative Power in America* (New York: Penguin, 2005), 177.

51. Devlin, "Contrasts in Presidential Campaign Commercials of 2000," 2341.

52. One elector in the District of Columbia left her ballot blank, protesting the fact that the District lacked voting status in the US Congress. Presumably, that electoral vote would have gone to Gore. David Stout, "The 43rd President: The Electoral College, The Electors Vote, and the Surprises Are Few," *New York Times*, December 19, 2000.

53. Jeffrey Toobin, *Too Close to Call: The Thirty-Six-Day Battle to Decide the 2000 Election* (New York: Random House, 2001), 280.

54. Ibid.

55. Shrum, *No Excuses*, xiv.

56. James Carville, "Karl Rove," *Time*, April 18, 2005, 113.

57. David E. Rosenbaum, "A Gephardt Staff Member Finds a New Home," *New York Times*, January 24, 2004.

58. His partners were Steve McMahon and Mark Squier, the son of media consultant Robert Squier.

59. Dennis W. Johnson, *Campaigning in the Twenty-First Century: A Whole New Ballgame?* (New York: Routledge, 2011), 6.

60. See Dennis W. Johnson, *No Place for Amateurs: How Political Consultants Are Reshaping American Democracy* (New York: Routledge, 2001), 139–40. From an insider's point of view, see Trippi, *The Revolution Will Not be Televised*. Michael Silberman was in charge of the Meetup campaign in the Dean operation.

61. Shrum, *No Excuses*, 325.

62. "Courage," Museum of the Moving Image, Living Room Candidate, http://www.livingroomcandidate.org/commercials/2004/filter/party (accessed May 2, 2014).

63. David W. Jones in Jamieson, ed., *Electing the President 2004*, 235.

64. Whouley quoted in Andrew E. Busch, "The Reemergence of the Iowa Caucuses: A New Trend, an Aberration, or a Useful Reminder?" in William G. Mayer, ed., *The Making of the Presidential Candidates 2008* (Lanham, Md.: Rowman & Littlefield, 2008), 39.

65. David M. Halbfinger and Adam Nagourney, "Kerry Dismisses Campaign Chief," *New York Times*, November 11, 2003.

66. Evan Thomas and staff of Newsweek, *Election 2004: How Bush Won and What You Can Expect in the Future* (New York: Public Affairs, 2004), 7; also Klein, *Politics Lost*, 206–7.

67. Ken Auletta, "Kerry's Brain," *The New Yorker*, September 20, 2004.

68. Klein, *Politics Lost*, 206–7.

69. Kerry quoted in Karen Tumulty, "The Miracle Worker," *Time*, March 8, 2004.

70. Rove, *Courage and Consequence*, 363.

71. Matthew Dowd in Jamieson, ed., *Electing the President 2004*, 24.

72. Donilon in ibid., 59.

73. Quoted in Thomas B. Edsall, *Building Red America: The New Conservative Coalition and the Drive for Permanent Power* (New York: Basic Books, 2006), 141.

74. "Troops," Museum of the Moving Image, Living Room Candidate, http://www.livingroomcandidate.org/commercials/2004 (accessed May 15, 2014).

75. "Windsurfer," Museum of the Moving Image, Living Room Candidate, http://www.livingroomcandidate.org/commercials/2004 (accessed May 15, 2014).

76. "This Land Is Your Land," lyrics written by Gregg and Evan Spiridellis, www.jibjab.com/originals/this_land, accessed December 27, 2013.

77. Many of the Internet parody sites were captured by the Institute for Politics, Democracy & the Internet, George Washington University, "Under the Radar and Over the Top: Online Political Videos in the 2004 Election."

78. Johnson, *No Place for Amateurs*, 141.

79. Paul Fahri, "Two Political Ads Share More than Fame and Controversy," *Washington Post*, September 7, 2004, A2.

80. For background on Swift Boat Veterans for Truth, see Albert L. May, "Swift Boat Vets in 2004: Press Coverage of an Independent Campaign," *First Amendment Law Review* 4 (2005): 79; and Kate Zernike and Jim Rutenberg, "Friendly Fire: The Birth of an Attack on Kerry," *New York Times*, August 20, 2004, A1; "Any Questions?" in Museum of the Moving Image, Living Room Candidate, http://www.livingroomcandidate.org/commercials/2004/filter/ind (accessed August 15, 2013).

81. Chris Landers, "Consultant Profile: Stevens Reed Curcio & Potholm," The Center for Public Integrity, September 26, 2006, www.publicintegrity.org/2006/09/26/6651/consultant-profile-stevens-reed-curcio-potholm (accessed May 3, 2014).

82. L. Patrick Devlin, "Contrasts in Presidential Campaign Commercials of 2004," *American Behavioral Scientist* 49, no. 2 (October 2005), 293.

83. Thomas, *Election 2004*, 120.

84. Chris LaCivita in Jamieson, ed., *Electing the President 2004*, 186.

85. Quoted in Ibid. Chris Landers, "Consultant Profile: Stevens Reed Curcio & Potholm."

86. Auletta, "Kerry's Brain."

87. Shrum, *No Excuses*, 489.

88. Rove, *Courage and Consequence*, 389–90.

89. McCarthy, Hennings, Whalen, Inc., website http://www.mhmediadc.com/larry-mccarthy.aspx (accessed August 12, 2014).

90. Brian McCabe in Jamieson, ed., *Electing the President 2004*, 179–83; Eric Boehlert, "The TV Ad that Put Bush over the Top," Salon, November 5, 2004, http://www.salon.com/2004/11/05/bush_ads_5/ (accessed May 19, 2014).

91. Shrum, *No Excuses*, 487.

92. Cutter would make a comeback in 2008, playing an important role as Michelle Obama's chief of staff, and then in several significant roles in the White House.
93. Thomas, *Election 2004*, 128–37.
94. Devlin, "Contrasts in Presidential Campaign Commercials of 2004," 279.
95. Ibid., 298–99.
96. Ibid., 281. Also on the team were media planner Mike Shannon, producer Ashley O'Connor, and Matthew Taylor.
97. Devlin, "Contrasts in Presidential Campaign Commercials of 2004," 299.
98. Thomas, *Election 2004*, 85.
99. Devlin, "Contrasts in Presidential Campaign Commercials of 2004," 312.
100. Ibid.
101. Terrence McCoy, "The Creepiness Factor: How Obama and Romney are Getting to Know You," *The Atlantic*, April 2012.
102. Devlin, "Contrasts in Presidential Campaign Commercials of 2004," 366.
103. Quoted in Edsall, *Building Red America*, 77.
104. David Paul Kuhn, "DNC Blunts GOP Microtargeting," *Politico*, May 23, 2008.
105. Edsall, *Building Red America*, 77.
106. Rove, *Courage and Consequence*, 365.
107. Ibid., 364.
108. Ibid., 365.
109. Ibid., 377.
110. Ibid.
111. Mehlman's decision to tell close friends and family was first reported in Marc Ambinder, "Bush Campaign Chief and Former RNC Chair Ken Mehlman: I'm Gay," *The Atlantic*, August 25, 2010; and Richard Socarides, "Ken Mehlman's Gay Marriage Mission," *The New Yorker*, February 26, 2013.
112. James Moore and Wayne Slater, *The Architect: Karl Rove and the Master Plan for Absolute Power* (New York: Crown, 2006), 72–75; and "Dan Gurley, from RNC Staffer to LGBT Activist," interview with Terry Gross, National Public Radio, May 6, 2009, http://www.npr.org/template/story/story.php?storyId=103847773 (accessed December 26, 2013).
113. Moore and Slater, *The Architect*, 135. Writing in 2010, Karl Rove said this about his father and his critics: "To this day, I have no idea if my father was gay. And, frankly, I don't care. He was my father, with whom I had a wonderful relationship and whom I deeply loved. The writers who are fascinated with whether my father was gay are really more interested in implying that all people who have gay relatives or friends must support same-sex marriage; otherwise they are bigots and hypocrites. And if one of these people happens to be Karl Rove, so much the better." Rove, *Courage and Consequence*, 20.
114. Moore and Slater, *The Architect*, 107.
115. Mark Leibovich, "Knock On Wood, Cross Your Fingers, and Don't Let Shrum Pay You a Compliment," *New York Times*," September 29, 2008.
116. Mark Crispin Miller, *Fooled Again: How the Right Stole the 2004 Election & Why They'll Steal the Next One Too (Unless We Stop Them)* (New York: Basic Books, 2005). Interview with Mark Crispin Miller and Mark Hertsgaard, "Was the 2004 Election Stolen? A Debate on Ohio One Year After Bush's Victory," interviewed by Amy Goodman and Juan Gonzalez, *Democracy Now!*, http://www.democracynow.org/2005/11/4/was_the_2004_election_stolen_a (accessed May 13, 2014).
117. Mark Hertsgaard, "Recounting Ohio. Was Ohio Stolen? You Might Not Like the Answer," *Mother Jones*, November 2005, http://www.motherjones.com/media/2005/11/recounting-ohio (accessed May 14, 2014).
118. Mellman in Jamieson, ed., *Electing the President 2004*, 138. On the reasons for Bush's victory, see also, James E. Campbell, "Why Bush Won the Presidential Election of 2004: Incumbency, Ideology, Terrorism and Turnout," *Political Science Quarterly* 120, no. 2 (Summer 2005): 219–41.

Chapter 18

Epigraph quotes from Napolitan in Joseph Napolitan, "An American in Paris," *Campaigns & Elections*, May/June 1989, 64; Schoen and Morris from Mark Stevenson, "America's Newest Export Industry: Political Advisers," Associated Press, January 29, 2000.

1. Larry J. Sabato, *The Rise of Political Consultants* (New York: Basic Books, 1981), 58.
2. Walter Shapiro, "Mad Men: Is the Golden Age of Political Consulting Over?" Review of *Alpha Dogs*, by James Harding (Farrar, Straus and Giroux, 2008), *Democracy: A Journal of Ideas*, Fall 2008, 107, http://democracyjournal.org/magazine/10/mad-men/.
3. John Maggs, "Not-So-Innocents Abroad," *National Journal*, June 17, 2000, 1906. On his work for Clinton and the international clients, see Stanley B. Greenberg, *Dispatches from the War Room: In the Trenches with Five Extraordinary Leaders* (New York: Thomas Dunne Books, 2009).
4. On the role and influence of political consultants internationally, see Gerald Sussman, *Global Electioneering: Campaign Consulting, Communications, and Corporate Financing* (Lanham, MD: Rowman & Littlefield, 2005); and Fritz Plasser, with Gunda Plasser, *Global Political Campaigning: A Worldwide Analysis of Campaign Professionals and Their Practices* (Westport, CT: Praeger, 2002).
5. See Samuel F. Huntington, *The Third Wave* (Norman: University of Oklahoma Press, 1996). Francis Fukuyama in the late 1980s wrote of the "end of history" and the achievement of liberal democracy throughout Europe, the Americas, Japan, and other countries. Fukuyama argued that all nations are bound, sooner or later, at this "end of history," with the emergence of liberal democratic institutions. Francis Fukuyama, *The End of History and the Last Man* (New York: Free Press, 1992), and his earlier essay, "The End of History?" *National Interest* 16 (Summer 1989): 3–18. For a more sobering view, see Benjamin R. Barber, *Jihad vs. McWorld: How Globalism and Tribalism are Reshaping the World* (New York: Ballantine Books, 1995). On patterns of modern campaigning, see David L. Swanson and Paolo Mancini, "Patterns of Modern Electoral Campaigning and Their Consequences," in Swanson and Mancini, eds., *Politics, Media, and Modern Democracy: An International Study of Innovations in Electoral Campaigning and Their Consequences* (Westport, CT: Praeger, 1996), 247–76.
6. Freedom House survey, "Freedom in the World, 1995–1996," reported in Barbara Crossette, "Globally, Majority Rules," *New York Times*, August 4, 1996; "Freedom in the World 2014," Freedom House, http://www.freedomhouse.org/report/freedom-world/freedom-world-2014#.Uov2nMdAKDA (accessed April 12, 2014).
7. For a general overview of role of television, see Lynda Lee Kaid and Christina Holtz-Bacha, "An Introduction to Parties and Candidates on Television," in Kaid and Holtz-Bacha, eds., *Political Advertising in Western Democracies* (Thousand Oaks, CA: SAGE, 1995), 1–7.
8. Margaret Scammel, *Designer Politics: How Elections Are Won* (New York: St. Martin's, 1995), 289.
9. Fritz Plasser, "Political Consulting Worldwide," in Dennis W. Johnson, ed., *Routledge Handbook of Political Management* (New York: Routledge, 2008), 24; and Plasser and Plasser, *Global Political Campaigning*, 241–43.
10. William R. Hamilton, interview by author, Washington, DC, May 4, 1995. Hamilton's firm, Hamilton & Staff, worked for candidates and parties in Canada, Greece, Sweden, Eastern Europe, and the Caribbean.
11. David Segal, "By the Numbers: Polling Firms Increasingly Turn to Business, Foreign Clients to Supplement Political Work," *Washington Post*, March 4,

1996, Business supplement, 12. In 2004, the Wirthlin Group was sold to Harris Interactive.

12. Walter Shapiro, "America's Dubious Export," *Time*, September 4, 1989, 72.

13. Napolitan, "An American in Paris," 64.

14. Quoted in Esther Schrader, "Mexico Imports American-Style Campaigning," *Los Angeles Times,* August 27, 1999, A1.

15. Writing in 1981, Larry Sabato stated that in no other country's elections have American political consultants played a more publicly prominent role than Venezuela. Sabato, *The Rise of Political Consultants,* 59. On Venezuela and the Americanization of campaigns, see Jose Antonio Mayobre, "Politics, Media, and Modern Democracy: The Case of Venezuela," in Swanson and Mancini, eds., *Politics, Media, and Modern Democracy,* 227–45. See discussion of campaign trends in Latin America, particularly Brazil, Chile, and Venezuela, in Alan Angell, Maria D'Alva Kinzo, and Diego Urbaneja, "Latin America," in David Butler and Austin Ranney, eds., *Electioneering: A Comparative Study of Continuity and Change* (Oxford: Clarendon Press, 1992), 43–69.

16. Walker Simon, "U.S. Advisers Play Role in Venezuelan Presidential Campaign," Reuters, November 30, 1988. Other early American consultants include David Doak, Robert Shrum, Ralph Murphine, F. Clifton White, Roger Ailes, Stanley Greenberg, Peter Schechter, and John Gorman.

17. Simon, "U.S. Advisers Play Role in Venezuelan Presidential Campaign."

18. Angell, D'Alva Kinzo, and Urbaneja, "Latin America," 63. The authors state that electoral costs rose in a "dizzy fashion" after the 1973 election, aided in part by huge increases in the value of oil. Daniel Drosdoff, "Image-Making Helped Lusinchi Victory," United Press International, December 5, 1983.

19. Thomas B. Edsall, "Branching Out with Burgeoning Influence," *Washington Post,* January 17, 1989.

20. Simon, "U.S. Advisers Play Role in Venezuelan Presidential Campaign."

21. Tom Ochs, interview by author, Washington, DC, April 11, 1995. Squier Knapp Ochs has created a partnership with another Democratic firm, the pollsters Penn + Schoen, to form Latin American Campaigns, Inc., with a satellite office in Buenos Aires. Latin American Campaigns Inc. claimed three of the five 1993 presidential elections in South America. "Squier, Penn and Schoen Go South," *Campaigns & Elections,* April/May 1993, 10.

22. Biographical sketch, Ralph Murphine, Board of Directors, American Association of Political Consultants, 2006, http://www.theaapc.com/content/aboutus/board/ralphmurphine.asp (accessed June 23, 2008).

23. Schrader, "Mexico Imports American-Style Campaigning."

24. National Democratic Institute, "NDI Activities in Latin America and the Caribbean: Mexico," October 6, 2000, from NDI website, www.ndi.org/latinamerica/mexico (accessed April 1, 2004).

25. Jorge I. Domínguez, "The Transformation of Mexico's Electoral and Party Systems, 1988–1997," in Jorge I. Domínguez and Alejandro Poiré, eds., *Toward Mexico's Democratization: Parties, Campaigns, Elections, and Public Opinion* (New York: Routledge, 1999), 9–10.

26. National Democratic Institute, "Statement of the NDI International Delegation to Mexico's July 2, 2000 Elections," Mexico City, July 3, 2000.

27. Michael Barone, "Mexico Votes—For Real," *Jewish World Review,* October 28, 1999, www.jewishworldreview.com/michael/barone102899.asp (accessed June 4, 2004).

28. Eric Olson and Laurie Freeman, "The Media's Influence in Mexico's Electoral Campaign," issue 5, *Mexico Election Monitor 2000* (Washington Office on Latin America, 2000).

29. Michael Riley, "TV Campaign Spectacle a First for Mexico," *Houston Chronicle,* May 21, 2000.

30. Ibid.

31. Esther Schrader, "Mexico Imports American-Style Campaigning," *Los Angeles Times*, August 27, 1999, A1.
32. Susan Ferris, "Mexico Gets Comic Relief as Presidential Candidates Hit Television Talk Show Circuit," Cox News Service, 1999, n.d.
33. Schrader, "Mexico Imports American-Style Campaigning."
34. After the election, Fox apologized to Labastida for calling him derogatory names. See Simeon Tegel, "Mexico's Voters Out to Get Shorty," *Times* (London), July 2, 2000; Michael Riley, "TV Campaign Spectacle a First for Mexico," *Houston Chronicle*, May 21, 2000, A26; Schrader, "Mexico Imports American-Style Campaigning," A1; Jose de Cordoba, "A Flashy Campaigner Shakes Up the Race for Mexico's President," *Wall Street Journal*, July 21, 2000, A1; "Mexico's Election Teaser: Who's the Most Macho," *Time*, June 30, 2000, http://content.time.com/time/magazine/article/0,9171,48910,00.html (accessed June 4, 2004); and especially Maggs, "Not-So-Innocents Abroad," 1906.
35. "Mexico's Presidential Elections American Political Style," *Salt Lake Tribune*, August 15, 1999, www.sltrib.com/1999/08151999/nation_w/15300.htm (accessed June 5, 2014).
36. Maggs, "Not-So-Innocents Abroad."
37. Molly Moore and John Anderson, "Mexican Power Shift Stirs Wide Celebration," *Washington Post*, July 4, 2000, A1.
38. Ibid.
39. Ibid.
40. Nicholas J. O'Shaughnessy, *The Phenomenon of Political Marketing* (London: Macmillan, 1990), 218.
41. Joseph Napolitan, *The Election Game and How to Win It* (New York: Doubleday, 1972), 254.
42. Ibid.
43. Margaret Scammel and Holli A. Semetko, "Political Advertising on Television: The British Experience," in Kaid and Holtz-Bacha, *Political Advertising in Western Democracies*, 31; see also Scammell, *Designer Politics*.
44. Michael Innes, "Arsenal of Democracy: Hired Guns Target International Clients," *Campaigns & Elections*, September 1992.
45. Dennis Kavanagh, *Election Campaigning: The New Marketing of Politics* (Oxford: Blackwell, 1995).
46. Innes, "Arsenal of Democracy."
47. William E. Schmidt, "By Jove! British Candidates, American Lingo," *New York Times*, March 21, 1992.
48. Peter Goldman, Thomas M. DeFrank, Mark Miller, Andrew Murr, and Tom Mathews, *Quest for the Presidency: 1992* (College Station: Texas A&M University Press, 1994), 518. In 1988, the Joseph Biden campaign for the presidency was sidetracked in part because of alleged plagiarism from a speech given by British Labour Leader Neil Kinnock.
49. Mary Matalin and James Carville, *All's Fair: Love, War, and Running for President* (New York: Random House, 1994), 374–76.
50. Ibid., 376–77.
51. Fred Barbash, "British Parties to Campaign American-Style," *Washington Post*, March 18, 1997, A1.
52. Ibid.
53. Dan Balz, "Once Again, Americans Doing Their Bit for Blair," *Washington Post*, May 5, 2005.
54. BBC News, "Labour Hire Obama Campaign Chief David Axelrod," April 18, 2014, http://www.bbc.com/news/uk-politics-27062278 (accessed April 19, 2014); Dan Balz, Griff Witte, and Karla Adam, "In U.K. Election's Wake, Questions on E.U., Scotland," *Washington Post*, May 8, 2015; Tim Ross, "Secrets of the Tories' Election 'War Room,'" *The Telegraph*, May 16, 2015, http://www.telegraph.co.uk/news/politics/11609570/Secrets-of-the-Tories-election-war-room.html (accessed May 22, 2015).
55. Sharon Moshavi, "Spin City," *The New Republic*, March 29, 1999, 10.

56. Greenberg, *Dispatches from the War Room*, 286.

57. Adam Nagourney, "Sound Bites over Jerusalem," *New York Times Magazine*, August 25, 1999, 44. On influence of American consultants in Israeli elections, see Dahlia Scheindlin and Israel Waismel-Manor, "Falafel and Apple Pie: American Consultants, Modernization and Americanization of Electoral Campaigns in Israel," in Johnson, ed., *Routledge Handbook on Political Management*, 317–31.

58. Nagourney, "Sound Bites over Jerusalem," 45; also, Stephen Rodrick, "Puppetmaster: The Secret Life of Arthur J. Finkelstein," *Boston Magazine*, October 1996, 62.

59. Lee Hockstader, "Cajun Ragin' in a New Home: James Carville Brings American-Style Politics to Israel," *Washington Post*, April 7, 1999, C1; William Schneider, "Why Bibi Struck Out," *National Journal*, May 22, 1999, 1438; Tracy Wilkinson, "Israel Shows Hallmarks of New Style of Politicking," *Los Angeles Times*, April 16, 1999, A5.

60. Nagourney, "Sound Bites over Jerusalem," 46.

61. On the 1999 elections: Larry Derfner, "Ehud Barak's Answer to Arthur Finkelstein," *Jerusalem Post*, December 18, 1998, 13; see also Greenberg, *Dispatches from the War Room*, 269–347, and Douglas E. Schoen, *The Power of the Vote: Electing Presidents, Overthrowing Dictators, and Promoting Democracy around the World* (New York: William Morrow, 2007), 90–98.

62. Cover picture accompanied this article, Nagourney, "Sound Bites over Jerusalem."

63. Nagourney, "Sound Bites over Jerusalem," 47.

64. Schoen, *The Power of the Vote*, 91.

65. Schneider, "Why Bibi Struck Out"; Shane D'Aprile, "Netanyahu's Obama Strategists," *Campaigns & Elections*, February 11, 2009; Julie Hirschfield Davis, "Former Obama Campaign Aide Now Works to Oust Netanyahu," *New York Times*, February 27, 2015; "Yesh Atid Strategist: Positive Campaign Proved Itself," *Jerusalem Post*, March 12, 2015, http://www.jpost.com/Israel-Elections/Yesh-Atid-strategist-Positive-campaign-proved-itself-393768 (accessed July 20, 2015); Raphael Ahren, "The Kingmaker's Kingmaker," *The Times of Israel*, February 26, 2013, http://www.timesofisrael.com/the-kingmakers-kingmaker/ (accessed July 20, 2015).

66. Sussman, *Global Electioneering*, 138.

67. On the 1991 USSR All-Union Referendum, see Dennis Polhill, "The Issue of a National Initiative Process," Initiative and Referendum Institute, University of Southern California, 2014, www.thenationalreferendum.org/polhill-national-initiative-institute-referendum-process (accessed May 16, 2016); Alessandra Stanley, "Moscow Journal: The Americans Who Saved Yeltsin (Or Did They?)," *New York Times*, July 8, 1996, A4.

68. Lee Hockstader, "American Advisers Work Quietly in Moscow to Help Incumbent," *Washington Post*, July 1, 1996, A11.

69. Michael Kramer, "Rescuing Boris: The Secret Story of How American Advisers Helped Yeltsin Win," *Time*, July 15, 1996, 28ff. The "Nightline" interview with Ted Koppel aired on July 8, 1996.

70. Ibid.

71. George Gorton, together with Richard Dresner, Joe Shumate, and Steve Moore, press conference, July 19, 1996, Washington, DC.

72. Gorton, press conference. The American consultants acknowledged that they never did have face-to-face contact with Yeltsin, and worked principally through his daughter, Tatyana Dyachenko.

73. Eleanor Randolph, "Americans Claim Role in Yeltsin Win," *Los Angeles Times*, July 9, 1996, A4.

74. Morris, *Behind the Oval Office*, 258–59. Morris notes that he and Dresner had been "best of friends" during the 1970s, but "mortal enemies" during most of the 1980s with the bitter breakup of their business partnership; at 258.

75. Ibid., 35.

76. Gorton press conference.

77. Lee Hockstader, "Yeltsin Paying Top Ruble for Positive News Coverage," *Washington Post*, June 30, 1996, A1.

78. Lee Hockstader and David Hoffman, "Yeltsin Campaign Rose from Tears to Triumph; Money, Advertising Turned Fortunes Around," *Washington Post*, July 7, 1996, A1.

79. *Spinning Boris*, directed by Roger Spottiswoode, written by Yuri Zeltser and Grace Cary Bickley.

80. Phil Noble, telephone interview with author, Charleston, SC, April 6, 1996.

81. Kim quoted in Michael Innes, "Arsenal of Democracy: Hired Guns Target International Clients," *Campaigns & Elections*, September 1992.

82. Gerald L. Curtis observes that some American political consultants have attempted to break into the Japanese election market, but "apparently with very little success." Gerald L. Curtis, "Japan," in Butler and Ranney, eds., *Electioneering*, 227; Plasser and Plasser, *Global Electioneering*, 15–46.

83. Darrell West, "America's Latest Export: Political Consultants," *Campaigns & Elections*, 10 (1) (1989), 17; and Napolitan interview, September 28, 2000. A magazine article two years after the election described Giscard d'Estaing's office having just three books on its shelf. Right next to Montaigne's *Essais* was Joseph Napolitan's *The Election Game*.

84. Ochs interview.

85. West, "America's Latest Export," 17.

86. Justine Hunter, "Washington Advice Termed Bad Choice for B.C. Interests," *Vancouver Sun*, April 13, 1995, B3. Premier Harcourt's office disputed the figure of 1,800, claiming that many were faxes and others were messages left for the Struble firm.

87. "Harcourt Used U.S. Writer, American Crafted Policy Speeches Documents Show," *Toronto Star*, March 20, 1995, A3.

88. "Harcourt Cleared," *Maclean's*, May 1, 1995, 17. Struble commented: "In retrospect, it probably shouldn't have been done that way and I deserve some of the blame," following accusations that Harcourt tried to hide his reliance "on an American spin doctor." Quoted in Michael Smyth, "U.S. Adviser Denies Role in NDP Policy," *Ottawa Citizen*, April 13, 1995, A20.

89. Schmidt, "By Jove! British Candidates, American Lingo," 11.

90. Peter Gwin, "Fear and Loathing on the European Campaign Trail: Political Consulting is Becoming a Global Business," *Europe*, October 1998, 380.

91. "Toward a Kinder, Gentler Aruba," *National Journal*, December 10, 1988.

92. Eleanor Clift, "Politics under the Palms: Consultants Find Life After Campaign '88—in Aruba," *Newsweek*, January 9, 1989, 27.

93. George Skelton, "Californians Pitched Political Message in Ukraine," *Los Angeles Times*, December 5, 1991.

94. West, "America's Latest Export," 20.

95. Siegel, "Spin Doctors to the World." On the Peruvian election, see Eugene Robinson, "Peruvian Dark Horse Aided by Evangelicals," *Washington Post*, April 11, 1990, A16; James Brooke, "Peru's New Frontrunner Vows to Shake-Up on Coca and Rebels," *New York Times*, April 15, 1990; Eugene Robinson, "Late-Rising Contender's Campaign Mystifies Many Peruvians," *Washington Post*, April 20, 1990, A19; Joseph Contreras, "Peru: Looking for a Miracle, Japanese Style," *Newsweek*, April 23, 1990; Pamela Constable, "Two Peru's Square Off in a Bitter Election," *Boston Globe*, June 10, 1990, 26; and Peter Hakim and Michael Jones, "Which President for Peru?" *Christian Science Monitor*, May 8, 1990, 18.

96. Ralph Murphine interview with author, October 15, 1995.

97. James Harding, *Alpha Dogs: The Americans Who Turned Political Spin into a Global Business* (New York: Farrar, Straus and Giroux, 2008), 190.

98. Richard Leiby, "Can Washington Campaign Tactics Translate in Iraq? Sam Patten and His Candidate Hope So," *Washington Post*, April 28, 2014.

99. Bonner, *Waltzing with a Dictator*, 395–97. West, "America's Latest Export," 20. Napolitan had represented Marcos earlier, but declined to do so in this election.

100. Shapiro, "America's Dubious Export," 72.

101. Kellyanne Fitzpatrick, at Graduate School of Political Management Forum on International Political Consulting, George Washington University, Washington, DC, December 5, 1994. Peter V. Miller wrote that polls in Nicaragua were viewed not as neutral social science instruments but as "propaganda weapons." See Miller, "Which Side Are You On? The 1990 Nicaraguan Poll 'Debacle,'" *Public Opinion Quarterly* 55 (1991): 281–302. Argentine political consultant Felipe Noguera, who more accurately predicted the preference for Chamorro, stated that poll misreadings stemmed, in part, from some American pollsters including "Americo-centric" questions, which came from a US perspective of Nicaragua as an American policy problem. Felipe Noguera "South Polls: What the Hell Happened in Nicaragua?" *Campaigns & Elections*, April/May 1990, 36.

102. West, "America's Latest Export."

103. John Aristotle Phillips, "Inside the Revolution: The Ukraine Story," *Campaigns & Elections*, February 2005, 44–45; Jean MacKenzie, "US Political Consultants Mucking Things Up Abroad," *GlobalPost*, February 3, 2013.

104. Hamilton interview.

105. Leonard Doyle, "Papandreou Scores a Convincing Win," *The Independent*, 11 October 1983, 8. Papandreou was represented by the American firm of Trippi, McMahon and Squier.

106. "Greece's Embattled Leader Calls in Clinton's Spin Doctor," *Sunday Times*, September 26, 1993. Greeks referred to this campaign between the 75-year-old Mitsotakis and the 74-year-old Papandreou as "the race of the dinosaurs."

107. Ibid. Humphreville had worked on several earlier campaigns with Carville; he resigned as executive director of the New York Stock Exchange Specialist Association and flew to Greece on August 30, 1993. "Humphreville Quits Specialist Associations for Politics," *Wall Street Letter*, August 30, 1993.

108. "Greece's Embattled Leader Calls in Clinton's Spin Doctor." Joining Carville in this race were Paul Begala and Mary Matalin—"An unholy political alliance" groused New Hampshire Democratic chairman Chris Spirou, who worked for Papandreou against Carville-Begala-Matalin. *Manchester Union-Leader*, October 19, 1993, reported in *American Political Hotline*.

109. "Greece's Embattled Leader Calls in Clinton's Spin Doctor." Carville's fee for managing the campaign was believed to be several hundred thousand dollars.

110. Doyle, "Papandreou Scores a Convincing Win." In an interview with Spyridon Rizopoulos, student at the Graduate School of Political Management, former President Mitsotakis stated that he thought James Carville did a magnificent job. When Carville came into the race, the party was well below the 40 percent level that it ultimately obtained in the election. Mitsotakis stated that his campaign should have given even greater emphasis on Papandreou's failing health. Constantine Mitsotakis, interviewed by Rizopoulos, Athens, January 4, 1995.

111. Catherine Foster, "Labor's Win in State Runs Counter to Australia's Conservative Tide," *Christian Science Monitor*, September 12, 1992.

112. Elisabeth Ryan Sullivan, "No Thanks, Yanks, for 'Willie Horton,'" *Philadelphia Inquirer*, November 29, 1992, A2.

113. Ibid. Melissa A. Haynes, a student from Australia in the Graduate School of Political Management, clarified and expanded upon several points concerning the Liberal Party advertisements.

114. On the speech, see Robert C. Roland and John M. Jones, *Reagan at Westminster: Foreshadowing the End of the Cold War* (College Station: Texas A&M University Press, 2010).

115. Joshua Muravchik, *Exporting Democracy: Fulfilling America's Destiny* (Washington, DC: AEI Press, 1991), 207.

116. Ibid., 216–17.
117. John M. Broder, "Political Meddling by Outsiders: Not New for U.S.," *New York Times*, March 31, 1997, A1.
118. Muravchik, *Exporting Democracy*, 210; National Democratic Institute, *Chile's Transition to Democracy: The 1988 Presidential Plebiscite* (Washington, DC: National Democratic Institute, 1988), passim. The CIA had a checkered history of manipulating Chilean elections. It had spent $4 million to help Eduardo Frei Montalva defeat Salvador Allende in the 1964 presidential elections. Then, nine years later, the CIA inspired a coup that toppled Allende, who had won power in a legitimate contest in 1970. Broder, "Political Meddling by Outsiders," A11.
119. R. Bruce McColm, president, International Republican Institute, testimony before US Congress, House Committee on Foreign Relations, Subcommittee on International Security, International Organizations, and Human Rights, August 1, 1994.
120. Ibid.
121. Ibid. The IRI maintains field offices in nine countries: Albania, Bulgaria, Cambodia, Kazakhstan, Romania, Russia (Moscow and St. Petersburg), Slovakia, South Africa, and Ukraine. International Republican Institute, *A Decade of Democracy, 1984–1994*, June 1994. The 1994 IRI budget of $6 million came from four different sources, the National Endowment for Democracy, Agency for International Development, AID/African Regional Electoral Assistance Fund (AREAF), and for the first time, private funding.
122. Nelson Mandela, *Long Walk to Freedom: The Autobiography of Nelson Mandela* (New York: Little, Brown, 1995).
123. The historical background to the South African elections is taken from Robert Mattes, "The Road to Democracy: From 2 February 1990 to 27 April 1994," in Andrew Reynolds, *Election '94 South Africa* (New York: St. Martin's, 1994), 1–22, and a 1994 report of the International Republican Institute, *South Africa: Campaign and Election Report*, April 26–29, 1994, ch. 1.
124. IRI Report, 22ff. One of the earliest and strongest supporters of the ANC was the Social Democratic Party of Sweden. Noble interview.
125. Ibid., 125.
126. National Democratic Institute, "NDI Helps Launch South African Election Support Project," *NDI Reports*, Winter/Spring 1993.
127. Christopher Matthews, "U.S.-Style Politics in S. Africa; Americans Offer Campaign Expertise," *San Francisco Examiner*, April 24, 1994, B10.
128. Lynne Duke, "Teaching the Baby Steps toward Democracy in South Africa," *Washington Post*, February 25, 1994, A13.
129. Ibid. McDougall was the only American on the International Election Commission.
130. Dinah Zeiger, "Denver Firm's Network Links S. Africa Voters," *Denver Post*, April 28, 1994.
131. Tom Lodge, "African National Congress," in Reynolds, ed., *Election '94 South Africa*, 27–28. In July 1993, 54 percent favored the ANC and 23 percent were uncommitted.
132. Greenberg, *Dispatches from the War Room*, 116.
133. Jessica Lee, "Mandela Calls on Top U.S. Strategists," *USA Today*, March 10, 1994, 7A. ANC officials had requested Greenberg's help through the National Endowment for Democracy.
134. Greenberg, *Dispatches from the War Room*, 112.
135. Scott Shepard, "U.S.-funded Media Whizzes Help Mandela," *Atlanta Journal and Constitution*, April 3, 1994, 8.
136. David Lauter, "Finger on the Pulse," *Washingtonian*, July 1994.
137. Ibid. Greenberg has also written two books on racial politics in the United States and two about race and labor policies in South Africa.
138. Shepard, "U.S.-Funded Media Whizzes Help Mandela."

139. Jon Sawyer, "Clinton's Pollster Aided Nelson Mandela's Election Campaign," *St. Louis Post-Dispatch,* June 16, 1994, 8A.

140. Matthews, "U.S.-Style Politics in S. Africa."

141. Sawyer, "Clinton's Pollster Aided Nelson Mandela's Election Campaign."

142. Stanley Greenberg, at Graduate School of Political Management Forum on South African Elections, George Washington University, Washington, DC, May 23, 1994.

143. Milton Morris, Joint Center for Political and Economic Studies, at GSPM South African Forum.

144. Kgosie Matthews, Washington Strategic Consulting Group, at GSPM South African Forum.

145. Shepard, "U.S.-Funded Media Whizzes Help Mandela." South African academics Daniel Silke and Robert Schrire wrote that the ANC used Applied Marketing and Communications, a division of Hunt Lascaris, one of South Africa's leading agencies, and drew advice from Greer and Greenberg. The National Party used its longtime advisers Saatchi & Saatchi, through their divisional representatives, Optimum. Silke and Schrire, "The Mass Media and the South African Election," in Reynolds, *Election '94 South Africa,* 133.

146. Matthews, "U.S.-Style Politics in S. Africa"; Ryan K. Walsh, "Lending South Africa an Expert Hand," *National Journal,* February 12, 1994, 374. Consultant Peter Kelly advised the Inkatha Freedom Party on the basics of running a campaign and met with the party's youth leadership to explain "what the word 'election' actually meant." Kelly's participation came through the NDI, while Republican consultants John Brockmeyer and Vada Hill were helping the Inkatha on behalf of the IRI. The Azanian People's Organization (AZAPO), which boycotted the election, received assistance from Democrat Ann Lewis and Republican Rita Levinson. All American political consultants who were under the auspices of the NDI and IRI signed agreements promising not to work for any South African parties after the election, and offered their services free of charge.

147. Shepard, "U.S.-Funded Media Whizzes Help Mandela."

148. For a detailed analysis of the results of the April 1994 election, see Andrew Reynolds, "The Results," in Reynolds, ed., *Election '94 South Africa,* 182–220.

149. Greenberg, GSPM Forum on South Africa.

150. Lee, "Mandela Calls on Top U.S. Strategists."

151. See Fritz Plasser, Christian Scheucher, and Christian Senft, "Is There a European Style of Political Marketing? A Survey of Political Managers and Consultants," in Bruce I. Newman, ed., *The Handbook of Political Marketing* (Thousand Oaks, CA: SAGE, 1999).

152. David Butler and Austin Ranney, "Conclusion," in Butler and Ranney, eds., *Electioneering,* 286.

Chapter 19

Epigraph quote from Thomas N. Edmonds, "Romney for President: the Last 20th-Century Campaign," in Dennis W. Johnson, ed., *Campaigning for President 2012: Strategy and Tactics* (New York: Routledge, 2013), 178.

1. From Obama's acceptance speech, November 4, 2008, http://www.youtube.com/watch?v=3K8GWCl7P7U (accessed March 15, 2014).

2. Diana Owen, "Media in the 2008 Election: 21st Century Campaign, Same Old Story," in Larry J. Sabato, ed., *The Year of Obama: How Barack Obama Won the White House* (New York: Longman, 2010), 167.

3. While twenty was a large number of candidates, recent elections had brought out plenty of candidates: in 2004, there were ten Democrats hoping to run

against incumbent George W. Bush; in 2000, there were two Democrats and ten Republicans running; in 1996, eleven Republicans were hoping to be chosen to go against incumbent Bill Clinton; in 1988, there were nine Democrats and six Republican candidates; in 1984, eight Democrats were ready to take on incumbent Ronald Reagan; and in 1976, there were fifteen Democrats and four Republicans, including the incumbent president Gerald Ford.

4. Video available from NBC, http://www.nbcnews.com/id/16720167/#.Ut6M-7807Jx (accessed January 21, 2007).

5. David Plouffe, *The Audacity to Win: The Inside Story and Lessons of Barack Obama's Historic Victory* (New York: Viking, 2009), 37.

6. Dan Balz and Haynes Johnson, *The Battle for America 2008: The Story of an Extraordinary Election* (New York: Viking, 2009), 149.

7. "Job Interview," http://www.youtube.com/watch?v=tjOuL5qwNIc (accessed July 1, 2014).

8. YouTube, December 27, 2006, http://www.youtube.com/watch?v=1etlZaf6zUw.

9. Julie Barko Germany, "The Online Revolution," in Dennis W. Johnson, ed., *Campaigning for President 2008* (New York: Routledge, 2009), 149. The "I Feel Pretty" video is on YouTube, http://www.youtube.com/watch?v=2AE847UXu3Q (accessed May 10, 2014).

10. See Tad Devine, "Obama Wins the Nomination: How He Did It," in Johnson, ed., *Campaigning for President 2008*, 31–43.

11. Ron Faucheux, "Why Clinton Lost," in Johnson, ed., *Campaigning for President 2008*, 47.

12. John Heilemann and Mark Halperin, *Game Change: Obama and the Clintons, McCain and Palin, and the Race of a Lifetime* (New York: HarperCollins, 2010), 17.

13. YouTube, http://www.youtube.com/watch?v=zz1wwhyVOXU (accessed May 10, 2014).

14. Plouffe, *The Audacity to Win*, 37.

15. Hillary Rodham Clinton, *Living History* (New York: Simon & Schuster, 2003), 513; see also Lois Romano, "Gatekeepers of Hillaryland," *Washington Post,* June 21, 2007.

16. Anne E. Kornbluth, "Clinton's Power Pointer," *Washington Post,* April 30, 2007.

17. Heilemann and Halperin, *Game Change*, 81–82.

18. Ibid., 81–83.

19. Joshua Green, "The Front-Runner's Fall," *The Atlantic*, September 2008; "Team of Rivals" characterization from Doris Kearn Goodwin, *Team of Rivals: The Political Genius of Abraham Lincoln* (New York: Simon & Schuster, 2005).

20. Heilemann and Halperin, *Game Change*, 265.

21. John McCormick, "Obama's Campaign Chief: Low Profile, High Impact," *Chicago Tribune,* June 9, 2008.

22. James A. Barnes, "Obama's Inner Circle," *National Journal*, March 31, 2008.

23. Ibid.

24. Peter Bell, "2008 Democratic Insiders Poll," *National Journal* (May 13, 2006), 6, 8.

25. Balz and Johnson, *The Battle for America 2008*, 104–105.

26. When she was twenty-nine years old, Vilmain began organizing for Michael Dukakis in the crucial 1988 Iowa Democratic presidential primary. She later became political director of EMILY's List in Washington, assisted Senator Herb Kohl in two of his Senate races, and was general consultant to Tom Vilsack. Alex MacGillis, "They Know How to Caucus: Teresa Vilmain and Other Experts in an Arcane Presidential Art," *Washington Post,* June 7, 2007. Later, at the 2011, Midwest Academy of Progressive Leadership Award ceremony, former president Bill Clinton praised Vilmain as "the gold standard of Democratic organizers in Iowa." Jackie Calmes, "Clinton Secret Weapon: Organization," *Wall Street Journal,* December 19, 2007; biographical sketch, "Teresa Vilmain," Institute

of Politics, Harvard University, http://www.iop.harvard.edu/teresa-vilmain; Clinton video for the Midwest Academy of Progressive Leadership Award http://www.youtube.com/watch?v=HNYCPkAIALk (accessed May 10, 2014).

27. Evan Thomas and staff of *Newsweek*, *"A Long Time Coming:" The Inspiring, Combative 2008 Campaign and the Historic Election of Barack Obama* (New York: Public Affairs, 2009), 26.

28. Balz and Johnson, *The Battle for America 2008*, 145.

29. Alter quoted in Norah McAlvanah, "What Phil Singer Cost Hillary," *Campaigns & Elections*, December 1, 2008.

30. Heilemann and Halperin, *Game Change*, 5.

31. Susan Davis, "Clinton Aide Met on Trade Deal," *Wall Street Journal*, April 4, 2008; Heilemann and Halperin, *Game Change*, 240–41.

32. On the ups and downs of the Republican primaries, see Tony Fabrizio, "McCain: From Frontrunner to Dead-in-the-Water to Nominee," in Johnson, ed., *Campaigning for President 2008*, 60–77. Senator George Allen, in an unguarded moment, referred to an Indian American campaign staffer working for his opponent, Jim Webb, as a "macaca." That term, unfamiliar to most Americans, was broadly interpreted as a racial slur and became a point of contention during the 2006 Virginia Senate race. "And let's give a welcome to Macaca here," Allen said pointing to the Webb staffer, S. R. Sidarth, "and welcome to American and to the real world of Virginia." This can be seen on Youtube, https://www.youtube.com/watch?v=r9oz0PMnKwI (accessed April 18, 2016).

33. Wayne P. Steger, Andrew J. Dowdle, and Randall E. Adkins, "Why Are Presidential Nomination Races So Difficult to Forecast?," in William G. Mayer and Jonathan Bernstein, eds., *The Making of the Presidential Candidates 2012* (Lanham, MD: Rowman & Littlefield, 2012), 3.

34. Michael D. Shear, "Head of 'The House': In Fred Thompson's Dining Room, Ken Rietz Helped Build a Campaign. Then the Chaos Began," *Washington Post*, November 13, 2007.

35. Chris Cillizza and Shailagh Murray, "The Man Who Helped Start Huckabee's Roll," *Washington Post*, December 2, 2007, A2.

36. For a profile on Myers, see Philip Rucker, "Beth Myers, Longtime Romney Adviser and Confidante, to Lead VP Search," *Washington Post*, April 16, 2012.

37. Balz and Johnson, *The Battle for America 2008*, 246.

38. Katharine Q. Seeley, "The McCain Shake-Up," *New York Times*, April 24, 2007.

39. Dan Balz and Anne E. Kornblut, "Top Aides Leave McCain Camp," *Washington Post*, July 11, 2007.

40. Fabrizio, "McCain," 77.

41. David Axelrod, *Believer: My Forty Years in Politics* (New York: Penguin, 2015), 295; YouTube, http://www.youtube.com/watch?v=0HXYsw_ZDXg (accessed May 10, 2014).

42. Heilemann and Halperin, *Game Change*, 359–64.

43. Elizabeth Bumiller and Michael Cooper, "Conservative Ire Pushes McCain from Lieberman," *New York Times*, August 30, 2008.

44. One of McCain's advisers said he would hear the candidate say this "lots of times." Robert Draper, "The Making (and Remaking) of McCain," *New York Times*, October 26, 2008.

45. Sarah Palin, *Going Rogue: An American Life* (New York: HarperCollins, 2009), 239.

46. Richard Wolffe, *Renegade: The Making of a President* (New York: Crown, 2009), 227.

47. Balz and Johnson, *The Battle for America 2008*, 360–61; Scott Shane, "Obama and the '60s Bomber: A Look at Crossed Paths," *New York Times*, October 8, 2008, 1.

48. Penn quoted in Wolffe, *Renegade*, 143.

49. Stanley B. Greenberg, *Dispatches from the War Room* (New York: Thomas Dunne, 2009), 107.

50. Pew Research Center for the People and the Press, "Obama Weathers the Wright Storm, Clinton Faces Credibility Problem," March 27, 2008, http://news-releases. uiowa.edu/2008/october/101408hawkpolltopline.pdf (accessed April 19, 2016). Texas Politics Project and the Government Department of the University of Texas poll of 550 registered voters, October 15–22, 2008, with a margin of error of +/-4.2 percent. Reported in Richard S. Dunham, "UT Poll Shows McCain, Cornyn with Comfortable Margins," *Houston Chronicle*, October 29, 2008. The nationwide figures come from the University of Iowa Hawkeye Poll, a tracking poll conducted October 1 to November 2 with a rolling sample of 60 respondents; 680 registered voters polled, with a margin of error of +/-3.5 percent. See Topline Results of Iowa poll, http://news-releases.uiowa.edu/2008/october/10148/ haepolltopline.pdf (accessed January 3, 2009).

51. Plouffe, *The Audacity to Win*, 247.

52. Joel Benenson interview with author, August 11, 2014.

53. Kate Kenski, Bruce W. Hardy, and Kathleen Hall Jamieson, *The Obama Victory: How Media, Money, and Message Shaped the 2008 Election* (New York: Oxford University Press, 2010), ch. 11.

54. "McCain Team Hiring Canvassers in Florida," *Washington Post*, October 14, 2008, A4.

55. Jose Antonio Vargas, "Obama's Wide Web," *Washington Post*, August 20, 2008, C1.

56. Peter Fenn, "Communication Wars: Television and New Media," in Johnson, ed., *Campaigning for President 2008*, 216.

57. Andrei Scheinkman, G. V. Xaquin, Alan McLean, and Stephen Westberg, "The Ad Wars," *New York Times*, May 23, 2012.

58. Ibid.

59. Abdon M. Pallasch, "Obama's 30-Minute Infomercial Covers All Bases," *Chicago Sun-Times*, October 30, 2008, quoted in Fenn, "Communication Wars," 215.

60. Jim Rutenberg, "Obama Infomercial: Closing Argument to the Everyman," *New York Times,* October 28, 2008.

61. Goff quoted in Amanda Fuchs Miller, ed., *Campaign for President: The Managers Look at 2012* (Lanham, MD: Rowman & Littlefield, 2013), 128.

62. Tom Edmonds, "The Romney Campaign," in Johnson, ed., *Campaigning for President 2012*, 172–95.

63. Mark Halperin and John Heilemann, *Double Down: Game Change in 2012* (New York: Penguin Press, 2013), 115.

64. On Barbour's decision not to run, see ibid., 113–22.

65. Jan van Lohuizen interviewed in John Ellis, "Bush Pollster Assesses GOP Presidential Campaign," *Business Insider,* July 12, 2011, http://www. businessinsider.com/bush-pollster-assesses-gop-presidential-campaign-2011-7 (accessed August 13, 2014).

66. Dan Balz, *Collision 2012: Obama vs. Romney and the Future of Elections in America* (New York: Viking, 2013), 128.

67. For an overview of the candidates, see Dennis W. Johnson, "The Election of 2012," in Dennis W. Johnson, ed., *Campaigning for President 2012: Strategy and Tactics* (New York: Routledge, 2013), 1–22.

68. Weaver quoted in Chris Jones, "Exclusive Interview: Jon Huntsman is Tired of Waiting," *Esquire*, June 15, 2011.

69. Paul Alexander, *Machiavelli's Shadow: The Rise and Fall of Karl Rove* (New York: Modern Times, 2008), 49–50.

70. Johnson, ed., *Campaigning for President 2012*, 261.

71. Rebecca Kaplan, "Perry Names Romney, Bain Capital as Vultures," CBS News, January 10, 2012.

72. Mike Allen and Evan Thomas, *Inside the Circus: Romney, Santorum, and the GOP Race,* Politico Playbook 2012, e-book, location 195 of 1278, http://www.politico. com/playbook-2012/family-tree/inside-the-circus/.

73. Holly Bailey, "Rick Perry Hires Bush's 2000 Campaign Manager in Staff Shake-Up," Yahoo News, October 24, 2011, http://news.yahoo.com/blogs/ticket/

rick-perry-hires-veteran-gop-operatives-campaign-shake-205923595.html (accessed May 19, 2014).

74. Block quoted in Miller, ed., *Campaign for President: The Managers Look at 2012*, 13.

75. For background on Rhoades, see Jason Horowitz, "Matt Rhoades, Romney Campaign's Under-the-Radar Chief," *Washington Post*, November 20, 2011.

76. David quoted in Miller, ed., *Campaign for President: The Managers Look at 2012*, 14.

77. "Rombo," from the BrabenderCox website, http://www.brabendercox.com/our-work.jsp?pageId=2161392240601235923006595 (accessed May 11, 2014).

78. See, for example, a radio ad toward the end of the campaign, featuring Romney himself, http://www.brabendercox.com/our-work.jsp?selectedVideoId=216139224 0601352106374177&pageId=2161392240601233885504337 (accessed May 11, 2014).

79. "Baggage" found at https://www.youtube.com/watch?v=YT2h9TEXePY (accessed April 24, 2014).

80. Stuart Stevens in Miller, ed., *Campaign for President: The Managers Look at 2012*, 192.

81. Joshua Green, "Obama's CEO: Jim Messina Has a President to Sell," *Bloomberg Businessweek*, June 14, 2102.

82. Ibid.

83. Pollsters included John Anzalone and Jeff Liszt (Anzalone Liszt Research), Joel Benenson (Benenson Strategy Group), David Binder (David Binder Research), Cornell Belcher (Brilliant Corners Research and Strategies), Diane Feldman (The Feldman Group), Lisa Grove (Grove Strategic Insight), and Paul Harstad (Harstad Strategic Research). Tad Devine, "Obama Campaigns for Re-election," in Johnson, ed., *Campaigning for President 2012*, 142. See Appendix A for a more complete list of Obama consultants.

84. Smoot is profiled in Matthew Mosk, "The $75 Million Woman," *Washington Post*, October 8, 2007.

85. The media team included Ann Liston (Adelstein Liston), Terry Walsh (Strategy Group), John Del Cecato (AKPD Media), Sergio Bendixen and Fernand Amandi (Bendixen & Amandi); Rich Davis and David Dixon (Dixon Davis Media Group), Mike Donilon, Ricki Fairley-Brown (DOVE Marketing), Clifford Franklin (FUSE Advertising), Jim Margolis (GMMB), James Aldrete (Message Audience and Presentation), and Mark Putnam (Putnam Partners). Devine, "Obama Campaigns for Re-election," in Johnson, ed., *Campaigning for President 2012*, 142. See Appendix A for a more complete list of Obama consultants.

86. Bird quoted in Miller, ed., *Campaign for President: The Managers Look at 2012*, 41–42.

87. Axelrod, *Believer*, 453.

88. Goff quoted in Miller, ed., *Campaign for President*, 127.

89. Sasha Issenberg, "How President Obama's Campaign Used Big Data to Rally Individual Voters," *MIT Technology Review*, December 19, 2012.

90. Ibid. Grisolano quote from Daniel Schulman, *Sons of Wichita: How the Koch Brothers Became America's Most Powerful and Private Dynasty* (New York: Grand Central Publishing, 2014), 325.

91. Goff in Miller, ed., *Campaign for President*, 128.

92. Zeynep Tufecki, "Beware the Smart Campaign," *New York Times*, November 17, 2012, A23; Michael Kranish, "The Story behind Mitt Romney's Loss in the Presidential Campaign to President Obama," *Boston Globe*, December 22, 2012, http://archive.boston.com/news/politics/2012/president/2012/12/23/the-story-behind-mitt-romney-loss-the-presidential-campaign-president-obama/2QWkUB9pJgVIi1mAcIhQjL/story.html. (accessed July 7, 2014).

93. Evan Tracey, "Political Advertising: When More Meant Less," in Johnson, ed., *Campaigning for President 2012*, 99.

94. Michael Cornfield, "Twelve for 2012: Consequential Choices by the Obama and Romney Presidential Campaigns," in Johnson, ed., *Campaigning for President 2012*, 229.

95. Axelrod quoted in Maggie Haberman, "Axelrod Says Ad Buy is $25 Million; Slams Rove and Kochs as Super PAC 'Contract Killers,'" *Politico*, May 7, 2012.

96. Elizabeth Wilner, "Ad Avalanche: 43,000 Political Spots a Day until November," *Advertising Age*, September 13, 2013. For an analysis of outside organizations in the 2008 and 2012 presidential campaigns, see Stephen K. Medvic, "Outside Voices: 527s, Political Parties, and Other Non-Candidate Groups," in Johnson, ed., *Campaigning for President 2008*, 189–209; Stephen K. Medvic, "Outside Voices: Super PACs, Parties, and Other Non-Candidate Actors," in Johnson, ed., *Campaigning for President 2012*, 151–71; Eric Lichtblau, "IRS Expected to Stand Aside as Nonprofits Increase Role in 2016 Race," *New York Times*, July 5, 2015.

97. 558 U.S. 310 (2010).

98. Schulman, *Sons of Wichita*, 325.

99. Jeff Zeleny and Jim Rutenberg, "G.O.P. 'Super PAC' Weighs Hard-Line Attack on Obama," *New York Times*, May 17, 2012; the proposal, obtained by the *Times*, was prepared by Davis's firm Strategic Perception, and was titled "The Defeat of Barack Hussein Obama: The Ricketts Plan to End His Spending for Good," http://www.nytimes.com/interactive/2012/05/17/us/politics/17donate-document.html (accessed May 10, 2014). The "metrosexual" line was penned by Davis's colleague Bill Kenyon; see Halperin and Heilemann, *Double Down*, 303–309, at 305.

100. Dan Balz, "A Most Poisonous Campaign," *Washington Post*, August 12, 2012; YouTube, https://www.youtube.com/watch?v=8b1go7uq4y8 (accessed May 17, 2016).

101. Burton quoted in Miller, ed., *Campaign for President: The Managers Look at 2012*, 149.

102. Putnam Partners website, http://www.putnampartners.net/portfolio.html (accessed July 1, 2014).

103. John C. Tedesco and Scott W. Dunn, "Political Advertising in the 2012 U.S. Presidential Election," in Robert E. Denton Jr., ed., *The 2012 Presidential Campaign: A Communication Perspective* (Lanham, MD: Rowman & Littlefield, 2014), 78; Evan Tracey, "Political Advertising: When More Meant Less," in Johnson, *Campaigning for President 2012*, 92–106.

104. Tim Dickinson, "The Obama Campaign's Real Heroes," *Rolling Stone*, December 7, 2012, http://www.rollingstone.com/politics/news/the-obama-campaigns-real-heroes-20121126 (accessed August 29, 2014).

105. Tedesco and Dunn, "Political Advertising in the 2012 U.S. Presidential Election," 91.

106. Tracey, "Political Advertising," 98.

107. Joel Benenson interview with author, August 11, 2014.

108. Maggie Halberman and Emily Schultheis, "The Man behind Mitt Romney's Poll Questions," *Politico*, November 4, 2012.

109. Curtis Gans, Center for the Study of the American Electorate, American University, report, November 8, 2012, noted in "Election Results 2012: Voter Turnout Lower than 2008 and 2004, Report Says," CNN Wire, http://www.abc15.com/dpp/news/national/election-results-2012-voter-turnout-lower-than-2008-and2004-report-says (accessed January 3, 2009).

110. Edmonds, "Romney for President," 190–91; also, John Dickerson, "Why Romney Never Saw It Coming," *Slate*, November 9, 2012, http://www.slate.com/articles/news_and_politics/politics/2012/11/why_romney_was_surprised_to_lose_his_campaign_had_the_wrong_numbers_bad.html (accessed July 7, 2014).

111. Mike Murphy, "Can This Party Be Saved?" *Time*, November 28, 2012.

112. Ashley Parker, "Romney Blames Loss on Obama's 'Gifts' to Minorities and Young," *The Caucus* (blog), *New York Times*, November 14, 2012, http://thecaucus.blogs.nytimes.com/2012/11/14/romney-blames-loss-on-obamas-gifts-to-minorities-and-young-voters/?ref=politics.

113. John Sides and Lynn Vavrek, *The Gamble: Choice and Chance in the 2012 Presidential Election* (Princeton, NJ: Princeton University Press, 2013), 224–25.

114. Ibid., 223.

115. Bruce I. Newman, *The Marketing Revolution in Politics: What Recent U.S. Presidential Campaigns Can Teach Us about Effective Marketing* (Toronto: University of Toronto Press, 2016), 158–59.

116. Daniel Fisher, "Inside the Koch Empire: How the Brothers Plan to Reshape America," *Forbes*, December 5, 2012. On the rise of the Koch brothers, see Schulman, *Sons of Wichita*; also, Jane Mayer, "Covert Operations," *The New Yorker*, August 30, 2010.

Chapter 20

Epigraph quote from Justice Kennedy, *Citizens United v. Federal Election Commission*, 558 U.S. 310 (2010). Online version available at http://www. supremecourt.gov/opinions/09pdf/08-205.pdf.

1. Thomas B. Edsall, "In Defense of Anonymous Political Giving," *New York Times*, March 18, 2014.

2. Ibid.; and Robert Maguire, "Dark Money Hits $100 Million with Help from Single Candidate Groups," October 9, 2014, http://www.opensecrets.org/news/2014/10/dark-money-hits-100-million-with-help-from-single-candidate-groups/ (accessed October 23, 2015).

3. Lee Aitken, "The Campaign Casino: Elections Have Become a Get-Rich-Quick Scheme, and the Press Is Missing the Story," Harvard University Kennedy School of Government, Shorenstein Center on Media, Politics and Public Policy, #D-83, February 2014, http://shorensteincenter.org/d83-aitken/ (accessed July 2, 2015).

4. Ibid.

5. Kennedy, *Citizens United v. FEC*.

6. President Barack Obama, State of the Union Address, January 27, 2010, White House website, http://www.whitehouse.gov/the-press-office/remarks-president-state-union-address (accessed August 22, 2014).

7. Wilner quoted in Ashley Parker, "Outside Money Drives a Deluge of Political Ads," *New York Times*, July 27, 2014.

8. Kenneth P. Vogel, *Big Money: 2.5 Billion Dollars, One Suspicious Vehicle, and a Pimp—On the Trail of the Ultra-Rich Hijacking American Politics* (New York: Public Affairs, 2014), 125.

9. Steven E. Billet, "The Rise and Impact of Monster PACs," in Dennis W. Johnson, ed., *Routledge Handbook on Political Management* (New York: Routledge, 2009), 139–50.

10. Ibid., 140.

11. *SpeechNow.org v. Federal Election Commission*, US District Court, District of Columbia (May 2010), http://www.fec.gov/law/litigation/speechnow.shtml (accessed October 5, 2015).

12. Ibid.

13. Center for Responsive Politics, "Super PACs," https://www.opensecrets.org/pacs/superpacs.php?cycle=2016 (accessed October 25, 2015)

14. Johnson quoted in Sean J. Miller, "Can Consultants Help the GOP Rebound?," *Campaigns & Elections*, February 19, 2013, http://www.campaignsandelections.com/magazine/1766/can-consultants-help-the-gop-rebound.

15. *McCutcheon et al. v. Federal Election Commission*, 572 U.S. ___ (2014). Online version available at http://www.supremecourt.gov/opinions/13pdf/12-536_e1pf. pdf; Matea Gold, "Wealthy Political Donors Seize on New Latitude to Give to Unlimited Candidates," *Washington Post*, September 2, 2014, citing spending analysis by Center for Responsive Politics, http://www.opensecrets.org/news/2013/09/mccutcheons-multiplying-effect-why/ (accessed December 7, 2015).

16. Breyer, *McCutcheon v. FEC*.

17. "Club Aims to Defeat Cranston, Hart, Dodd," *Los Angeles Times*, March 30, 1985, http://articles.latimes.com/1985-03-30/news/mn-29524_1_alan-cranston (accessed August 23, 2014).

18. "4 Men Accused of Election Fraud," *New York Times*, December 15, 1988.

19. American Crossroads, in Center for Responsive Politics, Opensecrets website, http://www.opensecrets.org/pacs/superpacs.php?cycle=2010 (accessed August 12, 2015).

20. Sunlight Foundation, "Non-Committee FEC Filers," April 11, 2014, http://reporting.sunlightfoundation.com/outside-spending/noncommittees/ (accessed July 22, 2014).

21. Byron Tau, "Crossroads Groups Fueled by Three Huge Donations," *Politico*, November 19, 2013, 19.

22. Center for Responsive Politics, "Election to Cost Nearly $4 Billion, CRP Projects, Topping Previous Midterms," http://www.opensecrets.org/news/2014/10/election-to-cost-nearly-4-billion-crp-projects-topping-previous-midterms/ (accessed December 17, 2014).

23. Editorial Board, "Dark Money Helped Win the Senate," *New York Times*, November 8, 2014.

24. McKinnon quoted in Ashley Parker, "Outside Money Drives a Deluge of Political Ads," *New York Times*, July 27, 2014.

25. Editorial Board, "Dark Money Helped Win the Senate."

26. Nicholas Confessore, Sarah Cohen, and Karen Yourish, "The Families Funding the 2016 Presidential Election," *New York Times*, October 10, 2015.

27. Republican National Committee, Growth and Opportunity Project, December 2012, http://goproject.gop.com/ (accessed October 18, 2015).

28. Trump quoted in Jill Lepore, "Politics and the New Machine," *The New Yorker* (November 16, 2015), 36.

29. Patrick Svitek, "Pro-Cruz SuperPACs Expect $31 Million First-Week Haul," *Texas Tribune*, April 8, 2015, http://www.texastribune.org/2015/04/08/3-super-pacs-set-back-cruzs-2016-campaign/ (accessed June 11, 2015).

30. Ed O'Keefe and Robert Costa, "How Jeb Bush's Campaign Ran Off Course before It Even Began," *Washington Post*, June 10, 2015.

31. Ibid., and Gregor Aisch and Karen Yourish, "Connecting the Dots behind the 2016 Presidential Candidates," *New York Times*, June 8, 2015.

32. Daniel Strauss, "The Power Players behind Chris Christie's Campaign," *Politico*, June 30, 2015, http://www.politico.com/story/2015/06/chris-christie-2016-campaign-staff-119587 (accessed December 3, 2015).

33. Katie Glueck, "The Power Players behind Rick Perry's Campaign," *Politico*, June 4, 2015, http://www.politico.com/story/2015/06/rick-perry-2016-camaign-staff-power-players-118640 (accessed November 17, 2015).

34. Katie Glueck, "The Power Players behind Marco Rubio's Campaign," *Politico*, April 13, 2015, http://www.politico.com/story/2015/04/the-power-players-behind-marco-rubios-campaign-116912 (accessed November 24, 2015).

35. Alexander Burns and Maggie Haberman, "The Invisible Primary," *Politico*, March 26, 2014.

36. Katie Glueck, "The Power Players behind Rand Paul's Campaign," *Politico*, April 7, 2015, http://www.politico.com/story/2015/04/rand-paul-2016-campaign-team-116715 (accessed November 27, 2015).

37. Katie Glueck, "The Power Players behind Scott Walker's Campaign," *Politico*, July 14, 2015, http://www.politico.com/story/2015/07/scott-walker-2016-campaign-staff-power-players-120086 (accessed November 27, 2015).

38. Philip Rucker and Matea Gold, "Carly Fiorina Actively Explores 2016 GOP Run but Faces Critics," *Washington Post*, November 25, 2014.

39. "John Kasich Presidential Campaign Key Staff and Advisor, 2016," *Ballotpedia*, n.d., http://ballotpedia.org/John_Kasich_presidential_campaign_key_staff_and_advisors,_2016 (accessed December 4, 2015).

40. Katie Glueck, "The Power Players behind Lindsey Graham's Campaign," *Politico*, June 15, 2015, http://www.politico.com/story/2015/06/

lindsey-graham-2016-campaign-staff-power-players-119015 (accessed December 4, 2015).

41. Katie Glueck, "The Power Players behind Ben Carson's Campaign," *Politico*, May 4, 2015, http://www.politico.com/story/2015/05/ben-carson-2016-campaign-staff-power-players-117598 (accessed December 4, 2015); Carson quoted in Steven Ginsberg and Robert Costa, "Ben Carson on the Brink: 'A Process Like This is Pretty Brutal,'" *Washington Post*, December 28, 2015.

42. Aaron Couch and Emmett McDermott, "Donald Trump Campaign Offered Actors $50 to Cheer for Him at Presidential Announcement," *Hollywood Reporter*, June 17, 2015, http://www.hollywoodreporter.com/news/donald-trump-campaign-offered-actors-803161 (accessed October 16, 2015). Gotham Government Relations and Communications, a New York-based consulting firm that had worked with Trump before, and partnered with Extra Mile, according to this report.

43. Patrick Healy and Maggie Haberman, "95,000 Words, Many of them Ominous, from Trump's Tongue," *New York Times*, December 5, 2015; Paul Schwartzman and Jenna Johnson, "It's not Chaos. It's Trump's Campaign Strategy," *Washington Post*, December 10, 2015.

44. Ben Schreckinger and Cate Martel, "The Man behind Trump's Run," *Politico*, July 22, 2015, http://www.politico.com/story/2015/07/man-behind-donald-trump-run-lewandowski-120443.html#sthash.mISEjIbh.dpuf (accessed October 16, 2015).

45. Tom Hamburger, "Cruz Campaign Credits Psychological Data and Analytics for Its Rising Success," *Washington Post*, December 13, 2015; Fred Davis, "The Power of Neuromarketing," *Campaigns & Elections*, August 18, 2014.

46. Bernie Sanders for President official website, n.d., https://berniesanders.com/issues/ (accessed December 4, 2015).

47. Jennifer Epstein and Mark Halperin, "An Inside Look at the Hillary Clinton Inner Circle," *Bloomberg News*, May 6, 2015, http://www.bloomberg.com/politics/articles/2015-05-06/an-inside-look-at-the-hillary-clinton-inner-circle (accessed October 3, 2015).

48. Ibid. See also, Eric M. Appleman's detailed presidential website, www.p2016.org .

49. Ballotpedia entries on O'Malley and Webb, https://ballotpedia.org/Martin_O'Malley_presidential_campaign_key_staff_and_advisors,_2016 and https://ballotpedia.org/Jim_Webb_presidential_campaign_key_staff_and_advisors,_2016 (accessed December 4, 2015).

50. Ballotpedia, "Lincoln Chafee Presidential Campaign Key Staff and Advisors," https://ballotpedia.org/Lincoln_Chafee_presidential_campaign_key_staff_and_advisors_experience,_2016 (accessed April 20, 2016).

51. Daniel Fisher, "Inside the Koch Empire: How the Brothers Plan to Reshape America," *Forbes*, December 5, 2012; see also Kenneth P. Vogel, "Koch World 2014," *Politico*, January 24, 2014, and Kenneth P. Vogel and Tarini Parti, "Inside Koch World," *Politico*, June 15, 2012.

52. Michael Isikoff, "Super PAC Backing Perry to Spend $55 Million to Beat Rivals, Documents Reveal," NBC News, September 6, 2011, http://www.nbcnews.com/id/44402386/#.VxbLZtQrLcs (accessed December 3, 2015).

53. Financial data from Center for Responsive Politics, http://www.opensecrets.org/pacs/indexpend.php?strID=C00573634&cycle=2016 (accessed December 3, 2015).

54. Spencer MacColl, "Capital Rivals: Koch Brothers vs. George Soros," Center for Responsive Politics, Open Secrets.org website, https://www.opensecrets.org/news/2010/09/opensecrets-battle—koch-brothers.html (accessed May 1, 2014); Peter H. Stone, "Sheldon Adelson Spent Far More on Campaign Than Previously Known," *Huffington Post*, December 3, 2012.

55. Matea Gold and Philip Rucker, "Billionaire Mogul Sheldon Adelson Looks for Mainstream Republican Who Can Win in 2016," *Washington Post*, March 25, 2014.

56. Dan Balz, "The 'Sheldon Primary' Is One Reason Americans Distrust the Political System," *Washington Post*, March 28, 2014.

57. Billy House, "Gingrich: Only Campaign Finance Reform Will Limit Billionaire Influence," *National Journal*, March 28, 2014. Jonathan Martin, "Sheldon Adelson is Poised to Give Donald Trump a Donation Boost," *New York Times*, May 13, 2016.

58. Matea Gold, "Koch-Backed Political Coalition, Designed to Shield Donors, Raised $400 million in 2012," *Washington Post*, January 5, 2014.

59. Noted in Jane Mayer, "Covert Operations: The Billion Brothers Who Are Waging a War against Obama," *The New Yorker*, August 30, 2010.

60. Ibid.

61. Vogel, "Koch World 2014."

62. Mike Allen and Jim Vandehei, "The Koch Brothers Secret Bank," *Politico*, September 11, 2013, http://www.politico.com/story/2013/09/behind-the-curtain-exclusive-the-koch-brothers-secret-bank-96669.html (accessed August 23, 2014) and Vogel, "Koch World 2014."

63. Vogel and Parti, "Inside Koch World"; see also Matea Gold, "Americans for Prosperity Plows Millions into Building Conservative Ground Force," *Washington Post*, October 6, 2014.

64. Nicholas Confessore, "Koch Brothers Budget of $889 Million for 2016 Is on Par with Both Parties' Spending," *New York Times*, January 26, 2015; see also Vogel, *Big Money*, ch. 1.

65. Matea Gold, "Billionaire Koch Brothers' Network Takes Cue from Obama's Playbook," *Washington Post*, July 29, 2015.

66. Kenneth P. Vogel, "The Koch Intelligence Agency," *Politico*, November 18, 2015.

67. Matea Gold, "Liberal Donors Eye New Strategy," *Washington Post*, May 5, 2014, A1.

68. Andrew Restuccia, "Tom Steyer Planning $100 million Campaign Push," *Politico*, February 18, 2014.

69. Data from Center for Responsive Politics, http://www.opensecrets.org/outsidespending/donor_stats.php (accessed May 17, 2016).

70. Nicholas Confessore, Sarah Cohen, and Karen Yourish, "The Families Funding the 2016 Presidential Election," *New York Times*, October 10, 2015.

71. Price quoted in Matea Gold, "It's Bold, but Legal: How Campaigns and Their Super PAC Backers Work Together," *Washington Post*, July 6, 2015.

72. Ibid.

73. Center for Responsive Politics, "2016 Outside Spending, by Super PAC," May 2016, https://www.opensecrets.org/outsidespending/summ.php?chrt=V&type=S (accessed May 17, 2016).

74. Shane Goldmacher, "Cruz's Silent Super PAC a Growing Worry for the Campaign," *Politico*, November 2, 2015, http://www.politico.com/story/2015/11/ted-cruz-silent-super-pacs-2016-215422 (accessed November 27, 2015).

Chapter 21

Epigraph quotes from Obama in video shown at the AAPC annual meeting, Washington, DC, in honor of Axelrod and Plouffe being inducted into that organization's Hall of Fame, April 6, 2013. Ryan quoted in Mark Leibovich, "Mitt Isn't Ready to Call It Quits," *New York Times Magazine*, September 30, 2014.

1. Maralee Schwartz, "Bad News for Consultants," *Washington Post*, October 8, 1989, A14.

2. Tobe quoted in Linda Williams, "The Selling of the Candidate," *Los Angeles Times*, June 6, 1988, E5.

3. Trump quoted in Michael W. Chapman, "Trump: Rove Gave Us Obama," CNS News, February 13, 2013, http://cnsnews.com/blog/michael-w-chapman/trump-rove-gave-us-obama (accessed October 29, 2015).

4. Clinton quoted in Richard Stengel and Eric Pooley, "Masters of the Message," *Time*, November 18, 1996, 18.

5. *Time*, September 2, 1996.

6. Lloyd Grove, "Taken under Advisement," *Washington Post*, August 31, 1996, D1.

7. Ibid.

8. Ed Rollins, with Tom DeFrank, *Bare Knuckles and Back Rooms* (New York: Broadway Books, 1996), picture caption, following p. 150.

9. Raymond D. Strother, *Falling Up: How a Redneck Helped Invent Political Consulting* (Baton Rouge: Louisiana State University Press, 2003), 206.

10. Caddell quoted in Charles S. Clark, "Political Consultants: Are Advisers and Handlers Harming Democracy?" *CQ Researcher* 6, no. 37 (October 4, 1996).

11. Ward Sinclair, "Political Consultants: The New Kingmakers Work Their Magic," *Washington Post*, June 5, 1982.

12. Ibid.

13. Rollins, *Bare Knuckles and Back Rooms,* 339.

14. Joseph Napolitan oral history, interviewed by John Franzén, American Association of Political Consultants Interview Collection, George Washington University Libraries, December 3, 1996, Part 2.

15. Herbert M. Baus, "Mr. Nixon, the Time Has Come to Bow Out," *Los Angeles Times*, February 26, 1974, A5.

16. Douglas E. Schoen and Patrick H. Caddell, "One and Done: To Be a Great President, Obama Should Not Seek Re-election in 2012," *Washington Post*, November 145, 2010.

17. Walter De Vries, "George and Mitt: Like Father, Like Son? Not Quite," October 15, 2012, s3.documentcloud.org/documents/468968/waltdevries.pdf; Michael Barbaro, "Romney Is Attacked by His Father's Longtime Aide," *New York Times*, October 15, 2012.

18. Mark McKinnon, "The Spin Doctor Is Out," *Texas Monthly*, November 1996, 130.

19. Manuel Roig-Franzia, "Mr. Homestretch," *Washington Post*, November 25, 2013, C5.

20. Ward Sinclair, "Stage Right and Stage Left, Consultants Setting Campaign Tones," *Washington Post*, May 11, 1982.

21. Eskew quoted in Jane Mayer, "Attack Dog: The Creator of the Willie Horton Ad Is Going All Out for Mitt Romney" *The New Yorker*, February 13, 2012.

22. McKinnon, "The Spin Doctor is Out," 130.

23. Joseph Napolitan, *1976 Journal of a Campaign Year*, unpublished manuscript, George Washington University, 64.

24. Gary Nordlinger interview with author, May 28, 2013.

25. Hank Sheinkopf, "Why Consultants?" GothamGazette.com, October 23, 2000, http://www.gothamgazette.com/iotw/polprofs/doc2.shtml (accessed August 22, 2014).

26. Sean J. Miller, "Is There Life after Consulting," *Campaigns & Elections*, November/December 2012, 37.

27. Lois Romano, "Horror Stories from the Campaign Front," *Washington Post*, February 26, 1984, C1.

28. Howard Blume, "Joe Cerrell Dies at 75," *Los Angeles Times*, December 4, 2010.

29. Douglas L. Bailey interview with author, Arlington, Virginia, February 6, 2013.

30. Pew Research Center for the People & the Press, "Don't Blame Us: The Views of Political Consultants," June 17, 1998, in conjunction with James Thurber and Candice Nelson of the Center for Congressional and Presidential Studies, American University, http://www.people-press.org/1998/06/17/dont-blame-us/. The poll was conducted between November 1997 and March 1998, N = 200.

James Thurber and David Dulio, "Industry Portrait: Political Consultants," *Campaigns & Elections*, July 1999, 28. See also, James A. Thurber and Candice Nelson, eds., *Campaign Warriors: Political Consultants in Elections* (Washington, DC: Brookings Institution Press, 2000).

31. See F. Christopher Arterton, "Professional Responsibility in Campaign Politics," unpublished paper for Conference on Professional Responsibility and Ethics in the Political Process, sponsored by the AAPC, Williamsburg, Virginia, March 24, 1991. On the discussion on ethics in politics, see, generally, Dennis W. Johnson, *Political Consultants and American Elections*, 3rd ed. (New York: Routledge, 2015), 283–86.

32. Paul Taylor, "In Politics of Attack, First Shots Often Backfire," *Washington Post*, July 10, 1990, A10.

33. Pew Research Center, "Don't Blame Us."

34. Peter Levine, "Consultants and American Political Culture," *Report from the Institute for Philosophy and Public Policy* 14, no. 3–4 (Summer/Fall 1994) (University of Maryland, School of Public Affairs).

35. Liza DePaulo, "The Scandal Sheet," *George*, December 1996, 102.

36. Eliza Newlin Carney, "Gold-Plated Guns for Hire," *National Journal*, June 6, 1998, 1296.

37. James Thurber, "Are Campaign Pros Destroying Democracy?" *Campaigns & Elections*, August 1998, 56.

38. Frank J. Murray, "Group to Condemn 'Push Poll' Methods: Settlement Targets Unethical Moves," *Washington Times*, June 24, 1996, A7.

39. Glenn Bolger and Bill McInturff, "'Push Polling' Stinks," *Campaigns & Elections*, August 1996, 70.

40. Johnson, *Political Consultants and American Elections*, 196–200.

41. George F. Bishop, *The Illusion of Public Opinion: Fact and Artifact in American Public Opinion Polls* (Lanham, MD: Rowman & Littlefield, 2005), 144.

42. Michael W. Traugott and Elizabeth C. Powers, "Did Public Opinion Support the Contract with America?" in *Election Polls, the News Media, and Democracy*, Paul J. Lavrakas and Michael W. Traugott, eds. (New York: Chatham House, 2000), 93–110.

43. Richard Morin, "Fifteen Minutes of Fame," *Washington Post*, August 28, 2000.

44. John Wagner, "This Just In from Channel Faux News," *Washington Post*, June 22, 2010, B1.

45. Shane Goldmacher, "NRCCF Launches Fake News Sites to Attack Democratic Candidates," *National Journal*, August 12, 2014; Shane Goldmacher, "Under Fire, GOP Adjusts Fake Democratic Websites," *National Journal*, February 17, 2014.

46. Spencer oral history, University of Virginia, 125

47. Mellman quoted in Adam Green, "The Pollies," *The New Yorker*, March 7, 2005.

48. Much of this analysis of twentieth- and twenty-first-century campaigning relies on Dennis W. Johnson, *Campaigning in the Twenty-first Century: Activists, Big Data, and Dark Money,* 2nd ed. (New York: Routledge, 2016).

49. Brian Franklin, "The Slow Boom of Campaign Technology," *Campaigns & Elections*, March/April 2013, 36.

50. Brian Franklin, telephone interview with author, April 16, 2014. Also, Impact Politics website, www.impactpolitics.com (accessed April 16, 2014), and Brian Franklin, "Seven Common New Media Mistakes," *Campaigns & Elections*, January 7, 2014.

51. Caroll Doherty, "Seven Things to Know about Polarization in America," Pew Research Center, June 12, 2014, http://www.pewresearch.org/fact-tank/2014/06/12/7-things-to-know-about-polarization-in-america/ (accessed August 24, 2014). The study is "Political Polarization in the American Public," June 12, 2014, http://www.people-press.org/2014/06/12/political-polarization-in-the-american-public/ (accessed August 24, 2014).

52. "Political Polarization in the American Public," 1.

INDEX